# PROGRAMMING IN
# BASIC
# FOR MICROCOMPUTERS

# PROGRAMMING IN
# BASIC
## FOR MICROCOMPUTERS

*Fourth Edition*

**Bruce Bosworth** ◆ **Harry L. Nagel**
**St. John's University**

# GLENCOE

Macmillan/McGraw–Hill

Lake Forest, Illinois   Columbus, Ohio   Mission Hills, California   Peoria, Illinois

Library of Congress Cataloging-in-Publication Data

Bosworth, Bruce.
    Programming in BASIC for microcomputers / Bruce Bosworth, Harry L.
Nagel. — 4th ed.
        p.   cm.
    Includes index.
    ISBN 0-02-800293-8 :
    1. BASIC (Computer program language)   2. Microcomputers-
-Programming.   3. Business—Data processing.   I. Nagel, Harry L.
II. Title.
QA76.73.B3B68   1992
005.26'2 — dc20                                                91-28079

Send all inquiries to:
GLENCOE DIVISION
Macmillan/McGraw-Hill
936 Eastwind Drive
Westerville, OH 43081

ISBN 0-02-800293-8

Printed in the United States of America.

1 2 3 4 5 6 7 8 9   COUR   99 98 97 96 95 94 93 92 91

# CONTENTS

# PREFACE

The fourth edition of *Programming in BASIC for Microcomputers* maintains the strengths of the previous three editions and is updated with new material, including the use of IBM personal computers and compatibles with MS DOS and IBM-MS BASIC. The emphasis of the fourth edition is on business applications with a nontechnical approach. Programming instruction begins very early in the text, using a statement-by-statement approach. Each BASIC statement is thoroughly explained and illustrated with actual program listings and output. Short cases reinforce the meaning of each statement. Each text chapter ends with a BASIC vocabulary summary, review questions, and graduated programming activities. The text contains more than three hundred review exercises and programming problems.

Major organizational changes in the fourth edition include moving string variables from Chapter 10 to Chapter 3 and introducing PRINT USING in Chapter 6 rather than Chapter 12. Data entry has been divided into two separate chapters, READ/DATA and INPUT.

This edition places greater emphasis on structured concepts and logic, program documentation, formatting, string usage, and software design. Topics new to the fourth edition include the following:

* DOS and BASIC commands
* on-screen editing
* function keys
* logic variables
* error trapping
* a new chapter illustrating all aspects of the PRINT USING statement

New statements or functions include: LOCATE, SPC, LINE INPUT, SWAP, IF/THEN/ELSE, ON ERROR, RESUME, ERR, ERL, CONT, RANDOMIZE TIMER, ASC, CHR$, SPACE$, STRING$, DATE$, TIME$, APPEND, and LINE INPUT #.

Chapters 1 through 11 provide sufficient material for a short course or an in-depth course in BASIC programming using a microcomputer. Chapters 12 through 16 present advanced aspects of BASIC, including extensive application problems and programming projects that can be used in a second course if desired.

The organization and flow of the text have been developed through many years of teaching an introductory course in programming and data processing. The text material has a logical sequence that builds and reinforces the knowledge and skills of the student.

Throughout the text the logic structures introduced and developed in previous chapters are reinforced in each successive chapter. This facilitates student learning and understanding of problem solving and program design. The end-of-chapter materials also provide strong reinforcement of the ideas covered. These materials include (1) a summary, of the concepts covered; (2) a BASIC vocabulary summary, which presents each keyword or function, its purpose, and an example; (3) review questions; and (4) programming activities. A diamond shape next to the exercise number designates those exercises whose solutions appear at the end of the text.

The end-of-text materials include Appendix A: Summary of Microcomputer Commands; Appendix B: Some Common BASIC Error Messages; Appendix C: Summary of Alt (Alternate) Key Functions; and Answers and Solutions to Selected Exercises.

Special thanks to Marjorie Lee, Kenny H. Du, Lisa DelCasale, Richard Gordon (our graduate assistants), and Michael B. Bosworth (student worker), all of whom helped prepare and process the programs and solutions for this edition. We would also like to thank our department secretary, Mrs. Mary Giuntini, for her assistance in many large and small ways.

# CHAPTER 1

# INTRODUCTION TO COMPUTERS, *BASIC*, AND STRUCTURED PROGRAMMING

Upon completing this chapter, you will be able to do the following:

- Understand what a program does.
- Identify the steps that go into developing a program in BASIC.
- Differentiate between a constant and a variable.
- See how a program's logic can be diagrammed using a flowchart.
- Discuss structured programming and the logic structures that help plan programming strategies for problem solving.

Ever since the early 1950s we have witnessed a rapid increase in the use of computers in our everyday lives. Today, computers are common in government, education, and business. Look at your driver's license or telephone bill. In all probability it was processed by computer. Examples like this are all around us.

To be useful, computers must be told not only what to do but also how to do it. This is the purpose of programming. A *program* is a detailed set of instructions that direct the computer to do its job. A *programmer* is a person who prepares such programs. Programs are typically referred to as *software*. *Hardware* constitutes the physical components of a computer system, that is, the equipment.

## COMPUTER LANGUAGES

There are a number of computer languages in which a programmer can write the detailed instructions needed to get the computer to work. The names of some of these languages are BASIC, C, C++, Pascal, FORTRAN, COBOL, Ada, Assembler, PL/1, APL, and Modula-2.

Learning how to program a computer is similar to learning a foreign language. In the BASIC language, however, you need to know only about 30 verb words, so vocabulary is no problem. Programming is like playing chess. There are only six different kinds of pieces on a chessboard but an almost infinite number of combinations of moves. Thus with the verb words in the BASIC language we can write programs to do such diverse things as

1. Help a person find a mate.
2. Prepare a payroll for a company, including writing the checks; determining the appropriate federal, state, and local tax deductions; and computing social security tax, pension deductions, and insurance deductions.
3. Process applications for credit cards to determine who is eligible.
4. Maintain a running balance of the inventory of a company with many products.
5. Explore different marketing strategies by creating a hypothetical environment to test them in.

## PURPOSE AND PLAN OF THIS TEXT

The programming language BASIC (*B*eginners *A*ll-purpose *S*ymbolic *I*nstruction *C*ode) is the most widely used with microcomputers. This book introduces you to the BASIC language one step at a time. The early chapters introduce simple programming concepts that, when applied, will build up your confidence and ability. In this way BASIC is easy to learn. If you take the time to study each chapter and to do the many review and programming exercises at the end of each one, you can move forward easily.

## MICROCOMPUTER *BASIC*

The BASIC language discussed in this text is the BASIC that has become the standard for microcomputers that are compatible with IBM PCs, PS/2s, and PS/1s. This BASIC was originally developed as Microsoft BASIC (MBASIC). In 1980 IBM adapted MBASIC for the IBM PC.

The programs in this text were all entered and processed using BASIC 3.0 and 4.0 as supplied by IBM. Users of other microcomputers with Disk BASIC should find the illustrations presented in the remainder of the text applicable to their systems as well.

Most text chapters conclude with a summary of the BASIC statements presented, along with the purpose and an example of each. These summaries can serve as a quick reference as you write your own BASIC programs.

## PROGRAMMING

*Programming* is the process of writing the step-by-step instructions that tell the computer what to do. Let's examine how programs are developed.

### Developing a Program

To develop a program and get it to work correctly, you should follow a series of steps.

1. *Defining the Problem*. What is the task to be done? What information and data must be collected to do the specified task? What is the output required?

2. *Planning*. Break the problem down into small components. Think about the steps that have to be taken to solve it. Typically, problem solving follows a simple, logical sequence of establishing (1) the data inputs; (2) the process, formula(s), or computation(s) required; and (3) the outputs to be produced. This approach can be generalized as input-process-output (I-P-O). Develop a rough flowchart to show the sequence of the steps to be taken.

3. *Coding*. Use BASIC statements to write out the step-by-step instructions needed in your program.

4. *Desk Checking*. Review your program for errors and bugs. Two types of errors can affect the execution of your program: syntax errors and logic errors. A syntax error might be a misspelled BASIC keyword or a missing punctuation mark. If such errors are not discovered when desk checking, they will be flagged by the computer—in the form of error messages—when you process or run your program. A logic error may involve the incorrect sequence of your program statements or the incorrect formulation of a processing expression. It is important to find logic errors when desk checking because the computer will not necessarily spot this kind of error. As a result, erroneous output may be produced.

5. *Program Testing*. Enter your program into the computer and run it. You might use several groups of test data for which you already know the answer. In this way you can compare output results with the known answer. Generally, most programs do not run successfully the first time. Possibly all of the errors were not discovered when desk checking. Also, new errors may have developed as you typed your program in. This is a good reason to check over your program before running it.

6.   *Debugging*. While at the computer, it may be possible to correct errors as indicated by the error messages—as well as to clear up any logic problems. You may cycle back to step 5 until you are satisfied with the results.

7.   *Documentation*. Once the program is complete and runs correctly, it should have support information for anyone else who may use it. This supporting documentation may include a final flowchart showing the sequence and logic of the program, a written description of the program outlining what it does and any special features it has, special instructions for using the program, a listing of the variables used in the program and what each one represents, or something similar.

- - - - - - - - - - - - - - - - - - - - - - - - - - - - - - - - - - - - - -

## CASE 1.1

**Problem**        **Selling Price Determination**
The proper pricing of goods or service is essential for a business to be successful. A program is needed that will derive the selling price of an item as the sum of its cost and markup.

**Data Input**     Test data to use is an item cost of $35 and a 50 percent markup.

**Process/Formulas**   To arrive at a selling price it is a common practice in many businesses to add a markup to the original cost of an item. The markup can be a percentage of the item cost, sufficient to provide a satisfactory profit after covering all expenses. The general formula for the selling price is:

Selling price = item cost + markup

where

Markup = a percent × item cost

**Output**         The output should appear as a report with headings identifying item cost, markup, and selling price and with the appropriate values under each heading.

- - - - - - - - - - - - - - - - - - - - - - - - - - - - - - - - - - - - - -

A program can be developed, following the steps described above, to produce the output desired in Case 1.1.

1.   *Define the Problem*. Write a program to find the selling price of an item, given the item cost and the markup percent.

2.   *Planning*. Let

$S$ = selling price

$C$ = item cost

$M$ = markup percent

then

$S = C + (M \times C)$

Data input includes values for $C$ and $M$. Compute the following in sequence:

a. Markup $= M \times C$

b. Add markup to the cost $C$ to derive $S$, the selling price.

What should be printed out? Output could be $S$, $C$, and the markup. In what order should it be generated? On the output, print the item cost, markup, and then the selling price.

Should the output have a heading? Form the output as follows:

Item Cost      Markup      Selling Price

The rough flowchart is shown in Figure 1.1. Note that the input, process, and output labels were placed on the flowchart only to reinforce the logic of problem solving. These labels are not usually included with the flowchart. (See Figure 1.6 for an explanation of the symbols used.)

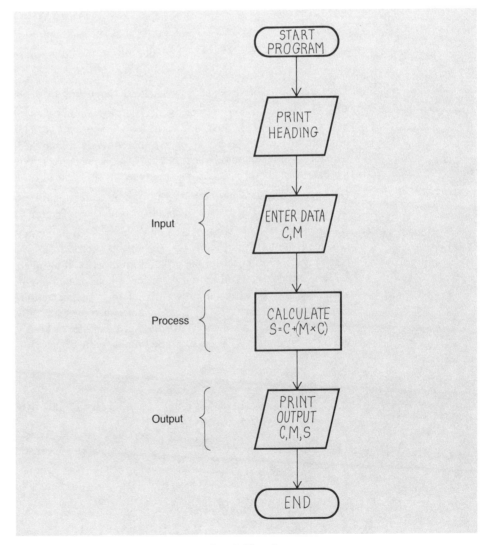

**FIGURE 1.1**   Case 1.1, Price Markup, Rough Flowchart

3.  *Coding*. Following the development outlined in step 2, write a BASIC program. (See Figure 1.2.)

4.  *Desk Checking*. Carefully review your handwritten program for syntax and logic errors. The program in Figure 1.2 has the following syntax errors:

| | |
|---|---|
| 20 READ C,M. | There should be no period (.) after M. |
| 30 LET S = C + (M × C) | × is not the multiplication symbol. Use *. |
| 60 DATA 50%, $35 | The symbols % and $ cannot be used with numeric data. |

The program also has the following logic errors:

| | |
|---|---|
| 50 END | END should be the highest-numbered line in the program (70 END, for instance); it should thus follow the DATA line. |
| 60 DATA 50%, $35 | This line is not logically consistent with the order of the items in line 20 (READ C, M). The cost data should precede the markup: 60 DATA 35, 50. |
| 60 DATA 50%, $35 | The value for M should be presented as a decimal— .50 (50%), not 50. |

These errors will become clearer when these statements are explained later in the text.

5.  *Program Testing*. Enter your desk-checked program into the computer using the test data $C = \$35$, $M = 50\%$, to see if $S = \$35 + .50 \times \$35 = \$52.50$. Run the program to see if it processes everything correctly. Figure 1.3 shows this program with the resulting output. Note that the answer is not correct. Why not? Because when the data was entered, 50 percent was typed as 5.0 instead of .50.

6.  *Debugging*. The data entry error is resolved by correcting line 60, and a new program run is produced. This time the output is correct. (See Figure 1.4.)

7.  *Documentation*. A flowchart based on the completed program (Figure 1.4) has been produced, as shown in Figure 1.5. Comments, in the form of remarks (REM statements), have been added to the program to describe it to other possible users (lines 1–7). Each data item in the program has a data name. These names can be listed alphabetically as part of the program's internal documentation, thus forming a data name dictionary (lines 4–7). Data names can represent constants or variables. A *constant* is a fixed data item. A *variable* is a data item whose value can be changed during the program's processing. Beginning with Chapter 3, and throughout the

```
10  PRINT "ITEM COST", "MARK UP", "SELLING PRICE"
20  READ C, M.
30  LET S = C + (M × C)
40  PRINT C, M, S
50  END
60  DATA 50%, $35
```

**FIGURE 1.2**   Case 1.1, Handwritten Price Markup Program

```
10 PRINT "ITEM COST", "MARKUP", "SELLING PRICE"
20 READ C, M
30 LET S = C + (M*C)
40 PRINT C, M, S
60 DATA 35, 5,0
70 END


RUN
ITEM COST          MARKUP              SELLING PRICE
  35                 5                    210
```

**FIGURE 1.3**  Program Testing, Case 1.1, Price Markup

```
1 REM       PROGRAM - PRICE MARKUP DETERMINATION
2 REM       PROGRAMMER - (name of person)   DATE - mm/dd/yy
4 REM       DATA NAMES - VARIABLE LIST
5 REM         C = ITEM COST
6 REM         M = % MARKUP
7 REM         S = SELLING PRICE
8 REM  ---------------------------
10 PRINT "ITEM COST", "MARKUP", "SELLING PRICE"
20 READ C, M
30 LET S = C + (M*C)
40 PRINT C, M, S
60 DATA 35, ,50
70 END


RUN
ITEM COST    MARKUP   SELLING PRICE
  35           ,5        52,5
```

**FIGURE 1.4**  Final Program, Case 1.1, Price Markup

remainder of this text, data names shown as part of program documentation will be placed in a variable list.

## Program Maintenance

Once a program is developed it must be maintained. Not all programs will need maintenance, but larger programs used in application areas on a regular basis may need to be revised. Revision can become necessary for several reasons: errors may have been discovered; new tasks or functions may be required; data or other items may need to be updated, removed, or changed; and so on. All such revisions are part of what is referred to as maintenance. Program maintenance requires the repetition of many of the steps listed for program development: coding, desk checking, testing, debugging, and documentation of all changes. The documentation of these maintenance changes should include an explanation of all revisions that have been made.

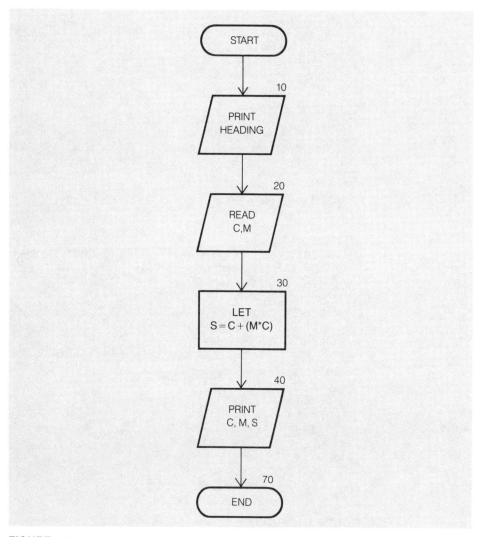

**FIGURE 1.5**   Flowchart for Figure 1.4, Case 1.1, Price Markup Program

## FLOWCHARTING

A useful aid in understanding a program is a diagram showing the logic, called a program flowchart. For simple programs a flowchart is not necessary because the logic is apparent. The more involved the program, however, the more necessary the flowchart.

Typically, a programmer will make a rough diagram (Figure 1.1) as a flowchart to help with the writing of the program. Ultimately, a final flowchart (Figure 1.5) will be developed showing the logic of the final program. This final flowchart serves as documentation so that at some later date you, or other programmers, can understand the program it represents.

The standard flowcharting symbols used in this book are defined in Figure 1.6. These symbols are part of a set of flowcharting symbols adopted by the American National Standards Institute (ANSI) to encourage common practices in program documentation.

## STRUCTURED PROGRAMMING

As programs get larger and more involved, the logic of a program often gets so confused that even the programmer is not sure how it works. To encourage good programming techniques, a concept called *structured programming* has emerged. The objectives of structured programming are to

**1.** Increase program clarity by reducing complexity.

**2.** Reduce program testing time.

**3.** Increase the programmer's productivity.

These objectives can be accomplished in part by developing a program that is well thought out logically before you start coding. Structured programming encourages a *top-down, modular approach* when designing a program. This approach is nothing more than good planning. That is, to solve a problem you have to break it down into steps, or modules. A structured program should incorporate these modules by using three basic control patterns: (1) simple sequence, (2) selection sequence, and (3) repetition sequence.

### Logic Structures

One of the main concepts of structured programming is that programs can be created by using only three basic control structures. These structures are illustrated in Figure 1.7.

**1.** The *simple sequence* is a structure that follows a sequential execution of statements. The program goes from one line to the next without a transfer or branch.

**2.** The *selection sequence* is exemplified by a comparison, or test. In this logic sequence, the computer performs a test to determine whether a condition is true or false. The result of the test is the execution of one of two statements. This structure is also called IF THEN ELSE and may be written without spaces: IF/THEN/ELSE. That is, *if* the condition is true, *then* execute the statement indicated, or *else* execute the other statement.

**3.** The *repetition sequence* provides for loops. A sequence of statements will be executed or repeated a specified number of times until a certain condition is met. This structure is called a DOWHILE; that is, *do* the statements *while* the condition is true.

These three structures should be sufficient to write any program. Several other structures have been developed for programming convenience. Two of these structures are DOUNTIL and CASE. (See Figure 1.8.)

**1.** The DOUNTIL structure is similar to the DOWHILE in providing a loop capability. The two structures differ as to when the condition is tested. The DOWHILE tests the condition *before* processing the statement, but the DOUNTIL tests the condition *after* the statement. With DOUNTIL the statement thus will be executed at least once. The loop will be repeated until the condition is true.

**2.** The CASE structure is an extension of the IF/THEN/ELSE structure (Figure 1.7). It is useful when there are several alternatives and only one is to be executed on the basis of the test condition.

In examining these control structures, you will find that each has only one entrance and one exit. This is significant. Programs written with these structures will have distinct

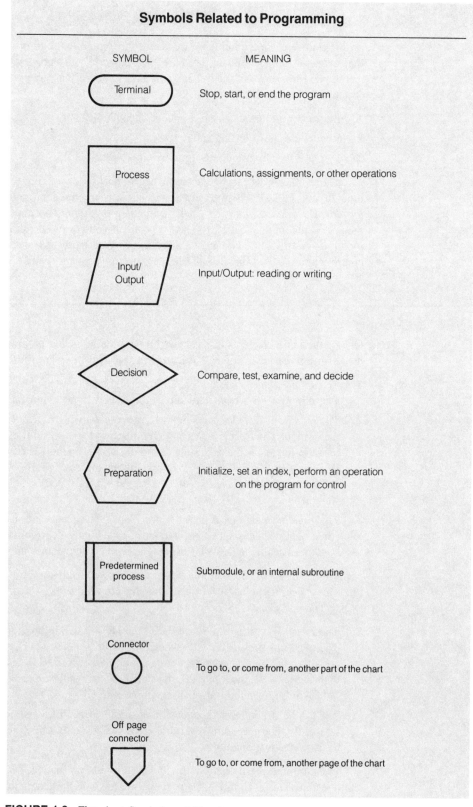

**FIGURE 1.6** Flowchart Symbols and Meanings

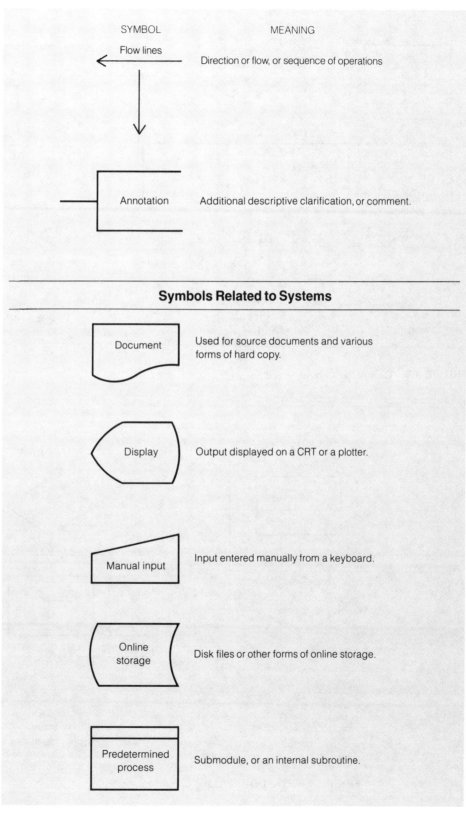

| SYMBOL | MEANING |
|--------|---------|
| Flow lines | Direction or flow, or sequence of operations |
| Annotation | Additional descriptive clarification, or comment. |

## Symbols Related to Systems

| | |
|--------|---------|
| Document | Used for source documents and various forms of hard copy. |
| Display | Output displayed on a CRT or a plotter. |
| Manual input | Input entered manually from a keyboard. |
| Online storage | Disk files or other forms of online storage. |
| Predetermined process | Submodule, or an internal subroutine. |

**FIGURE 1.6**  *continued*

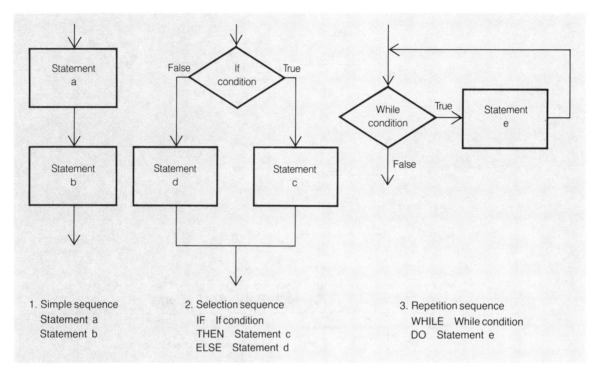

1. Simple sequence
   Statement a
   Statement b

2. Selection sequence
   IF   If condition
   THEN   Statement c
   ELSE   Statement d

3. Repetition sequence
   WHILE   While condition
   DO   Statement e

**FIGURE 1.7** Three Basic Control Structures

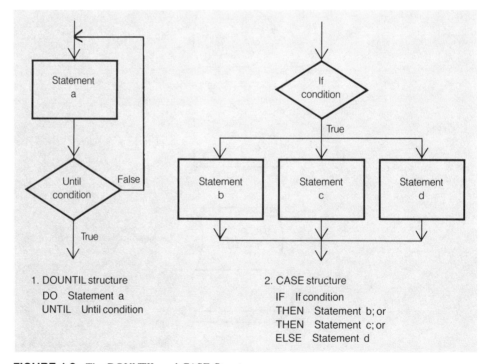

1. DOUNTIL structure
   DO   Statement a
   UNTIL   Until condition

2. CASE structure
   IF   If condition
   THEN   Statement b; or
   THEN   Statement c; or
   ELSE   Statement d

**FIGURE 1.8** The DOUNTIL and CASE Structures

blocks of statements, or *modules,* that can be followed easily by anyone looking at a program listing. In addition, such modules improve program testing and debugging by making it easier to locate the error.

## Logic Structures and Programming Strategies

Experienced programmers have learned to use logic structures in planning how to solve their programming problems. Before they begin to write any code, they try to match appropriate logic structures to the parts of the problem at hand. Logic structures provide programmers with standard approaches that can be used whenever applicable to solve the given problems. After a while programmers build up sets of strategies, based on these logic structures, for analyzing problems and constructing programs.

As you go through this text you will see these logic structures used and illustrated in both program examples and case application problem programs. You will learn that larger problems can be broken down into smaller subproblems. For these subproblems we use standardized solutions based on prior use of logic structures. At some point you will find yourself using these structures automatically as you develop your own programs.

## SUMMARY

Over the past 40 years, computers have become practically a necessity in government, education, and business. The largest area of computer growth is in microcomputers, or personal computers. Dozens of companies manufacture desktop or portable models. Microcomputers have become common items in the home.

All computers process data by following the steps of a program written in a specific language. The BASIC language is now widely used with microcomputers. It is easy to learn in comparison with other programming languages. However, the BASIC beginner still needs to learn the logic of programming.

Writing a program requires defining the problem, planning the sequence, coding, desk checking, testing, and documentation. With larger programs, program maintenance may be an added step after program development. Structured programming concepts can be used to develop good programming practices. Experience with logic structures can lead to programming strategies that make problem solving and programming easier.

## EXERCISES

**1.1**  What are some applications of computers?

**1.2**  What is meant by the term *computer program?*

**1.3**  What is meant by the terms *hardware* and *software?*

**1.4**  What steps should be followed to develop a program?

**1.5**  What is a syntax error? a logic error?

**1.6** What is the purpose of program flowcharting?

**1.7** What are the objectives of structured programming?

**1.8** Compare and contrast desk checking and program testing.

**1.9** Programs can be created using only three basic control structures. What are they?

**1.10** What control structure best describes the logic of Figure 1.4?

**1.11** How many conditions are tested with the selection sequence structure? How many with the CASE structure?

**1.12** What is the capability shared by both the DOUNTIL and DOWHILE structures?

**1.13** Create your own example to show an application of the CASE structure.

**1.14** Create your own example to show an application of the selection sequence.

## APPENDIX: SOME *BASIC* COMMANDS

Initially you should know four BASIC commands: LIST, RUN, LOAD, and SAVE. These commands are typical of those on most computers. You can type them directly each time you need one or, to save key strokes, press the appropriate function key, conveniently identified at the bottom of your screen (see Figure A1.1). Uppercase or lowercase characters are acceptable, as long as each command is spelled correctly.

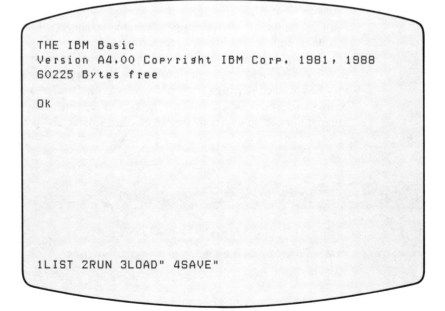

```
THE IBM Basic
Version A4.00 Copyright IBM Corp. 1981, 1988
60225 Bytes free

Ok




1LIST 2RUN 3LOAD" 4SAVE"
```

**FIGURE A1.1**  Screen Display after Loading BASIC, Showing the First Four of the Ten Function Keys.

1. LIST. After you have entered a program into the computer, or have loaded one that was previously saved, you can obtain a display of all the lines of the program by typing LIST, or using function key F1. Parts of a program can be listed using the following LIST commands, where *n* and *m* represent specific program line numbers:

   LIST *n* displays only line *n*

   LIST *n–* displays line *n* and all lines thereafter

   LIST *–n* displays all lines up to and including line *n*

   LIST *n–m* displays lines *n* to *m* inclusive

   If LIST is preceded by an L (LLIST), a hard copy is printed out, that is, the program is printed out on paper.

2. RUN. Entering the RUN command, by typing RUN or using the function key F2, will cause the program currently stored in the computer to be processed. Any syntax errors recognized by the computer will be indicated at this time. To process a program from a specific line *n* to the end, follow the command with the specific line number (RUN *n*). RUN 25, for example, will execute the program beginning with line 25.

3. LOAD. Programs that have been saved on diskette can be recalled by using the LOAD command. You can load from drive A, drive B, or drive C, as follows:

   Program on disk in drive A: use LOAD"A:progname"

   Program on disk in drive B: use LOAD"B:progname"

   Program in drive C: use LOAD"C:progname"

   Be sure to use the specific program name where *progname* is shown. *Caution:* Before you load a program, be sure any program you are currently working on is saved; otherwise it will be lost when you load a new program into the computer's memory.

4. SAVE. This command, when entered with a program name, will save your current program on a diskette. If no drive label is given, the computer will assume you want to save on the default drive. You can save programs using the naming conventions as follows:

   SAVE"A:progname" will save on diskette in drive A

   SAVE"B:progname" will save on diskette in drive B

   Be sure to use the specific program name where *progname* is shown. The BAS extension will automatically be added to the program name. *Caution:* Before you leave the computer or turn it off, be sure you save your work. Remember, every program you wish to retain must be saved on a diskette using the SAVE command. The BAS extension does not have to be given.

5. FILES. The FILES command is similar to the DOS DIR (directory) command. It will display a list of all of the programs/files on a particular drive while you are working with BASIC. If using drive A, enter FILES"A:"; for drive B enter FILES"B:"; and so on.

6. KILL. The KILL command in BASIC performs the same task as the DOS ERASE command.

   KILL"A:progname" will erase on diskette in drive A

   KILL"B:progname" will erase on diskette in drive B

   Be sure to use the specific program name where *progname* is shown.

7. NEW. This command will clear any program currently in computer memory. Because NEW will erase your current program, be sure you have saved your work before going on to another program. *Note:* If you find two programs are merged when listed, it is possible that you did not clear out the first program, using NEW, before entering the second program.

8. SYSTEM. The SYSTEM command allows you to return to DOS from BASIC. After you type and enter SYSTEM, the DOS prompt will appear.

---

## On-Screen Editing

As you begin creating a BASIC program, you may find it necessary to make corrections. Your keyboard includes several keys to help you edit. Among these are the cursor control, backspace, insert, delete, and escape keys. You can make corrections either while you are working on a current line, before you enter it, or later, by returning to a line you have already entered. Some additional aspects of screen editing follow.

*Changing Characters.* Use the left and right cursor keys and the End key to move on a line. Typing over existing characters causes them to be replaced. To enter it as a logical line, you must press the Enter key while on that line.

*Erasing Characters.* Use the left and right cursor keys and the End key to move on a line. To erase, place the cursor beneath the characters and press the Del (delete) key, then enter it as a logical line.

*Erasing Part of a Line.* Use the left and right cursor keys and the End key to move on a line. Position the cursor beneath the first character of the part of the line to be erased and press Ctrl-End. This will erase to the end of the line. Continue on the line, or enter it as a logical line.

*Canceling a Line.* Press the Esc (escape) key and the entire line you are typing will be erased.

It is beyond the scope of this appendix to go into the many other BASIC commands that are available. A summary of some BASIC commands can be found in Appendix A, located at the end of this text. For more details on these and other commands, refer to the BASIC manual appropriate to your computer.

# CHAPTER 2

# BEGINNING TO PROGRAM AND GENERATING SCREEN AND PRINTER OUTPUT

Upon completing this chapter, you will be able to do the following:

- See how easy it is to write and process a simple program using the PRINT and END statements.
- Understand the simple sequence logic structure.
- Explain the purpose of line numbers for each BASIC statement.
- Know how to display output on the screen and send output to the printer.
- Understand such BASIC commands as LIST, RUN, LOAD, and SAVE.
- Write and run programs that solve problems using computational operations and the PRINT statement.
- Know how to control output spacing using the comma, semicolon, TAB, and SPC functions.
- Document a program with the REM statement.
- Clear the screen display using CLS and plan output display using the LOCATE statement.

You can begin writing programs in the BASIC language almost immediately. Only two statements are required to generate output. This chapter shows how you can start programming using the PRINT and END statements. The third statement described in this chapter, REM, does not generate output.

You will also learn how output from a program can be printed on a printer, how output can be moved around the display screen, and how reports and results can be formatted in attractive and readable ways.

## PROGRAM STRUCTURE AND STATEMENT NUMBERS

A program in BASIC consists of a series of statements. Each statement is an instruction that stands alone as a single line. Each line in the program starts with a line number, which must be an integer, or whole number. These numbers are necessary to tell the computer the sequence of the program statements. Each line number is followed by a BASIC statement. Program 2.1 is a simple illustration of some BASIC statements and line numbering.

## PROGRAM 2.1   Line Numbering in a BASIC Program

```
10 REM AN ILLUSTRATION OF A BASIC PROGRAM
20 PRINT "BASIC IS NOT A DIFFICULT LANGUAGE TO LEARN"
30 PRINT
40 PRINT
50 END
```

The logic structure of this illustrative program, like the structure of the remaining programs in this chapter, follows the simple sequence described in Chapter 1. Recall that this sequence proceeds from one line to the next in the program without a branch or transfer in direction. Figure 2.1 shows this sequence.

Notice that every line in Program 2.1 has a different number. The numbers go from low to high. The available range is from 0 to 65529. It is suggested that you skip when numbering so additional programming statements can be inserted if necessary. Line numbering such as the following, for example, does not allow for easy changes or additions to the program:

1
2
3
4
5

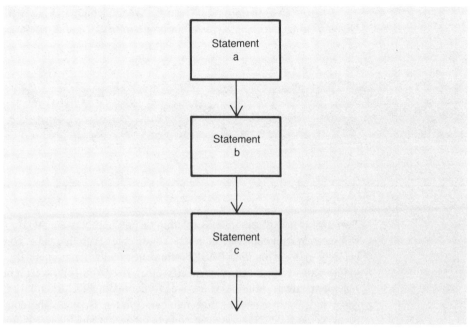

**FIGURE 2.1**   Simple Sequence Logic Structure

In this program, a line cannot be added between lines 3 and 4. If the line numbering had been expanded, however, a line could be added between existing lines if desired:

    10
    20
    30
    40
    50

In this example a line 25 can be inserted between lines 20 and 30.

BASIC has two useful commands, AUTO and RENUM, to help you with line numbering. These are discussed in the next section.

A line in a program can be replaced by typing the number of the existing line followed by the new text, and then pressing Enter. To delete an existing program line, type only the line number followed by Enter. Listing the program will show that the line has been deleted. A DELETE command can also be used to erase program lines. Table 2.1 summarizes this command.

**TABLE 2.1**   DELETE Command

| COMMAND | EFFECT AND EXAMPLES |
|---------|---------------------|
| DELETE line | DELETE 20 deletes program line 20 |
| DELETE line– | DELETE 30– deletes line 30 to the end of the program |
| DELETE –line | DELETE –40 deletes all program lines up to and including 40 |
| DELETE line–line | DELETE 10–20 deletes program lines 10 through 20 inclusive |

To erase an entire program, type the BASIC command NEW. Be careful when using NEW. You may accidentally erase a program that you did not save but wanted to retain.

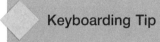

**Keyboarding Tip**     To save key strokes, use the combination of Alt plus D keys to produce the command DELETE.

## Line Number Commands

Two useful BASIC commands relating to line numbers are AUTO and RENUM. AUTO will provide automatic line numbers as you enter each line. This command is typed once, before you begin entering BASIC statements, and will automatically display line numbers in intervals of 10, unless you specify otherwise. You follow each number with a BASIC statement, always ending your line by depressing the Return key. To stop the AUTO command from generating line numbers, you must press the combination of Ctrl and Break keys. If AUTO produces a line number that already exists for some other program line, an asterisk (*) will appear next to the line number as a warning. To avoid accidentally replacing the existing line, press Enter. AUTO will generate the next line number in the sequence.

RENUM enables you to renumber a program automatically in increments of 10, unless you specify otherwise. You can type this command as often as needed when working on a program. The LIST command (see the appendix to Chapter 1) is often used to let you examine and check the numbering sequence of your program.

Table 2.2 provides the general form of the AUTO and RENUM commands.

**TABLE 2.2**  Line Number Commands

| COMMAND | EFFECT AND EXAMPLES |
| --- | --- |
| AUTO | Displays line numbers starting with 10, by 10 |
| AUTO number,increment | AUTO 20,5 generates line numbers 20, 25, 30, 35, . . . |
| AUTO ,increment | AUTO ,5 generates line numbers 0, 5, 10, 15, . . . |
| AUTO number, | AUTO 100, generates line numbers 100, 110, 120, . . . unless a previous AUTO increment other than 10 has been set |
| RENUM | Renumbers all lines beginning with the first one, starting with the number 10 and increasing by 10 (10, 20, 30, . . .) |
| RENUM number,,increment | RENUM 50,,20 renumbers the entire program starting with 50 (50, 70, 90, . . .) |
| RENUM new,old,increment | RENUM 100,90,5 renumbers existing lines from 90 up so they begin at 100 incrementing by 5 (100, 105, 110, . . .); lines prior to line 90 remain unchanged |

**Keyboarding Tip**   To save key strokes, use the Alt and A key combination to enter and display the AUTO command.

## THE END STATEMENT

Every program written in BASIC should conclude with a statement indicating termination. The END statement does this. It should be assigned the highest line number in the program.

The general form of this statement is

line # END

For example, 999 END is a complete END statement.

Although most microcomputers will permit a program to process without an END statement, your final program listing is not complete without it. The END statement serves to indicate the physical boundary where the program terminates.

## THE PRINT STATEMENT

The PRINT statement produces printed output. In general this statement can be used within a program in three different ways: (1) labeling and providing headings, (2) carrying out computations where it is not necessary to store and identify the computation, and (3) showing the end result of the computation carried out as a separate operation using a LET statement (see Chapter 5). In this chapter, only the first two uses will be covered.

The PRINT statement has the general form

$$\text{line \# PRINT} \begin{cases} \text{labels or headings} \\ \text{computations} \\ \text{values or numbers} \\ \text{combinations of the above} \end{cases}$$

### Printing Literals

A literal is an expression, label, heading, or term made up of alphabetic or numeric characters or a combination of both. For example, a description of a part and the number of units in stock could be made up of alphabetic and numeric characters as illustrated by the following:

| ALPHABETIC | NUMERIC | COMBINATION |
|---|---|---|
| Red Pins: Stock | 1458 | Red Pins: Stock 1,458 |

Both alphabetic and numeric literals can be printed by placing the items to be printed within quotation marks:

5 PRINT ''RED PINS:STOCK 1,458''

A numeric can also be printed without being placed in quotes as long as it does not include any special characters, such as commas:

5 PRINT 1458

Because both the display and keyboard have upper- and lowercase capability, either upper- or lowercase characters can be placed within the quotes:

7 PRINT ''Green Pins:Stock 3,542''

Programs 2.2 through 2.4 illustrate literal printing.

The output for each program is found after the word RUN. This word is a *system command* that is typed on the computer keyboard and causes the program to be executed, that is, to be processed by the computer.* RUN is a standard command for most micro-computers.

---

## PROGRAM 2.2   Printing Alphabetic and Numeric Literals

```
5 PRINT "RED PINS:STOCK 1,458"
9 END

RUN
RED PINS:STOCK 1,458
```

---

## PROGRAM 2.3   Printing a Numeric Literal without Quotes

```
5 PRINT "RED PINS:STOCK"
6 PRINT "1458"
7 PRINT 1458
9 END

RUN
RED PINS:STOCK
1458
 1458
```

---

Program 2.2 shows the combined alphabetic and numeric literal. Program 2.3 illustrates that a numeric does not have to be quoted to be printed. Note that when a numeric is printed without quotes, the number output is indented one space to allow for a plus sign ( + ) that is not printed. Negative numbers have the minus sign ( − ) printed in the first position.

Program 2.4 includes a line (line 7) that contains both uppercase and lowercase characters. The output results after RUN reflect the contents of that statement.

---

*Appendix A, at the end of this book, describes the system commands that appear in this text. These commands are generally similar to those in most other systems. It is always a good idea to read the appropriate system manual so that you understand all system commands.

## PROGRAM 2.4    Printing Uppercase and Lowercase Characters

```
5 PRINT "RED PINS:STOCK 1,458"
7 PRINT "Green Pins:Stock 3,542"
9 END

RUN
RED PINS:STOCK 1,458
Green Pins:Stock 3,542
```

You will find that if you type a BASIC keyword in lowercase characters, when you list the program it will appear in uppercase. All keywords by convention are in uppercase.

It is a common error to forget the quotes when using the PRINT statement. An error message, such as ''Illegal expression,'' may indicate that this occurred.* Check the PRINT statement if such a message appears. Even though the PC permits a program to process with the end quotes missing, your program is still not complete without them (see Appendix B for more on error messages).

A blank space should be placed after a keyword, as shown in the programs thus far. You may find the error message ''Syntax error in '' if the space is not provided. For example, if the statement

7 PRINT1458

were included in Program 2.3, the error message

Syntax error in 7

would be displayed at the end of the program. The correct statement has a blank space between the keyword PRINT and the data value 1458.

Extra blank spaces on both sides of a keyword are ignored by the computer. They do not become part of any output spacing. Blanks that are included within the quotes, however, are *not* ignored; they result in a space for each blank as part of the output. To see this effect, refer back to Programs 2.2 and 2.3 and the resulting output.

## USING BASIC COMMANDS

Most program illustrations in this text include only a single BASIC command, that is RUN. In practice, however, you use many commands while at the computer—SAVE, LOAD, LIST, RENUM, and DELETE, for example. To illustrate the use of some of these commands, let's reexamine Program 2.3. Note that in the following discussion no drive label is given for the SAVE or LOAD commands because the default drive in the illustration is A.

---

*After running a program, you may find that the output contains a message indicating that something is wrong with your program. Such error messages direct you to correct whatever is wrong. Since messages differ from system to system, study the system manual for the appropriate error messages and their meanings. Also, see Appendix B.

```
(a) LIST
    5 PRINT "RED PINS;STOCK"
    6 PRINT "1458"
    7 PRINT 1458
    9 END

(b) SAVE "PG2-3"

(c) NEW

(d) LIST

(e) LOAD"PG2-3"

(f) LIST
    5 PRINT "RED PINS;STOCK"
    6 PRINT "1458"
    7 PRINT 1458
    9 END

(g) RENUM

(h) LIST
    10 PRINT "RED PINS;STOCK"
    20 PRINT "1458"
    30 PRINT 1458
    40 END

(i) 35 PRINT "BLUE PINS"
    38 PRINT "STOCK 1200"

(j) LIST
    10 PRINT "RED PINS;STOCK"
    20 PRINT "1458"
    30 PRINT 1458
    35 PRINT "BLUE PINS"
    38 PRINT "STOCK 1200"
    40 END

    LIST 10-30
    10 PRINT "RED PINS;STOCK"
    20 PRINT "1458"
    30 PRINT 1458

    LIST 30-
    30 PRINT 1458
    35 PRINT "BLUE PINS"
    38 PRINT "STOCK 1200"
    40 END

    LIST -30
    10 PRINT "RED PINS;STOCK"
    20 PRINT "1458"
    30 PRINT 1458

(k) DELETE 10-20

(l) LIST
    30 PRINT 1458
    35 PRINT "BLUE PINS"
    38 PRINT "STOCK 1200"
    40 END

(m) SAVE"PG2-3"
```

**FIGURE 2.2** Using BASIC Commands When Programming

Figure 2.2 displays the program (referred to as PG2–3) first being listed by LIST (*a*), followed by the command SAVE''PG2–3'' (*b*). Then NEW is entered (*c*) followed by LIST (*d*) to show that we no longer have the program to work with. Since the program was saved, it can be loaded from the diskette (LOAD''PG2–3'') (*e*) and listed once again (*f*). A RENUM (*g*) is followed by a LIST (*h*) to display the result. Two lines (*i*) are then added to the program. Selected LIST commands (*j*) display segments of the revised program. A DELETE (*k*) erases two lines, followed by another LIST (*l*) to check the program. Finally, the program is saved (*m*) again in its latest form.

Using the combination of the Shift and PrtSc keys, for PCs—or the PrtSc key, for PS/1s and PS/2s—will produce a printed copy of your program and output from the screen. You can get a hard copy listing of your program by using LIST preceded by L (that is, LLIST). You can also display a list of your saved diskette files by entering FILES, for drive A, when drive A is the default drive, or FILES''B:'', for drive B.

---

**Keyboarding Tip**   To save key strokes, you can enter and display the BASIC keyword PRINT by using the Alt and P key combination. Another key stroke-saving technique is to enter a question mark (?) as a substitute for the keyword PRINT. When the program is listed, the ? is converted to PRINT.

---

## CONSTANTS

A *constant* is a value or data name that remains fixed while your program is being processed. Many computations use formulas that incorporate constant values. For example, compound interest is found using the formula $A = P(1 + r)^n$, where $P$ is the principal or starting amount, $r$ is the interest rate, $n$ is the number of time periods, and $A$ is the final result. The ''1'' in this formula is a constant. Following are some examples of numeric constants in BASIC:

| | | |
|---|---|---|
| −6.345 | .005214 | 3.1416 |
| 105138 | 2.71828 | 2 |

Program 2.5 illustrates the use of the compound interest formula (with constants in the formula) to determine the total cost of a $3000 loan, at 8 percent interest, compounded yearly for 6 years.

---

**PROGRAM 2.5   Finding Compound Interest: Constant Values**

```
20 PRINT 3000*(1.0 + .08)^6
30 END

RUN
 4760.624
```

The symbols * and ^ represent the operations multiplication and exponentiation, respectively. These operations are explained in the next sections.

When processing numerical data in BASIC, leading plus and minus signs and decimal points appropriate to the numbers being used are acceptable. Here are some unacceptable data values:

| | |
|---|---|
| $100 | The dollar sign is not permitted. |
| − 58.32.6 | Two decimal points are not allowed. |
| 4,356 | A comma between characters is not allowed. |
| 228 − | The minus sign should not be at the end. |

---

## E Notation

Printed values are generally limited to six character spaces, plus a decimal point if required.* For numbers that exceed these space limits, E notation may result. This scientific notation indicates that the number to the left of the E should be multiplied by 10 raised to the power of the number after the E. For example, the value 2,000,000 in E notation is 2.0E6. The interpretation, $2 \times 10^6$, tells us to multiply the 2 by 10 raised to the sixth power, which is the same as adding six zeros after the 2, or 2,000,000.

If the number after the E is positive, move the decimal point to the right the number of places shown after the E to return to the full value equivalent. So for 2.0E6 we move the decimal point six places to the right:

2.000000.

A value such as .00000456 in E notation would be expressed as $4.56E-6$. The E followed by a minus sign means that the value on the left is divided by 10 raised to the power to the right of the minus sign. In this example we have

$$\frac{4.56}{10^6} \quad \text{or} \quad \frac{4.56}{1000000}$$

To return from an E minus notation to the full decimal equivalent, move the decimal point to the left the number of places indicated by the number after the E minus. So for $4.56E-6$ we move the decimal point six places to the left:

.000004.56

Numerical data in E notation can be included in a PRINT statement. Program 2.6 shows data in line 5 in E notation; line 10 shows data that is very small in value. The output illustrates what happens when these types of data are printed.

## PROGRAM 2.6    Printing with E Notation

```
5 PRINT 5.5E5,.283E-2
10 PRINT -.00000456
99 END
```

---

*Space limitation differs from system to system.

```
RUN
 550000            .00283
 -4.56E-06
```

## COMPUTATIONAL OPERATIONS

To direct the computer to perform a computation, the correct symbols must be used. These symbols in BASIC are shown in Table 2.3.

Besides knowing the symbols for computations, the programmer must know how the computer evaluates expressions. The order of priority is as follows: first, any exponentiations; second, any multiplications or divisions; and third, any additions or subtractions. An expression is evaluated from left to right, following the order just described. Some examples are shown in Table 2.4.

Notice in the first example of Table 2.4 that subtraction is done before the addition. This sequence is because these two operations are on the same level, and the operation that comes first, going from left to right, is performed first. In the second example, going from left to right and by order of priority, the exponentiation operations are carried out first and second, the division third, and the addition last. In the third example, going from left to right, the division is done first, the multiplication next, and the subtraction last.

Another important concept is the use of parentheses in an expression. Operations that are placed within parentheses will be performed before those that are not in parentheses.

**TABLE 2.3**  Computations with BASIC

| OPERATION | *BASIC* SYMBOL | ARITHMETIC EXAMPLES | *BASIC* |
|-----------|----------------|---------------------|---------|
| Exponentiation | ^ | $X^2$, $17^{1/2}$ | X^2, 17^.5 |
| Multiplication | * | $A \times B$, $2.14 \times D$ | A*B, 2.14*D |
| Division | / | $\dfrac{50}{Z}$, $L \div M$ | 50/Z, L/M |
| Addition | + | $A + B + C$, $15 + X$ | A+B+C, 15+X |
| Subtraction | − | $X - Y$, $B - 1.5$ | X−Y, B−1.5 |

**TABLE 2.4**  Order of Operations

| EXPRESSION | *BASIC* | SEQUENCE OF OPERATIONS |
|------------|---------|------------------------|
| 1. $A^2 - B + 4$ | A^2−B+4 | [1] [2] [3]<br>A^2−B+4 |
| 2. $X + Y^2/Y^3$ | X+Y^2/Z^3 | [4] [1][3][2]<br>X+Y^2/Z^3 |
| 3. $3/P - A \times C$ | 3/P−A*C | [1] [3] [2]<br>3/P−A*C |

**TABLE 2.5**  Order of Operations with Parentheses

| EXPRESSION | BASIC | SEQUENCE |
|---|---|---|
| 1. $a^2 + \dfrac{b}{2a}$ | A^2+B/(2*A) | ② ④ ③ ①<br>A^2+B/(2*A) |
| 2. $P \times (1 + r)^n$ | P*(1+R)^N | ③ ① ②<br>P*(1+R)^N |
| 3. $(2 + X) \times (Y - 4)$ | (2+X)*(Y−4) | ① ③ ②<br>(2+X)*(Y−4) |
| 4. $K \times \dfrac{(L + M)^2}{4}$ | K*((L+M)^2/4) | ④ ① ②③<br>K*((L+M)^2/4) |

The sequencing described above will still apply to items in the parentheses. Table 2.5 shows several examples. Notice that in each example of Table 2.5, the sequence of evaluation would change if the parentheses were not present. The computer would interpret the expression without parentheses as follows:

**1.**  $a^2 + \dfrac{b}{2} \times a$

**2.**  $P \times 1 + r^n$

**3.**  $2 + X \times Y - 4$

**4.**  $K \times L + \dfrac{M^2}{4}$

The resulting expressions are now very different from their original forms. Table 2.6 shows how incorrect answers can result when parentheses are not used.

Note that in the fourth BASIC example of Table 2.5, K*((L+M)^2/4), the expression L+M, within parentheses is itself enclosed in parentheses. The inner expression, L+M, is evaluated first, followed by the remaining items within the outer parentheses. Thus, if parentheses are *nested*, the innermost set of parentheses is evaluated first and then the next outer set, and so on, until all parentheses have been eliminated.

**TABLE 2.6**  Correct and Incorrect Use of Parentheses

| EXPRESSION | CORRECT BASIC | RIGHT ANSWER | INCORRECT BASIC | WRONG ANSWER |
|---|---|---|---|---|
| 1. $a^2 + \dfrac{b}{2a}$ | 5^2+4/(2*5) | 25.4 | 5^2+4/2*5 | 35 |
| 2. $P \times (1 + r)^n$ | 200*(1+.1)^2 | 242 | 200*1+.1^2 | 200.01 |
| 3. $(2 + X) \times (Y - 4)$ | (2+50)*(10−4) | 312 | 2+50*10−4 | 498 |
| 4. $K \times \dfrac{(L + M)^2}{4}$ | 3*((4+2)^2/4) | 27 | 3*4+2^2/4 | 13 |

## Computational Printing

We can use the PRINT statement to direct the computer to perform computations. All of the symbols and operations described so far can be incorporated in a PRINT statement. Programs 2.7–2.9 demonstrate computational printing using the information from Case 2.1.

### CASE 2.1

**Problem**

**Sales Tax Collection**
The tax on sales in a certain state is 5 percent of the total value of the items purchased. Write a program that will calculate the total sales tax.

**Data Input**      Two items were purchased for $5 and $10. Tax is 5%.

**Process/Formulas**  Total sales tax = sum of all items purchased × tax rate

**Output**      Display only the total sales tax.

Program 2.7 illustrates a solution to the problem of Case 2.1.

### PROGRAM 2.7    A Single Computational PRINT Statement

```
2 PRINT (5+10)*.05
10 END

RUN
.75
```

The output of Program 2.7 is a result of the computation performed based on line 2 of the program. Only the tax on the total is printed out. Note the use of parentheses to ensure that the addition is carried out first, then the multiplication.

The desired output usually has headings or labels. Programs 2.8 and 2.9 show how headings and labels can be printed. Observe that both programs show that more than one computation is possible in the PRINT statement (line 40).

### PROGRAM 2.8    Printing Headings, Multiple PRINT Computations

```
10 PRINT "TOTAL","TAX"
20 PRINT "SALES","TOTAL"
40 PRINT (5+10),(5+10)*.05
50 END
```

```
RUN
TOTAL          TAX
SALES          TOTAL
 15             .75
```

## PROGRAM 2.9 Underlining Headings, Multiple PRINT Computations

```
10 PRINT "TOTAL","TAX"
20 PRINT "SALES","TOTAL","GRAND TOTAL"
30 PRINT "------------------------------------------"
40 PRINT (5+10),(5+10)*.05,(5+10)+(5+10)*.05
50 END

RUN
TOTAL          TAX
SALES          TOTAL          GRAND TOTAL
------------------------------------------
 15             .75            15.75
```

Observe that none of the computations carried out with the PRINT statement in Programs 2.8 and 2.9 has quotation marks around it. A computation placed in quotes would result in the quoted expression being treated as a literal, not a computation.

Often the appearance of computer output would be improved by the use of blank lines. You can achieve this by inserting a PRINT statement, as shown in Program 2.10, line 60. For every blank PRINT in a program, a line is skipped. By properly inserting blank PRINT statements, you can skip as many lines as desired.

## PROGRAM 2.10 Skipping Lines Using the PRINT Statement

```
20 PRINT "TOTAL SALES"
40 PRINT "------------------"
60 PRINT
80 PRINT 5+10+20
90 END

RUN
TOTAL SALES
------------------

 35
```

A flowchart for Program 2.10 is shown in Figure 2.3. This flowchart shows the simple sequence logic that is the structure of all the programs in this chapter. Such flowcharts are also part of the documentation that accompanies completed programs. The

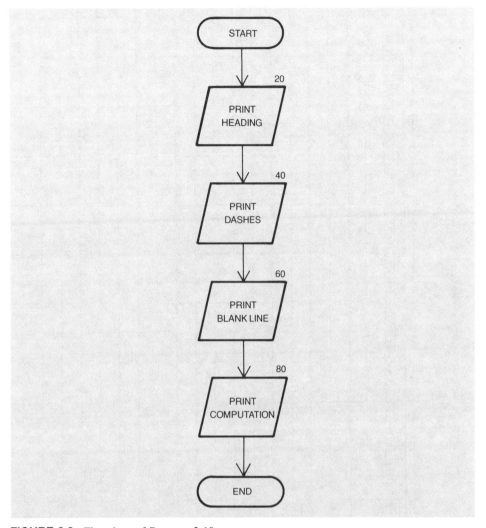

**FIGURE 2.3**   Flowchart of Program 2.10

shapes of the flowchart symbols for START, PRINT, and END are part of a set of standard symbols described in Chapter 1 (Figure 1.6).

In actual practice the flowchart of Figure 2.3 would not include symbols such as 40 and 60. These are shown for illustrative purposes only. The programmer would use a layout form such as the one shown in Figure 2.4 when writing the program.

## OUTPUT SPACING

A video display usually has 80 characters of output per line. When a PRINT statement indicates that more than one item will be printed on a line, the spacing is regulated by the computer. Two punctuation marks—the comma and the semicolon—can be used in the PRINT statement to control how the output is spaced.

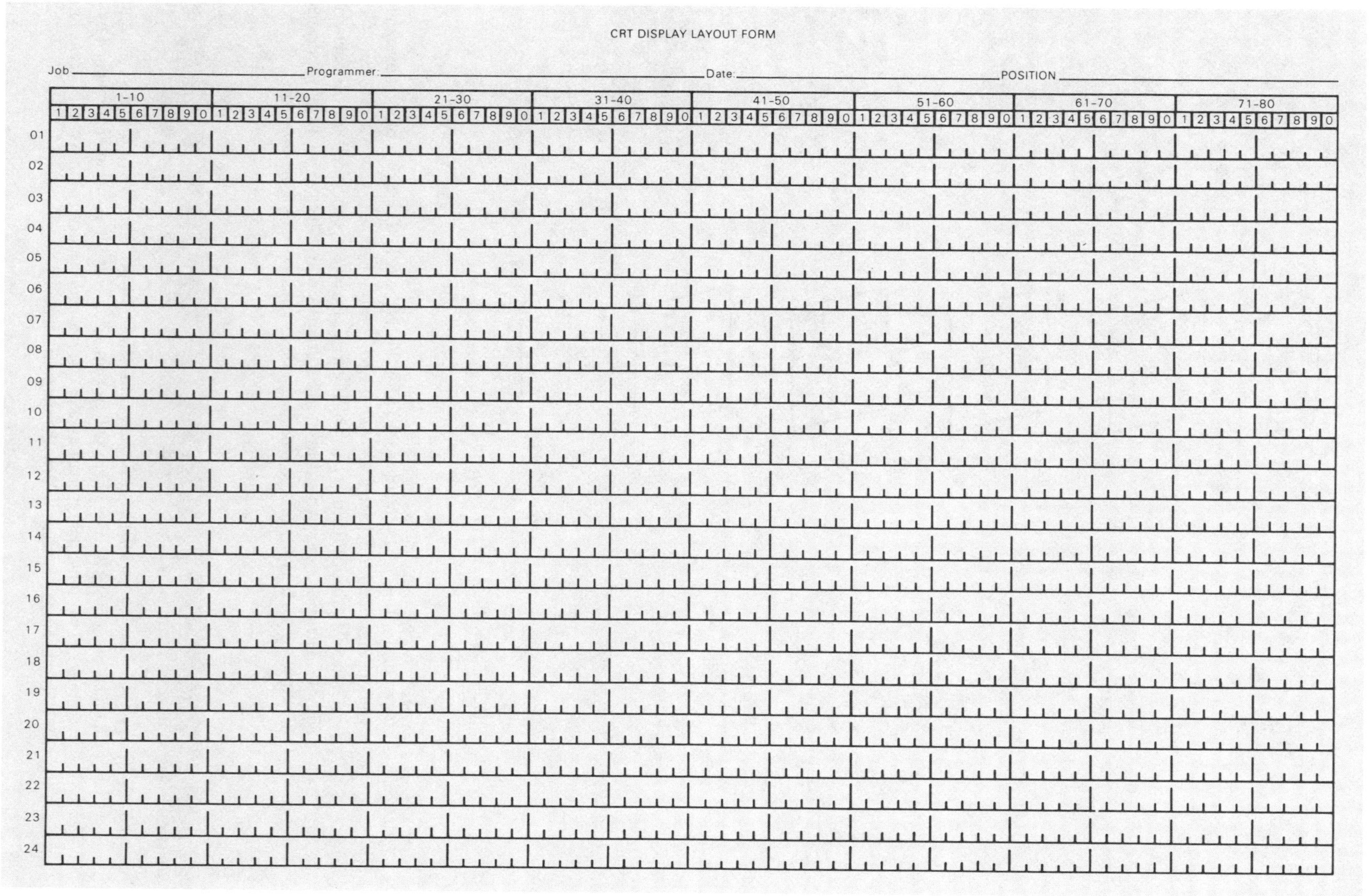

**FIGURE 2.4** Display Layout Form

## The Comma

With a screen display of 80 characters per line, *fields* of 14 characters can be defined by using a comma in a PRINT statement. In both Programs 2.8 and 2.9, the output spacing is based on the commas in lines 10, 20, and 40. In each program the literal headings and computational prints have been separated by commas.

Using PC BASIC you will have five fields with a total of 80 spaces available for each output line. The first four fields each have 14 spaces and the fifth field has the remaining 24 spaces. Program 2.11 generates output that identifies all five print fields.

---

**PROGRAM 2.11   Print Field Positions Using Commas**

```
5 PRINT "PRINT POSITION SHOWN BY NUMBERS BELOW"
10 PRINT
20 PRINT "12345678901234567890123456789012345678901234567890123456789012345678 90"
30 PRINT "FIELD 1","FIELD 2","FIELD 3","FIELD 4","FIELD 5"
40 END

RUN
PRINT POSITION SHOWN BY NUMBERS BELOW

12345678901234567890123456789012345678901234567890123456789012345678 90
FIELD 1        FIELD 2        FIELD 3        FIELD 4        FIELD 5
```

The location of each of the five print fields can be summarized as follows:

| PRINT FIELD | STARTING AND ENDING POSITION FROM LEFT MARGIN |
|---|---|
| 1 | 1–14 |
| 2 | 15–28 |
| 3 | 29–42 |
| 4 | 43–56 |
| 5 | 57–80 |

Literals and negative values will be printed starting at the left of the field. Positive values are printed one space farther to the right to allow for a plus sign that is not printed. The blank space for the suppressed plus sign is in the same column position as the negative sign. The output of Program 2.9 illustrates the starting positions of literals and numerics.

You may wish to skip a field to have output spaced across the entire page. Field skipping can be accomplished by using quotation marks enclosing a blank space, as shown in line 5 of Program 2.12.

---

**PROGRAM 2.12   Skipping Fields**

```
5 PRINT "FIELD 1"," ","FIELD 3"," ","FIELD 5"
10 END

RUN
FIELD 1                        FIELD 3                        FIELD 5
```

The quoted blank for field skipping will work on all systems. PC BASIC will also permit field skipping without a quoted blank, using only the comma as a field spacer. For example, the following line will produce the same result as line 5 of Program 2.12:

5 PRINT "FIELD 1",,"FIELD 3",,"FIELD 5"

The comma can also be used to continue output printing on one line, combining the information from two or more PRINT statements. If a PRINT statement ends with a "dangling comma," the output will not advance to the next line. Instead, the output of the next PRINT statement will follow on the same line as the preceding output but it will start in the next available print field. This continuation is shown in Program 2.13.

**PROGRAM 2.13   Commas at the End of a PRINT Statement**

```
5 PRINT "GROSS WAGE",
10 PRINT "+ OVERTIME",
15 PRINT "= TOTAL WAGE",
20 PRINT "- TAXES",
25 PRINT "= NET WAGE"
99 END

RUN
GROSS WAGE    + OVERTIME    = TOTAL WAGE  - TAXES       = NET WAGE
```

Note that the output from Program 2.13 is spaced according to the five print field positions we described earlier.

## The Semicolon

When a semicolon is used in a PRINT statement between positive numerical data, two blank spaces will be placed between the printed output. One blank is from the semicolon; the other represents the positive sign. If a semicolon is followed by a negative numeric, only one blank space will result. Using the semicolon instead of the comma enables output to be "packed" on a line. This packing is shown in the output of Program 2.14. Line 25 of the program shows various numerical values separated by semicolons.

**PROGRAM 2.14   Printing Packed Output Using the Semicolon**

```
25 PRINT 1;2;3;4;5;6;7;8;9;10;100;2000;-888;12.6+83
99 END

RUN
 1  2  3  4  5  6  7  8  9  10  100  2000 -888  95.6
```

Program 2.15 shows a mixture of commas and semicolons in PRINT statements.

## PROGRAM 2.15    Mixing Commas and Semicolons

```
5 PRINT 100/2;100/3,100/4;100/5
10 PRINT 100/2,100/3;100/4;100/5
99 END

RUN
 50    33.33333                  25    20
 50               33.33333  25    20
```

When the semicolon is used with literals, it does *not* provide extra spacing. The effect of a semicolon between literals is the same as that of a hyphen in a word break at the end of a line. If the semicolon is at the end of a PRINT statement, the output will not advance. Program 2.16 shows what can happen to the output when the semicolon is used between literals.

## PROGRAM 2.16    The Semicolon between Literals

```
10 PRINT "BETWEEN LITERALS" ; "THE SEMICOLON"
20 PRINT "DOES NOT PROVIDE SPACING."
99 END

RUN
BETWEEN LITERALSTHE SEMICOLON
DOES NOT PROVIDE SPACING.
```

Program 2.17 shows the ''dangling semicolon'' at the end of line 10 with the resulting output.

## PROGRAM 2.17    Semicolon at the End of a PRINT Statement

```
10 PRINT "THERE ARE FIFTY STATES IN THE UNITED STATES OF A";
20 PRINT "MERICA."
99 END

RUN
THERE ARE FIFTY STATES IN THE UNITED STATES OF AMERICA.
```

Extra spacing is needed to correct the output of Program 2.16. Spacing can be added by using blanks within the quotes, as shown in lines 20 and 30 of Program 2.18.

## PROGRAM 2.18   The Semicolon between Literals with Spacing

```
10 PRINT "TO USE THE ; WITH LITERALS";
20 PRINT " YOU CAN PROVIDE";
30 PRINT " THE EXTRA SPACES NEEDED."
99 END

RUN
TO USE THE ; WITH LITERALS YOU CAN PROVIDE THE EXTRA SPACES NEEDED.
```

To understand the spacing that results when literals and numerics are separated by semicolons, study Program 2.19. When a literal is followed by either numerics or a computation, with a semicolon between them, the printed output will show a single space after the literal if the numeric/computation is positive and no space if it is negative. When a numeric/computation occurs before a literal and they are separated by a semicolon, a single space will appear between them on the printed output.

## PROGRAM 2.19   The Semicolon between Literals and Numerics

```
10 PRINT "ENDING INVENTORY";200-15;"UNITS"
99 END

RUN
ENDING INVENTORY 185 UNITS
```

## THE *REM* STATEMENT

Often it is desirable to provide statements within the written program that spell out in some detail the purpose of the program or of various sections. These remark (REM) statements are part of program documentation. This kind of documentation is useful to the programmer and to others who want to review and better understand the program.

Lines 5, 10, and 30 in Program 2.20 illustrate how comments are put into a program using REM statements. The output is not affected by these statements because they are ignored by the computer. The apostrophe (') can be used in place of REM. See line 30.

The REM statement has the general form

line # REM

followed by any characters of the computer's character set:

line # REM $\left\{\begin{array}{l}\text{programmer's name, date, job description, variable list,}\\\text{comments about sections of code, etc.}\end{array}\right.$

It is a good habit to include REM statements for any work you submit. You should include your name, the class/section, the date, and the exercise number.

## PROGRAM 2.20   REM Statements in a Program

```
5 REM THIS PROGRAM WAS WRITTEN BY I. SABO IN BASIC
10 REM IT ILLUSTRATES SOME ASPECTS OF PRINTING.
20 PRINT "SALES TAX IS";5;"% OF TOTAL"
30 'COMPUTATIONAL PRINT IN LINE 40.
40 PRINT "TOTAL $";(25+30+5)*1.05
99 END

RUN
SALES TAX IS 5 % OF TOTAL
TOTAL $ 63
```

Program 2.21 uses the information in Case 2.2 to illustrate several functions of the PRINT statement. Note the REM documentation included in the program.

## CASE 2.2

**Problem**

**Annual Bond Interest Determination**

An investor with a bond portfolio wants to know the annual interest on each separate bond. A program is needed to determine the interest for a group of corporate bonds.

**Data Input**

The following data represents the par value and annual interest rates for a bond portfolio.

| TOTAL PAR VALUE | INTEREST RATE |
|---|---|
| $4000 | 6 1/4% |
| 7000 | 7 5/8 |
| 3000 | 6 1/2 |
| 8000 | 8 1/8 |

**Process/Formulas**

The annual interest on corporate bonds is found as follows:

Annual interest = par value × annual interest rate

**Output**

The output display should have column headings identifying the total par value, interest rate, and annual interest for each bond. All data output should follow the example provided here:

```
  TOTAL        INTEREST        ANNUAL
PAR VALUE        RATE         INTEREST
------------------------------------------
$4000          6 1/4%         $ 250
 ----          -----           ----
 ----          -----           ----
 ----          -----           ----
```

Program 2.21 calculates the interest for each bond in Case 2.2. Later we will see that it is possible to solve problems such as this with less involved PRINT statements.

## PROGRAM 2.21   Case 2.2, Computing Bond Interest with PRINT

```
5 REM  PROGRAM - CASE 2.2, COMPUTING BOND INTEREST
15 REM PROGRAMMER- (name of person)  DATE - mm/dd/yy
25 REM -----------------------------------------------
35 PRINT "  TOTAL","INTEREST"," ANNUAL"
45 PRINT "PAR VALUE","  RATE","INTEREST"
55 PRINT "-------------------------------------------"
65 PRINT "$4000","6 1/4%","$";4000*.0625
75 PRINT "$7000","7 5/8%","$";7000*.07625
85 PRINT "$3000","6 1/2%","$";3000*.065
95 PRINT "$8000","8 1/8%","$";8000*.08125
105 END

RUN
   TOTAL          INTEREST        ANNUAL
PAR VALUE          RATE          INTEREST
-------------------------------------------
$4000           6 1/4%          $ 250
$7000           7 5/8%          $ 533.75
$3000           6 1/2%          $ 195
$8000           8 1/8%          $ 650
```

## OUTPUT TO A PRINTER

The typical microcomputer system, in addition to having a video display terminal, also has a printer attached. Using the PRINT statement in a BASIC program may produce output on the screen only. To produce printer output you need to use a PRINT statement with the prefix L. The form of the LPRINT statement is exactly the same as that of the PRINT statement. In Program 2.22 an LPRINT statement replaces each PRINT statement of Program 2.21.

## PROGRAM 2.22   Case 2.2, Computing Bond Interest with LPRINT

```
5 REM CASE 2.2, COMPUTING BOND INTEREST
15 REM PROGRAMMER- (name of person)  DATE - mm/dd/yy
25 REM -----------------------------------------------
35 LPRINT "  TOTAL","INTEREST"," ANNUAL"
45 LPRINT "PAR VALUE","  RATE","INTEREST"
55 LPRINT "-------------------------------------------"
65 LPRINT "$4000","6 1/4%","$";4000*.0625
75 LPRINT "$7000","7 5/8%","$";7000*.07625
85 LPRINT "$3000","6 1/2%","$";3000*.065
95 LPRINT "$8000","8 1/8%","$";8000*.08125
105 END
```

```
RUN
```

```
    TOTAL          INTEREST        ANNUAL
    PAR VALUE       RATE           INTEREST
    ------------------------------------------------
    $4000          6 1/4%          $ 250
    $7000          7 5/8%          $ 533.75
    $3000          6 1/2%          $ 195
    $8000          8 1/8%          $ 650
```

The PRINT statement sends output to the screen and the LPRINT statement sends output to the printer. You can write a program and observe the results on the screen and then change each PRINT to an LPRINT, or add LPRINTs to produce the required output format on the printer paper. For example, Program 2.23 produces the two outputs shown; the first on the screen and the second as a hard copy on the printer. When planning your output you must consider the output devices of your system.

## PROGRAM 2.23   Screen and Printer Output

```
10 REM 1. SCREEN OUTPUT WITH PRINT
20 REM 2. PRINTER OUTPUT WITH LPRINT
30 PRINT "SCREEN OUTPUT"
40 PRINT 1991,1992,1993,1994,1995
50 PRINT "END OF SCREEN OUTPUT"
55 REM
60 LPRINT "PRINTER OUTPUT"
70 LPRINT 1991,1992,1993,1994,1995
75 LPRINT "------","------","------","------","------"
80 LPRINT "END OF PRINTER OUTPUT"
90 END
```

```
RUN
SCREEN OUTPUT
 1991          1992          1993          1994          1995
END OF SCREEN OUTPUT
```

```
PRINTER OUTPUT
 1991          1992          1993          1994          1995
 ------        ------        ------        ------        ------
END OF PRINTER OUTPUT
```

## OUTPUT FORMATTING CONTROLS

In our discussion so far, output spacing has been controlled by the comma, which produces wide fields, and the semicolon, which packs output. Both the comma and semicolon produce displays and printed results according to fixed spacing specifications. We often need to produce output in the form of reports or tables, however, that require more flexible spacing than the comma and semicolon can provide. In BASIC the TAB function and SPC (space) function provide flexibility for both printed and display results.

### The TAB Function

The TAB function, in conjunction with the PRINT statement, allows us to specify in which column, from the left side of the display, we want the output to start appearing. The form for using this function is

$$\text{line \# PRINT TAB(n);} \begin{cases} \text{labels or headings} \\ \text{computations} \\ \text{values or numbers} \\ \text{combinations of the above} \end{cases}$$

The $n$ within parentheses is an integer or expression that indicates to the computer the column position for placement of the output items that follow the semicolon. All positions are from the left margin or edge of the screen. The computer display starts a line with $n$ as the first column position. The $n$ for the last column on a line is usually 80. Using TAB, we could print a heading such as "MARCH SALES REPORT" beginning in column position 36 with the statement

10 PRINT TAB(36);"MARCH SALES REPORT"

TAB will cause the first 35 spaces from the left to be skipped, with the output starting in column 36. Note the semicolon following TAB(36). A comma in that position would have caused "MARCH SALES REPORT" to be printed in column 43 (that is, the fourth field) because that is the next available field after column 36. The TAB statement should therefore always be used with a semicolon. Program 2.24 illustrates the TAB function.

## PROGRAM 2.24   The TAB Function

```
10 PRINT TAB(5);"JAN."; TAB(15);"FEB."; TAB(25);"MARCH"
20 PRINT "---------------------------------"
30 END

RUN
    JAN.      FEB.      MARCH
---------------------------------
```

As you can see in Program 2.24, several tabs can be placed within a single program, with semicolons separating the items to be displayed. The output spacing is controlled by the values placed in each tab of line 10. Thus, JAN. is printed starting in column 5, FEB. starting in column 15, and MARCH starting in column 25. Note that the three output tabs have increasing column numbers, allowing enough space for the literals to be printed out. If your output has more characters than the number of columns available because you have not correctly specified the *n* values in the TAB statement, you may get some unexpected output displays. An example of such a display is shown in Program 2.25.

## PROGRAM 2.25   The TAB Function with Incorrect Specification

```
10 PRINT TAB(5);"JANUARY"; TAB(10);"FEBRUARY"; TAB(15);"MARCH"
20 PRINT "--------------------------------"
30 END

RUN
    JANUARY
         FEBRUARY
              MARCH
--------------------------------
```

Program 2.25 shows that when insufficient space is allowed (placing tabs at 5, 10, and 15, in this case), the PRINT statement places each literal on a separate line. If the tabs had been specified as 5, 15, 25, there would have been enough space for all three months to be displayed on a single line.

The TAB function works with LPRINT in the same way it does with PRINT. Where PRINT TAB is used for display output, LPRINT TAB is used for printer output. Lines 70 and 75 of Program 2.26 illustrate the LPRINT TAB.

## PROGRAM 2.26   LPRINT and TAB

```
10 REM 1. SCREEN OUTPUT WITH PRINT
20 REM 2. PRINTER OUTPUT WITH LPRINT
30 PRINT "SCREEN OUTPUT"
40 PRINT "JAN.","FEB.","MARCH"
50 PRINT "END OF SCREEN OUTPUT"
55 REM
60 LPRINT "PRINTER OUTPUT"
70 LPRINT TAB(11); "JAN.","FEB.","MARCH"
75 LPRINT TAB(11); "----","----","-----"
80 LPRINT "END OF PRINTER OUTPUT"
90 END

RUN
SCREEN OUTPUT
JAN.            FEB.            MARCH
END OF SCREEN OUTPUT
```

```
PRINTER OUTPUT
            JAN,            FEB,            MARCH
            ----            ----            -----
END OF PRINTER OUTPUT
```

As we have mentioned, because the TAB function gives greater flexibility in design-ing output displays, you can produce neater and more attractive printed reports or output results. Program 2.27 represents a revision of Program 2.21, for Case 2.2, incorporating the TAB function to create more attractive output.

---

**PROGRAM 2.27  Case 2.2, Computing Bond Interest, Output with TAB**

```
5 REM  PROGRAM - CASE 2.2, COMPUTING BOND INTEREST
15 REM PROGRAMMER- (name of person)  DATE - mm/dd/yy
25 REM ---------------------------------------------
45 PRINT TAB(5);"TOTAL PAR VALUE";TAB(25);"INTEREST RATE";TAB(45);"ANNUAL INTERE
ST"
55 PRINT TAB(5);"------------------------------------------------------"
65 PRINT TAB(9);"$4000";TAB(29);"6 1/4%";TAB(49);"$";4000*.0625
75 PRINT TAB(9);"$7000";TAB(29);"7 5/8%";TAB(49);"$";7000*.07625
85 PRINT TAB(9);"$3000";TAB(29);"6 1/2%",TAB(49);"$";3000*.065
95 PRINT TAB(9);"$8000";TAB(29);"8 1/8%",TAB(49);"$";8000*.08125
98 PRINT TAB(5);"------------------------------------------------------"
105 END

RUN
    TOTAL PAR VALUE      INTEREST RATE        ANNUAL INTEREST
    ---------------------------------------------------------
        $4000             6 1/4%              $ 250
        $7000             7 5/8%              $ 533,75
        $3000             6 1/2%              $ 195
        $8000             8 1/8%              $ 650
    ---------------------------------------------------------
```

One major advantage of the TAB function, as illustrated by the output of Program 2.27, is that we can specify that fields be larger or smaller than 14 columns. Originally Program 2.21 required two lines for the heading labels because there was not enough column space to fit each of the column headings on one line. Using TAB (lines 65–95) with PRINT in Program 2.27 allows the heading labels to appear on a single line and results in more attractive spacing for the output. In addition, the use of TAB has expanded the column space to 20. Note that line 45 is longer than the 80 columns of the display and thus extends onto a second line when the program is listed. This is not a printing error; longer line listings may appear in other chapters of this text as well.

## The SPC Function

Whereas the TAB function allows us flexible spacing using the left margin as a guideline, the SPC function permits us to specify the number of blank spaces to be placed between output items. SPC is used in conjunction with a PRINT or LPRINT statement in the same way as the TAB is. The form for using this function is

$$\text{line \# PRINT SPC(n);} \begin{cases} \text{labels or headings} \\ \text{computations} \\ \text{values or numbers} \\ \text{combinations of the above} \end{cases}$$

The *n* within parentheses is an integer that indicates to the computer the number of blank spaces to place between output items that follow the semicolon. Program 2.28 shows the SPC function in line 30 with three labels: JAN., FEB., and MARCH. The program also has the same three labels in line 40 with the TAB function.

---

**PROGRAM 2.28    The SPC and TAB Functions**

```
10 PRINT "12345678901234567890123456789012345678901234567890   SPC FUNCTION SPACING"
30 PRINT SPC(5);"JAN.";SPC(10);"FEB.";SPC(10);"MARCH"
35 PRINT
40 PRINT TAB(5);"JAN.";TAB(15);"FEB.";TAB(25);"MARCH"
60 PRINT "12345678901234567890123456789012345678901234567890   TAB FUNCTION SPACING"
70 END

RUN
12345678901234567890123456789012345678901234567890   SPC FUNCTION SPACING
     JAN.           FEB.          MARCH
     JAN.        FEB.       MARCH
12345678901234567890123456789012345678901234567890   TAB FUNCTION SPACING
```

The output for Program 2.28 shows that line 30, with the SPC function, causes 5, 10, and 10 blank spaces to be produced preceding the three labels. In comparison, the same three labels print beginning in columns 5, 15, and 25 as a result of the tabs in line 40.

The SPC and TAB functions can be placed together in a single PRINT statement. Program 2.29 is a revision of Program 2.27 (based on Case 2.2) with SPC(14) functions replacing TAB(29) and TAB(49) functions in lines 65–95.

---

**PROGRAM 2.29    Case 2.2, Computing Bond Interest, Output with SPC Function**

```
5 REM   PROGRAM - CASE 2.2, COMPUTING BOND INTEREST
15 REM PROGRAMMER- (name of person)   DATE  - mm/dd/yy
25 REM ------------------------------------------
45 PRINT TAB(5);"TOTAL PAR VALUE";SPC(5);"INTEREST RATE";SPC(5);"ANNUAL INTEREST"
```

```
55 PRINT TAB(5);"--------------------------------------------------------"
65 PRINT TAB(9);"$4000";SPC(14);"6 1/4%";SPC(14);"$";4000*.0625
75 PRINT TAB(9);"$7000";SPC(14);"7 5/8%";SPC(14);"$";7000*.07625
85 PRINT TAB(9);"$3000";SPC(14);"6 1/2%";SPC(14);"$";3000*.065
95 PRINT TAB(9);"$8000";SPC(14);"8 1/8%";SPC(14);"$";8000*.08125
98 PRINT TAB(5);"--------------------------------------------------------"
105 END

RUN
     TOTAL PAR VALUE     INTEREST RATE     ANNUAL INTEREST
     -----------------------------------------------------
            $4000            6 1/4%            $ 250
            $7000            7 5/8%            $ 533.75
            $3000            6 1/2%            $ 195
            $8000            8 1/8%            $ 650
     -----------------------------------------------------
```

## DISPLAY CONTROLS

Up to this point, program output has generally been displayed on the screen starting from the left margin position at column one. A program's output can also be displayed at other locations on the screen. A display screen can be viewed as a sheet of graph paper with a grid of 25 rows and 80 columns. Using the LOCATE statement we can instruct the computer to position a program's output at a specific location, by row and column, on the screen. To do this we will need two BASIC statements; CLS (clear screen) and LOCATE.

## The CLS Statement

Because the display screen has a limited size, it can fill up very fast with a program's output, listings, and assorted commands. Once you have developed a program for actual use, it is usually desirable to have a clean or clear screen for output results. This is easily accomplished by placing a CLS statement as one of the beginning lines in a program. The form for this statement is

line # CLS

For example, if the first program line is 10 CLS, any display on the screen will be cleared when RUN is entered. The screen will be blank until output from the program starts to be displayed. See Program 2.30 for an example.

## The LOCATE Statement

Points on the display screen can be identified with coordinates based on rows and columns. For our purposes we will use the four corners as extreme locations when using the LOCATE statement. The upper left corner is 1,1; or row 1, column 1; the upper right corner is 1,80; or row 1, column 80; the lower left corner is 25,1; or row 25, column 1; and the lower right corner is 25,80; or row 25, column 80.

The LOCATE statement uses the row and column coordinates. It has the form

line # LOCATE r,c

The $r$ is a row specification from 1 to 25, and the $c$ is a column specification from 1 to 80. Output begins in this column location. If we wanted to locate a heading on the screen five lines down from the top and starting twenty columns over, an appropriate LOCATE statement to precede the PRINT line containing the heading would be

25 LOCATE 5,20

In Program 2.30, the LOCATE statement (line 25) causes the heading in line 30 to be positioned on the screen five lines down and twenty columns from the left margin. The original program and the word RUN were cleared off the screen by the use of line 10 CLS.

## PROGRAM 2.30    The CLS and LOCATE Statements

```
10 CLS
25 LOCATE 5,20
30 PRINT"TABLE A-1   POPULATION BY REGION"
95 END
```

```
            TABLE A-1   POPULATION BY REGION
```

Programs that incorporate the LOCATE statement should have a CLS statement as well. If not, your output results may be intermixed with whatever else is on the screen in the positions specified by the LOCATE coordinates.

The LOCATE statement increases our flexibility in displaying output results. It allows us to move in two directions on the screen, that is, both horizontally and vertically; without it we can move only horizontally. Program 2.31 is a revision of Program 2.29 (Case 2.2) with LOCATE statements added (lines 40, 50, 60, 70, 80, 90, and 96). These lines were added to center the output in the middle of the screen. Note that line 30 is a CLS statement to ensure that the screen is clear.

**Keyboarding Tip**    To save key strokes, use the Alt and L key combination to enter and display the BASIC keyword LOCATE.

## PROGRAM 2.31 Case 2.2, Computing Bond Interest, Output with LOCATE

```
5 REM   PROGRAM - CASE 2.2, COMPUTING BOND INTEREST
15 REM PROGRAMMER- (name of person)   DATE - mm/dd/yy
25 REM ---------------------------------------------
30 CLS
40 LOCATE 10,15
45 PRINT "TOTAL PAR VALUE";SPC(5);"INTEREST RATE";SPC(5);"ANNUAL INTEREST"
50 LOCATE 11,15
55 PRINT "-----------------------------------------------------"
60 LOCATE 12,15
65 PRINT SPC(5);"$4000";SPC(14);"6 1/4%";SPC(14);"$";4000*.0625
70 LOCATE 13,15
75 PRINT SPC(5);"$7000";SPC(14);"7 5/8%";SPC(14);"$";7000*.07625
80 LOCATE 14,15
85 PRINT SPC(5);"$3000";SPC(14);"6 1/2%";SPC(14);"$";3000*.065
90 LOCATE 15,15
95 PRINT SPC(5);"$8000";SPC(14);"8 1/8%";SPC(14);"$";8000*.08125
96 LOCATE 16,15
98 PRINT "-----------------------------------------------------"
105 END
```

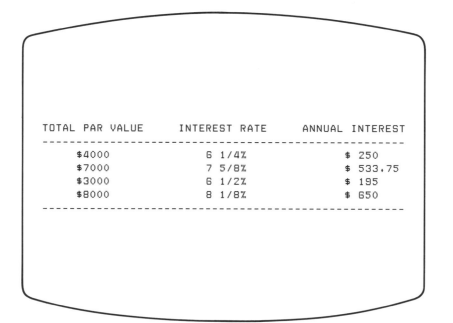

```
TOTAL PAR VALUE      INTEREST RATE     ANNUAL INTEREST
----------------------------------------------------------
        $4000           6 1/4%           $ 250
        $7000           7 5/8%           $ 533.75
        $3000           6 1/2%           $ 195
        $8000           8 1/8%           $ 650
----------------------------------------------------------
```

## Planning Output Displays

To assist in planning output displays, you can use layout worksheets such as the one
shown in Figure 2.4 (p. 32). The worksheet enables you to position and view the output
before coding. Note that the layout form covers the screen area typical of most displays,

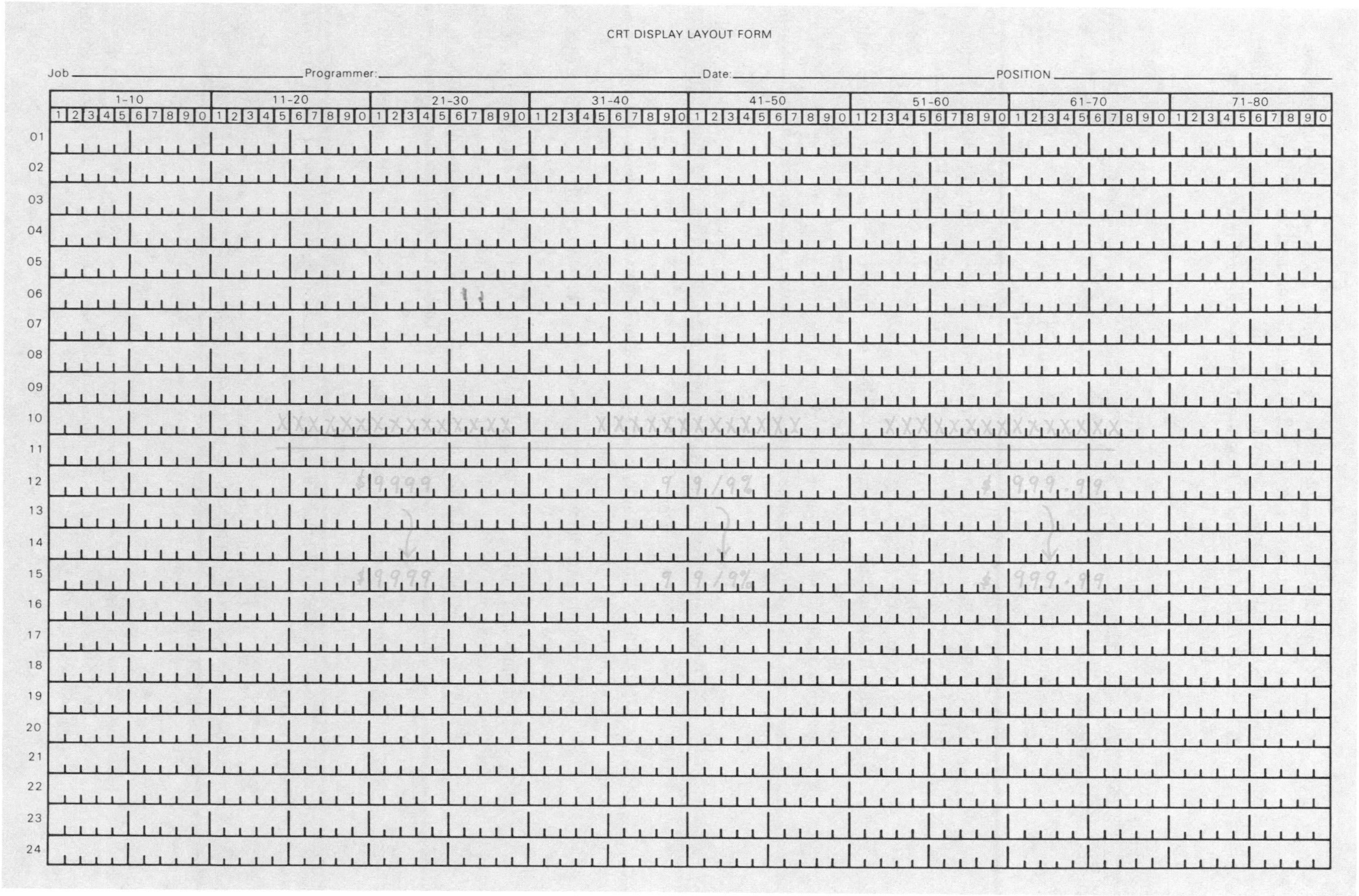

**FIGURE 2.5** Display Layout Form, Program 2.31

that is, 24 rows down by 80 columns across.* Figure 2.5 shows a layout worksheet filled in as part of the planning for Program 2.31. This layout sheet shows the output occupying rows 10–15 and beginning in column 15. Literals are represented by *X*s and numerics by 9s. The LOCATE statements in Program 2.31 are written to match the display as planned using the layout worksheet.

## SUMMARY

A program in BASIC consists of statements. Each statement begins with a line number. Every BASIC program should have one END statement, which must have the highest line number in the program. A block of statements can form a simple sequence logic structure.

Statement line numbers can be generated automatically using the AUTO command. A DELETE command can be used to erase program lines. Lines in a program can be renumbered using the RENUM command. Other useful commands include SAVE, LOAD, NEW, RUN, LIST, and LLIST.

PRINT statements can generate alphabetic, numeric, and alphanumeric output. Upper- and lowercase characters can be intermixed as output. PRINT statements can also perform computations. Output is printed from the left margin.

To direct the computer to perform computations, you must understand the following rules:

1. Higher order operations are performed before lower order ones. The order of priority is (1) exponentiation, (2) multiplication and division, (3) addition and subtraction.

2. Expressions are evaluated from left to right.

3. Operations within parentheses are performed before those outside parentheses according to the order priority in rule 1.

4. With multiple parentheses, the order of evaluation starts with the innermost parentheses and proceeds outward.

Commas in a PRINT statement will typically generate output spacing in five fields. The first four fields contain 14 character spaces each; the fifth field includes the remaining 24 spaces. A comma at the end of a PRINT statement will not advance the output to the next line if space is available on the current line. The next PRINT statement will use any available space and then continue to a new line if it is needed.

Semicolons in a PRINT statement leave

1. One blank space if placed after a numeric.

2. No blank spaces if placed after a quoted item and before another quoted item or a numeric.

Remarks in the form of REM statements provide comments and descriptions (documentation) about a program. They can be placed anywhere in the program. They do not generate output.

---

*Although the LOCATE command will accept a row designation of 25, the worksheet shows only 24 rows. The 25th row is reserved for the function key definitions. This row can be erased from the screen with the KEY OFF command (see Appendix A).

On computers that are connected to a printer, the LPRINT statement must be used in a program to produce printed output. This statement performs all the functions of the PRINT statement but results go to the printer, not the screen.

Output formatting can be controlled with the TAB and SPC functions to change print field size. Using the CLS statement clears the display screen. LOCATE statements can position output on the screen using row and column coordinates. A screen display layout form can help you plan your output.

## BASIC VOCABULARY SUMMARY

| Statement | Purpose | Example |
|---|---|---|
| CLS | Clears screen | 10 CLS |
| END | Last statement of a program | 290 END |
| LOC (Alt + L key) | Positions output at screen coordinates | 60 LOCATE 3,5 |
| LPRINT | Sends output to a printer | 30 LPRINT ''SALES REPORT'' |
| PRINT (Alt + P key or ?) | Prints literals and values | 25 PRINT ''# Units''; 3542 |
| REM or ' | Provides remarks in a program | 40 REM Payroll Program |
| SPC | Provides blank spaces in output | 30 PRINT SPC(10);''$500'' |
| TAB | Specifies exact print position of output on a line | 90 PRINT TAB(20);''Feb.'' |

| Command | Purpose |
|---|---|
| AUTO (Alt + A key) | Automatically numbers lines as program is entered. |
| CLS | Clears screen |
| DELETE (Alt + D key) | Erases lines in a program |
| LIST (Function key F1) | Displays a listing of program lines |
| LLIST | Sends to printer a hard copy listing of program lines |
| LOAD (Function key F3) | Loads a program into memory (LOAD''progname'') |
| NEW | Erases current program from memory |
| RENUM | Renumbers lines of the entire program |
| RUN (Function key F2) | Executes the current program in memory |
| SAVE (Function key F4) | Saves the program in memory (SAVE''progname'') |

## Review Questions

♦ **2.1** For the information listed, write a PRINT statement in BASIC that generates one line of output.
   a. Earnings for 3rd quarter
   b. In field two, Division; in field four, Sales
   c. A heading with each of the following items in a separate field: name, social security number, date of birth, number of dependents.

**2.2** In each case write a single PRINT statement that generates one line of output.
   a. "NAME" in the second field, "HOURS" in the third field, and "RATE" in the fifth field.
   b. The three months "JAN.", "FEB.", and "MARCH" tabbed in column positions 15, 25, and 35 respectively.
   c. The column headings "Division 1", "Division 2", and "Division 3", with 10 spaces between them, beginning in column position 15.
   d. The same headings from question c, placed alone on the screen in line 10, starting in column position 5.

**2.3** The following PRINT statements contain errors; correct them.
   a. 10 PRINT FINANCIAL REPORT
   b. 20 "PRINT INVENTORY LEVEL"
   c. 30 "JANUARY"
   d. "40 PRINT CURRENT ASSETS"
   e. PRINT "HELP"
   f. PRINT 279, UNITS
   g. 50 PRINT 10 + 62.5 =
   h. 60 PRINT 20(485,000)

♦ **2.4** Convert these values from E notation:
   a. $528E-5$
   b. $.0153E-5$
   c. $4.68E6$
   d. $3.41791E-2$
   e. $7531E7$
   f. $-1.23658E-2$

**2.5** Which of the following constants are acceptable in BASIC?
   a. $-.00567$
   b. $+8.1302$
   c. $1,281.3$
   d. $2.61-E3$
   e. $161.00$
   f. $+\$28.56$
   g. $\$+28.56$
   h. $-459176$

**2.6** Write the following expressions using BASIC notations:
   a. $\frac{1}{2} bh$
   b. $b^2 - 4ac$
   c. $P(r + 1)^n$
   d. $t^{2n+2}$
   e. $6XY$
   f. $X^2 + 2XY + Y^2$
   g. $g - n + K$
   h. $.80^5$
   i. $-0.2X^3 + 10X$
   j. $.35X \div 200$

♦ **2.7**  Rewrite each of the following expressions in BASIC symbols and notation. Solve the expressions manually for the values $a = 5$, $b = 3$, $c = 4$, $d = 2$.

a. $\dfrac{b - 2}{d + a}$

b. $c^2 - \dfrac{b}{2 + a}$

c. $\dfrac{b}{3}ac$

d. $a(b + 1)^d$

e. $\dfrac{2a}{b + d} - \dfrac{a - b}{d^2}$

f. $5^d - \dfrac{a}{-b + c}$

g. $-abc^d$

h. $\dfrac{(-abc)^d}{5^d}$

**2.8**  What will the following programs print if all of the parentheses are removed from the computational PRINT statements?

a. Program 2.7

```
2 PRINT (5+10)*.05
10 END

RUN
 .75
```

b. Program 2.8

```
10 PRINT "TOTAL","TAX"
20 PRINT "SALES","TOTAL"
40 PRINT (5+10),(5+10)*.05
50 END

RUN
TOTAL          TAX
SALES          TOTAL
 15             .75
```

c. Program 2.9

```
10 PRINT "TOTAL","TAX"
20 PRINT "SALES","TOTAL","GRAND TOTAL"
30 PRINT "--------------------------------------"
40 PRINT (5+10),(5+10)*.05,(5+10)+(5+10)*.05
50 END

RUN
TOTAL          TAX
SALES          TOTAL          GRAND TOTAL
--------------------------------------
 15             .75            15.75
```

d. Program 2.10

```
20 PRINT "TOTAL SALES"
40 PRINT "------------------"
60 PRINT
80 PRINT (5+10+20)
90 END

RUN
TOTAL SALES
------------------
 35
```

---

Programming Activities

♦ **2.9** **Purpose** To use PRINT and simple output formatting.

**Problem** Write and run a program that will show your name, address, and course number.

**Output** Your output should have this format:
Name-
Address- as many lines as needed
Course-

**2.10** **Purpose** To use PRINT, computational PRINT, and simple output formatting.

**Problem** Use the digits in your social security number as data. Write and run a program that will
a. print out the number
b. sum up the digits of the number
c. calculate the average of all the digits
d. show the sum of all the digits squared

**Data** Your social security number.

**Output** Your output should have this format:

```
S.S. # IS 111-22-3456
SUM IS          25
AVERAGE IS      2.777778
SUM SQUARED IS 625
```

**2.11** **Purpose** To use computational PRINT and simple output formatting.

**Problem** Write and run a program to calculate the total of a sale where:

Total = sales price + sales price × tax rate

**Data** Sales are $5, $10, and $15. The tax rate is 5 percent.

**Output** Your output should have this format:

```
SALES           TAX             TOTAL
--------------------------------------
5               .25             5.25
10              .5              10.5
15              .75             15.75
```

♦ **2.12** **Purpose** To use computational PRINT, simple output formatting, commas, and semicolons.

**Problem** Redo exercise 2.11 with dollar signs ($) in the output.

**Output** Your output should have this format:

```
SALES           TAX             TOTAL
--------------------------------------
$ 5             $ .25           $ 5.25
$ 10            $ .5            $ 10.5
$ 15            $ .75           $ 15.75
```

**2.13** **Purpose** To use computational PRINT, simple output formatting, commas, and semicolons.

**Problem** Redo exercise 2.11 with the output below.

**Output** Your output should have this format:

```
SALES   $ 5       $ 10      $ 15
TAX     $ .25     $ .5      $ .75
------------------------------
TOTAL   $ 5.25    $ 10.5    $ 15.75
```

**2.14** **Purpose** To use computational PRINT and simple output formatting.

**Problem** Write and run a program to calculate the area of a triangle by using the expression $1/2bh$, where $b$ is the base dimension and $h$ is the height of the triangle.

**Data**

| TRIANGLE | BASE | HEIGHT |
|---|---|---|
| 1 | 5 | 7 |
| 2 | 10.5 | 6.2 |
| 3 | 100 | 78 |

**Output** Your output should have this format:

```
BASE        HEIGHT        AREA
 5            7           17.5
10.5         6.2          32.55
100          78           3900
```

**2.15** **Purpose** To use computational PRINT and simple output formatting.

**Problem** Write and run a program to find the two roots of an equation, $aX^2 + bX + c$, using the quadratic formula:

$$X = \frac{-b \pm (b^2 - 4ac)^{1/2}}{2a}$$

**Data** $a = 2$, $b = 5$, and $c = 3$.

**Output** Output should consist of two lines, each with one answer.

**2.16** **Purpose** To use computational PRINT and simple output formatting.

**Problem** Redo exercise 2.15 so that the output shows all values $a$, $b$, $c$, and $X$ with labels.

**Output** Your output should have this format:

```
A= 2              B= 5              C= 3
FIRST ROOT        SECOND ROOT
-1                -1.5
```

**◆ 2.17** **Purpose** To use computational PRINT and simple output formatting.

**Problem** Write and run a program to evaluate each of the following expressions:

a. $a + \dfrac{b}{c}$

b. $\dfrac{a + b}{c}$

c. $\dfrac{(a + b)^2}{c}$

d. $a^2 + \dfrac{b}{c}$

**Data**   $a = 3, b = 6, c = 3$.

**Output**   Output should consist of four lines, each with one answer.

**2.18**   **Purpose**   To use computational PRINT and simple output formatting.

**Problem**   Redo exercise 2.17 so that the output shows each of the expressions that were evaluated, the values used, and the final answer.

**Output**   Your output should have this format:

```
A= 3                   B= 6                   C= 3
A+B/C= 5
(A+B)/C= 3
(A+B)^2/C= 27
A^2+B/C= 11
```

**2.19**   **Purpose**   To use the PRINT for simple word processing.

**Problem**   Many marketing promotions consist of computerized letters sent through the mail. Write a program that generates the following letter:

Today's Date

Dear Student:

    Stop by the computer lab for a demonstration of the computer equipment being used. Before coming, please read the chapters in the text that I have assigned. I'm looking forward to seeing you in the lab.

_____

Your Instructor

**Data**   Use today's date and your instructor's name.

**Output**   Your output should as appear shown in the problem description.

**◆ 2.20**   **Purpose**   To use computational PRINT, LPRINT, simple output formatting, and REM.

**Problem**   Write and run a program to calculate the area of a triangle by using the expression $1/2bh$, where $b$ is the base dimension and $h$ is the height of the triangle. Include REM statements in the program describing the problem and the program.

**Data**

| TRIANGLE | BASE | HEIGHT |
|---|---|---|
| 1 | 5 | 7 |
| 2 | 10.5 | 6.2 |
| 3 | 100 | 78 |

**Output**   Your output should be both display and hard copy with this format:

```
BASE        HEIGHT        AREA
 5           7             17.5
 10.5        6.2           32.55
 100         78            3900
```

**2.21**   **Purpose**   To use computational PRINT, LPRINT, and output formatting with SPC and TAB functions.

**Problem** In accounting, one measure of a company's financial condition is the current ratio. This ratio is computed as current assets divided by current liabilities. Following are several years' data for the GIGO Computer Company, Inc. Write and run a program to find the current ratio.

**Data**

|                     | 1989   | 1990   | 1991   |
|---------------------|--------|--------|--------|
| Current Assets      | $3700  | $4000  | $4500  |
| Current Liabilities | $1600  | $1000  | $1500  |

**Output** Your output should display on the screen and also generate a hard copy. Output should follow this format:

```
                         1989      1990      1991
                        ------    ------    ------
CURRENT ASSETS          $ 3700    $ 4000    $ 4500
CURRENT LIABILITIES     $ 1600    $ 1000    $ 1500
CURRENT RATIO           2.3125    4         3
```

**2.22** **Purpose** To use computational PRINT, LPRINT, and output formatting with SPC.

**Problem** Redo exercise 2.21 so that the output follows the format below.

**Output** Your output should display on the screen and also generate a hard copy. Output should follow this format:

```
                             CURRENT
             ----------------------------------------
             ASSETS         LIABILITIES          RATIO
             ----------------------------------------
     1989    $ 3700         $ 1600              2.3125
     1990    $ 4000         $ 1000              4
     1991    $ 4500         $ 1500              3
```

**2.23** **Purpose** To do complex problem solving with computational PRINT, LPRINT, and output formatting with the SPC function.

**Problem** A firm estimates that 5 years from now it will need $2 million to purchase some new equipment. To accumulate this sum, the firm decides to set aside an amount each year. The firm can earn 9 percent compounded annually on its cash. To find the amount that must be deposited at the end of each of the 5 years to accumulate the $2 million, use the following formula:

$$A = F\left[\frac{r}{(1 + r)^n - 1}\right]$$

where $A$ is the amount to be deposited at the end of $n$ years, with the annual interest rate of $r$, and $F$ is the future sum needed. Write a program that will find $A$. Include REM statements in your program.

**Data** Use the data values provided in the problem statement.

**Output** Your output should display on the screen and also generate a hard copy. Output should follow this format:

```
AMOUNT        FUTURE SUM     INTEREST RATE      YEARS
----------------------------------------------------
$ 334184.7   $ 2000000          9%               5
```

**2.24** **Purpose** To do complex problem solving with computational PRINT and format with SPC.

**Problem** A present value problem asks this question: What amount could be invested at 15 percent compounded annually that will grow to $300,000 or more at the end of five years? Write and run a program that will find the present value $P$. To find the answer, use this formula:

$$P = \frac{F}{(1 + r)^n}$$

where $P$ is the present value, $F$ is the future amount needed, $r$ is the annual rate of interest (a decimal), and $n$ is the length of the period.

**Data** Use the data values provided in the problem statement.

**Output** Your output should display on the screen. The heading is preceded by 15 blank spaces, and each output line that follows is preceded by 10 blank spaces. Output should follow this format:

```
              PRESENT VALUE ANALYSIS
         ----------------------------------
         FUTURE AMOUNT NEEDED IS $300,000
         INTEREST RATE IS 15%
         PERIOD- 5 YEARS
         THE PRESENT VALUE IS $ 149153
```

**2.25** **Purpose** To use PRINT, CLS, and LOCATE for screen formatting.

**Problem** Write and run a program that will display the information provided on this display layout form:

**Output**  Your output should display on the screen the items on the layout form in the positions indicated.

**2.26**  **Purpose**  To do complex problem solving with computational PRINT and output formatting with LOCATE.

**Problem**  Redo exercise 2.23 with the output specifications given below.

**Data**  Use the data values provided in exercise 2.23.

**Output**  Your output should display on the screen starting in row 15, column 10. The output has this format:

```
AMOUNT          FUTURE SUM    INTEREST RATE    YEARS
----------------------------------------------------
$ 334184.7    $2000000            9%             5
```

# CHAPTER 3

# DATA ENTRY:
# *READ/DATA*

Upon completing this chapter, you will be able to do the following:

* Explain the difference between numeric and nonnumeric variable names and data types.
* Understand how data can be assigned to variables using the READ statement.
* Solve programming problems by using a simple sequence logic structure of READ/DATA, PRINT, and END.
* See how it is possible to reread data with the RESTORE statement.
* Recognize the difference between single and double precision.

Chapter 2 showed how we can use the PRINT statement to generate specific output based on numeric data that is placed in PRINT statements. Only limited amounts of data can be placed into a program using the PRINT statement, however. To enter larger amounts of data into a program we can use the READ/DATA statements. In this chapter we will see how numerical data can be entered into a BASIC program and assigned to variables by means of the READ/DATA statements.

## BASIC VARIABLES

A *variable* represents a value that is not fixed. In the compound interest formula $A = P(1 + r)^n$, where $P$ is the principal or starting amount, $r$ is the interest rate, $n$ is the number of time periods, and $A$ is the final result, the components $P$, $r$, and $n$ represent factors that can change and thus are variables. For compound interest we may want to find the value of $A$ for numerous sets of variables $P$, $r$, and $n$. For example,

| $P$ | $r$ | $n$ |
|------|-----|---------|
| $1000 | 5% | 5 years |
| 2000 | 6 | 10 |
| 4000 | 8 | 12 |

In the BASIC that can be processed on any computer, including microcomputers, any single alphabetic letter from A to Z, or any alphabetic letter followed by a numeric value from 0 (zero) to 9, may be used to specify a numeric variable. This gives a total of 286 possibilities for variable names: 26 single letters, plus 10 times 26 combinations of A0 to A9, . . . , Z0 to Z9. Some examples of acceptable variable names are

| | | | | |
|-----|-----|-----|-----|-----|
| *A* | *B* | *X* | *Z*3 | *B*2 |
| *C*9 | *F*1 | *D*5 | *X*7 | *M*8 |

Some examples of unacceptable variable names are

| | |
|-----|-----|
| 5*X* | The alphabetic character must be first. |
| *B* − | The alphabetic must stand alone or be followed by a numeric. |

With the BASIC on many microcomputers it is also possible to have a numeric variable name of two-letter sequences, such as *AA*, *BB*, *SU*, *NT*, . . . , *ZZ*, and so on.

In Microsoft BASIC, variable names may be any length; however, only the first 40 characters are significant. The characters allowed in a variable name are letters, numbers, and the decimal point. The first character, however, must always be a letter.

Thus, for example, a variable name made up of 40 letter *A*s is a valid variable and is different from a variable made up of 39 *A*s followed by a letter *B*. A variable name made up of 41 letter *A*s is also valid but is not distinguishable from a variable made up of 40 *A*s followed by a *B*. Some versions of Microsoft BASIC do not allow variables longer than 40 characters. In any case, it is unlikely that you will ever need such large variable names to write any of the programs in this book.

The following are some examples of valid variable names in Microsoft BASIC:

| | |
|---|---|
| SALES | THE.SUM.OF.25.SALES |
| SUMOFSALES | JOE |
| SUM.OF.SALES | A22 |

The following are not valid variable names:

| | |
|---|---|
| 50ITEMS | The first character must be a letter. |
| TOTAL.OF.1,000 | A comma is not a valid character. |

Another restriction on variable names is that they cannot be a keyword, although a keyword may be imbedded in the variable name. Therefore, REM is not a valid variable name but REMBRANDT is.

Certain special characters may appear at the end of the variable name to signify what may be stored in the variable. These special characters and their meanings are listed in Table 3.1.

A disadvantage of using double precision variables is that they require twice as much computer memory storage as single precision numbers and four times as much storage as integers. Also, computations in double precision take longer.

**TABLE 3.1**  Types of Variable Names

| SYMBOL | EXAMPLE | MEANING |
|---|---|---|
| $ | NAME$ | String—Can store any string of characters, e.g., NAME$ = ''JOHN DOE'' |
| % | NUMBER% | Integer—Can contain only integer values in the range of $-32,768$ to $+32,767$ |
| ! or no symbol | SMALL! or SUM | Single precision—Can contain any number with a precision of 7 digits |
| # | GNP87# | Double precision—Can contain numbers with a precision of 16 digits |

## THE *READ* AND *DATA* STATEMENTS

The general forms for the READ and DATA statements follow:

line # READ variable name list
line # DATA data list

Each variable name except the last in the READ statement is followed by a comma. No punctuation is required at the end of the READ statement. The items in the DATA statement are also separated by commas. Like the READ statement, the DATA statement requires no ending punctuation.

Program 3.1 illustrates the READ/DATA statements. The READ A, B in line 10 will cause the values in line 15 to be assigned to the variables $A$ and $B$, respectively. Variable $A$ will take on the value 5, and variable $B$ will take on the value 10.

## PROGRAM 3.1   READ/DATA Statements

```
5 REM THIS PROGRAM ADDS TWO NUMBERS
10 READ A,B
15 DATA 5,10
40 PRINT "A=";A;"B=";B;"SUM=";A+B
99 END

RUN
A= 5 B= 10 SUM= 15
```

If we're interested in finding the sum of another set of numbers, say 7 and 12, we could simply replace line 15 with 15 DATA 7, 12 and then run the program to produce a new result.

The variable names and items in READ/DATA statements have to be matched on a sequential one-for-one basis. Thus if we have three values, we could write three variable names:

10 READ X, Y, Z
20 DATA 10, −6, 5.2

$X$ is set equal to 10, $Y$ is set equal to −6, and $Z$ is set equal to 5.2. If there were additional data in line 20, say

20 DATA 10, −6, 5.2, 16, 38

the values 16 and 38 would not be read, since only three variables are specified in line 10. If the data were

20 DATA 10, −6

the program execution would terminate because the data set has only two items but the READ statement requests values for three variables. An "Out of data in 10" message would appear as output. Programs 3.2 and 3.3 illustrate what happens when the program has excess or insufficient data.

## PROGRAM 3.2   Excess Data

```
5 PRINT "X","Y","Z"
10 READ X,Y,Z
15 DATA 10,-6,5.2,16,38
20 PRINT X,Y,Z
99 END

RUN
X               Y               Z
   10             -6              5.2
```

## PROGRAM 3.3  Insufficient Data

```
5 PRINT "X","Y","Z"
10 READ X,Y,Z
15 DATA 10,-6
20 PRINT X,Y,Z
99 END


RUN
X               Y               Z
OUT OF DATA IN 10
```

Program 3.4 shows various READ/DATA statement arrangements. Note that because the computer matches variables and data on a sequential one-for-one basis, breaking up the READ or DATA statements does not change the output.

## PROGRAM 3.4  READ/DATA Statement Arrangements

```
(a) 10 READ A,B,C         (c)  5 READ A
    15 DATA 5                 10 READ B
    16 DATA -7                20 READ C
    18 DATA 9                 30 DATA 5,-7,9
    20 PRINT A,B,C            35 PRINT A,B,C
    40 END                    40 END

    RUN                       RUN
      5    -7     9             5    -7     9

(b) 10 READ A             (d) 10 READ A,B,C
    15 DATA 5, -7             20 DATA 5,-7
    20 READ B,C              30 DATA 9
    25 DATA 9                 35 PRINT A,B,C
    30 PRINT A,B,C           40 END
    40 END
                              RUN
    RUN                         5    -7     9
      5    -7     9
```

As shown in Program 3.4, the DATA statement can be placed either before or after the READ statement, as long as it is before the END statement. This point is made in Program 3.5. The output for Programs 3.5a–d is the same, regardless of where the DATA statement is located. If the data list is to be changed, it is easier to have the data in statements just before the END statement (Program 3.5c). This is the most common approach. If you want to keep track of your data, place it immediately following the corresponding READ (Program 3.5b).

## PROGRAM 3.5    Positions of the DATA Statement

```
(a) 5 REM DATA BEFORE READ
    10 DATA 15,6,7
    20 READ A,A1,A2
    30 PRINT A,A1,A2
    40 END

    RUN
     15            6            7
```

```
(b) 5 REM DATA IMMEDIATELY AFTER READ
    20 READ A,A1,A2
    25 DATA 15,6,7
    30 PRINT A,A1,A2
    40 END

    RUN
     15            6            7
```

```
(c) 5 REM DATA JUST BEFORE THE END
    20 READ A,A1,A2
    30 PRINT A,A1,A2
    35 DATA 15,6,7
    40 END

    RUN
     15            6            7
```

```
(d) 5 REM DATA BEFORE AND AFTER READ
    10 DATA 15
    15 READ A,A1,A2
    20 DATA 6
    30 PRINT A,A1,A2
    35 DATA 7
    40 END

    RUN
     15            6            7
```

Printing a variable *before* a value has been assigned to it can, on some systems, result in an error message such as "Undefined variable in line #." In Microsoft BASIC, undefined variables are assigned a value of zero. Program 3.6 illustrates the printing of an undefined variable, $A$, in line 10. Line 20 causes the value assigned to $A$ by line 15 to be correctly printed out as 381.

PROGRAM 3.6   Printing an Undefined Variable

```
 5 DATA 381
10 PRINT A
15 READ A
20 PRINT A
40 END

RUN
 0
 381
```

Since the computer retains only the current value of a variable, a PRINT statement containing a variable will result in output of the current value only. Program 3.7 illustrates this point. Line 10 of the program reads variable $A$ twice, first assigning $A = 7$ and then $A = 3$. When line 20 (the PRINT statement) is executed, the value of $A$ that is printed out is 3, as shown by the output.

PROGRAM 3.7   Printing the Current Value

```
10 READ A,B,C,A
20 PRINT A;B;C;A
30 DATA 7,9,6,3
40 END

RUN
 3   9   6   3
```

In the previous chapter, numerical data in E notation was introduced. Data in E format can be assigned to variables in the same way as ordinary data values. Program 3.8 illustrates this point. Line 10 of the program reads values that are in E notation from the data list in line 20. Line 30 will print out the value in E format if it exceeds six character spaces; otherwise the output result is an ordinary numerical value.

PROGRAM 3.8   Data in E Notation

```
10 READ A,B,C,D
20 DATA 1E5, 4.56E-2, 2.5E8, .65E4
30 PRINT A,B,C,D
40 END

RUN
 100000        .0456        2.5E8        6500
```

The logic structure of the preceding programs, as well as the remaining programs in this chapter, follows the simple sequence described in Chapter 1. Recall that this sequence proceeds from one line to the next in the program without a branch or transfer in direction. The simple sequence logic structure is illustrated in Chapter 2 (Figure 2.1).

The use of the READ/DATA statements in a programming application is shown in Program 3.9. This program is based on Case 3.1.

## CASE 3.1

**Problem**

**Calculation of Total Profit**
Create a program that will calculate total profit.

**Data Input**

The data values needed are the number of units sold (225), the cost per unit ($6.50), and the selling price ($10).

**Process/Formulas**

Total profits ($T$) is found by subtracting total cost from total revenue. Total revenue is found by multiplying revenue per unit ($P$) times the number of units sold ($U$); and total cost is obtained by multiplying the cost of each unit sold ($C$) times the number of units sold. This formula is represented symbolically as $T = P \times U - C \times U$.

**Output**

The output display should have the form of a report, as shown here:

```
          TOTAL PROFIT REPORT

NUMBER OF UNITS SOLD 225
PRICE PER UNIT 10              COST PER UNIT 6.5
TOTAL REVENUE 2250
LESS TOTAL COST 1462.5
------------------------------------------------
TOTAL PROFIT 787.5
```

Program 3.9 obtains the total revenue, total cost, and total profit based on the data supplied in Case 3.1.

---

**PROGRAM 3.9    Case 3.1, Finding Total Profit, READ/DATA Statements**

```
5 REM CASE 3.1, FINDING TOTAL PROFITS
6 REM PROGRAMMER- (name of person) DATE - mm/dd/yy
7 REM       TOTAL PROFITS = TOTAL REVENUE - TOTAL COST
9 REM       VARIABLE LIST - P, C, U
10 REM            P=PRICE PER UNIT, C=COST PER UNIT,
15 REM            U=# UNITS SOLD AND BOUGHT
16 REM -------------------------------------------------
30 READ P, C, U
40 DATA 10, 6.50, 225
```

```
65 PRINT
68 PRINT
70 PRINT TAB(10); "TOTAL PROFIT REPORT"
75 PRINT
80 PRINT "NUMBER OF UNITS SOLD";U
85 PRINT "PRICE PER UNIT";P,"COST PER UNIT";C
90 PRINT "TOTAL REVENUE";P*U
92 PRINT "LESS TOTAL COST";C*U
95 PRINT "-------------------------------------------"
100 PRINT "TOTAL PROFIT";P*U-C*U
199 END

RUN
          TOTAL PROFIT REPORT

NUMBER OF UNITS SOLD 225
PRICE PER UNIT 10               COST PER UNIT 6.5
TOTAL REVENUE 2250
LESS TOTAL COST 1462.5
------------------------------------------------
TOTAL PROFIT 787.5
```

Program 3.9 demonstrates one advantage of using READ/DATA statements. Specifically, when the program is generalized so that it can be used over and over again—with different sets of data each time—only the data lines have to be changed. If computational PRINT statements were used instead of the READ/DATA statements, it would be impractical as well as troublesome to change the program for each new set of data.

## THE *RESTORE* STATEMENT

It is sometimes necessary to reread data previously read in a program. Data once read cannot be read again unless the DATA lines are repeated or a RESTORE statement is used. The RESTORE statement has the form

line # RESTORE

This statement causes the data initially read from storage to be replaced in storage. Program 3.10 shows a simple program using RESTORE. The data was initially read in and corresponds to the variables *A*, *B*, and *C*. The RESTORE in line 20 restores the data beginning with the first data value in the first data statement, line 10. A partial RESTORE from a point in the data list *after* the first data value is not possible on most computers. Line 25 causes the data 1, 2, 3 to be assigned to the variables *X*, *Y*, and *Z*, respectively.

## PROGRAM 3.10   RESTORE Statement

```
1 PRINT "A","B","C"
5 READ A,B,C
10 DATA 1
12 DATA 2,3
```

```
15 PRINT A,B,C
16 PRINT
20 RESTORE
22 PRINT "X","Y","Z"
25 READ X,Y,Z
30 PRINT X,Y,Z
99 END

RUN
A         B         C
  1         2         3

X         Y         Z
  1         2         3
```

If the RESTORE statement were not inserted at line 20, the READ statement at line 25 could not be executed because no data would be available to read.

In the case that follows, RESTORE is used to assign a single set of data to a variable list other than the one initially read.

- - - - - - - - - - - - - - - - - - - - - - - - - - - - - - - - - - - - - - - -

## CASE 3.2

**Problem**

**Comparing Linear Equations**

A linear equation in two variables is a straight line when plotted on graph paper. Linear equations have wide business application in areas such as price theory, break-even analysis, and linear programming. Write a program comparing different forms of linear equations.

**Data Input**

In the formulas below, use the data values of 30, 100, and 20 for the variable $x$, the constant term, and the slope, respectively. Only a single DATA statement is needed; make use of RESTORE to reread the data as necessary.

**Process/Formulas**

Symbolically, linear equations are presented in two general forms:

**1.** $y = a + bx$     where $b$ is the slope, $a$ is a constant, and $x$ is a variable
**2.** $y = mx + b$     where $m$ is the slope, $b$ is a constant, and $x$ is a variable

To show that both forms would produce the same answer for $y$, we substitute the given data into each equation.

**Output**

The output display should show both equations indented 10 spaces from the left margin. Each equation should be on a separate line with a blank line between them.

- - - - - - - - - - - - - - - - - - - - - - - - - - - - - - - - - - - - - - - -

Program 3.11 computes the value of $y$ for both forms of the linear equation in Case 3.2. Note that the first READ, in line 25, assigns 100 to $A$, 20 to $B$, and 30 to $X$. The RESTORE in line 40 makes the data list in line 27 available for the next READ. Line 50 reads only the constant value ($B = 100$) and the slope ($M = 20$). The value for $X$ does not have to be assigned again, since there is to be no change to this variable.

## PROGRAM 3.11    Case 3.2, Linear Equations

```
10 REM CASE 3.2, LINEAR EQUATION FORMS
12 REM PROGRAMMER- (name of person)    DATE - mm/dd/yy
14 REM VARIABLE LIST-  A,B,X,M
16 REM A=CONSTANT
17 REM B=SLOPE FIRST, THEN CONSTANT
18 REM X=VARIABLE
19 REM M=SLOPE
20 REM -------------------------------------------
25 READ A,B,X
26 PRINT
27 DATA 100,20,30
30 PRINT TAB(10); "Y = A + B*X =";A+B*X
40 RESTORE
50 READ B,M
55 PRINT
60 PRINT TAB(10); "Y = M*X + B =";M*X+B
90 END

RUN
          Y = A + B*X = 700

          Y = M*X + B = 700
```

## VARIABLE TYPES

The programs presented so far that include READ/DATA assignments have all used single precision numeric data variables. At the beginning of this chapter, Table 3.1 described several other variable types: string, integer, and double precision. These variable types are illustrated in the programs that follow.

Program 3.12 illustrates the four different types of variables. Each variable type is assigned the same data value, 1.23456789. Note that variable A! (or simply A) loses some precision (1.234568 instead of 1.23456789) and that variable A% drops everything to the right of the decimal point, leaving just a 1. The double precision variable A# reproduces the data value as is. A$, the string variable, also reproduces the data value, but no arithmetic operations can be performed with it since it is a nonnumeric string variable. Once a data item is assigned to a string, it cannot be treated as a numeric in computations.

## PROGRAM 3.12    Different Variable Types

```
4 REM A! = SINGLE PRECISION NUMERIC VARIABLE, A# = DOUBLE PRECISION VARIABLE
6 REM A% = INTEGER VARIABLE, A$ = STRING VARIABLE
10 READ A!, A#, A%, A$
20 DATA 1.23456789, 1.23456789, 1.23456789, 1.23456789
30 PRINT "ORIGINAL DATA VALUE - 1.23456789"
40 PRINT "SINGLE PREC.", "DOUBLE PREC.", "INTEGER", "STRING"
50 PRINT A!, A#, A%, A$
60 END
```

```
RUN
ORIGINAL DATA VALUE - 1.23456789
 SINGLE PREC.  DOUBLE PREC.  INTEGER    STRING
  1.234568     1.23456789       1      1.23456789
```

String and literal nonnumeric data items can be assigned to variables in the same way as for numeric data items. Numeric data is stored in the computer because it is assigned to numeric variables, and, nonnumeric data is stored because it is assigned to string variables. When you use string variables in READ statements, the nonnumeric data items in the DATA statement are assigned on a sequential one-for-one basis, as shown in Program 3.13.

## PROGRAM 3.13    String Variables

```
5 REM ASSIGNMENT OF STRING DATA WITH READ
10 READ NME$, ADD$, CITY$
20 DATA SANDY SMITH, 101 TULIP LANE, SOMEPLACE 90099
30 PRINT NME$
40 PRINT ADD$
50 PRINT CITY$
60 END

RUN
SANDY SMITH
101 TULIP LANE
SOMEPLACE 90099
```

As with numeric data, excess string data in a DATA statement beyond the READ variable list will be ignored. The number of data items must agree with the number of string variables in the READ statement. If there are too few data items for the READ variable list, an error message—"Out of data in line #"—will be displayed.

Program 3.14 further illustrates how strings of characters are read into string variables and stored in the computer. Line 30 of this program shows that both string and numeric variables can be placed together in a single READ statement. It is essential that the data items in the DATA statement appear in the same sequence as the variable types in the READ statement.

## PROGRAM 3.14    String and Numeric Variables

```
10 REM N$ = NAME, S$ = SOC. SECURITY NUMBER
20 REM H = NUMBER HOURS WORKED, R = RATE PER HOUR
30 READ N$, S$, H, R
40 DATA SHELDON HERTZ, 123-45-6789, 40, 6.75
50 PRINT N$, S$, H, R, H*R
60 END

RUN
SHELDON HERTZ 123-45-6789      40            6.75           270
```

The values of the string variables in the DATA statement must be enclosed in quotation marks if there is an embedded comma in the string of characters. For example, if the name is to be written as ''HERTZ,SHELDON'', the DATA statement would have to be written as in Program 3.15. If there were no quotes around the name, the computer would say ''Syntax error in 40'', because variable N$ would be set equal to ''HERTZ'', variable S$ would be set equal to ''SHELDON'', and the string of characters ''123–45–6789'' could not be set equal to a numeric variable $H$.

## PROGRAM 3.15    String Data in Quotes

```
10 REM N$ = NAME, S$ = SOC. SECURITY NUMBER
20 REM H = NUMBER HOURS WORKED, R = RATE PER HOUR
30 READ N$, S$, H, R
40 DATA "HERTZ,SHELDON", 123-45-6789, 40, 6.75
50 PRINT N$, S$, H, R, H*R
60 END

RUN
HERTZ,SHELDON 123-45-6789     40           6.75           270
```

The syntax error of trying to assign a nonnumeric data item to a numeric variable type is illustrated in Program 3.16. The displayed message directs your attention to the DATA line, indicating that there may be a mismatch between data item types and the variable types in the READ line. It is easy to see that the literal MARCH cannot be assigned to the numeric data variable NUM. To correct the error, either the items in the DATA statement or the variables in the READ statement must be switched. Until then, the program will not be able to complete the processing.

## PROGRAM 3.16    Data Mismatch—Syntax Error

```
10 REM SYNTAX ERROR - DATA MISMATCH
20 READ LIT$, NUM
30 DATA 889, MARCH
40 PRINT LIT$, NUM
50 END

RUN
Syntax error in 30
```

## SUMMARY

A variable can be used to store numeric or literal data. Variable names can be up to 40 characters in length and can be made up of letters, numeric digits, and the decimal point. The first character must always be a letter. A variable name can have as the last character a $, indicating that it can store string data; a %, indicating that it can store only integers;

a ! (or no symbol), indicating that it can store single precision data, or numbers with a precision of 7 digits; or a #, indicating that it can store double precision numbers, or numbers with a precision of 16 digits.

Values can be assigned to variables using the READ/DATA statements. Sufficient data must be entered to agree with the variable list in the READ. Too little data will result in an error message.

A RESTORE statement allows a program's DATA statements to be reread.

A READ/DATA, PRINT statement pattern in a program forms a simple sequence logic structure.

## BASIC VOCABULARY SUMMARY

| Statement | Purpose | Example |
|-----------|---------|---------|
| DATA | Stores the values of variables that are read by the READ statement. | 90 DATA 1.45,John,2.3E7 |
| READ | Assigns values to variables from data stored in a DATA statement. | 30 READ J,N$,Q# |
| RESTORE | Allows data stored in the DATA statement to be reread by a subsequent READ statement. | 50 RESTORE |

## EXERCISES

### Review Questions

**3.1** Which of the following are *unacceptable* BASIC numeric variables? Why?
a. X11     c. -M5     e. PI     g. K9     i. SUM3     k. 5UM!
b. I3     d. C.2     f. N     h. D+8     j. REM     l. TOTAL%

**3.2** Which of the following are *acceptable* BASIC string variables? Why?
a. A$1     c. NM$     e. END$     g. 5$     i. X%$
b. JAY9$     d. D3/5$     f. ITM$     h. $1,000     j. L.5.Y$

**3.3** Use appropriate variables and notation to write a BASIC expression that will give you net pay, which is gross pay less a deduction equal to 22 percent of gross pay.

♦ **3.4** In inventory analysis we attempt to find what is called the *economic order quantity*. This quantity can be calculated using the following formula:

$$\sqrt{\frac{2 \times \text{annual required units} \times \text{cost per order}}{\text{Cost per unit of item} \times \text{percent carrying cost}}}$$

Rewrite this expression with symbols and notation acceptable to BASIC. It is helpful to note that the square root of a number is equal to that number raised to the one-half power.

**3.5**  The Cobb-Douglas production function, often encountered in macroeconomics, has the form

Output $= A \times L^{\alpha} \times K^{1-\alpha}$

where $A$ is technical progress, $L$ is the employed labor force, $K$ is the stock of capital for production, $\alpha$ (alpha) is the fraction of total output earned by labor, and $1 - \alpha$ is the fraction of total output earned by capital. Write the function as an expression in BASIC. Remember that $\alpha$ is not an acceptable BASIC symbol.

♦ **3.6**  What output will result from the following program?

```
10 DATA 60,4,20
20 READ A, B, C
30 PRINT A + B + C/B
40 PRINT (A/B)*C + B
99 END
```

**3.7**  What will the following program (Program 3.7) print if
a. line 10 is changed to 10 READ A,B,C,A1
b. line 30 is changed to 30 DATA 7,9,6

```
10 READ A,B,C,A
20 PRINT A;B;C;A
30 DATA 7,9,6,3
40 END
```

**3.8**  What output will result from each of the following programs?

```
a. 5 READ A          b. 5 READ A,A         c. 5 READ G,E,O,R,G,E
   10 PRINT A;          10 PRINT A,A          10 DATA 1,2,3,4,5,6
   15 DATA -32          20 PRINT A;           20 PRINT G;E;O;R;G;E
   20 READ A            25 PRINT A            99 END
   25 PRINT A           30 DATA -32,7
   30 DATA 7            99 END
   99 END
```

**3.9**  What will the following program print when it is run?

```
10 READ A$, A, A%, A#
20 DATA 1.23, 1.23, 1.23, 1.23
30 PRINT A$, A, A%, A#
40 END
```

**3.10**  What will the following program print when it is run with each of the given data lines?

```
10 READ A$, A, A%, A#
20 DATA
30 PRINT A$, A, A%, A#
40 END
```

a.  20 DATA 1.23E1, 1.23E1, 1.23E1, 1.23E1
b.  20 DATA 27E-3, 27E-3, 27E-3, 27E-3

**3.11**    What would the following programs do if the RESTORE statements were omitted?

♦ a.  Program 3.10

```
1 PRINT "A","B","C"
5 READ A,B,C
10 DATA 1
12 DATA 2,3
15 PRINT A,B,C
16 PRINT
20 RESTORE
22 PRINT "X","Y","Z"
25 READ X,Y,Z
30 PRINT X,Y,Z
99 END
```

b.  Program 3.11

```
10 REM CASE 3.2, LINEAR EQUATION FORMS
12 REM PROGRAMMER- (name of person) DATE - mm/dd/yy
14 REM VARIABLE LIST- A,B,X,M
16 REM A=CONSTANT
17 REM B=SLOPE
18 REM X=VARIABLE
19 REM M=SLOPE
20 REM ------------------------------------------------
25 READ A,B,X
27 DATA 100,20,30
30 PRINT TAB(10); "Y = A + B*X =";A+B*X
40 RESTORE
50 READ B,M
60 PRINT TAB(10); "Y = M*X + B =";M*X+B
90 END
```

**3.12**    a. What will the output for the program below look like?

b. What will the program print if all of the RESTORE statements are removed?

```
10 READ A,B,C
20 DATA 2,4,6
30 PRINT (A + B)/C,
40 RESTORE
50 READ B,A,C
60 PRINT (A + B)/C,
70 RESTORE
80 READ C,A,B
90 PRINT (A + B)/C,
100 RESTORE
110 READ C,B,A
120 PRINT (A + B)/C,
130 RESTORE
140 READ A,C,B
150 PRINT (A + B)/C,
199 END
```

**3.13**    a. What will the following program print when it is run?

```
10 DATA 1,2
15 READ A,B,C
20 DATA 6,7,8,9
```

```
25 READ D,E
30 RESTORE
35 PRINT A,B,C,D,E
40 READ C,A,D
45 PRINT A,B,C,D,E
50 END
```

b. What will the above program print if the RESTORE statement is removed?
c. What will the above program print if only line 40 is removed?

## Programming Activities

● ● ● ● ● ●♦ **3.14**   **Purpose**  To use READ/DATA statements with numeric data, computational PRINT, and simple output formatting.

**Problem**  Write and run a program to calculate the total of a sale where:

Total = sales price + sales price × tax rate

**Data**  Sales are $5, $10, and $15. The tax rate is 5 percent.

**Output**  Your output should have this format:

```
SALES   TAX     TOTAL
  5       ,25     5,25
 10       ,5     10,5
 15       ,75    15,75
```

● ● ● ● ● ● **3.15**   **Purpose**  To use READ/DATA statements with numeric data, computational PRINT, and simple output formatting.

**Problem**  Write and run a program to calculate the area of three triangles where:

Area = 1/2 base × height

**Data**

| TRIANGLE | BASE | HEIGHT |
|----------|------|--------|
| 1 | 5 | 7 |
| 2 | 10.5 | 6.2 |
| 3 | 100 | 78 |

**Output**  Your output should have this format:

```
BASE    HEIGHT   AREA
  5       7       17,5
 10,5     6,2     32,55
100      78       3900
```

● ● ● ● ● ● **3.16**   **Purpose**  To use READ/DATA statements with numeric data, computational PRINT, and simple output formatting.

**Problem**  Write and run a program to find the two roots of an equation, $aX^2 + bX + c$, using the quadratic formula. That is,

$$X = \frac{-b \pm (b^2 - 4ac)^{1/2}}{2a}$$

**Data**   $a = 2, b = 5, c = 3$

**Output**    Output should consist of two lines, each with one answer.

```
FIRST ROOT  -1
SECOND ROOT -1.5
```

**3.17**    **Purpose**    To use READ/DATA statements with numeric data, computational PRINT, LPRINT, simple output formatting, and REM.

**Problem**    Below is a set of investments that are to be increased by the same three rates: 7 percent, 7½ percent, and 8¼ percent. Write a program that will increase this set of investments by these rates, using REM statements to describe both the problem and the program.

**Data**    One-year investments: $3,000; $10,000; $12,500; $17,000

**Output**    Your output should be both display and hard copy with this format:

```
INVESTMENT   7% INC.   7.5% INC.   8.25% INC.
  3000        3210       3225        3247.5
 10000       10700      10750       10825
 12500       13375      13437.5     13531.25
 17000       18190      18275       18402.5
```

**3.18**    **Purpose**    To use READ/DATA statements with numeric data, computational PRINT, LPRINT, and output formatting with SPC and TAB functions.

**Problem**    In accounting, one measure of a company's financial condition is the current ratio. This ratio is computed as current assets divided by current liabilities. Write and run a program to find the current ratio for the data below.

**Data**

|  | 1988 | 1989 | 1990 |
|---|---|---|---|
| Current assets | $370,000 | $400,000 | $450,000 |
| Current liabilities | 160,000 | 100,000 | 150,000 |

**Output**    Your output should display on the screen and also generate a hard copy. Output should follow this format:

```
                       1988      1989      1990
                     --------  --------  --------
CURRENT ASSETS       $370000   $400000   $450000
CURRENT LIABILITIES  $160000   $100000   $150000
CURRENT RATIO         2.3125   4         3
```

**3.19**    **Purpose**    To do complex problem solving using READ/DATA statements, numeric data, computational PRINT, and simple output formatting.

**Problem**    The Cobb-Douglas production function often encountered in macroeconomics has the form

Output $= A \times L^{\alpha} \times K^{1-\alpha}$

where $A$ is technical progress, $L$ is the employed labor force, $K$ is the stock of capital for production, $\alpha$(alpha) is the fraction of total output earned by labor, and $1 - \alpha$ is the fraction of total output earned by capital. If $A$ is 15, $L$ is 500, $K$ is 250, and $\alpha$ is .5, write a program that reads in this data and computes output. Remember that $\alpha$ is not an acceptable BASIC symbol.

**Data**  Use the data values provided in the problem statement.

**Output**  Output should follow this format:

```
TECH,PROG, LABOR CAPITAL ALPHA OUTPUT
 15          500   250    ,5    5303,299
```

**3.20**  **Purpose**  To use READ/DATA statements with numeric data, computational PRINT, and output formatting with SPC and TAB functions.

**Problem**  A balance sheet in accounting is divided into two parts. On the left are the assets and on the right are the liabilities and capital. Assets consist of current plus fixed assets. Suppose the XYZ Company has current assets of $45,000, fixed assets of $78,000, current liabilities of $32,000, and capital of $91,000. Write a program that reads in this data and prepares a balance sheet with a heading and labels for all the items mentioned, including totals for both parts.

**Data**  Use the data values provided in the problem statement.

**Output**  Your output should have this format:

```
              XYZ COMPANY BALANCE SHEET
        ASSETS                LIABILITIES AND CAPITAL
   CURRENT ASSETS 45000          LIABILITIES   32000
   FIXED ASSETS   78000          CAPITAL       91000
                  -----                        -----
   TOTAL ASSETS  123000          TOTAL LIAB,  123000
```

**3.21**  **Purpose**  To use the READ/DATA and RESTORE statements, numeric data, and simple output formatting.

**Problem**  Write a program having a single DATA statement:

100 DATA 2,4,6,8,10

Assign the following numbers to the designated variables:

| Variable: | A | B | C | D | E | F | G | X |
|---|---|---|---|---|---|---|---|---|
| Number: | 2 | 4 | 6 | 8 | 2 | 6 | 8 | 4 |

**Data**  The data is provided above in the problem description.

**Output**  Your output should have this format:

```
A B C D
2 4 6 8

E F G X
2 6 8 4
```

**3.22**  **Purpose**  To use READ/DATA statements with string and numeric data. To use the computational PRINT and simple output formatting.

**Problem**  Real estate brokers are often compensated on a straight commission basis. Their total earnings are computed this way:

$$\left( \begin{array}{c} \text{value of real} \\ \text{estate property sold} \end{array} \right) \times \left( \begin{array}{c} \text{commission} \\ \text{rate \%} \end{array} \right) = \left( \begin{array}{c} \text{commission} \\ \text{on sale} \end{array} \right)$$

Write and run a program that computes the commissions for the data given below, based on a 6 percent commission rate on all property sold.

**Data**

| PERSON | PROPERTY SOLD | PERSON | PROPERTY SOLD |
|--------|---------------|--------|---------------|
| A.Smith | $140,000 | J.Jenkins | $176,250 |
| | 162,500 | | 140,500 |
| | 147,500 | | 157,500 |

**Output**  Your output should have this format:

```
PERSON          PROP, SOLD        COMMISSION
A, Smith          140000            8400
                  162500            9750
                  147500            8850
J, Jenkins        176250           10575
                  140500            8430
                  157500            9450
```

. . . . . . **3.23**  **Purpose**  To use READ/DATA statements with string and numeric data. To use the computational PRINT and simple output formatting.

**Problem**  The United Computer Company pays its salespersons a monthly salary of $1000 plus 1½ percent commission for equipment sold during the month. The data below shows the sales figures by salesperson for last month. Write a program that will calculate the total salary (base salary of $1000 plus commission rate of .015).

**Data**

| SALESPERSON | AMOUNT SOLD |
|-------------|-------------|
| M. Worth | $13,600 |
| K. Gray | 22,000 |
| S. Legan | 9,800 |
| B. Hinz | 24,500 |

**Output**  Your output should have this format:

```
SALESPERSON      AMOUNT SOLD        SALARY
M, Worth           13600            1204
K, Gray            22000            1330
S, Legan            9800            1147
B, Hinz            24500            1367,5
```

. . . . . . **3.24**  **Purpose**  To use READ/DATA statements with string and numeric data. To use the computational PRINT and simple output formatting.

**Problem**  The ABC Company has four divisions selling various products. Management wants to know what percentage of total sales volume is generated by each division. Below are the gross sales figures by division for the past year. Write a program that reads in the sales data and generates a table as output. The table should (1) show the data listed below with total sales and with a third column headed ''% OF TOTAL'' and (2) show the percentage for each division (that is, division sales/total × 100).

| Data | DIVISION | SALES (MILLION $) |
|------|----------|-------------------|
|      | West     | 3.85              |
|      | South    | 8.62              |
|      | North    | 4.57              |
|      | East     | 3.81              |

**Output**   Your output should have this format:

```
DIVISION          SALES(MIL.$)          % OF TOTAL
West                  3.85              18.46523
South                 8.62              41.34293
North                 4.57              21.91847
East                  3.81              18.27338
------------------------------------------------
Totals               20.85              100
```

**3.25**   **Purpose**   To use READ/DATA statements with string and numeric data. To use the computational PRINT and simple output formatting.

**Problem**   The ABC Company (see exercise 3.24) anticipates that, for this year and the next 2 years, sales in each division will grow above last year's sales by the following percentage growth rates:

|         | LAST YEAR-1 | THIS YEAR-2 | NEXT YEAR-3 | YEAR AFTER-4 |
|---------|-------------|-------------|-------------|--------------|
| Percent | 100.0       | 108.0       | 114.2       | 121.3        |

Write a program that will generate for each of the divisions the expected sales for the years involved.

**Data**   The data for year 1 is as follows:

| DIVISION | SALES (MILLION $) |
|----------|-------------------|
| West     | 3.85              |
| South    | 8.62              |
| North    | 4.57              |
| East     | 3.81              |

**Output**   Your output should have this format:

```
          THREE YEAR SALES FORECAST - ABC COMPANY
                  MILLIONS OF DOLLARS
DIVISION     YEAR 1      YEAR 2         YEAR 3      YEAR 4
----------------------------------------------------------
West          3.85       4.158          4.3967      4.67005
South         8.62       9.3096         9.84404     10.45606
North         4.57       4.935601       5.21894     5.543411
East          3.81       4.1148         4.35102     4.62153
----------------------------------------------------------
```

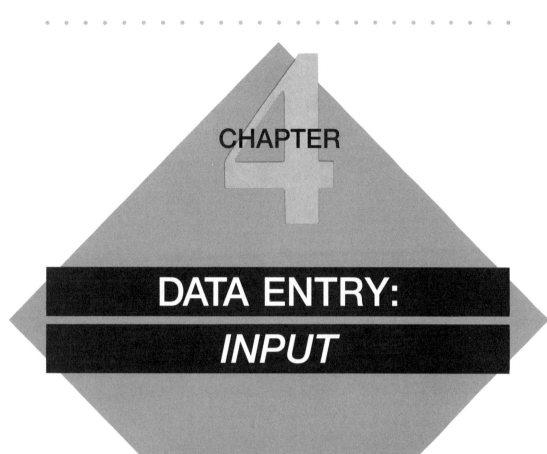

CHAPTER

4

# DATA ENTRY:

## *INPUT*

Upon completing this chapter, you will be able to do the following:

- Develop an interactive or conversational program with data being entered from the keyboard using the INPUT statement.
- Explain the difference between the READ/DATA and INPUT statements.
- Solve programming problems by using a simple sequence logic structure of INPUT, PRINT, and END.
- Understand the different forms of the INPUT statement and how to use them in a problem-solving program.
- See how it is possible to assign a line of information to a string variable with the LINE INPUT statement.

In Chapter 3 we saw how variables were given values with the READ/DATA statements. In this chapter we will learn how variables can be assigned values using the INPUT statement. With the INPUT statement, data is not part of the program but rather is supplied by the person at the keyboard when the program is run.

## THE *INPUT* STATEMENT

Using a microcomputer allows you to carry out a "conversation" with the computer via the program being run. Such conversational programming permits direct and almost immediate response from the computer. Real time systems, such as airlines reservation systems, use this kind of *interactive programming*.

To write a program permitting a dialogue between the program user and the computer, replace the READ/DATA statements with an INPUT statement. This statement has the form

line # INPUT $\begin{cases} \text{variable list/data names} \\ \text{prompt followed by a variable} \end{cases}$

Table 4.1 provides some examples of the forms that the INPUT statement can take.

**TABLE 4.1**  Forms of the INPUT statement

| STATEMENT | EXPLANATION |
| --- | --- |
| 10 INPUT A | Outputs a question mark (?) that requires a single numeric data entry from the keyboard. |
| 20 INPUT A, B\$ | Outputs a ? that requires a numeric data entry and a string data entry from the keyboard. |
| 30 INPUT "What is the date";DT\$ | Prompt in quotes is followed by a ? that requires a string data entry from the keyboard. |
| 40 INPUT "Enter two numbers", N1,N2 | Prompt in quotes is not followed by a ? but requires two numeric data entries from the keyboard. |
| 50 LINE INPUT "Enter Address"; AD\$ | Permits keyboard string entry that can include characters such as , / -. Prompt is not followed by a ?. |

---

| **Keyboarding Tip** | To save key strokes, you can type the Alt plus I key combination to enter and display the keyword INPUT. |

---

Several examples illustrating the INPUT statement are shown in Programs 4.1–4.4.

## PROGRAM 4.1    INPUT Statement without a Prompt

```
10 INPUT A,B
20 PRINT "SUM OF";A;"AND";B;"IS";A+B
99 END

RUN
 ?5,10
SUM OF 5 AND 10 IS 15
```

When the INPUT statement is executed by the computer, a question mark (?) appears as the initial output, as shown in Program 4.1. The programmer or program user must then type in the values for *A* and *B*. In this case, 5 and 10 are typed in, separated by a comma and without any ending punctuation. When the enter key is depressed, after the data has been typed in, the program resumes execution with line 20.

Note that the inputting of data is similar to the placement of data in a DATA statement.

The programmer can use another type of INPUT statement to have the computer print a prompting message before the question mark. An example of an INPUT statement with a prompt string is illustrated in Program 4.2.

## PROGRAM 4.2    INPUT with Prompt String Question

```
10 INPUT "What are the two numbers"; A,B
20 PRINT "SUM OF";A;"AND";B;"IS";A+B
99 END

RUN
What are the two numbers? 5,10
SUM OF 5 AND 10 IS 15
```

If the program user fails to type in all of the data needed to conform to the INPUT statement, an error message, ''Redo from start'', will appear indicating that more data is needed. This is shown in Figure 4.1. Figure 4.2 shows what happens when too much data is typed. The error message, ''Redo from start'' has occurred because the data input does

```
RUN
Type in the two numbers: 5
?Redo from start
Type in the two numbers: 5,10
SUM OF 5 AND 10 IS 15
```

**FIGURE 4.1** Insufficient Data Inputted to Program 4.3

```
RUN
Type in the two numbers: 5,10,25
?Redo from start
Type in the two numbers: 5,10
SUM OF 5 AND 10 IS 15
```

**FIGURE 4.2** Excess Data Inputted to Program 4.3

not conform to the variable list in line 10 of Program 4.3. Once the data is typed in and conforms to the variable list, the execution of the program continues as though no error was made.

If the prompt string message is not in the form of a question, a comma may be used instead of the semicolon in the INPUT statement to suppress the question mark, as illustrated in Program 4.3.

## PROGRAM 4.3  INPUT with Prompt String Message

```
10 INPUT "Type in the two numbers: ", A,B
20 PRINT "SUM OF";A;"AND";B;"IS";A+B
99 END

RUN
Type in the two numbers: 5,10
SUM OF 5 AND 10 IS 15
```

To assign a string of characters that contains a comma to a variable, you must enclose the string in quotes. For example, if you want to assign ''Brooklyn, New York'' to variable A$ using the input statement INPUT A$, you would have to type ''Brooklyn, New York'' (within quotation marks) after the ?; otherwise, the computer would assume that you were inputting strings for two variables—''Brooklyn'' and ''New York''—and the error message ''? Redo from start'' would result.

Program 4.4 illustrates keyboard entry of string data in response to an INPUT prompt for two string data items.

## PROGRAM 4.4   INPUT with Prompt for String Data

```
5 INPUT "Enter your I.D. number and Course Code:", ID$, CODE$
10 INPUT "What is your name, and age"; NM$, AG
15 PRINT "I.D. Number-"; ID$, "COURSE CODE:"; CODE$
20 PRINT "NAME- "; NM$, "AGE- "; AG; "years old"
99 END


RUN
Enter your I.D. number and Course Code:3542, CIS 201
What is your name, and age? Sandy Jones, 21
I.D. Number-3542               COURSE CODE:CIS 201
NAME- Sandy Jones             AGE- 21 years old
```

Since application programs are often used by people other than the programmers who write them, an INPUT statement in a program should be preceded by some instructions that will explain to the user the format of the data to be inputted. Otherwise, the ? could be meaningless to the program user when it appears. Thus the programmer should write additional PRINT statements (lines 15–35), as shown in Program 4.5, which is a conversational version of Program 3.9 (see Chapter 3).

## PROGRAM 4.5   Case 3.1, Finding Total Profit, INPUT Statement

```
5 REM CASE 3.1, FINDING TOTAL PROFITS
6 REM PROGRAMMER- (name of person)   DATE - mm/dd/yy
7 REM            TOTAL PROFITS = TOTAL REVENUE - TOTAL COST
8 REM             VARIABLE LIST- P, C, U
9 REM              P=PRICE PER UNIT
10 REM             C=COST PER UNIT
11 REM             U=# UNITS SOLD AND BOUGHT
12 REM -------------------------------------------------------
13 PRINT
15 PRINT TAB(15); "INSTRUCTIONS"
20 PRINT TAB(15); "------------"
25 PRINT "TO GENERATE OUTPUT FROM THE TOTAL PROFIT PROGRAM"
30 PRINT "WHEN THE ? APPEARS, TYPE AFTER IT THE ITEMS INDICATED"
35 PRINT "EACH SEPARATED BY A COMMA: "
38 PRINT "-----------------------------------------------------"
40 INPUT "What is the Price/Unit, Cost/Unit, & # Units sold";P,C,U
65 PRINT
70 PRINT TAB(10); "TOTAL PROFIT REPORT"
75 PRINT
80 PRINT "NUMBER OF UNITS SOLD";U
85 PRINT "PRICE PER UNIT";P,"COST PER UNIT";C
90 PRINT "TOTAL REVENUE";P*U
92 PRINT "LESS TOTAL COST";C*U
95 PRINT "---------------------------------------------"
100 PRINT "TOTAL PROFIT";P*U-C*U
199 END
```

```
RUN

              INSTRUCTIONS
              ------------
TO GENERATE OUTPUT FROM THE TOTAL PROFIT PROGRAM
WHEN THE ? APPEARS, TYPE AFTER IT THE ITEMS INDICATED
EACH SEPARATED BY A COMMA:
-----------------------------------------------------
What is the Price/Unit, Cost/Unit, & # Units sold? 10, 6.50, 225

           TOTAL PROFIT REPORT

NUMBER OF UNITS SOLD 225
PRICE PER UNIT 10            COST PER UNIT 6.5
TOTAL REVENUE 2250
LESS TOTAL COST 1462.5
---------------------------------------------
TOTAL PROFIT 787.5
```

## LINE INPUT

Another method for inputting strings of characters that contain commas is by using the LINE INPUT statement. The form of the LINE INPUT statement is similar to that of the INPUT statement except that only one variable can be used to assign whatever is typed on the line. See Program 4.6.

## PROGRAM 4.6   LINE INPUT Statement

```
10 LINE INPUT  "What is your address? "; A$
20 PRINT A$
30 END

RUN
What is your address?  Brooklyn, N.Y.  11230
Brooklyn, N.Y. 11230
```

Note that the LINE INPUT statement does not generate a question mark like the INPUT statement does. Thus the statement 10 LINE INPUT ''What is your address'';A$ will not print any question mark, nor will it leave a space before the response. A space or a question mark must be included in the prompt string. The LINE INPUT statement can also be used without a prompt string but since there is no prompt whatsoever, it is not very practical in most circumstances. Note that it is not necessary to enclose Brooklyn, N.Y. 11230 in quotes even though a comma is embedded in the string of characters. This is because the entire line that is input is assigned to variable A$. A semicolon following the words LINE INPUT will not cause the output to advance to the next line when the Enter key is pressed after the response. Thus in Program 4.6, 10 LINE INPUT; ''What is your address? '';A$ would print Brooklyn, N.Y. 11230 immediately after the response. This is shown in Program 4.7.

## PROGRAM 4.7   LINE INPUT without Carriage Return

```
10 LINE INPUT; "What is your address? "; A$
20 PRINT A$
30 END

RUN
What is your address? Brooklyn, N.Y. 11230 Brooklyn, N.Y. 11230
```

There is no limit to the types or numbers of INPUT statements that can be placed in a program. Multiple INPUT statements are illustrated by lines 15 (a LINE INPUT), 20, and 25 in Program 4.8, which is based on Case 4.1.

## CASE 4.1

**Problem**  **Analysis of Weekly Inventory**
As one part of controlling and analyzing its inventory system, the ABC Company has an interactive program that is run each week to produce an inventory analysis report.

**Data Input**  The program requires that the inventory level of the previous week be input, as well as the number of units sold each day of the current week.

**Process/Formulas**  Ending inventory = beginning inventory − units sold during the week

**Output**  The program should produce a display showing daily sales, beginning inventory, number of units sold for the week, and ending inventory.

## PROGRAM 4.8   Case 4.1, Inventory Analysis, Multiple INPUTs

```
4 REM CASE 4.1  INVENTORY ANALYSIS
5 REM PROGRAMMER- (name of person)   DATE - mm/dd/yy
6 REM VARIABLE LIST-D$,I,M,T,W,TH,F
7 REM D$ = DATE
8 REM I=BEGINNING INVENTORY
9 REM M=MONDAY SALES
10 REM T=TUESDAY SALES
11 REM W=WEDNESDAY SALES
12 REM TH=THURSDAY SALES
13 REM F=FRIDAY SALES
14 REM -------------------------------------------
```

```
15 LINE INPUT "WHAT IS THIS WEEK'S ENDING DATE ?"; D$
20 INPUT "WHAT IS BEGINNING INVENTORY"; I
25 INPUT "WHAT WERE SALES FOR EACH DAY OF THE WEEK";M, T, W, TH, F
30 PRINT
32 PRINT TAB(15);"*** INVENTORY ANALYSIS REPORT ***
33 PRINT TAB(19);"WEEK ENDING "; D$
40 PRINT
45 PRINT TAB(25); "DAILY SALES"
50 PRINT TAB(25); "-----------"
55 PRINT "MON.","TUES.","WED.","THUR.","FRI."
60 PRINT M,T,W,TH,F
62 PRINT
65 PRINT SPC(10); "BEG. INV.";I;"UNITS"
70 PRINT SPC(10); "NUMBER OF UNITS SOLD THIS WEEK";M+T+W+TH+F
75 PRINT SPC(10); "ENDING INVENTORY";I-(M+T+W+TH+F)
99 END


RUN
WHAT IS THIS WEEK'S ENDING DATE ?March 5, 1989
WHAT IS BEGINNING INVENTORY? 150
WHAT WERE SALES FOR EACH DAY OF THE WEEK? 20,30,15,25,10

                *** INVENTORY ANALYSIS REPORT ***
                    WEEK ENDING March 5, 1989

                        DAILY SALES
                        -----------
MON.            TUES.           WED.            THUR.           FRI.
 20              30              15              25              10


        BEG. INV. 150 UNITS
        NUMBER OF UNITS SOLD THIS WEEK 100
        ENDING INVENTORY 50
```

A program can contain both READ/DATA and INPUT statements. The conversational part of the program will be based on the variable list of the INPUT statements. Other data required for the program can be entered by the READ/DATA statements.

Program 4.9 shows a program that converts miles to kilometers. The conversion factor is 1.609 kilometers to a mile. This constant is entered into the program by the READ in line 10. The INPUT statement is used to enter the number of miles to be converted to kilometers, since that will change each time. The READ/DATA statements are used for the constant factor.

## PROGRAM 4.9  A Program with Both READ/DATA and INPUT Statements

```
10 READ K
20 DATA 1.609
30 INPUT "ENTER NUMBER OF MILES TO CONVERT TO KILOMETERS"; M
35 PRINT
40 PRINT M;"MILES IS EQUIVALENT TO";K*M;"KILOMETERS"
50 END
```

```
RUN
ENTER NUMBER OF MILES TO CONVERT TO KILOMETERS? 250

    250 MILES IS EQUIVALENT TO 402.25 KILOMETERS
```

Another example of a program containing both READ/DATA and INPUT statements is Program 4.10, based on Case 4.2.

- - - - - - - - - - - - - - - - - - - - - - - - - - - - - - - - - - -

## CASE 4.2

**Problem**    **Individual Retirement Account Computations**
An individual retirement account (IRA) permits an annual investment contribution, at a fixed rate of interest, for a specific period of time. The formula below is used to calculate the accumulation for such an account. Write an interactive-conversational program to compute the accumulation.

**Data Input**    Interactively enter the annual contribution and number of years for the investment, using a contribution of $1500 for 10 years at a fixed rate of 7.5%. Simple instructions should be provided for the data entry.

**Process/Formulas**  The total accumulation for an IRA account is calculated by the formula

$$F = A \left[ \frac{(1 + R)^N - 1}{R} \right]$$

where $F$ is the total, $A$ is the amount paid into the account each year for $N$ years, and $R$ is the rate of interest. For purposes of accuracy use double precision variables.

**Output**    The program should produce a display of all data values entered as well as the total accumulation.

- - - - - - - - - - - - - - - - - - - - - - - - - - - - - - - - - - -

Treating $R$ as a constant and $A$ and $N$ as variables to be entered by an INPUT statement, Program 4.10 supplies the answer. The flowchart for this program is shown in Figure 4.3. It illustrates the simple sequence logic structure of the programs in this chapter.

Note that the output for Program 4.10 shows two sets of results. The second set was obtained by running the program again with a different set of inputs for $A$ and $N$.

Also observe the dangling semicolon at the end of line 80. This symbol causes the INPUT question mark to appear on the same line as the output of the PRINT statement. This query technique for interactive data entry, with questions and responses, is important for users who may have no knowledge of programming. It also reflects good program design and is important if users are going to accept the programs being offered them.

Because programs of a financial nature require a high degree of accuracy, double precision variables should be used, as in Program 4.10.

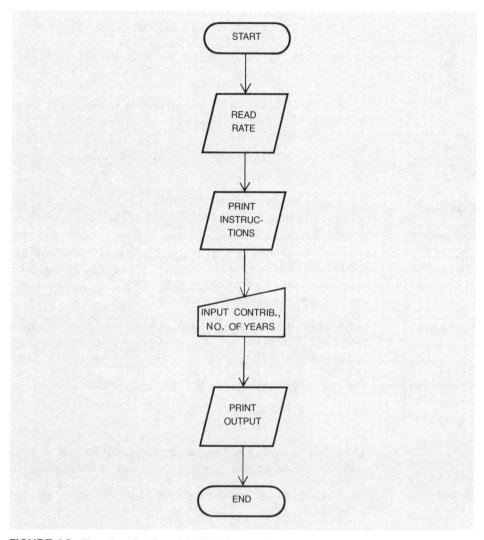

**FIGURE 4.3** Flowchart for Case 4.2, IRA Account Program 4.10

## PROGRAM 4.10 Case 4.2, IRA Accumulation with READ/DATA and INPUT

```
5 REM CASE 4.2, PROGRAM TO FIND THE ACCUMULATION IN AN IRA ACCOUNT
6 REM PROGRAMMER- (name of person)   DATE - mm/dd/yy
7 REM VARIABLE LIST-R#,A#,N#
8 REM R# = COMPOUNDED RATE PER YEAR
9 REM A# = YEARLY CONTRIBUTION OF $
10 REM N# = NUMBER OF YEARS
12 REM -------------------------------------------------
15 READ R#
20 DATA 7.5
25 PRINT
30 PRINT "INSTRUCTIONS: TYPE ITEMS REQUESTED AND THEN ENTER-"
70 PRINT SPC(20);"WHAT IS THE ANNUAL CONTRIBUTION, AND HOW MANY YEARS"
```

```
80 PRINT SPC(20); "WILL IT BE PAID IN";
90 INPUT A#,N#
105 PRINT SPC(20);"******* IRA ANALYSIS *******"
110 PRINT SPC(15);"YEARLY CONTRIBUTION OF $";A#;"FOR";N#;"YEARS"
120 PRINT SPC(15);"COMPOUNDED AT";R#;"% EACH YEAR, GENERATES A TOTAL"
130 PRINT SPC(15);"IRA ACCOUNT OF $";A##(((1 + R#/100)^N# - 1)/R#/100))
140 END

RUN

INSTRUCTIONS: TYPE ITEMS REQUESTED AND THEN ENTER-
              WHAT IS THE ANNUAL CONTRIBUTION, AND HOW MANY YEARS
              WILL IT BE PAID IN? 1500,10
              ******* IRA ANALYSIS *******
         YEARLY CONTRIBUTION OF $1500 FOR 10 YEARS
         COMPOUNDED AT 7.5% EACH YEAR, GENERATES A TOTAL
         IRA ACCOUNT OF $ 21220.64590454102


RUN

INSTRUCTIONS: TYPE ITEMS REQUESTED AND THEN ENTER-
              WHAT IS THE ANNUAL CONTRIBUTION, AND HOW MANY YEARS
              WILL IT BE PAID IN? 1000,15
              ******* IRA ANALYSIS *******
         YEARLY CONTRIBUTION OF $ 1000 FOR 15 YEARS
         COMPOUNDED AT 7.5% EACH YEAR, GENERATES A TOTAL
         IRA ACCOUNT OF $ 26118.38976542155
```

## SUMMARY

Values can be assigned to variables using the INPUT statement. The LINE INPUT statement will assign to a single string variable whatever is typed on a single line.

Interactive or conversational programs use the INPUT statement. When data is typed in response to an input statement, it must be typed in exact conformance with the variable format. Too much or too little data will result in an error message.

An INPUT, PRINT statement pattern in a program forms a simple sequence logic structure.

## BASIC VOCABULARY SUMMARY

| Statement | Purpose | Examples |
|---|---|---|
| INPUT (Alt + I key) | Values to be assigned to a variable from a source external to the program | 10 INPUT N$,A |
| LINE INPUT | Assigns the contents of a line typed when the program is run to a single string variable | 10 LINE INPUT A$ |

## EXERCISES

### Review Questions

**4.1**  How does the INPUT statement with a semicolon (;) after the prompt differ from the INPUT statement with a comma (,) after the prompt?

**4.2**  Compare and contrast the INPUT statement with the LINE INPUT statement.

**4.3**  Compare and contrast the READ/DATA and INPUT statements when there is excess data.

**4.4**  Compare and contrast the READ/DATA and INPUT statements when there is insufficient data.

**4.5**  What would the following program (Program 4.8) print if the variables in lines 25, 60, 70, and 75 were changed to M, T, W, T, F?

```
4 REM CASE 3.3,  INVENTORY ANALYSIS
5 REM PROGRAMMER- (name of person)  DATE - mm/dd/yy
6 REM VARIABLE LIST-D$,I,M,T,W,TH,F
7 REM D$ = DATE
8 REM I=BEGINNING INVENTORY
9 REM M=MONDAY SALES
10 REM T=TUESDAY SALES
11 REM W=WEDNESDAY SALES
12 REM TH=THURSDAY SALES
13 REM F=FRIDAY SALES
14 REM -------------------------------------------
15 LINE INPUT "WHAT IS THIS WEEKS ENDING DATE ?"; D$
20 INPUT "WHAT IS BEGINNING INVENTORY"; I
25 INPUT "WHAT WERE SALES FOR EACH DAY OF THE WEEK";M, T, W, TH, F
30 PRINT
32 PRINT TAB(15);"*** INVENTORY ANALYSIS REPORT ***
33 PRINT TAB(19);"WEEK ENDING "; D$
40 PRINT
45 PRINT TAB(25); "DAILY SALES"
50 PRINT TAB(25); "-----------"
55 PRINT "MON.","TUES.","WED.","THUR.","FRI."
60 PRINT M,T,W,TH,F
62 PRINT
65 PRINT SPC(10); "BEG. INV.";I;"UNITS"
70 PRINT SPC(10); "NUMBER OF UNITS SOLD THIS WEEK";M+T+W+TH+F
75 PRINT SPC(10); "ENDING INVENTORY";I-(M+T+W+TH+F)
99 END
```

### Programming Activities

**4.6**  **Purpose**  To use appropriate INPUT statements with numeric data, computational PRINT, simple output formatting, and REM.

**Problem**  Below is a set of investments that are to be increased by the same three interest rates: 7 percent, 7½ percent, and 8¼ percent. Write an interactive program that will increase this set of investments by these three rates. Include REM statements in the program describing the problem and the program.

**Data** One-year investments: $3,000; $10,000; $12,500; $17,000

**Output** Your output should display this format:

```
ENTER  4  INVESTMENTS 3000,  10000,  12500,  17000
ENTER  3  INTEREST  RATES  (.dd)  .07,  .075,  .0825
INVESTMENT      7% INC.    7.5% INC. 8.25% INC.
  3000           3210        3225       3247.5
 10000          10700       10750      10825
 12500          13375       13437.5    13531.25
 17000          18190       18275      18402.5
```

♦ **4.7** **Purpose** To use READ/DATA, an INPUT statement with numeric data, computational PRINT, and simple output formatting.

**Problem** A mathematical property states that for a set of data the sum of the deviations about its mean is equal to zero; or $\Sigma(X_i - \mu) = 0$, where $\Sigma$ is the sum of, $X_i$ is each data value, and $\mu$ is the average or mean of all the $X_i$. For the data below, write and run a program that illustrates this property. (*Hint:* First have the program compute the mean, then input the mean.)

**Data** Use the values 5, −3, 7, 8, −2.

**Output** Your output should display with this format:

```
RUN
THE MEAN IS: 3
ENTER THE COMPUTED VALUE OF THE MEAN: 3
THE SUM OF THE DEVIATION ABOUT THE MEAN IS: 0
```

**4.8** **Purpose** To use READ/DATA, an INPUT statement with numeric data, computational PRINT, and simple output formatting.

**Problem** A measure of variation in statistics is called the *standard deviation*. It has the formula

$$\sigma = \sqrt{\frac{\Sigma(X_i - \mu)^2}{N}}$$

where $N$ is number of data values. Write an interactive program to find the standard deviation for the data below. *Note:* $\sqrt{X} = X^{1/2}$. The program should first compute the mean and then call for it to be entered interactively.

**Data** Use the values 5, −3, 7, 8, −2.

**Output** Your output should display with this format:

```
RUN
THE MEAN IS: 3
ENTER THE COMPUTED VALUE OF THE MEAN: 3
THE STANDARD DEVIATION IS: 4.604347
```

♦ **4.9**　**Purpose**　To use appropriate INPUT statements with string and numeric data. To use the computational PRINT and simple output formatting.

**Problem**　The United Computer Company pays its salespersons a monthly salary of $1000 plus 1½ percent commission for equipment sold during the month. The data below shows the sales figures by person for last month. Write an interactive program that will produce a table containing the data plus an additional column that shows the total salary plus commission on sales.

**Data**

| SALESPERSON | AMOUNT SOLD |
|---|---|
| M. Worth | $13,500 |
| K. Gray | 21,000 |
| S. Legan | 9,600 |
| B. Hinz | 24,400 |

**Output**　Your output should have this format:

```
RUN
ENTER 4 SALESPERSONS NAMES: M. WORTH, K. GRAY, S. LEGAN, B. HINZ
ENTER THE AMOUNT SOLD FOR EACH PERSON: 13500, 21000, 9600, 24400

SALESPERSON     AMOUNT SOLD        SALARY
  M. WORTH         13500           1202.5
  K. GRAY          21000           1315
  S. LEGAN          9600           1144
  B. HINZ          24400           1366
```

**4.10**　**Purpose**　To use the LINE INPUT and INPUT statements with string and numeric data. To use the computational PRINT and simple output formatting.

**Problem**　Salespersons are paid straight commissions using this formula to determine total earnings for a given period:

Commission = (amount sold − returns) × (commission rate)

Write an interactive program to compute such commissions.

**Data**　Test your program with the following data items:

| SALESPERSON | AMOUNT SOLD | RETURNS |
|---|---|---|
| O'Hara, Sally | $11,200 | $800 |
| Cohen, Jack | $ 9,400 | $600 |

The commission rate is 11%.

**Output**　The output display should follow this format:

```
ENTER FIRST EMPLOYEE'S NAME: O'hara, Sally
ENTER SECOND EMPLOYEE'S NAME: Cohen, Jack
ENTER THE AMOUNT SOLD BY EACH PERSON: 11200, 9400
ENTER THE RETURNS FOR EACH PERSON: 800, 600

SALESPERSON     AMOUNT SOLD   RETURNS   COMMISSIONS
O'Hara, Sally      11200        800        1144
Cohen, Jack         9400        600         968
```

**4.11** **Purpose** To do complex problem solving using appropriate INPUT statements, numeric data, computational PRINT, and simple output formatting.

**Problem** The Cobb-Douglas production function has the form

$$\text{Output} = A \times L\alpha \times K^{1-\alpha}$$

where $A$ is technical progress, $L$ is the employed labor force, $K$ is the stock of capital for production, $\alpha$ (alpha) is the fraction of total output earned by labor, and $1 - \alpha$ is the fraction of total output earned by capital. If $A$ is 15, $L$ is 500, $K$ is 250, and $\alpha$ is .5, write an interactive program that enters in this data and computes output.

**Data** Use the data values provided in the problem statement. Data entry should be interactive.

**Output** Your output display should follow this format:

```
WHAT IS THE VALUE OF A? 15
WHAT IS THE VALUE OF L? 500
WHAT IS THE VALUE OF K? 250
WHAT IS THE VALUE OF ALPHA? .5
A= 15 L= 500 K= 250 A1= .5
OUTPUT= 5303.299
```

**4.12** **Purpose** To do complex problem solving using appropriate INPUT statements, numeric data, computational PRINT, double precision, LPRINT, and simple output formatting.

**Problem** A firm estimates that 5 years from now it will need $2 million to purchase some new equipment. To accumulate this sum, management decides to set aside an amount each year. The firm can earn 9 percent compounded annually on its cash. To find the amount that must be deposited at the end of each of the 5 years to accumulate the $2 million, use the following formula:

$$A = F \frac{r}{(1 + r)^n - 1}$$

where $A$ is the amount to be deposited at the end of $n$ years, with the annual interest rate of $r$, and $F$ is the future sum needed. Write an interactive conversational program that will find $A$.

**Data** Use the data values provided in the problem statement. Data entry should be interactive.

**Output** Your output should display on the screen and also generate a hard copy. Output should follow this format:

```
WHAT IS THE NUMBER OF YEARS? 5
WHAT IS THE ANNUAL INTEREST RATE (.dd)? .09
WHAT IS THE FUTURE SUM NEEDED? 2000000
F= 2000000 R= .09 N= 5
AMOUNT TO BE DEPOSITED PER YEAR IS $ 334184.7080809896
```

• • • • • • **4.13** **Purpose** To do complex problem solving using appropriate INPUT statements with numeric data, computational PRINT, double precision, and simple output formatting, with the SPC function.

**Problem** A present value problem asks this question: What amount could be invested at 15 percent compounded annually that will grow to $300,000 or more at the end of five years? Write and run an interactive conversational program that will find the present value $P$. To find the answer, use this formula:

$$P = \frac{F}{(1 + r)^n}$$

where $P$ is the present value, $F$ is the future amount needed, $r$ is the annual rate of interest (a decimal), and $n$ is the length of the period.

**Data** Use the data values provided in the problem statement. Data entry should be interactive.

**Output** Your output should display on the screen. Each output line is preceded by ten blank spaces. Output should follow this format:

```
WHAT IS THE NUMBER OF YEARS? 5
WHAT IS THE ANNUAL INTEREST RATE (.dd)? .15
WHAT IS THE FUTURE AMOUNT NEEDED? 300000
N= 5 R= .15 F= 3000000
THE PRESENT VALUE P=$ 149153.0293757541
```

# CHAPTER 5

# SIMPLE SEQUENCE STRUCTURES AND ASSIGNMENT STATEMENTS

Upon completing this chapter, you will be able to do the following:

- Understand how the LET statement is used to assign numeric and nonnumeric data to variables.
- Use the LET statement to evaluate expressions to be used in problem-solving programs.
- Explain the difference between the LET and the SWAP statements.
- Solve programming problems by using a simple sequence logic structure of READ/DATA, LET, PRINT, END.
- Solve programming problems by using a simple sequence logic structure of INPUT, LET, PRINT, END.

In the previous chapters we studied how to assign values to variables with the READ/ DATA and INPUT statements. Another way to assign values to variables is to use the LET statement. The LET statement is also used to evaluate expressions.

In this chapter we will see how the LET statement is used for both of these functions. The simple sequence logic structure of READ/DATA, PRINT, END described in the preceding chapters will be further developed. Programs presented here follow the simple sequence structure of READ/DATA, LET, PRINT, END.

## THE *LET* STATEMENT

The form of the LET statement is

$$\text{line \# LET \{variable\}} = \begin{Bmatrix} \text{constant or} \\ \text{variable or} \\ \text{expression} \end{Bmatrix}$$

The LET statement evaluates the expression on the right side of the equal sign and assigns that value to the variable on the left side of the equal sign. An expression here means any variable or constant or a valid combination of variables, constants, and operators ($+$, $-$, $*$, $/$, and $\char94$).

For string variables the form of the LET statement is

$$\text{line \# LET \{string variable\}} = \begin{Bmatrix} \text{string variable} \\ \text{or} \\ \text{``literal item''} \end{Bmatrix}$$

Some examples of the LET statement are shown in Table 5.1. A discussion of the examples follows.

Example 1 of Table 5.1 assigns the value of 5 to variable $N$, even if $N$ had some other value before the execution of line 100.

Example 2 evaluates the expression $A * X \char94 2 + B * X + C$ and assigns the value of that expression to the variable $Y$. The variables $A$, $B$, $C$, and $X$ must have been assigned values before the execution of line 100. The previous value of variable $Y$, if any, would be replaced by the value of the expression.

In example 3 the value of variable $B$ is assigned to variable $A$. That is, if variable $A$ had the value of 2 and variable $B$ had the value of 3, after line 100 is executed both variables have the value of 3.

Example 4 differs from example 3 in that the value of variable $A$ is assigned to variable $B$. Thus if variable $A$ had the value of 2 and variable $B$ had the value of 3, after line 100 in this example both variables would have the value of 2.

Example 5 requires variable $J$ to have been defined previously. It takes the old value of variable $J$, adds 1 to that value, and assigns that increased value to the variable $J$. So if variable $J$ had the value of 10 before line 100, then after line 100 is executed variable $J$ has the value of 11.

**TABLE 5.1**   Examples of the LET Statement

| STATEMENT | EXPLANATION |
| --- | --- |
| 1. 100 LET N = 5 | Assigns numeric value 5 to $N$. |
| 2. 100 LET Y = A*X^2 + B*X+C | Expression on the right is evaluated. Result is assigned and stored in $Y$. |
| 3. 100 LET A = B | Value assigned and stored as $B$ is assigned to $A$. |
| 4. 100 LET B = A | Value assigned and stored as $A$ is assigned to $B$. |
| 5. 100 LET J = J + 1 | Increments the previous value of $J$ by a constant 1, reassigning the increase to $J$. |
| 6. 100 LET T = T + X | Increments the previous value of $T$ by the value in variable $X$, reassigning the increase to $T$. |
| 7. 100 LET AN$ = ''Yes'' | Assigns quoted literal to string variable AN$. |
| 8. 100 LET CTY$ = NM$ | String assigned and stored as NM$ is assigned to CTY$. |
| 9. 100 LET C$ = A$ + B$ | Combines strings A$ and B$ to form C$ (*concatenation*). |

It is important to remember that the symbol '' = '' in the BASIC language does not mean ''is equal to.'' Example 5 clearly demonstrates this, since $J$ is never equal to $J + 1$. The symbol '' = '' means, rather, ''assign the value on the right to the variable on the left.''

Example 6 requires that the variable $T$ be previously assigned a value. The value of $X$ is added to $T$. The new result is then reassigned to $T$, causing it to increase. If $T$ were equal to 25 before line 100, and $X$ is currently 15, the new value assigned and stored in $T$ would be 40, replacing the prior value of 25.

Although examples 5 and 6 demonstrate adding values to the variables on the right side of the expression, values can be subtracted as well. The statements can read 100 LET $C = C - 1$ or 100 LET $S = S - A$, for example.

Example 7 assigns the string item ''Yes'' to the string variable AN$. The quotation marks are necessary.

In example 8, the literal stored in NM$ is assigned to the string variable CTY$. Now, the same literal is stored by two different variables.

Example 9 shows the process of *concatenation*, which means ''joining together string items to create a new string.'' Thus if A$ = ''LABEL 1'' and B$ = ''LABEL 2'', C$ would be ''LABEL 1 LABEL 2''.

Table 5.2 shows some examples of *invalid* LET statements. These examples are all invalid because the left side of the = must contain only a single variable that matches the data type on the right side. Also note that while $A = B + C$ is the same as $B + C = A$ in mathematics, in the BASIC language

LET $A = B + C$

is a valid statement, but

LET $B + C = A$

is invalid. When this type of invalid LET statement is processed, an error message (''Syntax error in   '') will be displayed followed by the statement line that contains the error. Program 5.1 illustrates the LET statement.

**TABLE 5.2** Examples of Invalid LET Statements

| STATEMENT | EXPLANATION |
|---|---|
| 50 LET 5 = N | Left side of = must contain a single variable. |
| 50 LET A + B^2*C = Y | Left side of = must contain a single variable. |
| 50 LET J + 1 = J | Left side of = must contain a single variable. |
| 50 LET "NO" = R$ | A string variable must be on the left side of =. |
| 50 LET A = B$ | A string cannot be assigned to a numeric variable. |
| 50 LET D$ = D# | A numeric variable cannot be assigned to a string variable. |

## PROGRAM 5.1   The LET Statement

```
10 READ A,B,C
15 LET X=A+B+C
20 PRINT X,X^2,X^3
25 DATA 1,2,3
30 END

RUN
 6              36              216
```

Note that in Program 5.1 it would have been possible to omit line 15 and replace line 20 with the statement shown in Figure 5.1.

```
20 PRINT A+B+C, (A+B+C)^2, (A+B+C)^3
```

**FIGURE 5.1** PRINT without Using LET in Program 5.1

One advantage of Program 5.1 is that it avoids the lengthy statement in Figure 5.1. Another advantage is that the statement in Figure 5.1 requires the computer to add $A + B + C$ three times. The computer does not remember the sum of $A$, $B$, and $C$ unless it is assigned to a variable. Thus Program 5.1 requires fewer computations than a program with the statement shown in Figure 5.1.

Another application of the LET statement arises when lengthy computations are required. Suppose we wish to compute the value of

$$\frac{A^2 + B^2}{C(B - A)} \div \frac{(D - A)B}{C^2 - D^2}$$

Figure 5.2 shows us how. However, an easier way is illustrated in Figure 5.3.

```
10 PRINT ((A^2+B^2)/(C*(B-A)))/(((D-A)*B)/(C^2-D^2))
```

**FIGURE 5.2** Lengthy Computations without Using LET

```
10 LET N1 = A^2 + B^2
15 LET D1 = C*(B-A)
20 LET N2 = (D-A)*B
25 LET D2 = C^2 - D^2
30 PRINT (N1/D1)/(N2/D2)
```

**FIGURE 5.3**  Lengthy Computations Using LET

Programs with statements like those in Figure 5.3 are much less prone to error than programs with statements like the one in Figure 5.2.

Program 5.2 has no practical application, but it does illustrate some of the features of the LET statement.

## PROGRAM 5.2    Several LET Statements

```
10 READ A,B,C,D
20 LET C=A
30 LET A=B+C
40 LET D=A+D
50 LET B=A
60 PRINT A,B,C,D
70 DATA 1,2,3,4
80 END

RUN
 3                 3                 1                 7
```

The variables changed as follows:

| LINE | A | B | C | D |
|------|---|---|---|---|
| 10 | 1 | 2 | 3 | 4 |
| 20 | 1 | 2 | 1 | 4 |
| 30 | 3 | 2 | 1 | 4 |
| 40 | 3 | 2 | 1 | 7 |
| 50 | 3 | 3 | 1 | 7 |

Note that the order in which the statements are executed makes a considerable difference in the final output.

Consider Program 5.3. This program consists of the identical statements of Program 5.2, but the output is completely different.

## PROGRAM 5.3    The Order of the LET Statements

```
10 READ A,B,C,D
20 LET B=A
30 LET A=B+C
40 LET C=A
```

```
50 LET D=A+D
60 PRINT A,B,C,D
70 DATA 1,2,3,4
80 END

RUN
 4              1              4              8
```

If we have the statement

10 LET X = A + 1

and *A* has not been given a value previously, an error message may be printed such as "Undefined variable accessed on line 10", referring to variable *A*. Microsoft BASIC, though, will automatically assign the value zero to any undefined variable.

Suppose you desire to switch the assigned values of variables *A* and *B* (that is, to reassign the value of variable *A* to variable *B*, and to reassign the value of variable *B* to variable *A*). It is not possible to do this with a program like Program 5.4.

## PROGRAM 5.4   Improper Value Switching

```
10 READ A, B
15 DATA 1, 2
20 LET A=B
30 LET B=A
40 PRINT A, B
50 END

RUN
 2              2
```

Notice that Program 5.4 prints two 2s. To properly accomplish the switching, we can first assign the value of variable *A* to another (dummy) variable and then perform the switch, as is done in Program 5.5 (line 25). Program 5.6 shows how we can exchange the values of two variables without using a dummy variable.

## PROGRAM 5.5   Proper Value Switching Using a Dummy Variable

```
10 READ A,B
15 DATA 1,2
20 PRINT A,B
25 LET D=A
30 LET A=B
35 LET B=D
40 PRINT A,B
50 END

RUN
 1              2
 2              1
```

## THE SWAP STATEMENT

Another, simpler way of exchanging the values of two variables is the SWAP statement. The general form of the SWAP statement is

line # SWAP variable1, variable2

Both variables must be the same type; that is, they both must be string, integer, single precision, or double precision variables.

The SWAP statement is illustrated in Program 5.6.

## PROGRAM 5.6    Value Switching Using the SWAP Statement

```
5 REM EXCHANGING VALUES WITH SWAP STATEMENT
10 READ A,B
15 DATA 1,2
20 PRINT A,B
30 SWAP A,B
40 PRINT A,B
50 END

RUN
 1              2
 2              1
```

In the same way that the SWAP statement is used to exchange numeric data values between variables, it can also be used with string variables. Line 30 of Program 5.7 shows how literal data items can be switched from one string variable (J$ to F$) to another.

## PROGRAM 5.7    Switching Strings Using the SWAP Statement

```
5 REM EXCHANGING STRINGS WITH SWAP STATEMENT
10 READ J$, F$
15 DATA JANUARY, FEBRUARY
20 PRINT J$, F$
30 SWAP J$, F$
40 PRINT J$, F$
50 END

RUN
JANUARY        FEBRUARY
FEBRUARY       JANUARY
```

These examples of value and string switching provide some of the logic and background needed to write programs that sort data, as described in Chapter 14.

The expression on the right of the LET statement must match the variable (either number or string) on the left, but they may differ in the type of numeric variable and expression. Thus the LET statement 10 LET I% = A# is valid because each variable represents data stored in numeric form. The statement 10 LET A$ = A# is not valid, however, because A# is a double precision numeric variable and A$ is a string variable. Let's look at Program 5.8.

## PROGRAM 5.8   Matching and Mismatching Variables with LET

```
10 REM A# = DOUBLE PRECISION VARIABLE, A = SINGLE PRECISION VARIABLE
20 REM A% = INTEGER VARIABLE, A$ = STRING VARIABLE
30 LET A# = 1.751619278#
40 LET A = A#
50 LET A% = A#
60 PRINT "ORIGINAL DATA VALUE - 1.751619278"
70 PRINT "DOUBLE PREC.", "SINGLE PREC.", "INTEGER"
80 PRINT A#, A, A%
90 LET A$ = A#
100 END

RUN
ORIGINAL DATA VALUE - 1.751619278
DOUBLE PREC.    SINGLE PREC.    INTEGER
 1.751619278     1.751619          2

Type mismatch in 90
```

Note that the integer variable A% is rounded to the nearest whole number, changing it from 1.751619278 to 2. Also, the single precision variable A causes the original double precision value to be rounded to the nearest seven digits, or 1.751619.

## Logic Structures

The logic structure of the preceding programs, as well as the remaining programs in this chapter, follows the simple sequence described in Chapter 1. You will recall that this sequence goes from one line to the next in the program without a branch or transfer in direction. The simple sequence logic structure was illustrated in Chapter 2 (Figure 2.1).

Applications of LET statements are given in Cases 5.1 and 5.2.

## CASE 5.1

**Problem**

**Calculation of Merchandise Inventory Turnover Ratio**

One method of measuring inventory management is to find the merchandise inventory turnover ratio and compare it to the ratio of prior years or with similar industry measures. This ratio can be computed by taking the cost of goods sold and dividing it by the average inventory. The first step is to obtain the average inventory. This is done by taking the sum of the beginning and ending inventory and dividing by 2.

Create a program that will determine average inventory and the merchandise inventory turnover ratio.

**Data Input**  Over a period of time your business sold $24,000 worth of goods. If the beginning period inventory was $2,000 and the ending period inventory was $1,000, what is the inventory turnover at cost?

**Process/Formulas**  The merchandise inventory ratio is found using these formulas:

$$\text{Average inventory} = \frac{\text{beginning inventory} + \text{ending inventory}}{2}$$

$$\text{Merchandise inventory turnover ratio} = \frac{\text{cost of goods sold}}{\text{average inventory}}$$

**Output**  The output should display the following items on separate lines: cost of goods sold, beginning inventory, ending inventory, average inventory, and the merchandise inventory turnover ratio.

Program 5.9 shows how the merchandise inventory turnover ratio for Case 5.1 can be obtained using only LET statements. These statements are found in lines 50–100.

## PROGRAM 5.9   Case 5.1, Merchandise Inventory Turnover Ratio Using LET

```
4 REM CASE 5.1, PROGRAM TO CALCULATE MERCHANDISE
5 REM INVENTORY TURNOVER AT COST
6 REM PROGRAMMER- (name of person)   DATE- mm/dd/yy
7 REM VARIABLE LIST- C,B,E,I,A,T
8 REM C=COST OF GOODS SOLD
9 REM B=BEGINNING INVENTORY
10 REM E=ENDING INVENTORY
11 REM I=BEG. INVENTORY & END. INVENTORY
12 REM A=AVERAGE INVENTORY
13 REM T=MERCHANDISE INVENTORY TURNOVER AT COST
15 REM ------------------------------------
50 LET C=24000
60 LET B=2000
70 LET E=1000
80 LET I=B+E
90 LET A=I/2
100 LET T=C/A
110 PRINT "COST OF GOODS SOLD $" ;C
120 PRINT "BEG. INVENTORY $";B
130 PRINT "END. INVENTORY $";E
```

```
140 PRINT "AVERAGE INVENTORY $";A
150 PRINT
160 PRINT "MERCHANDISE INVENTORY TURNOVER AT COST";T
170 END

RUN
COST OF GOODS SOLD $ 24000
BEG. INVENTORY $ 2000
END. INVENTORY $ 1000
AVERAGE INVENTORY $ 1500

MERCHANDISE INVENTORY TURNOVER AT COST 16
```

Program 5.10 also calculates the merchandise inventory turnover ratio, but this program uses only READ/DATA statements (lines 50 and 60) to place the data into the program rather than LET statements as in Program 5.9.

## PROGRAM 5.10   Case 5.1, Merchandise Inventory Turnover Ratio, READ/DATA

```
5 REM CASE 5.1, CALCULATING MERCHANDISE
6 REM INVENTORY TURNOVER AT COST
7 REM PROGRAMMER- (name of person)   DATE - mm/dd/yy
8 REM VARIABLE- C,B,E,I,A,T
9 REM C=COST OF GOODS SOLD
10 REM B=BEG. INVENTORY
11 REM E=END. INVENTORY
12 REM I=BEG. INVENTORY & END. INVENTORY
13 REM A=AVERAGE INVENTORY
14 REM T=MERCHANDISE INVENTORY TURNOVER AT COST
15 REM ----------------------------------------
50 READ C,B,E
60 DATA 24000,2000,1000
70 LET I=B+E
80 LET A=I/2
90 LET T=C/A
100 PRINT "COST OF GOODS SOLD $";C
110 PRINT "BEG. INVENTORY $";B
120 PRINT "END. INVENTORY $";E
130 PRINT "AVERAGE INVENTORY $";A
140 PRINT
150 PRINT "MERCHANDISE INVENTORY TURNOVER AT COST";T
160 END

RUN
COST OF GOODS SOLD $ 24000
BEG. INVENTORY $ 2000
END. INVENTORY $ 1000
AVERAGE INVENTORY $ 1500

MERCHANDISE INVENTORY TURNOVER AT COST 16
```

## CASE 5.2

**Problem**  **Straight-Line Depreciation Determination**

One method of determining the depreciation of an item is by the straight-line approach. In this approach, annual depreciation is found by dividing the cost of the item (less any salvage) by the estimated years of life of the item. Create an interactive-conversational program to determine annual depreciation.

**Data Input**  Suppose at the start of the year the XYZ Construction Company purchases a piece of equipment that costs $36,000. The useful life of this type of equipment is three years. At the end of that time, the resale or salvage value is $ 1,200. These items should be entered interactively in response to an appropriate set of user instructions.

**Process/Formulas**  Straight-line depreciation is found using this formula:

$$\frac{\text{Cost } - \text{ salvage value}}{\text{Estimated years of life}} = \text{depreciation per year}$$

**Output**  The output from the program will include the item cost, salvage value, estimated years of life, and the annual depreciation.

Program 5.11 computes the annual depreciation. This conversational program uses an INPUT statement in line 110 to request the required values for the program. Line 120 calculates cost less salvage, and line 130 finds the depreciation. If another depreciation result is needed, we can type RUN again and the program will start over.

The flowchart for Program 5.11 is shown in Figure 5.4 (p. 107). Note the numbers placed in the upper right-hand corner of the flowchart symbols. These numbers correspond to the line numbers of the program. They provide a means of cross-reference between the flowchart and the program.

## PROGRAM 5.11  Case 5.2, Depreciation, Using LET and INPUT Statements

```
5 REM CASE 5.2, CONVERSATIONAL PROGRAM FOR STRAIGHT LINE
6 REM DEPRECIATION DETERMINATION
7 REM PROGRAMMER- (name of person)  DATE - mm/dd/yy
8 REM VARIABLE LIST-C,V,L,T,D
9 REM C=COST
10 REM V=SALVAGE VALUE
11 REM L=USEFUL LIFE
12 REM T=COST SUBTRACT SALVAGE VALUE
13 REM D=ANNUAL DEPRECIATION
15 REM -----------------------------------------------
50 PRINT "****STRAIGHT LINE DEPRECIATION DETERMINATION****"
60 PRINT
65 PRINT "INSTRUCTIONS:"
70 PRINT "TYPE IN THE FOLLOWING ITEMS EACH SEPARATED"
80 PRINT "BY A , : COST, SALVAGE VALUE (TYPE 0 IF NONE)"
```

```
90 PRINT "AND EST, YEARS OF LIFE";
100 PRINT
110 INPUT"PLEASE ENTER ITEMS:"; C,V,L
120 LET T=C-V
130 LET D=T/L
140 PRINT
150 PRINT "WITH A COST OF $";C;", A SALVAGE VALUE OF $";V
160 PRINT "AND A USEFUL LIFE OF";L;"YEARS"
165 PRINT
170 PRINT "THE ANNUAL DEPRECIATION FOR THIS ITEM IS $";D
180 END

RUN
****STRAIGHT LINE DEPRECIATION DETERMINATION****

INSTRUCTIONS:
TYPE IN THE FOLLOWING ITEMS EACH SEPARATED
BY A , : COST, SALVAGE VALUE (TYPE 0 IF NONE)
AND EST, YEARS OF LIFE

PLEASE ENTER ITEMS:36000, 1200, 3

WITH A COST OF $ 36000 , A SALVAGE VALUE OF $ 1200
AND A USEFUL LIFE OF 3 YEARS

THE ANNUAL DEPRECIATION FOR THIS ITEM IS $ 11600
```

## Concatenation

String variables can be joined using the LET statement. This joining is done by addition, as illustrated in Program 5.12. Note how the LET statement in line 30 joins string data items A$ and B$ to form C$, a single literal reading HELLO THERE. Since strings can also be in the form of characters, such as asterisks (*) or dashes (-), we can join them together as well, as in line 80. Blank spaces can also be assigned to a string, as in line 60 and joined together with other strings.

**PROGRAM 5.12   Adding String Variables—Concatenation**

```
10 LET A$ = "HELLO "
20 LET B$ = "THERE"
30 LET C$ = A$ + B$
40 PRINT A$, B$, C$
50 LET D$ = "-------"
60 LET E$ = "       "
70 LET F$ = "*******"
80 LET G$ = F$ + E$ + D$ + E$ + F$
90 PRINT G$
100 END

RUN
HELLO           THERE           HELLO THERE
*******         -------         *******
```

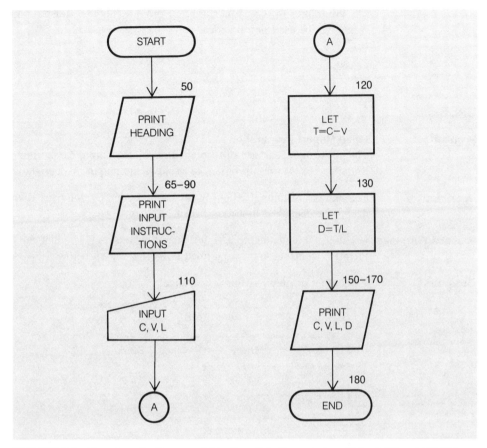

**FIGURE 5.4**  Flowchart for Program 5.11, Case 5.2, Depreciation, Using LET and INPUT
Statements

By assigning special characters to string variables using the LET statement, we can
construct output displays that have lines or column separators. Program 5.13 illustrates
that it is easier to assign the literal items ''¦'' and ''-'' to strings than to place the
characters directly into PRINT statements each time they are needed.

## PROGRAM 5.13    String Assignments for Output Format Displays

```
10 LET V$ = "¦"
20 LET D$ = "------------"
30 PRINT V$; "HEADING 1    "V$; "HEADING 2    ";V$; "HEADING 3    ";V$
35 LET X$ = V$+D$+V$+D$+V$+D$+V$
40 PRINT X$
50 PRINT X$
60 PRINT X$
70 END

RUN
¦HEADING 1    ¦HEADING 2    ¦HEADING 3    ¦
¦------------¦------------¦------------¦
¦------------¦------------¦------------¦
¦------------¦------------¦------------¦
```

Program 5.14, based on Case 5.3, provides another illustration of how string assignments can be used in a practical way.

. . . . . . . . . . . . . . . . . . . . . . . . . . . . . . . . . . .

## CASE 5.3

**Problem**

**Lined Report Preparation**
The physical appearance of displayed or printed output can be improved by adding lines to the results. Write a program to produce the output display shown below.

**Data Input**

The number of units (000's) for any two months, by company division (I and II), is the data to be displayed in a report form.

**Process/Formulas**

Use the LET statement to assign a line of characters (''-'') that can be repeated in several PRINT statements to create a lined output as shown below.

**Output**

The output display has this appearance:

```
------------------------------------
                  MONTHS
------------------------------------
DIVISION     JAN,          FEB,
------------------------------------
I            120           140
------------------------------------
II           135           150
------------------------------------
```

. . . . . . . . . . . . . . . . . . . . . . . . . . . . . . . . . . .

Program 5.14 illustrates how the output display for Case 5.3 can be produced. Line 20 assigns a sequence of underline characters to the string variable LN$. When this string variable is used with PRINT statements 70, 90, 110, 130, and 150, it generates the required displayed effect.

## PROGRAM 5.14   Case 5.3, Displayed Report Form

```
2 REM CASE 5.3 INVENTORY REPORT
4 REM PROGRAMMER- (name of person)  DATE - mm/dd/yy
6 REM
8 REM    VARIABLE LIST - IC$, UN, PR, DVI
10 REM            LN$ = LINE
12 REM            MN1$, MN2$ = MONTH STRING
14 REM            D1, D2, D3, D4 = UNITS (000'S)
16 REM ---------------------------------------------------
20 LET LN$ = "-----------------------------------------"
30 READ MN1$, MN2$
```

```
40 DATA JAN,, FEB,
50 READ D1, D2, D3, D4
60 DATA 120, 140, 135, 150
70 PRINT LN$
80 PRINT TAB(20); "MONTHS"
90 PRINT LN$
100 PRINT "DIVISION", MN1$, MN2$
110 PRINT LN$
120 PRINT "I", D1, D2
130 PRINT LN$
140 PRINT "II", D3, D4
150 PRINT LN$
```

```
RUN
----------------------------------------
                    MONTHS
----------------------------------------
DIVISION      JAN,          FEB,
----------------------------------------
I              120           140
----------------------------------------
II             135           150
----------------------------------------
```

## SUMMARY

The LET statement, like the READ and INPUT statements, can be used to assign constant values to variables. In addition, the LET statement can be used to evaluate expressions and assign numeric data values or string items to variables.

The SWAP statement is used to exchange the values, or character strings, of two variables.

A READ/DATA, LET, and PRINT statement pattern in a program form a simple sequence logic structure.

## BASIC VOCABULARY SUMMARY

| Statement* | Purpose | Examples |
| --- | --- | --- |
| LET | Assigns numeric values, or character strings, to variables, from the right side of the "=" to the left side. | 10 LET X = 5<br>20 LET T = T + 1<br>30 LET A = B * 2/C<br>40 LET N$ = "AJAX"<br>50 LET P$ = L$ + M$ |
| SWAP | Causes contents of two variables to be exchanged. | 25 SWAP X, Y<br>35 SWAP A$, B$ |

*The keyword LET is not required in Microsoft BASIC.

Review Questions

**5.1** Compare and contrast the LET statement with READ/DATA.

**5.2** Find all of the syntax errors in the following LET statements:
a. 10 LET X + Y = Z
b. 20 LET S = "SUM OF", A + B
c. 30 LET "ANS." = (2 + X) − Y
d. 40 LET R = "X + 9"
e. 50 LET 2AVE = (X + Y)/2
f. 60 LET A + B + C " = " SUM
g. 70 LET C$ = A + B
h. 80 LET DAT$ = 3/6/90
i. 90 LET L2 = L$ + M$

♦ **5.3** Show what the following program will print when it is run:

```
10 READ A,B,C,D
15 DATA 1,2
20 LET X = A + B
25 LET B = X + A
30 LET A = X^B/C*A - 5
35 DATA 4,5,6
40 PRINT A,B,C,X
45 END
```

♦ **5.4** What will the program in exercise 5.3 print if lines 25 and 30 are interchanged?

**5.5** Correct the following program:

```
10 READ A + B
20 LET 5 = C
30 PRINT X
40 LET A + B + C = X
50 DATA 12,16,9,3,8,10
90 END
```

**5.6** Look at the following program. What results will it produce? Can you suggest any revisions?

```
20 LET I = P*(1 + R)^N
30 LET P = 2000
40 LET R = .085
50 LET N = 6
60 PRINT P,R,N,I
90 END
```

**5.7** Trace the values of the variables A, B, C, and D for the following program (Program 5.3) as was done in the text for Program 5.2.

```
10 READ A,B,C,D
20 LET B=A
30 LET A=B+C
40 LET C=A
50 LET D=A+D
60 PRINT A,B,C,D
70 DATA 1,2,3,4
80 END
```

♦ **5.8**  Rewrite Program 3.9 (Case 3.1) using LET statements to evaluate total revenue, total cost, and total profit. Assign total revenue to the variable $T1$, total cost to $T2$, and total profit to $T$.

```
5 REM CASE 3.1, FINDING TOTAL PROFITS. TOTAL PROFITS = TOTAL
6 REM REVENUE - TOTAL COST
7 REM PROGRAMMER- (name of person)  DATE - mm/dd/yy
10 REM WHERE P=PRICE PER UNIT, C=COST PER UNIT,
15 REM AND U=# UNITS SOLD AND BOUGHT
16 REM -------------------------------------------
30 READ P,C,U
40 DATA 10,6,50,225
65 PRINT
68 PRINT
70 PRINT "TOTAL PROFIT REPORT"
75 PRINT
80 PRINT "NUMBER OF UNITS SOLD";U
85 PRINT "PRICE PER UNIT";P,"COST PER UNIT";C
90 PRINT "TOTAL REVENUE";P*U
92 PRINT "LESS TOTAL COST";C*U
95 PRINT "------------------------------------"
100 PRINT "TOTAL PROFIT";P*U-C*U
199 END
```

**5.9**  Rewrite Program 4.8 (Case 4.1) using LET statements to evaluate the number of units sold ($N$) this week and the ending inventory ($E$).

```
5 REM CASE 4.1, INVENTORY ANALYSIS
6 REM PROGRAMMER- (name of person)  DATE - mm/dd/yy
7 REM VARIABLE LIST-I,M,T,W,T1,F
8 REM I=BEGINNING INVENTORY
9 REM M=MONDAY SALES
10 REM T=TUESDAY SALES
11 REM W=WEDNESDAY SALES
12 REM T1=THURSDAY SALES
13 REM F=FRIDAY SALES
14 REM -------------------------------------------
15 INPUT "WHAT IS BEGINNING INVENTORY?";I
20 INPUT "WHAT WERE SALES FOR EACH DAY OF THE WEEK?";M,T,W,T1,F
30 PRINT
35 PRINT "BEG. INV.";I;"UNITS"
40 PRINT
45 PRINT "              DAILY SALES"
50 PRINT "            ----------  "
55 PRINT "MON.","TUES.","WED.","THUR.","FRI."
60 PRINT M,T,W,T1,F
65 PRINT
70 PRINT "NUMBER OF UNITS SOLD THIS WEEK";M+T+W+T1+F
75 PRINT "ENDING INVENTORY";I-(M+T+W+T1+F)
99 END
```

## Programming Activities

**5.10**  **Purpose**  To use READ/DATA and LET statements with numeric data and the simple sequence logic structure for simple output formatting.

**Problem**  Write and run a program that reads in values for $A$, $B$, $C$, and $D$ and then calculates

$$Y = \frac{(A + B)^\wedge 2}{C^\wedge 2 + D^\wedge 2} \div \frac{1/D + 1/B}{C^\wedge A - B}$$

Use LET statements to evaluate each of the numerators and denominators.

**Data**  Use the data values $A = 1$, $B = 2$, $C = 3$, $D = 4$.

**Output**  Your output should display on the screen and follow this format:

```
RUN
A               B               C               D               Y
-------------------------------------------------------------------
1               2               3               4              .48
```

**5.11**  **Purpose**  To use READ/DATA, LET, and SWAP statements with numeric data and the simple sequence logic structure for simple output formatting.

**Problem**  Write and run a program that reads values into variables $A$, $B$, and $C$ and then moves $B$ to $A$, $C$ to $B$, and $A$ to $C$.

**Data**  Use the data values $A = 1$, $B = 2$, $C = 3$.

**Output**  Your output should display on the screen and follow this format:

```
RUN
A               B               C
1               2               3
2               3               1
```

**5.12**  **Purpose**  To do complex problem solving using appropriate READ/DATA statements, numeric data, and LPRINT for simple output formatting.

**Problem**  The Cobb-Douglas production function has the form

$$\text{Output} = A \times L^\alpha \times K^{1 - \alpha}$$

where $A$ is technical progress, $L$ is the employed labor force, $K$ is the stock of capital for production, $\alpha$ is the fraction of total output earned by labor, and $1 - \alpha$ is the fraction of total output ($O$) earned by capital. If $A$ is 15, $L$ is 500, $K$ is 250, and $\alpha$ is .5, write a program that reads in this data and computes output.

**Data**  Use the data values provided in the problem statement.

**Output**  Your output should display on the screen and also generate a hard copy. Output should follow this format:

```
RUN
    OUTPUT      A       L       K       X
    5303.299    15     200     250      .5
```

**5.13**  **Purpose**  To use READ/DATA and LET statements with numeric data and the simple sequence logic structure for simple output formatting.

**Problem**  Gross profit margin is used by businesses to measure the profitability of their products or services. It is often expressed as a percentage based on the difference between selling price and the cost of producing the product or service. The gross profit margin can be expressed as

$$GPM = \frac{SP - \text{cost}}{SP}$$

where *GPM* is the gross profit margin, *SP* is the selling price of the item, and cost is the production cost of making the item. Using the LET statement and data entry with the READ statement, write and run a program to determine the gross profit margin for a product that has a selling price of $34.95 and a production cost of $27.50.

**Data**  Use the data values provided in the problem statement.

**Output**  Your output should display on the screen and follow this format:

```
RUN
PRICE IS $ 34.95
COST IS  $ 27.5
THE GROSS MARGIN IS 21.31617%
```

**5.14**  **Purpose**  To use INPUT and LET statements with numeric data and the simple sequence logic structure for simple output formatting.

**Problem**  Using interactive data entry and the gross profit margin formula defined in exercise 5.13, write and run a program to determine the gross profit margin for a product that has a selling price of $34.95 and a production cost of $27.50.

**Data**  Use the data values provided in the problem statement.

**Output**  Your output should display on the screen and follow this format:

```
RUN
ENTER THE PRICE AND THE COST
WHAT IS THE PRICE ? 34.95
WHAT IS THE COST ? 27.5
THE GROSS MARGIN IS  21.31617%
```

**◆ 5.15**  **Purpose**  To use READ/DATA and LET statements with numeric data and the simple sequence logic structure for simple output formatting.

**Problem**  What amount could be invested at 15 percent compounded annually that will grow to $300,000 or more at the end of five years? Write and run a program that will find the present value *P*. To find the answer, use this formula:

$$P = \frac{F}{(1 + r)^n}$$

where *P* is the present value, *F* is the future amount needed, *r* is the annual rate of interest (a decimal), and *n* is the length of the period.

**Data**  Use the data values provided in the problem statement.

**Output**    Your output should display on the screen and follow this format:

```
RUN
FUTURE AMOUNT IS $ 300000
ANNUAL RATE OF INTEREST IS 15 %
TIME PERIOD IS 5 YEARS
THE PRESENT VALUE IS $ 149153
```

**5.16**    **Purpose**    To use appropriate INPUT statements with numeric data and the simple sequence logic structure for simple output formatting.

**Problem**    What amount could be invested at 15 percent compounded annually that will grow to $300,000 or more at the end of five years? Using this data and the formula given in exercise 5.15, write and run an interactive conversational program that will find the present value *P*.

**Data**    Use the data values provided in the problem statement. Remember that data entry should be interactive.

**Output**    Your output should display on the screen and follow this format:

```
RUN
WHAT IS THE FUTURE AMOUNT NEEDED ? 300000
WHAT IS THE ANNUAL RATE OF INTEREST? .15
WHAT IS THE TIME PERIOD ? 5
THE PRESENT VALUE IS $ 149153
```

**5.17**    **Purpose**    To use READ/DATA and LET statements with numeric data, the simple sequence logic structure, double precision, and LPRINT for simple output formatting.

**Problem**    A firm estimates that five years from now it will need $2 million to purchase some new equipment. To accumulate this sum, the firm decides to set aside an amount each year. The firm can earn 9 percent compounded annually on its cash. To find the amount that must be deposited at the end of each of the five years to accumulate the $2 million, the following formula is used:

$$A = F \left[ \frac{r}{(1 + r)^n - 1} \right]$$

where *A* is the amount to be deposited at the end of *n* years, *r* is the annual interest rate, and *F* is the future sum needed. Write and run a program that will find *A*.

**Data**    Use the data values provided in the problem statement.

**Output**    Your output should display on the screen and also generate a hard copy. Output should follow this format:

```
RUN
              A                          F            R          N
- - - - - - - - - - - - - - - - - - - - - - - - - - - - - - - - - - - -
    334184.7080809896              2000000         .09          5
```

**5.18**    **Purpose**    To use READ/DATA and LET statements with numeric data and the simple sequence logic structure for simple output formatting.

**Problem**    An individual retirement account (IRA) permits an annual contribution of up to $2,000 a year. The total accumulation for such an account is calculated by the formula

$$F = A \left[ \frac{(1 + R)^N - 1}{R} \right]$$

where $F$ is the total, $A$ is the amount paid into the account each year for $N$ years, and $R$ is the rate of interest. If $1,500 a year is put into an IRA at 7.5 percent compounded annually for 10 years, what is the total accumulation? Write and run a program to find the answer.

**Data**    Use the data values provided in the problem statement.

**Output**    Your output should display on the screen and follow this format:

```
RUN

       F                A             R             N
-------------------------------------------------------
   21220.65           1500          .075          10
```

**5.19**    **Purpose**    To do complex problem solving using READ/DATA and LET statements with numeric data and the simple sequence logic structure for simple output formatting.

**Problem**    To compute the monthly payment necessary to amortize (pay off) a loan given the principal amount $P$, the yearly interest rate $Y$, and the term of the loan in $N$ years, the formula below is used:

$$A = \frac{PR(1 + R)^M}{(1 + R)^M - 1}$$

where

$$R = \frac{Y}{12}$$

$$M = 12N$$

Write and run a program to find the monthly payment for a 20-year loan of $20,000, having an annual interest rate of 14 percent, where $A$ is the monthly amount, $P$ is the principal amount, $R$ is the monthly interest rate, $M$ is the number of months over which the payments are to be made, $Y$ is the annual interest rate, and $N$ is the number of years.

**Data**    Use the data values provided in the problem statement.

**Output**    Your output should display on the screen and follow this format:

```
RUN
LOAN AMOUNT $ 20000
ANNUAL RATE OF INTEREST    14 %
YEARS OF THE LOAN    20
THE MONTHLY PAYMENT IS $ 248.7043
```

**5.20** **Purpose** To do complex problem solving using appropriate INPUT and LET statements with numeric data and the simple sequence logic structure for simple output formatting.

**Problem** Using the formula given in exercise 5.19, write and run a program to find the monthly payment for a 20-year loan of $20,000, having an annual interest rate of 14 percent, where $A$ is the monthly amount, $P$ is the principal amount, $R$ is the monthly interest rate, $M$ is the number of months over which the payments are to be made, $Y$ is the annual interest rate, and $N$ is the number of years.

**Data** Use the data values provided in the problem statement. Data entry is interactive.

**Output** Your output should display on the screen and follow this format:

```
RUN
-------------------------------------------
WHAT IS THE LOAN AMOUNT ? 20000
WHAT IS THE ANNUAL RATE OF INTEREST ? .14
HOW MANY YEARS IS THE LOAN ? 20
-------------------------------------------
THE MONTHLY PAYMENT IS $ 248.7043
```

**5.21** **Purpose** To use the simple sequence logic structure and string and numeric data for simple output formatting.

**Problem** Write and run a program to read in the employee name, hours worked, and hourly rate. Your program should output a table showing the name, salary (number of hours × hourly rate), federal tax (20 percent of salary), social security tax (.05478 × salary), and net salary (that is, gross salary − all deductions).

**Data**

| EMPLOYEE NAME | HOURS WORKED | RATE |
|---|---|---|
| Brown, A. | 37 | $4.50 |

**Output** Your output should have this format:

```
RUN
----------------------------------------------------------------
EMPLOYEE        SALARY       FED.TAX      S.S.TAX      NET SALARY
----------------------------------------------------------------
Brown, A.       166.5        33.3         9.120869     124.0791
----------------------------------------------------------------
```

♦ **5.22** **Purpose** To use appropriate INPUT statements, the simple sequence logic structure, and string and numeric data for simple output formatting.

**Problem** Write and run a program using interactive data entry to input the employee name, hours worked, and hourly rate. Using the information given in exercise 5.21, your program should output a table showing the name, salary, federal tax, social security tax, and net salary.

**Data**

| EMPLOYEE NAME | HOURS WORKED | RATE |
|---|---|---|
| Brown, A. | 37 | $4.50 |

**Output**    Your output should have this format:

```
RUN
ENTER EMPLOYEE NAME Brown, A,
ENTER NUMBER OF HOURS WORKED AND RATE 37, 4.50
-------------------------------------------------------------
EMPLOYEE      SALARY      FED.TAX      S.S.TAX      NET SALARY
-------------------------------------------------------------
Brown, A,      166.5       33.3       9.120869      124.0791
-------------------------------------------------------------
```

**5.23**    **Purpose**  To use the simple sequence logic structure and string and numeric data for simple output formatting.

**Problem**  The ABC Company has four divisions selling various products. Management wants to know what percent of total sales volume is generated by each division. Below are the gross sales figures by division for the last year. Write and run a program that reads values into variables $D1$, $D2$, $D3$, and $D4$ (the amounts sold by the four divisions of the company) and prints as output a table that shows (1) the total sales of each division and (2), using a third column headed "% of TOTAL," the percent of total sales represented by each division. (Use [division sales/total] $\times$ 100 to find the percent of total sales.)

**Data**

| DIVISION | SALES (MILLION $) |
|----------|-------------------|
| West | 2.85 |
| South | 7.62 |
| North | 3.57 |
| East | 2.81 |

**Output**    Your output should have this format:

```
RUN
DIVISION        AMOUNT SOLD    % OF TOTAL
-----------------------------------------
WEST              2.85         16.91395
SOUTH             7.62         45.22256
NORTH             3.57         21.18695
EAST              2.81         16.67656
-----------------------------------------
```

# CHAPTER 6

# FORMATTING OUTPUT

Upon completing this chapter, you will be able to do the following:

- Understand how to design output displays using numeric and string data formatting.
- Use the various forms of the PRINT USING statement to enhance the output of programming problem solutions.
- Explain the difference between the PRINT statement and PRINT USING statement for output display.
- Continue to develop programming problem solutions using a simple sequence logic structure of READ/DATA, LET, PRINT USING, END.
- Continue to develop programming problem solutions using a simple sequence logic structure of INPUT, LET, PRINT USING, END.

In this chapter you will see how it is possible to produce output with greater flexibility than was previously available with the PRINT statement and TAB function. With the use of a PRINT USING statement, you can produce output that is formatted to include dollar signs, embedded commas, right justification, a specific number of decimal places, and other useful features.

## THE *PRINT USING* STATEMENT

Program 6.1 is a copy of the program to find total profit, which was described in Case 3.1 (Chapter 3). The output report produced was formatted by the PRINT statements in lines 70–100. The numeric contents of the report are displayed in a very simple manner. For example, the price, cost, revenue, and other items are not preceded by a $. Some numbers have no decimal places (the price is 10, and the total revenue is 2250); others have one (the cost per unit is 6.5). The alignment of the output is left justified; that is, the values 225, 6.5, 2250, and 787.5 all align on the character that is most to the left, as do the 10 and 1462.5.

## PROGRAM 6.1   Output Generated with PRINT Statements

```
5 REM CASE 3.1, FINDING TOTAL PROFITS
6 REM PROGRAMMER- (name of person)  DATE - mm/dd/yy
7 REM              TOTAL PROFITS = TOTAL REVENUE - TOTAL COST
9 REM              VARIABLE LIST - P, C, U, REV, TC, PROF
10 REM             P=PRICE PER UNIT, C=COST PER UNIT,
15 REM             U=# UNITS SOLD AND BOUGHT
16 REM             REV=REVENUE = P*U
17 REM             TC=TOTAL COST = C*U
18 REM             PROF=TOTAL PROFIT = REV-TC
20 REM -------------------------------------------------------
30 READ P, C, U
40 DATA 10, 6.50, 225
45 LET REV = P*U
50 LET TC = C*U
55 LET PROF = REV - TC
65 PRINT
68 PRINT
70 PRINT TAB(10); "TOTAL PROFIT REPORT"
75 PRINT
80 PRINT "UNITS SOLD",U
85 PRINT "PRICE PER UNIT",P
87 PRINT "COST PER UNIT",C
90 PRINT "TOTAL REVENUE", REV
92 PRINT "LESS TOTAL COST", TC
```

```
95 PRINT "-----------------------------------------------"
100 PRINT "TOTAL PROFIT", PROF
199 END

RUN


                   TOTAL PROFIT REPORT

UNITS SOLD         225
PRICE PER UNIT                      10
COST PER UNIT      6.5
TOTAL REVENUE      2250
LESS TOTAL COST                    1462.5
-------------------------------------------------
TOTAL PROFIT       787.5
```

Now look at the difference in the output for Program 6.2.

## PROGRAM 6.2   Output Generated with PRINT USING Statements

```
10 REM CASE 3.1, FINDING TOTAL PROFITS
20 REM PROGRAMMER- (name of person)  DATE - mm/dd/yy
30 REM            TOTAL PROFITS = TOTAL REVENUE - TOTAL COST
40 REM            VARIABLE LIST - P, C, U, REV, TC, PROF
50 REM            P = PRICE PER UNIT, C=COST PER UNIT,
60 REM            U=# UNITS SOLD AND BOUGHT
70 REM            REV=REVENUE = P*U
80 REM            TC=TOTAL COST = C*U
90 REM            PROF=TOTAL PROFIT = REV-TC
100 REM -----------------------------------------------------
110 READ P, C, U
120 DATA 10, 6.50, 225
130 LET REV = P*U
140 LET TC = C*U
150 LET PROF = REV - TC
160 PRINT
170 PRINT
180 PRINT TAB(10); "TOTAL PROFIT REPORT"
190 PRINT
200 PRINT USING "UNITS SOLD    ###"; U
210 PRINT USING "PRICE PER UNIT        $$###.##"; P
220 PRINT USING "COST PER UNIT         $$###.##"; C
230 PRINT USING "TOTAL REVENUE       $$#,###.##"; REV
240 PRINT USING "LESS TOTAL COST    -$$#,###.##"; TC
250 PRINT         "---------------------------------------"
260 PRINT USING "TOTAL PROFIT        $$#,###.##"; PROF
270 END

RUN
```

```
          TOTAL  PROFIT  REPORT
UNITS  SOLD              225
PRICE  PER  UNIT                    $10.00
COST  PER  UNIT                      $6.50
TOTAL  REVENUE                    $2,250.00
LESS  TOTAL  COST               - $1,462.50
-----------------------------------------
TOTAL  PROFIT                      $787.50
```

The output of Program 6.1 and Program 6.2 is identical in the information it conveys. However, it is very different in the way it is formatted. In Program 6.2 the output values are now right justified, that is, they align on the character that is most to the right of each item. The $ that precedes the items enhance the overall appearance of the monetary values. Every dollar value has two decimal places shown, even if the original value was given with less than two (for example, 10 or 6.5). All of the decimal values are aligned on the decimal point. Items greater than 999 are formatted so that an embedded comma is correctly placed, as in $2,250.00. These and other revised output features are the result of using PRINT USING statements in lines 200–240 and 260.

The general form of the PRINT USING statement is

line # PRINT USING ''format'' ; variable(s) list

The format may be placed directly in the PRINT USING statement or may be assigned as a string variable. If it is not assigned to a string variable, the format must be placed in quotes. Some examples of PRINT USING have already appeared in Program 6.2. Table 6.1 provides additional examples to illustrate how the format can be specified.

As shown in Table 6.1, the format is made up of special characters, such as #, that have unique meanings. Format design must take into account whether your output is numeric or string. First we examine how numerics can be formatted; then we demonstrate formatting of string output.

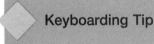

**Keyboarding Tip**   To save keystrokes, enter the keyword PRINT USING by first typing the ALT plus P key combination to display PRINT and then by typing the ALT plus U key combination to display USING.

## FORMATTING NUMBERS

Many special format characters can help you design an output that has a more formal and complete appearance. Table 6.2 lists the characters that control output formats associated with the PRINT USING statement for numeric data values.

The next several programs illustrate the use of the format control characters shown in Table 6.2. You will notice that a number of these programs have comments alongside some of the program statements. These comments are similar to REM statements (see Chapter 2) in the sense that they are not processed. A single apostrophe (') sets the comment apart from the statement. Such comments can be useful as part of your program documentation.

**TABLE 6.1** Forms of the PRINT USING Statement

| STATEMENT | EXPLANATION |
|---|---|
| **Numeric Data** | |
| 20 PRINT USING "#####"; A | The print zone for variable $A$ is specified by # characters enclosed in quotation marks. The zone for $A$ will allow up to five digits and no decimals. Decimals are rounded to the nearest whole integer. |
| 40 PRINT USING "##### ##.##"; A, B | Print zones for variables $A$ and $B$ are specified by # characters enclosed in quotation marks. Five digits are allowed for variable $A$; four digits for variable $B$, which include two for decimals. $B$ values are rounded to the nearest hundredth, and $A$ values are rounded to the nearest whole number. Spaces between character zones are included in the output. |
| 60 LET F$ = "#####"<br>70 PRINT USING F$; A | The format for the print zone is first assigned to a string variable F$ and then placed in the PRINT USING statement. |
| 80 LET F$ = "#####"<br>90 PRINT USING F$; A, B | The format is assigned to F$. Both of the output zones for variables $A$ and $B$ are the same five character spaces on the same line next to each other. |
| 100 LET F$ = "#####    ##.##"<br>110 PRINT USING F$; A, B | The format is assigned to F$. The output zones for variables $A$ and $B$ are not the same (five integer spaces for $A$; four spaces for $B$, which include two for decimals). Spaces between character zones are included in the output. |
| **Nonnumeric or String Data** | |
| 20 PRINT USING "\      \"; CO$ | The print zone for string variable CO$ is specified by the number of spaces between the backslashes plus two more. |
| 30 PRINT USING "\ \ \    \"; A$, B$ | Print zones for string variables A$ and B$ are specified by the number of spaces between the backslashes plus two more. |
| 40 LET FT$ = "\ \ \  \"<br>80 PRINT USING FT$; A$, B$ | As with numerics above, one or more print zones can be assigned to a string FT$ and then placed in the PRINT USING statement. |

## Numeric Formats within the PRINT USING Statement

Program 6.3 shows how the numeric format is placed in quotation marks after the keyword PRINT USING. It is separated from the variable *NUM* by a semicolon. Line 30 establishes a print zone for an integer value of up to seven character spaces. When the value 12345, assigned to the variable *NUM,* prints out, three blank spaces precede the numeral. Two spaces are left from the format of seven spaces; the other is the implied plus (+) sign. Lines 40 and 50 show the format containing two and three decimal spaces, respectively. Although the original data value (*NUM* = 12345) contained no decimal

**TABLE 6.2**   PRINT USING Numeric Control Characters

| CHARACTER | PURPOSE | EXAMPLE | VALUE | OUTPUT |
|---|---|---|---|---|
| # | Provides space for one digit. Need as many as largest number. Extras count as blank spaces. Output is right justified. | # #### #### | 5.3 142 9118 | 5 142 9118 |
| . | Specifies a decimal point location in a numeric zone. Zeros are added when there is no decimal character. Numbers are rounded to fit into decimal spaces. Data is decimally aligned within a field. | #.# ##.### ##.## ##.# | 5 12.448 12.448 12.448 | 5.0 12.448 12.45 12.4 |
| , | Specifies location of comma in a numeric zone. Comma will not output unless number of characters is sufficient. | #,### ##,### #,###,### | 999 4788 54200 | 999 4,788 54,200 |
| $ | Provides that dollar sign will be printed exactly as given. Unused #s are blank. | $#### $##,###.## | 5 8682.5 | $5 $ 8,682.50 |
| $$ | Specifies that a single $ will appear before the leftmost digit. Floats the $. | $$#### $$#,###.## | 5 8682.5 | $5 $8,682.50 |
| ** | Specifies that leading blanks and/or spaces will be filled with *. Asterisk protection feature. | **#### **##,###.## | 5 8682.5 | *****5 ***8,682.50 |
| **$ | Specifies that leading spaces and/or blanks will be filled with *. First character before numeric is a $. Combines $$ and ** control character features. | **$#### **$##,###.## | 5 8682.5 | *****$5 ***$8,682.50 |
| + | At the beginning of the format, causes the sign ( + or − ) of the number to be printed out before the number. At the end of the format, it causes the sign of the number to be printed after the number. | +#### +#### ####+ ####+ | +5 −5 +5 −5 | +5 −5 5+ 5− |
| − | At the end of the format, causes negative numbers to be printed with a trailing −. | ####− ####− | 5 −5 | 5 5− |

part, when processed with a decimal format, two or three zeros are placed in the designated decimal places.

If the number is too large for the format, the error is indicated with a % symbol. Thus, in the last line of the output, a percent symbol (%) leads the value 12345, indicating an error due to insufficient spaces in the format of line 60. Only four #### characters follow PRINT USING in that line for a data value that needs at least five spaces.

## PROGRAM 6.3 PRINT USING Numeric Formats

```
10 READ NUM
20 DATA 12345
25                                      'Comments:
30 PRINT USING "#######"; NUM          'integer field
40 PRINT USING "#######.##"; NUM        'field with 2 decimal places
50 PRINT USING "#######.###"; NUM       'field with 3 decimal places
60 PRINT USING "####"; NUM              'field too small for 5 place number
90 END

RUN
    12345
    12345.00
    12345.000
%12345
```

The PRINT USING format can result in numeric values being rounded when such rounding may be not desirable. In Program 6.4, for example, the value of *NUM* = 12345.67 is placed into a format without decimal spaces in line 30. This results in output with a value of 12346, since *NUM* has been rounded up in this case. Lines 40 and 50 show how the format can be set up to include as many decimal places as are needed for the data that will be processed by the program. It is important that you correctly format the zone specifications to agree with the data values being printed out.

## PROGRAM 6.4 PRINT USING Numeric Formats, Rounding

```
10 READ NUM
20 DATA 12345.67
25                                      'Comments:
30 PRINT USING "#######"; NUM          'field without decimal places rounds
40 PRINT USING "#######.##"; NUM        'field with 2 decimal places
50 PRINT USING "#######.###"; NUM       'field with 3 decimal places
90 END

RUN
    12346
    12345.67
    12345.670
```

More than one numeric data value can follow a single PRINT USING format zone specification. In line 30 of Program 6.5, for instance, NUM1 and NUM2 both use the decimal format ###,###.##. Note that this format also contains an embedded comma for values greater than 999.99. Observe the second line of output: the data values 12345.67 and 987 have become 12,345.67 and 987.00. Adding two dollar symbols to the beginning of the format in line 30 establishes a new format (line 50). This format causes all numeric output to have a floating dollar sign as a leading character.

## PROGRAM 6.5    PRINT USING Numeric Formats, Comma and Floating $

```
10 READ NUM1, NUM2
20 DATA 12345.67, 987
22                                          'Comments:
25 PRINT NUM1, NUM2                         'ordinary print statement
30 PRINT USING "  ###,###.##"; NUM1, NUM2   'field with comma & 2 decimal places
50 PRINT USING "$$###,###.##"; NUM1, NUM2   'floating dollar $ signs
90 END

RUN
  12345.67      987
    12,345.67       987.00
  $12,345.67      $987.00
```

When negotiable instruments such as checks are printed, it is important to prevent possible alterations by making the blank spaces in front of the numeric dollar amount unusable. One way to fill up excess blanks in a numeric field is to use a floating dollar sign (see Program 6.5). Another approach is to fill all leading unused spaces in a format with asterisks. This is called *asterisk protection*. It prevents anyone from increasing the amount by typing in additional numbers. Program 6.6 illustrates in line 50 how two ** characters are placed in the format. The resulting output shows all extra blanks filled with asterisks, plus two additional asterisk characters. Note that this second line of output appears crowded, since all character spaces have been filled. To improve the appearance, leading or trailing spaces can be included in the format, as shown in lines 70 and 80. The last two lines of output now have the additional blank spaces between data values.

## PROGRAM 6.6    PRINT USING Numeric Formats, Asterisk Protection

```
10 READ NUM1, NUM2
20 DATA 1234.56, 987
30                                          'Comments:
40 PRINT NUM1, NUM2                         'ordinary print statement
45 PRINT
50 PRINT USING "**#,###.##"; NUM1, NUM2     'asterisk protection
60 PRINT USING "**$#,###.##"; NUM1, NUM2    'asterisks & dollar sign
65 PRINT
70 PRINT USING "    **#,###.##"; NUM1, NUM2 'leading spaces, asterisks
80 PRINT USING "    **$#,###.##"; NUM1, NUM2 'leading spaces, * & $ sign
90 END

RUN
  1234.56         987

**1,234.56****987.00
**$1,234.56****$987.00

  **1,234.56    ****987.00
  **$1,234.56    ****$987.00
```

It is possible to format output to control how plus and minus signs are printed. These signs can be printed in a leading position—in front of the numeric value—or in a trailing position—after the numeric value. A plus sign placed as the first character in the format (Program 6.7, line 50) will cause the sign of the value ( + or − ) to be displayed, as shown in the second line of program output. These signs can also trail the values displayed by putting a plus sign at the end of the format, as in line 60. The result can be seen in the third line of output, where the values have a trailing + and −, respectively. To display a trailing minus sign only, place a minus at the end of the format, as shown in line 70. The result of this format is shown in the last line of output (987.00−).

## PROGRAM 6.7   PRINT USING Numeric Formats, Leading and Trailing Signs

```
10 READ NUM1, NUM2
20 DATA 1234.56, -987
30                                      'Comments:
40 PRINT NUM1, NUM2                     'ordinary print statement
50 PRINT USING "  +#,###.## "; NUM1, NUM2  'display + or - sign
60 PRINT USING "   #,###.##+"; NUM1, NUM2  'display + or - at end
70 PRINT USING "   #,###.##-"; NUM1, NUM2  'display trailing -, no +
90 END

RUN
  1234.56        -987
  +1,234.56       -987.00
  1,234.56+       987.00-
  1,234.56        987.00-
```

So far our program illustrations have shown a single format included within the quotations marks. It is possible, though, to include more than one format in the quotation marks. This is helpful with output design because not every numeric requires the same treatment. Some numbers need a leading dollar sign, some need an asterisk protection, and others need no asterisk protection. Some values need only a few spaces, whereas others need more. Decimal spacing requirements may also differ from one numeric value to another. The format flexibility of the PRINT USING statement is illustrated in Program 6.8.

## PROGRAM 6.8   PRINT USING Numeric Formats, Multiple Print Zones

```
10 READ NUM1, NUM2
20 DATA 1234.56, 987
30                                      'Comments:
40 PRINT NUM1, NUM2                     'ordinary print
60 PRINT USING "*###,###.##    $$###.##"; NUM1, NUM2 '2 fields & variables
80 PRINT 35421.96, -2.3724             'ordinary print
100 PRINT USING "+$$##,###.##   +#,###"; 35421.96,-2.3724 '2 fields & values
110 END
```

```
RUN
 1234.56         987
***1,234.56      $987.00
 35421.96        -2.3724
 +$35,421.96     -2.372
```

Lines 60 and 100 each contain two different format specifications. Line 60 produces the second output line, in which the first data value has leading asterisks and an embedded comma. The second data value has a *currency format*, consisting of a leading dollar sign and two decimal places. Line 100 also contains multiple formats and produces the last line of program output. Note that the last data value, $-2.3724$, is rounded to $-2.372$ because the format only contains three decimal places.

We have already seen in Program 6.6 that we can include blank spaces in the format so printed output is not crowded. In addition to leading or trailing blanks, literals can be included in the format as well. Lines 60, 80, and 110 in Program 6.9 illustrate the use of literals to enhance output displays.

## PROGRAM 6.9    PRINT USING Numeric Formats, Leading and Trailing Literals

```
10 READ AMT, UN
20 DATA 1234.56, 2987
30                                        'Comments:
40 PRINT AMT, UN
60 PRINT USING "AMOUNT DUE **$#,###.##"; AMT    'leading literals
80 PRINT USING "####   UNITS"; UN               'trailing literals
100                                  'leading & trailing literals
110 PRINT USING "For #,###  Units at $$#.## per unit ...$$####,###.##"; UN,5,UN*5
120 END

RUN
 1234.56        2987
AMOUNT DUE **$1,234.56
2987   UNITS
For 2,987  Units at $5.00 per unit ... $14,935.00
```

The output from Program 6.9 begins with the original data values ($AMT = 1234.56$, and $UN = 2987$) in their unformatted design. Lines 60 and 80 cause the second and third lines of output, which show literals before (AMOUNT DUE) and after (UNITS) the respective numeric values. The last line of output displays literals and numerics inter-mixed as a result of the formatting in line 110. This line contains formats for the variable $UN$ (#,###), the numeric value 5 ($$#.##), and the computational result of the operation $UN \times 5$ ($$###,###.##).

Program 6.10, which is based on Case 6.1, provides a more comprehensive illustration of the PRINT USING statement.

## CASE 6.1

**Problem**          **Earnings Per Share Computations**
Earnings per share are one measure of corporate profitability that is commonly referred to in financial press reports and included in corporate annual reports. Write a program that will generate the earnings per share for a company.

**Data Input**       The following data represents the net income and number of shares outstanding for two years:

|                               | 1990        | 1989        |
|-------------------------------|-------------|-------------|
| Net income                    | $1,582,000  | $1,235,000  |
| Number of shares outstanding  | 250,000     | 240,000     |

**Process/Formulas** Earnings per share are determined by dividing net income by the number of shares outstanding.

**Output**           The output display should be completely formatted, and earnings per share should have two decimal places. The final display should have this appearance:

```
                                        1990          1989
                                        ----          ----
Net income ....................    $1,582,000    $1,235,000
                                   ==========    ==========
Shares of stock outstanding ...       250,000       240,000
                                   ==========    ==========
Earnings per share ............        $x.dd         $x.dd
```

---

## PROGRAM 6.10   Case 6.1 Earnings Per Share

```
10 REM CASE 6.1 EARNINGS PER SHARE COMPUTATIONS
20 REM PROGRAMMER- (name of person)  DATE - mm/dd/yy
30 REM      VARIABLE LIST -
40 REM         NI1, NI2 = NET INCOME EACH YEAR
50 REM         SHO1, SHO2 = SHARES OF COMMON STOCK OUTSTANDING
60 REM         EPS1, EPS2 = EARNINGS PER SHARE = NET INCOME/SHARES
70 REM -------------------------------------------------------------------
100 LET A1$ ="                                      1990          1989"
110 LET A2$ ="                                      ----          ----"
120 LET A3$ ="Net income ....................    $$###,###,###  $$###,###,###"
130 LET A4$ ="                                   ==========    =========="
140 LET A5$ ="Shares of stock outstanding ...       ###,###       ###,###"
160 LET A6$ ="Earnings per share ............        $$##.##       $$##.##"
170 READ NI1, NI2, SHO1, SHO2
180 DATA 1582000, 1235000, 250000, 240000
190 LET EPS1 = NI1/SHO1
200 LET EPS2 = NI2/SHO2
210 PRINT A1$
```

```
220 PRINT A2$
230 PRINT USING A3$; NI1, NI2
240 PRINT A4$
250 PRINT USING A5$; SHO1, SHO2
260 PRINT A4$
270 PRINT USING A6$; EPS1, EPS2
280 END

RUN
                                    1990          1989
                                    - - - -       - - - -
Net income ....................  $1,582,000   $1,235,000
                                 ==========   ==========
Shares of stock outstanding ...     250,000      240,000
                                 ==========   ==========
Earnings per share ...........       $6.33        $5.15
```

The output from Program 6.10 satisfies the requirements of Case 6.1. Lines 230, 250, and 270 are the essential PRINT USING format statements that cause the numeric output to appear as it does. Note that the PRINT lines 210, 220, 240, and 260, which precede the PRINT USING statements, serve to position the output away from the left margin in a uniform way.

Line 130 illustrates a useful assignment technique. Rather than repeat the literal within quotation marks in a PRINT statement each time it is needed for output, assign the literal to a variable that allows you to place the variable in the PRINT statement instead. This technique is used in lines 240 and 260.

Case 6.2 and Program 6.11 provide another illustration of the PRINT USING formatting capabilities.

## CASE 6.2

**Problem**         **Price Earnings Ratio Computations**
The business and financial press often cite a company's price-earnings ratio on common stock as a measure of profitability and an indicator of investment worthiness. Write a program that will generate the price-earnings ratio for a company.

**Data Input**      The following data represents the market price per share of common stock and the earnings per share on common stock for two years:

|                        | 1990      | 1989      |
|------------------------|-----------|-----------|
| Market price per share | $146.20   | $113.50   |
| Earnings per share     | $ 12.64   | $ 11.35   |

**Process/Formulas**  Price-earnings ratios are computed by dividing the market price per share of common stock at a specific date by the annual earnings per share.

**Output**          The output display should be completely formatted. Market price per share and earnings per share should be in currency format (each with two decimal places and a leading dollar sign). The price-earnings ratios should have one decimal place. Dollar values should be right justified, with decimal points aligned. The final display should have this appearance:

```
                                              1990       1989
                                              ----       ----
        Market price per share .......      $146.20    $113.50
                                            =======    =======
        Earnings per share      .......      $12.64     $11.35
                                            =======    =======
        Price-earnings ratio    .......       xx.d       xx.d
```

· · · · · · · · · · · · · · · · · · · · · · · · · · · · · · · · · · · · · · · · · · · · ·

## PROGRAM 6.11    Case 6.2 Price-Earnings Ratio

```
10 REM CASE 6.2 PRICE-EARNINGS RATIO COMPUTATIONS
20 REM PROGRAMMER- (name of person)  DATE - mm/dd/yy
30 REM PRICE-EARNINGS RATIO = MARKET PRICE PER SHARE/EARNINGS PER SHARE
40 REM     VARIABLE LIST -
50 REM         A1$ - A6$ = FORMATS
60 REM         MPPS1, MPPS2 = MARKET PRICE PER SHARE
70 REM         EPS1, EPS2 = EARNINGS PER SHARE
80 REM         PER1, PER2 = PRICE-EARNINGS RATIO
85 REM           PER = MARKET PRICE PER SHARE/EARNINGS PER SHARE
90 REM -------------------------------------------------------
100 READ MPPS1, MPPS2, EPS1, EPS2
110 DATA 146.20, 113.50, 12.64, 11.35
120 LET PER1 = MPPS1/EPS1
130 LET PER2 = MPPS2/EPS2
140 LET A1$ ="                                   1990       1989"
150 LET A2$ ="                                   ----       ----"
160 LET A3$ ="     Market price per share .......   $$###.##   $$###.##"
170 LET A4$ ="                                     =======    ======="
180 LET A5$ ="     Earnings per share     .......   $$##.##    $$##.##"
190 LET A6$ ="     Price-earnings ratio   .......    ##.#       ##.#"
200 PRINT A1$
210 PRINT A2$
220 PRINT USING A3$; MPPS1, MPPS2
230 PRINT A4$
240 PRINT USING A5$; EPS1, EPS2
250 PRINT A4$
260 PRINT USING A6$; PER1, PER2
270 END

RUN
                                              1990       1989
                                              ----       ----
        Market price per share .......      $146.20    $113.50
                                            =======    =======
        Earnings per share      .......      $12.64     $11.35
                                            =======    =======
        Price-earnings ratio    .......       11.6       10.0
```

The output from Program 6.11 meets the requirements of Case 6.2. Lines 220, 240, and 260 are the relevant PRINT USING format statements that cause the numeric output to appear as it does. The PRINT lines 200, 210, 230, and 250, which precede the PRINT USING statements, position the display output uniformly away from the left margin.

As in Program 6.10, line 170 eliminates the need to repeat the literal each time it is needed for output. By assigning the literal to a variable, we can then use the variable in a PRINT statement instead (see lines 230 and 250).

## Logic Structures

As in earlier chapters, the logic structure of the preceding illustrative and case programs, as well as the remaining programs in this chapter, follows the simple sequence described in Chapter 1. This sequence proceeds from one line to the next in the program without a branch or transfer in direction. The simple sequence logic structure is illustrated in Chapter 2 (Figure 2.1).

Program 6.12, using the information from Case 6.3, incorporates many of the ideas of PRINT USING formatting described so far.

## CASE 6.3

**Problem**

**Creating a Check-Writing Program**
Write a program that will print on a blank check all the items that are required.

**Data Input**

The data input consists of the date, the payee, and the dollar amount in both numerics and words. These items correspond to the check shown at the end of Program 6.12. All data items should be entered interactively.

**Process/Formulas** The process for the required program includes interactive data entry and data validation. *Validation* usually requires the examination of data for correctness against certain criteria: the screen display value should agree with the value on the source document, and the data values entered should agree with the format specified.

**Output**

The output for the program will be a screen display of all the data input entered so that it can be validated for correctness before the check is printed. A check using the layout and numeric format **#,###.##, which includes the asterisk protection feature, is printed out each time the program is processed.

## PROGRAM 6.12   Case 6.3 Check-Writing Program

```
10 REM CASE 6.3  CHECK-WRITING PROGRAM
20 REM PROGRAMMER- (name of person)  DATE- mm/dd/yy
30 REM      VARIABLE LIST -
50 REM      AMT = NUMERIC AMOUNT FOR THE CHECK
60 REM      AMT$ = AMOUNT IN WORDS
65 REM      D$ = DATE
70 REM      FMT$ = FORMAT STRING
80 REM      PAY$ = PAYEE
85 REM      PR$ = INPUT VARIABLE TO "PAUSE" PROGRAM EXECUTION
90 REM -----------------------------------------------------
100 REM    SEGMENT TO ENTER CHECK INFORMATION
110 LET FMT$ = "**#,###.##"
120 CLS
130 INPUT "1. Date    mm/dd     "; D$
```

```
140 INPUT "2. Pay to the order of "; PAY$
150 INPUT "3. Dollar Amount (numerics) "; AMT
160 INPUT "4. Enter Amount (words) "; AMT$
170 REM
180 REM     SEGMENT TO PRINT TO SCREEN
190 PRINT
200 PRINT "== ITEMS TO BE PRINTED OUT ON THE CHECK- PLEASE EXAMINE =="
210 PRINT
220 PRINT SPC(5);"DATE "; D$";/91
230 PRINT SPC(5);"PAY TO THE ORDER OF "; PAY$,
240 PRINT USING FMT$; AMT
250 PRINT SPC(5); AMT$;"/100 DOLLARS"
260 PRINT
270 REM
280 REM LINE 300 GIVES OPTION TO PRINT OR NOT TO PRINT THE CHECK IF IT IS WRONG
290 REM
300 INPUT "TO PRINT CHECK, PRESS ENTER- OTHERWISE CONTROL-BREAK", PR$
310 REM
320 REM     SEGMENT TO PRINT OUT CHECK ON PRINTER
330 REM
340 LPRINT TAB(37);D$; "       91"
350 LPRINT "    "
360 LPRINT TAB(3); PAY$, TAB(49);
370 LPRINT USING FMT$; AMT
380 LPRINT "   "
390 LPRINT AMT$;"/100"
400 REM
410 PRINT
420 PRINT SPC(10);"******** CHECK WRITER TERMINATED ********"
430 PRINT SPC(15); "TO WRITE ANOTHER CHECK ENTER RUN"
990 END

RUN
1. Date      mm/dd      ? 11/20
2. Pay to the order of  ? ABC CO.
3. Dollar Amount (numerics) ? 1100.25
4. Enter Amount (words) ? ELEVEN-HUNDRED & 25
```

```
== ITEMS TO BE PRINTED OUT ON THE CHECK- PLEASE EXAMINE ==

      DATE 11/20/91
      PAY TO THE ORDER OF ABC CO.          **1,100.25
      ELEVEN-HUNDRED & 25/100 DOLLARS

TO PRINT CHECK, PRESS ENTER- OTHERWISE CONTROL-BREAK

      ******** CHECK WRITER TERMINATED ********

          TO WRITE ANOTHER CHECK ENTER RUN
```

The output of Program 6.12 correctly produces the results required by Case 6.3. One output is the screen display; the other is the formatted check with asterisk protection (because of line 110). Data is entered interactively as a result of lines 130–160. All data is then displayed on the screen for checking because of lines 220–250. If the data entered is not correct, line 300 provides a ''pause'' so that a Control Break can be executed. This will enable the data to be reentered correctly after another run. Otherwise, any response to the line 300 INPUT prompt will cause processing to continue. The result will be a printed check based on the LPRINTs in lines 340–390. When the program completes its task, a message is displayed on the screen as a result of lines 420 and 430.

A program such as this one, which allows reentry of data before the final processing occurs, is said to be *forgiving*. That is, it permits the data entry to be repeated without the ''penalty'' of producing incorrect output. In this particular program, *data entry checking* is performed visually, by human eye. In later chapters (see Chapter 8, for example) we will see how data entry checking can be built into a program as well. We will also see that the awkward Control Break used in Program 6.12 can be replaced by appropriate program logic and design using statements discussed in forthcoming chapters.

## FORMATTING STRINGS

Just as there are many useful special format characters for numeric data, there are also format characters for nonnumeric or string (literal) data. Table 6.3 lists the characters that control output formats associated with the PRINT USING statement for nonnumeric data. As with numeric control characters, nonnumeric characters are enclosed in quotation marks. For a review of format and statement forms, refer back to Table 6.1.

Programs 6.13 through 6.17 illustrate the nonnumeric formats of Table 6.3. The string formats F1$, F2$, and F3$ in lines 20–40 of Program 6.13 show the exclamation and backslash characters enclosed in quotation marks as required. The program output shows the first, first two, and first three characters of the string data value EMPLOYEE NAME. These outputs were caused by the PRINT USING statements of lines 60–80.

**TABLE 6.3** PRINT USING String Control Characters

| CHARACTER | PURPOSE | STRING EXAMPLE | OUTPUT |
|---|---|---|---|
| ! (Exclamation mark) | Causes only the first character of a string as output. | ABC | A |
| \ \ (Backslashes— no spaces) | Causes only the first two characters of a string as output. | MARCH | MA |
| \n spaces\ | Causes (n + 2) characters of a string as output. Output is left-justified. A longer string will be cut down from the right; any extra spaces are placed at the end. | | |
| \   \ | n = 1. Outputs three characters. | WEST | WES |
| \     \ | n = 2. Outputs four characters. | SOUTH | SOUT |
| \       \ | n = 4. Outputs six characters. | AUGUST | AUGUST |
| & (Ampersand) | Causes string to output exactly as it is. String field length is variable rather than fixed. | NORTH JULY XYZ CO | NORTH JULY XYZ CO |

## PROGRAM 6.13   PRINT USING String Formats, " ! ", and " \ \ " Characters

```
10 LET WORD$ = "EMPLOYEE NAME"    'Comments:
20 LET F1$ = "!"                  'displays first character of a string
30 LET F2$ = "\\"                 'displays first two string characters
40 LET F3$ = "\ \"                'displays first three string characters
50 PRINT WORD$
60 PRINT USING F1$; WORD$
70 PRINT USING F2$; WORD$
80 PRINT USING F3$; WORD$
90 END

RUN
EMPLOYEE NAME
E
EM
EMP
```

The purpose of Program 6.14 is to show how string formats can be mixed and how longer variable lists can be included in the PRINT USING statements. The output for this program is based on displaying parts of the string variables N1$ (SANDY) and N2$ (RICHMOND). The formats are specified in lines 50–90. The PRINT USING statements, lines 100–140, first output the first characters of each data string. This output is then followed by various other string parts, as indicated in the comment lines of the program. Note that leading or trailing blank spaces in the format quotation marks are also part of the output results.

## PROGRAM 6.14    PRINT USING String Formats, Mixed String Formats

```
10  READ N1$, N2$
20  DATA SANDY, RICHMOND
30  PRINT N1$, N2$
40  PRINT                        'Comments:
50  LET F1$ = " !"               'displays first character of each string
60  LET F2$ = " \\"              'displays first two string characters
70  LET F3$ = " \  \"            'displays first four string characters
80  LET F4$ = "  \  \ !"         'displays four and one string characters
90  LET F5$ = " !\  \ "          'displays one and four string characters
100 PRINT USING F1$; N1$, N2$
110 PRINT USING F2$; N1$, N2$
120 PRINT USING F3$; N1$, N2$
130 PRINT USING F4$; N1$; N2$
140 PRINT USING F5$; N1$, N2$
150 END

RUN
SANDY           RICHMOND

 S R
 SA RI
 SAND RICH
  SAND R
 S RICH
```

The ampersand character (&) used in a format allows for output of string data exactly as it appears. The output space is thus considered variable, being the length of the string, rather than being set by a specific number of spaces as when backslashes ( \ \ ) are used. Program 6.15 shows several PRINT USING statements that include a string format comprised of & characters. Three string data items are assigned to V1$, V2$, and V3$ by the READ statement in line 10. The first output line shows these three strings as produced by the PRINT statement in line 40. The next four output lines are based on the PRINT USING statements 60, 80, 100, and 130. Note how the output spacing is controlled by the placement of the & within the format quotation marks. With three &s no space is provided for output in line 60. Line 80 shows spacing between & with output no longer crowded. The last two output lines are variations that are described by the program comments.

## PROGRAM 6.15    PRINT USING String Formats, " & " Characters

```
10  READ V1$, V2$, V3$
20  DATA SMALL.STRING.., LARGE..STRING..., VERY.LARGE..STRING.....
30  PRINT                        'Comments:
40  PRINT V1$, V2$, V3$          'Ordinary string output
50  PRINT
60  PRINT USING "&&&"; V1$, V2$, V3$          'insert and pack no spacing
70  PRINT
80  PRINT USING " &  &  &"; V1$, V2$, V3$     'insert with spacing
```

```
90 PRINT
100 PRINT USING "1. &   2. &   3. &"; V1$, V2$, V3$   'insert between literals
110 PRINT
120 LET F$ =   "a. &  b. &  c. &"                     'format string with &
130 PRINT USING F$; V1$, V2$, V3$                     'format string in statement
140 PRINT
150 END

RUN

SMALL.STRING..               LARGE..STRING...         VERY.LARGE..STRING.....

SMALL.STRING..LARGE..STRING...VERY.LARGE..STRING.....

 SMALL.STRING.. LARGE..STRING... VERY.LARGE..STRING.....

1. SMALL.STRING.. 2. LARGE..STRING... 3. VERY.LARGE..STRING.....

a. SMALL.STRING.. b. LARGE..STRING... c. VERY.LARGE..STRING.....
```

Two cases, 6.4, and 6.5, illustrate some aspects of string format characters.

## CASE 6.4

| | |
|---|---|
| **Problem** | **Changing Names to Initials** <br> A college instructor has a list of class names in last-name, first-name order. The list is to be modified by a program so that the student's initials will be printed out. |
| **Data Input** | The program will read a list of names in the format <br><br> DATA SMITH, PETER |
| **Process/Formulas** | The initials for each name can be obtained by using a string format character (!) that will output the first character of a string. |
| **Output** | For each name in last, first sequence, the first- and last-name initials (F.L.) will be printed out. |

Program 6.16 serves only as a model, or prototype, for Case 6.4 because it will do only a single conversion each time rather than an entire list of names. In the next chapter we will learn how to process efficiently many sets of data. However, this program does illustrate how names in one form can be converted to initials. The program takes a single name, as shown by the output, and produces the first initial of each name part by means of a PRINT USING statement in line 60. The format, "!.!.", specifies that the first character of each string data value is to be printed followed by a period.

## PROGRAM 6.16 Case 6.4, Changing Names to Initials

```
10 REM CASE 6.4  NAME LIST CONVERSION
15 REM PROGRAMMER- (name of person)  DATE - mm/dd/yy
20 REM
25 REM     VARIABLE LIST
30 REM     LTN$ = LAST NAME
35 REM     FTN$ = FIRST NAME
40 REM ----------------------------------------
45 READ LTN$, FTN$
50 PRINT LTN$, FTN$
55 DATA SMITH, PETER
60 PRINT USING "!.!.";FTN$, LTN$
65 END

RUN
SMITH          PETER
P.S.
```

## CASE 6.5

**Problem**

**Dividing Telephone Numbers into Parts**

A market research firm wants to analyze a list of names and telephone numbers by area code. A program is needed to extract and produce a list of area codes only.

**Data Input**

The data items are to be read in as a string. A typical item has the form

(area code) telephone number

**Process/Formulas**

To separate the area code from the rest of the phone number, use the string format character backslash ($\setminus$ $\setminus$) with the appropriate number of spaces as part of a PRINT USING statement.

**Output**

The printed results will appear as, for example, AREA CODE (914).

Program 6.17 provides only a partial solution to Case 6.5. In its current form this program can process only a limited amount of data. You will learn that BASIC statements introduced in the next few chapters can be used to upgrade the program to do larger data sets. To extract area codes from a telephone number, the format AC$ is used in line 70. Since the area code consists of the first five characters of the telephone number—(123), for example—the format uses the backslash with three blank spaces. Three blanks, plus the two provided automatically by the format characters, result in the desired effect. The first output line shows each telephone number in its original form; the second output line displays the extracted area codes.

## PROGRAM 6.17 Case 6.5, Separating Area Codes from Telephone Numbers

```
10 REM CASE 6.5  AREA CODE EXTRACTION
15 REM PROGRAMMER- (name of person)  DATE - mm/dd/yy
20 REM
25 REM     VARIABLE LIST -
30 REM     TN1$ = TELEPHONE NUMBER 1
35 REM     TN2$ = TELEPHONE NUMBER 2
40 REM      T$ = LITERAL LABEL
45 REM -------------------------------------------
50 LET T$ = "TEL. NO. "
55 READ TN1$, TN2$
60 DATA (617)828-8350, (714)841-6199
65 PRINT T$; TN1$, T$; TN2$
70     LET AC$ = "AREA CODE \     \      "
75     PRINT USING AC$;TN1$, TN2$
80 END

RUN
TEL. NO. (617)828-8350        TEL. NO. (714)841-6199
AREA CODE (617)               AREA CODE (714)
```

## COMBINING NUMERIC AND STRING FORMATS

If data consists of a mixture of numeric and string items, we can design formats that take such mixtures into account. Program 6.18 shows how both numeric and string format characters can be combined into a single format statement (lines 20, 30, and 35). Depending on the data types and output displays required, these lines suggest the many variations that are possible when mixing formats.

## PROGRAM 6.18 PRINT USING Mixing Numeric and String Formats

```
10                                          'Comments:
20 LET FMT1$ = "\       \  #####.##"        'formats for literal
30 LET FMT2$ = "$$###,###.##  \     \"       'and numeric data
35 LET FMT3$ = " ####.##  \       \ $$##,###.##"
40 READ MN$, TOT, AMT                       'variable list
50 DATA MAR, 1, 3542, 23000
55 PRINT
60 PRINT USING FMT1$; MN$, TOT        'literal-string & numeric
65 PRINT
70 PRINT USING FMT2$; AMT, MN$        'numeric & literal-string
75 PRINT
80 PRINT USING FMT3$; TOT, MN$, AMT   'numeric, literal-string, numeric
99 END
```

```
RUN

MAR, 1    3542,00

 $23,000,00   MAR, 1

 3542,00   MAR, 1    $23,000,00
```

## SOME FORMAT DESIGN ERRORS

When constructing a string format, it is important to remember to provide enough space between the backslashes to ensure that the output specifications for a given problem are correct. If an entire string is to be produced as output and too little space is provided, the output is *truncated*, or cut off. The output in Program 6.19 illustrates this error. In this program the variable CA$ represents a customer's account AC123. A format specification in line 20 does provide enough space between the backslashes to produce the first output line. However, note that the second output line shows the customer account as only AC1. This truncated output is because the format specification in line 30 is too small. Only a single blank space was provided between the slashes, when at least three were needed. As a result, the customer's account was cut from five characters down to three.

## PROGRAM 6.19   PRINT USING: Some Format Errors

```
10                                      'Comments:
20 LET FMT1$ = "\    \    $##,###"      'enough spacing for data
30 LET FMT2$ = "\ \     $##,###"        'too little literal-string space
40 READ CA$, AMT                        'string & numeric variables
50 DATA AC123, 23000
60 PRINT USING FMT1$; CA$, AMT
65 PRINT
70 PRINT USING FMT2$; CA$, AMT
75 PRINT
80 PRINT USING FMT2$; AMT, CA$          'data types do not match FMT2$
99 END

RUN
AC123   $23,000

AC1     $23,000

Type mismatch in 80
```

You will recall that when a numeric data item does not fit into the field specification, an error character (%) is displayed to warn you about the problem. With string formats no such warning is displayed. Therefore, you must visually check your output against the output design requirements to be sure your program is doing what it should.

The last line of output for Program 6.19 displays the error message "Type mismatch in 80." To find the cause of this error, first look at line 80. The data types to be printed are a numeric, AMT, and a string, CA$. Since this is a PRINT USING statement, we need to check the format FMT2$ in line 30. This format shows the specification "\ \ $##,###" for a string followed by a numeric data item. Clearly the error is a mismatch between the format and the variable list in the PRINT USING statement. Here is the mismatch:

Format specification:  String \ \  Numeric $##,###

PRINT USING variable list:  Numeric AMT  String CA$

When constructing programs, always be sure to check that your output variable list in PRINT USING statements agrees with the sequence of the data types in the format statements.

An additional illustration of combining numeric and string formats is provided by Case 6.6 and Program 6.20.

## CASE 6.6

**Problem**  **Formatting an Inventory Report**
A program is required to produce a neatly formatted inventory report.

**Data Input**  The data items for the report include an item code, the number of units currently in stock for the item, and the price at cost. The data list for the program follows the same order. A data line looks like this:

160 DATA AX89-B, 4259, 2.75

**Process/Formulas**  To derive the dollar value at cost for the inventory on hand, we need to compute:

Dollar value (DVI) = number of units in stock (UN) × price per unit (PR)

**Output**  The report should show the following items in the format shown below:

```
**** INVENTORY REPORT ****

ITEM CODE   NO. UNITS   PRICE   DOLLAR VALUE
-------------------------------------------
 AX89-B       4,259     $2.75    $11,712.25
```

The output from Program 6.20 clearly reflects the requirements of Case 6.6. The essential line of this program is the format line 120. The mixture of string and numeric format characters results in an attractive output display.

Note that the opening quotation marks in lines 105–125 are aligned vertically. Having all of these output-related lines lined up helps you visualize the appearance of the final display.

## PROGRAM 6.20    Case 6.6, Formatting an Inventory Report

```
10 REM CASE 6.6 INVENTORY REPORT
20 REM PROGRAMMER- (name of person)   DATE - mm/dd/yy
30 REM
40 REM     VARIABLE LIST-
45 REM          H$   = HEADING OF REPORT
50 REM          IC$  = ITEM CODE
60 REM          UN   = NUMBER OF UNITS IN STOCK
70 REM          PR   = PRICE PER UNIT
80 REM          DVI  = DOLLAR VALUE OF ITEMS IN STOCK
90 REM          FMT$ = FORMAT FOR REPORT
95 REM          L$   = STRING VARIABLE FOR UNDERLINE
100 REM ------------------------------------------------------------
105 LET H$ =    "     ITEM CODE    NO. UNITS    PRICE    DOLLAR VALUE"
110 LET L$ =    "     ------------------------------------------------"
120 LET FMT$ = "       \         \   ##,###     $$##.##    $$###,###.##"
125 PRINT      "               **** INVENTORY REPORT  ****"
126 PRINT
130 PRINT H$
140 PRINT  L$
150 READ IC$, UN, PR
160 DATA AX89-B, 4259, 2.75
170 LET DVI  = UN * PR
180 PRINT USING FMT$; IC$, UN, PR, DVI
190 END

RUN
                **** INVENTORY REPORT  ****

     ITEM CODE    NO. UNITS     PRICE    DOLLAR VALUE
     --------------------------------------------------
        AX89-B       4,259      $2.75     $11,712.25
```

## SUMMARY

The appearance of a program's output, in both its displayed and printed form, can be enhanced by the PRINT USING statement. The statement permits the formatting of numeric data and string data. The number of character spaces for a numeric can be specified by using a pound character (#). Various control characters for numeric data permit great flexibility for output. You can set the number of decimal places needed, round numbers to any number of decimal places, have commas embedded in large numbers, have dollar signs printed, add an asterisk protection feature, and have leading and trailing plus and minus signs printed. All numeric output can be right justified to conform to standard accounting and report practices.

The use of control characters for string data enables you to control the placement and length of the output for labels, names, and headings. The most useful control character for string data is the backslash (\ \). The number of spaces it contains determines the output field size for a string.

The format part of the PRINT USING statement can be contained in quotation marks. Numeric and string PRINT USING formats can be combined in a single statement. Common errors include making the output print fields too small by not allowing enough room in the formats. Care must also be taken to avoid mismatching the data types in the format with the variable types in the PRINT USING statement.

## BASIC VOCABULARY SUMMARY

| Statement | Purpose | Examples |
|---|---|---|
| LPRINT USING | Prints numeric or string output to a printer using a format specification. | 80 LET F$ = "$$#,###.##" <br> 90 LPRINT USING F$; A, B |
| PRINT USING (Alt + P key, Alt + U key) | Prints numeric or string output to a display using a format specification. | 40 LET FT$ = "\ \" <br> 50 PRINT USING FT$; CO$ |

## EXERCISES

### Review Questions

**6.1** The following PRINT USING statements contain errors. Identify each error and provide a suitable correction. (There may be more than one suitable correction.)
a. 30 PRINT USING ###; TOT
b. 40 PRINT USING "###.#     ##"; X1
c. 50 PRINT USING "##     ##   ##"; A1, A2, A3, A4
d. 60 PRINT USING "#           #"; DIV$
e. 70 PRINT USING \ \     \ \; N1$, N2$
f. 80 PRINT USING "###  \      \"; DT$, SUM

**6.2** The following groups of statements contain one or more errors. Identify each error and provide a suitable correction. (There may be more than one suitable correction.)
a. 10 LET F1$ = #####
   20 PRINT USING F1; AMT
♦ b. 30 LET F2$ = "###.##"
   40 PRINT USING F2$; IVT$
c. 50 LET F3$ = "\     \   $###.##"
   60 PRINT USING NUM1, NUM$
♦ d. 70 LET F4$ = "\    \    \"
   80 PRINT USING F4$; D1$, D2$
e. 10 READ N1, N2
   15 DATA 123, 5.678
   20 PRINT USING " ## "; N1, N2

**6.3**   For each of the following output values shown, provide a suitable set of format control characters in the space provided:

| OUTPUT | FORMAT CONTROL CHARACTERS |
|---|---|
| a.       15 | |
| b.      12.789 | |
| c.    39,156.5 | |
| d.   $  10.00 | |
| e.  $1,538.62 | |
| f.  **10,567.37 | |
| g.  **$10,567.37 | |
| h.  + 2,135.42 | |
| i.   $587.65- | |

**6.4**   What will the following programs print as output when they are processed? Show the output exactly as it would appear after RUN.

```
a. 10 LET X$="####       #,###,#  +###,### *****,###,##    $$#,###,##"
   20 READ A,B,C,D,E
   30 DATA 1234.567,1234.67,1.234567,12.34567,345.6789
   40 PRINT X$
   50 PRINT USING X$;A,B,C,D,E
   60 END

b. 10 LET X$="#  ###       #,###,#  +###,### *****,###,##    $$#,###,##"
   20 READ A,B,C,D,E
   30 DATA -4.321,98765.4,-1e3,2.345e-2,1234.5
   40 PRINT X$
   50 PRINT USING X$;A,B,C,D,E
   60 END

c. 10 LET X$="#,###-  **$#,###,#   $##,###,###   ##,###,##+    $$#,###"
   20 READ A,B,C,D,E
   30 DATA 1234.567,1234.67,1.234567,12.34567,345.6789
   40 PRINT X$
   50 PRINT USING X$;A,B,C,D,E
   60 END
```

**6.5**   What will the following programs print as output when they are processed? Show the output exactly as it would appear after RUN.

```
a. 10 LET X$="\   \    !   \\         &        \     \"
   20 READ A$,B$,C$,D$,E$
   30 DATA A,BC,DEF,GHIJ,KLMNO
   40 PRINT X$
   50 PRINT USING X$;A$;B$,C$,D$,E$
   60 END

b. 10 LET X$="\ \    !   \\         &        \     \"
   20 READ A$,B$,C$,D$,E$
   30 DATA A,BC,DEF,GHIJ,KLMNO
   40 PRINT X$
   50 PRINT USING X$,E$,D$,A$,B$,C$
   60 END
```

**6.6**   For the following program, provide the LET statement that will cause the name to be printed in the first 13 spaces, the rate and salary to be printed correct to two decimal places with dollar signs, and the hours to be printed correct to one decimal place.

```
10 LET A$ = "NAME           RATE    HOURS    SALARY"
20 READ N$, R, H
30 PRINT A$
```

```
40 PRINT USING B$; N$, R, H, H*R
50 DATA "I. GREEN", 20.53, 40.5
60 END
```

The program's output should have this appearance:

```
RUN
NAME          RATE      HOURS      SALARY
I. GREEN      20.53     40.5       831.47
```

♦ **6.7**  Add statements to the program shown in exercise 6.6 so that it will process the DATA for three employees. Use the following additional DATA statement:

51 DATA ''M. HEIGH'', 10.45, 35, ''D. HIMBER'', 30.79, 22.28

The program's output should have this appearance:

```
RUN
NAME          RATE      HOURS      SALARY
I. GREEN      20.53     40.5       831.47
M. HEIGH      10.45     35.0       365.75
D. HIMBER     30.79     22.3       686.00
```

**6.8**  Add to the program in exercise 6.7 so that it will total the number of hours worked and the salaries. Use PRINT USING statements to print the word ''TOTALS'' under the name and the totals lined up under the appropriate column. The program's output should have this appearance:

```
RUN
NAME          RATE      HOURS       SALARY
I. GREEN      20.53     40.5        831.47
M. HEIGH      10.45     35.0        365.75
D. HIMBER     30.79     22.3        686.00
TOTALS                  97.8     $1,883.22
```

**6.9**  Add to the program in exercise 6.8 one LET statement and two PRINT USING statements that will underline the column headings and the body of the report. The program's output should have this appearance:

```
RUN
NAME          RATE      HOURS      SALARY
----------------------------------------
I. GREEN      20.53     40.5       831.47
M. HEIGH      10.45     35.0       365.75
D. HIMBER     30.79     22.3       686.00
----------------------------------------
TOTALS                  97.8    $1,883.22
```

**6.10**  Add to the program in exercise 6.9 one LET statement and one PRINT USING statement to change the headings as follows:

| EMPLOYEE | HOURLY | NUMBER OF | GROSS |
| NAME | RATE | HOURS | SALARY |

The program's output should have this appearance:

```
RUN
EMPLOYEE        HOURLY        NUMBER OF        GROSS
NAME            RATE          HOURS            SALARY
-------------------------------------------
I. GREEN        20.53         40.5               831.47
M. HEIGH        10.45         35.0               365.75
D. HIMBER       30.79         22.3               686.00
-------------------------------------------
TOTALS                        97.8          $1,883.22
```

## Programming Activities

**6.11**  **Purpose**  To use the simple sequence logic structure, numeric data, and PRINT USING statement for output formatting.

**Problem**  Write and run a program to calculate the total of a sale using the formula below:

Total = sales price + sales price × tax rate

**Data**  Sales are $5, $10, and $15. The tax rate is 5 percent.

**Output**  Your output should have this format:

```
RUN
SALES           TAX           TOTAL
$ 5.00          $ 0.25        $ 5.25
$10.00          $ 0.50        $10.50
$15.00          $ 0.75        $15.75
```

**6.12**  **Purpose**  To use the simple sequence logic structure, numeric data, and PRINT USING statement for output formatting.

**Problem**  Write and run a program to calculate the area of these triangles using the formula below:

Area = 1/2(base × height)

**Data**

| TRIANGLE | BASE | HEIGHT |
|----------|------|--------|
| 1 | 5 | 7 |
| 2 | 10.5 | 6.2 |
| 3 | 100 | 78 |

**Output**  Your output should have this format:

```
BASE            HEIGHT          AREA
   5.0             7.0             17.5
  10.5             6.2             32.6
 100.0            78.0          3,900.0
```

**6.13**  **Purpose**  To use the simple sequence logic structure, numeric data, and LPRINT USING statement for output formatting.

**Problem** Write a program that will increase the set of investments shown below by the same three interest rates, first by 7 percent, then by 7½ percent, and then by 8¼ percent. Include REM statements in the program describing the problem and the program.

**Data** One-year investments: $3,000; $10,000; $12,500; $17,000

**Output** Your output should be in both displayed and hard copy form. It should follow this format:

```
INVESTMENT      7% INC.        7.5% INC.       8.25% INC.
-----------------------------------------------------------
$  3,000.00    $  3,210.00    $  3,225.00    $  3,247.50
$ 10,000.00    $ 10,700.00    $ 10,750.00    $ 10,825.00
$ 12,500.00    $ 13,375.00    $ 13,437.50    $ 13,531.25
$ 17,000.00    $ 18,190.00    $ 18,275.00    $ 18,402.50
```

**6.14 Purpose** To use the simple sequence logic structure, numeric data, and LPRINT and PRINT USING statements for output formatting.

**Problem** In the field of accounting, one measure of a company's financial condition is the current ratio. This ratio is computed as current assets divided by current liabilities. Write and run a program to find the current ratio using the data below.

**Data**

|                     | 1988       | 1989       | 1990       |
|---------------------|------------|------------|------------|
| Current assets      | $370,000   | $400,000   | $450,000   |
| Current liabilities | $160,000   | $100,000   | $150,000   |

**Output** Your output should display on the screen and also generate a hard copy. Output should follow this format:

```
                         1988        1989        1990
                       --------    --------    --------
CURRENT ASSETS        $ 370,000   $ 400,000   $ 450,000
CURRENT LIABILITIES   $ 160,000   $ 100,000   $ 150,000
CURRENT RATIO              2.3         4.0         3.0
```

**6.15 Purpose** To use the simple sequence logic structure; numeric data; and SPC, TAB, and PRINT USING statement for output formatting.

**Problem** A balance sheet in accounting is divided into two parts. On the left are the assets and on the right are the liabilities and capital. Assets consist of current plus fixed assets. Suppose the XYZ Company has current assets of $45,000, fixed assets of $78,000, current liabilities of $32,000, and capital of $91,000. Write a program that reads in this data and prepares a balance sheet with a heading, labels for each item mentioned, and totals for both parts.

**Data** Use the data values provided in the problem statement.

**Output** Your output should have this format:

```
                    XYZ COMPANY BALANCE SHEET
            ASSETS                   LIABILITIES AND CAPITAL
CURRENT ASSETS  $ 45,000        LIABILITIES    $ 32,000
FIXED ASSETS       78,000       CAPITAL           91,000
                --------                        --------
TOTAL ASSETS    $123,000        TOTAL LIAB.    $123,000
```

**6.16**  **Purpose**  To use the simple sequence logic structure, string and numeric data, and PRINT USING statement for output formatting.

**Problem**  Write and run a program that reads in an employee's number, hours worked, and the hourly rate and that outputs a table showing the employee's number, salary (number of hours × hourly rate), federal tax (20 percent of salary) social security tax (.05478 × salary), and net salary (that is, gross salary − all deductions).

**Data**  Employee number (a string), 3542; hours worked, 37; and rate, $4.50.

**Output**  Your output should have this format:

```
EMPLOYEE #   HOURS   RATE    SALARY    FED.TAX   S.S.TAX   NET SALARY
   3542        37    $4.50   $166.50   $33.30    $9.12     $124.08
```

**6.17**  **Purpose**  To use the simple sequence logic structure, string and numeric data, and PRINT USING statement for output formatting.

**Problem**  Real estate brokers are often compensated on a straight commission basis. Their total earnings are computed this way:

$$\text{Commission on sale} = \frac{\text{value of real estate}}{\text{property sold}} \times \frac{\text{commission}}{\text{rate }\%}$$

If there is a 6 percent commission rate on all property sold, write and run a program that computes the commissions for the data given below.

**Data**

| PERSON | PROPERTY SOLD | PERSON | PROPERTY SOLD |
|--------|---------------|--------|---------------|
| A. Smith | $140,000 | J. Jenkins | $176,250 |
| | 162,500 | | 140,500 |
| | 147,500 | | 157,500 |

**Output**  Your output should have this format:

```
PERSON          PROP. SOLD    COMMISSION
------------------------------------
A. Smith        $140,000      $ 8,400
                $162,500      $ 9,750
                $147,500      $ 8,850
J. Jenkins      $176,250      $10,575
                $140,500      $ 8,430
                $157,500      $ 9,450
------------------------------------
```

◆ **6.18**  **Purpose**  To use the simple sequence logic structure, string and numeric data, and PRINT USING statement for output formatting.

**Problem**  The United Computer Company pays its salespersons a monthly salary of $1,000 plus 1½ percent commission for equipment sold during the month. The data below shows the sales figures by salesperson for last month. Write and run a program that computes the total monthly salary for each salesperson.

**Data**

| SALESPERSON | AMOUNT SOLD |
|-------------|-------------|
| M. Worth | $ 13,600 |
| K. Gray | 22,000 |
| S. Legan | 9,800 |
| B. Hinz | 24,500 |

**Output**   Your output should have this format:

```
SALESPERSON      AMOUNT SOLD        SALARY
------------------------------------------
  M. Worth         $13,600        $1,204.00
  K. Gray          $22,000        $1,330.00
  S. Legan         $ 9,800        $1,147.00
  B. Hinz          $24,500        $1,367.50
------------------------------------------
```

**6.19   Purpose**   To use the simple sequence logic structure, string and numeric data, and PRINT USING statement for output formatting.

**Problem**   The ABC Company has four divisions that sell various products. Management wants to know what percent of total sales volume is generated by each division. Below are the gross sales figures by division for the last year. Write and run a program that reads in the sales data and generates as output a table that shows (1) the total sales of each division, (2) using a third column headed "% of TOTAL," the percent of total sales represented by each division (use division sales/total $\times$ 100 to find the percent of total sales), and (3) the total sales and percents for all divisions.

**Data**

| DIVISION | SALES (MILLION $) |
|----------|-------------------|
| West     | 3.85              |
| South    | 8.62              |
| North    | 4.57              |
| East     | 3.81              |

**Output**   Your output should have this format:

```
-------------------------------------------
DIVISION      SALES(MIL.$)      % OF TOTAL
-------------------------------------------
  West          $ 3.85            18.5
  South         $ 8.62            41.3
  North         $ 4.57            21.9
  East          $ 3.81            18.3
-------------------------------------------
  TOTALS        $20.85           100.0
-------------------------------------------
```

**6.20   Purpose**   To use the simple sequence logic structure, string and numeric data, and PRINT USING statement for output formatting.

**Problem**   The ABC Company (see exercise 6.19) anticipates that for this year and the next two years sales in each division will exceed last year's sales by the following percentage growth rates:

|         | LAST YEAR-1 | THIS YEAR-2 | NEXT YEAR-3 | YEAR AFTER-4 |
|---------|-------------|-------------|-------------|--------------|
| Percent | 100.0       | 108.0       | 114.2       | 121.3        |

Write and run a program that will generate for each of the divisions the expected sales for the years involved.

**Data**    The data for year 1 is as follows:

| DIVISION | SALES (MILLION $) |
|----------|-------------------|
| West | 3.85 |
| South | 8.62 |
| North | 4.57 |
| East | 3.81 |

**Output**    Your output should have this format:

```
------------------------------------------------
        THREE YEAR SALES FORECAST - ABC COMPANY
                 MILLIONS OF DOLLARS
------------------------------------------------
DIVISION    YEAR 1      YEAR 2      YEAR 3      YEAR 4
------------------------------------------------
West         3.85        4.16        4.40        4.67
South        8.62        9.31        9.84       10.46
North        4.57        4.94        5.22        5.54
East         3.81        4.11        4.35        4.62
------------------------------------------------
```

**6.21** **Purpose**    To use appropriate INPUT statements with numeric data, double precision, the simple sequence logic structure, and PRINT USING statement for output formatting.

**Problem**    A firm estimates that five years from now it will need $2 million to purchase some new equipment. To accumulate this sum, the firm has decided to set aside an amount each year. The firm can earn 9 percent compounded annually on its cash. To find the amount that must be deposited at the end of each of the five years to accumulate the $2 million, the following formula is used:

$$A = F \left[ \frac{r}{(1 + r)^n - 1} \right]$$

where $A$ is the amount to be deposited at the end of $n$ years, $r$ is annual interest rate, and $F$ is the future sum needed. Write and run an interactive conversational program that will find $A$.

**Data**    Use the data values provided in the problem statement. Remember that data entry should be interactive.

**Output**    Your output should display on the screen and also generate a hard copy. Output should follow this format:

```
RUN
WHAT IS THE NUMBER OF YEARS? 5
WHAT IS THE ANNUAL INTEREST RATE (.dd)? .09
WHAT IS THE FUTURE SUM NEEDED? 2000000

F = $ 2,000,000    R = .09      N = 5 YEARS

AMOUNT TO BE DEPOSITED PER YEAR IS   $334,184.71
```

**6.22** **Purpose**    To use appropriate INPUT statements with numeric data, double precision, the simple sequence logic structure, and PRINT USING statement for output formatting.

**Problem** What amount could be invested at 15 percent compounded annually that will grow to $300,000 or more at the end of five years? Write and run an interactive conversational program that will find the present value $P$. To find the answer, use this formula:

$$P = \frac{F}{(1 + r)^n}$$

where $P$ is the present value, $F$ is the future amount needed, $r$ is the annual rate of interest (a decimal), and $n$ is the length of the period.

**Data** Use the data values provided in the problem statement. Remember that data entry should be interactive.

**Output** Your output should display on the screen and follow this format:

```
RUN
WHAT IS THE NUMBER OF YEARS? 5
WHAT IS THE ANNUAL INTEREST RATE (.dd)? .15
WHAT IS THE FUTURE AMOUNT NEEDED? 300000
N = 5 YEARS   R = .15   F =   $300,000
THE PRESENT VALUE IS $149,153.03
```

# CHAPTER

# 7

# SIMPLE
# BRANCHING
# LOGIC

Upon completing this chapter, you will be able to do the following:

- Develop problem solutions using a simple looping structure that incorporates the GOTO statement.
- Understand that too many GOTO statements in a program indicate poor design and "spaghetti code."
- Learn how to write a program that performs the tasks of counting and accumulation.
- Recognize and understand the meaning of the "Out of data" message.
- Explain how the logic error of an "infinite loop" can occur and how to correct such errors.
- Continue to develop programming problem solutions using a simple sequence logic structure of READ/DATA, LET, PRINT USING, repeating itself in a GOTO loop.

If the only capabilities of computers were to carry out statements like PRINT, READ/DATA, LET, and INPUT, the importance of computers would be similar to the importance of electronic calculators. The branching statements to be introduced in this chapter and in chapters 8, 9, and 10 give computers their immense power.

In all of the programs in the previous chapters, the statements were executed sequentially following a simple sequence logic; that is, the first statement to be executed was the first statement in the program, the second statement executed was the second statement in the program, and so on, until the END statement was encountered. Branching statements change this simple sequence of statement execution. There are two types of branching statements. The type discussed in this chapter is the unconditional branch—the GOTO statement.

## THE GOTO STATEMENT

The form of the GOTO statement is

line #1 GOTO line #2

When line 1 is encountered, the next statement to be executed is line 2. Line 2 may have a higher number than line 1, in which case we wish to skip some statements; or, as in Table 7.1, line 2 may have a lower number than line 1, in which case we want to repeat a number of statements.

We never need to have statements like

100 GOTO 101

101

Statement 100 accomplishes nothing, since the next statement to be executed would be 101 anyway.

Examples of the GOTO statement are shown in Table 7.1.

**TABLE 7.1** Examples of the GOTO Statement

| STATEMENT | EXPLANATION |
| --- | --- |
| 10 READ AMT, NM$<br>20 -----<br>30 -----<br>. . .<br>90 GOTO 10 | The sequence up to line 90 is processed repeatedly until there is no more data for the read. |
| 100 GOTO 200<br>110 -----<br>120 -----<br>. . .<br>200 PRINT ''ANS. = ''; ANS | Execution of line 100 causes a branch to line 200. All lines in between will be skipped over. |

**Keyboarding Tip**    To save keystrokes, you can enter and display the keyword GOTO by typing the Alt plus G key combination.

Consider Program 7.1, which presents an example of how the GOTO statement changes the simple sequence of the execution of the statements.

## PROGRAM 7.1    GOTO Statement

```
10 READ X
15 PRINT X, X^2, X^3
20 GOTO 10
25 DATA 2,4,5,10,8,-3
30 END

RUN
  2              4              8
  4             16             64
  5             25            125
 10            100           1000
  8             64            512
 -3              9            -27
Out of DATA in 10
```

In line 10 the READ X assigns the number 2 to the variable $X$. The PRINT statement on line 15 then prints the numbers 2, 4, and 8. The GOTO 10 on line 20 tells the computer to execute line 10 again. This time, the READ X assigns the number 4 to variable $X$ because the first number in the DATA statement, the number 2, has already been read. The program then prints the current values of $X$, $X^2$, and $X^3$; namely, 4, 16, and 64. When the GOTO 10 is encountered a second time, it again sends the computer looping back to line 10 to read another value of $X$. This repetitive procedure continues until there are no more numbers in the DATA statement. When the computer is told to read a number from the DATA statement and all of the numbers in the DATA statement have already been read, the computer prints ''Out of data'' in the line that tries to do the reading. Program 7.1 is an example of what is called a *loop*. See the flowchart for this program in Figure 7.1, and note the simple sequence READ, PRINT that is to be repeated until all of the data is used up.

The GOTO statement changes the normal sequence of the execution of the statements. It tells the computer what the next statement to be executed is. Program 7.1 will work for as many numbers as there are in the DATA statement(s). We are beginning to see the power of the computer.

Program 7.2 has no practical importance other than to illustrate the GOTO statement. The statements are executed in the following order: 10, 15, 45, 50, 35, 40, 55, 60, 20, 30, and 99, resulting in the printing of the statement ''EVERY GOOD PERSON DOES FINE.''

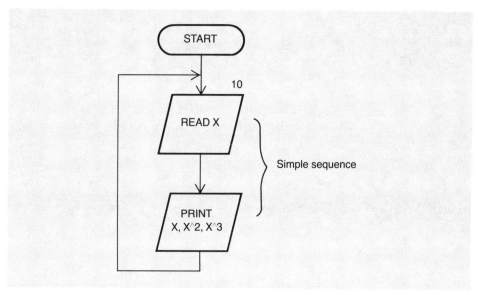

**FIGURE 7.1** Flowchart of Program 7.1

## PROGRAM 7.2   Several GOTO Statements

```
10 PRINT "EVERY";
15 GOTO 45
20 PRINT " FINE";
30 GOTO 99
35 PRINT " PERSON";
40 GOTO 55
45 PRINT " GOOD";
50 GOTO 35
55 PRINT " DOES";
60 GOTO 20
99 END

RUN
EVERY GOOD PERSON DOES FINE
```

Case 7.1 shows a program that uses a GOTO loop sequence of operation.

. . . . . . . . . . . . . . . . . . . . . . . . . . . . . . . . . . . . . . . . . .

## CASE 7.1

**Problem**            **Price List Revision**
Because of increased labor and raw materials costs, the Global Manufacturing Company has decided to revise its prices on several items. The new price for each item is to be 6.6 percent above the current price. A program to derive the revised prices needs to be created.

**Data Input**

The data to be processed consists of item identification numbers (treat as nonnumerics) and current prices. This data is shown below under Output.

**Process/Formulas**  A repetitive process is to be used so that each current price is increased by 6.6 percent to derive a revised price.

**Output**

The output for the program should have the following appearance:

```
ITEM              CURRENT              REVISED
NUMBER              PRICE                PRICE
------------------------------------------
  218             $200.00             $213.20
  233           $1,456.00           $1,552.10
  345             $545.00             $580.97
  367             $248.00             $264.37
  401             $225.00             $239.85
  406             $179.00             $190.81
  407           $1,000.00           $1,066.00
  557             $267.00             $284.62
  679             $470.00             $501.02
  887             $359.00             $382.69
```

Program 7.3, using a GOTO loop, generates a revised price list for Case 7.1.

## PROGRAM 7.3   Case 7.1, Revising Price List

```
10 REM CASE 7.1   PRICE LIST REVISION
20 REM PROGRAMMER- (name of person)   DATE - mm/dd/yy
30 REM
40 REM      VARIABLE LIST - A$, B$, C$, IN$, CP, RP
50 REM          A$, B$ = HEADINGS
60 REM          C$ = FORMAT
70 REM          IN$ = ITEM NUMBER
80 REM          CP = CURRENT PRICE
90 REM          RP = REVISED PRICE = CP * 1.066
100 REM -------------------------------------------------
110 LET A$= "ITEM              CURRENT              REVISED"
120 LET B$= "NUMBER              PRICE                PRICE"
130 LET C$= "\      \      $$##,###.##      $$##,###.##"
140 PRINT   A$
150 PRINT   B$
155 PRINT   "------------------------------------------"
160    READ IN$, CP
170    LET RP = CP*1.066
180    PRINT USING C$; IN$, CP, RP
190 GOTO 160
195 DATA 218,200,233,1456,345,545,367,248
200 DATA 401,225,406,179,407,1000
210 DATA 557,267,679,470,887,359
220 END
```

```
RUN
ITEM              CURRENT              REVISED
NUMBER              PRICE                PRICE
----------------------------------------
 218            $200.00              $213.20
 233          $1,456.00            $1,552.10
 345            $545.00              $580.97
 367            $248.00              $264.37
 401            $225.00              $239.85
 406            $179.00              $190.81
 407          $1,000.00            $1,066.00
 557            $267.00              $284.62
 679            $470.00              $501.02
 887            $359.00              $382.69
Out of DATA in 160
```

## Logic Structures

Use of the GOTO statement provides a simple and convenient way for transferring control in a program. When used in a loop structure, as in Program 7.3, where a simple sequence is being executed repeatedly, it can process large amounts of data values or items very easily. Figure 7.2 shows this idea as a loop that will end when there is no more data to process.

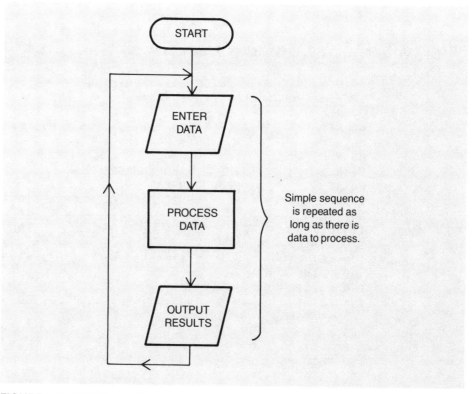

**FIGURE 7.2**  GOTO Loop Structure

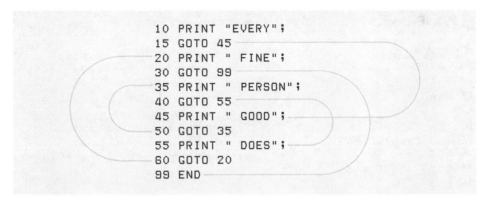

**FIGURE 7.3**   Spaghetti Code, Program 7.2

In larger programs, excess use of the GOTO statement can lead to difficulty in understanding a program. This can even be true for small programs (see program 7.2, for example). A program that contains excessive GOTO statements is often referred to as *spaghetti code* because the lines of flow can be visualized as strands of spaghetti. Figure 7.3 illustrates Program 7.2 as an example of spaghetti code.

Too many GOTO statements may also result in transfers that cause various errors in logic. Specifically, when a line is deleted or a statement is changed, it is important to check to see if it is a line or statement being transferred to by one or more GOTO statements. If so, does the deletion or change lead to some error? Remember that all changes must be examined to determine the total effect on the program's logic.

Other looping structures are described in later chapters. These structures help us avoid excess use of the GOTO statement and enable us to end our programs with "elegance" instead of with an "Out of data" error message.

## Program Appearance and Indenting

In Program 7.3 note the use of *indentation* to separate the repeated simple sequence logic structure (lines 160–180) from the rest of the code. It is recommended that you indent statements inside a control structure or loop, especially in larger programs. Indenting the code helps make the program more readable. It also produces code that clearly indicates the logic structures of the program. This clarity is helpful when you are debugging errors that show up during the testing phase of program development.

## COUNTING AND ACCUMULATING

Program 7.4 illustrates how the LET statement can be used to either count items or accumulate values.

## PROGRAM 7.4 A Counter and an Accumulator

```
5 LET C=0                       'initialize C the counter
10 LET S=0                      'initialize S the accumulator
12 PRINT "C","X","S"
15 READ X                       'read data values
18     LET C=C+1                'count data values
20     LET S=S+X                'accumulate (sum) values of X
25     PRINT C,X,S
30 GOTO 15                      'repeat the READ, LET, PRINT sequence
35 DATA 7,3,5,6,1
99 END

RUN
C                  X                 S
  1                7                 7
  2                3                 10
  3                5                 15
  4                6                 21
  5                1                 22
Out of DATA in 15
```

Variable $C$ in Program 7.4, at line 18, is being used to count the number of times the program cycles through the GOTO loop. Each time line 18 is executed, a constant value of 1 is added to the prior value of $C$. Line 5 gives $C$ an initial value of 0. This defining of a variable is often referred to as *initialization*.

Although microcomputers will set all variables to zero when the RUN command is entered to process a program, it is still good form to show the initialization of variables when your program has a counter or accumulator. Including initialization in the program improves the program's documentation. If you choose not to code the initialization, provide a remark (REM) telling the reader the initial values of the variables. To be consistent, initialization of counters and accumulators is shown throughout this text where required.

Variable $S$ is used in Program 7.4 to accumulate the sum (hence the variable name $S$) of the values in the DATA statement. The purpose of line 10 is to give $S$ an initial value of 0 so that it can be used to accumulate the values of variable $X$ in line 20.

When line 15 is executed the first time, the variable $X$ is assigned the value 7. In line 20, variable $S$, which was 0 because of line 10, becomes 7, since $0 + 7 = 7$. Line 25 prints the values of $X$ and $S$, which are both 7, along with $C$, the counter, which is 1.

The GOTO 15 on line 30 transfers the program to line 15, which causes the value of $X$ to be changed to 3 from 7, since the second entry in the DATA statement is 3. Line 20 now changes the value of $S$ from 7 to 10, since $7 + 3 = 10$. Note that $S$ did not become zero again since line 10 was only executed the first time. Line 25 then prints the current values of $C$, $X$, and $S$, which are now 2, 3, and 10, respectively. This program will continue until all of the numbers in the DATA statement have been read. When GOTO 15 is then encountered, the computer attempts to read another value for $X$ from the DATA

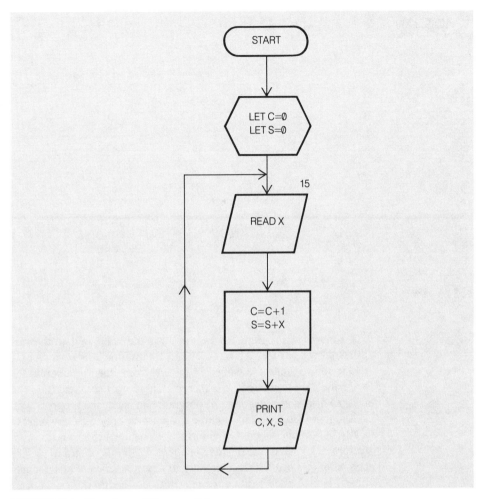

**FIGURE 7.4**   Flowchart of Program 7.4

statement and, since there is no more data, the computer says ''Out of data in 15.'' Figure 7.4 is a flowchart of Program 7.4.

## The Infinite GOTO Loop

Program 7.5 is another illustration of the GOTO statement. The program as shown has a logic error that causes an *infinite loop* to occur. Specifically, the program will not end, as did the prior programs that ran out of data. The execution of Program 7.5 will not stop unless the ''plug is pulled out'' (actually, you should never pull out the computer's plug) or the computer reaches a number that is too large. Termination of an infinite loop is achieved manually using the Ctrl and Break keys together.

## PROGRAM 7.5 An Infinite Loop

```
10 LET X=1                     'start X at 1
15 PRINT X, X^2, X^3, X^.5, 1/X   'print operations on X
20     LET X=X+1               'increment X by 1
25 GOTO 15                     'repeat lines 15-20
99 END
```

```
RUN
1                 1              1           1            1
2                 4              8           1.414213     .5
3                 9              27          1.732051     .3333334
4                 16             64          2            .25
5                 25             125         2.236068     .2
6                 36             216         2.44949      .1666667
7                 49             343         2.645751     .1428571
8                 64             512         2.828427     .125
^C
Break in 15
```

Line 10 of Program 7.5 assigns an initial value of 1 to the variable $X$. Line 15 then prints the value of 1, $1^2$, $1^3$, $\sqrt{1}$, and 1/1. In line 20 the value of $X$ is increased by 1 so that it now assumes the value 2. Line 25 returns the execution to line 15 where 2, $2^2$, $2^3$, $\sqrt{2}$, and 1/2 are printed. $X$ is then increased by 1 to 3 and the process is repeated. Note that the data is generated in this program and hence the program will never run out of data as Program 7.1 did. Thus, with a program of only five statements, we can get, theoretically, an infinite amount of information; namely, the squares, cubes, square roots, and reciprocals of all of the positive integers. With this program we see the real power of the computer. We can tell the computer to repeat a series of statements an infinite number of times. Unlike people, the computer does not get tired.

An infinite loop structure is an example of poor design. Infinite loops should be avoided because they will not terminate under program control; rather, they need to be stopped by user or programmer intervention. Table 7.2 shows some other infinite loop situations. Note that in the examples shown, the loops do not contain a READ statement.

Program 7.6, which is based on Case 7.2, provides another illustration of the GOTO statement.

· · · · · · · · · · · · · · · · · · · · · · · · · · · · · · · · · · · · · · · · ·

## CASE 7.2

**Problem** **Simple Interest Calculations**
A program is required to calculate the simple interest on several loans.

**Data Input** The data to be processed consists of the principal amount, the interest rate in decimal form, and the time in months. Six sets of data are to be processed (see below under Output).

**Process/Formulas** A repetitive process is to be used. To calculate simple interest use the following formula:

Interest = principal $\times$ rate $\times$ time

where the interest is the amount charged for the loan, the principal is the amount borrowed, the rate is the annual percentage charge, and the time is the fractional part of a year. A counter should be used, with the count variable acting as the loan number in the output.

**Output**

The program output should have the following appearance:

```
LOAN    PRINCIPAL   RATE-%  TIME        INTEREST

  1     $1,200.00   7.00%   7 MONTHS    $ 49.00
  2       $850.00   9.50%   6 MONTHS    $ 40.38
  3    $11,250.00   9.25%   9 MONTHS    $780.47
  4     $8,566.50  11.75%   4 MONTHS    $335.52
  5     $2,500.00  10.50%   8 MONTHS    $175.00
  6       $925.75   8.25%   5 MONTHS    $ 31.82
```

**TABLE 7.2** Examples of Infinite GOTO Loops

| EXAMPLES | EXPLANATION |
|---|---|
| 10 LET AMT= N *W<br>20 PRINT AMT, N, W<br>. . .<br>90 GOTO 10 | Line 10 will recalculate the same thing each time, and line 20 will cause the same result to be printed over and over again. |
| 10 LET AMT= N *W<br>20 PRINT AMT N, W<br>. . .<br>90 GOTO 20 | Line 10 is processed once. Line 20 will cause the same result to be printed over and over again. |
| 100 GOTO 200<br>. . .<br>200 PRINT "A= "; A<br>220 GOTO 100 | Execution of line 100 causes a branch to 200, skipping all the lines in between. Line 220 causes a transfer to line 100, creating a never-ending loop. In this example, line 200 will print each time the loop cycles. |
| 500 GOTO 500 | Line 500 causes an infinite loop without any physical indication, such as screen output. This usually occurs as the result of a typographical error or an error in a line-number change. |
| 50 INPUT TOT<br>. . .<br>90 GOTO 50 | Line 50 will continue to request data for input over and over again. Lines that follow 50 will be processed. Pressing the Ctrl and Break keys together will terminate the loop. |

## PROGRAM 7.6   Case 7.2, Calculating Interest on Loans

```
10 REM CASE 7.2  FINDING INTEREST ON LOANS
15 REM PROGRAMMER- (name of person)  DATE - mm/dd/yy
20 REM     VARIABLE LIST - A1$, A2$, I, L, P, R, T
25 REM         A1$ = HEADING
```

```
30 REM            A2$ = FORMAT
32 REM            I  = INTEREST
35 REM            L  = LOAN NUMBER
40 REM            P  = PRINCIPAL
45 REM            R  = INTEREST RATE-%
50 REM            T  = TIME
60 REM -------------------------------------------------
65 LET A1$ = "LOAN     PRINCIPAL     RATE-%     TIME       INTEREST"
70 LET A2$ = "   #      $$#,###.##    ##.##%    ## MONTHS   $###.##"
75 LET L=1
80 PRINT A1$
85 PRINT
90 READ P, R, T
95      LET I=P*(R/100)*(T/12)
100     PRINT USING A2$; L, P, R, T, I
105     LET L=L+1
110 GOTO 90
115 DATA 1200,7,7,850,9.5,6
120 DATA 11250,9.25,9,8566.50,11.75,4
125 DATA 2500,10.5,8,925.75,8.25,5
130 END

RUN
LOAN     PRINCIPAL     RATE-%     TIME       INTEREST

  1     $1,200.00      7.00%     7 MONTHS   $  49.00
  2       $850.00      9.50%     6 MONTHS   $  40.38
  3    $11,250.00      9.25%     9 MONTHS   $780.47
  4     $8,566.50     11.75%     4 MONTHS   $335.52
  5     $2,500.00     10.50%     8 MONTHS   $175.00
  6       $925.75      8.25%     5 MONTHS   $  31.82
Out of DATA in 90
```

Program 7.6 shows how the interest for the given loans can be calculated. A counter is used in this program (line 105) instead of including the loan number with the data. Note that in line 95, the interest rate is converted into decimal form by dividing by 100, and the time ($T$) is divided by 12 to obtain the fractional part of the year.

## Data Structures and Styling

Sometimes you can style your data items to improve their readability and correspondence to the READ statement. For example, the DATA statements (lines 115 to 125) in Program 7.6 could have been structured as:

115 DATA 1200,7,7

118 DATA 850,9.5,6

120 DATA [and so on]

Such concerns about appearance and style help make your program easier to understand in terms of logic and processing sequence.

Case 7.3 and Program 7.7 illustrate this idea of data structure and styling.

## CASE 7.3

**Problem**      **Payroll Report Preparation**
A company would like to have a program-generated payroll report. For each employee, this report should include his or her name, social security number, hours worked during the week, pay rate, and gross salary.

**Data Input**   Data inputs include the string items of name and social security number and the numeric values of hours and rate. (See below under Output.) Style each line of data so its structure represents a single employee's data list. This will facilitate any future changes that may occur.

**Process/Formulas** The process is repetitive. Salary is computed as:

Salary = number of hours × hourly rate

**Output**       The output display should be formatted as follows:

| NAME | S.S.NUMBER | HOURS | RATE | SALARY |
|------|------------|-------|------|--------|
| J.SUTTON | 123-45-6789 | 40 | $15.55 | $662.00 |
| E.KAPLAN | 352-31-7896 | 35 | $7.70 | $269.50 |
| R.NENNER | 098-76-5321 | 41 | $3.80 | $155.80 |
| B.SIROTA | 212-17-6034 | 50 | $10.50 | $525.00 |
| P.KAMBER | 696-40-3117 | 30 | $8.50 | $255.00 |

Program 7.7 carries out the requirements for Case 7.3. To format the output correctly according to the case specifications, a PRINT USING statement is used in line 205. This statement defines two string zones and three numeric zones. Double dollar signs ($$) produce the floating dollar signs before each rate and salary value. The horizontal lines between each row of output were achieved by the string assignment in line 175 and the print statement in lines 190 and 210.

## PROGRAM 7.7    Case 7.3, Payroll Report Generation

```
100 REM CASE 7.3  PAYROLL REPORT
105 REM PROGRAMMER- (name of person)   DATE - mm/dd/yy
110 REM
115 REM      VARIABLE LIST - F$, H, H$, L$, N$, R, SA, S$
120 REM          F$ = FORMAT
125 REM          H = HOURS WORKED
130 REM          H$ = HEADING
135 REM          L$ = UNDERLINE
140 REM          N$ = EMPLOYEE NAME
145 REM          R = RATE PER HOUR
150 REM          SA = SALARY = H * R
```

```
155 REM           S$ = SOCIAL SECURITY NUMBER
160 REM -------------------------------------------------------
165 REM
170 LET H$ = "     NAME          S.S.NUMBER     HOURS    RATE         SALARY"
175 LET L$ = "----------------------------------------------------------------"
180 LET F$ = " \              \     \              \     ##    $$##.##    $$###.##"
185 PRINT H$
190 PRINT L$
195 READ N$, S$, H, R
200     LET SA = H*R
205     PRINT USING F$; N$, S$, H, R, SA
210     PRINT L$
215 GOTO 195
220 DATA J.SUTTON, 123-45-6789, 40, 15.55
225 DATA E.KAPLAN, 352-31-7896, 35, 7.70
230 DATA R.NENNER, 098-76-5321, 41, 3.80
235 DATA B.SIROTA, 212-17-6034, 50, 10.50
240 DATA P.KAMBER, 696-40-3117, 30, 8.50
245 END
```

```
RUN
    NAME           S.S.NUMBER       HOURS     RATE        SALARY
    -------------------------------------------------------------
    J.SUTTON       123-45-6789        40    $15.55      $622.00
    -------------------------------------------------------------
    E.KAPLAN       352-31-7896        35    $7.70       $269.50
    -------------------------------------------------------------
    R.NENNER       098-76-5321        41    $3.80       $155.80
    -------------------------------------------------------------
    B.SIROTA       212-17-6034        50    $10.50      $525.00
    -------------------------------------------------------------
    P.KAMBER       696-40-3117        30    $8.50       $255.00
    -------------------------------------------------------------
Out of DATA in 195
```

## SUMMARY

The GOTO statement transfers control unconditionally to the statement indicated by the specified line number, instead of to the next statement in sequence. GOTO causes the computer to repeat a number of steps or to skip them. The GOTO statement can create a loop structure, which repeats a process many times. Too many GOTO statements should be avoided to prevent spaghetti code. The contents of a loop structure can be indented to improve program clarity.

## BASIC VOCABULARY SUMMARY

| Statement | Purpose | Examples |
|---|---|---|
| GOTO<br>(Alt + G key) | Transfers control to statements above or below, without any conditions. | 20 READ A$, B, C<br>· · ·<br>150 GOTO 20<br><br>250 GOTO 400<br>400 END |

## Review Questions

**♦ 7.1**   What would the following program (Program 7.1) do if line 20 were changed to
a. 20 GOTO 15?
b. 20 GOTO 30?

```
10 READ X
15 PRINT X, X^2, X^3
20 GOTO 10
25 DATA 2,4,5,10,8,-3
30 END
RUN
 2              4              8
 4             16             64
 5             25            125
10            100           1000
 8             64            512
-3              9            -27
Out of DATA in 10
```

**7.2**   What would the following program (Program 7.1) do if a RESTORE statement were added on
a. Line 5?
b. Line 12?
c. Line 17?
d. Line 22?
e. Line 27?

```
10 READ X
15 PRINT X, X^2, X^3
20 GOTO 10
25 DATA 2,4,5,10,8,-3
30 END

RUN
 2              4              8
 4             16             64
 5             25            125
10            100           1000
 8             64            512
-3              9            -27
Out of DATA in 10
```

**7.3**   What would the following program (Program 7.2) do if
a. Only line 15 were removed?
b. Only line 30 were removed?
c. Only line 40 were removed?
d. Only line 50 were removed?
e. Only line 60 were removed?
f. All of the GOTO statements in lines 15, 30, 40, 50, and 60 were removed?

```
10 PRINT "EVERY";
15 GOTO 45
20 PRINT " FINE";
30 GOTO 99
35 PRINT " PERSON";
40 GOTO 55
45 PRINT " GOOD";
50 GOTO 35
55 PRINT " DOES";
60 GOTO 20
99 END

RUN
EVERY GOOD PERSON DOES FINE
```

**7.4**   a. What is wrong with the following statement?
             100 GOTO 100
         b. What would happen if this statement were the first statement in a program?

**7.5**   How would the output of the following program (Program 7.3) change if the comma between the first two numbers in the DATA statement in line 195 were changed to a decimal point?

195 DATA 218.200,233,1456,345,545,367,248

```
40 REM        VARIABLE LIST - A$, B$, C$, IN$, CP, RP
50 REM           A$, B$ = HEADINGS
60 REM           C$ = FORMAT
70 REM           IN$ = ITEM NUMBER
80 REM           CP = CURRENT PRICE
90 REM           RP = REVISED PRICE = CP * 1.066
100 REM  --------------------------------------------------
110 LET A$="ITEM          CURRENT          REVISED"
120 LET B$="NUMBER          PRICE            PRICE"
130 LET C$=" \     \    $$##,###.##      $$##,###.##"
140 PRINT A$
150 PRINT B$
155 PRINT "---------------------------------------"
160    READ IN$, CP
170    LET RP = CP*1.066
180    PRINT USING C$; IN$, CP, RP
190 GOTO 160
195 DATA 218,200,233,1456,345,545,367,248
200 DATA 401,225,406,179,407,1000
210 DATA 557,267,679,470,887,359
220 END

RUN
ITEM          CURRENT          REVISED
NUMBER          PRICE            PRICE
---------------------------------------

 218          $200.00          $213.20
 233        $1,456.00        $1,552.10
 345          $545.00          $580.97
 367          $248.00          $264.37
 401          $225.00          $239.85
 406          $179.00          $190.81
 407        $1,000.00        $1,066.00
 557          $267.00          $284.62
 679          $470.00          $501.02
 887          $359.00          $382.69
```

**7.6**   What would the following program (Program 7.3) do if
a. A line 158 DATA 100 were added?
b. A line 215 DATA 100 were added?
c. A line 161 RESTORE were added?
d. A line 185 RESTORE were added?
e. A line 195 RESTORE were added?
f. Line 190 were changed to 190 GOTO 155?
g. Line 190 were changed to 190 GOTO 170?

```
40 REM       VARIABLE LIST - A$, B$, C$, IN$, CP, RP
50 REM            A$, B$ = HEADINGS
60 REM            C$ = FORMAT
70 REM            IN$ = ITEM NUMBER
80 REM            CP = CURRENT PRICE
90 REM            RP = REVISED PRICE = CP * 1.066
100 REM ----------------------------------------------------
110 LET A$="ITEM          CURRENT          REVISED"
120 LET B$="NUMBER         PRICE            PRICE"
130 LET C$=" \     \    $$##,###.##      $$##,###.##"
140 PRINT A$
150 PRINT B$
155 PRINT "-------------------------------------------"
160     READ IN$, CP
170     LET RP = CP*1.066
180     PRINT USING C$; IN$, CP, RP
190 GOTO 160
195 DATA 218,200,233,1456,345,545,367,248
200 DATA 401,225,406,179,407,1000
210 DATA 557,267,679,470,887,359
220 END
```

```
RUN
ITEM              CURRENT              REVISED
NUMBER             PRICE                PRICE
-------------------------------------------
 218              $200.00              $213.20
 233            $1,456.00            $1,552.10
 345              $545.00              $580.97
 367              $248.00              $264.37
 401              $225.00              $239.85
 406              $179.00              $190.81
 407            $1,000.00            $1,066.00
 557              $267.00              $284.62
 679              $470.00              $501.02
 887              $359.00              $382.69
```

**7.7**   What would the following program (Program 7.4) do if
a. Line 35 were changed to 35 DATA 1,2,3,4,5,6?
♦ b. Line 30 were changed to 30 GOTO 10?
c. Line 30 were changed to 30 GOTO 20?
d. Line 30 were changed to 30 GOTO 25?
♦ e. Line 30 were changed to 30 GOTO 99?
f. Line 20 were changed to 20 LET X = X + S?
g. Line 20 were changed to 20 LET S = S + X^2?
h. A line 40 were added that read 40 DATA $-4, -9, -8, -1$?
♦ i. Line 30 were eliminated?
♦ j. Line 20 were eliminated?
k. A RESTORE statement were added on line 16?

```
 5 LET C=0
10 LET S=0
12 PRINT "C", "X", "S"
15 READ X
18     LET C=C+1
20     LET S=S+X
25      PRINT C, X, S
30 GOTO 15
35 DATA 7,3,5,6,1
99 END

RUN
C                   X                   S
 1                  7                   7
 2                  3                   10
 3                  5                   15
 4                  6                   21
 5                  1                   22
```

**7.8** What would the following program (Program 7.5) do if
 a. Line 10 were changed to 10 LET X = 5?
 b. Line 20 were changed to 20 LET X = X + 2?
 c. Line 25 were changed to 25 GOTO 10?
 d. Line 25 were changed to 25 GOTO 20?

```
10 LET X=1
15      PRINT X, X^2, X^3, X^.5, 1/X
20 LET X=X+1
25 GOTO 15
99 END
RUN
 1          1          1          1          1
 2          4          8          1.414213   .5
 3          9          27         1.732051   .3333334
 4          16         64         2          .25
^C
Break in 15
```

**7.9** What changes are necessary to revise the program below so that the output prints the results for
 a. Only the even numbers? (*Hint:* Lines 10 and 20 must be changed.)
 b. Only the odd numbers?
 c. The numbers 5, 10, 15, 20, . . . ?

```
10 LET X=1
15 PRINT X, X^2
20 LET X=X+1
25 GOTO 15
99 END

RUN
 1          1
 2          4
 3          9
 4          16
 5          25
^C
Break in 15
```

**7.10**  What would the following program (Program 7.6) do if line 110 GOTO 90 were changed to

a. 110 GOTO 75?          d. 110 GOTO 95?

b. 110 GOTO 80?          e. 110 GOTO 100?

c. 110 GOTO 85?          f. 110 GOTO 115?

```
20 REM       VARIABLE LIST-A1$, A2$, L, P, R, T, I
25 REM             A1$ = HEADING
30 REM             A2$ = FORMAT
35 REM             L = LOAN NUMBER
40 REM             P = PRINCIPAL
45 REM             R = INTEREST RATE-%
50 REM             T = TIME
55 REM             I = INTEREST
60 REM -------------------------------------------------------
65 LET A1$ = "LOAN       PRINCIPAL     RATE-%     TIME        INTEREST"
70 LET A2$ = "   #     $$#,###.##     ##.##%     # MONTHS    $###.##"
75 LET L=1
80 PRINT A1$
85 PRINT
90     READ P, R, T
95     LET I=P*(R/100)*(T/12)
100    PRINT USING A2$; L, P, R, T, I
105    LET L=L+1
110 GOTO 90
115 DATA 1200,7,7,850,9.5,6
120 DATA 11250,9.25,9,8566.50,11.75,4
125 DATA 2500,10.5,8,925.75,8.25,5
130 END


RUN
LOAN       PRINCIPAL     RATE-%     TIME        INTEREST

  1       $1,200.00      7.00%     7 MONTHS    $ 49.00
  2         $850.00      9.50%     6 MONTHS    $ 40.38
  3      $11,250.00      9.25%     9 MONTHS    $780.47
  4       $8,566.50     11.75%     4 MONTHS    $335.52
  5       $2,500.00     10.50%     8 MONTHS    $175.00
  6         $925.75      8.25%     5 MONTHS    $ 31.82
```

## Programming Activities

**7.11**  **Purpose**  To use the simple branching logic structure, numeric data, LPRINT, and PRINT USING statements for output formatting.

**Problem**  The current ratio is an accounting measure of a company's financial condition. This ratio is found by dividing current assets by current liabilities. Write and run a program that will find the current ratio for each year presented under Data below.

**Data**

| YEAR | CURRENT ASSETS | CURRENT LIABILITIES |
|------|----------------|---------------------|
| 1988 | $500,000 | $400,000 |
| 1989 | $160,000 | $120,000 |
| 1990 | $950,000 | $320,000 |
| 1991 | $600,000 | $300,000 |

**Output**  Your output should display on the screen and also generate a hard copy. Output should follow this format:

```
              CURRENT      CURRENT       CURRENT
      YEAR    ASSETS       LIABILITIES   RATIO
      --------------------------------------------
      1988    $500,000     $400,000      1.25
      1989    $160,000     $120,000      1.33
      1990    $950,000     $320,000      2.97
      1991    $600,000     $300,000      2.00
```

**7.12**  **Purpose**  To use the simple sequence logic structure, numeric data, and PRINT USING statement for output formatting.

**Problem**  For the data given below, write and run a program to find the percent of increase for each month shown. That is, (2nd yr − 1st yr)/1st yr × 100 for each month.

**Data**

|  |  | **MONTH** |  |
|---|---|---|---|
| **UNITS SOLD:** | **1** | **2** | **3** |
| 1st yr | 400 | 450 | 440 |
| 2nd yr | 500 | 575 | 600 |

**Output**  Your output should have this format:

```
                                    MONTH
      ----------------------------------------------------------
      UNITS SOLD              1              2              3
      ----------------------------------------------------------
      FIRST YEAR             400            450            440
      SECOND YEAR            500            575            600
      ----------------------------------------------------------
      % INCREASE            25.00          43.75          36.36
```

**7.13**  **Purpose**  To use the simple branching logic structure, numeric data, double precision variables, and PRINT USING statement for output formatting.

**Problem**  Write and run a program to find the total accumulation for six Individual Retirement Accounts (see Case 4.2). Use the formula:

$$F = A\left[\frac{(1 + R)^N - 1}{R}\right]$$

Include REM statements in the program describing the problem and the program. Use double precision variables.

**Data**  $A$ is \$1,000 and \$1,500; $R$ is 8½ percent; and $N$ is 10, 15, and 20 years. Note that $R$ is fixed, and each $A$ will have three different periods of $N$ years each.

**Output**  Your output should have this format:

```
      AMOUNT     YEARS   RATE      TOTAL
      ------------------------------------------
      $1,000      10     0.085    $14,835.11
      $1,500      10     0.085    $22,252.67
      $1,000      15     0.085    $28,232.30
      $1,500      15     0.085    $42,348.45
      $1,000      20     0.085    $48,377.08
      $1,500      20     0.085    $72,565.62
```

**◆ 7.14**

**Purpose** To use the simple branching logic structure, string and numeric data, and PRINT USING statement for output formatting.

**Problem** The United Computer Company pays its salespersons a monthly salary of $1,000 plus 1½ percent commission for equipment sold during the month. The data below shows the sales figures by salesperson for last month. Write and run a program that computes the total monthly salary plus commission for each salesperson.

**Data**

| SALESPERSON | AMOUNT SOLD |
|-------------|-------------|
| M. Worth | $13,500 |
| K. Gray | 21,000 |
| S. Legan | 9,600 |
| B. Hinz | 24,400 |

**Output** Your output should have this format:

```
SALESPERSON        AMT SOLD      SALARY+COMM.
-----------------  ---------     -----------

M. WORTH           $13,500       $1,202.50
K. GRAY            $21,000       $1,315.00
S. LEGAN           $ 9,600       $1,144.00
B. HINZ            $24,400       $1,366.00
```

**7.15**

**Purpose** To use the simple branching logic structure, string and numeric data, and PRINT USING statement for output formatting.

**Problem** The ABC Company (see exercises 6.19 and 6.20) anticipates that for this year and the next two years, sales in each division will exceed last year's sales by the following percentage growth rates.

| | LAST YEAR-1 | THIS YEAR-2 | NEXT YEAR-3 | YEAR AFTER-4 |
|---------|-------------|-------------|-------------|--------------|
| Percent | 100.0 | 108.0 | 114.2 | 121.3 |

Write and run a program that will generate for each of the divisions the expected sales for years involved.

**Data** The data for year 1 is as follows:

| DIVISION | SALES (MILLION $) |
|----------|-------------------|
| West | 3.85 |
| South | 8.62 |
| North | 4.57 |
| East | 3.81 |

**Output** Your output should have this format:

```
            THREE YEAR SALES FORECAST- ABC COMPANY

DIVISION        YEAR 1      YEAR 2      YEAR 3      YEAR 4
--------------------------------------------------------------
WEST            3.85        4.16        4.40         4.67
SOUTH           8.62        9.31        9.84        10.46
NORTH           4.57        4.94        5.22         5.54
EAST            3.81        4.11        4.35         4.62
```

**7.16**

**Purpose** To use the simple branching logic structure, string and numeric data, and PRINT USING statement for output formatting.

**Problem**   A large retail establishment uses a wage payment plan of straight salary at $300.00 per week, plus a commission of 10 percent of the amount of merchandise each employee sells. Using the information given below, write and run a program that completes the table shown by computing commissions and total earnings.

**Data**

| EMPLOYEE NUMBER | REGULAR SALARY | AMOUNT SOLD |
|---|---|---|
| 1015 | $300.00 | $500.00 |
| 1068 | 300.00 | 580.00 |
| 1135 | 300.00 | 485.00 |
| 1359 | 300.00 | 610.50 |
| 2370 | 300.00 | 450.00 |

Note that the employee number is treated as a string data item.

**Output**   Your output should have this format:

```
EMPLOYEE      REGULAR      AMOUNT      COMMISSION    TOTAL
NUMBER        SALARY       SOLD                      EARNINGS
--------------------------------------------------------------
    1015      $300.00      $500.00       $50.00      $350.00
    1068      $300.00      $580.00       $58.00      $358.00
    1135      $300.00      $485.00       $48.50      $348.50
    1359      $300.00      $610.50       $61.05      $361.05
    2370      $300.00      $450.00       $45.00      $345.00
```

**7.17**   **Purpose**   To use the simple branching logic structure, string and numeric data, and PRINT USING statement for output formatting.

**Problem**   Write and run a program that reads in employee names, hours worked, and the hourly rate and that outputs a table showing the employee names, salary (number of hours × hourly rate), federal tax (20 percent of salary), social security tax (.05478 × salary), and net salary (that is, gross salary − all deductions).

**Data**

| EMPLOYEE NAME | HOURS WORKED | RATE |
|---|---|---|
| Brown, A. | 37 | $4.50 |
| Levine, C. | 35 | 5.25 |
| Bean, L.L. | 39 | 4.75 |
| Engle, M. | 34 | 4.00 |
| Stone, J. | 43 | 6.00 |

**Output**   Your output should have this format with dollar amounts rounded to the nearest penny.

```
EMPLOYEE   HOURS   RATE    SALARY    FED.TAX   S.S.TAX    NET
  NAME                                                   SALARY

Brown, A.   37    $4.50   $166.50    $33.30     $9.12   $124.08
Levine, C.  35    $5.25   $183.75    $36.75    $10.07   $136.93
Bean, L.L.  39    $4.75   $185.25    $37.05    $10.15   $138.05
Engle, M.   34    $4.00   $136.00    $27.20     $7.45   $101.35
Stone, J.   43    $6.00   $258.00    $51.60    $14.13   $192.27
```

# CHAPTER

# 8

# SELECTION
# SEQUENCE
# LOGIC AND
# DECISION MAKING

Upon completing this chapter, you will be able to do the following:

- Understand the many forms of the IF/THEN statement.
- Develop an understanding of a more complicated logic structure that includes controlled looping and decision making, or selection.
- Write programs that use an end of data test.
- Write programs that use the IF/THEN/ELSE statement.
- Include processing controls in programs.
- Understand the differences between the simple IF/THEN statement and the logical IF/THEN statement.
- Use logical variables as another means of comparison and testing.
- Write programs that can compare string items.
- Continue to develop programming problem solutions using iteration and decision-making structures.

In Chapter 7 we saw how the GOTO statement could be used to create a loop that results in a process or task being repeated until all the data is exhausted. Programs 7.3 and 7.7 illustrate the GOTO statement loop sequence. In this chapter we show how the unconditional GOTO loop sequence can be modified under conditions specified by the IF/THEN statement. We also discuss and illustrate decision making using IF/THEN statements.

Several forms of the IF/THEN statement are examined. These include IF/THEN line number, IF/THEN clause statement, IF/THEN/ELSE, and the logical IF/THEN.

## IF/THEN LINE NUMBER STATEMENT

Although the GOTO statement branches unconditionally (that is, no matter what), the IF/THEN statement branches only if a particular condition is true. Otherwise, it will not branch but will execute the next statement in the sequence. Thus, it will only branch conditionally.

The general form of the IF/THEN statement is

line #1 IF {expression 1} relationship {expression 2} THEN line #2

A *relationship* may be a comparison or test between variables, constants, expressions, and so forth. Table 8.1 shows several kinds of simple relationships.

An example of an IF/THEN statement is

50 IF N = 10 THEN 80
60

Statement 50 instructs us to test if the variable $N$ is equal to the number 10. If it is, then execute line 80 next. If the variable $N$ is not equal to the number 10, then execute the next statement in sequence (the one following this IF), which is 60 in this example. Other examples of the IF/THEN line number statement are shown in Table 8.2.

**TABLE 8.1** Examples of Comparison-Test Relations

| SYMBOL | EXAMPLE | MEANING |
|---|---|---|
| $<$ | $A < B$ | $A$ is less than $B$. |
| $<=$ | $X <= 5$ | $X$ is less than or equal to 5. |
| $>$ | $A + B > C$ | $A + B$ is greater than $C$. |
| $>=$ | $Y >= P + 5$ | $Y$ is greater than or equal to $P + 5$. |
| $=$ | $N = 10$ | $N$ is equal to 10. |
| $<>$ | $J + K <> L + M$ | $J + K$ is not equal to $L + M$. |

**TABLE 8.2**  IF/THEN Line Number Statements

| STATEMENT | EXPLANATION |
|---|---|
| 10 IF X > Y THEN 30<br>20 ----<br>30 ---- | Test if numeric variable *X* is greater than numeric variable *Y*. Go to line 30 if it is; go to the next line, 20, if it is not. |
| 85 IF AMT = −999 THEN 400<br>90 ----<br>400 ---- | Test if numeric variable *AMT* is equal to the numeric −999. Go to line 400 if it is; go to the next line, 90, if it is not. |
| 60 IF AN$ = BN$ THEN 90<br>70 -----<br>90 ----- | Compare two string items. If they are the same, go to line 90; if they are not the same, go to the next line, 70. |
| 20 -----<br>30 -----<br>125 IF R$ <> "YES" THEN 20<br>150 ----- | Compare the string variable R$ with the literal "YES". If they are not the same, loop back to line 20; otherwise go to the next line, 150. |

**Keyboarding Tip**    To save keystrokes, you can enter and display the keyword THEN by typing the Alt plus T key combination.

A variation of the IF/THEN statement is the IF/GOTO statement. Most PC dialects of BASIC permit the optional use of the GOTO in place of the THEN. Thus the statement

25 IF A > B THEN 40

could be written as

25 IF A > B GOTO 40

and work without error. We do *not* recommend the use of this optional form, however. It is awkward and can cause confusion when reading longer programs. Also, as we pointed out in Chapter 7, too many GOTO statements may imply a spaghetti code logic that should be avoided. By placing GOTOs in the IF/THEN statement, you increase rather than reduce the potential for confusion in your program.

A decision-making structure is illustrated by Program 8.1 using an IF/THEN statement.

## PROGRAM 8.1    The IF/THEN Statement

```
10 REM DECISION MAKING
30 REM THIS PROGRAM READS TWO NUMBERS
40 REM AND PRINTS THE LARGER OF THE TWO
50 READ A,B
60    IF A>B THEN 90
```

```
70        PRINT B
80 GOTO 110
90        PRINT A
100 DATA 7,3
110 END

RUN
 7
```

In line 50, Program 8.1 assigns the number 7 to variable *A* and the number 3 to variable *B*. Then *A* is compared to *B* in line 60. Since *A* is greater than *B*, the next statement to be executed is line 90, which prints the value of *A*. If the DATA statement in line 100 were to read 100 DATA 4, 12, variable *A* would be assigned the value 4 and variable *B* would be 12. Then because the condition *A* > *B* would not be true, when line 60 was encountered, line 90 would *not* be executed next; instead line 70 would be executed next, which prints the value of *B* (12). The GOTO 110 in line 80 prevents the variable *A* from also being printed when *B* is the larger number.

Note that in the flowchart in Figure 8.1 the diamond-shaped box has two lines coming from it. The one to the right with a YES over it points to the instruction that should be

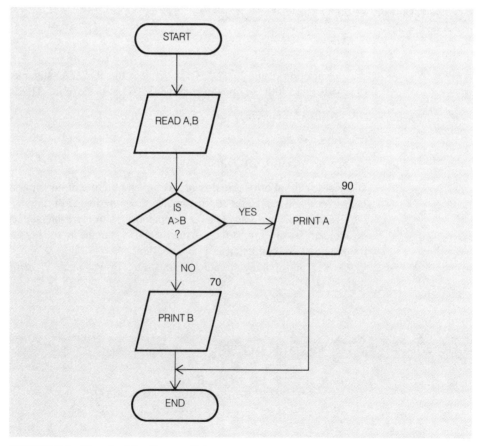

**FIGURE 8.1** Flowchart for Program 8.1

executed if the relationship $A > B$ is true. That is, if $A$ is greater than $B$ then PRINT A. If the relationship is false, if $A$ is less than $B$ or equal to $B$, the line below the diamond-shaped box indicates that the next statement to be executed is PRINT B.

## Logic Structures

The IF/THEN statement enables us to design programs and evaluate programming problems in terms of several logic structures. These include iterative structures for looping, as well as selection, or decision-making, structures that enable tests and comparisons to be performed. Figure 8.2 shows these types of structures.

The structures in Figure 8.2 should be used as a guide to organize your thinking on how to solve particular programming problems. When looking at a particular problem, ask yourself, "Which structure fits the problem?" Then use the appropriate BASIC statements to write the program details.

Figure 8.2 reveals that the DOWHILE and DOUNTIL are similar in the sense that they both provide a loop capability. However, they are different in the sense that the DOWHILE loop will test the condition *before* processing the statement, and the DOUNTIL loop will test the condition *after* the statement. This means that the statement in Figure 8.2(b) must be processed at least once.

Program 8.2, based on Case 8.1, illustrates the use of the IF/THEN statement in a simple decision-making situation.

## CASE 8.1

| | |
|---|---|
| **Problem** | **Determining Students' Honor List** |
| | A program is to be written to produce an honor list of all students with at least a 3.0 cumulative grade index. |
| **Data Input** | The data to be processed to test the program consists of each student's identification number and grade index. Use the following data values: 1234,3.5, 9876,2.9, 1768,3.0, 1357,2.8. |
| **Process/Formulas** | A repetitive process is to be used so that each grade index is tested to determine if it is at least 3.0. |
| **Output** | The output should be those students' identification numbers that correspond to a grade index of at least 3.0. |

## PROGRAM 8.2   Case 8.1, Students' Honor List

```
10 REM CASE 8.1, LISTING HONOR STUDENTS-DECISION MAKING
15 REM PROGRAMMER-(name of person) DATE-mm/dd/yy
16 REM    VARIABLE LIST- N,G
17 REM        N = STUDENT NO.
18 REM        G = GRADE
```

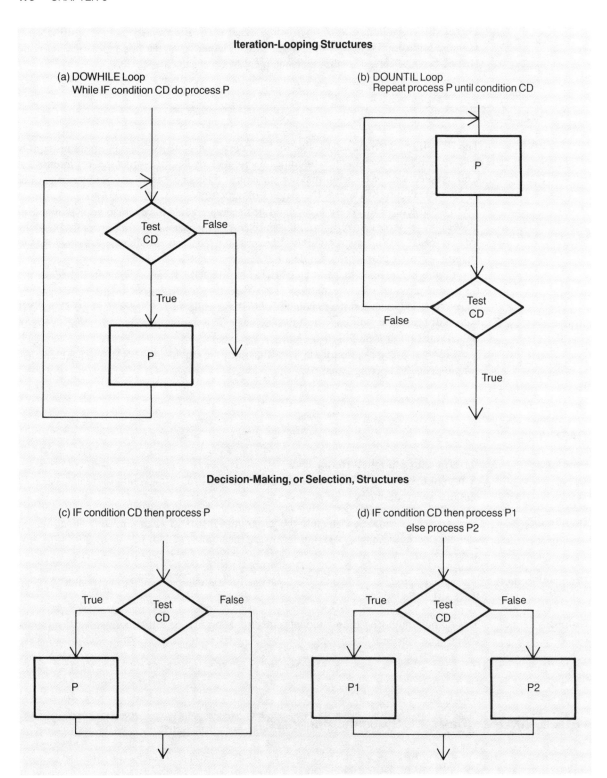

**Iteration-Looping Structures**

(a) DOWHILE Loop
   While IF condition CD do process P

(b) DOUNTIL Loop
   Repeat process P until condition CD

**Decision-Making, or Selection, Structures**

(c) IF condition CD then process P

(d) IF condition CD then process P1
   else process P2

**FIGURE 8.2** Iteration-Looping and Decision-Making, or Selection, Structures

```
20 REM ------------------------------------
30 READ N,G
40    IF G>= 3 THEN 50
45 GOTO 30
50    PRINT N
55 GOTO 30
60 DATA 1234,3.5, 9876,2.9, 1768,3.0, 1357,2.8
65 END

RUN
 1234
 1768
Out of DATA in 30
```

A flowchart for Program 8.2 is shown in Figure 8.3.

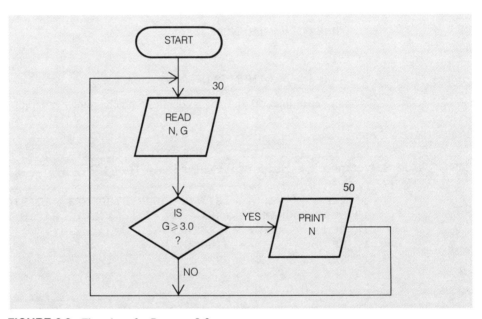

**FIGURE 8.3**   Flowchart for Program 8.2

## IF/THEN CLAUSE STATEMENT

The IF/THEN line number statement is only one of several forms of the IF/THEN statement. Instead of having a direction to transfer to a specific line number, the IF/THEN statement can include a specific clause. Such a clause is a BASIC statement. The form of this type of IF/THEN statement is

line # IF {expression 1} relationship {expression 2} THEN clause

If the relationship is true, the clause will be executed and then the next line is also executed. If the relationship is false, only the next line will be executed. Table 8.3 provides examples of this form of IF/THEN statement.

**TABLE 8.3** IF/THEN Clause Statement

| STATEMENT | EXPLANATION |
|---|---|
| 10 IF X > Y THEN PRINT X<br>20 ----- | Test if numeric variable *X* is greater than numeric variable *Y*. If it is, print *X* before going to the next line; if it is not, go to the next line without printing *X*. |
| 85 IF AMT = −999 THEN END<br>90 ----- | Test if numeric variable *AMT* is equal to the numeric −999. Go to END if it is; if not go to the next line. |
| 125 IF A < B THEN LET C = C + 1<br>150 ----- | Test if numeric variable *A* is less than numeric variable *B*. If it is, increase *C* by one; if it is not, go to the next line. |
| 60 IF AN$ = BN$ THEN PRINT "MATCH"<br>70 ----- | Compare two string items. If they are the same, print "MATCH"; if they are not, go to the next line. |

Program 8.3 shows the IF/THEN clause statement incorporated into Program 8.2. By revising line 40 in the original program from

40 IF G>= 3 THEN 50

to

40 IF G>= 3 THEN PRINT N

we can delete lines 50 and 55, producing a much simpler program.

## PROGRAM 8.3 Case 8.1, Students' Honor List—Revised

```
10 REM CASE 8.1, LISTING HONOR STUDENTS-DECISION MAKING
15 REM PROGRAMMER-(name of person) DATE mm/dd/yy
16 REM     VARIABLE LIST- N,G
17 REM        N = STUDENT NO.
18 REM        G = GRADE
20 REM  ----------------------------------------
30 READ N,G
40    IF G>= 3 THEN PRINT N
45 GOTO 30
60 DATA 1234,3.5, 9876,2.9, 1768,3.0, 1357,2.8
65 END

RUN
 1234
 1768
Out of DATA in 30
```

The revised program does exactly the same thing as the original. It does not change the flowchart in Figure 8.3 (except the 50 above the PRINT N symbol is no longer needed). With the revised line 40, if the test relationship is true, the student number is printed and then we proceed to line 45 to cycle the loop one more time. If the test relationship is false, the program proceeds to the next line and cycles back one more time.

## IF/THEN/ELSE STATEMENT

Another form of the IF/THEN statement adds an ELSE clause to the form just described. The form of this type of IF/THEN statement is

line # IF {expression 1} relationship {expression 2} THEN clause 1 ELSE clause 2

If the test relationship is true, the THEN clause 1 is executed and the ELSE clause 2 is ignored. If the test relationship is false, the THEN clause 1 is ignored and the ELSE clause 2 is executed. In either case, the program then continues to the next line.

Table 8.4 provides examples of this form of the IF/THEN statement.

◆ **Keyboarding Tip**    To save keystrokes, you can enter and display the keyword ELSE by typing the Alt plus E key combination.

The IF/THEN clause statement has been incorporated into Program 8.3 to produce Program 8.4. Adding the ELSE clause to line 40 in Program 8.4 changes it from

40 IF G> = 3 THEN PRINT N

to

40 IF G> = 3 THEN PRINT N;"*HONOR LIST*" ELSE PRINT N; "NON-HONORS"

and enables two different print results to be shown: those getting honors, and those not eligible.

**TABLE 8.4**  IF/THEN/ELSE Statements

| STATEMENT | EXPLANATION |
|---|---|
| 10 IF X > Y THEN PRINT X ELSE PRINT Y<br>20 ----- | Test if numeric variable $X$ is greater than numeric variable $Y$. If it is, the program will print $X$ and then go to line 20; if it is not, the program will print $Y$ and then go to line 20. |
| 85 IF AMT = −999 THEN END ELSE 50 | Test if numeric variable $AMT$ is equal to the numeric −999. The program will end if it is; if it is not, the program will branch to line 50. |
| 25 IF A < B THEN LET B = 0 ELSE PRINT A<br>50 ----- | Test if numeric variable $A$ is less than numeric variable $B$. If it is, the program will set $B$ to zero and go to line 50; if it is not, the program will print $A$ and then go to line 50. |
| 60 IF AN$ = BN$ THEN PRINT " = " ELSE END<br>70 ----- | Compare two string items. If they are the same, the program will print " = " and go to line 70; if they are not, the program will end. |

## PROGRAM 8.4   Case 8.1, Students' Honor List—Revised with ELSE Clause

```
10 REM CASE 8.1, LISTING HONOR STUDENTS-DECISION MAKING
15 REM PROGRAMMER (name of person) DATE- mm/dd/yy
16 REM     VARIABLE LIST- N,G
17 REM        N = STUDENT NO.
18 REM        G = GRADE
20 REM ---------------------------
30 READ N,G
40    IF G>= 3 THEN PRINT N;" * HONOR LIST *" ELSE PRINT N; "    NON-HONORS "
45 GOTO 30
60 DATA 1234,3.5, 9876,2.9, 1768,3.0, 1357,2.8
65 END

RUN
 1234 * HONOR LIST *
 9876    NON-HONORS
 1768 * HONOR LIST *
 1357    NON-HONORS
Out of DATA in 30
```

Be careful when using the ELSE form of the IF/THEN statement. The examples in Table 8.4 demonstrate that with the addition of the ELSE clause the IF/THEN statement becomes very powerful in the sense that it can carry out three different tasks. These include a test comparison and two other operations, one following the THEN and one after the ELSE. Don't assume that all programs must use such statements. Sometimes the simple IF/THEN with additional statements is just as effective as a more involved IF/THEN/ELSE statement.

## REPETITION LOGIC STRUCTURES

Recall that parts (a) and (b) of Figure 8.2 illustrated the DOWHILE and DOUNTIL loop structures. These structures provide us with the logic to carry out repetitive processing tasks. The next few programs illustrate such tasks. For example, Program 8.5 will process all the data items in the program as a DOUNTIL. In that program, a certain number of iterations have been completed before the program sequence is changed because of the specified IF/THEN test conditions.

## PROGRAM 8.5   Summing Numbers and Their Squares

```
5   REM  LOOP REPETITION - DOUNTIL
10 REM  THIS PROGRAM READS 5 NUMBERS FROM THE DATA STATEMENT
20 REM  AND PRINTS THE NUMBERS, THE SQUARES OF THE NUMBERS,
30 REM  AND THE SUMS OF THE NUMBERS AND THEIR SQUARES.
40 LET S=0
45 LET S2=0
50 LET N=1
55 READ X
```

```
60    LET S=S+X           'accumulate X values
65    LET S2=S2+X^2        'accumulate X values squared
70    PRINT X,X^2
75    IF N=5 THEN 90       'is the count at five?
80         LET N=N+1       'counter is incremented
85 GOTO 55
90 PRINT "---","---"
95 PRINT S,S2
100 DATA 7,3,5,6,1
999 END
```

```
RUN
  7              49
  3               9
  5              25
  6              36
  1               1
 ---             ---
 22             120
```

Variables $S$ and $S2$ accumulate the sum of the numbers and the sum of the squares of the numbers, respectively. These sums are initialized to zero in lines 40 and 45. Variable $N$ is used as a counter to count the number of data values that have been read in. $N$ is initialized to 1 before the first number is read in. Lines 60 and 65 accumulate the sum and the sum of the squares of the numbers, and line 70 prints the number and its square. In line 75, we test if $N = 5$. That is, we see if we are finished processing all five numbers. If $N$ is not 5, we proceed to line 80, where 1 is added to the variable $N$. Then we go back to line 55 to read the next number from the DATA statement. We repeat this process until all five numbers have been read, at which time $N$ is equal to 5 and control is transferred to line 90.

Program 8.5 is a typical illustration of a program designed to do something a fixed number of times. The flowchart of this program appears in Figure 8.4.

Sometimes we may not know exactly how many times we are to perform an operation, but we want to keep performing it until we have read all of the data. This situation is illustrated in Program 8.6.

## PROGRAM 8.6   Testing DATA to End Program

```
5   REM LOOP REPETITION - DOWHILE
10  REM THIS PROGRAM ACCOMPLISHES THE SAME THING AS
15  REM PROGRAM 8.5 BUT WITH AN END OF DATA TEST
40  LET S=0
45  LET S2=0
50  READ X
55     IF X=999 THEN 80        'end of data test
60         LET S=S+X
65         LET S2=S2+X^2
70         PRINT X,X^2
75  GOTO 50
80  PRINT "---","---"
```

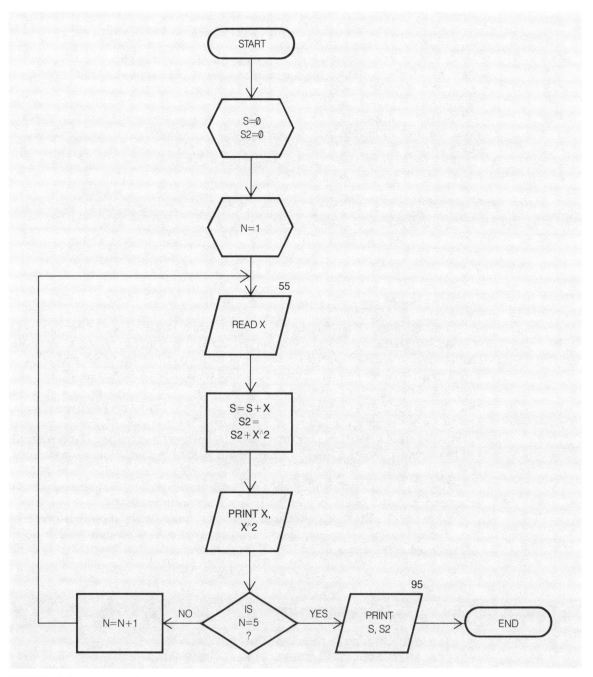

**FIGURE 8.4**  Flowchart for Program 8.5

```
85 PRINT S,S2
90 DATA 7,3,5,6,1,999
999 END

RUN
   7              49
   3               9
   5              25
   6              36
   1               1
 ---             ---
  22             120
```

Note that Program 8.6 has the same output as Program 8.5. Program 8.5 works for any five numbers in the DATA statement. Program 8.6 will work for all numbers in the DATA statement except the number 999. Thus, if line 90 were changed to

   90 DATA 7,2,3,999,4,1

the numbers 4 and 1 would not be read by the program, since as soon as the 999 were encountered the totals would be printed. Similarly, if there were 50 numbers followed by a 999 in the DATA statement, all 50 numbers would be processed.

   Any number can be used to signal the end of the data. Thus, if line 55 were changed to

   55 IF X = 1000 THEN 80

and the DATA statement were

   90 DATA 7,3,5,6,1,1000

the output would also be identical to the output of Programs 8.5 and 8.6.

   This end-of-data value is also called a *flag*. The flag obviously should be a value that is *not* found in the DATA list itself, such as $-99$ or $-9999$, for example.

## Program Appearance and Indenting

We can improve a program's appearance by indenting program statements to create *white space*. In the previous chapter we illustrated how the contents of a GOTO loop may be indented so the program statements being repeated by the loop are clearly identified. The use of indentation also appears in the programs in this chapter. We indented and aligned the statements in Program 8.5 that made up a simple sequence logic under the READ statement. Statements under the IF/THEN statement are further indented, as shown in both Programs 8.5 and 8.6. Figure 8.5 shows these two programs with suggested guidelines for indenting. There are no set rules for indenting statements. Usually an indent of only three or four spaces from the left is sufficient. Examine the programs in this chapter to see how you can make your programs clearer in their presentation and easier to understand. Case 8.2 shows an application of the IF/THEN statement.

```
40 LET S=0
45 LET S2=0
50 LET N=1
55 READ X
60     LET S=S+X
65     LET S2=S2+X^2
70     PRINT X,X^2
75     IF N=5 THEN   90
80        LET N=N+1
85 GOTO 55
90 PRINT "---","---"
95 PRINT S,S2
100 DATA 7,3,5,6,1
999 END
```

White space — Indent simple logic sequence
Indent statement(s) under IF

```
40 LET S=0
45 LET S2=0
50 READ X
55    IF X=999 THEN 80
60       LET S=S+X
65       LET S2=S2+X^2
70       PRINT X,X^2
75 GOTO 50
80 PRINT "---","---"
85 PRINT S,S2
90 DATA 7,3,5,6,1,999
999 END
```

White space — Indent simple logic sequence under IF

**FIGURE 8.5**  Some Indentation Guidelines

## CASE 8.2

**Problem**        **Earnings Computations**
Each month the ABC Company computes the monthly earnings for each of its salespersons. A program performs this task, taking into account a bonus possibility for those salespersons selling over $5,000.

**Data Input**     Last month the sales of the nine salespersons were as follows:

| SALESPERSON | MONTHLY SALES | SALESPERSON | MONTHLY SALES |
|---|---|---|---|
| 1 | $4,000 | 6 | $6,050 |
| 2 | 6,250 | 7 | 8,300 |
| 3 | 4,750 | 8 | 3,500 |
| 4 | 4,800 | 9 | 9,625 |
| 5 | 7,125 | | |

**Process/Formulas**  A repetitive process is to be used. Decision testing is required to determine if a bonus is applicable. Monthly earnings are computed as 20 percent of total sales plus a bonus of 12½ percent of any amount sold in excess of $5,000. The program terminates as a result of an end of data test.

**Output**    Output follows this format:

```
PERSON  1  NO BONUS THIS MONTH   EARNINGS     $800.00
PERSON  2  BONUS     $156.25     EARNINGS   $1,406.25
PERSON  3  NO BONUS THIS MONTH   EARNINGS     $950.00
```

Program 8.7 shows how earnings and bonuses can be found. Note that the program ends when the number $-9999$ is encountered in the DATA statement using the *end of data test* in line 25. In this program we could not use the number 999 to signal the end of the data, as we did in Program 8.6, because it is possible for a salesperson to sell exactly $999 worth of merchandise, which would cause the program to end prematurely. A flowchart for Program 8.7 appears in Figure 8.6.

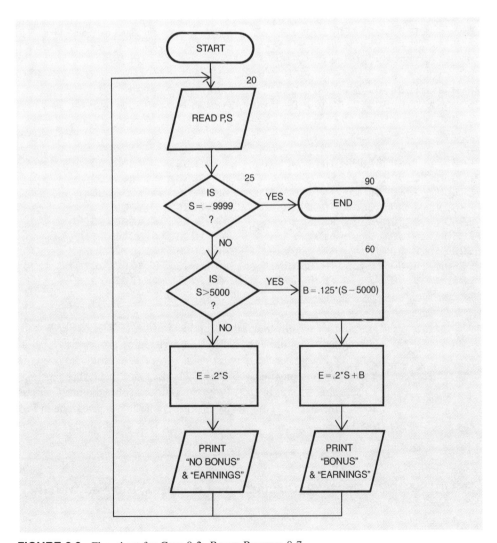

**FIGURE 8.6**  Flowchart for Case 8.2, Bonus Program 8.7

## PROGRAM 8.7   Case 8.2, Calculation of Bonuses

```
2   REM CASE 8.2, CALCULATING BONUSES
4   REM PROGRAMMER - (name of person)   DATE - mm/dd/yy
6   REM     VARIABLE LIST - B,E,P,S,A$,B$
8   REM          B=BONUS
10 REM          E=EARNINGS
12 REM          P=PERSON NUMBER
14 REM          S=MONTHLY SALES
16 REM ---------------------------------------------
17 LET A$ = "PERSON ## NO BONUS THIS MONTH   EARNINGS $$##,###.##"
18 LET B$ = "PERSON ## BONUS $$#,###.##      EARNINGS $$##,###.##"
20 READ P,S
25    IF S =-9999 THEN 90                'end of data test
35       IF S> 5000 THEN 60              'test for the bonus
40       LET E=.2*S
45       PRINT USING A$; P, E
50 GOTO 20
60    LET B=.125*(S-5000)                'computation of the bonus
65    LET E=.2*S+B
70    PRINT USING B$; P, B, E
75 GOTO 20
80 DATA 1,4000, 2,6250, 3,4750, 4,4800, 5,7125
85 DATA 6,6050, 7,8300, 8,3500, 9,9625, 0,-9999
90 END

RUN
PERSON  1 NO BONUS THIS MONTH   EARNINGS    $800.00
PERSON  2 BONUS    $156.25      EARNINGS  $1,406.25
PERSON  3 NO BONUS THIS MONTH   EARNINGS    $950.00
PERSON  4 NO BONUS THIS MONTH   EARNINGS    $960.00
PERSON  5 BONUS    $265.63      EARNINGS  $1,690.63
PERSON  6 BONUS    $131.25      EARNINGS  $1,341.25
PERSON  7 BONUS    $412.50      EARNINGS  $2,072.50
PERSON  8 NO BONUS THIS MONTH   EARNINGS    $700.00
PERSON  9 BONUS    $578.13      EARNINGS  $2,503.13
```

Earlier we illustrated the usefulness of the IF/THEN/ELSE statement for simplifying a program. Examine Program 8.8, a revision of Program 8.7, as it applies to Case 8.2. Altering line 35 for the new program allows us to eliminate one complete segment of the previous program (lines 60–75). This does not mean that the first program solution to Case 8.2 is wrong. In fact, Program 8.7 does solve the problem correctly. But if we can reduce the size and complexity of a program, as we have done in Program 8.8, we should do it.

## PROGRAM 8.8   Case 8.2, Calculation of Bonuses, Revised with IF/THEN/ELSE

```
2   REM CASE 8.2, CALCULATING BONUSES
4   REM PROGRAMMER-(name of person) DATE-mm/dd/yy
6   REM     VARIABLE LIST- B,E,P,S
8   REM          B=BONUS
```

```
10 REM        E=EARNINGS
12 REM        P=PERSON NO.
14 REM        S=MONTHLY SALES
16 REM -----------------------------------------
20 READ P,S
25    IF S =-9999 THEN 90    'end of data test
35       IF S> 5000 THEN B=.125*(S-5000) ELSE B = 0  'test for the bonus
40       LET E=.2*S + B
45    PRINT USING "PERSON ## BONUS $$#,###.##     EARNINGS $$#,###.##"; P,B,E
50 GOTO 20
80 DATA 1,4000, 2,6250, 3,4750, 4,4800, 5,7125
85 DATA 6,6050, 7,8300, 8,3500, 9,9625, 0,-9999
90 END


RUN
PERSON 1   BONUS       $0.00    EARNINGS      $800.00
PERSON 2   BONUS     $156.25    EARNINGS    $1,406.25
PERSON 3   BONUS       $0.00    EARNINGS      $950.00
PERSON 4   BONUS       $0.00    EARNINGS      $960.00
PERSON 5   BONUS     $265.63    EARNINGS    $1,690.63
PERSON 6   BONUS     $131.25    EARNINGS    $1,341.25
PERSON 7   BONUS     $412.50    EARNINGS    $2,072.50
PERSON 8   BONUS       $0.00    EARNINGS      $700.00
PERSON 9   BONUS     $578.13    EARNINGS    $2,503.13
```

In Program 8.8 both the person number (*P*) and the monthly sales (*S*) are placed in the data lines. An alternate approach would be to use a counter to generate the person number (*P*), as provided by lines 18 and 28 in Program 8.9.

## PROGRAM 8.9    Case 8.2, Calculation of Bonuses, IF/THEN/ELSE and Counter

```
2   REM CASE 8.2, CALCULATING BONUSES
4   REM PROGRAMMER - (name of person) DATE - mm/dd/yy
6   REM    VARIABLE LIST - B,E,P,S
8   REM        B=BONUS
10  REM        E=EARNINGS
12  REM        P=PERSON NO.
14  REM        S=MONTHLY SALES
16  REM -----------------------------------------------
18 LET P = 0                 'initialize person counter to 0
20 READ S
25    IF S =-9999 THEN 90    'end of data test
28       LET P = P + 1       'counter for person number
35       IF S> 5000 THEN B=.125*(S-5000) ELSE B = 0        'test for the bonus
40       LET E=.2*S + B
45    PRINT USING "PERSON ## BONUS $$#,###.##     EARNINGS $$#,###.##"; P,B,E
50 GOTO 20
80 DATA 4000, 6250, 4750, 4800, 7125
85 DATA 6050, 8300, 3500, 9625, -9999
90 END


RUN
PERSON 1   BONUS       $0.00    EARNINGS      $800.00
PERSON 2   BONUS     $156.25    EARNINGS    $1,406.25
PERSON 3   BONUS       $0.00    EARNINGS      $950.00
PERSON 4   BONUS       $0.00    EARNINGS      $960.00
```

```
PERSON 5   BONUS    $265.63    EARNINGS   $1,690.63
PERSON 6   BONUS    $131.25    EARNINGS   $1,341.25
PERSON 7   BONUS    $412.50    EARNINGS   $2,072.50
PERSON 8   BONUS      $0.00    EARNINGS     $700.00
PERSON 9   BONUS    $578.13    EARNINGS   $2,503.13
```

. . . . . . . . . . . . . . . . . . . . . . . . . . . . . . . . . . . . . . . . . . .

## CASE 8.3

**Problem**

### Retirement Eligibility Determination

The ACME Company wishes to print a list of the employee numbers of all employees who are eligible for retirement. For retirement eligibility, any one of the following conditions must be satisfied:

1. The employee must be at least 65 years old.

2. The employee must have worked at least 30 years with the company.

3. The employee must be over 60 years old and have worked at least 25 years with the company.

4. The employee must be over 55 years old, have worked at least 20 years with the company, and have a salary of at least $30,000 per year. (This last condition amounts to early retirement for executives.)

A program is required to produce the retirement list.

**Data Input**

The following data values will be processed by the program:

| EMPLOYEE NUMBER | AGE | YEARS EMPLOYED | SALARY |
|---|---|---|---|
| 1234 | 40 | 5 | $12,500 |
| 1235 | 61 | 25 | 15,000 |
| 1236 | 56 | 21 | 30,000 |
| 1237 | 71 | 15 | 18,000 |
| 1238 | 62 | 19 | 41,000 |
| 1239 | 59 | 30 | 11,000 |
| 1240 | 20 | 10 | 10,000 |
| 1241 | 56 | 22 | 29,000 |
| 1242 | 57 | 18 | 31,000 |
| 1243 | 62 | 24 | 35,000 |

**Process/Formulas**    A repetitive process is to be used. Using the conditions specified above, decision testing is required to determine who is eligible for retirement. The program terminates as a result of an end of data test.

**Output**    Output is a list of employee numbers.

. . . . . . . . . . . . . . . . . . . . . . . . . . . . . . . . . . . . . . . . . . .

Program 8.10 will read an employee's number, age, years employed with the company, and salary. It will then determine if he or she is eligible for retirement. If an employee is eligible for retirement, it will cause his or her number to be printed. If an employee is not eligible, the process will go on to the next employee and will continue until the data for all the employees has been processed. The DATA in line 160 for the last employee is followed by zeros to signal the program to end. Note that we need data (zeros, or zero for *N* and any numbers for *A*, *Y*, *S*) for all four of the variables (*N*, *A*, *Y*, and *S*) because line 30 reads all four variables.

The program uses the variables *N*, employee number; *A*, employee's age; *Y*, years employed with the company; and *S*, employee's salary.

Because there are many decisions in this program, we may want to draw a flowchart (see Figure 8.7) before writing the program. Once the flowchart is complete, writing the program and working through the logic of it should follow readily.

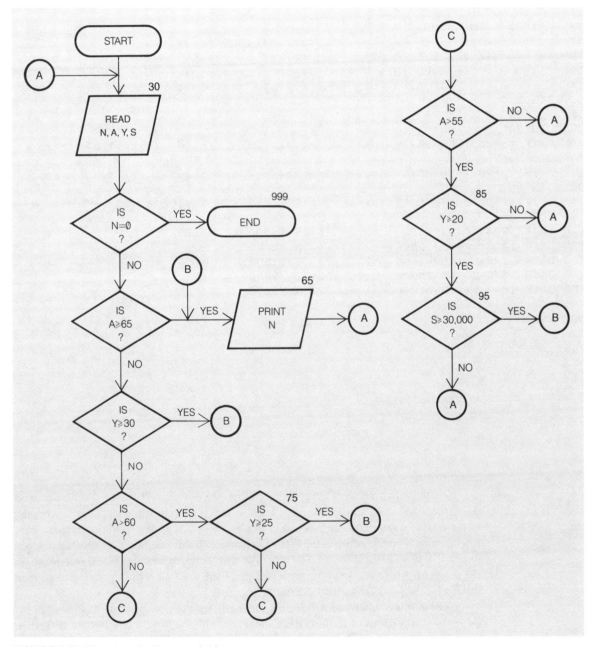

**FIGURE 8.7**  Flowchart for Program 8.10

## PROGRAM 8.10   Case 8.3, Eligibility for Retirement

```
10 REM CASE 8.3, IDENTIFYING ELIGIBILITY FOR RETIREMENT
15 REM   PROGRAMMER- (name of person)   DATE - mm/dd/yy
16 REM      VARIABLE LIST- A,N,S,Y
17 REM          A=EMPLOYEE'S AGE
18 REM          N=EMPLOYEE NO.
19 REM          S=EMPLOYEE'S SALARY
20 REM          Y=YEARS EMPLOYED WITH THE COMPANY
25 REM -------------------------------------------
30 READ N,A,Y,S
35    IF N=0 THEN 999
40       IF A>=65 THEN 65          'at least 65 years old
45          IF Y>=30 THEN 65       'worked at least 30 years
50             IF A>60 THEN 75     'over 60 years old
55                IF A>55 THEN 85  'over 55 years old
60 GOTO 30
65    PRINT N
70 GOTO 30
75    IF Y>=25 THEN 65     'over 60 years old & worked at least 25 years
80 GOTO 55
85    IF Y>=20 THEN 95     'over 55 years old & worked at least 20 years
90 GOTO 30
95    IF S>=30000 THEN 65 'over 55 & 20+ years & $30,000+ salary
100 GOTO 30
110 DATA 1234,40,5,12500,    1235,61,25,15000
120 DATA 1236,56,21,30000,   1237,71,15,18000
130 DATA 1238,62,19,41000,   1239,59,30,11000
140 DATA 1240,20,10,10000,   1241,56,22,29000
150 DATA 1242,57,18,31000,   1243,62,24,35000
160 DATA 0,0,0,0
999 END

RUN
  1235
  1236
  1237
  1239
  1243
```

Note the way the flow of the program follows the flowchart (Figure 8.7). We first read the variables $N$, $A$, $Y$, and $S$ in line 30. Then we test if $N = 0$. If it does, there is a branch to the end. If it does not, we proceed to test if $A >= 65$. If this condition is true, there is a branch to line 65, which is the PRINT statement. If this condition is false, we proceed to test if $Y >= 30$, and so on. You will note that there are four GOTO 30 statements in the program. Also observe in the flowchart that there are four arrows pointing to an A in the circles, which refer to the "READ N, A, Y, S" in line 30.

Later in this chapter you will learn a more efficient way to carry out this program by using the comparisons of the IF/THEN statement with the logical OR and the IF/THEN statement with the logical AND (Case 8.7 and Program 8.19).

## PROCESSING CONTROLS

The IF/THEN statement has wide use in programs that incorporate *processing controls*. These controls are written into programs to ensure that abnormal or undesirable actions do not occur during processing. We examine three control applications: counting records, sequence checking, and reasonableness tests.

## Counting Records

Counting records is a very common type of processing control. To be sure all documents or records that are to be entered are in fact entered, the computer is programmed to count each document in a batch of documents to be processed. This initial batch count is compared with the number of documents actually entered to determine if any records or documents were missed during processing. This control process is illustrated by Case 8.4.

## CASE 8.4

**Problem**

**Processing Controls, Counting Documents**

A large insurance company has much of its claims data entered from forms through cathode ray tube (CRT) terminals. Terminal operators are given batches of up to 25 documents to be processed.

An operator must enter two items from each document: an account number and an amount. The amounts must be totaled. In addition to the batch of documents, the operator receives a document count to be entered before processing starts.

A program is required that will count the number of documents actually processed and compare the count to the given batch count.

**Data Input**

Data entry is interactive. It consists of an account number and an amount.

**Process/Formulas**

A repetitive process is to be used. Decision testing is required to compare the number of documents actually processed with the batch count. The program terminates as a result of an end of data test.

**Output**

Output can indicate Too many documents have been entered, please check; or Check for # skipped document(s); or Batch control count # equals the number of documents entered. Since the last message indicates that there are no processing mistakes, the amount total is printed out.

Program 8.11 shows how document counts can be incorporated into a program. Before data items are entered for processing, the operator must respond to line 40, "How many documents in the batch." Line 55, INPUT A, A1, requests the required data items from each document. A test is performed in line 65 to determine if the operator has finished processing the batch of documents. Line 70, LET T = T + 1, is the counter of the records processed. This count is compared with the initial number of documents value,

*B*, entered earlier. If we test line 85, B = T, and determine *B* does not equal *T*, it means that either too many or too few documents have been processed. Too many documents will produce the printed message shown by the first output. This result occurs because the test in line 100, IF B < T THEN 115, is true. When this test is *not* true, it means that too few documents have been processed; that is, an operator may have skipped some data. As a result, a message such as the one shown in the second output is printed. If all counts are equal, if *B* = *T*, processing continues to completion, producing the third output shown.

## PROGRAM 8.11   Case 8.4, Insurance Forms, Document Count

```
10 REM CASE 8.4, PROCESSING CONTROLS, DOCUMENT COUNT
15 REM PROGRAMMER- (name of person)  DATE - mm/dd/yy
16 REM     VARIABLE LIST A,A1,B,S1,T
17 REM          A=ACCOUNT NO.
18 REM          A1=AMOUNT
19 REM          B=# OF DOCUMENTS
20 REM          S1=TOTAL AMOUNT
21 REM          T=# OF ENTRIES
25 REM ------------------------------------------------
30 LET T = 0        'start count at zero
35 LET S1 = 0       'start amount at zero
40 INPUT "HOW MANY DOCUMENTS IN THE BATCH "; B
50 PRINT "TYPE -99, -99 WHEN THE BATCH IS COMPLETED"
55 INPUT "ENTER ACCT. NO., AMOUNT ", A, A1
65    IF A= -99 THEN 85      'end of INPUT test
70       LET T = T + 1       'count the entries
75       LET S1 = S1 + A1    'accumulate amount
80 GOTO 55
85 IF B = T THEN 130             'is the actual count = to the batch count?
90    PRINT "BATCH CONTROL COUNT";B;" DOES NOT EQUAL ";
95    PRINT "NUMBER OF ENTRIES";T
100      IF B < T THEN 115    'is batch count less than the actual count?
105         PRINT "CHECK FOR"; B - T "SKIPPED DOCUMENT(S)"
110 GOTO 999
115      PRINT T - B; "TOO MANY DOCUMENTS HAVE BEEN ";
120      PRINT "ENTERED, PLEASE CHECK."
125 GOTO 999
130 PRINT "BATCH CONTROL COUNT ";B;" EQUALS THE ";
135 PRINT "NUMBER DOCUMENTS ENTERED."
140 PRINT
145 PRINT "AMOUNT TOTAL IS"; S1
999 END

RUN
HOW MANY DOCUMENTS IN THE BATCH? 2
TYPE -99, -99 WHEN THE BATCH IS COMPLETED
ENTER ACCT. NO., AMOUNT 123,40
ENTER ACCT. NO., AMOUNT 234,60
ENTER ACCT. NO., AMOUNT 133,40
ENTER ACCT. NO., AMOUNT -99, -99
BATCH CONTROL COUNT 2 DOES NOT EQUAL NUMBER OF ENTRIES 3
 1 TOO MANY DOCUMENTS HAVE BEEN ENTERED, PLEASE CHECK.
```

```
RUN
HOW MANY DOCUMENTS IN THE BATCH? 5
TYPE -99, -99 WHEN THE BATCH IS COMPLETED
ENTER ACCT. NO., AMOUNT 123,40
ENTER ACCT. NO., AMOUNT 234,60
ENTER ACCT. NO., AMOUNT 133,40
ENTER ACCT. NO., AMOUNT -99, -99
BATCH CONTROL COUNT 5 DOES NOT EQUAL NUMBER OF ENTRIES 3
CHECK FOR 2 SKIPPED DOCUMENT(S)

RUN
HOW MANY DOCUMENTS IN THE BATCH? 3
TYPE -99, -99 WHEN THE BATCH IS COMPLETED
ENTER ACCT. NO., AMOUNT 123,40
ENTER ACCT. NO., AMOUNT 234,60
ENTER ACCT. NO., AMOUNT 133,50
ENTER ACCT. NO., AMOUNT -99, -99
BATCH CONTROL COUNT 3 EQUALS THE NUMBER DOCUMENTS ENTERED.

AMOUNT TOTAL IS 150
```

---

### Sequence Checking

Sequence checking is another form of processing control. It can be used to ensure that documents containing input data are processed in the correct sequence. In many processing operations, the original source document has a preprinted sequential document number. Such document numbers are useful because they provide a means of accounting for all source documents. In addition, they provide a means of identifying specific documents if an error or customer complaint arises.

The need for sequence checking as a program control, presented in Case 8.5, is shown in Program 8.12.

## CASE 8.5

**Problem**

**Processing Controls, Sequence Checking**

The Central General Hospital keeps track of drug prescriptions written each week for outpatients of the hospital by requiring the use of multiple-copy prescription pads with sequence numbers. One copy goes to the patient; the other copy is kept for record keeping and internal controls. Each week the hospital's copies are processed to count the number of narcotic and nonnarcotic prescriptions written over the period. The source documents are sequenced by number. A missing number suggests that either the document was skipped, the document number was entered incorrectly, or a document is missing. Whatever the case, a message is generated, indicating that some action is necessary.

A program is to be written that will carry out a sequence check for a batch of documents.

**Data Input**

The program assumes that data is entered in data lines by sequence number ($N$), along with a code number ($C$) of either 0, for a nonnarcotic prescription, or 1, for a narcotic prescription. A set of test data looks like this:

1245,0, 1246,1, 1248,1, 1249,0, 1252,1

**Process/Formulas** A repetitive process is to be used. Decision testing is required to determine if a document is missing from those being processed. The program terminates as a result of an end of data test.

**Output** The output will consist of the document number and the code (0 or 1) as well as a missing document message when the condition exists. Other outputs will include the total number of documents processed, the number of narcotic and nonnarcotic prescriptions, and the number of documents missing.

---

## PROGRAM 8.12 Case 8.5, Central General Hospital, Sequence Checking

```
10 REM CASE 8.5, PROCESSING CONTROLS, SEQUENCE CHECKING
15 REM PROGRAMMER- (name of person) DATE mm/dd/yy
16 REM      VARIABLE LIST- C,M,N,T1,T2,X
17 REM          C=CODE NO.:0=NON NARCOTIC, 1=NARCOTIC
18 REM          M=# OF MISSING DOCUMENTS
19 REM          N=SEQUENCE NUMBER
20 REM          T1=# OF TOTAL DOCUMENTS
21 REM          T2=# OF NARCOTICS
22 REM          X=THE FIRST SEQUENCE NO.
25 REM  ----------------------------------------------
30 LET T1=0        'start document count at zero
35 LET T2=0        'start narcotic count at zero
40 LET M=0         'start missing document count at zero
45 PRINT "NUMBER", "NARC.=1, NON-NARC.=0"
46 PRINT "----------------------------------"
50 READ X          'enter first sequence number
65 RESTORE
70 READ N,C        'enter sequence number and code
75 REM TEST FOR END OF DATA
80    IF N= -99 THEN 170    'end of data test
90      IF N <> X THEN 125 'are the document & sequence number different?
95      PRINT N,C
100         LET X=N+1       'increment sequence number by 1
110         LET T1=T1+1     'count documents
115         LET T2=T2+C     'count narcotics
120 GOTO 70
125    PRINT "* NOTE- DOCUMENT(S) MISSING* "; N-X
135    LET M=M+(N-X)              'count missing documents
140 GOTO 95
170 PRINT "----------------------------------"
175 PRINT "TOTALS:";T1;"DOCUMENTS"
180 PRINT "NARCOTIC";T2;"OTHER";T1-T2
185 PRINT "MISSING";M
187 DATA 1245,0,1246,1,1248,1,1249,0,1252,1
188 DATA -99,-99
190 END
```

```
RUN
NUMBER          NARC.=1 , NON-NARC.=0
-------------------------------------
  1245            0
  1246            1
* NOTE- DOCUMENT(S) MISSING* 1
  1248            1
  1249            0
* NOTE- DOCUMENT(S) MISSING* 2
  1252            1
-------------------------------------
TOTALS: 5 DOCUMENTS
NARCOTIC 3 OTHER 2
MISSING 3
```

Note how line 135 keeps track of the number of missing documents, and how line 115 counts just the $C$s adding up all the narcotics, since $C = 0$ or $C = 1$.

---

## Reasonableness Tests

Reasonableness tests are a third type of processing control that can be included in programs. Such tests are used to determine if something unusual, unlikely, or logically inconsistent has occurred. Two examples are petty cash disbursements should not exceed $100 and the number of units of a certain shipped item is usually in the range of 1,000–2,000 units.

In a situation where a reasonableness test fails, the program will cause some type of "unreasonable" information report to be printed out. This exception report can be reviewed to determine if a data entry error has been made, if some illegal processing is being attempted (a computer embezzlement scheme), or whatever. There is an increasing awareness of the possibilities of computer crime and computer fraud, and one purpose of processing controls is to prevent such activities. Case 8.6 illustrates the application of reasonableness tests.

· · · · · · · · · · · · · · · · · · · · · · · · · · · · · · · · · · · ·

## CASE 8.6

**Problem**

**Processing Controls, Reasonableness Tests**

A large manufacturing company has hundreds of employees who are paid weekly wages based on an hourly rate and the number of hours worked. As one part of a large payroll program, there are several reasonableness tests applied to weekly pay before a check is issued. This program segment performs three tests: (1) Is gross wage above $625? (This first test is based on the premises that there is a 40-hour week, that the maximum hourly wage is $10 per hour, and that overtime pay is at time and a half but is never more than 15 hours per week.) (2) Is overtime more than 15 hours per week? (3) Is the hourly pay more than $10 per hour?

**Data Input**     The test data to be read by the program is as follows:

| NUMBER | WAGE | HOURS |
|--------|------|-------|
| 1 | 6 | 45 |
| 2 | 15 | 52 |
| 3 | 20 | 30 |
| 4 | 5 | 56 |
| 5 | 10 | 39 |
| 6 | 8 | 48 |
| 7 | 12 | 51 |
| 8 | 15 | 60 |

**Process/Formulas**  A repetitive process is to be used. Decision testing is required based on the three conditions stated in the problem.

**Output**     Printed outputs will include the format shown below, along with the possibility of one or more messages indicating that a reasonableness test has been exceeded.

```
EMPLOYEE 1 GROSS WAGE    $285.00
EMPLOYEE 2 GROSS WAGE    $870.00 NOTE-EXCESS WAGES/RATE
EMPLOYEE 3 GROSS WAGE    $600.00 NOTE-EXCESS WAGES/RATE
EMPLOYEE 4 GROSS WAGE    $320.00 NOTE-EXCESS OVERTIME
```

Program 8.13 shows how the reasonableness tests of Case 8.6 can be carried out. Line 75 tests to see if the overtime hours exceed 15. If they do, a note is printed out, indicating that some action should be taken to see why excess overtime is being reported. Maybe there is a data entry error, maybe this was an exceptional case of overtime, and so forth. Line 90 tests to see if wages exceeded a limit of $625, and line 95 tests to see if the hourly rate is above $10. If either is true, a note is printed out, indicating that either wages are in excess of the limit, the wage rate is too high, or both items are unreasonable and have to be looked at.

### PROGRAM 8.13    Case 8.6, Employee Payroll, Reasonableness Tests

```
10 REM CASE 8.6, PROCESSING CONTROLS, REASONABLENESS TESTS
11 REM                    EMPLOYEE PAYROLL
15 REM PROGRAMER- (name of person)  DATE- mm/dd/yy
16 REM     VARIABLE LIST-H,N,R,T,W
17 REM        H=HOURS
18 REM        N=EMPLOYEE NO.
19 REM        R=WAGE RATE
20 REM        T=OVERTIME
21 REM        W=GROSS WAGE
25 REM  ------------------------------------------
30 READ N,R,H
35    IF N=-99 THEN 140           'end of data test
40       IF H>40 THEN 60          'more than 40 hours?
45          LET W=R*H             'compute wage with no overtime
50          PRINT USING "EMPLOYEE # GROSS WAGE $$#,###.## "; N,W;
55    GOTO 90
```

```
60        LET T=H-40                  'compute hours above 40
65        LET W=R*40+(1.5*(R*T))      'compute wages including overtime
70        PRINT USING "EMPLOYEE # GROSS WAGE $$#,###.## "; N,W;
75          IF T>15 THEN 85           'check if more than 15 o.t. hours
80    GOTO 90
85      PRINT "NOTE-EXCESS OVERTIME ";
90        IF W>625 THEN 110           'check if wages are above $625.00
95          IF R>10 THEN 110          'check if rate is above maximum $10/hr
100             PRINT
105 GOTO 30
110     PRINT "NOTE-EXCESS WAGES/RATE"
115 GOTO 30
120 DATA 1,6,45,2,15,52,3,20,30
125 DATA 4,5,56,5,10,39,6,8,48
130 DATA 7,12,51,8,15,60
135 DATA -99,0,0
140 END

RUN
EMPLOYEE 1 GROSS WAGE     $285.00
EMPLOYEE 2 GROSS WAGE     $870.00 NOTE-EXCESS WAGES/RATE
EMPLOYEE 3 GROSS WAGE     $600.00 NOTE-EXCESS WAGES/RATE
EMPLOYEE 4 GROSS WAGE     $320.00 NOTE-EXCESS OVERTIME
EMPLOYEE 5 GROSS WAGE     $390.00
EMPLOYEE 6 GROSS WAGE     $416.00
EMPLOYEE 7 GROSS WAGE     $678.00 NOTE-EXCESS WAGES/RATE
EMPLOYEE 8 GROSS WAGE   $1,050.00 NOTE-EXCESS OVERTIME NOTE EXCESS WAGES/RATE
```

A revised program for Case 8.6 appears as Program 8.14. The purpose of this revision is to show how we can shorten the original program by combining statements and tasks by using the IF/THEN clause and IF/THEN/ELSE. Observe how the revised program uses line 33, IF N = −99 THEN END, to replace line 35 of the original program, which was IF N = −99 THEN 140. Also, note how the IF/THEN/ELSE in line 40 of the revised program performs the tasks of lines 40, 45, and 65 in the original program. In the revised program, lines 75, 90, and 95 are IF/THEN clause statements that combine testing with PRINT, thus avoiding three GOTO transfers of the original program. Overall we get a more logical flow with fewer transfers and fewer lines of code.

## PROGRAM 8.14   Case 8.6, Payroll, Revised with IF/THEN and IF/THEN/ELSE

```
10 REM CASE 8.6, PROCESSING CONTROLS, REASONABLENESS TESTS
11 REM                    EMPLOYEE PAYROLL
15 REM PROGRAMMER- (name of person) DATE - mm/dd/yy
16 REM    VARIABLE LIST-H,N,R,T,W
17 REM        H=HOURS
18 REM        N=EMPLOYEE NO
19 REM        R=WAGE RATE
20 REM        T=OVERTIME
21 REM        W=GROSS WAGE
25 REM -------------------------------------------
30 READ N,R,H
33    IF N = -99 THEN END
35    LET T = H-40              'compute o.t. hours
40        IF H>40 THEN LET W = R*40+(1.5*(R*T)) ELSE LET W=R*H   'test o.t.
```

```
50      PRINT USING "EMPLOYEE # GROSS WAGE $$#,###.## "; N,W;
75      IF T>15 THEN PRINT "NOTE-EXCESS OVERTIME ";    'test overtime
90        IF W>625 THEN PRINT "NOTE-EXCESS WAGES ";    'test excess wages
95          IF R>10 THEN PRINT "NOTE-EXCESS RATE ";    'test excess rate
100            PRINT
115 GOTO 30
120 DATA 1,6,45, 2,15,52, 3,20,30
125 DATA 4,5,56, 5,10,39, 6,8,48
130 DATA 7,12,51, 8,15,60
135 DATA -99,0,0
140 END

RUN
EMPLOYEE 1 GROSS WAGE    $285.00
EMPLOYEE 2 GROSS WAGE    $870.00 NOTE-EXCESS WAGES NOTE-EXCESS RATE
EMPLOYEE 3 GROSS WAGE    $600.00 NOTE-EXCESS RATE
EMPLOYEE 4 GROSS WAGE    $320.00 NOTE-EXCESS OVERTIME
EMPLOYEE 5 GROSS WAGE    $390.00
EMPLOYEE 6 GROSS WAGE    $416.00
EMPLOYEE 7 GROSS WAGE    $678.00 NOTE-EXCESS WAGES NOTE-EXCESS RATE
EMPLOYEE 8 GROSS WAGE  $1,050.00 NOTE-EXCESS OVERTIME NOTE-EXCESS WAGES
NOTE-EXCESS RATE
```

## LOGICAL IF/THEN STATEMENT

The IF/THEN statement performs a test that, if true, will cause a transfer of control or sequence in a program to change. This concept was illustrated earlier in this chapter in Program 8.1, for example. If the test condition is not true, processing control will continue to the very next line after the IF/THEN test. In Program 8.15, values of the variables $A$, $B$, and $C$ are being compared to determine if $A$ is greater than either $B$ or $C$. The program makes use of two separate IF/THEN comparisons: line 30 $A > B$ and line 35 $A > C$. The logical IF/THEN statement will allow you to have more than one comparison on a single line.

## PROGRAM 8.15   IF/THEN Test to Compare A to B and C

```
10 REM IF THEN COMPARISON
15 PRINT " A   B   C"
20 READ A,B,C
30   IF A > B THEN 50
35     IF A > C THEN 50
40       PRINT USING " ## ## ##   A IS NOT GREATER THAN B OR C"; A,B,C
45 GOTO 20
50       PRINT USING " ## ## ##   A IS GREATER THAN EITHER B OR C"; A,B,C
55 GOTO 20
60 DATA 25,12,30, 31,40,15, 15,20,24
65 DATA 22,28,30, 50,25,20, 85,85,85
70 END
```

```
RUN
 A  B  C
 25 12 30   A IS GREATER THAN EITHER B OR C
 31 40 15   A IS GREATER THAN EITHER B OR C
 15 20 24   A IS NOT GREATER THAN B OR C
 22 28 30   A IS NOT GREATER THAN B OR C
 50 25 20   A IS GREATER THAN EITHER B OR C
 85 85 85   A IS NOT GREATER THAN B OR C
Out of DATA in 20
```

## Logical OR

The logical OR takes this form:

line # IF (comparison) OR (comparison) THEN line #

Only one comparison on either side of the OR must be true for the whole IF statement to be true. The sequence would then transfer to the line # indicated after the THEN. Program 8.16 is a modified version of Program 8.15 using an IF/THEN statement with the logical OR operation in line 30 to replace the two IF/THEN statements in Program 8.15.

### PROGRAM 8.16    Logical OR, IF/THEN Test to Compare A to B and C

```
10 REM LOGICAL OR, IF THEN COMPARISON
15 PRINT " A   B   C"
20 READ A,B,C
30    IF A > B OR A > C THEN 50          'a logical OR test
40        PRINT USING " ## ## ##   A IS NOT GREATER THAN B OR C"; A,B,C
45 GOTO 20
50        PRINT USING " ## ## ## A IS GREATER THAN EITHER B OR C"; A,B,C
55 GOTO 20
60 DATA 25,12,30, 31,40,15, 15,20,24
65 DATA 22,28,30, 50,25,20, 85,85,85
70 END

RUN
 A  B  C
 25 12 30   A IS GREATER THAN EITHER B OR C
 31 40 15   A IS GREATER THAN EITHER B OR C
 15 20 24   A IS NOT GREATER THAN B OR C
 22 28 30   A IS NOT GREATER THAN B OR C
 50 25 20   A IS GREATER THAN EITHER B OR C
 85 85 85   A IS NOT GREATER THAN B OR C
Out of DATA in 20
```

## Logical AND

The logical AND takes this form:

line # IF (comparison) AND (comparison) THEN line #

The comparisons on both sides of the AND must be true for the whole IF statement to be true. Line 30 in Program 8.17 is an example of the logical AND. The program shown seeks to determine if the values for three variables *A*, *B*, and *C* are all equal. Although this program is similar to Program 8.16, it uses a logical AND *not* the logical OR.

## PROGRAM 8.17   Logical AND, IF/THEN Test to Compare A, B, and C

```
10 REM LOGICAL AND, IF THEN TEST
20 READ A,B,C
30    IF A=B AND B=C THEN 50           'a logical AND test
35        PRINT "A B AND C ARE NOT ALL =",A;B;C
45 GOTO 20
50        PRINT "A B AND C ARE ALL =", A;B;C
55 GOTO 20
60 DATA 86,30,50, 29,29,29, 79,79,12
65   DATA 12,14,20, 42,42,42, 21,35,35
70   END

RUN
A B AND C ARE NOT ALL =        86    30    50
A B AND C ARE ALL =            29    29    29
A B AND C ARE NOT ALL =        79    79    12
A B AND C ARE NOT ALL =        12    14    20
A B AND C ARE ALL =            42    42    42
A B AND C ARE NOT ALL =        21    35    35
Out of DATA in 20
```

The advantage of the logical AND as shown by Program 8.17 is further illustrated by the approach taken in Program 8.18. *Without* using the logical AND to determine whether all three variables *A*, *B*, and *C* are equal, this program needs an additional IF test in line 46 and another GOTO in line 48.

## PROGRAM 8.18   IF/THEN Test to Compare A, B, and C without Logical AND

```
10 REM IF THEN TEST, IS A = B = C?
20 READ A,B,C
30    IF A = B THEN 46
35        PRINT "A B AND C ARE NOT ALL =",A;B;C
45 GOTO 20
46    IF B = C THEN 50
48 GOTO 35
50        PRINT "A B AND C ARE ALL =",A;B;C
55 GOTO 20
60 DATA 86,30,50, 29,29,29, 79,79,12
65 DATA 12,14,20, 42,42,42, 21,35,35
70 END
```

```
RUN
A B AND C ARE NOT ALL =        86  30  50
A B AND C ARE ALL =            29  29  29
A B AND C ARE NOT ALL =        79  79  12
A B AND C ARE NOT ALL =        12  14  20
A B AND C ARE ALL =            42  42  42
A B AND C ARE NOT ALL =        21  35  35
Out of DATA in 20
```

Case 8.7 illustrates the logical OR and AND statements. This case is identical to Case 8.3.

## CASE 8.7

**Problem**

**Retirement Eligibility Determination**

For an employee to be eligible for retirement, he or she must satisfy one of the following conditions:

1. The employee must be at least 65 years old, or have been with the company at least 30 years.

2. The employee must be over 60 years old and have worked at least 25 years with the company.

3. The employee must be over 55 years old, have worked at least 20 years with the company, and have a salary of at least $30,000 per year. (This last condition amounts to early retirement for executives.)

A program is required to produce the retirement list.

**Data Input**

The following data values will be processed by the program:

| EMPLOYEE NUMBER | AGE | YEARS EMPLOYED | SALARY |
| --- | --- | --- | --- |
| 1234 | 40 | 5 | $12,500 |
| 1235 | 61 | 25 | 15,000 |
| 1236 | 56 | 21 | 30,000 |
| 1237 | 71 | 15 | 18,000 |
| 1238 | 62 | 19 | 41,000 |
| 1239 | 59 | 30 | 11,000 |
| 1240 | 20 | 10 | 10,000 |
| 1241 | 56 | 22 | 29,000 |
| 1242 | 57 | 18 | 31,000 |
| 1243 | 62 | 24 | 35,000 |

**Process/Formulas**  A repetitive process is to be used. Using the conditions specified above, decision testing is required to determine who is eligible for retirement. The program terminates as a result of an end of data test.

**Output**  Output is a list of employee numbers.

Program 8.19 evaluates a data list (see Case 8.3) to determine which employees are eligible for retirement. In this program, line 30 tests for the OR requirement of condition 1 above. For the AND requirements of conditions 2 and 3, lines 40 and 45 perform the appropriate tests.

## PROGRAM 8.19  Case 8.7, Eligibility for Retirement

```
1 REM CASE 8.7, VERIFYING THE ELIGIBILITY
2 REM PROGRAMMER- (name of person)   DATE - mm/dd/yy
3 REM      VARIABLE LIST- A,N,Y,S
4 REM           A=AGE
5 REM           N=EMPLOYEE NO.
6 REM           Y=YEARS EMPLOYED
7 REM           S=SALARY
8 REM  -------------------------------------------
10 READ  N,A,Y,S
20   IF N = 0 THEN 170                    'end of data test
30   IF A >=65 OR Y >=30 THEN 60          'over 65 OR at least 30 years
40    IF A >=60 AND Y >=25 THEN 60        'over 60 AND at least 25 years
45     IF A >55 AND Y >=20 AND S >=30000 THEN 60   'early retirement
50 GOTO 10
60     PRINT N
70 GOTO 10
110 DATA 1234,40,5,12500,   1235,61,25,15000
120 DATA 1236,56,21,30000,  1237,71,15,18000
130 DATA 1238,62,19,41000,  1239,59,30,11000
140 DATA 1240,20,10,10000,  1241,56,22,29000
150 DATA 1242,57,18,31000,  1243,62,24,35000
160 DATA 0,0,0,0
170 END

RUN
 1235
 1236
 1237
 1239
 1243
```

## LOGICAL VARIABLES

Logical variables are variables that have relational expressions assigned to them. If the relationship is false, the value of variable will be zero. If the relationship is true, the value of the variable will be $-1$. The general form for the assignment of a relationship to a logical variable is

line # LET logical variable = relational expression

Any numeric variable can be a logical variable. The value of 0 or $-1$ is assigned to the variable by the computer depending upon the truth or falseness of the relational expression. Relational expressions can take on any of the test relationships we have already seen

**TABLE 8.5** Logical Variables and Relational Expressions

| STATEMENT | EXPLANATION |
|---|---|
| 10 LET A = X > Y | A is assigned a value of $-1$ if the test is true; if the test is false, A is assigned a value of 0. |
| 20 LET B = J+1 <= K + 1 | B is assigned a value of $-1$ if the test is true; if the test is false, B is assigned a value of 0. |
| 30 LET C = S>=5 OR T>=15 | C is assigned a value of $-1$ if one or the other test is true; if both tests are false; C is assigned a value of 0. |
| 40 LET D = M<=.8 AND N>=.12 | D is assigned a value of $-1$ if both tests are true; if even one test is false, D is assigned a value of 0. |

with the IF/THEN statement, including the logical IF/THEN. Table 8.5 provides examples of logical variables and relational expressions.

Observe Program 8.20. Values of A and B are read and examined by line 30, LET L = A > B, to determine if A is greater than B. The result of the test determines the value assigned to the logical variable L. If the test is false, the value of L will be 0; if the test is true, the value of L will be $-1$. Line 50 (IF L THEN) will print out the message "A>B" whenever the IF test is true; that is, when L = $-1$. When the test is *not* true, the ELSE message "A<=B" is printed.

## PROGRAM 8.20   Logical Variables, Test to Compare A > B

```
5 REM LOGICAL VARIABLES
8 PRINT " A              B              L          A>B OR A<=B"
9 PRINT "-----------------------------------------------------------"
20 READ A, B
30    LET L = A>B        'logical test:set L= -1 if true, L = 0 if false
40      PRINT A,B,L,
50       IF L THEN PRINT "A>B" ELSE PRINT "A<=B"
60 GOTO 20
70    DATA 12,11, 12,13, 5,5, .9,.5, 2.5,-5.3, -25,-7.2
90 END
```

```
RUN
 A              B              L          A>B OR A<=B
-------------------------------------------------------
 12            11            -1           A>B
 12            13             0           A<=B
  5             5             0           A<=B
  .9            .5           -1           A>B
 2.5           -5.3          -1           A>B
-25            -7.2           0           A<=B
Out of DATA in 20
```

Logical variables can be used to simplify complicated conditions. By using logical variables, Program 8.21 repeats the tests performed in Program 8.19. Here are the key statement segments of both programs that are involved:

**PROGRAM 8.19**
30 IF A >=65 OR Y >=30 THEN 60
40 IF A >=60 AND Y >=25 THEN 60
45 IF A >55 AND Y >=20 AND S >=30000 THEN 60

**PROGRAM 8.21**
12 LET J = A>=65
14 LET K = Y>=30
16 LET L = A>=60 AND Y>=25
18 LET M = A> 55 AND Y>=20 AND S>=30000
35 IF J OR K OR L OR M THEN 60

---

**PROGRAM 8.21   Case 8.7, Eligibility for Retirement Using Logical Variables**

```
1 REM CASE 8.7, VERIFYING THE ELIGIBILITY with Logical Variables
2 REM PROGRAMMER- (name of person)   DATE- mm/dd/yy
3 REM     VARIABLE LIST- A,N,Y,S
4 REM         A=AGE
5 REM         N=EMPLOYEE NO.
6 REM         Y=YEARS EMPLOYED    S=SALARY
7 REM         J, K, L, M = LOGICAL VARIABLES (-1 = TRUE, 0 = FALSE)
8 REM ------------------------------------------------------------
10 READ N,A,Y,S
11    IF N = 0 THEN 170             'end of data test
12       LET J = A>=65             'over 65 logical test -1 or 0
14       LET K = Y>=30             'over 30 logical test -1 or 0
16       LET L = A>=60 AND Y>=25    'over 60 AND over 25 logical test -1 or 0
18       LET M = A>55 AND Y>=20 AND S>=30000    'early retirement
35        IF J OR K OR L OR M THEN 60  'is J or K or L or M = -1? then eligible
50 GOTO 10
60     PRINT N
70 GOTO 10
110 DATA 1234,40,5,12500,    1235,61,25,15000
120 DATA 1236,56,21,30000,   1237,71,15,18000
130 DATA 1238,62,19,41000,   1239,59,30,11000
140 DATA 1240,20,10,10000,   1241,56,22,29000
150 DATA 1242,57,18,31000,   1243,62,24,35000
160 DATA 0,0,0,0
170 END

RUN
 1235
 1236
 1237
 1239
 1243
```

Logical variables can also be combined to create additional logical variables. In Program 8.16 line 30,

IF A > B OR A > C THEN 50

has been rewritten in Program 8.22 as

22 LET J = A>B
24 LET K = A>C
26 LET L = J OR K
30 IF L THEN 50

Note how the logical variable L in line 26 combines the variables J and K of lines 22 and 24, respectively.

## PROGRAM 8.22   Logical Variables to Compare A to B or C

```
10 REM LOGICAL VARIABLES, IF THEN COMPARISON
12 REM IN A SET OF THREE VALUES A,B, & C, IS A GREATER THAN EITHER B OR C?
15 PRINT " A B C"
20 READ A,B,C
22    LET J = A>B        'logical variable J (= -1 true, or = 0 false)
24    LET K = A>C        'logical variable K (= -1 true, or = 0 false)
26    LET L = J OR K     'logical variable L (is J OR K true)
30    IF L THEN 50       'if L is true (= -1) then goto line 50
40       PRINT USING " ## ## ##   A IS NOT GREATER THAN B OR C"; A,B,C
45 GOTO 20
50       PRINT USING " ## ## ##   A IS GREATER THAN EITHER B OR C"; A,B,C
55 GOTO 20
60 DATA 25,12,30, 31,40,15, 15,20,24
65 DATA 22,28,30, 50,25,20, 85,85,85
70 END

RUN
 A  B  C
 25 12 30   A IS GREATER THAN EITHER B OR C
 31 40 15   A IS GREATER THAN EITHER B OR C
 15 20 24   A IS NOT GREATER THAN B OR C
 22 28 30   A IS NOT GREATER THAN B OR C
 50 25 20   A IS GREATER THAN EITHER B OR C
 85 85 85   A IS NOT GREATER THAN B OR C
Out of DATA in 20
```

## STRING COMPARISONS

Up to this point we have only seen how the IF/THEN statement is used to test or compare numeric data values. Such tests are comparisons and can also be performed on nonnumeric, or literal data (see Tables 8.2–8.4). An example of such a test is provided by Program 8.23. This program illustrates how a test of a literal entry ''YES'' or ''NO'' can be used to exit an INPUT loop sequence.

## PROGRAM 8.23   String Comparisons

```
10 REM IF THEN TEST OF LITERAL ITEM
20 INPUT "ENTER TWO DATA VALUES: ",A,B
25    LET SUM = A + B
30    PRINT " SUM IS"; SUM
35    PRINT "------------------------------"
45    INPUT "DO YOU WISH TO CONTINUE-RESPOND YES OR NO?"; R$
50 IF R$ = "YES" OR R$ = "yes" THEN 20    'a string comparison
60 PRINT " THIS DATA ENTRY SESSION IS OVER"
90 END

RUN
ENTER TWO DATA VALUES: 5,3
 SUM IS 8
------------------------------
DO YOU WISH TO CONTINUE-RESPOND YES OR NO? yes
ENTER TWO DATA VALUES: 87,13
 SUM IS 100
------------------------------
DO YOU WISH TO CONTINUE-RESPOND YES OR NO? no
 THIS DATA ENTRY SESSION IS OVER
```

Line 50 tests the string entry ''YES'' or ''yes'' with a logical OR. If anything other than these two string responses are entered, the test will be false, thus causing line 60 to be executed and bringing about the termination of the program.

Note that the string test item or items *must* be placed in quotation marks as shown in line 50, or a syntax error message will result when the line is processed.

Earlier in this chapter the end of data test was described and illustrated using a numeric flag with a value of 999, $-99$, or $-9999$ for example. At times when the data list contains nonnumeric, or string data items, we may have to perform the end of data test using a string comparison. Such a comparison can be generalized as

line #1 IF string variable = ''string flag'' THEN line #2

Look at Program 8.24. The end of data test is in line 20 where the test is given as

20 IF NM$ = ''EOD'' THEN 90

In order for this test to work, the data list, line 60, must contain a string item that when processed by the READ statement matches the string item in the IF test. Thus, when the string data item EOD in line 60 is read and assigned to the string variable NM$ in line 10 and then evaluated by the IF/THEN statement in line 20, the program moves to line 90, the END statement.

## PROGRAM 8.24   String Comparison, End of Data Test

```
5  REM END OF DATA TEST USING A STRING COMPARISON
10 READ NM$, A
20    IF NM$ = "EOD" THEN 90    'string comparison end of DATA test
30    PRINT NM$, A
```

```
40 GOTO 10
50 DATA NANCY,400, TERRY,250, STACEY 500
60 DATA EOD,0
90 END

RUN
NANCY          400
TERRY          250
STACEY         500
```

## SUMMARY

The IF/THEN statement transfers control to the statement indicated by the line number only if a certain condition is true. If the condition is not true, the statement following the IF/THEN statement is executed next. The relationships used in expressing conditions that can be tested are $>$, $>=$, $<$, $<=$, $=$, and $<>$.

The IF/THEN statement enables us to construct programs that contain DOWHILE or DOUNTIL loop structures. Decision making can be carried out in a program by using one or more forms of the IF/THEN statement.

The IF/THEN statement can take several forms. It can be an IF/THEN line number, IF/THEN clause, or IF/THEN/ELSE.

Processing controls can be built into a program by using the IF/THEN statement.

Logical comparisons can be made with the IF/THEN statement by using the AND or the OR.

Logical variables can be assigned relational expressions and can be used with the IF/THEN statement.

Testing and comparisons can be performed on numeric and nonnumeric (string) data.

## BASIC VOCABULARY SUMMARY

| Statement | Purpose | Examples |
|---|---|---|
| IF/THEN line #<br>IF/THEN clause<br>IF/THEN/ELSE<br>(Alt + T Key,<br>Alt + E Key) | Transfers control to other lines, statements or clauses, after a test relationship is evaluated. | 10 IF X > Y THEN 30<br>60 IF AN$ = BN$ THEN 90<br>70 IF T1 <= T2 THEN PRINT T1<br>85 IF AMT = −999 THEN END ELSE 50<br>90 IF A >= 65 OR Y >= 30 THEN 60 |
| LET | Assigns −1 (true) or 0 (false) from a relational expression on the right side of the = to a logical variable on the left side of the =. | 15 LET J = A>=65<br>30 LET B = X > Y |

Review Questions

**8.1**  What is wrong with the following statement?

50 IF A > B THEN 50

♦ **8.2**  What would happen to Program 8.1 (shown below) if
a.  Line 50 were changed to 50 READ B,A?
b.  Line 80 were omitted?

```
10 REM DECISION MAKING
30 REM THIS PROGRAM READS TWO NUMBERS
40 REM AND PRINTS THE LARGER OF THE TWO
50 READ A,B
60    IF A>B THEN 90
70        PRINT B
80 GOTO 110
90        PRINT A
100 DATA 7,3
110 END

RUN
 7
```

**8.3**  What would Program 8.2 (shown below) do if
a.  Line 40 were changed to 40 IF G < 3 THEN 30?
b.  Line 45 were omitted?
c.  Line 55 were omitted?
d.  Line 45 were omitted and line 40 were changed to
    40 IF G < 3 THEN 30?

```
10 REM CASE 8.1, LISTING HONOR STUDENTS- DECISION MAKING
15 REM PROGRAMMER- (name of person)  DATE mm/dd/yy
16 REM    VARIABLE LIST- N,G
17 REM        N=STUDENT NO.
18 REM        G=GRADE
20 REM ------------------------------------------
30 READ N,G
40    IF G>= 3 THEN 50
45 GOTO 30
50    PRINT N
55 GOTO 30
60 DATA 1234,3.5, 9876,2.9, 1768,3.0, 1357,2.8
65 END

RUN
 1234
 1768
Out of DATA in 30
```

The next three exercises relate to Program 8.5 (shown here).

```
5   REM LOOP REPETITION - DOUNTIL
10  REM THIS PROGRAM READS 5 NUMBERS FROM THE DATA STATEMENT
20  REM AND PRINTS THE NUMBERS, THE SQUARES OF THE NUMBERS
30  REM AND THE SUMS OF THE NUMBERS AND THEIR SQUARES.
40  LET S=0
45  LET S2=0
50  LET N=1
55  READ X
60     LET S=S+X
65     LET S2=S2+X^2
70     PRINT X,X^2
75     IF N=5 THEN 90
80        LET N=N+1
85  GOTO 55
90  PRINT "---", "---"
95  PRINT S,S2
100 DATA 7,3,5,6,1
999 END

RUN
 7              49
 3               9
 5              25
 6              36
 1               1
---             ---
 22             120
```

**8.4** What will Program 8.5 do when each of the following changes is made? (Each part of this exercise is independent of the others.)

a. Line 75 is changed to 75 IF N <> 5 THEN 90.

b. Line 75 is changed to 75 IF N <= 5 THEN 90.

c. Line 75 is changed to 75 IF N <> 5 THEN 80.

d. Line 75 is changed to 75 IF N >= 5 THEN 90.

e. Line 75 is changed to 75 IF N > 5 THEN 90.

**8.5** What will Program 8.5 do when each of the following changes is made? (Each part of this exercise is independent of the others.)

a. Line 85 is changed to 85 GOTO 50.

b. Line 85 is changed to 85 GOTO 60.

c. Line 85 is changed to 85 GOTO 65.

d. Line 85 is changed to 85 GOTO 70.

**8.6** What will Program 8.5 do when each of the following changes is made? (Each part of this exercise is independent of the others.)

a. Line 75 is moved to line 58.

b. Line 80 is changed to 80 LET N = N + 2.

c. Line 80 is changed to 80 LET N = N + 3.

**8.7** What will Program 8.6 (shown below) do when each of the following changes is made? (Each part of this exercise is independent of the others.)

a. Line 75 is changed to 75 GOTO 40.

b. Line 75 is changed to 75 GOTO 45.

c. Line 75 is changed to 75 GOTO 55.

d. Line 55 is changed to 55 IF X = 999 THEN 999.

♦ e. Line 55 is moved to line 72.

```
5   REM LOOP REPETITION - DOWHILE
10 REM THIS PROGRAM ACCOMPLISHES THE SAME THING AS
15 REM PROGRAM 8.5 BUT WITH AN END OF DATA TEST.
40 LET  S=0
45 LET  S2=0
50 READ X
55    IF  X=999 THEN  80
60        LET  S=S+X
65        LET  S2=S2+X^2
70        PRINT X,X^2
75 GOTO 50
80 PRINT "---","---"
85 PRINT S,S2
90  DATA 7,3,5,6,1,999
999 END

RUN
 7              49
 3               9
 5              25
 6              36
 1               1
 ---           ---
 22            120
```

**8.8** Rewrite Program 8.3 (shown below) so that only the numbers of those students whose grade index is less than 3.0 will be printed. The program should print an appropriate heading.

```
10 REM CASE 8.1, LISTING HONOR STUDENTS- DECISION MAKING
15 REM PROGRAMMER- (name of person)  DATE mm/dd/yy
16 REM    VARIABLE LIST- N,G
17 REM        N=STUDENT NO.
18 REM        G=GRADE
20 REM ------------------------------------------
30 READ N,G
40    IF G>= 3 THEN PRINT N
45 GOTO 30
60  DATA 1234,3.5, 9876,2.9, 1768,3.0, 1357,2.8
65  END

RUN
 1234
 1768
Out of DATA in 30
```

**8.9** We want the following program to read 5 numbers from the DATA statement and PRINT the sum. Three lines are missing. What are they? Include the appropriate line numbers. Use the counter variable *C* to stop reading and print the sum.

```
5    LET C = 1
10   LET S = 0
20   READ X
30   DATA 4,2,7,3,7
40   LET C = C + 1
50   PRINT S
60   END
```

**8.10**   A school would like to print a list of the numbers of all students who have at least a 3.0 cumulative grade index. Each student number is followed by the corresponding grade index in the DATA statement of the following program. Two lines are missing. What are they? You should use the last two data elements to end your program.

```
10    READ N,G
20    GO TO 10
30    PRINT N
40    GO TO 10
50    DATA 1234,3.1, 2468,1.75, 1357,2.2, 0,0
60    END
```

**8.11**   The program below was developed to process a large number of data values. The desired results should include the total or sum of the values being read in and the average of the values being processed.
a. What output is processed from this program?
b. How should the program be revised to produce the desired results?

```
3   LET N = 0
5   LET S1 =0
10  READ S
20  IF S = -999 THEN 75
30     LET S1 = S1 + S
40     LET N = N + 1
50     LET S2 = S1/N
70  GOTO 10
75     PRINT "TOTAL"; S1, "AVERAGE";S2
80  DATA 15,7,8,3,5
100 END
```

The next two exercises relate to Program 8.7 below:

```
2   REM CASE 8.2, CALCULATING BONUSES
4   REM PROGRAMMER - (name of person)  DATE - mm/dd/yy
6   REM     VARIABLE LIST - B,E,P,S,A$,B$
8   REM        B=BONUS
10  REM        E=EARNINGS
12  REM        P=PERSON NUMBER
14  REM        S=MONTHLY SALES
16  REM -------------------------------------------------
17  LET A$ = "PERSON ## NO BONUS THIS MONTH  EARNINGS $$###,###.##"
18  LET B$ = "PERSON ## BONUS $$##,###.##    EARNINGS $$###,###.##"
20  READ P,S
25     IF S =-9999 THEN 90
35       IF S> 5000 THEN 60
40       LET E=.2*S
45     PRINT USING A$; P, E
50  GOTO 20
60     LET B=.125*(S-5000)
65     LET E=.2*S+B
70     PRINT USING B$; P, B, E
75  GOTO 20
80  DATA 1,4000, 2,6250, 3,4750, 4,4800, 5,7125
85  DATA 6,6050, 7,8300, 8,3500, 9,9625, 0,-9999
90  END
```

```
RUN
PERSON  1 NO BONUS THIS MONTH   EARNINGS     $800.00
PERSON  2 BONUS    $156.25      EARNINGS   $1,406.25
PERSON  3 NO BONUS THIS MONTH   EARNINGS     $950.00
PERSON  4 NO BONUS THIS MONTH   EARNINGS     $960.00
PERSON  5 BONUS    $265.63      EARNINGS   $1,690.63
PERSON  6 BONUS    $131.25      EARNINGS   $1,341.25
PERSON  7 BONUS    $412.50      EARNINGS   $2,072.50
PERSON  8 NO BONUS THIS MONTH   EARNINGS     $700.00
PERSON  9 BONUS    $578.13      EARNINGS   $2,503.13
```

**8.12** Modify Program 8.7 so that the sum of all of the sales, bonuses, and earnings are printed. The output should look like this:

| PERSON | SALES | BONUS | EARNINGS |
|--------|-------|-------|----------|
| 1 | $ 4,000 | $    0.00 | $    800.00 |
| 2 | $ 6,250 | $  156.25 | $ 1,406.25 |
| . . . | . . . | . . . | . . . |
| 9 | $ 9,625 | $  578.13 | $ 2,503.13 |
| TOTALS | $xx,xxx | $x,xxx.xx | $xx,xxx.xx |

**8.13** To Program 8.7 add the following processing controls

**1.** A counter to check that data for all nine employees has been processed.

**2.** A reasonableness test that produces an asterisk (*) at the end of the output for each employee earning more than $2,000.

The next seven exercises relate to Program 8.10 below:

```
10  REM CASE 8.3, IDENTIFYING ELIGIBILITY FOR RETIREMENT
15  REM   PROGRAMMER- (name of person)  DATE - mm/dd/yy
16  REM      VARIABLE LIST- A,N,S,Y
17  REM         A=EMPLOYEE'S AGE
18  REM         N=EMPLOYEE NO.
19  REM         S=EMPLOYEE'S SALARY
20  REM         Y=YEARS EMPLOYED WITH THE COMPANY
25  REM -------------------------------------------------
30  READ N,A,Y,S
35     IF N=0 THEN 999
40        IF A>=65 THEN 65
45           IF Y>=30 THEN 65
50              IF A>60 THEN 75
55                 IF A>55 THEN 85
60  GOTO 30
65     PRINT N
70  GOTO 30
75     IF Y>=25 THEN 65
80  GOTO 55
85     IF Y>=20 THEN 95
90  GOTO 30
95     IF S>=30000 THEN 65
100 GOTO 30
110 DATA 1234,40,5,12500,   1235,61,25,15000
120 DATA 1236,56,21,30000,  1237,71,15,18000
130 DATA 1238,62,19,41000,  1239,59,30,11000
140 DATA 1240,20,10,10000,  1241,56,22,29000
150 DATA 1242,57,18,31000,  1243,62,24,35000
160 DATA 0,0,0,0
999  END
```

```
RUN
 1235
 1236
 1237
 1239
 1243
```

**8.14** Revise Program 8.10 so that the output will have this format:

```
ELIGIBLE EMPLOYEE    AGE    YEARS EMPLOYED    SALARY

        1235          61          25          $15,000
```

Be sure to include all the relevant data for each employee.

**8.15** Revise Program 8.10 so that counters are included in the program to derive the number of all employees and the number of eligible employees. The counts are to be printed out at the end of the list of employee numbers.

**8.16** Rewrite Program 8.10 to test for the following conditions for retirement:

1. Age of the employee must be at least 62.
2. Age of the employee must be at least 60, and the years employed at the company must be at least 20.
3. Years employed at the company must be at least 25.
4. Age of the employee must be at least 58, years employed at the company must be at least 20, and salary must be at least $25,000.

**8.17** Revise Program 8.10 to include program statements that will perform a sequence check on the employee number (see Program 8.12 for an example).

**8.18** Rewrite Program 8.10 utilizing the logical IF/THEN and IF/THEN clause statements where possible.

**8.19** Rewrite Program 8.10 using logical variables (see Program 8.21 for an example).

**8.20** Rewrite Program 8.10 so that data entry is interactive and conversational. The input query should require the data entry of all the READ variables $N$, $A$, $Y$, and $S$. The output response should show the employee number followed by a message that states "eligible" or "not eligible" for retirement. The program should terminate by using a "YES" or "NO" response to the query "DO YOU WISH TO CONTINUE?" (see Program 8.23 for an example).

## Programming Activities

**8.21** **Purpose** To use the DOUNTIL loop sequence logic structure.

**Problem** Write and run a program to print the sum of the odd numbers between 7 and 33 inclusive.

**Data** Use a counter to generate the odd numbers.

**Output** Your output should have this format:

```
THE SUM IS xxx
```

**8.22** **Purpose** To use the decision-making, or selection, logic structure and numeric data.

**Problem** Write and run a program to read any three different numbers, and print out the largest of the three.

**Data** Use your own three data values.

**Output** Your output should have this format:

THE LARGEST VALUE IS xxx

**8.23** **Purpose** To use the decision-making, selection, logic structure and numeric data.

**Problem** Write and run a program to read any three different numbers, to test and compare them using the logical IF/THEN, and to print out the median of the three. (The median is the middle value; for example, of the numbers, 8, 12, 3, the median is 8.)

**Data** Use your own three data values.

**Output** Your output should have this format:

DATA VALUES xxx    xxx    xxx
THE MEDIAN VALUE IS xxx

**8.24** **Purpose** To use the DOWHILE loop repetition logic structure to process numeric data values.

**Problem** Write and run a program to read at least 10 numbers until the end of data list −999 is encountered. The program is to compute the average of the numbers. (The average is the sum of the values divided by the total number of data values.) Use a LET counter to count the number of values processed and a LET accumulator to sum the data values.

**Data** Use these data values: 25, 15, 70, 48, 2, 11, 16, 16, 15, 20, 21, 19, 21, 39, 47.

**Output** Your output should have this format:

DATA VALUES 25   15   75 , , , 47
THE AVERAGE IS xxx,xx

**8.25** **Purpose** To use the DOWHILE loop repetition logic structure to process numeric data values and to use the IF/THEN statement for decision selection.

**Problem** Write and run a program to read 10 numbers until the end of data list −999 is encountered. The numbers represent grades in a programming examination. The program is to compute the average passing grade, the average failing grade, and the class average. A grade of 60 or above is passing.

**Data** Use these data values:

100 DATA 60,59,40,88,98,75,90,72,82,77,−99

**Output** Your output should have this format:

AVG, PASSING GRADE 80,25
AVG, FAILING GRADE 49,50
CLASS AVG,          74,10

**8.26**  **Purpose**  To use the DOWHILE loop repetition logic structure to process numeric data values; to perform decision selection; and to use the IF/THEN clause statement where practical.

**Problem**  Write and run a program that reads in a product number, unit price, and quantity ordered. The program is to find the discount to be given and the total dollar amount for each order. A discount of 10 percent is given on all orders of at least 100 items. The amount is equal to price times quantity less discount. There is no discount on orders of fewer than 100 items.

**Data**  Use these data values:

100 DATA 101,2,250, 210,6,95, 330,3,110, −99,0, 0

**Output**  Your output should have this format:

```
NUMBER      PRICE      QUANTITY   DISCOUNT   AMOUNT
  101       $2.00        250       $50.00    $450.00
  210       $6.00         95         0.00    $570.00
  330       $3.00        110       $33.00    $297.00
```

**8.27**  **Purpose**  To use the decision-making, or selection, logic structure and the logical IF/THEN statement to process groups of numeric data.

**Problem**  Write and run a program to read groups of four numbers in order to test and compare the numbers within each group to determine if they are equal to each other.

**Data**  Use several sets of your own data values including these:

3,4,4,4, 9,9,9,9

**Output**  For each set of data values, your output should have this format:

```
VALUES x x x x ARE EQUAL TO EACH OTHER
```

or

```
VALUES x x x x ARE NOT EQUAL TO EACH OTHER
```

**8.28**  **Purpose**  To use the DOWHILE loop repetition logic structure to process numeric data values and to use the IF/THEN clause statement, the logical IF/THEN statement, and the IF/THEN/ELSE statement, where possible.

**Problem**  Write and run a program that will compute federal and state tax deductions based on the gross wage conditions given below. Design the program so that it will also determine the total amount of deductions and the net wage after all taxes are deducted from the gross wage.

| FEDERAL TAX DEDUCTION | | STATE TAX DEDUCTION | |
|---|---|---|---|
| **Gross Wage** | **%** | **Gross Wage** | **%** |
| Less than or equal to $200 | 15 | Less than or equal to $200 | 2 |
| Greater than $200 but less than $301 | 20 | Greater than $200 | 3 |
| Greater than $300 | 22 | | |

**Data**  Use these data values: $200, $350, $300, $250, $100, and $500. Have a separate data line for the end of data test value −999.

**Output**    Your output should have this format:

```
GROSS        FEDERAL      STATE       TOTAL          NET
WAGE         TAX          TAX         DEDUCTIONS     WAGE
$200.00      $ 30.00      $  4.00     $ 34.00        $ 166.00
$350.00      $ 77.00      $ 10.50     $ 87.50        $ 262.50
 . . .        . . .        . . .       . . .          . . .
$500.00      $110.00      $ 15.00     $ 125.00       $ 375.00
```

**8.29    Purpose**    To use the DOUNTIL loop repetition logic structure to process numeric data values and string items and find column totals using the LET statement as an accumulator.

**Problem**    The following table shows the first-quarter sales of the EXACT Company, by division. Sales are in thousands of dollars.

| DIVISION | JANUARY | FEBRUARY | MARCH |
|----------|---------|----------|-------|
| WEST | $1,000 | $  750 | $  750 |
| SOUTH | 1,200 | 800 | 1,000 |
| NORTH | 1,200 | 500 | 1,200 |
| EAST | 1,500 | 1,050 | 950 |

Write and run a program that derives the total sales for each month.

**Data**    Use the data values shown in the table above. Have a separate data line for the end of data (EOD) test value.

**Output**    Your output should have this format:

```
DIVISION    JAN.       FEB.        MAR.
------------------------------------------
WEST        $1,000     $  750     $  750
SOUTH       $1,200     $  800     $1,000
NORTH       $1,200     $  500     $1,200
EAST        $1,500     $1,050     $  950
------------------------------------------
TOTALS      $4,900     $3,100     $3,900
```

**8.30    Purpose**    To use the DOUNTIL loop repetition logic structure to process numeric data values and to use the IF/THEN clause and IF/THEN/ELSE where possible.

**Problem**    The bank your company uses for checking employs the following method for determining checking account charges each month:

**1.**   If the end-of-the month balance is $400 or more, there is no charge for the month regardless of the number of checks written.

**2.**   If the end-of-the month balance is less than $400, there is $.25 per check charge for checks written during the month.

These charges are automatically deducted from the balance in the account. There is already a $500 starting balance from the previous month to be carried over to month 1. At the end of the month the balance in the account reflects the deductions for all checks written and for any charges made against the account plus the additions for all deposits made. Write and run program that will carry out the computations required to produce the output shown below.

**Data**  Use these data values:

| MONTH | AMOUNT OF EACH CHECK WRITTEN | DEPOSITS |
|---|---|---|
| 1 | $25,$500,$300,$75,$20, $10,$1,500,$200,$900 | $300,$200,$1,000,$1,500 |
| 2 | $575,$500,$75,$725,$50, $65,$300,$55,$25 | $750,$1,200,$800 |
| 3 | $30,$1,200,$45,$55,$700, $1,500,$400 | $500,$1,800,$1,200 |
| 4 | $1,075,$125,$350,$60, $1,440,$560,$200,$150 | $1,500,$1,000,$1,600 |
| 5 | $75,$1,025,$750,$35,$25, $165,$450,$565,$120 | $1,250,$1,700,$1,800 |

A DATA statement is organized as follows:

1000 DATA 25, 500, 300, 75, 20, 10, 1500, 200, 900, $-99$
1100 DATA 300, 200, 1000, 1500, $-99$, etc.

**Output**  Your output should have this format:

| MONTH | CHECKS WRITTEN | ENDING BALANCE | MONTHLY CHARGE |
|---|---|---|---|
| 1 | $X,XXX.XX | $X,XXX.XX | $XX.XX |
| 2 | $X,XXX.XX | $X,XXX.XX | $XX.XX |
| ... | ... | ... | ... |
| 5 | $X,XXX.XX | $X,XXX.XX | $XX.XX |

· · · · · · · **8.31**  **Purpose**  To use the DOUNTIL loop repetition logic structure to process numeric data values entered in an interactive and conversational manner. Data entry terminates with an end of data test. The IF/THEN clause should be used where possible. Logical variables may also be incorporated into the program.

**Problem**  Many airlines have computerized reservation systems for their flights. As reservations are taken, the number of seats available begins to decline. It is important to be forewarned when the number of seats on a particular flight gets low so as to prevent overbooking. Suppose Goodflight Airlines has three daily flights as follows:

| FLIGHT NO. | NO. SEATS AVAILABLE AT THIS HOUR |
|---|---|
| 381 | 25 |
| 402 | 15 |
| 283 | 30 |

In the last four hours the following number of reservations have been made for each of these flights:

| HOUR | NO. SEATS RESERVED PER FLIGHT | | |
|---|---|---|---|
| | 381 | 402 | 283 |
| 1 | 5 | 7 | 0 |
| 2 | 7 | 1 | 2 |
| 3 | 5 | 3 | 3 |
| 4 | 5 | 2 | 5 |

Assume that at the end of every hour these figures are fed into the computer by a clerk to get an update on the seats available. If for any flight the number of available seats is 10 or less, a warning for that flight is printed out by the computer. Your job is to write and run a conversational program that a nonprogramming clerk can use at the end of each hour to obtain the current seating status for each flight.

**Data**  Use the data values shown in the table above.

**Output**  The output for this program should be fully labeled in a format that you have designed.

**8.32**  **Purpose**  To use the DOUNTIL loop repetition logic structure to process numeric data values and perform decision selection. Data entry terminates with an end of data test. The IF/THEN clause, the logical IF/THEN, and the IF/THEN/ELSE should be used where possible. Logical variables may also be incorporated into the program.

**Problem**  A bank that issues credit cards uses the following standards to determine applicant eligibility.

**1.**  A person must have a salary of more than $25,000 per year.

**2.**  A person must have an annual salary of more than $20,000 and pay rent that amounts to less than one-quarter of a month's salary.

**3.**  A person must have an annual salary of more than $15,000 and be living at the same address for more than five years.

**4.**  A person must have an annual salary of $10,000 or more, be living at the same address for at least five years, and be employed at the same job for at least three years.

All applicants who do not meet at least one of these four standards are rejected. Write and run a program that will read 10 persons' application numbers, annual salaries, rents, years employed at the same job, and years living at the same address. Have the computer print the application numbers of people who are eligible for a credit card. The program should also count the number of applicants and the number of those eligible for a credit card and to compute the acceptance ratio, that is, number eligible divided by the number of all applicants times 100.

**Data**  Use the data values shown in the table below. Have a separate data line for the end of data test value.

| APPLICATION NUMBER | SALARY | RENT | YEARS EMPLOYED | YEARS RESIDING |
|---|---|---|---|---|
| 605 | $21,000 | $560 | 4 | 5 |
| 610 | 18,000 | 500 | 10 | 14 |
| 614 | 35,000 | 750 | 2 | 10 |
| 656 | 11,000 | 280 | 20 | 19 |
| 678 | 15,500 | 400 | 6 | 2 |
| 692 | 8,000 | 200 | 10 | 11 |
| 694 | 32,000 | 850 | 3 | 3 |
| 697 | 12,500 | 375 | 4 | 6 |
| 698 | 40,000 | 950 | 15 | 8 |
| 700 | 20,000 | 395 | 5 | 5 |

**Output**    Your output will be a list of application numbers that have satisfied any one of the eligibility conditions specified above, the number of applicants, the number eligible for a credit card, and the acceptance ratio. Your output should have this format:

```
Eligible Applicants
  xxx
  xxx
  xxx
Number of Applicants  xxx
Number of Eligible Applicants xxx
Acceptance Ratio  xx.xx%
```

**8.33**  **Purpose**  To use the DOUNTIL loop repetition logic structure to process numeric data values and to perform decision selection with the IF/THEN statement. Data entry terminates with an end of data test.

**Problem**  Write and run a program that reads in an employee's number; the number of his or her dependents; the number of hours that he or she worked during the week; the hourly rate that applies; and a code number of 0, 1, or 2 to indicate that the employee carries no insurance, personal insurance only, or family insurance, respectively.

Have the computer calculate the employee's gross wages. This is calculated by the number of hours times the hourly rate if the number of hours worked is 40 hours or less. If the number of hours worked is greater than 40, the employee should receive 1½ times the hourly rate for the additional hours above 40. The taxes deducted from the gross wages should be according to the following table:

| NUMBER OF DEPENDENTS | PERCENT DEDUCTED |
|---|---|
| 0 | 28 |
| 1 | 26 |
| 2 | 24 |
| 3 | 22 |
| 4 | 20 |
| 5 | 18 |
| 6 | 16 |
| 7 or more | 14 |

The amount of insurance deducted should be calculated according to the following table:

| CODE | MEANING | AMOUNT DEDUCTED |
|---|---|---|
| 0 | No insurance | $ 0 |
| 1 | Insurance for self only | 5 |
| 2 | Insurance for family | 10 |

Once all of the deductions have been determined, the net pay should be calculated.

**Data**  In addition to the information given above (tax deductions and insurance deductions), use the data values shown in the table below. Have a separate data line for the end of data test value −999.

| EMPLOYEE NO. | DEPENDENTS | HOURS WORKED | HOURLY RATE | INSURANCE CODE |
|---|---|---|---|---|
| 6044 | 0 | 37 | $4.50 | 1 |
| 4411 | 2 | 42 | 4.75 | 2 |
| 7158 | 1 | 40 | 4.10 | 2 |
| 1142 | 0 | 47 | 4.50 | 1 |
| 6482 | 8 | 45 | 4.80 | 2 |
| 1231 | 4 | 50 | 5.50 | 1 |
| 7111 | 2 | 40 | 4.00 | 1 |
| 1421 | 5 | 42 | 4.60 | 2 |
| 8421 | 7 | 38 | 4.25 | 2 |
| 1333 | 0 | 41 | 4.80 | 0 |

**Output**   Your output should include column totals as shown in this format:

```
EMPLOYEE     GROSS        TAX        INSURANCE
NUMBER       WAGES      DEDUCTED     DEDUCTED      NET PAY
-------------------------------------------------------------
   6044     $166.50     $46.42        $5.00       $114.88
   4411     $204.25     $49.02       $10.00       $145.23
   7158     $164.00     $42.64       $10.00       $111.36
   1142     $227.25     $63.63        $5.00       $158.62
   6482     $228.00     $31.92       $10.00       $186.08
   1231     $302.50     $60.50        $5.00       $237.00
   7111     $160.00     $38.40        $5.00       $116.60
   1421     $197.80     $35.60       $10.00       $152.20
   8421     $161.50     $22.61       $10.00       $128.89
   1333     $199.20     $55.78        $0.00       $143.42
-------------------------------------------------------------
 TOTALS  $2,010.00    $446.72       $70.00     $1,494.28
```

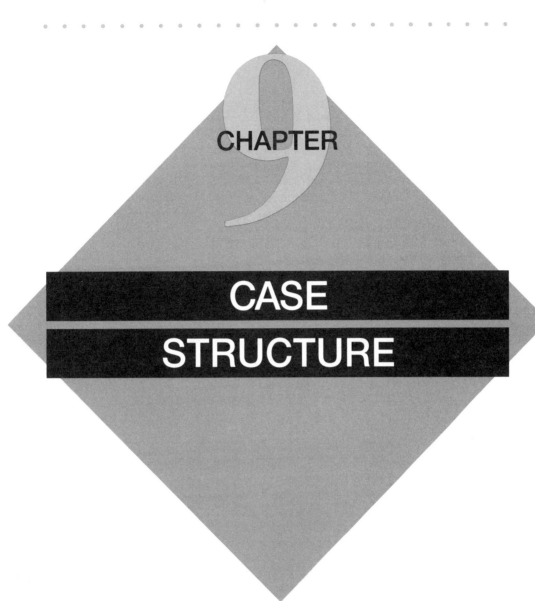

# CHAPTER 9

## CASE

## STRUCTURE

Upon completing this chapter, you will be able to do the following:

- Recognize the difference between decision making using the IF/THEN statement and using the computed GOTO or ON/GOTO statement.
- Understand how the CASE structure of programming logic differs from previously discussed decision-making logic structures.
- Recognize problem applications that can use the CASE structure as a means of problem solution.
- Develop on-screen conversational/interactive menus based on the CASE structure.
- Use the STOP statement and the CONT (continue) command correctly in a program, particularly as part of the testing phase in program development.
- Continue to develop programming problem solutions using the CASE structure.

In Chapter 8 we saw how the unconditional GOTO loop sequence can be modified under conditions specified by the IF/THEN statement. We also saw how decision making using IF/THEN statements is accomplished. In this chapter we examine another sequence structure. This structure is often referred to as the *ON/GOTO, or computed GOTO,* and is given the general name *CASE structure.* CASE structure assumes that the decision-making problem at hand has several choices, such as would be the case in a multiple choice question for which only one answer is correct.

Also discussed in this chapter are the STOP statement and the CONT command. Both can be useful in debugging programs.

## THE CASE STRUCTURE

A case situation exists when there are more than two choices to be made and these choices can be represented as options on a scale of 1, or 2, or 3, or 4, or 5, and so forth. Figure 9.1 illustrates CASE structure. It is an extension of the IF/THEN/ELSE previously discussed

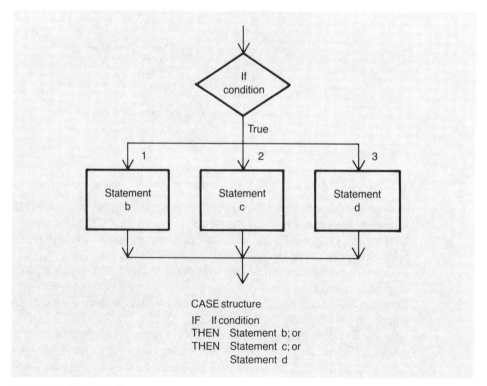

**FIGURE 9.1** CASE Structure

in Chapter 8. CASE structure is useful when there are several choices, but only one can be processed on the basis of the test condition.

## THE ON/GOTO STATEMENT

To carry out the logic shown in Figure 9.1, we can make use of the ON/GOTO statement. This statement tests to determine if a particular variable or expression has an integer value of 1, or 2, or 3, or 4, and so forth. If the test condition is found to be an integer value within a specified range of possibilities, the program will transfer control to the line associated with that value.

The form of the ON/GOTO statement is

$$\text{line \# ON} \begin{Bmatrix} \text{variable} \\ \text{or} \\ \text{expression} \end{Bmatrix} \text{GOTO line \#, line \#, line \#, line \#, . . . , line\#}$$

where the value of the variable or expression is an integer 1, 2, 3, 4, . . . , 255. This integer determines the line number to which the program transfers. For example, if the integer is 2, the program proceeds to the second number in the line number list after the GOTO and then transfers to the line with that number. If the integer were 8, the program would proceed to the eighth number in the line number list after the GOTO and then transfer to the line with that number. Specific examples of ON/GOTO statements are shown in Table 9.1.

**TABLE 9.1** ON/GOTO Statements

| STATEMENT | EXPLANATION |
|---|---|
| 100 ON A GOTO 50,200,75,30,80,90 | Branch to line 50 if $A = 1$, to line 200 if $A = 2$, to line 75 if $A = 3$, to line 30 if $A = 4$, to line 80 if $A = 5$, and to line 90 if $A = 6$. |
| 50 ON M + 1 GOTO 80,80,110,200,250 | Branch to line 80 if the expression $M + 1$ equals either 1 or 2, to line 110 if it equals 3, to line 200 if it equals 4, and to line 250 if it equals 5. Branch to line 80 would also be effected if $M = 0$ or 1 (since $M + 1 = 1$ or 2), to line 110 if $M = 2$, and so forth. |
| 25 ON (X + Y)/2 GOTO 50,60,70,70,80 | Branch to line 50 if the expression $(X + Y)/2$ equals 1, to line 60 if it equals 2, to line 70 if it equals either 3 or 4, and to line 80 if it equals 5. When an expression has a fractional part, it is rounded to the nearest integer value to make a line determination. For example, 2.1 would be rounded to 2 but 2.8 would be rounded to 3. |

In any of the examples in Table 9.1, if the value of the variable or expression is less than 1, or if it is more than the last possible value corresponding to line number positions, control will pass to the statement immediately following the ON/GOTO statement.

An illustration of the ON/GOTO, or computed GOTO, statement appears in Program 9.1. As each of the first four integer values in data line 60 is processed, control transfers to the line number associated with the integer value of $X$. Note that when $X = 3.5$, the program transfers control to line 40 where "FOUR" is printed because 3.5 is rounded up to 4. When $X = 1.4$ is processed, it is rounded down to 1, causing line 30 to print "ONE." When $X = 5$ is processed by line 15, the number "TWO" is printed since that is the statement *after* the ON/GOTO in line 15, and 5 is out of the range of $X$. The value of $X$ was limited to 1, 2, 3, or 4 because there were only four line numbers (30,20,50,40) following the ON/GOTO in line 15.

The flowchart in Figure 9.2 illustrates Program 9.1 and the idea of the CASE structure.

It is important to remember that on the IBM PC and other computers, *no* error message is displayed when the ON/GOTO value is out of range. Rather, processing will continue to the next statement after the ON/GOTO, possibly causing erroneous output results similar to the one in Program 9.1. In planning your program, anticipate a way to handle the situation when the test value is not in the specified range.

If the test variable or expression is either greater than 255 or less than or equal to $-.5$, however, an "Illegal function call in #" results, where # is the line number of the ON/GOTO.

## PROGRAM 9.1   Computed GOTO Statement

```
10 READ X
15    ON X GOTO 30,20,50,40
20      PRINT X;"TWO"
25 GOTO 10
30      PRINT X;"ONE"
35 GOTO 10
40      PRINT X;"FOUR"
45 GOTO 10
50      PRINT X;"THREE"
55 GOTO 10
60 DATA 3,1,4,2,1,4,2,8,3,5,2,2,5
99 END

RUN
 3 THREE
 1 ONE
 4 FOUR
 2 TWO
```

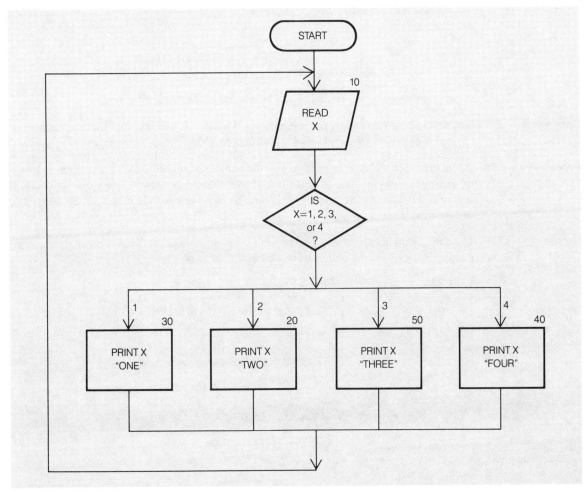

**FIGURE 9.2**  Flowchart for Program 9.1, CASE Structure

```
1.4 ONE
2.8 THREE
3.5 FOUR
2.2 TWO
5 TWO
Out of DATA in 10
```

Program 9.2, based on Case 9.1, illustrates an application of the ON/GOTO statement and CASE logic.

## CASE 9.1

**Problem**

**Decision Making and Determining Action to Take**
A certain state will take the following actions against the owners of motor vehicles who have at least one outstanding parking violation.

| NUMBER OF VIOLATIONS | ACTION |
|---|---|
| 1 or 2 | Send polite warning letter. |
| 3 | Send strong letter. |
| 4 | Send to collection agency. |
| 5 | Revoke registration. |

A program needs to be written to produce a list of the required actions.

**Data Input**     The data to be processed by the program reads a data list that includes the license number ($L$) and the number of unpaid parking violations ($N$).

**Process/Formulas** A repetitive process is to be used so that the number of unpaid parking violations is tested to determine what action, as described above, should be taken. The required decision testing is based on the number of violations being an integer value of 1, or 2, or 3, or 4, or 5 or more.

**Output**     The output should consist of a list showing the license number, the number of outstanding parking tickets, and the action to be taken. For example,

```
LICENSE              TICKETS            ACTION
-------------------------------------------------
   30903                2              POLITE WARNING
   49943                1              POLITE WARNING
```

---

## PROGRAM 9.2   Case 9.1, Parking Violations, Computed GOTO Statement

```
10 REM CASE 9.1, PARKING VIOLATIONS LISTING
20 REM PROGRAMMER- (name of person)    DATE - mm/dd/yy
30 REM     VARIABLE LIST-L,N
40 REM        L=LICENSE NUMBER
50 REM          N=# OF UNPAID PARKING TICKETS
60 REM --------------------------------------------
70 PRINT "LICENSE","TICKETS","ACTION"
80 PRINT "--------------------------------------------------"
90 READ L,N
100     IF L = -99 THEN 250             'end of DATA test
110        IF N>=5 THEN 190             'test for 5 or more violations
120           ON N GOTO 130,130,150,170   'test for 1 or 2,3,4
130              PRINT L,N,"POLITE WARNING"
140 GOTO 90
150              PRINT L,N,"STRONG LETTER"
160 GOTO 90
170              PRINT L,N,"COLLECTION AGENCY"
180 GOTO 90
190              PRINT L,N,"REVOKE REGISTRATION"
200 GOTO 90
210 DATA 30903,2,49943,1,98760,8,20989,3
220 DATA 17603,2,33344,1,45655,1,98789,5
230 DATA 77777,6,87676,4,36476,3
240 DATA -99,0
250 END
```

```
RUN
LICENSE         TICKETS         ACTION
--------------------------------------------------------
  30903           2             POLITE WARNING
  49943           1             POLITE WARNING
  98760           8             REVOKE REGISTRATION
  20989           3             STRONG LETTER
  17603           2             POLITE WARNING
  33344           1             POLITE WARNING
  45655           1             POLITE WARNING
  98789           5             REVOKE REGISTRATION
  77777           6             REVOKE REGISTRATION
  87676           4             COLLECTION AGENCY
  36476           3             STRONG LETTER
```

Sometimes you may encounter a situation in which the decision data has a lower value beginning at zero and increasing as an integer 1, 2, 3, 4, and so forth. One treatment would be to "trap" the zero value with an IF test before the ON/GOTO is processed. Another approach would be to add a 1 to the ON/GOTO variable forcing the range to begin at 1.

Look at Program 9.3. It is a revision of Program 9.2 and assumes that some data will be a license number with no (zero) violations. For example, see the last data items in each data line (210–230). Note how line 120 was changed from $N$ in Program 9.2 to $N + 1$. It now appears as

120 ON N + 1 GOTO 125, 130, 130, 150, 170

and has an additional line transfer to 125 for "NO ACTION TAKEN."

---

**PROGRAM 9.3   Case 9.1, Parking Violations, Computed GOTO Statement, Revision**

```
10 REM CASE 9.1, PARKING VIOLATIONS LISTING
20 REM PROGRAMMER- (name of person)   DATE - mm/dd/yy
30 REM    VARIABLE LIST-L,N
40 REM       L=LICENSE NUMBER
50 REM       N=# OF UNPAID PARKING TICKETS
60 REM -------------------------------------------------
70 PRINT "LICENSE","TICKETS","ACTION"
80 PRINT "-------------------------------------------------"
90 READ L,N
100     IF L = -99 THEN 250               'end of DATA test
110       IF N>=5 THEN 190                 'test for 5 or more violations
120         ON N+1 GOTO 125,130,130,150,170 'use N+1 to change 0 to 1
125             PRINT L,N,"NO ACTION TAKEN"
128 GOTO 90
130             PRINT L,N,"POLITE WARNING"
140 GOTO 90
150             PRINT L,N,"STRONG LETTER"
160 GOTO 90
170             PRINT L,N,"COLLECTION AGENCY"
180 GOTO 90
```

```
190                PRINT L,N,"REVOKE REGISTRATION"
200 GOTO 90
210 DATA 30903,2,49943,1,98760,8,20989,3,35425,0
220 DATA 17603,2,33344,1,45655,1,98789,5,23702,0
230 DATA 77777,6,87676,4,36476,3
240 DATA -99,0
250 END

RUN
LICENSE         TICKETS         ACTION
------------------------------------------------
  30903            2            POLITE WARNING
  49943            1            POLITE WARNING
  98760            8            REVOKE REGISTRATION
  20989            3            STRONG LETTER
  35425            0            NO ACTION TAKEN
  17603            2            POLITE WARNING
  33344            1            POLITE WARNING
  45655            1            POLITE WARNING
  98789            5            REVOKE REGISTRATION
  23702            0            NO ACTION TAKEN
  77777            6            REVOKE REGISTRATION
  87676            4            COLLECTION AGENCY
  36476            3            STRONG LETTER
```

In the last three programs, we illustrated situations where the ON/GOTO variable or expression conformed to a series of integer values (1, 2, 3, . . .), as given by the data lists.

Case 9.2 illustrates how the computed GOTO statement can be used to determine if the value of an ON/GOTO expression is within a particular range when the expressions are *not* integers to begin with.

. . . . . . . . . . . . . . . . . . . . . . . . . . . . . . . .

## CASE 9.2

**Problem**

**Determining Union Dues**

A union charges its members dues based on their salary as given in the following table.

| MONTHLY SALARY | DUES |
|---|---|
| $ 0–499.99 | $ 5 |
| 500.00–999.99 | 8 |
| 1,000.00–1,499.99 | 12 |
| 1,500.00–1,999.99 | 16 |
| 2,000.00–2,499.99 | 20 |
| 2,500.00–2,999.99 | 25 |
| 3,000.00 and over | 30 |

A computer program is needed to prepare a report showing each member's name, salary, and union dues charged with totals for salary and union dues.

**Data Input**

There are nine union members, and last month their salaries were as follows:

| NAME | SALARY | NAME | SALARY |
|------|--------|------|--------|
| BURNS | $2,235.62 | DALE | $ 666.22 |
| COSTA | $3,645.52 | EGAN | $1,499.99 |
| CONTI | $ 357.75 | KANE | $1,776.76 |
| CONNOR | $2,545.03 | PAPPAS | $2,485.71 |
| CURRY | $1,111.11 | | |

**Process/Formulas**  A repetitive process is to be used. Decision testing is required to determine the amount of union dues. To carry out this test, the monthly salary is converted to a code (1 to 6) using the expression (salary/500 + .5). The program terminates as a result of an end of data test.

**Output**  Output follows this format:

```
NAME            SALARY           UNION DUES
----------------------------------------------
BURNS           $2,235.62           $20
COSTA           $3,645.52           $30
CONTI           $   357.75          $ 5
CONNOR          $2,545.03           $25
CURRY           $1,111.11           $12
DALE            $   666.22          $ 8
EGAN            $1,499.99           $12
KANE            $1,776.76           $16
PAPPAS          $2,485.71           $20
                ---------           ----
TOTALS          $16,323.71          $148
```

Program 9.4 provides a solution to Case 9.2. Note how the computed GOTO in line 100,

100 ON (SA/500 + .5) GOTO 105,115,125,135,145,155

is able to determine the appropriate union dues. For example, if the salary is $2,235.62, the computation (2,235.62/500 + .5) is (4.47124 + .5) which equals 4.97124. Since the ON/GOTO rounds to the nearest integer value, the result is a value of 5. This is the value that correctly produces the $20 union dues to the given salary. The .5 in the expression ensures that the correct integer value is obtained. In this example, if the .5 were not included in the expression, the computer would round 4.47124 down to 4, causing the dues to be $16 instead of $20.

**PROGRAM 9.4    Case 9.2, Union Dues Determination, Computed GOTO Statement**

```
10 REM CASE 9.2, DETERMINING UNION DUES
15 REM PROGRAMMER- (name of person)  DATE - mm/dd/yy
20 REM    VARIABLE LIST-
25 REM       EN$=EMPLOYEE NAME
30 REM       F$=FORMAT FOR PRINT USING
35 REM       SA=SALARY
```

```
40 REM          TS=TOTAL SALARY
45 REM          TUD=TOTAL UNION DUES
50 REM          UD=UNION DUES
55 REM -------------------------------------------
60 LET H1$= "NAME            SALARY        UNION DUES"
65 LET H2$= "-------------------------------------------"
70 LET F$ = " \              \ $#,###.##        $##"
72 LET L$ = "                   ---------       ----"
74 LET F1$ ="  TOTALS        $##,###.##        $###"
75 LET TS=0
80 LET TUD=0
82 PRINT H1$
84 PRINT H2$
85 READ EN$, SA
90     IF EN$= "EOD" THEN 190                'end of DATA test
95        IF SA >= 3000 THEN 165             '$3000 and over test
100          ON (SA/500 + .5) GOTO 105,115,125,135,145,155   'set code: 1-6
105                LET UD= 5
110             GOTO 170
115                LET UD= 8
120             GOTO 170
125                LET UD= 12
130             GOTO 170
135                LET UD= 16
140             GOTO 170
145                LET UD= 20
150             GOTO 170
155                LET UD= 25
160             GOTO 170
165             LET UD= 30
170             PRINT USING F$;EN$,SA,UD
175             LET TS = TS + SA
180             LET TUD = TUD + UD
185 GOTO 85
190 PRINT L$
195 PRINT USING F1$; TS, TUD
200 DATA BURNS,2235.62, COSTA,3645.52
205 DATA CONTI,357.75, CONNOR,2545.03
210 DATA CURRY,1111.11, DALE,666.22
215 DATA EGAN,1499.99, KANE,1776.76
220 DATA PAPPAS,2485.71
225 DATA EOD,0
299 END


RUN
NAME            SALARY        UNION DUES
----------------------------------------
 BURNS          $2,235.62          $20
 COSTA          $3,645.52          $30
 CONTI          $   357.75         $ 5
 CONNOR         $2,545.03          $25
 CURRY          $1,111.11          $12
 DALE           $   666.22         $ 8
 EGAN           $1,499.99          $12
 KANE           $1,776.76          $16
 PAPPAS         $2,485.71          $20
                ---------          ----
  TOTALS        $16,323.71         $148
```

**THE MENU CONCEPT**

As more and more people use computers, the programs that make them work must be designed so that it is easy for the user to perform various tasks. One design concept that can be incorporated into programs to make them easy to use is that of the *menu*. This often leads to the statement that a program is *menu driven*. In this way a user is given a choice of tasks that can be performed with the computer. Such choices are typical when ordering from a restaurant menu such as the one shown in Figure 9.3. As with menu-driven

## Appetizers

| | |
|---|---|
| Escargot .................................... 6.95 | Mussels Marinara |
| Shrimp Cocktail........................... 7.50 | (sweet or hot) ................................... 5.50 |
| Clams on the Halfshell ............... 6.95 | Zucchini Styx ............................. 4.50 |
| Clams Casino ............................ 7.50 | Garlic Bread ............................... 3.75 |

## Entrees

### Fish

| | |
|---|---|
| Shrimp Scampi ..........................13.95 |
| Shrimp Parmesan ......................12.95 |
| Seafood Combo .........................13.95 |
| Broiled Scallops .........................12.50 |
| Scallops Scampi ........................13.50 |
| Scallops Parmesan ....................12.95 |
| Stuffed Flounder ........................11.95 |
| Broiled Filet of Sole ...................11.25 |
| Fried Sole Parmesan..................10.95 |

### Pasta

Linguine with Red Clam Sauce ... 9.95
Linguine with White Clam Sauce  9.95
Linguine with Shrimp & Scallops
Marinara ...................................13.95
Fettuccine Alfredo ...................... 9.95
Fettuccine with Escargot &
Spinach......................................13.95
Tortellini Alfredo with Broccoli .....11.95

### Meat

| | |
|---|---|
| New York Sirloin Steak ..............13.95 | Veal Piccata ..............................12.95 |
| Steak and Scampi ......................15.95 | Veal Marsala .............................12.95 |
| Open Sliced Steak .....................11.95 | Veal Parmesan..........................12.95 |

### Soups

| | |
|---|---|
| Minestrone................................. 2.75 |
| Soup of the Day ......................... 2.95 |

### Beverages

| | |
|---|---|
| Coffee........................................... .75 |
| Tea................................................ .75 |
| Milk ............................................... .75 |

All Entrees include Salad, Bread, and Choice of Potato

**FIGURE 9.3**  A Restaurant Menu

programs, there is usually a main menu that lists all the broad categories offered, such as appetizers, entrees, soups, and beverages (see Figure 9.3). Each main menu item can have either a simple list of items under it for selection (such as beverages: coffee, tea, or milk) or a group of subitems, each one with its own simple list of items for selection. In Figure 9.3 the entrees show three subitems (fish, pasta, and meat), each with a simple list of items under it.

Figure 9.4 provides an overview of how a main menu at a restaurant can be broken down to submenus. An example of a program-generated menu is the display in Figure 9.5.

To incorporate menus into programs, use of the ON/GOTO statement is suggested. This statement is a conditional transfer based on the integer value of a variable beginning with the value of 1. Depending on the variable value—1, 2, 3, . . . , and so forth—a transfer is made within a program corresponding to the user's choice. Case 9.3 illustrates how the ON/GOTO can be used in a menu-type program.

## CASE 9.3

**Problem**  **Building an Accounts Receivable Menu**
A company would like to have the computer handle its accounts receivable transactions, such as entering cash received, sending monthly statements, printing sales journals, and so forth.

A conversational menu-driven program is to be developed. The initial program development starts with the menu and is only a part of what would be a much larger program.

**Data Input**  The data input will be the numbers 1, 2, 3, 4, 5, or 6 to correspond to the following choices:

    1 TO ENTER NEW CUSTOMER

    2 TO ENTER INVOICE

    3 TO ENTER CASH RECEIVED

    4 TO PRINT STATEMENTS

    5 TO PRINT SALES JOURNAL

    6 TO STOP

**Process/Formulas**  A repetitive process is to be used that includes the CASE structure. Decision testing is required to determine which menu task is to be performed by the computer. The program terminates when the user selects menu item 6. Decision testing is used to prevent a value out of the data input range (1 to 6) from being processed.

**Output**  Because this is only a partial program, the output will only reflect testing of the menu sequence. After a menu selection has been made, an output statement for that selection will be displayed.

Program 9.5 provides the initial structure for Case 9.3. After RUN the user must enter the type of transaction the computer is to perform via the INPUT statement in line 70. For

MAIN MENU
APPETIZERS
ENTREES
SOUPS
BEVERAGES
List of items
FISH
PASTA
MEAT
List of items
List of items
List of items
List of items
List of items

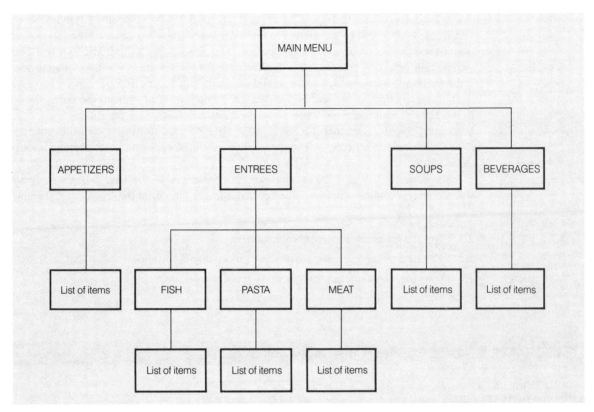

**FIGURE 9.4** Overview of Restaurant Menu Structure

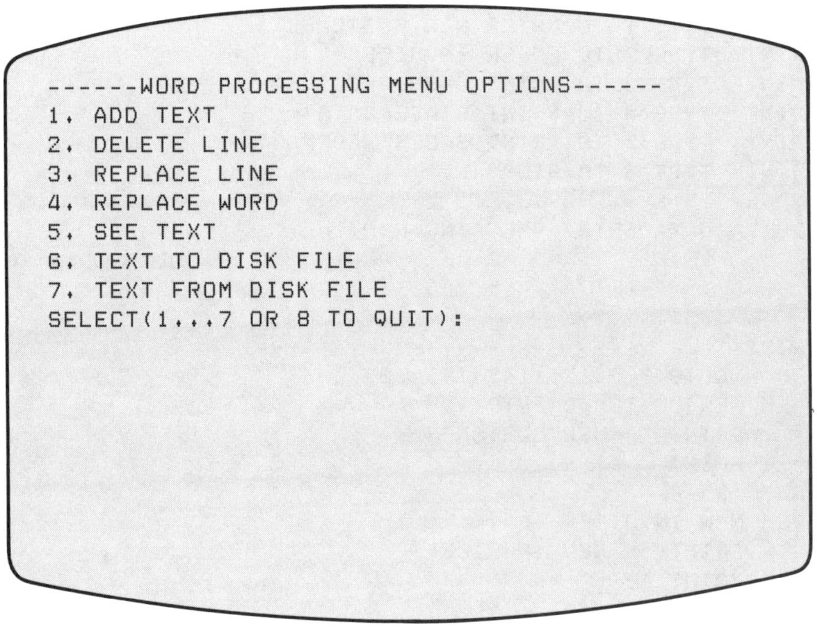

------WORD PROCESSING MENU OPTIONS------
1. ADD TEXT
2. DELETE LINE
3. REPLACE LINE
4. REPLACE WORD
5. SEE TEXT
6. TEXT TO DISK FILE
7. TEXT FROM DISK FILE
SELECT(1...7 OR 8 TO QUIT):

**FIGURE 9.5** A Menu Display

example, if a new customer is to be entered, the user would respond by typing a 1, in which case control will be transferred to line 105. Lines 105–120 might be used to request the customer's name, address, phone number, salesperson, credit limit, and so forth. This information would be entered into a file for later use. (Files are covered in Chapter 15.) If the number 3 were typed, control would be transferred to line 145, where the program might then request the customer's number, the amount of the payment, the date, and so forth. This information would also be entered into the system for later use.

Lines 75–90 ensure that if a menu value of less than 1 or greater than 6 is entered, it is trapped and not processed. The user is then given the opportunity to reenter a correct menu value.

Sometimes there may be a *submenu*. For instance, if the user wishing to print statements types in the number 4, the computer might then print the following submenu:

**1.** Type all statements.

**2.** Type statement for a particular customer.

**3.** Type statements that have a balance of more than $50.00 only.

**4.** Type statements that are two or more months overdue.

---

### PROGRAM 9.5   Case 9.3, Accounts Receivable Menu

```
5 REM CASE 9.3, BUILDING AN ACCOUNTS RECEIVABLE MENU
10 REM PROGRAMMER- (name of person)   DATE - mm/dd/yy
15 REM     VARIABLE LIST-
20 REM         A=MENU OPTION NUMBER
25 REM -------------------------------------------------
30 PRINT
35 PRINT "ACCOUNTS RECEIVABLE PROGRAM"
40 PRINT "TYPE 1 TO ENTER NEW CUSTOMER"
45 PRINT "TYPE 2 TO ENTER INVOICE"
50 PRINT "TYPE 3 TO ENTER CASH RECEIVED"
55 PRINT "TYPE 4 TO PRINT STATEMENTS"
60 PRINT "TYPE 5 TO PRINT SALES JOURNAL"
65 PRINT "TYPE 6 TO STOP"
70 INPUT "ENTER 1, 2, 3, 4, 5, OR 6 :",A
72 REM    DATA ENTRY CHECKING ROUTINE
75        IF A>=1  AND  A<=6  THEN 95         'out of range check for INPUT
80            PRINT "* PLEASE ENTER ONLY VALUES FROM 1 TO 6 *"
90            GOTO 70
95 PRINT "------------------------------"
100 ON A GOTO 105,125,145,165,185,205
105 REM NEW CUSTOMER ENTRY
110      PRINT "  NEW CUSTOMER"
115      PRINT
120 GOTO 35
125 REM NEW INVOICE
130      PRINT "  NEW INVOICE"
135      PRINT
140 GOTO 35
145 REM CASH RECEIVED
```

```
150     PRINT "  CASH RECEIVED"
155     PRINT
160 GOTO 35
165 REM PRINTING STATEMENTS
170     PRINT "  STATEMENTS"
175     PRINT
180 GOTO 35
185 REM PRINTING SALES JOURNAL
190     PRINT "  SALES JOURNALS"
195     PRINT
200 GOTO 35
205 PRINT " ALL ACCOUNTS RECEIVABLE TRANSACTIONS COMPLETED"
210 END

RUN

ACCOUNTS RECEIVABLE PROGRAM
TYPE 1 TO ENTER NEW CUSTOMER
TYPE 2 TO ENTER INVOICE
TYPE 3 TO ENTER CASH RECEIVED
TYPE 4 TO PRINT STATEMENTS
TYPE 5 TO PRINT SALES JOURNAL
TYPE 6 TO STOP
ENTER 1, 2, 3, 4, 5, OR 6 :3
---------------------------------
  CASH RECEIVED

ACCOUNTS RECEIVABLE PROGRAM
TYPE 1 TO ENTER NEW CUSTOMER
TYPE 2 TO ENTER INVOICE
TYPE 3 TO ENTER CASH RECEIVED
TYPE 4 TO PRINT STATEMENTS
TYPE 5 TO PRINT SALES JOURNAL
TYPE 6 TO STOP
ENTER 1, 2, 3, 4, 5, OR 6 :8
* PLEASE ENTER ONLY VALUES FROM 1 TO 6 *
ENTER 1, 2, 3, 4, 5, OR 6 :5
---------------------------------
  SALES JOURNALS

ACCOUNTS RECEIVABLE PROGRAM
TYPE 1 TO ENTER NEW CUSTOMER
TYPE 2 TO ENTER INVOICE
TYPE 3 TO ENTER CASH RECEIVED
TYPE 4 TO PRINT STATEMENTS
TYPE 5 TO PRINT SALES JOURNAL
TYPE 6 TO STOP
ENTER 1, 2, 3, 4, 5, OR 6 :1
---------------------------------
  NEW CUSTOMER

ACCOUNTS RECEIVABLE PROGRAM
TYPE 1 TO ENTER NEW CUSTOMER
TYPE 2 TO ENTER INVOICE
```

```
TYPE 3 TO ENTER CASH RECEIVED
TYPE 4 TO PRINT STATEMENTS
TYPE 5 TO PRINT SALES JOURNAL
TYPE 6 TO STOP
ENTER 1, 2, 3, 4, 5, OR 6 :0
* PLEASE ENTER ONLY VALUES FROM 1 TO 6 *
ENTER 1, 2, 3, 4, 5, OR 6 :2
---------------------------------
  NEW INVOICE

ACCOUNTS RECEIVABLE PROGRAM
TYPE 1 TO ENTER NEW CUSTOMER
TYPE 2 TO ENTER INVOICE
TYPE 3 TO ENTER CASH RECEIVED
TYPE 4 TO PRINT STATEMENTS
TYPE 5 TO PRINT SALES JOURNAL
TYPE 6 TO STOP
ENTER 1, 2, 3, 4, 5, OR 6 :6
---------------------------------
 ALL ACCOUNTS RECEIVABLE TRANSACTIONS COMPLETED
```

## THE STOP STATEMENT

The STOP statement does just what its name implies—it stops the program. If the END statement is on line 999, a STOP statement anywhere in the program is the same as a GOTO 999. However, there are some differences between the STOP statement and the END statement. There can be several STOP statements anywhere in the program, but there should be only one END statement and it should be the last executable statement in the program. Also, it is possible to continue the execution of the program beginning with the line number after the STOP statement. When the END statement is used, it is not possible to continue the program; the program must be run from the beginning.

The form of the STOP statement is

line # STOP

An example of the STOP statement is line 80 in Program 9.6. (Instead of 80 STOP, we could have used 80 GOTO 110, which would have done the same thing and is identical to what was done in Program 8.1.)

## PROGRAM 9.6   The STOP Statement

```
5 REM THE SAME PROGRAM AS 8.1 WITH A STOP
10 REM DECISION MAKING
30 REM THIS PROGRAM READS TWO NUMBERS
40 REM AND PRINTS THE LARGER OF THE TWO
50 READ A,B
60    IF A>B THEN 90
70      PRINT B
80 STOP
90      PRINT A;
```

```
100 DATA 3,7
110 END

RUN
7
Break in 80
```

Note that after the STOP statement is processed, the message "Break in 80" is displayed.

In responding to Case 9.4, Program 9.7 illustrates how several STOP statements can be included in a program.

- - - - - - - - - - - - - - - - - - - - - - - - - - - - - - - - - - - - - - - -

## CASE 9.4

**Problem**   **Credit-Limit Checking**

A conversational program is needed to determine the status of an individual's credit account. A credit account can be in any one of four states: at the limit, near the limit (defined as being within $50 of the limit), over the limit, or below the limit (OK).

**Data Input**   Data entry is interactive. It consists of an account number, the amount due, and the credit limit.

**Process/Formulas**   A decision process is to be used. Decision testing is required to compare the amount due with the credit limit for the account. The program terminates after an account is processed.

**Output**   Output shows the account number and one of four messages: At limit, Near limit within, Over limit by, and OK - Below the limit by. Each message is followed by a dollar amount relating to the message.

- - - - - - - - - - - - - - - - - - - - - - - - - - - - - - - - - - - - - - - -

Program 9.7 carries out the requirements for Case 9.4. Line 45 requests the user to enter the relevant data values for testing. Lines 50, 60, 70, and 80 carry out the appropriate decision test as well as cause a message and dollar amount to be printed. After the decision test is performed correctly, the next statement to be processed is a STOP. This statement in lines 55, 65, and 75 terminates any further processing by the program.

## PROGRAM 9.7   Case 9.4, Credit-Limit Checking, STOP Statements

```
10 REM CASE 9.4, CREDIT LIMIT CHECKING
15 REM PROGRAMMER- (name of person)  DATE - mm/dd/yy
20 REM     VARIABLE LIST- N, A, L
25 REM       N= ACCOUNT NUMBER
30 REM       A= AMOUNT DUE
35 REM       L= CREDIT LIMIT
40 REM -------------------------------------------------
45 INPUT "ENTER ACCOUNT NUMBER, AMOUNT DUE, AND CREDIT LIMIT:", N, A, L
50   IF A=L THEN PRINT N; " AT LIMIT $"; L ELSE 60
```

```
55 STOP
60    IF L-A>0 AND L-A<=50 THEN PRINT N; " NEAR LIMIT WITHIN $"; L-A ELSE 70
65 STOP
70    IF A>L THEN PRINT N; " OVER LIMIT BY $"; A-L ELSE 80
75 STOP
80       PRINT N;" OK - BELOW THE LIMIT BY $"; L-A
85 STOP
90 END

RUN
ENTER ACCOUNT NUMBER, AMOUNT DUE, AND CREDIT LIMIT:123,600,500
 123 OVER LIMIT BY $ 100
Break in 75

RUN
ENTER ACCOUNT NUMBER, AMOUNT DUE, AND CREDIT LIMIT:234,250,500
 234 OK - BELOW THE LIMIT BY $ 250
Break in 85

RUN
ENTER ACCOUNT NUMBER, AMOUNT DUE, AND CREDIT LIMIT:345,475,500
 345 NEAR LIMIT WITHIN $ 25
Break in 65

RUN
ENTER ACCOUNT NUMBER, AMOUNT DUE, AND CREDIT LIMIT:456,800,800
 456 AT LIMIT $ 800
Break in 55
```

## THE CONT COMMAND

After a STOP statement has been executed, it is possible to resume processing by entering the CONT (continue) command. This command can be typed on the keyboard followed by ENTER or activated by pressing the function key F5.

Both the STOP statement and CONT command can be used for debugging a program. For example, if a program causes strange output values to appear for variables or expressions in a line, we can stop the program with a STOP statement, examine the current values of the variable or expression with a PRINT statement, and then resume processing with a CONT command.

The usefulness of the CONT command is illustrated by Programs 9.8 and 9.9.

## PROGRAM 9.8   Examination of Processing

```
10 LET X = 1
20 LET X = X + 1
30 IF X < 50 THEN 20
40 LET T = X^2 + 2*X + 6
50 PRINT T
55 END

RUN
 2606
```

Suppose we are not sure how the output 2606 was obtained in Program 9.8. We need to determine what value of $X$ was processed by line 40. A STOP has been added in line 45 of Program 9.9. After the break, we can examine the value of the variable $X$ with a PRINT statement *without* a line number. A direct statement such as

PRINT X
50

shows the value of $X$ to be 50. We can then resume execution of the rest of the program with the CONT command. In Program 9.9 the statement following the STOP (line 50) is processed next. Once you have debugged a program using the STOP-PRINT sequence, the STOP statement is removed.

## PROGRAM 9.9    Examination of Processing with STOP, PRINT, and CONT

```
10 LET X = 1
20 LET X = X + 1
30 IF X < 50 THEN 20
40 LET T = X^2 + 2*X + 6
45 STOP
50 PRINT T
55 END

RUN
Break in 45

PRINT X
 50

CONT
 2606
```

## SUMMARY

The computed GOTO enables us to design programs using a CASE structure. The computed GOTO statement (ON/GOTO) allows control to be transferred to any one of several statements based on the current value of a particular variable or expression.

Menu-driven programs can be designed using the computed GOTO statement.

The STOP statement stops the program's execution, just as a GOTO to the END statement does.

The CONT command makes it possible to resume processing after a STOP has been executed. Both the STOP and CONT can be used for program debugging.

## BASIC VOCABULARY SUMMARY

| Statement | Purpose | Examples |
|---|---|---|
| ON/GOTO line # (Alt + G key = GOTO) | Transfers control to another line, or statement, after the integer value of a variable or expression is tested and evaluated. | 100 ON A GOTO 50,200,75,300,320<br>50 ON M + 1 GOTO 80,80,110,200<br>85 ON (X + Y)/2 GOTO 50,60,70,70,80 |
| STOP | Stops program execution. | 90 STOP |
| CONT | Resumes processing after a STOP statement. | CONT |

## EXERCISES

### Review Questions

**9.1** Making use of the ON/GOTO statement, rewrite the following program segment.

```
20 READ A
32    IF A = 0 THEN 100
34    IF A = 1 THEN 150
36    IF A = 2 THEN 150
37    IF A = 3 THEN 210
38    IF A = 4 THEN 210
39    IF A >= 5 THEN 250
```

**9.2** Write a single BASIC statement so that a program goes to line 600 if *J* equals 60, line 100 if *J* equals 61, and line 200 if *J* equals 62.

**9.3** Look at the following program:

```
10 LET I=1
15 ON I GOTO 40,20,30
20 PRINT "IS",
25 GOTO 45
30 PRINT "EASY"
35 GOTO 45
40 PRINT "PROGRAMMING",
45 LET I=I+1
50 IF I<=3 THEN 15
55 END
```

a. What will it print when it is run?
b. If line 55 END is replaced with line 55 STOP, what will be printed after a run?
c. How would you change line 15 so the program will print ''Is programming easy''?

**9.4** Using the program in exercise 9.3, what would be printed each time if line 15 is changed to the following?
a. 15 ON I + 1 GOTO 40,20,30      c. 15 ON 3*1 GOTO 40,20,30
♦ b. 15 ON 2*1 GOTO 40,20,30      d. 15 ON I^.5 GOTO 40,20,30

**9.5**  What will Program 9.1 (shown below) do if line 15 is changed to the following?
a.  15 ON X GOTO 30,20,50,40,99
◆ b.  15 ON X GOTO 30,20,50,40,10
c.  15 ON X GOTO 30,20,50,40,20

```
10 READ X
12   IF X = -99 THEN 99
15      ON X GOTO 30,20,50,40
20         PRINT X;"TWO"
25 GOTO 10
30      PRINT X;"ONE"
35 GOTO 10
40      PRINT X;"FOUR"
45 GOTO 10
50      PRINT X;"THREE"
55 GOTO 10
60 DATA 3, 1, 4, 2, 1.4, 2.8, 3.5, 2.2, 5
70 DATA -99
99 END

RUN
 3 THREE
 1 ONE
 4 FOUR
 2 TWO
 1.4 ONE
 2.8 THREE
 3.5 FOUR
 2.2 TWO
 5 TWO
```

## Programming Activities

**♦ 9.6**  **Purpose**  To use the CASE structure and loop repetition logic to process numeric data values and perform decision selection with the ON/GOTO statement. Data entry terminates with an end of data test.

**Problem**  Write and run a program that reads 10 account numbers, each followed by the number of months during which no payment has been made. Have the computer print the account number, the number of months overdue, and the appropriate action for each, as given in the following table:

| NUMBER OF MONTHS OVERDUE | ACTION |
|---|---|
| 0 | none |
| 1 | gentle reminder |
| 2 or 3 | strong reminder |
| 4 or more | lawyer's letter |

**Data**  In addition to using the information given above, use the data values shown in the table below. Have a separate data line for the end of data test value −999.

| ACCOUNT NUMBER | MONTHS | ACCOUNT NUMBER | MONTHS |
|---|---|---|---|
| 2370 | 2 | 2182 | 8 |
| 3542 | 3 | 1352 | 5 |
| 2372 | 0 | 1519 | 1 |
| 8282 | 1 | 2315 | 2 |
| 3838 | 4 | 1820 | 0 |

**Output**   Your output should have this format:

```
ACCOUNT NUMBER      MONTHS NO PAYMENT        ACTION TO BE TAKEN
-------------------------------------------------------------
    2370                   2                 STRONG REMINDER
    3542                   3                 STRONG REMINDER
    2372                   0                 NONE
    8282                   1                 GENTLE REMINDER
    3838                   4                 LAWYER'S LETTER
    2182                   8                 LAWYER'S LETTER
    1352                   5                 LAWYER'S LETTER
    1519                   1                 GENTLE REMINDER
    2315                   2                 STRONG REMINDER
    1820                   0                 NONE
```

**9.7**   **Purpose**   To use the CASE structure and loop repetition logic to process numeric data values and perform decision selection with the ON/GOTO statement. Data entry terminates with an end of data test.

**Problem**   Write and run a program that reads in an employee's number; the number of his or her dependents; the number of hours that he or she worked during the week; the hourly rate that applies; and a code number of 0, 1, or 2 to indicate that the employee carries no insurance, personal insurance only, or family insurance, respectively.

Have the computer calculate the employee's gross wages. This is calculated by the number of hours × the hourly rate if the number of hours worked is 40 hours or less. If the number of hours worked is greater than 40, the employee should receive $1\frac{1}{2}$ times the hourly rate for the additional hours above 40. The taxes deducted from the gross wages should be according to the following table:

| NUMBER OF DEPENDENTS | PERCENT DEDUCTED |
|---|---|
| 0 | 28 |
| 1 | 26 |
| 2 | 24 |
| 3 | 22 |
| 4 | 20 |
| 5 | 18 |
| 6 | 16 |
| 7 or more | 14 |

The amount of insurance deducted should be calculated according to the following table:

| CODE | MEANING | AMOUNT DEDUCTED |
|---|---|---|
| 0 | No insurance | $ 0 |
| 1 | Insurance for self only | 5 |
| 2 | Insurance for family | 10 |

Once all of the deductions have been determined, the net pay should be calculated.

**Data** In addition to the information given above (tax deductions and insurance deductions), use the data values shown in the table below. Have a separate data line for the end of data test value $-999$.

| EMPLOYEE NO. | DEPENDENTS | HOURS WORKED | HOURLY RATE | INSURANCE CODE |
|---|---|---|---|---|
| 6044 | 0 | 37 | $4.50 | 1 |
| 4411 | 2 | 42 | $4.75 | 2 |
| 7158 | 1 | 40 | $4.10 | 2 |
| 1142 | 0 | 47 | $4.50 | 1 |
| 6482 | 8 | 45 | $4.80 | 0 |
| 1231 | 4 | 50 | $5.50 | 1 |
| 7111 | 2 | 40 | $4.00 | 1 |
| 1421 | 5 | 42 | $4.60 | 2 |
| 8421 | 7 | 38 | $4.25 | 2 |
| 1333 | 0 | 41 | $4.80 | 0 |

**Output** Your output should include column totals as shown in this format:

```
EMPLOYEE      GROSS        TAX      INSURANCE
NUMBER        WAGES      DEDUCTED    DEDUCTED        NET PAY
------------------------------------------------------------

  6044      $166.50      $46.62      $5.00         $114.88
  4411      $204.25      $49.02     $10.00         $145.23
  7158      $164.00      $42.64     $10.00         $111.36
  1142      $227.25      $63.63      $5.00         $158.62
  6482      $228.00      $31.92      $0.00         $196.08
  1231      $302.50      $60.50      $5.00         $237.00
  7111      $160.00      $38.40      $5.00         $116.60
  1421      $197.80      $35.60     $10.00         $152.20
  8421      $161.50      $22.61     $10.00         $128.89
  1333      $199.20      $55.78      $0.00         $143.42
------------------------------------------------------------

 TOTAL    $2,010.00     $446.72     $60.00       $1,504.28
```

**9.8** **Purpose** To use the CASE structure and loop repetition logic to process inputted data values and perform decision selection with the ON/GOTO statement.

**Problem** Write and run an interactive program *segment* that displays the menu below and provides for a user response from the keyboard.

```
-----------HELP SCREEN MENU OPTIONS-----------
TO GET HELP SELECT THE ITEM YOU WANT EXPLAINED
        1. HOW TO ADD TEXT.
        2. HOW TO DELETE LINES.
        3. HOW TO REPLACE LINES.
        4. HOW TO COPY LINES.
        5. HOW TO MOVE LINES.
        6. QUIT THE HELP MENU
-----------------------------------------------
```

**Data** Input values are 1, 2, 3, 4, 5, 6, corresponding to the menu.

**Output**    Your screen display should have this format:

```
-----------HELP SCREEN MENU OPTIONS-----------
TO GET HELP SELECT THE ITEM YOU WANT EXPLAINED
        1. HOW TO ADD TEXT.
        2. HOW TO DELETE LINES.
        3. HOW TO REPLACE LINES.
        4. HOW TO COPY LINES.
        5. HOW TO MOVE LINES.
        6. QUIT THE HELP MENU.
-----------------------------------------------
INSTRUCTIONS: PLEASE SELECT(1...5 OR 6 TO QUIT):? 3

HELP ITEM 3. TO REPLACE LINES . . .

-----------HELP SCREEN MENU OPTIONS-----------
TO GET HELP SELECT THE ITEM YOU WANT EXPLAINED
        1. HOW TO ADD TEXT.
        2. HOW TO DELETE LINES.
        3. HOW TO REPLACE LINES.
        4. HOW TO COPY LINES.
        5. HOW TO MOVE LINES.
        6. QUIT THE HELP MENU.
-----------------------------------------------
INSTRUCTIONS: PLEASE SELECT(1...5 OR 6 TO QUIT):? 6
```

# CHAPTER 10

## SUBROUTINES

Upon completing this chapter, you will be able to do the following:

- Know the purpose of a subroutine.
- Construct a program that incorporates one or more subroutines.
- Understand how the GOSUB and RETURN statements work.
- Recognize error messages and know their meaning.
- Build "error trapping" into a program using the ON ERROR GOTO, ERR, ERL, and RESUME statements.

In Chapter 9 we learned about the *CASE structure*. In this chapter, another structure, the *subroutine,* is discussed. Subroutines are useful when developing larger programs and when simplifying programs that have redundant or repetitive code segments.

The GOSUB and RETURN statements are used to write subroutines. Other statements and variables that are examined and illustrated in this chapter include ON ERROR GOTO, ERR, ERL, and RESUME.

## SUBROUTINES

A subroutine is usually a set of statements placed apart from a main program. It is most commonly used when a program has repetitive or redundant lines of code performing the same task throughout the program. We can take that task and set it aside as a subroutine, "calling" for it each time it is required by the logic of the program. Another use of subroutines is in the design of very large programs. In such programs we can break long segments into smaller components, or subroutines. One advantage of doing this is that it is more effective to test and debug a smaller part of the program. Another advantage of using subroutines is that the final listing has a more structured appearance, thus improving the readability of the program.

A subroutine is constructed using two statements—GOSUB, which causes a transfer to the subroutine, and RETURN, which causes the transfer back to the statement immediately following the GOSUB. The form of the GOSUB statement is

line # GOSUB line #

The form of the RETURN statement is

line # RETURN

Figure 10.1 illustrates how a subroutine is structured, as indicated by the numbered sequence.

Because of its repetitive printing task, Program 10.1 illustrates a program that can make good use of the subroutine concept. Throughout the program two PRINT statements repeat themselves, performing the same tasks (see lines 25, 30, 40, 45, 55, 60, 70, 75, 85, 90, and 100, 105).

A subroutine for this print task is created in Program 10.2, thus reducing the overall size of the original program while still maintaining all of the necessary printing. Within Program 10.2, the subroutine is found in lines 200–210. In the main part of the program, the redundant lines of Program 10.1 have been replaced with GOSUB 200 in lines 25, 40, 55, 70, 85, and 100. When a GOSUB is encountered, the computer internally stores the number of the line following the GOSUB statement. In this way, when the RETURN is processed at the end of the subroutine, control is transferred back to the proper line. For example, when 25 GOSUB 200 is executed, line number 35 is stored in the computer's memory. When the RETURN in line 210 is processed, control is transferred back to line 35, since that is the line immediately following the GOSUB instruction.

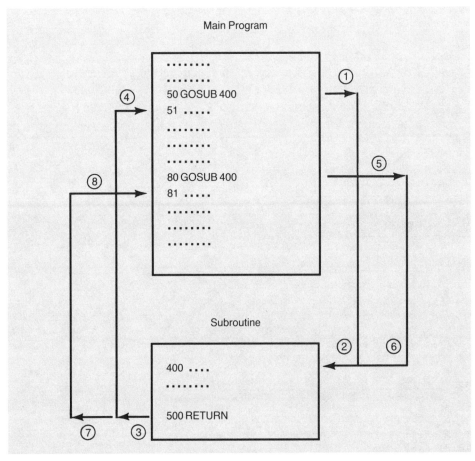

**FIGURE 10.1**   The Subroutine Structure

---

## PROGRAM 10.1   Repetitive Printing Tasks, No Subroutine

```
10 REM PROGRAM WITHOUT SUBROUTINE
15 READ NM$, AD$, CT$, SZ$, TL$
20    IF NM$ = "EOD" THEN 130
25        PRINT "----------------------------"
30        PRINT
35        PRINT NM$
40        PRINT "----------------------------"
45        PRINT
50        PRINT AD$
55        PRINT "----------------------------"
60        PRINT
65        PRINT CT$
70        PRINT "----------------------------"
75        PRINT
80        PRINT SZ$
85        PRINT "----------------------------"
```

```
90        PRINT
95        PRINT TL$
100       PRINT "------------------------------"
105       PRINT
110 GOTO 15
115 DATA J. SMITH,"123 STATE ST.", ANYTOWN1, STATE1    12345, (718) - 990-6399
120 DATA B. JONES,"58-31 FIRST ST.", ANYTOWN2, STATE2  54312, (914) - 654-1234
125 DATA "EOD", A, B, C, D
130 END

RUN
------------------------------

J. SMITH
------------------------------

123 STATE ST.
------------------------------

ANYTOWN1
------------------------------

STATE1    12345
------------------------------

(718) - 990-6399
------------------------------

------------------------------

B. JONES
------------------------------

58-31 FIRST ST.
------------------------------

ANYTOWN2
------------------------------

STATE2  54312
------------------------------

(914) - 654-1234
------------------------------
```

## PROGRAM 10.2 Repetitive Printing Tasks, Using a Subroutine

```
10 REM PROGRAM WITH SUBROUTINE
15 READ NM$, AD$, CT$, SZ$, TL$
20     IF NM$ = "EOD" THEN 330
25         GOSUB 200
35             PRINT NM$
40         GOSUB 200
50             PRINT AD$
55         GOSUB 200
65             PRINT CT$
70         GOSUB 200
80             PRINT SZ$
```

```
85          GOSUB 200
95              PRINT TL$
100         GOSUB 200
110 GOTO 15
115 DATA J. SMITH,"123 STATE ST.", ANYTOWN1, STATE1    12345, (718) - 990-6399
120 DATA B. JONES,"58-31 FIRST ST.", ANYTOWN2, STATE2  54312, (914) - 654-1234
125 DATA "EOD", A, B, C, D
190 REM ****    SUBROUTINE    ****
192 REM
195 REM
200    PRINT "------------------------------"
205    PRINT
210         RETURN
215 REM
330 END


RUN
------------------------------

J. SMITH
------------------------------

123 STATE ST.
------------------------------

ANYTOWN1
------------------------------

STATE1    12345
------------------------------

(718) - 990-6399
------------------------------

------------------------------

B. JONES
------------------------------

58-31 FIRST ST.
------------------------------

ANYTOWN2
------------------------------

STATE2  54312
------------------------------

(914) - 654-1234
------------------------------
```

Another example of a program that can use a subroutine is shown by Program 10.3. It is a partial program, but its purpose is to print two messages, each surrounded by asterisks, like this:

```
*****************************************
*                                       *
*     WELCOME TO EPSILON SOFTWARE        *
*                                       *
*****************************************
```

```
****************************************
*                                      *
*  THANK YOU FOR USING EPSILON SOFTWARE *
*                                      *
****************************************
```

The first message is printed at the beginning of the program and the second is printed at the end.

## PROGRAM 10.3   Beginning and Ending Messages, No Subroutine

```
10  PRINT "****************************************"
15  PRINT "*                                      *"
20  PRINT "*         WELCOME TO EPSILON SOFTWARE        *"
25  PRINT "*                                      *"
30  PRINT "****************************************"
100 REM        ¦   The Body   ¦
120 REM        ¦    of the    ¦
130 REM        ¦   Program    ¦
200 PRINT "****************************************"
210 PRINT "*                                      *"
220 PRINT "* THANK YOU FOR USING EPSILON SOFTWARE *"
230 PRINT "*                                      *"
240 PRINT "****************************************"
250 END

RUN
****************************************
*                                      *
*         WELCOME TO EPSILON SOFTWARE        *
*                                      *
****************************************
****************************************
*                                      *
* THANK YOU FOR USING EPSILON SOFTWARE *
*                                      *
****************************************
```

We can rewrite Program 10.3 using a subroutine and the GOSUB, RETURN, and STOP statements. The result is Program 10.4.

## PROGRAM 10.4   Beginning and Ending Messages, Using a Subroutine

```
10 LET X$= "        WELCOME TO EPSILON SOFTWARE        "
20 GOSUB 2000
100 REM        ¦   The Body   ¦
120 REM        ¦    of the    ¦
130 REM        ¦   Program    ¦
```

```
200 LET X$=    "THANK YOU FOR USING EPSILON SOFTWARE"
210 GOSUB 2000
220 STOP
1090 REM    ---------- SUBROUTINE ----------
2000 PRINT "****************************************"
2010 PRINT "*                                      *"
2020 PRINT "* "; X$; TAB(40);"*"
2030 PRINT "*                                      *"
2040 PRINT "****************************************"
2045 RETURN
2050 END


RUN
****************************************
*                                      *
*      WELCOME TO EPSILON SOFTWARE      *
*                                      *
****************************************
****************************************
*                                      *
* THANK YOU FOR USING EPSILON SOFTWARE *
*                                      *
****************************************
Break in 220
```

When the GOSUB 2000 in line 20 of Program 10.4 is encountered, the computer places the next line number (line 100) in a special memory location. Program control transfers to line 2000, and the subroutine is processed with the beginning message printed out. When the RETURN statement in line 2045 is encountered, the computer transfers control back to line 100 and erases the contents of the special memory location.

When the next GOSUB 2000 is encountered in line 210, the line number 220 is put in the special memory location. Control is again transferred to line 2000, and the subroutine is processed with the ending message printed out. The RETURN in line 2045 causes the control to transfer back to line 220, since it is the line number currently stored in memory. The last statement processed is line 220 STOP. It causes the ''Break in 220'' to appear after the last line of output.

Before each GOSUB was processed in Program 10.4, a string statement was assigned to the variable X$ (lines 10 and 200). Thus the subroutine (lines 2000–2045) will print whatever message is contained in X$ and surround it by a box of asterisks.

Note the use of a STOP statement in line 220. Generally a STOP or transfer to the END statement is placed after the main program and before the subroutine in order to prevent an *extra,* and erroneous, processing of the subroutine. If such an error does occur, the message

RETURN without GOSUB in line #

appears, indicating that the RETURN did not know where to go back to since a GOSUB did not cause a line number to be stored in memory. Figure 10.2 shows how the output from Program 10.4 would appear if the STOP in line 220 were removed from the program. The result is an extra processing of the subroutine, as shown by the second ''Thank you . . . '' message followed by the error message ''RETURN without GOSUB in 2045.''

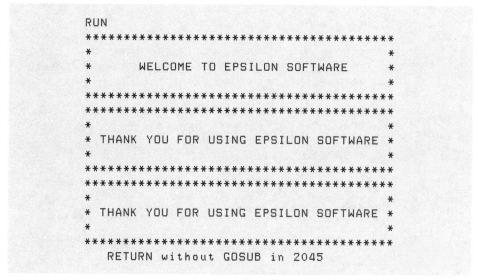

**FIGURE 10.2** Subroutine Error, Missing STOP statement in Program 10.4

As we said earlier, the second application of subroutines is to aid in the writing of large computer programs. For example, if we are writing a payroll program, we could write one subroutine to determine FICA taxes; others to determine federal, state, and city income taxes; another to determine insurance deductions; and so forth. Each of the subroutines can be written independently of the main program and checked individually. In this case, the main program would consist primarily of a series of GOSUB statements. This type of programming is part of structured programming.

Case 10.1 provides an illustration of this application of subroutines.

## CASE 10.1

**Problem**

**Processing Tasks Using Subroutines**

The Luce Candy Company of New York City sells products at a discount, depending on the amount purchased, and collects sales tax based on the location of the purchaser, as given in the following tables. (The location code is explained under Data Input.)

**DISCOUNT PERCENTAGES**

| Amount of Order | Discount |
|---|---|
| Less than $100 | 0 |
| From $100 to $499 | 5% |
| More than $499 | 10% |

**SALES TAX PERCENTAGES**

| Location of Purchaser | Location Code | Sales Tax |
|---|---|---|
| New York City | 1 | 8% |
| New York State | 2 | 4% |
| Out of state | 3 | 0% |

A program is to be written and run that uses the above information to determine the discounts taken, sales tax, and net amount after discounts and taxes are deducted and to total the amount, discount, sales tax, and net amount columns.

**Data Input**    The data consists of a customer account I.D. number, a location code (1 = city, 2 = state, 3 = out of state), and the amount of the order. A data line looks like this:

180 DATA 632,3,512,314,2,480,711,1,400,342,2,65,759,1,550

**Process/Formulas** A repetitive process is to be used. The discount, sales tax, and total computations will be carried out in separate subroutines. Decision testing is required to determine discounts and the sales tax to be taken. The program terminates as a result of an end of data test.

**Output**    The output should look like the table below:

| I.D. | AMOUNT | DISCOUNT | SALES TAX | NET AMOUNT |
|------|--------|----------|-----------|------------|
| 632 | $   512.00 | $ 51.20 | $  0.00 | $   460.80 |
| 314 | $   480.00 | $ 24.00 | $18.24 | $   474.24 |
| 711 | $   400.00 | $ 20.00 | $30.40 | $   410.40 |
| 342 | $    65.00 | $  0.00 | $ 2.60 | $    67.60 |
| 759 | $   550.00 | $ 55.00 | $39.60 | $   534.60 |
| TOTALS | $2,007.00 | $150.20 | $90.84 | $1,947.64 |

Program 10.5 reads (line 120) the customer's account I.D. number, location code (1 = city, 2 = state, 3 = out of state), and the amount of the order, and then prints a table showing the customer's account I.D., amount of order, discount, sales tax, and net amount. It also prints on a separate line at the bottom the total amount ordered, total discount, total sales tax, and total net amount. There are separate subroutines to calculate the discount, to calculate the tax, and to accumulate the totals.

Note that the use of subroutines improves program clarity and avoids unnecessary branching. These features are part of structured programming.

## PROGRAM 10.5    Case 10.1, Structured Program Using Subroutines

```
10 REM CASE 10.1, STRUCTURED PROGRAM USING SUBROUTINES
15 REM   PROGRAMMER- (name of person)   DATE - mm/dd/yy
20 REM      VARIABLE LIST-A,A1,C,D,D1,M,N,N1,T,T1
25 REM       A=AMOUNT OF ORDER
30 REM       A1=TOTAL AMOUNT
35 REM       C=INTEGER FOR IDENTIFYING LOCATION OF PURCHASER
40 REM       D=DISCOUNT
45 REM       D1=TOTAL DISCOUNT
50 REM       M=ACCOUNT I.D. NUMBER
55 REM       N=NET AMOUNT
60 REM       N1=TOTAL NET AMOUNT
62 REM       T=SALES TAX
65 REM       T1=TOTAL SALES TAX
70 REM -------------------------------------------------------------
75 LET A$= "  I.D.      AMOUNT    DISCOUNT    SALES TAX    NET AMOUNT"
```

```
80 LET B$= "  ###      $#,###.##      $###.##      $##.##      $#,###.##"
85 LET C$= "TOTALS    $#,###.##      $###.##      $##.##      $#,###.##"
87 LET D$= "--------------------------------------------------------------"
90 PRINT A$
95 PRINT D$
100 REM INITIALIZATION OF VARIABLES FOR TOTALS
105 READ A1, D1, T1, N1
110 DATA 0, 0, 0, 0
115 REM **** MAIN ROUTINE ****
120 READ M,C,A
125     IF M = -999 THEN 165       'end of DATA test
130         GOSUB 200              'determine discount
135         GOSUB 225              'determine sales tax
140         LET N=A-D+T
145         GOSUB 265              'accumulate totals
150         PRINT USING B$;M,A,D,T,N
155 GOTO 120
160 REM **********************
165 PRINT D$
170 PRINT USING C$;A1,D1,T1,N1
175 GOTO 305                       'go to the END
180 DATA 632,3,512,314,2,480,711,1,400
185 DATA 342,2,65,759,1,550
190 DATA -999,0,0
195 REM ****  SUBROUTINE TO DETERMINE DISCOUNT  ****
200     IF A<100 THEN LET D = 0
205     IF A>= 100 AND A<500 THEN LET D = .05 * A
210     IF A>= 500 THEN LET D=.1*A
215         RETURN
220 REM ****  SUBROUTINE TO DETERMINE SALES TAX  ****
225     ON C GOTO 250, 240, 230
230             LET T=0
235         RETURN
240             LET T =.04*(A-D)
245         RETURN
250             LET T =.08*(A-D)
255         RETURN
260 REM ****  SUBROUTINE TO ACCUMULATE TOTALS  ****
265         LET D1=D1+D
270         LET A1=A1+A
275         LET T1=T1+T
280         LET N1=N1+N
285         RETURN
305 END
```

```
RUN
 I.D.     AMOUNT    DISCOUNT    SALES TAX    NET AMOUNT
--------------------------------------------------------
 632   $   512.00   $ 51.20     $ 0.00      $   460.80
 314   $   480.00   $ 24.00     $18.24      $   474.24
 711   $   400.00   $ 20.00     $30.40      $   410.40
 342   $    65.00   $  0.00     $ 2.60      $    67.60
 759   $   550.00   $ 55.00     $39.60      $   534.60
--------------------------------------------------------
TOTALS  $2,007.00   $150.20     $90.84      $1,947.64
```

## NESTED SUBROUTINES

It is possible for one subroutine to cause the computer to branch to another subroutine. This is illustrated by Program 10.6.

## PROGRAM 10.6    Nested Subroutines

```
10 READ A, B, C, D
15 DATA 3, 4, 0, 0
17 PRINT " A"," B"," C"," D"
18    PRINT A,B,C,D
20 GOSUB 100
25      PRINT A,B,C,D
30 GOSUB 200
35      PRINT A,B,C,D
40 GOTO 300
100    LET C=A+B
105    GOSUB 200
107    LET C=C-1
110    RETURN
200       LET D=D+1
205        RETURN
300 END
RUN
 A              B              C              D
 3              4              0              0
 3              4              6              1
 3              4              6              2
```

The statements in Program 10.6 are executed in the following sequence:

10, 15, 17, 18, 20, 100, 105, 200, 205, 107, 110, 25, 30, 200, 205, 35, 40, 300

Note that the RETURN in 205 transfers back first to 107 and then to 25. As before, the RETURN always transfers back to the statement following the most recently executed GOSUB statement. That is, each GOSUB statement that is executed puts into that special memory location (actually, an array) the line number of the following statement. If a second GOSUB is encountered before a RETURN statement, the line number of the statement following the second GOSUB statement is also put into that array. Then, when a RETURN is encountered, the last line number to be put into the array is the one to which control is transferred; in other words, the last-in, first-out principle.

## THE ON ERROR GOTO STATEMENT

If an error occurs during the execution of a program, the program stops and an error message appears on the screen. For example, if the program attempts to print something using the printer and the printer is *not* turned on, an error message will appear on the screen as it does in Program 10.7.

## PROGRAM 10.7   Error Message

```
5 REM PRINTER NOT READY ERROR MESSAGE
10 LPRINT "THIS IS A TEST"
20 STOP
200 END

RUN
Device Fault in 10  ◄──────────── screen message with printer turned off

RUN
THIS IS A TEST      ◄──────────── printer message with printer turned on
```

Once the error has occurred, the program stops and cannot be continued. The ON ERROR GOTO statement allows the programmer to report the error to the user and to suggest the appropriate corrective action. This statement and appropriate error numbers, along with the RESUME statement, enable us to build into a program an ''error trap'' that will then allow the program to continue where it left off.

The form of the ON ERROR GOTO statement is

line #1 ON ERROR GOTO line #2

This ON ERROR GOTO statement should be near the beginning of the program so that it can trap all of the errors that may occur. A statement such as

10 ON ERROR GOTO 200

instructs the computer to transfer to line 200 when an error occurs. At line 200 the program will have an appropriate statement or statements to examine the error condition and instruct the user on what action is to be taken next. To carry out this examination of the error condition, the programmer, in anticipation of such an error, builds into the program a trap using the various error numbers that are described next.

## ERROR NUMBERS

Whenever an error occurs, BASIC gives values to the variables ERR and ERL. ERR is a numeric variable that contains a reference to the *type of error* that has occurred. Table 10.1 contains all of these error numbers and what they represent.

Note that error 25, device fault, occurs in Program 10.7. The message may not mean much to the person using the program. However, the ON ERROR GOTO statement transferring in the program to an appropriate logical IF test allows the programmer to test for the type of error that has occurred and advises the user on how to proceed.

ERL is a numeric variable that contains the *line number* where the error has occurred. Used in conjunction with the ERR variable, the programmer can determine, in many cases, the exact cause and location of the error and the necessary corrective action.

A typical IF test for the kind of device fault error mentioned above might be

100 IF ERR = 25 AND ERL = 10 THEN PRINT ''PLEASE TURN ON THE PRINTER''

**TABLE 10.1**  Error Numbers and Messages

| ERR | MESSAGE | ERR | MESSAGE |
|---|---|---|---|
| 1 | NEXT without FOR | 25 | Device fault |
| 2 | Syntax error | 26 | FOR without NEXT |
| 3 | RETURN without GOSUB | 27 | Out of paper |
| 4 | Out of data | 29 | WHILE without WEND |
| 5 | Illegal function call | 30 | WEND without WHILE |
| 6 | Overflow | 50 | FIELD overflow |
| 7 | Out of memory | 51 | Internal error |
| 8 | Undefined line number | 52 | Bad file number |
| 9 | Subscript out of range | 53 | File not found |
| 10 | Duplicate definition | 54 | Bad file mode |
| 11 | Division by zero | 55 | File already open |
| 12 | Illegal direct | 57 | Device I/O error |
| 13 | Type mismatch | 58 | File already exists |
| 14 | Out of string space | 61 | Disk full |
| 15 | String too long | 63 | Bad record number |
| 16 | String formula too complex | 64 | Bad file name |
| 17 | Can't continue | 66 | Direct statement in file |
| 18 | No RESUME | 67 | Too many files |
| 19 | RESUME without error | 68 | Device unavailable |
| 22 | Missing operand | 69 | Communications buffer overflow |
| 23 | Line buffer overflow | 70 | Disk write protect |
| 24 | Device timeout | | |

The RESUME statement then allows the program to continue after corrective action has been taken.

## THE RESUME STATEMENT

The RESUME statement has the following forms:

    line # RESUME
    line # RESUME NEXT
    line # RESUME line #

In the first case, RESUME will continue execution beginning with the line # that caused the error. In the second, RESUME NEXT will continue with the line immediately following the line that caused the error. In the third, RESUME line # will continue with the specified line number.

## ERROR TRAPPING

Program 10.8 takes Program 10.7 and incorporates the ideas discussed above to build into the program an error trapping segment using an ON ERROR GOTO, IF ERR AND ERL, and RESUME statements.

## PROGRAM 10.8   ERROR TRAPPING

```
2 ON ERROR GOTO 100        'go to trap if printer NOT on
10 LPRINT "THIS IS A TEST"  'print message if printer IS on
20 STOP
100 IF ERR=25 AND ERL=10 THEN PRINT "PLEASE TURN ON THE PRINTER"
110 PRINT "PRESS ENTER TO CONTINUE"
120 INPUT A$
130 RESUME
200 END

RUN
PLEASE TURN ON THE PRINTER  ◄——————— with printer turned off
PRESS ENTER TO CONTINUE     ◄——————— printer turned on and Enter key is depressed
Break in 20

RUN
THIS IS A TEST              ◄——————— is printed on the printer
Break in 20
```

The ON ERROR GOTO 100 in line 2 will transfer control to line 100 as soon as any error is detected. In line 100, a logical IF/THEN test is performed to determine if the error is number 25 (device fault) and also if the error has occurred in line 10. When the program was run, the printer was deliberately turned off so the program could *not* perform the LPRINT "THIS IS A TEST" statement in line 10, and an error condition was sensed. The ON ERROR GOTO statement in line 2 then instructed the computer to perform the test in line 100. Since the IF/THEN clauses were both true, the program executed the statement

PRINT "PLEASE TURN ON THE PRINTER"

"PRESS ENTER TO CONTINUE" is the instruction given the operator in line 110. Line 120 pauses the program by assigning a blank character that is typed to the dummy variable A$. As soon as ENTER is typed, the RESUME in line 130 continues the execution of the program with line 10. (A 130 RESUME 10 would have accomplished the same result.)

After the printer was turned on and Enter was depressed, the program printed "This is a test" on the printer and then proceeded to line 20 where the program stopped.

Several error tests may be performed back to back. For example, we may add the following line to Program 10.8 to also test if the printer is out of paper.

102 IF ERR = 27 AND ERL = 10 THEN PRINT "PUT PAPER IN PRINTER"

Then, if the printer is turned on but it is out of paper, an appropriate correction will be suggested to the operator.

SUMMARY

The GOSUB and RETURN statements are used to write subroutines. A subroutine is useful when you have a series of statements that are to be executed more than once in a program (not in a loop) or when a very large program is being written and it is desired to write and test the different parts of the program independently.

The ON ERROR GOTO statement allows error trapping in a program. This statement, when combined with the ERR error numbers and ERL error line, allows for an error test in a program to suggest corrective action.

The RESUME statement allows the program to continue after the error test corrective action has taken place.

## BASIC VOCABULARY SUMMARY

| Statement | Purpose | Examples |
| --- | --- | --- |
| GOSUB | Transfers control to a subroutine. | 60 GOSUB 400 |
| RETURN | Causes the transfer of control back to the line following the GOSUB. | 500 RETURN |
| ON ERROR GOTO | Performs an error test, and transfers to a specified line. | 10 ON ERROR GOTO 250 |
| RESUME | Causes a program to continue after an error has been detected. | 130 RESUME<br>140 RESUME NEXT<br>150 RESUME 20 |

## EXERCISES

### Review Questions

**10.1**  What will the following program print when it is run?

```
10 READ N
15 DATA 5
20 GOSUB 40
25     PRINT N,X,Y
30 GOSUB 70
35 STOP
40 REM-SUBROUTINE A
45     LET X=N^2
50     GOSUB 70
55     LET Y=X/Z
60     LET X=X+2
65     RETURN
70 REM-SUBROUTINE B
75        LET Z=X*N
80        PRINT N,X,Z
85        RETURN
90 END
```

**10.2** What is the error message for each of these error codes?

a. 1          d. 13
b. 2          e. 22
c. 3          f. 26

Illustrate each error with an example.

**10.3** Compare the purpose of the STOP, CONT, and RESUME statements.

**10.4** Revise Program 10.8 shown below to include an error trap for the printer's being out of paper.

```
2 ON ERROR GOTO 100       'go to trap if printer NOT on
10 LPRINT "THIS IS A TEST"  'print message if printer IS on
20 STOP
100 IF ERR=25 AND ERL=10 THEN PRINT "PLEASE TURN ON THE PRINTER"
110 PRINT "PRESS ANY KEY TO CONTINUE"
120 INPUT A$
130 RESUME
200 END
```

## Programming Activities

**10.5** **Purpose** To use the DOUNTIL loop repetition logic structure to process numeric data values and string items, to find row totals using the LET statement as an accumulator, and to use a subroutine to print out table lines.

**Problem** The following table shows the first four months of sales data for each division of the ABC Company. Sales are in thousands of dollars.

| DIVISION | JANUARY | FEBRUARY | MARCH | APRIL |
|----------|---------|----------|-------|-------|
| WEST     | $1,000  | $ 750    | $ 750 | $900  |
| SOUTH    | 1,200   | 800      | 1,000 | 850   |
| NORTH    | 1,200   | 500      | 1,200 | 950   |
| EAST     | 1,500   | 1,050    | 950   | 900   |

Write and run a program that derives the total sales for each division.

**Data** Use the data values shown in the table above.

**Output** Your output should look like the table below. Make use of a subroutine to produce the dashed lines in the output.

```
------------------------------------------------------------------------------
DIVISION        JAN.        FEB.        MAR.        APRIL       TOTAL
------------------------------------------------------------------------------
WEST            $1,000      $   750     $   750     $   900     $3,400
------------------------------------------------------------------------------
SOUTH           $1,200      $   800     $1,000      $   850     $3,850
------------------------------------------------------------------------------
NORTH           $1,200      $   500     $1,200      $   950     $3,850
------------------------------------------------------------------------------
EAST            $1,500      $1,050      $   950     $   900     $4,400
------------------------------------------------------------------------------
```

**10.6** **Purpose** To use the subroutine logic structure to process numeric data values and to enter data interactively using the INPUT statement.

**Problem** To compute the monthly payment necessary to amortize (pay off) a loan given the principal amount $P$, the yearly interest rate $Y$, and the term of the loan in $N$ years, using the formula given below:

$$A = \frac{P \times R(1 + R)^M}{(1 + R)^M - 1}$$

$$R = \frac{Y}{12}$$

$$M = 12N$$

where $A$ is the monthly amount, $P$ is the principal amount, $R$ is the monthly interest rate, $M$ is the number of months over which the payments are to be made, $Y$ is the annual interest rate, and $N$ is the term of the loan in years.

Write and run a program to find the monthly payment for the data below. Design your program to include three subroutines: one for data entry, one for computations, and one for output. Provide the user with a conversational ("YES" or "NO") continuation option as shown in the output below.

**Data** Use these data values:

| P | Y | N |
|---|---|---|
| $100,000 | 11% | 15 years |
| $ 50,000 | 10% | 30 years |

Remember that data entry should be interactive.

**Output** Your output should look like the results below:

```
ENTER THE LOAN AMOUNT, INTEREST RATE, AND YEARS: 100000, .11, 15
    AMOUNT       RATE   YEARS      PAYMENT
$100,000.00      0.11    15      $1,136.60

DO YOU WISH TO CONTINUE: ENTER Y= YES OR N= NO? Y
ENTER THE LOAN AMOUNT, INTEREST RATE, AND YEARS: 50000, .10, 30

    AMOUNT       RATE   YEARS      PAYMENT
$ 50,000.00      0.10    30      $438.79

DO YOU WISH TO CONTINUE: ENTER Y= YES OR N= NO? N
```

**10.7** **Purpose** To use error trapping with the ON ERROR GOTO statement and the ERR variable and to use the DOWHILE loop repetition logic structure to process numeric data values and string items.

**Problem** Write and run a program that reads in the data below. The program will print out the data as shown in the output below. Use a GOTO-READ loop logic. Provide for error trapping for the out of data condition so that the program can resume processing with a message that states "All of the data has been processed."

**Data**   Use the data values shown in the table below:

| DIVISION | JANUARY | FEBRUARY |
|----------|---------|----------|
| WEST | $1,000 | $  750 |
| SOUTH | 1,200 | 800 |
| NORTH | 1,200 | 500 |
| EAST | 1,500 | 1,050 |

**Output**   Your output should have this format:

```
DIVISION            JANUARY          FEBRUARY
---------------------------------

   WEST             $1,000          $   750
   SOUTH            $1,200          $   800
   NORTH            $1,200          $   500
   EAST             $1,500          $1,050
---------------------------------

All of the data has been processed
```

# CHAPTER

## 11

## LOOPING

Upon completing this chapter, you will be able to do the following:

* Carry out repetitive operations using the FOR/NEXT statement.
* Create a FOR/NEXT loop structure in a problem solution program.
* Understand how nested FOR/NEXT loops are structured.
* Explain how nested FOR/NEXT loops operate.
* Create a nested FOR/NEXT loop structure in a problem solution program.

In Chapter 8 we saw how a GOTO loop sequence can be controlled to repeat a process a number of times under conditions specified by the IF/THEN statement. In this chapter we examine a simpler way to perform an operation or several operations a specified number of times. Specifically, we illustrate how repetitive operations using the FOR/NEXT statements can be carried out using simple looping structures and nested looping structures.

## THE FOR/NEXT STATEMENTS

The generalized form of the FOR statement is

$$\text{line \# FOR (variable)} = \left\{ \begin{array}{l} \text{constant} \\ \text{variable} \\ \text{expression} \end{array} \right\} \text{TO} \left\{ \begin{array}{l} \text{constant} \\ \text{variable} \\ \text{expression} \end{array} \right\} \text{STEP} \left\{ \begin{array}{l} \text{constant} \\ \text{variable} \\ \text{expression} \end{array} \right\}$$

The word FOR must be followed by some variable. This variable will be initialized to the value on the right of the equal sign ( = ). The previous value of the variable, if any, will be lost.

A constant, variable, or expression must follow the equal sign ( = ) and then the word TO. The variable, as well as any variables in the expressions, must have been previously given values. The STEP part of the statement is optional. If not included, the FOR variable will automatically increase by 1. The addition of a STEP makes it possible to change this increment to fractional (decimal) values, integers other than one, or negative values. A negative STEP is only used when the starting value of the loop is greater than the ending value.

The form of the NEXT statement is

line # NEXT variable

For each FOR statement in a program there should exist *one and only one* NEXT statement using the same variable designation. The NEXT statement serves to give the loop structure a physical lower boundary.

The FOR statement can also be viewed as having a counter, a starting value, an ending value, and an optional increment.

line # FOR loop variable-counter = starting value TO ending value STEP incremental value

If the value of the counter is greater than or equal to the ending value, program execution continues with the statement following the NEXT statement.

To introduce the FOR/NEXT statements, Program 11.1 was written to print the numbers 1 through 10, using a GOTO loop structure and an IF/THEN statement.

## PROGRAM 11.1    Printing the Numbers 1 through 10 Using IF/THEN

```
10 LET N=1
15 PRINT N;
20    LET N=N+1
25    IF N>10 THEN 35
30 GOTO 15
35 END

RUN
 1  2  3  4  5  6  7  8  9  10
```

Program 11.2 is a revision of Program 11.1. It uses the FOR/NEXT statements.

## PROGRAM 11.2    Printing the Numbers 1 through 10 Using FOR/NEXT

```
10 FOR N= 1 TO 10
15    PRINT N;
20 NEXT N
25 END

RUN
 1  2  3  4  5  6  7  8  9  10
```

The FOR statement in line 10 initializes the variable $N$ to 1. Line 15 then prints the number 1. The NEXT statement in line 20 increases $N$ by 1 and tests whether $N$ is greater than 10. If $N$ is less than or equal to 10, as in the case of this program, execution will continue with the line following the FOR statement. Thus, the number 2 will be printed by line 15. This will continue until the variable $N$ is finally greater than 10, at which time execution will continue with the statement following the NEXT statement, which in this case is the END statement.

Suppose we wished to have the computer print all the odd numbers between 1 and 10. One way to accomplish this is to alter Program 11.1 by replacing line 20 with

20 LET N = N + 2

That is, the variable $N$ is increased by 2 rather than by 1. This change can also be accomplished with the FOR/NEXT statements by replacing line 10 in Program 11.2 with

10 FOR N = 1 TO 10 STEP 2

in Program 11.3. That is, if we wish the index variable $N$ to be changed by any number other than the number 1, we can add the word STEP at the end of the FOR statement and specify by how much we would like the index variable to be changed. Note that Program 11.2 would stop printing with the number 10, while Program 11.3 would stop printing with the number 9. The difference in logic is that Program 11.2 increases $N$ by 1, prints $N$, and then tests $N$ to see if it is greater than 10; Program 11.3 increases $N$ by 2.

## PROGRAM 11.3   Printing Odd Numbers from 1 to 10 Using FOR/NEXT and STEP

```
10 FOR N = 1 TO 10 STEP 2
15     PRINT N;
20 NEXT N
25 END

RUN
 1   3   5   7   9
```

Several examples of FOR/NEXT statements are shown in Table 11.1.

**TABLE 11.1**   FOR/NEXT Statements

| STATEMENT | EXPLANATION |
|---|---|
| 15 FOR N = 1 TO 10 <br> · · · <br> 50 NEXT N | Repeat the statements between lines 15 and 50 ten times. Let *N* start at 1 and increase by 1 until it reaches 10. When *N* is greater than 10, processing continues to the statement following line 50. |
| 20 FOR N = 1 TO 10 STEP 2 <br> · · · <br> 60 NEXT N | Repeat the statements between lines 20 and 60 as long as the index variable *N* is less than or equal to 10. Let *N* start at 1 and increase by 2 (that is 1,3,5,7,9) toward 10. If *N* is greater than 10, processing continues to the statement following line 60. |
| 75 FOR KT = 20 TO M STEP .5 <br> · · · <br> 150 NEXT KT | Repeat the statements between lines 75 and 150 until the variable *KT* exceeds *M*. Let *KT* start at 20 and increase to *M* by .5. When *KT* is greater than *M*, processing continues with the statement following line 150. The value of *M* must be greater than 20 and must have been assigned prior to line 75. |
| 100 FOR V = B1 TO E1 STEP U <br> · · · <br> 180 NEXT V | Repeat the statements between lines 100 and 180. The loop starts at *B*1 and continues until the variable *V* is greater than the upper limit *E*1. When *V* is greater than *E*1, processing continues with the statement following line 180. All values of *B*1, *E*1, and *V* must have been assigned prior to line 100. *V* is increased by *U* each time the loop is executed until the value of *E*1 is exceeded. |
| 200 FOR E = A+B TO C+5 STEP D*2 <br> · · · <br> 270 NEXT E | Repeat the statements between lines 200 and 270. The loop starts at *A+B* and continues until the variable *E* is greater than the upper limit *C+5*, at which time processing continues to the statement following line 270. All values of *A*, *B*, *C*, and *D* must have been assigned prior to line 200. *E* is increased by *D*\*2 each time the loop is executed until the value of *C+5* is exceeded. |
| 310 FOR P = 100 TO 50 STEP −5 <br> · · · <br> 380 NEXT P | Repeat the statements between lines 310 and 380. The loop initializes variable *P* at 100 and continues to decrease *P* by the STEP decrement −5. The loop ends when the value of *P* goes below the lower limit of 50, at which time processing continues with the statement following line 380. |

We will now rewrite Program 8.5 (shown below) by using the FOR/NEXT statements eliminating the counter, IF/THEN, and GOTO statements. Note that the output in Program 11.4 is identical to that of Program 8.5.

```
10 REM THIS PROGRAM READS 5 NUMBERS FROM THE DATA STATEMENT
20 REM AND PRINTS THE NUMBERS, THE SQUARES OF THE NUMBERS,
30 REM AND THE SUMS OF THE NUMBERS AND THEIR SQUARES.
40 LET S=0
45 LET S2=0
50 LET N=1
55 READ X
60      LET S=S+X
65      LET S2=S2+X^2
70      PRINT X,X^2
75      IF N=5 THEN 90
80          LET N=N+1
85 GOTO 55
90 PRINT "---", "---"
95 PRINT S,S2
100 DATA 7,3,5,6,1
999 END

RUN
 7              49
 3               9
 5              25
 6              36
 1               1
---            ---
 22            120
```

**PROGRAM 11.4   Rewriting Program 8.5 Using the FOR/NEXT Statements**

```
10 REM THIS PROGRAM READS 5 NUMBERS FROM THE DATA STATEMENT
20 REM AND PRINTS THE NUMBERS, THE SQUARES OF NUMBERS,
30 REM AND THE SUMS OF THE NUMBERS AND THEIR SQUARES.
40 LET S=0
45 LET S2=0
50 FOR N = 1 TO 5
55      READ X
```

```
60      LET S=S+X
65      LET S2=S2+X^2
70      PRINT X,X^2
75 NEXT N
90 PRINT "---", "---"
95 PRINT S,S2
100 DATA 7,3,5,6,1
999 END

RUN
  7                  49
  3                   9
  5                  25
  6                  36
  1                   1
 ---                 ---
 22                 120
```

## The DOUNTIL Structure

The FOR/NEXT loop structure in Microsoft BASIC follows a DOUNTIL structure. A DOUNTIL structure, as with the FOR/NEXT loop examples described above, is shown in Figure 11.1. In a DOUNTIL structure, a test is performed *after* a statement is processed. This is shown in Program A of Figure 11.1. The FOR/NEXT in Program B functions in a similar way. The loop variable serves as a counter. If $N$ is greater than the upper limit of the FOR statement, processing continues with the statement following the NEXT. As long as $N$ is equal to or less than 10, the loop will continue to print $N$. The statements within a FOR/NEXT loop will be repeated until the test condition is true as shown in the flowchart in Figure 11.2 (p. 272).

## A FOR/NEXT Caution

Because the FOR/NEXT loop has a decision test at the end of the loop, the counter loop variable will have increased beyond the upper limit of the FOR statement when processing continues after the NEXT statement. This means that the final value of the loop variable is not necessarily the upper limit, and, if used in a later part of your program, the final results could be incorrect. Look at Program 11.5. The values for the loop variable $N$ go from 1 to 10 and are correctly printed as such. You might assume that the final value for $N$ that is stored by the computer is 10. Later in your program you might wish to use this value of $N$ believing it to be equal to 10. In fact, the final value for $N$ is *not* 10, but 11! Look at the output of the program. As described above, the loop-variable counter is greater than the upper FOR limit when the loop process is over. Depending on the STEP option, the exit value for the loop variable is generally an additional increment of 1. Be careful with the final value of the loop variable when writing your programs and performing computations.

**PROGRAM A**

```
5    REM DOUNTIL STRUCTURE
10   LET N=1
30   PRINT N;
40      LET N=N+1
45          IF N>10 THEN 60
50   GOTO 30
60   END

RUN
 1   2   3   4   5   6   7   8   9   10
```

**PROGRAM B**

```
5    REM DOUNTIL STRUCTURE
10   FOR N= 1 TO 10
15       PRINT N;
20   NEXT N
25   END

RUN
 1   2   3   4   5   6   7   8   9   10
```

**FIGURE 11.1**   DOUNTIL Structure

## PROGRAM 11.5   FOR/NEXT Caution, Last Value for Loop Variable

```
5   REM ** CAUTION ON THE LAST LOOP VALUE **
10  FOR N= 1 TO 10
15      PRINT N;
20  NEXT N
22  PRINT
23  PRINT N    'N value outside the loop is 10 + 1 or 11
25  END

RUN
 1  2  3  4  5  6  7  8  9  10
 11
```

### Program Appearance and Indentation

In chapter 8 we pointed out that by indenting the contents of a GOTO loop, we improve the clarity of the program listing (see Figure 8.5). All the programs in this chapter show indentation of the contents of a FOR/NEXT loop. For example, if you examine

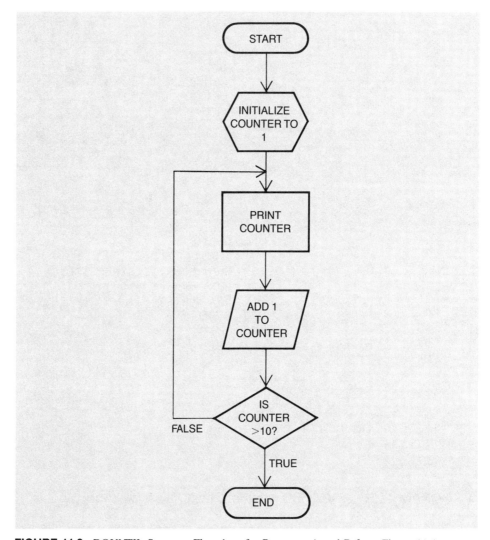

**FIGURE 11.2** DOUNTIL Structure Flowchart for Programs A and B from Figure 11.1

Programs 11.2–11.5 you will find that the contents of a loop are indented several spaces to produce a block of white space that clearly shows the FOR/NEXT statements.

Throughout the remainder of this chapter, and in the remaining chapters of the book, we indent statements following the illustrations of Chapters 8–11.

The FOR/NEXT statements permit a process to be repeated as many times as specified in the FOR statement. In Case 11.1, three different sets of data are processed within a single program using the FOR and NEXT statements.

## CASE 11.1

**Problem**

**Fast-Food Chain Sales Analysis**
A fast-food chain has three geographic regions each with a different number of stores in it. A program provides a monthly sales report by calculating the total sales per region and the average amount of sales per region.

**Data Input**  The data to be processed by the program consists of a data list for each region. Each data list has an end of data value of $-99$. Last month's sales for each region were:

| REGION | STORE SALES (IN THOUSANDS OF $) | | | | | |
|--------|------|------|------|------|------|------|
| 1 | 40 | 20 | 50 | 60 | | |
| 2 | 50 | 40 | 55 | 35 | 70 | 65 |
| 3 | 35 | 46 | 25 | | | |

**Process/Formulas**  A repetitive FOR/NEXT loop process is to be used so that the sales data for each store in each region is totaled by region. The average sales are derived by dividing the total sales for a region by the number of stores in the region.

**Output**  Using the format shown below, the output will show for each region the sales for each store, the total, and the average sales.

```
REGION #  ##  ## , , , ##  TOTAL ###  AVERAGE ##.##
```

Program 11.6 produces the results desired. The FOR/NEXT loop (lines 30–150) is set to repeat the accumulation processes for each set of data. Each DATA statement ends with a $-99$ value to trigger the IF/THEN in line 80, which transfers control to line 130. When the third DATA statement is completed, the program execution ends. Note that there is no ''Out of data'' message because the program's logic ensures that, after all the data has been read, control will pass to line 150 and then finally to line 190. The flowchart in Figure 11.3 diagrams the logic of Program 11.6.

## PROGRAM 11.6   Case 11.1, Sales Analysis, FOR/NEXT Statement

```
10 REM CASE 11.1, ANALYZING FAST-FOOD CHAIN SALES
15 REM PROGRAMMER- (name of person) DATE mm/dd/yy
16 REM     VARIABLE LIST-
17 REM          A=STORE SALES
18 REM          AVE = AVERAGE,T/C
19 REM          C=COUNTS THE # OF STORES BY REGION
22 REM          I=REGION #
23 REM          T=TOTAL SALES FOR EACH REGION
25 REM -------------------------------------------
30 FOR I = 1 TO 3
40     LET C = 0
50     LET T = 0
60     PRINT "REGION";I;
70     READ A
80         IF A= -99 THEN 130  'test for the end of each DATA list
90             LET C = C+1      'count the items
100            LET T = T+A      'accumulate A values
110            PRINT A;
120    GOTO 70
130        LET AVE = T/C               'calculate the average
132        PRINT TAB(35);
135        PRINT USING "TOTAL ###   AVERAGE ##.##"; T,AVE
150 NEXT I
```

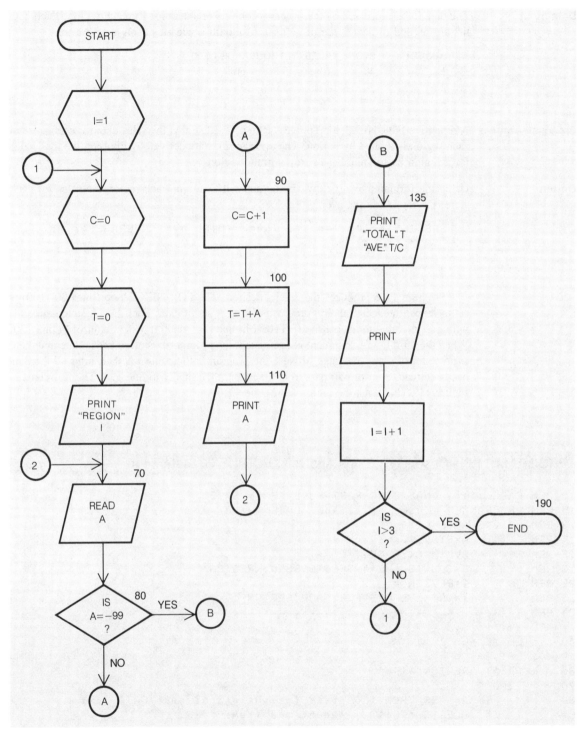

**FIGURE 11.3** Flowchart for Program 11.6, Case 11.1, Fast-Food Chain Sales Analysis

```
160 DATA 40,20,50,60,-99
170 DATA 50,40,55,35,70,65,-99
180 DATA 35,46,25,-99
190 END

RUN
REGION 1  40  20  50  60            TOTAL 170  AVERAGE 42,50
REGION 2  50  40  55  35  70  65  TOTAL 315  AVERAGE 52,50
REGION 3  35  46  25                TOTAL 106  AVERAGE 35,33
```

Another illustration of the FOR/NEXT statements is found in Program 11.7, which is based on Case 11.2. This case describes a situation in which the FOR/NEXT loop should never be completed.

. . . . . . . . . . . . . . . . . . . . . . . . . . . . . . . . . . . . . . . .

## CASE 11.2

**Problem**          **Inventory Search**
In order to obtain the current inventory level for 1 of 10 products, an interactive and conversational program is used. This program will search data lists that contain product numbers and current inventory amounts and match the inputted product number to the product number in the program data lists.

**Data Input**       Suppose we have 10 product numbers, each followed in a DATA statement by the amount of that product in inventory. A salesperson will input a product number, and we want the computer to print the amount of that product in inventory. If the salesperson inputs an incorrect product number (that is, one that is not listed in the DATA statements), he or she will be informed of this and allowed to try again. When the salesperson has completed asking questions, he or she can type in zero (0) for the product number, signaling the computer that data entry is completed.

**Process/Formulas** A repetitive FOR/NEXT loop process is to be used. Decision testing is required to determine if a product number is in a data list. To terminate the program, the user types a zero (0) in response to an INPUT query.

**Output**           Output follows this format:

```
WHAT IS THE PRODUCT NUMBER (TYPE 0 TO END)? 3311
  THE AMOUNT OF PRODUCT 3311 IN INVENTORY IS 500

WHAT IS THE PRODUCT NUMBER (TYPE 0 TO END)? 1122
: NO SUCH PRODUCT NUMBER AS 1122 TRY AGAIN :
```

. . . . . . . . . . . . . . . . . . . . . . . . . . . . . . . . . . . . . . . .

## PROGRAM 11.7   Case 11.2, Inventory Search, FOR/NEXT Statements

```
10 REM CASE 11,2, INVENTORY SEARCH
12 REM PROGRAMMER- (name of person)  DATE- mm/dd/yy
14 REM    VARIABLE LIST-
16 REM        A=AMOUNT OF INVENTORY
```

```
18 REM        F1$,F2$=PRINT USING FORMATS
20 REM        N=PRODUCT NUMBER FROM KEYBOARD
22 REM        P=PRODUCT NUMBER FROM DATA LIST
24 REM -----------------------------------------------------------
30 LET F1$ = " THE AMOUNT OF PRODUCT ####  IN INVENTORY IS ####"
35 LET F2$ = ": NO SUCH PRODUCT NUMBER AS ##### TRY AGAIN : "
40 INPUT "WHAT IS THE PRODUCT NUMBER (TYPE 0 TO END)"; N
45      IF N=0 THEN END              'end of INPUT test, is N=0?
50          FOR I= 1 TO 10
55              READ P,A
60                  IF P=N THEN 85      'is INPUT number same as DATA?
65          NEXT I
70          PRINT USING F2$; N            'message when INPUT and DATA
75          PRINT                             'are not the same
80          GOTO 95
85              PRINT USING F1$; P,A       'when P = N print P and A
90              PRINT
95          RESTORE                     'start DATA list from beginning
100 GOTO 40
105 DATA 1234,100,2345,150,1345,50,1432,75,3214,25,4321,10
110 DATA 3241,250,2233,80,1144,200,3311,500
115 END

RUN
WHAT IS THE PRODUCT NUMBER (TYPE 0 TO END)? 2345
 THE AMOUNT OF PRODUCT 2345 IN INVENTORY IS 150

WHAT IS THE PRODUCT NUMBER (TYPE 0 TO END)? 3311
 THE AMOUNT OF PRODUCT 3311 IN INVENTORY IS 500

WHAT IS THE PRODUCT NUMBER (TYPE 0 TO END)? 1122
: NO SUCH PRODUCT NUMBER AS 1122 TRY AGAIN :

WHAT IS THE PRODUCT NUMBER (TYPE 0 TO END)? 2233
 THE AMOUNT OF PRODUCT 2233 IN INVENTORY IS 80

WHAT IS THE PRODUCT NUMBER (TYPE 0 TO END)? 1144
 THE AMOUNT OF PRODUCT 1144 IN INVENTORY IS 200

WHAT IS THE PRODUCT NUMBER (TYPE 0 TO END)? 3313
: NO SUCH PRODUCT NUMBER AS 3313 TRY AGAIN :

WHAT IS THE PRODUCT NUMBER (TYPE 0 TO END)? 0
```

Note that in Program 11.7 we do not wish to complete the FOR/NEXT loop 10 times. If the program does complete the loop without branching out from it, this would mean that we have not found a product number in the DATA statements that matches the one that was in the INPUT statement.

Thus we see that we can branch out of a FOR/NEXT loop. However, we should never branch into a FOR/NEXT loop from the outside. For example, if we would have a GOTO 55 on line 47 or on line 75, it would cause an error message to be printed out. We *can*

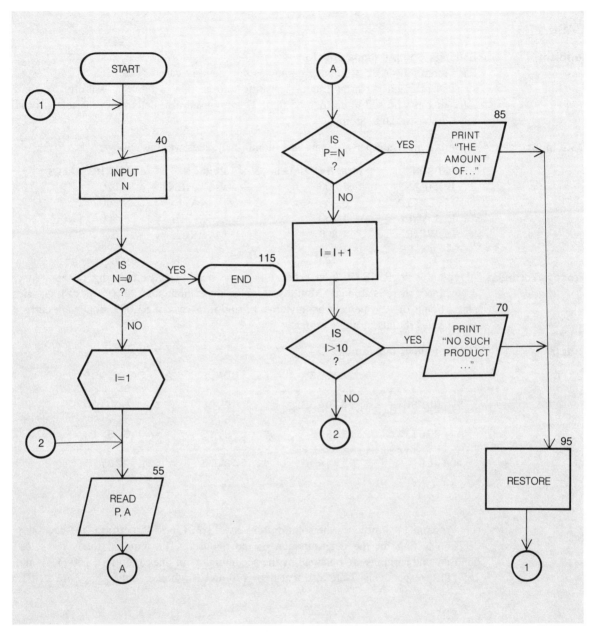

**FIGURE 11.4**   Flowchart for Program 11.7, Case 11.2, Inventory Search

branch to a statement in a FOR/NEXT loop from some other statement in the same loop without any difficulty. (See, for example, Program 11.11.)

A flowchart that helps to explain the logic of Program 11.7 for Case 11.2 is shown in Figure 11.4.

Case 11.3 offers another illustration that incorporates the FOR/NEXT loop structure. In addition to decision testing, Case 11.3 also requires that several different totals be calculated.

. . . . . . . . . . . . . . . . . . . . . . . . . . . . . . . . . . . . .

## CASE 11.3

**Problem**        **Earnings Computations and Totals**

Each month the ABC Company computes the monthly earnings of each of its salespersons. A program performs this task, taking into account a bonus possibility for those salespersons who sell more than $5,000. This program also determines the totals for all sales, bonuses, and earnings.

**Data Input**     There are nine salespersons, and last month their sales were as follows:

| PERSON | MONTHLY SALES | PERSON | MONTHLY SALES |
|---|---|---|---|
| B. GLASS | $ 4,000 | J. COHEN | $6,050 |
| M. LACEY | 6,250 | D. KAYE | 8,300 |
| E. LANE | 4,750 | S. RACHE | 3,500 |
| L. WINE | 4,800 | M. BRET | 9,625 |
| A. JONES | 7,125 | | |

**Process/Formulas** A repetitive FOR/NEXT loop process is to be used. Decision testing is required to determine if there is a bonus. Monthly earnings are computed as 20 percent of total sales plus a bonus of 12½ percent on any amount sold in excess of $5,000. Totals are derived for all sales, bonuses, and earnings.

**Output**         Output follows this format:

```
     NAME          SALES          BONUS          EARNINGS

------------------------------------------------------------
    B. GLASS       $4,000      $      0.00      $     800.00
     . . .          . . .          . . .            . . .
    M. BRET        $9,625      $    578.13      $   2,503.13
------------------------------------------------------------
    TOTALS        $54,400      $1,543.75       $12,423.75
```

. . . . . . . . . . . . . . . . . . . . . . . . . . . . . . . . . . . . .

Program 11.8 provides the solution for Case 11.3. Line 145 performs the necessary decision testing for the determination of the bonuses. The required totals for sales, bonuses, and earnings are obtained by the accumulators in lines 155 (TS), 160 (TB), and 165 (TE), respectively. Note also that lines 170 and 185 both use the same format, F$.

## PROGRAM 11.8   Case 11.3, Earnings Computations with Totals, FOR/NEXT

```
10 REM CASE 11.3, CALCULATING EARNINGS
15 REM PROGRAMMER- (name of person)  DATE- mm/dd/yy
20 REM     VARIABLE LIST-
25 REM         B=BONUS    TB=TOTAL BONUSES
30 REM         E=EARNINGS TE=TOTAL EARNINGS
35 REM         F$, F1$ = PRINT USING FORMATS
40 REM         P$=PERSON NAME
45 REM         S=MONTHLY SALES  TS=TOTAL SALES
55 REM     ----------------------------------------
100 LET TS=0
105 LET TB=0
110 LET TE=0
```

```
115 LET F$=   "  \                      \  $##,###      $#,###.##      $##,###.##"
118 LET F1$= "---------------------------------------------------------------"
120 PRINT       "    NAME              SALES          BONUS        EARNINGS"
125 PRINT F1$                                              'print dashes
130 FOR P = 1 TO 9
135     READ P$, S                                        'read name & sales
145         IF S> 5000 THEN B=.125*(S-5000) ELSE B = 0    'test for bonus
150             LET E=.2*S + B                            'earnings plus bonus
155             LET TS = TS + S                           'accumulate sales
160             LET TB = TB + B                           'accumulate bonuses
165             LET TE = TE + E                           'accumulate earnings
170                 PRINT USING F$; P$, S, B, E
175 NEXT P
180 PRINT F1$                                             'print dashes
185 PRINT USING F$; "TOTALS", TS, TB, TE
190 DATA B. GLASS,4000, M. LACEY,6250, E. LANE,4750
195 DATA L. WINE,4800, A. JONES,7125, J. COHEN,6050
200 DATA D. KAYE,8300, S. RACHE,3500, M. BRET,9625
245 END
```

```
RUN
    NAME              SALES          BONUS        EARNINGS
    ----------------------------------------------------------
    B. GLASS          $ 4,000      $     0.00    $     800.00
    M. LACEY          $ 6,250      $   156.25    $   1,406.25
    E. LANE           $ 4,750      $     0.00    $     950.00
    L. WINE           $ 4,800      $     0.00    $     960.00
    A. JONES          $ 7,125      $   265.63    $   1,690.63
    J. COHEN          $ 6,050      $   131.25    $   1,341.25
    D. KAYE           $ 8,300      $   412.50    $   2,072.50
    S. RACHE          $ 3,500      $     0.00    $     700.00
    M. BRET           $ 9,625      $   578.13    $   2,503.13
    ----------------------------------------------------------
TOTALS                $54,400      $1,543.75     $12,423.75
```

## NESTED FOR/NEXT LOOPS

A FOR/NEXT loop will repeat a process or task as given by a sequence of statements. It is possible to place a FOR/NEXT loop within another FOR/NEXT loop to create a structure called a *nested loop*. Look at Program 11.9.

## PROGRAM 11.9    Nested Loops

```
10 FOR I= 1 TO 3
15     FOR J= 1 TO 5
20         PRINT I;J,
25     NEXT J
30 NEXT I
35 END

RUN
    1   1        1   2        1   3        1   4        1   5
    2   1        2   2        2   3        2   4        2   5
    3   1        3   2        3   3        3   4        3   5
```

In this program, a nested loop situation is created by having one FOR/NEXT loop (lines 15–25) contained entirely within another FOR/NEXT loop (lines 10–30).

The inner loop (lines 15–25) is indented slightly to improve the readability of the program and to give the program a structured look.

Note that in Program 11.9 the variable *J* goes from 1 to 5 each time variable *I* assumes a value. Note also that the NEXT J statement comes *before* the NEXT I statement. This is necessary because the FOR J = 1 TO 5 statement is *after* the FOR I = 1 TO 3 statement.

The output further aids in understanding how the nested loops are working. First the outer loop FOR statement in line 10 is executed. The value of *I* = 1 is fixed. This can be seen in the first row of output. The inner loop FOR statement in line 15 is executed and varies *J* from 1 to 5, while *I* is fixed at 1. Again look at the first line of output. Line 20, the PRINT statement, generates the fixed value of the outer loop and the varying values of the inner loop. Each row of output follows a similar pattern. The row value derived from the outer loop is fixed, while the column value derived from the inner loop varies.

Nested loop operations can also be seen in Programs 11.10 and 11.11. Program 11.10 prints a 5 × 5 multiplication table.

## PROGRAM 11.10   A 5 x 5 Multiplication Table

```
10 FOR I=1 TO 5
15     FOR J=1 TO 5
20          PRINT I*J,
25     NEXT J
30 NEXT I
35 END

RUN
  1          2          3          4          5
  2          4          6          8          10
  3          6          9          12         15
  4          8          12         16         20
  5          10         15         20         25
```

Program 11.11 prints a 10 × 10 table of 0s with 1s along the major diagonal.

## PROGRAM 11.11   Branching in a FOR/NEXT Loop

```
10 FOR I=1 TO 10
15     FOR J=1 TO 10
20          LET X=0
25          IF I<>J THEN 35
30              LET X=1
35              PRINT X;
```

```
40      NEXT J
45        PRINT
50  NEXT I
55  END

RUN
  1  0  0  0  0  0  0  0  0  0
  0  1  0  0  0  0  0  0  0  0
  0  0  1  0  0  0  0  0  0  0
  0  0  0  1  0  0  0  0  0  0
  0  0  0  0  1  0  0  0  0  0
  0  0  0  0  0  1  0  0  0  0
  0  0  0  0  0  0  1  0  0  0
  0  0  0  0  0  0  0  1  0  0
  0  0  0  0  0  0  0  0  1  0
  0  0  0  0  0  0  0  0  0  1
```

Line 25 of Program 11.11 illustrates the fact that we can branch from one part of a FOR/NEXT loop to another part of the same loop without difficulty. Observe that the PRINT statement on line 45 causes a line feed. Without line 45, line 35 will continue to print 0s and 1s until the entire line is filled.

Case 11.4 illustrates the concept of nested FOR/NEXT loops.

## CASE 11.4

**Problem**

**Three-Year Sales Projection**

Each year the planning department for a large corporation prepares a three-year projection of sales that is broken down by division. The actual projection is generated by a computer program that uses the current year's sales as a base for projecting sales over the next three years.

**Data Input**

The following sales figures are for this year:

| DIVISION | SALES (MILLION $) |
|---|---|
| 1 | $5.25 |
| 2 | 6.10 |
| 3 | 4.75 |
| 4 | 8.70 |
| 5 | 6.75 |
| 6 | 3.30 |

**Process/Formulas**  A repetitive nested FOR/NEXT loop process is to be used. The company is assuming a 12 percent growth rate compounded annually. The compounding formula is:

$$P = S (1 + R)^Y$$

where $P$ is the projected sales, $S$ is the sales for the current year, $R$ is the growth rate, and $Y$ is the projection year (1, 2, or 3).

**Output**    The output should look like the table below:

```
------------------------------------------------
        DIVISIONS SALES PROJECTIONS - MILLIONS $
------------------------------------------------
           CURRENT          PROJECTION YEARS
DIVISION    YEAR        1          2          3
------------------------------------------------
    1      $5.25      $5.88    $ 6.59     $ 7.38
    .  .  .      .  .  .     .  .  .    .  .  .    .  .  .
------------------------------------------------
```

Program 11.12 generates a table with the required projections. This table is derived by the nested FOR/NEXT loops in the program. The outer loop (lines 150 and 195) represents each of the six divisions. The inner loop (lines 170 and 185) supplies the value for the variable *Y*, which is found in the compounding formula in line 175. Note the placement of line 160 between the FOR statements. Because of this PRINT statement, the division numbers are outputted as part of the table.

A flowchart showing the logic of Program 11.12 is shown in Figure 11.5.

## PROGRAM 11.12    Case 11.4, Sales Projection, Nested FOR/NEXT Loops

```
10 REM CASE 11.4, SALES PROJECTIONS
12 REM PROGRAMMER- (name of person) DATE - mm/dd/yy
14 REM     VARIABLE LIST
16 REM         D=DIVISION #
18 REM         L$=DASHES
20 REM         P=PROJECTED SALES
22 REM         R=GROWTH RATE
24 REM         S=SALES
26 REM         Y=YEAR
28 REM -------------------------------------------
100 LET L$ = "--------------------------------------------------"
105 PRINT L$
110 PRINT     "     DIVISIONS SALES PROJECTIONS - MILLIONS $"
115 PRINT L$
120 PRINT     "          CURRENT          PROJECTION YEARS"
130 PRINT "DIVISION","YEAR",1,2,3
135 PRINT L$
140 LET R=.12                          'growth rate of 12%
150 FOR D=1 TO 6                        'outer loop for each division
155     READ S                         'read current sales
160     PRINT USING " #          $##,##"; D,S,
```

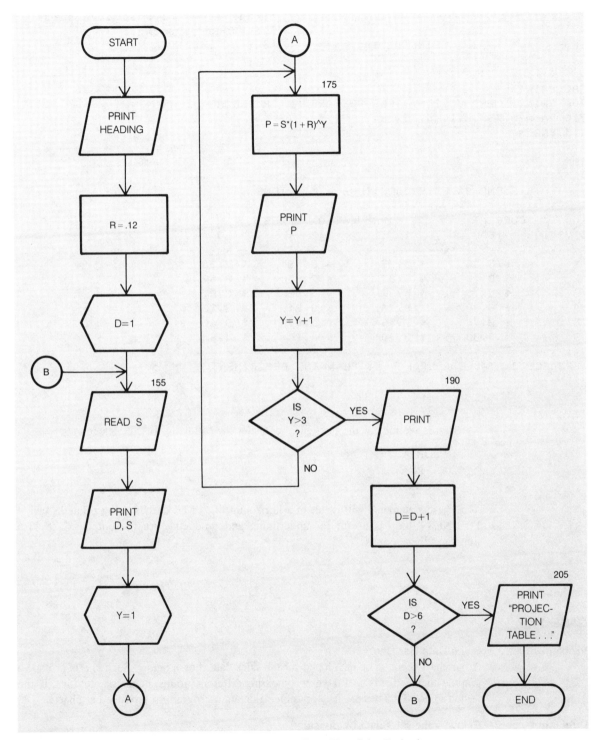

**FIGURE 11.5** Flowchart for Program 11.12, Case 11.4, Three-Year Sales Projection

```
170      FOR Y=1 TO 3                        'inner loop for projected sales
175          LET P=S*(1+R)^Y                 'compounding formula
180          PRINT USING "   $##.##"; P,     'output results
185      NEXT Y
195 NEXT D
200 PRINT L$
205 PRINT " PROJECTION TABLE PREPARED BY PLANNING DEPARTMENT"
210 DATA 5.25, 6.1, 4.75, 8.7, 6.75, 3.3
215 END
```

```
RUN
-----------------------------------------------------------
     DIVISIONS SALES PROJECTIONS - MILLIONS $
-----------------------------------------------------------
        CURRENT              PROJECTION YEARS
DIVISION  YEAR        1            2            3
-----------------------------------------------------------
  1       $ 5.25     $ 5.88      $ 6.59      $ 7.38
  2       $ 6.10     $ 6.83      $ 7.65      $ 8.57
  3       $ 4.75     $ 5.32      $ 5.96      $ 6.67
  4       $ 8.70     $ 9.74      $10.91      $12.22
  5       $ 6.75     $ 7.56      $ 8.47      $ 9.48
  6       $ 3.30     $ 3.70      $ 4.14      $ 4.64
-----------------------------------------------------------
PROJECTION TABLE PREPARED BY PLANNING DEPARTMENT
```

Before we look at the next case, consider the following BASIC statements:

10 FOR A = 1 TO 60
20    PRINT "-";
30 NEXT A

These statements will result in a horizontal line of 60 dashes being printed. Such a FOR/NEXT loop is useful for underlining and producing graphic output. Case 11.5 illustrates these points.

## CASE 11.5

**Problem**

**Sales Data Bar Chart**
A bar chart needs to be developed for the sales data shown below. Such charts provide a graphic display that is useful when comparing different groups, items, or activities. Using nested FOR/NEXT loops, it is possible to create a program to produce bar charts.

**Data Input**

Below is the sales data by division:

| DIVISION | SALES (MILLION $) |
|---|---|
| 1 | $15 |
| 2 | 22 |
| 3 | 18 |
| 4 | 30 |

**Process/Formulas** A repetitive nested FOR/NEXT loop process is to be used. The length of the bars in the chart is set by the amount of the sales (in millions of dollars). If sales are \$20 million, the length of the bar is 20 characters. Each character is printed as '' = '' to produce a bar.

**Output** The bar chart output should be formatted like this:

```
                    SALES DATA - BAR CHART
-------------------------------------------------------
          DIVISION 1 :===============:      15
             . . .              . . .              . . .
```

Program 11.13 produces a bar chart for the data supplied. The underlined heading is a result of the FOR/NEXT loop in lines 20–30. The bars are produced by the FOR/NEXT statements in lines 55–65. The lengths of the bars are determined by a variable, *D*, read by the statement 45 READ D. The outer loop (lines 40 and 80) controls how many data values will be read and graphed.

**PROGRAM 11.13   Case 11.5, Sales Data Bar Chart, Nested FOR/NEXT Loop**

```
1 REM CASE 11.5, DEVELOPING A BAR CHART
2 REM PROGRAMMER- (name of person)  DATE - mm/dd/yy
3 REM    VARIABLE LIST-A,D,I
4 REM        A=COUNTER
5 REM        D=SALES
6 REM        I=DIVISION #
8 REM -------------------------------------------------
15 PRINT " ","SALES DATA - BAR CHART"
20 FOR A = 1 TO 50             'loop for dashes
25     PRINT "-";
30 NEXT A
35 PRINT
40 FOR I= 1 TO 4               'outer loop for each division
45     READ D                  'bar length set by D
50     PRINT "DIVISION";I;":";
55     FOR A = 1 TO D           'inner loop prints each bar
60         PRINT "=";
65     NEXT A
70     PRINT ":    ";D
80 NEXT I
85 DATA 15, 22, 18, 30
90 END

RUN
              SALES DATA - BAR CHART
-------------------------------------------------------
DIVISION 1 :===============:    15
DIVISION 2 :======================:    22
DIVISION 3 :==================:    18
DIVISION 4 :==============================:    30
```

There is no limit to the number of levels of nesting, as long as no inner loop overlaps any outer loop. Figure 11.6 illustrates valid and invalid nested FOR/NEXT loop structures. When a program with an invalid FOR/NEXT loop is processed, an error message

NEXT without FOR in line #

will be generated.

Programs 11.14 and 11.15 illustrate the two *valid* loops shown in Figure 11.6.

## PROGRAM 11.14   Three Nested Loops

```
10 FOR I= 1 TO 2
15     FOR J= 12 TO 14
20         FOR K = 26 TO 29
25             PRINT I;J;K,
30         NEXT K
32         PRINT
35     NEXT J
37     PRINT
40 NEXT I
45 END

RUN
 1   12   26      1   12   27      1   12   28      1   12   29
 1   13   26      1   13   27      1   13   28      1   13   29
 1   14   26      1   14   27      1   14   28      1   14   29
 2   12   26      2   12   27      2   12   28      2   12   29
 2   13   26      2   13   27      2   13   28      2   13   29
 2   14   26      2   14   27      2   14   28      2   14   29
```

## PROGRAM 11.15   Three Nested Loops

```
10 FOR I= 1 TO 2
15     FOR J= 12 TO 14
20         PRINT I;J,
25     NEXT J
27     PRINT
30     FOR K=26 TO 29
35         PRINT I;K,
40     NEXT K
42     PRINT
45 NEXT I
50 END

RUN
 1   12      1   13      1   14
 1   26      1   27      1   28      1   29
 2   12      2   13      2   14
 2   26      2   27      2   28      2   29
```

Case 11.6 illustrates three levels of nesting.

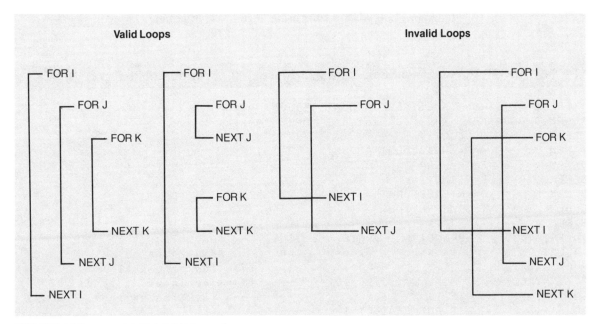

**FIGURE 11.6**  Nested FOR/NEXT Loop Structures

## CASE 11.6

**Problem**

**Investment Determination Table**

A bank wishes to print a table of the amounts of money generated when various principals are invested at different interest rates for a variety of time periods. Using the data below, such a table can be created with a program having three levels of nested FOR/NEXT loops.

**Data Input**

Each loop corresponds to these data values:

| PRINCIPAL | RATE | TIME (YEARS) |
|---|---|---|
| $1,000 $2,000 | 7%, 8%, 9% | 5, 10, 15, 20 |

**Process/Formulas**

A repetitive nested FOR/NEXT loop process with three levels is to be used. The compounding formula is:

$$\text{Amount} = P(1 + R)^t$$

where $P$ is the principal, $R$ is the interest rate, and $t$ is the time in years.

**Output**

The output should be formatted like the table below:

```
PRINCIPAL   RATE    TIME      AMOUNT
  $1,000    0.070     5    $  1,402.55
  $1,000    0.070    10    $  1,967.15

  . . .     . . .   . . .      . . .
  $2,000    0.090    15    $  7,284.97
  $2,000    0.090    20    $ 11,208.83
```

Program 11.16 prints a table using three levels of nesting.

---

**PROGRAM 11.16    Case 11.6, Determining Investment Amount, Nested FOR/NEXT**

```
1 REM CASE 11.6, INVESTMENT AMOUNT DETERMINATION
2 REM PROGRAMMER- (name of person)  DATE- mm/dd/yy
3 REM     VARIABLE LIST-
4 REM        AMT=INVESTMENT AMOUNT
5 REM        FMT$=FORMAT
6 REM        P=PRINCIPAL
7 REM        R=INTEREST RATE
8 REM        T=TIME PERIOD
9 REM -------------------------------------------------
10 PRINT        " PRINCIPAL    RATE      TIME        AMOUNT"
15 LET FMT$ = "   $#,###      #.###      ##        $###,###.##"
20 FOR P=1000 TO 2000 STEP 1000              'loop for principal
25    FOR R=.07 TO .0901 STEP .01            'loop for interest rates
30       FOR T=5 TO 20 STEP 5                'loop for time periods
35          LET AMT=P*(1+R)^T
40          PRINT USING FMT$; P,R,T,AMT
43       NEXT T
45       PRINT
50    NEXT R
55    PRINT
60 NEXT P
70 END
RUN
 PRINCIPAL    RATE       TIME       AMOUNT
  $1,000     0.070        5      $ 1,402.55
  $1,000     0.070       10      $ 1,967.15
  $1,000     0.070       15      $ 2,759.03
  $1,000     0.070       20      $ 3,869.69

  $1,000     0.080        5      $ 1,469.33
  $1,000     0.080       10      $ 2,158.93
  $1,000     0.080       15      $ 3,172.17
  $1,000     0.080       20      $ 4,660.96

  $1,000     0.090        5      $ 1,538.62
  $1,000     0.090       10      $ 2,367.36
  $1,000     0.090       15      $ 3,642.48
  $1,000     0.090       20      $ 5,604.42


  $2,000     0.070        5      $ 2,805.10
  $2,000     0.070       10      $ 3,934.30
  $2,000     0.070       15      $ 5,518.07
  $2,000     0.070       20      $ 7,739.38

  $2,000     0.080        5      $ 2,938.66
  $2,000     0.080       10      $ 4,317.85
  $2,000     0.080       15      $ 6,344.34
  $2,000     0.080       20      $ 9,321.92
```

| $2,000 | 0.090 | 5 | $ 3,077.25 |
| $2,000 | 0.090 | 10 | $ 4,734.73 |
| $2,000 | 0.090 | 15 | $ 7,284.97 |
| $2,000 | 0.090 | 20 | $11,208.83 |

The PRINT statements on lines 45 and 55 improve the readability of the output by skipping lines whenever the interest rate and principal change. Note that the upper limit in line 25 is .0901 to ensure that the 9% rule will be processed, since $R$ is not an integer.

## SUMMARY

Whenever an operation needs to be performed a fixed number of times, the FOR/NEXT statement should be used. The FOR/NEXT statements are equivalent to a LET, an IF THEN, and a GOTO. The STEP option allows the programmer to increase the index variable by numbers other than 1.

FOR/NEXT loops may be nested. Such loops are permissible as long as they don't overlap.

## BASIC VOCABULARY SUMMARY

| Statement | Purpose | Examples |
|---|---|---|
| FOR<br>(Alt + F Key) | Specifies the number of times a repetitive process will occur. | 20 FOR M = 1 TO 20<br>20 FOR M = 5 TO 20 STEP 2<br>20 FOR M = 50 TO 20 STEP − 5<br>20 FOR M = A TO B<br>20 FOR M = A TO B STEP C<br>20 FOR M = A + 1 TO B*2 STEP C/4 |
| NEXT<br>(Alt + N Key) | Is the last statement of the program segment that the FOR will repeat. | 300 NEXT M |

## EXERCISES

### Review Questions

**11.1** The following statements contain either syntax or logic errors. Correct all of these errors.

a. 20 FOR A − 1 TO TEN
b. 30 FOR B = 5T090
c. 40 FOR C = 10 TO 20 STEP 30
d. 50 FOR D = 50 TO 500 STEP − 25
e. 60 FOR E = .5 TO .75 STEP .5

**11.2** What does the error message in the program below indicate? What corrective action is required?

```
10 FOR I = 1 TO 5
20     FOR J = 1 TO 3
30         PRINT I;J,
40     NEXT I
50 NEXT J
60 END


NEXT without FOR in 50
```

**◆ 11.3** If we run the following program, what output will it have?

```
10 READ A,B,C
15 FOR I = A TO B/C STEP C*A
20     PRINT I;
25 NEXT I
30 DATA 1, 10, 1
35 END
```

**11.4** What will happen in the program presented in exercise 11.3 if line 30 is changed as follows?
a. 30 DATA 2, 12, 1
b. 30 DATA .5, 5, 1
c. 30 DATA 10, 1, −.5
d. 30 DATA 1,2,3

**11.5** What would Program 11.4 (shown below) do if
a. Line 50 is changed to 50 FOR N = 1 TO 5 STEP 2?
b. Line 50 is changed to 50 FOR N = 1 TO 5 STEP 3?
c. Lines 50 and 75 are changed as follows:
  50 FOR X = 1 TO 5
  75 NEXT X
d. Line 60 is changed to 60 LET N = N + X?
e. Line 50 is moved to 30?
f. Line 50 is moved to 42?
g. Line 50 is moved to 57?
h. Line 50 is moved to 62?
i. Line 50 is moved to 67?
j. Line 50 is moved to 72?
k. Line 75 is moved to 52?
l. Line 75 is moved to 57?
m. Line 75 is moved to 62?
n. Line 75 is moved to 67?
o. Line 75 is moved to 92?
p. Line 50 is changed to 50 FOR N = 1 TO 10 STEP 2?
q. Line 50 is changed to 50 FOR N = 61 TO 70?

```
40 LET S=0
45 LET S2=0
50 FOR N = 1 TO 5
55     READ X
```

```
60      LET S=S+X
65      LET S2=S2+X^2
70      PRINT X,X^2
75 NEXT N
90 PRINT "---", "---"
95 PRINT S,S2
100 DATA 7,3,5,6,1
999 END

RUN
  7               49
  3                9
  5               25
  6               36
  1                1
---              ---
 22              120
```

**11.6**  What would Program 11.7 (shown below) do if
a. Line 50 is changed to
   50 FOR I = 11 TO 20?
b. Line 50 is changed to
   50 FOR I = 1 TO 20?
c. The RESTORE statement on line 95 is changed to a REM?
d. Line 80 is changed to 80 GO TO 40?

For each of the above parts, assume that the same numbers are input, as in the illustration.

```
30 LET F1$ = " THE AMOUNT OF PRODUCT #### IN INVENTORY IS ####"
35 LET F2$ = ": NO SUCH PRODUCT NUMBER AS ##### TRY AGAIN :"
40 INPUT "WHAT IS THE PRODUCT NUMBER (TYPE 0 TO END)"; N
45      IF N=0 THEN END
50         FOR I= 1 TO 10
55            READ P,A
60               IF P=N THEN 85
65         NEXT I
70         PRINT USING F2$; N
75         PRINT
80         GOTO 95
85               PRINT USING F1$;P,A
90               PRINT
95         RESTORE
100 GOTO 40
105 DATA 1234,100,2345,150,1345,50,1432,75,3214,25,4321,10
100 DATA 3241,250,2233,80,1144,200,3311,500
115 END

RUN
WHAT IS THE PRODUCT NUMBER (TYPE 0 TO END)? 2345
 THE AMOUNT OF PRODUCT 2345 IN INVENTURY IS 150

WHAT IS THE PRODUCT NUMBER (TYPE 0 TO END)? 3313
: NO SUCH PRODUCT NUMBER AS 3313 TRY AGAIN :

WHAT IS THE PRODUCT NUMBER (TYPE 0 TO END)? 0
```

◆ **11.7** Revise Program 11.6 (shown below) with the necessary steps to print the grand total for the entire company and the average for all three regions.

```
30 FOR I = 1 TO 3
40    LET C = 0
50    LET T = 0
60    PRINT "REGION";I;
70    READ A
80       IF A = -99 THEN 130
90          LET C = C+1
100         LET T = T+A
110            PRINT A;
120    GOTO 70
130    LET AVE = T/C
132    PRINT TAB (35);
135    PRINT USING "TOTAL ### AVERAGE ##.##"; T;AVE
150 NEXT I
160 DATA 40,20,50,60,-99
170 DATA 50,40,55,35,70,65,-99
180 DATA 35,46,25,-99
190 END

RUN
REGION 1 40 20 50 60              TOTAL 170   AVERAGE 42.50
REGION 2 50 40 55 35 70 65        TOTAL 315   AVERAGE 52.50
REGION 3 35 46 25                 TOTAL 106   AVERAGE 35.33
```

**11.8** Revise Program 11.13 shown below so that the horizontal lines in the output are twice as long.

```
15 PRINT " ","SALES DATA - BAR CHART"
20 FOR A = 1 TO 50
25    PRINT "-";
30 NEXT A
35 PRINT
40 FOR I = 1 TO 4
45    READ D
50    PRINT "DIVISION";I;":";
55    FOR A = 1 TO D
60       PRINT "=";
65    NEXT A
70    PRINT ":    ";D
80 NEXT I
85 DATA 15,22,18,30
90 END

RUN
                SALES DATA - BAR CHART
------------------------------------------------------
DIVISION 1 :===============:   15
DIVISION 2 :======================:   22
DIVISION 3 :==================:   18
DIVISION 4 :==============================:   30
```

**11.9**  What will the following program print when it is run?

```
10 FOR I = 1 TO 20 STEP 6
15     FOR J = 3 TO 10 STEP 2
20         PRINT I;J,
25     NEXT J
30     PRINT
35 NEXT I
40 END
```

**11.10**  What will the following program print when it is run?

```
10 FOR I = 1 TO 11 STEP 3
15     FOR J = 5 TO -1 STEP -2
20         FOR K = 2 TO 3 STEP .25
25             PRINT I;J;K,
30         NEXT K
35         PRINT
40     NEXT J
45     PRINT
50 NEXT I
55 END
```

## Programming Activities

**11.11**  **Purpose**  To use the FOR/NEXT loop logic structure.

**Problem**  Write and run a program that will print all of the even integer numbers between 1 and 20.

**Data**  Data values are provided by the FOR statement.

**Output**  Your output should follow this format:

```
2   4   6   8   10   12   14   16   18   20
```

**11.12**  **Purpose**  To use the FOR/NEXT loop logic structure, numeric data, and LPRINT and PRINT USING for output formatting.

**Problem**  The current ratio is an accounting measure of a company's financial condition. This ratio is computed by dividing current assets by current liabilities. Write and run a program to find the current ratio, using the data from the table below.

**Data**

| YEAR | CURRENT ASSETS | CURRENT LIABILITIES |
|------|----------------|---------------------|
| 1988 | $500,000 | $400,000 |
| 1989 | 160,000 | 120,000 |
| 1990 | 950,000 | 320,000 |
| 1991 | 600,000 | 300,000 |

**Output** Your output should display on the screen and also generate a hard copy. Output should follow this format:

```
            CURRENT      CURRENT        CURRENT
YEAR        ASSETS       LIABILITIES    RATIO
------------------------------------------------------
1988        $500,000     $400,000       1.25
1989        $160,000     $120,000       1.33
1990        $950,000     $320,000       2.97
1991        $600,000     $300,000       2.00
```

**11.13** **Purpose** To use the FOR/NEXT loop logic structure, numeric data, and PRINT USING statement for output formatting.

**Problem** For the data given below, write and run a program to find the percent of increase for each month shown. That is, percent increase = (2nd yr − 1st yr)/1st yr × 100 for each month shown.

**Data**

| | MONTH | | |
|---|---|---|---|
| UNITS SOLD | 1 | 2 | 3 |
| 1st yr | 400 | 450 | 440 |
| 2nd yr | 500 | 575 | 600 |

**Output** Your output should have this format:

```
                        MONTH
--------------------------------------
UNITS SOLD      1       2       3
--------------------------------------
FIRST YEAR     400     450     440
SECOND YEAR    500     575     600
--------------------------------------
% INCREASE    25.00   43.75   36.36
```

**♦ 11.14** **Purpose** To use the FOR/NEXT loop logic structure, numeric data, and PRINT USING statement for output formatting.

**Problem** For the information given below write and run a program that will output this information and calculate and compute a fourth column that shows the ending inventory. (Ending inventory is determined by subtracting the units sold from beginning inventory.)

**Data**

| ITEM | BEGINNING INVENTORY | UNITS SOLD | ENDING INVENTORY |
|---|---|---|---|
| 1 | 250 | 40 | — |
| 2 | 700 | 75 | — |
| 3 | 600 | 280 | — |

**Output** Your output should have this format:

```
ITEM   BEGINNING INVEN.   UNITS SOLD   ENDING INVEN.
----------------------------------------------------
 1           250              40            210
 2           700              75            625
 3           600             280            320
```

**11.15** **Purpose** To use the FOR/NEXT logic structure to process numeric data values and perform decision selection and use the IF/THEN statement for decision making.

**Problem** Write and run a program that reads in a product number, unit price, and quantity ordered. The program is to find the discount to be given and the total dollar amount for each order. A discount of 10 percent is given on all orders of 100 items or more. There is no discount on orders of fewer than 100 items. The total dollar amount is equal to price times quantity less discount.

**Data** Use these data values:

| NUMBER | PRICE | QUANTITY |
|--------|-------|----------|
| 101 | $2 | 250 |
| 210 | 6 | 95 |
| 330 | 3 | 110 |

**Output** Your output should have this format:

```
Number   Price    Quantity    Discount    Amount
  101    $2.00      250        $50.00      $450.00
  210    $6.00       95        $ 0.00      $570.00
  330    $3.00      110        $33.00      $297.00
```

**11.16  Purpose** To use the FOR/NEXT loop logic structure to process numeric data values and to use the IF/THEN statement for decision making.

**Problem** Write and run a program that will compute federal and state tax deductions based on the gross wage conditions given below. Design the program so that it will also determine the total amount of deductions and the net wage after all taxes are deducted from the gross wage.

| FEDERAL DEDUCTION | | STATE DEDUCTION | |
|-------------------|---|-----------------|---|
| Gross Wage | % | Gross Wage | % |
| Less than or equal to $200 | 15 | Less than or equal to $200 | 2 |
| Greater than $200 but less than or equal to $300 | 20 | Greater than $200 | 3 |
| Greater than $300 | 22 | | |

**Data** Use these data values: $200, $350, $300, $250, $100, and $500.

**Output** Your output should have this format:

```
GROSS      FEDERAL     STATE      TOTAL         NET
WAGE       TAX         TAX        DEDUCTIONS    WAGE
$200.00    $ 30.00     $  4.00    $ 34.00       $166.00
$350.00    $ 77.00     $ 10.50    $ 87.50       $262.50
$300.00    $ 60.00     $  9.00    $ 69.00       $231.00
$250.00    $ 50.00     $  7.50    $ 57.50       $192.50
$100.00    $ 15.00     $  2.00    $ 17.00       $ 83.00
$500.00    $110.00     $ 15.00    $125.00       $375.00
```

**11.17  Purpose** To use the FOR/NEXT logic structure to process numeric data and to find column totals using the LET statement as an accumulator and the PRINT USING statement for output formatting.

**Problem** Write and run a program that will print out all the data shown below along with the total number of units produced for each year. Your program should be able to process data for 25 plants. Test it with the limited data supplied. The output should have appropriate headings.

**Data**  Use the data values shown below to test your program:

**UNITS PRODUCED**

| Plant | 1989 | 1990 |
|-------|------|------|
| 1 | 2,400 | 2,900 |
| 2 | 3,000 | 3,100 |
| 3 | 2,500 | 3,000 |
| 4 | 3,000 | 3,200 |
| Totals | x,xxx | x,xxx |

**Output**  Your output should have this format:

```
              UNITS PRODUCED
         -----------------
PLANT        1989        1990
-----------------------------
    1       2,400       2,900
    2       3,000       3,100
    3       2,500       3,200
    4       3,000       3,200
-----------------------------
TOTAL      10,900      12,200
```

**11.18**  **Purpose**  To use the FOR/NEXT logic structure to process numeric data values and to use the IF/THEN statement for decision selection.

**Problem**  Write and run a program to read 10 numbers. The numbers are grades in a programming examination. The program is to compute the average passing grade, the average failing grade, and the class average. A grade of 60 or above is passing.

**Data**  Use these data values:

100 DATA 60,59,40,88,98,75,90,72,82,77

**Output**  Your output should have this format:

```
AVG. PASSING GRADE   80.25
AVG. FAILING GRADE   49.50
CLASS AVERAGE        74.10
```

**11.19**  **Purpose**  To use the FOR/NEXT logic structure, string and numeric data, and the PRINT USING statement for output formatting.

**Problem**  A large retail establishment uses a wage payment plan of straight salary, $300 per week, plus a commission of 10 percent on the amount of merchandise each employee sells. Using the information given below, write and run a program that completes the table shown by computing commissions and total earnings.

| Data | EMPLOYEE NUMBER | REGULAR SALARY | AMOUNT SOLD |
|------|-----------------|----------------|-------------|
|      | 1015            | $300.00        | $500.00     |
|      | 1068            | 300.00         | 580.00      |
|      | 1135            | 300.00         | 485.00      |
|      | 1359            | 300.00         | 610.50      |
|      | 2370            | 300.00         | 450.00      |

Note that the employee number is treated as a string data item.

**Output**  Your output should have this format:

```
EMPLOYEE        REGULAR      AMOUNT                    TOTAL
NUMBER          SALARY       SOLD        COMMISSION    EARNINGS
------------------------------------------------------------------

1015            $300.00      $500.00     $50.00        $350.00
1068            $300.00      $580.00     $58.00        $358.00
1135            $300.00      $485.00     $48.50        $348.50
1359            $300.00      $610.50     $61.05        $361.05
2370            $300.00      $450.00     $45.00        $345.00
```

♦ **11.20**  **Purpose**  To use the FOR/NEXT logic structure, string and numeric data, and the PRINT USING statement for output formatting.

**Problem**  The ABC Company has four divisions that sell various products. Management wants to know what percent of total sales volume is generated by each division. Below are the gross sales figures by division for the year.

Write and run program that reads in the sales data and generates as output a table that shows (1) the total sales of each division, (2) a third column headed ''% OF TOTAL'' (use division sales/total sales × 100 to find the percent of total sales), and (3) the totals of the sales and percents for all divisions at the bottom. The last column should total 1.0.

| Data | DIVISION | SALES (MILLION $) |
|------|----------|-------------------|
|      | WEST     | $2.85             |
|      | SOUTH    | 7.62              |
|      | NORTH    | 3.57              |
|      | EAST     | 2.81              |

**Output**  Your output should have this format:

```
DIVISION       SALES       % OF TOTAL
-------------------------------------

WEST           2.85        0.17
SOUTH          7.62        0.45
NORTH          3.57        0.21
EAST           2.81        0.17
-------------------------------------

TOTALS         16.85       1.00
```

♦ **11.21**  **Purpose**  To use the FOR/NEXT logic structure to process numeric data values and string items and find column totals using the LET statement as an accumulator and the PRINT USING statement for output formatting.

**Problem** The following table shows the first-quarter sales for each division of the EXACT Company. Sales are in thousands of dollars.

| DIVISION | JAN. | FEB. | MAR. |
|----------|------|------|------|
| WEST | $1,000 | $ 750 | $ 750 |
| SOUTH | 1,200 | 800 | 1,000 |
| NORTH | 1,200 | 500 | 1,200 |
| EAST | 1,500 | 1,050 | 950 |

Write and run a program that derives the total sales for each month.

**Data** Use the data values shown in the table above.

**Output** Your output should look like this:

```
DIVISION            JAN,         FEB,          MAR,
-------------------------------------------------------
WEST              $1,000      $    750      $    750
SOUTH             $1,200      $    800      $1,000
NORTH             $1,200      $    500      $1,200
EAST              $1,500      $1,050       $    950
-------------------------------------------------------
TOTALS            $4,900      $3,100       $3,900
```

• • • • • • **11.22** **Purpose** To use the FOR/NEXT logic structure, string and numeric data, and the PRINT USING statement for output formatting.

**Problem** United Computer pays its salespersons a monthly salary of $1,000 plus 1½ percent commission for equipment sold during the month. The table below shows the sales figures by salesperson for last month.

Write and run a program that will print out the above information and a column that shows the total salary plus commission on sales.

**Data**

| SALESPERSON | AMOUNT SOLD |
|-------------|-------------|
| M. Worth | $13,500 |
| K. Gray | 21,000 |
| S. Legan | 9,600 |
| B. Hinz | 24,400 |

**Output** Your output should have this format:

```
SALESPERSON     AMT SOLD      SALARY+COMM
-------------------------------------------------
M, Worth        $13,500       $1,202,50
K, Gray         $21,000       $1,315,00
S, Legan        $ 9,600       $1,144,00
B, Hinz         $24,400       $1,366,00
-------------------------------------------------
TOTAL           $68,500       $5,027,50
```

• • • • • • **11.23** **Purpose** To use the FOR/NEXT loop logic structure, numeric data, and the ON/GOTO for decision testing and to use the PRINT USING statement for output formatting.

**Problem** Write and run a program that reads 10 account numbers, each followed by the number of months during which no payment has been made. Have the computer print the account number, the number of months no payment has been received, and the appropriate action for each, as given in the following table:

| NUMBER OF MONTHS OVERDUE | ACTION |
|---|---|
| 0 | None |
| 1 | Gentle reminder |
| 2 or 3 | Strong reminder |
| 4 or more | Lawyer's letter |

**Data**   Test your program using the following data:

| ACCOUNT NUMBER | MONTHS | ACCOUNT NUMBER | MONTHS |
|---|---|---|---|
| 2370 | 2 | 2182 | 8 |
| 3542 | 3 | 1352 | 5 |
| 2372 | 0 | 1519 | 1 |
| 8282 | 1 | 2315 | 2 |
| 3838 | 4 | 1820 | 0 |

**Output**   Your output should have this format:

```
ACCOUNT NUMBER    MONTHS NO PAYMENT    ACTION TO BE TAKEN
-------------------------------------------------------
     2370                 2            STRONG REMINDER
     3542                 3            STRONG REMINDER
     2372                 0            NONE
     8282                 1            GENTLE REMINDER
     3838                 4            LAWYER'S LETTER
     2182                 8            LAWYER'S LETTER
     1352                 5            LAWYER'S LETTER
     1519                 1            GENTLE REMINDER
     2315                 2            STRONG REMINDER
     1820                 0            NONE
```

**11.24**   **Purpose**   To use the FOR/NEXT loop logic structure, numeric data, and the ON/GOTO for decision testing and to use the PRINT USING statement for output formatting.

**Problem**   Write and run a program to revise a price list. Each product is assigned a code that represents a specific percentage increase over the current price. (The new price equals the old price multiplied by the percent of increase.) The code and percentage increase are shown below.

**Data**

| CODE | % INCREASE |
|---|---|
| 1 | 5.5 |
| 2 | 6.25 |
| 3 | 7.75 |
| 4 | 8.15 |

Test your program with this data:

| PRODUCT NUMBER | CURRENT PRICE | CODE |
|---|---|---|
| 123 | 7.49 | 2 |
| 456 | 8.38 | 1 |
| 159 | 17.49 | 3 |
| 215 | 10.00 | 4 |

**Output** Your output should have this format:

```
PRODUCT          CURRENT        CODE      NEW
NUMBER            PRICE                  PRICE
-----------------------------------------------
  123           $ 7.49           2      $ 7.96
  456           $ 8.38           1      $ 8.84
  159           $17.49           3      $18.85
  215           $10.00           4      $10.82
```

**11.25** **Purpose** To use the nested FOR/NEXT loop logic structure and numeric data.

**Problem** Write and run a program to create a bar chart like the one shown in the output below (see Case 11.5).

**Data** Use the following sales data from last week for the United Store chain:

| Store 1 | $1,200 | Store 4 | $1,600 |
|---------|--------|---------|--------|
| Store 2 | 1,900 | Store 5 | 1,900 |
| Store 3 | 2,100 | Store 6 | 2,200 |

(*Hint:* The program should scale down the data by dividing by a constant large enough so that the bars can fit on the display.)

**Output** Your output should look like this:

```
        SALES DATA - BAR CHART
           UNITED STORE CHAIN
    --------------------------------------
    STORE 1 :============:   1200
    STORE 2 :==================:  1900
    STORE 3 :====================:   2100
    STORE 4 :================:  1600
    STORE 5 :==================:  1900
    STORE 6 :====================:  2200
```

**11.26** **Purpose** To use the nested FOR/NEXT loop logic structure and interactive data entry.

**Problem** Write and run a program that causes the computer to print out a form like the one shown below as many times as the user requests. The form is fixed, and the user is prompted to enter the number of times the form should be printed.

**Data** Data entry, the number of times the form is to be printed, is from the keyboard.

**Output** Your data entry and output should look like this:

```
HOW MANY COPIES OF THE FORM ARE REQUIRED?  2

CUSTOMER NAME              ADDRESS      TEL. NO.
------------------------------------------------
1
------------------------------------------------
2
------------------------------------------------
3
------------------------------------------------
```

```
4
    ------------------------------------------------
5
    ------------------------------------------------
    CUSTOMER NAME              ADDRESS       TEL. NO.
    ------------------------------------------------
1
    ------------------------------------------------
2
    ------------------------------------------------
3
    ------------------------------------------------
4
    ------------------------------------------------
5
    ------------------------------------------------
```

**11.27**  **Purpose**  To use the nested FOR/NEXT loop logic structure, computational operations, and the PRINT USING statement for output.

**Problem**  Write and run a program that will develop a compound interest table using the formula

$$I = (1 + r)^n$$

Going across the top of the table, the interest rate $r$ will increase from 8 to 9 percent by $\frac{1}{4}$ percent increments. Going down the left margin, the number of years $n$ will go from 1 to 10.

**Data**  Use the FOR statements to set the interest rate, $r$, and the number of years, $n$.

**Output**  Your output should look like this:

```
                COMPOUND INTEREST TABLE
    -------------------------------------------------
       N       8.0%    8.25%    8.5%    8.75%    9.0%
    -------------------------------------------------
       1       1.080   1.083   1.085   1.088   1.090
       2       1.166   1.172   1.177   1.183   1.188
       3       1.260   1.268   1.277   1.286   1.295
       4       1.360   1.373   1.386   1.399   1.412
       5       1.469   1.486   1.504   1.521   1.539
       6       1.587   1.609   1.631   1.654   1.677
       7       1.714   1.742   1.770   1.799   1.828
       8       1.851   1.885   1.921   1.956   1.993
       9       1.999   2.041   2.084   2.127   2.172
      10       2.159   2.209   2.261   2.314   2.367
    -------------------------------------------------
```

**11.28**  **Purpose**  To use the nested FOR/NEXT loop logic structure, computational operations, and the PRINT USING statement for output.

**Problem**  Using the compound interest formula given in exercise 11.27, write and run a program that will output three tables, each one for a 10-year period. In the first table, the interest rate, $r$, should increase from 10 to 11 percent; in the second, $r$ should increase from 11 to 12 percent; and in the third, $r$ should increase from 12 to 13 percent. In each case the increment is ¼ percent. The last of the three tables to be produced is shown below as an example of how your output should look.

**Data**   The outer loop sets up the three tables. The inner loops use the FOR statements to set the interest rates, $r$, and the number of years, $n$.

**Output**   Your output should look like this:

```
        TABLE 3  12% TO 13% BY 1/4% FOR 10 YEARS
        -------------------------------------------------------
        N      12.00%   12.25%   12.50%   12.75%   13.00%
        -------------------------------------------------------
        1      1.1200   1.1225   1.1250   1.1275   1.1300
        2      1.2544   1.2600   1.2656   1.2713   1.2769
        3      1.4049   1.4144   1.4238   1.4333   1.4429
        4      1.5735   1.5876   1.6018   1.6161   1.6305
        5      1.7623   1.7821   1.8020   1.8221   1.8424
        6      1.9738   2.0004   2.0273   2.0545   2.0820
        7      2.2107   2.2455   2.2807   2.3164   2.3526
        8      2.4760   2.5205   2.5658   2.6118   2.6584
        9      2.7731   2.8293   2.8865   2.9448   3.0040
        10     3.1058   3.1759   3.2473   3.3202   3.3946
        -------------------------------------------------------
```

♦ **11.29**   **Purpose**   To use the nested FOR/NEXT loop logic structure and decision testing.

**Problem**   Write and run a program that will print a 10 × 10 table with zeros everywhere except along the major and minor diagonals. Those positions should contain 1s. If the program is written properly, the computer will print an "X" of 1s in a field of 0s. See the output below as an example.

**Data**   Use the FOR statements to set the values for each loop.

**Output**   Your output should look like this:

```
1  0  0  0  0  0  0  0  0  1
0  1  0  0  0  0  0  0  1  0
0  0  1  0  0  0  0  1  0  0
0  0  0  1  0  0  1  0  0  0
0  0  0  0  1  1  0  0  0  0
0  0  0  0  1  1  0  0  0  0
0  0  0  1  0  0  1  0  0  0
0  0  1  0  0  0  0  1  0  0
0  1  0  0  0  0  0  0  1  0
1  0  0  0  0  0  0  0  0  1
```

# ARRAYS,

# LISTS,

# AND TABLES

Upon completing this chapter, you will be able to do the following:

- Contrast the differences between ordinary variable types and subscripted variable types.
- Create a program that assigns data to a one-dimensional list or array as subscripted items.
- Explain the purpose of dimensioning and the DIM statement.
- Create a program that assigns data to a two-dimensional table as subscripted items.
- Develop a program solution to a problem using subscripted variables for both numeric and nonnumeric data.

n previous chapters, each variable could contain only one numeric or string value at a time. Frequently, it is desirable to treat a set of data items in an array as a list or a table with one variable name and have subscripts to distinguish each of the data items in the set. In this chapter we discuss the advantages of using arrays and how they are programmed in BASIC.

## SUBSCRIPTED VARIABLES

A subscripted variable could be $B_1$ ($B$ sub 1) or $M_{25}$ ($M$ sub 25). The letters $B$ and $M$ are the names of groups of similar items. Such a group of similar items having a single name is referred to as a one-dimensional *array*.

With subscripted variables a complete storage area is set aside for the values that are read in. This storage area has a single name, and each value in the array has a subscript, or index, giving it a position in the storage area. If 10 values were to be treated as an array having a common name, $N$, read in and assigned by subscripting, Figure 12.1 would represent the storage area being discussed.

In Figure 12.1 the subscripts show that position in the array follows from left to right (low to high). The subscripts are always whole numbers, never fractions or decimals.

Now that you understand what subscripted variables are, you need to know how they are programmed in BASIC.

Suppose a company has insurance policies in various amounts for its 10 senior executives. We can assign a single variable name to these policies, say $P$. The mathematical notation and the BASIC notation for these 10 policies are as follows:

| MATHEMATICAL | BASIC | POLICY FACE VALUE |
|---|---|---|
| $P_1$ | P(1) | $20,000 |
| $P_2$ | P(2) | 25,000 |
| $P_3$ | P(3) | 15,000 |
| . . . | . . . | . . . |
| $P_{10}$ | P(10) | 26,000 |

The subscript in the mathematical notation is written slightly below the variable name. Since the keyboard does not permit such a notation, the subscript identification number is

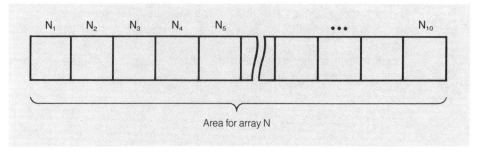

**FIGURE 12.1** Storage Area for an Array with Subscripts

**TABLE 12.1**  Subscripted Numeric Variables

| VARIABLE NOTATION | EXPLANATION |
|---|---|
| B(1) | A subscripted variable for a numeric data item to be placed in a one-dimensional array $B$, location 1. |
| TOT(25) | A subscripted variable for a numeric data item to be placed in a one-dimensional array $TOT$, location 25. |
| SUM(I) | A subscripted variable for a numeric data item to be placed in a one-dimensional array $SUM$, location I. |

placed in parentheses next to the variable name. When these policy amounts are read into the computer, each is assigned to a location referred to by the $P$ and given a position with a specific (unique) identification number, or index. In this way P(1) will be set equal to $20,000, P(2) will be set equal to $25,000, and so on, through P(10).

Subscripted variables can be used for both numeric, and nonnumeric, or string, data. Several examples of numeric subscripted variables are shown in Table 12.1. Subscripted string variables are described later in this chapter.

Examples of acceptable subscripts are S(4), X2(37), M(I + 6), L(2*J), and E(B − 1). Thus, a subscript can be any expression that uses the operators ^, *, /, +, and −. In addition, it is possible to subscript a subscripted variable so that if B(I) is a value, we can have the variable N(B(I)).

## A Subscript Caution

Subscript values should be positive integers. If they are not, some systems will truncate the subscript [T(4.5) will become T(4), for example]; other systems will round to the nearest integer [X(7.9) will become X(8), for example]. Using PC/Microsoft BASIC, you will find that subscript values that are not integers are rounded to the nearest whole integer. For example, R(4.2) is rounded down to R(4), while R(5.9) is rounded up to R(6).

For the 10 insurance policies described above, a simple program illustrating how values are read, printed, and stored as subscripted variables is shown in Program 12.1. The FOR/NEXT loop provides the identification numbers for each of the $P$ variables. When line 15, READ P(I), is executed, each data value gets the same variable name, $P$, but a different identification number. To print out the values of these variables we need a PRINT statement, as shown in line 20.

## PROGRAM 12.1   Reading, Printing, and Storing Subscripted Variables

```
10 FOR I= 1 TO 10
15    READ P(I)
20    PRINT P(I);
25 NEXT I
30 DATA 20000,25000,15000,16500,18500
35 DATA 32000,19500,17500,22000,26000
99 END

RUN
 20000  25000  15000  16500  18500  32000  19500  17500  22000  26000
```

The 10 values in Program 12.1 form an array named *P*. Each value is now stored in a specific location, P(1), . . . , P(10). If lines 15 and 20 in Program 12.1 had been

15 READ P
20 PRINT P;

the output obtained would have been the same. The difference in programs is reflected in the variables used. An "ordinary" variable such as *P* provides only a single storage location for a single value at any one time. The subscripted variable P(I) provides a storage area that can contain more than a single value at any one time. In addition, specific values of a subscripted array can be printed and used in subsequent processing if necessary. With the ordinary-variable approach mentioned above, it would not be possible to print out a specific *P* value, say the fourth or sixth value. Line 27 in Program 12.2 shows how the fourth, sixth, second, and seventh policy values are printed out because each has been assigned to a subscripted variable, which has its own storage location in memory.

## PROGRAM 12.2   Printing Specific Array Values

```
10 FOR I = 1 TO 10
15    READ P(I)
20    PRINT P(I);
25 NEXT I
26 PRINT
27 PRINT P(4), P(6), P(2), P(7)
30 DATA  20000,25000,15000,16500,18500
35 DATA  32000,19500,17500,22000,26000
99 END

RUN
 20000   25000   15000   16500   18500   32000   19500   17500   22000   26000
 16500           32000           25000           19500
```

At times, subscripted variables may be stated directly rather than using FOR/NEXT loops to give identification numbers. Values may be assigned to subscripted variables by using one of the following:

READ/DATA statements,

10 READ M(1), M(2), M(3)
20 DATA 2,3,70

INPUT statement,

10 INPUT M(1),M(2),M(3)

or LET statements,

10 LET M(1) = 2
20 LET M(2) = 3
30 LET M(3) = 70

Note that in Program 12.2 it would have been possible to replace lines 10, 15, 20, and 25 with the two statements

10 READ P(1),P(2),P(3),P(4),P(5),P(6),P(7),P(8),P(9),P(10)
20 PRINT P(1),P(2),P(3),P(4),P(5),P(6),P(7),P(8),P(9),P(10)

## DIMENSIONING

When subscripted variables are read into the computer, they are placed in storage with a specific memory location. You are permitted up to 10 "free" subscripted variables for each of the variable names in your program. However, since total storage available is limited, if you have more than 10 subscripted variables you must reserve storage space for them in the computer. Such reservations are made by using a DIM (dimension) statement at the start of your program. This statement is illustrated within the discussion of lists and tables that follows.

## Lists

A single column or row of values comprises a list or array. Such a list was formed by the 10 policies in Program 12.2. Since the list did not have more than 10 values, no dimension statement was required. If the list were larger, a DIM statement in the following form would be needed:

line # DIM variable name (number of storage spaces desired)

Several examples of the DIM statement are shown in Table 12.2. Example 2 demonstrates that the full form of the dimension statement is

line # DIM variable name 1(# of spaces), variable name 2(# spaces), . . .

## A Dimensioning Caution

When a subscripted variable name is used without a DIM statement, the maximum value of the subscript is assumed to be 10. If the value of the subscript within your program is greater than 10, the error message "Subscript out of range" will appear.

Program 12.3 illustrates how a list of 20 data items is dimensioned, placed into an array, and then printed out. These data items are the amounts of 20 insurance policies.

**TABLE 12.2**  Examples of the Dimension Statement

| STATEMENT | EXPLANATION |
|---|---|
| 1.  20 DIM B(35) | The maximum number of storage locations for the variable $B$ is 35 numbers, or 36 when you include the location B(0). (See OPTION BASE at the end of this chapter.) |
| 2.  40 DIM B(35), KT(20), MO1(42) | Multiple data lists or arrays can be dimensioned within a single DIM statement. |

## PROGRAM 12.3 Dimensioning for a List of 20 Insurance Policies

```
5   DIM P(20)
11 FOR I = 1 TO 20
15    READ P(I)
30 NEXT I
32 PRINT "POLICY",   "AMOUNT",   "POLICY",   "AMOUNT"
33 PRINT "-------------------------------------------------"
34 FOR I= 1 TO 10
35     PRINT I,"$";P(I),I+10,"$";P(I+10)
38 NEXT I
40 DATA 20000,25000,15000,16500,18500
42 DATA 32000,19500,17500,22000,26000
45 DATA 18000,22000,16500,21500,22500
50 DATA 20000,18500,17000,19500,28000
99 END
```

```
RUN
POLICY          AMOUNT          POLICY          AMOUNT
------------------------------------------------------
  1            $ 20000          11            $ 18000
  2            $ 25000          12            $ 22000
  3            $ 15000          13            $ 16500
  4            $ 16500          14            $ 21500
  5            $ 18500          15            $ 22500
  6            $ 32000          16            $ 20000
  7            $ 19500          17            $ 18500
  8            $ 17500          18            $ 17000
  9            $ 22000          19            $ 19500
 10            $ 26000          20            $ 28000
```

Line 5 indicates that 20 storage areas are to be reserved for variable $P$. If the DIM statement were left out of the program, an error message would occur during the running of the program. The DIM specification should always be equal to or greater than the size of the data list. Overdimensioning is permissible; underdimensioning is an error. Note the use of the variable designation $P(I + 10)$ in line 35. With this designation, the program prints out the 11th through the 20th policy amounts on the same line as it prints the 1st through the 10th.

## Program Appearance and Indentation

In Chapter 11 we pointed out that clarity of the program listing is improved by indenting the contents of a FOR/NEXT loop. All the programs in this chapter show indentation of the contents of a FOR/NEXT loop. For example, if you examine Programs 12.1–12.18, you will find the contents of a loop are indented four or more spaces to produce a block of white space that clearly shows the FOR/NEXT statements.

Throughout the remainder of this chapter and in the remaining chapters of the book, we indent statements following the illustrations of Chapters 8–11.

Program 12.4, using the information of Case 12.1, incorporates the concepts of dimensioning and subscripted numeric variables.

. . . . . . . . . . . . . . . . . . . . . . . . . . . . . . . . . . .

## CASE 12.1

**Problem**

**Estimate of Average Charge Account Sale**

The B and N Department Store Company wants to estimate the average amount of a charge sale as well as the percent of charges that are above the average.

**Data Input**

The following data to be processed is a random sample of 15 charges that were recorded one day last week.

| CHARGE | AMOUNT | CHARGE | AMOUNT |
|--------|--------|--------|--------|
| 1 | $ 3.47 | 9 | $33.21 |
| 2 | 97.74 | 10 | 57.60 |
| 3 | 16.76 | 11 | 18.18 |
| 4 | 12.56 | 12 | 25.62 |
| 5 | 55.59 | 13 | 23.42 |
| 6 | 16.22 | 14 | 52.36 |
| 7 | 84.42 | 15 | 37.85 |
| 8 | 63.01 | | |

**Process/Formulas**

A repetitive FOR/NEXT loop process is to be used, with the 15 charges placed into a subscripted array. All of the charges will be totaled, and an average calculated. The average is derived by dividing the total dollar amount by the number of charges. The percent of charges above the average is determined by counting those charges that are above the average and dividing by 15.

**Output**

The output will show the sample total, the estimated average charge, and the percent of charges above the average. The output should look like this:

```
CHARGE          AMOUNT
-----------------------

   1               $3.47
   2              $97.74
   . . .           . . .
  14              $52.36
  15              $37.85
                --------
SAMPLE TOTAL    $XXX.XX
EST.AVE.CHARGE    $X.XX
PERCENT OF CHARGES ABOVE THE AVERAGE   XX.XX %
```

. . . . . . . . . . . . . . . . . . . . . . . . . . . . . . . . . . .

Program 12.4 shows how the desired results for Case 12.1 can be obtained. With subscripting, all that is needed is a loop, such as the one in lines 75–85, and a comparison test, such as the one in line 80. Comments within the program explain what some of the statements do. A flowchart for the program is shown in Figure 12.2.

## PROGRAM 12.4    Case 12.1, Percent of Charges above the Average

```
1 REM CASE 12.1, ESTIMATING AVERAGE CHARGE ACCOUNT SALE
2 REM PROGRAMMER- (name of person)  DATE- mm/dd/yy
3 REM     VARIABLE LIST-
4 REM      A1=AVERAGE CHARGE
5 REM      C(I)=AMOUNT OF A CHARGE SALE
6 REM      H1$, H2$, H3$ = FORMATS
7 REM      I=LOOP INDEX
8 REM      T1=TOTAL CHARGES
9 REM      T2=COUNTER FOR # OF CHARGES ABOVE AVERAGE
10 REM -----------------------------------------
11 DIM C(15)
12 LET H1$="CHARGE          AMOUNT "
13 LET H2$="----------------------"
14 LET H3$="  ##            $$##.## "
25 PRINT H1$
30 PRINT H2$
35 LET T1=0
40 LET T2=0
45 FOR I = 1 TO 15
50    READ C(I)                   'read and store charges
55    PRINT USING H3$; I,C(I)
60    LET T1= T1+C(I)        'determine the sum of all charges
65 NEXT I
70 LET A1 = T1/15
75 FOR I= 1 TO 15                 'loop to test if the charge is
80    IF C(I)>A1 THEN LET T2=T2+1 'greater than the average and
85 NEXT I                         'count it
90 PRINT " "," --------"
95 PRINT USING   "SAMPLE TOTAL   $$####.## ";T1
100 PRINT USING "EST.AVE.CHARGE  $$###.## ";A1
105 PRINT USING "PERCENT OF CHARGES ABOVE THE AVERAGE  ##.## %"; (T2/15)*100
110 DATA 3.47,97.74,16.76,12.56,55.59
115 DATA 16.22,84.42,63.01,33.21,57.60
120 DATA 18.18,25.62,23.42,52.36,37.85
125 END
```

```
RUN
CHARGE          AMOUNT
----------------------
   1              $3.47
   2             $97.74
   3             $16.76
   4             $12.56
   5             $55.59
   6             $16.22
   7             $84.42
   8             $63.01
   9             $33.21
  10             $57.60
  11             $18.18
  12             $25.62
  13             $23.42
  14             $52.36
  15             $37.85
                --------
SAMPLE TOTAL    $598.01
EST.AVE.CHARGE  $39.87
PERCENT OF CHARGES ABOVE THE AVERAGE  40.00 %
```

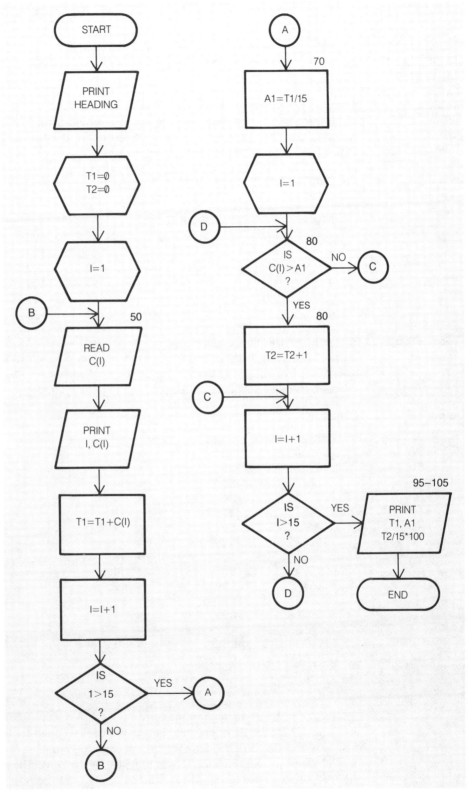

**FIGURE 12.2**  Flowchart for Program 12.4, Case 12.1, B and N Department Store Company

A problem may have multiple data lists. Case 12.2 is such a situation.

## CASE 12.2

**Problem**

**Computing the Market Value of an Investment Portfolio**

An investment advisor wants to compute the current market value of one investment portfolio. For each of the 12 stocks in the portfolio, the advisor knows the number of shares held and the current market price (see below).

**Data Input**

The number of shares held for each of the 12 stocks and their current market price are listed below:

| STOCK | # SHARES | MARKET PRICE | STOCK | # SHARES | MARKET PRICE |
|-------|----------|--------------|-------|----------|--------------|
| 1 | 300 | $ 50 | 7 | 500 | $ 77 |
| 2 | 400 | 42 | 8 | 100 | 98 |
| 3 | 500 | 32 | 9 | 800 | 52 |
| 4 | 900 | 5 | 10 | 100 | 49 |
| 5 | 300 | 31 | 11 | 400 | 80 |
| 6 | 500 | 17 | 12 | 800 | 83 |

**Process/Formulas** A repetitive FOR/NEXT loop process is to be used, with the number of shares and the market price, each being stored in a separate subscripted array. The portfolio value is determined by multiplying the number of shares of each stock, $N$, by its current market price, $P$, and then summing up the products to get a total, $T$.

**Output**

Output follows this format:

```
STOCK        # SHARES       MARKET PRICE
  1            300            $ 50
  2            400            $ 42
  3            500            $ 32
  4            900            $  5
  5            300            $ 31
  6            500            $ 17
  7            500            $ 77
  8            100            $ 98
  9            800            $ 52
 10            100            $ 49
 11            400            $ 80
 12            800            $ 83
-----------------------------------------------------
    PORTFOLIO VALUE           $263,300
```

Program 12.5 illustrates how the current total market value for the stocks in Case 12.2 is obtained. Note the DIM statement in line 30 that is required for the two lists, $N$ and $P$. Also note that line 30 provides overdimensioning for variables $N$ and $P$ since there are only 12 securities and room for 15 was provided by the DIM. The program contains four FOR/NEXT loops in a series. The first loop (lines 60–80) reads in the number of shares; the second loop (lines 90–110) reads in the market price; the third loop (lines 120–150) causes the printing of stock numbers, number of shares, and market price and then accumulates the market price times the number of shares. The last loop results in printing dashes to underline across the page (lines 160–180).

---

**PROGRAM 12.5   Case 12.2 Current Market Value of Stock Portfolio**

```
10 REM CASE 12.2, COMPUTING THE MARKET VALUE OF AN INVESTMENT PORTFOLIO
15 REM PROGRAMMER- (name of person)  DATE- mm/dd/yy
16 REM    VARIABLE LIST-
17 REM        A$,B$ = FORMATS
19 REM        I=# OF STOCK AND LOOP INDEX
20 REM        N(I)=# OF SHARES
21 REM        P(I)=MARKET PRICE
22 REM        T=TOTAL CURRENT VALUE
25 REM -----------------------------------
30 DIM N(15),P(15)
32 LET A$ = "STOCK      # SHARES     MARKET PRICE"
34 LET B$ = "  ##          ###          $ ##"
40 PRINT A$
50 LET T=0
60 FOR I = 1 TO 12     'loop to read the number of shares
70    READ N(I)
80 NEXT I
90 FOR I = 1 TO 12     'loop to read the market prices
100    READ P(I)
110 NEXT I
120 FOR I = 1 TO 12          'loop to print and accumulate
130    PRINT USING B$;I,N(I),P(I)
140    LET T = T+N(I)*P(I)     'number of shares x price per share
150 NEXT I
160 FOR I= 1 TO 40            'loop to print dashes
170    PRINT "-";
180 NEXT I
190 PRINT
200 PRINT USING "    PORTFOLIO VALUE   $$###,### ";T
210 DATA 300,400,500,900,300,500,500,100,800,100,400,800
220 DATA 50,42,32,5,31,17,77,98,52,49,80,83
230 END

RUN
STOCK     # SHARES    MARKET PRICE
  1          300        $ 50
  2          400        $ 42
  3          500        $ 32
  4          900        $  5
  5          300        $ 31
  6          500        $ 17
  7          500        $ 77
  8          100        $ 98
  9          800        $ 52
 10          100        $ 49
 11          400        $ 80
 12          800        $ 83
-----------------------------------------
    PORTFOLIO VALUE       $263,300
```

Program 12.6 is a simple illustration of how it is possible to have values assigned to subscripted variables using the INPUT statement (line 20). Note how line 35 causes the inputted values to be printed out in reverse sequence.

## PROGRAM 12.6 Subscripting Variables Using the INPUT Statement

```
10 FOR I= 1 TO 5
20    INPUT A(I)
25 NEXT I
30 PRINT
35 FOR I=5 TO 1 STEP -1
40    PRINT A(I);
50 NEXT I
99 END

RUN
? 22
? 25
? 38
? 46
? 59

   59   46   38   25   22
```

Case 12.3 is based on the idea of using the INPUT statement to assign values to subscripted variables.

## CASE 12.3

**Problem**

**Generating a Sales Report, Conversational Program**

Town Food Stores, Inc., has a sophisticated management information system (MIS) that keeps track of daily operations for its 13 stores. At the end of each day, each store telephones the total daily receipts to the clerk in the main computer room. The clerk then responds to a conversational program that requests the sales figures for each store. This information is stored, and a daily summary giving a total for all the stores is printed out.

**Data Input**

The data values are entered interactively in response to an INPUT prompt. Today's sales figures are:

| STORE | SALES | STORE | SALES |
|-------|-------|-------|-------|
| 1 | $3,696 | 2 | $4,281 |
| 3 | 5,650 | 4 | 6,969 |
| 5 | 3,854 | 6 | 4,955 |
| 7 | 5,724 | 8 | 1,695 |
| 9 | 7,864 | 10 | 1,947 |
| 11 | 4,417 | 12 | 5,092 |
| 13 | 2,611 | | |

**Process/Formulas** A repetitive FOR/NEXT loop process is to be used, with daily sales being assigned to a subscripted array. These values are then accumulated to produce a daily total.

**Output** A hard copy report is generated showing the sales for each store and a summary total for the entire day. Input and output for both the screen display and hard copy follows this format:

**DATA ENTRY**

```
INSTRUCTIONS: PLEASE TYPE IN THE DAILY SALES
FOR EACH STORE AFTER ? MARK.
STORE 1  ? 3696
STORE 2  ? 4281
STORE 3  ? 5650
STORE 4  ? 6969
STORE 5  ? 3854
STORE 6  ? 4955
STORE 7  ? 5724
STORE 8  ? 1695
STORE 9  ? 7864
STORE 10 ? 1947
STORE 11 ? 4417
STORE 12 ? 5092
STORE 13 ? 2611
```

**HARD COPY OUTPUT**

```
TODAY'S SALES REPORT
--------------------
STORE           SALES
--------------------
   1        $ 3,696
   2        $ 4,281
   3        $ 5,650
   4        $ 6,969
   5        $ 3,854
   6        $ 4,955
   7        $ 5,724
   8        $ 1,695
   9        $ 7,864
  10        $ 1,947
  11        $ 4,417
  12        $ 5,092
  13        $ 2,611
--------------------
TOTAL       $58,755
```

Program 12.7 shows a conversational program that carries out the objectives of Case 12.3. Line 90, INPUT D(I), is within a FOR/NEXT loop that causes values to be assigned to variables D(1)–D(13).

Note how the INPUT query is preceded by instructions for the user. Every INPUT in an applications program should have instructions, or a prompt before it, containing some message for program users. This gives users a better understanding of what they have to do when entering data.

## PROGRAM 12.7 Case 12.3, Town Food Stores, Inc., Conversational Program

```
10 REM CASE 12.3, GENERATING A SALES REPORT
15 REM PROGRAMMER- (name of person)  DATE- mm/dd/yy
16 REM     VARIABLE LIST-D,S1,I
17 REM         A0$,A1$,A2$,A3$,A4$ = FORMATS
18 REM         D(I)=DAILY SALES
19 REM         S1=TOTAL SALES
20 REM         I=LOOP INDEX AND STORE NUMBER
25 REM --------------------------------
30 DIM D(15)
40 PRINT "INSTRUCTIONS: PLEASE TYPE IN THE DAILY SALES"
50 PRINT "FOR EACH STORE AFTER ? MARK."
60 LET S1 = 0
61 LET A0$= "TODAY'S SALES REPORT"
62 LET A1$= "--------------------"
63 LET A2$= "STORE         SALES"
64 LET A3$= " ##        $$##,###"
66 LET A4$= "TOTAL      $$##,###"
70 FOR I= 1 TO 13        'loop for INPUT data entry
80     PRINT "STORE";I;
90     INPUT D(I)
100    LET S1 =S1+D(I)  'accumulate daily sales
100 NEXT I
115 LPRINT
120 LPRINT A0$
130 LPRINT A1$
145 LPRINT A2$
147 LPRINT A1$
150 FOR I = 1 TO 13      'loop to print out report contents
160     LPRINT USING A3$; I, D(I)
170 NEXT I
180 LPRINT A1$
190 LPRINT USING A4$;S1  'prints out the total
200 END


RUN
INSTRUCTIONS: PLEASE TYPE IN THE DAILY SALES
FOR EACH STORE AFTER THE ? MARK.
STORE 1 ? 3696
STORE 2 ? 4281
STORE 3 ? 5650
STORE 4 ? 6969
STORE 5 ? 3854
STORE 6 ? 4955
STORE 7 ? 5724
STORE 8 ? 1695
STORE 9 ? 7864
STORE 10 ? 1947
STORE 11 ? 4417
STORE 12 ? 5092
STORE 13 ? 2611
```

Screen display

```
TODAY'S SALES REPORT
--------------------
STORE           SALES
--------------------
  1           $3,696
  2           $4,281
  3           $5,650
  4           $6,969
  5           $3,854
  6           $4,955
  7           $5,724
  8           $1,695
  9           $7,864
 10           $1,947
 11           $4,417
 12           $5,092
 13           $2,611
--------------------
TOTAL        $58,755
```

Printer output

Case 12.4 illustrates the use of a subscripted array instead of using a computed GOTO statement when data values are coded 0, 1, 2, . . . , and so forth. In such a situation the index of the array (1, 2, 3, . . . , and so forth) is matched with the data value codes (1, 2, 3, . . . , and so forth) to process the item stored in the array location.

## CASE 12.4

**Problem**

**Generating a Payroll Report**
As part of a payroll report, a company wishes to print out the salary (hours × hourly rate), federal tax, and net pay, along with the totals. The federal tax deducted is based on the number of dependents claimed, as shown in the following table:

| DEPENDENTS | TAX RATE |
|---|---|
| 0 | .20 |
| 1 | .18 |
| 2 | .15 |
| 3 | .11 |
| 4 | .08 |
| 5 or more | .05 |

**Data Input**

The data values to be processed are contained in the following lists:

| NAME | HOURS WORKED | HOURLY RATE | NUMBER OF DEPENDENTS |
|---|---|---|---|
| A. BRIE | 30 | $ 4.50 | 4 |
| S. HERTZ | 45 | 4.00 | 2 |
| J. THURM | 25 | 5.00 | 3 |
| L. SACHS | 40 | 7.50 | 5 |
| D. LENT | 45 | 10.00 | 5 |
| A. SENT | 35 | 6.00 | 1 |
| J. RINDER | 30 | 4.50 | 0 |

**Process/Formulas**  A repetitive FOR/NEXT loop process is to be used, with tax rates being assigned to a subscripted array. Another FOR/NEXT loop processes the employee data to determine salary (hours $\times$ hourly rate), tax, and net pay (salary $-$ tax). The tax is determined by multiplying the appropriate tax rate, as adjusted for the number of dependents, times the salary. Totals are derived for all of the salaries, taxes deducted, and net pay.

**Output**  The output follows this format:

```
NAME         SALARY       TAX        NET PAY

A. BRIE     $135.00     $10.80      $124.20
S. HERTZ    $180.00     $27.00      $153.00
J. THURM    $125.00     $13.75      $111.25
L. SACHS    $300.00     $15.00      $285.00
D. LENT     $450.00     $22.50      $427.50
A. SENT     $210.00     $37.80      $172.20
J. RINDER   $135.00     $27.00      $108.00

TOTALS    $1,535.00    $153.85    $1,381.15
```

Program 12.8 reads the tax rates into an array $P$ and can determine the appropriate tax rate with line 180 and without using the computed GOTO or IF/THEN tests. Thus, if someone claims three dependents, his or her tax rate is P(D) or P(3), which is 11%.

## PROGRAM 12.8   Case 12.4, Net Pay Using Coded Tax Rates

```
10 REM CASE 12.4, PAYROLL REPORT CALCULATIONS: SALARY
11 REM             TAX DEDUCTION, NET PAY, AND TOTALS
12 REM PROGRAMMER- (name of person)  DATE- mm/dd/yy
13 REM    VARIABLE LIST-
14 REM        A$,B$,C$,T$= FORMATS
15 REM        D=# OF DEPENDENTS
16 REM        E$=EMPLOYEE NAME
17 REM        H=HOURS
18 REM        I,C=COUNTER
19 REM        P(I)=TAX RATE
20 REM        P=NET PAY, P1=TOTAL NET PAY
22 REM        R=RATE
23 REM        S=SALARY, S1=TOTAL SALARY
25 REM        T=TAX, T1=TOTAL TAX
27 REM -----------------------------
30 LET S1=0
40 LET T1=0
50 LET P1=0
55         LET T$ = "NAME          SALARY        TAX         NET PAY"
60         LET A$ = "\            \  $###.##       $##.##        $###.##"
70         LET B$ = "TOTALS     $#,###.##      $###.##      $#,###.##"
```

```
 80 FOR I= 0 TO 5           'note: loop index starts at 0
 90     READ P(I)           'enter tax rate
100 NEXT I
110 DATA .20,.18,.15,.11,.08,.05
120 PRINT T$
130 PRINT
140 FOR C=1 TO 7                'loop for processing
150     READ E$,H,R,D
160     LET S=H*R                'determine salary
170     IF D>5 THEN LET D = 5
180        LET T=S*P(D)    'find tax
190        LET P=S-T        'net pay
200        LET S1=S1+S       'total salary
210        LET T1=T1+T       'total tax
220        LET P1=P1+P       'total net pay
230        PRINT USING A$;E$,S,T,P
240 NEXT C
250     DATA A. BRIE,30,4.50,4, S. HERTZ,45,4,2
255     DATA J. THURM,25,5,3, L. SACHS,40,7.50,5
260     DATA D. LENT,45,10,6, A. SENT,35,6,1, J. RINDER,30,4.50,0
270        PRINT
280        PRINT USING B$; S1,T1,P1
290 END


RUN
NAME            SALARY        TAX          NET PAY

A. BRIE        $135.00      $10.80        $124.20
S. HERTZ       $180.00      $27.00        $153.00
J. THURM       $125.00      $13.75        $111.25
L. SACHS       $300.00      $15.00        $285.00
D. LENT        $450.00      $22.50        $427.50
A. SENT        $210.00      $37.80        $172.20
J. RINDER      $135.00      $27.00        $108.00

TOTALS     $1,535.00     $153.85      $1,381.15
```

## Tables

Many times, data takes the form of a table that is simply several lists grouped together. Rather than reading each list as a separate variable, it is easier to treat them all as a single variable with two subscripts instead of one. In this manner we have a table with one subscript representing the row locations and the other subscript representing the column locations. Table 12.3 shows examples of numeric variables with two subscripts.

As was the case with lists, tables containing data must be appropriately dimensioned to reserve storage space. The general form of the statement to be used is:

line # DIM variable name(# rows, # columns)

Table 12.4 shows examples of the dimension statement for array tables.

**TABLE 12.3**   Subscripted Numeric Variables—Tables

| VARIABLE NOTATION | EXPLANATION |
| --- | --- |
| B(1,6) | A subscripted variable for a numeric data item to be placed in a two-dimensional array *B*, row 1, column 6. |
| TOT(25,2) | A subscripted variable for a numeric data item to be placed in a two-dimensional array *TOT*, row 25, column 2. |
| SUM(I,J) | A subscripted variable for a numeric data item to be placed in a two-dimensional array *SUM*, row I, column J. |

**TABLE 12.4**   Examples of the Dimension Statement—Tables

| STATEMENT | EXPLANATION |
| --- | --- |
| 1. 20 DIM C(5,8) | The maximum number of storage locations for the table variable *C* is 5 rows, and 8 columns. Can be 6 rows and 9 columns if we include C(0,0). See OPTION BASE at end of chapter. |
| 2. 40 DIM B(35,50), TL3(20,20) | Several tables can be dimensioned within a single DIM statement. |
| 3. 60 DIM MO(35,50), X2(40) | Tables and lists can be dimensioned within a single DIM statement. |

Suppose the Better Gum Company has test marketed a new chewing gum in five types of outlets (candy stores, gum machines, supermarkets, and so forth) in three regions for the period of one month and had obtained the following sales figures in dozens of units sold:

|  | REGION | | |
| --- | --- | --- | --- |
| TYPE OF OUTLET | 1 | 2 | 3 |
| 1 | 15 | 17 | 13 |
| 2 | 18 | 15 | 16 |
| 3 | 12 | 18 | 15 |
| 4 | 14 | 15 | 14 |
| 5 | 17 | 12 | 13 |

This table data has five rows with three columns. If the table is given the name Table G, a program can then be written to read in and store the table. The reading of the table will follow a row-by-row sequence, going from left to right across each row, column by column. The operation of nested loops does this reading process for us. In Program 12.9 the outer loop (bounded by lines 20 and 60) provides the row designation, and the inner loop (lines 30–50) provides the column designation.

Line 10 in Program 12.9 shows the appropriate dimension, G(5,3), for a 5 × 3 table. The data in line 70 shows each row in sequence.

## PROGRAM 12.9    Reading and Storing a 5 × 3 Table

```
10 DIM G(5,3)
20 FOR I=1 TO 5            'outer loop for the rows
30     FOR J = 1 TO 3 'inner loop for the columns
40              READ G(I,J)
50     NEXT J
60 NEXT I
65 PRINT G(3,2),G(5,1)
70 DATA 15,17,13, 18,15,16, 12,18,15, 14,15,14, 17,12,13
99 END

RUN
 18               17
```

When the program is executed, each data value is represented by the variable name followed by a unique identification number corresponding to its row, $I$, and column, $J$, location. Variable $G(3,2)$ is assigned the value 18, variable $G(5,1)$ is assigned the value 17, and similarly for the rest of the data. The PRINT statement in line 65 shows how the values of individual subscripted variables such as $G(3,2)$ and $G(5,1)$ can be printed out. To print all of Table G, a PRINT statement, such as line 45, PRINT $G(I,J)$ in Program 12.10, is required. Figure 12.3 shows Table G with its subscripted variables and their values.

To obtain a total for *all* of the data in Table G and row totals, two accumulators need to be added to Program 12.9. To accomplish the task, lines 12, 23, 42, and 52 are added to the program. The revised program and resulting output are shown as Program 12.10.

Line 12 initializes the accumulator (T1) and line 52 computes the grand total. Line 23 initializes the row accumulator (R) and line 42 computes the outlet (row) totals. The PRINT statement in line 55 causes the row totals to be printed. The PRINT statement in line 65 causes the grand total (224) to be printed. A flowchart of Program 12.10 is shown in Figure 12.4.

|  |  | J: Columns | | |
|---|---|---|---|---|
|  |  | 1 | 2 | 3 |
| Rows | 1 | G(1,1)=15 | G(1,2)=17 | G(1,3)=13 |
|  | 2 | G(2,1)=18 | G(2,2)=15 | G(2,3)=16 |
| G(I,J) | 3 | G(3,1)=12 | G(3,2)=18 | G(3,3)=15 |
|  | 4 | G(4,1)=14 | G(4,2)=15 | G(4,3)=14 |
|  | 5 | G(5,1)=17 | G(5,2)=12 | G(5,3)=13 |

**FIGURE 12.3**    Table G Variables and Values

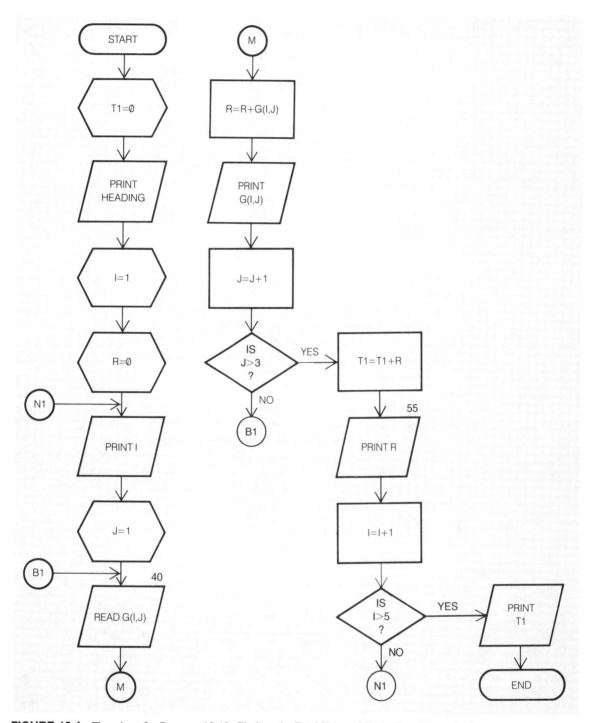

**FIGURE 12.4** Flowchart for Program 12.10, Finding the Total Value of Table G and Row Totals

## PROGRAM 12.10   Finding the Total Value of Table G and Row Totals

```
10 DIM G(5,3)
12 LET T1 = 0
14 PRINT TAB(28); "REGION"
15 PRINT
16 PRINT "OUTLET",1,2,3,"OUTLET TOTALS"
17 PRINT
20 FOR I = 1 TO 5
23      LET R=0
25      PRINT I,
30      FOR J = 1 TO 3
40          READ G(I,J)
42          LET R=R+G(I,J)
45          PRINT G(I,J),
50      NEXT J
52      LET T1=T1+R
55      PRINT R
60 NEXT I
62 PRINT
65 PRINT TAB(20);"TOTAL SALES FOR ALL REGIONS",T1
69 DATA 15,17,13, 18,15,16, 12,18,15, 14,15,14, 17,12,13
99  END
```

```
RUN
                            REGION

OUTLET         1            2            3            OUTLET TOTALS

   1          15           17           13            45
   2          18           15           16            49
   3          12           18           15            45
   4          14           15           14            43
   5          17           12           13            42

              TOTAL SALES FOR ALL REGIONS              224
```

After values have been read in and stored as a table, it is possible to manipulate them. For instance, it may be desired to retrieve a part of a table. This can be accomplished by changing the starting point of the nested loops. Program 12.11 shows how the sales data for outlets 3–5 in regions 2 and 3 of the Better Gum Company's test marketing could be printed out. Lines 70 and 80 are responsible for the partial output of Table G. The outer loop restricts printing to rows 3–5, while the inner loop restricts printing to columns 2 and 3.

## PROGRAM 12.11   Printing Out Part of Table G

```
10 DIM G(5,3)
20 FOR I = 1 TO 5
30      FOR J = 1 TO 3
40          READ G(I,J)
```

```
50        NEXT J
60 NEXT I
69 DATA 15,17,13, 18,15,16, 12,18,15, 14,15,14, 17,12,13
70  FOR I = 3 TO 5      'outer loop for rows 3, 4, 5
80        FOR J = 2 TO 3      'inner loop for columns 2, 3
90            PRINT G(I,J),
100       NEXT J
110       PRINT
115 NEXT I
199 END

RUN
 18            15
 15            14
 12            13
```

To obtain a specific row or column of a table that has already been read in and stored (such as Table G), several approaches can be used. With only a few columns, a statement such as

73 PRINT G(2,1),G(2,2),G(2,3)

would output the values of row 2 of Table G (18, 15, and 16, respectively). This could have also been done with the following statements:

77 FOR J = 1 TO 3
78      PRINT G(2,J),
80 NEXT J

Notice that G(2,J) holds the printing to row 2, while the columns, $J$, vary from 1 to 3. The same approach could be used to obtain a single column of a table. To print out the third column of Table G would require the following statements:

84 FOR I = 1 TO 5
85      PRINT G(I,3)
86 NEXT I

Although the rows will vary from 1 to 5, the PRINT G(I,3) ensures that printing is fixed on the third column. Program 12.12 summarizes these ideas based on Program 12.9 which was shown earlier.

## PROGRAM 12.12   Printing Out a Row and Column of Table G

```
10 DIM G(5,3)
20 FOR I = 1 TO 5
30     FOR J = 1 TO 3
40             READ G(I,J)
50     NEXT J
60 NEXT I
69 DATA 15,17,13, 18,15,16, 12,18,15, 14,15,14, 17,12,13
70 PRINT
```

```
71 PRINT "OUTLET 2:"
73 PRINT G(2,1),G(2,2),G(2,3)        'row 2, columns 1, 2, 3
76 PRINT "OUTLET 2:"
77 FOR J = 1 TO 3
78      PRINT G(2,J),               'row 2, columns J = 1, 2, 3
80 NEXT J
81 PRINT
82 PRINT "REGION 3:"
84 FOR I = 1 TO 5
85      PRINT G(I,3)                'rows I = 1, 2, 3, 4, 5, column 3
86 NEXT I
199 END


RUN
OUTLET 2:
 18        15        16
OUTLET 2:
 18        15        16
REGION 3:
 13
 16
 15
 14
 13
```

Case 12.5 requires a single program that uses data in the form of two tables and one list.

. . . . . . . . . . . . . . . . . . . . . . . . . . . . . . . . . . . .

## CASE 12.5

**Problem**

**Gross Wage Computations**
The Computer Components Company pays its workers according to the number of units of each type of component (A, B, or C) they have assembled. The gross wage for each worker is to be determined.

**Data Input**

The data values are the piecework rates and the worker output for the last two weeks. The piecework rate is as follows:

| Component | A | B | C |
|---|---|---|---|
| Rate per unit | $.25 | $.35 | $.50 |

Output for the last two weeks is as follows:

| WORKER | WEEK 1 COMPONENTS | | | WEEK 2 COMPONENTS | | |
|---|---|---|---|---|---|---|
| | A | B | C | A | B | C |
| 1 | 200 | 100 | 20 | 185 | 110 | 22 |
| 2 | 150 | 125 | 30 | 160 | 115 | 25 |
| 3 | 320 | 75 | 15 | 275 | 100 | 30 |
| 4 | 275 | 100 | 15 | 275 | 90 | 20 |
| 5 | 100 | 200 | 10 | 150 | 150 | 10 |

**Process/Formulas** Using nested FOR/NEXT loops, each week of data values is to be treated as a table. The piecework rates are to be treated as an array using a single FOR/NEXT loop process. A nested FOR/NEXT loop will process the weekly data to determine the total gross wage for each worker. The gross wage for each worker is computed by taking the total output of each type of component produced during both weeks and multiplying it by the respective component piecework rate. The results of each of these multiplications for components A, B, and C are then totaled to derive the gross wage for each worker.

**Output** The output should look as follows:

```
WORKER 1      GROSS WAGE      $190.75
WORKER 2      GROSS WAGE      $189.00
WORKER 3      GROSS WAGE      $232.50
WORKER 4      GROSS WAGE      $221.50
WORKER 5      GROSS WAGE      $195.00
```

Program 12.13 shows how two tables (one for each week) and one list (the rates) are used to obtain the gross wage per worker.

## PROGRAM 12.13  Case 12.5, Gross Wage Calculations

```
10 REM 12.5, COMPUTING GROSS WAGE FOR FIVE WORKERS
15 REM PROGRAMMER- (name of person)  DATE- mm/dd/yy
16 REM     VARIABLE LIST-
17 REM          A(I,J)=TOTAL # OF COMPONENTS FINISHED - TABLE
18 REM          G=GROSS WAGE
19 REM          I,J=COUNTER
20 REM          R(J)=RATE PER UNIT - LIST
21 REM          W1(I,J)=# OF COMPONENTS FINISHED BY WORKER IN WEEK 1 TABLE
22 REM          W2(I,J)=# OF COMPONENTS FINISHED BY WORKER IN WEEK 2 TABLE
25 REM --------------------------------------------------------------
30 DIM W1(5,3),W2(5,3),A(5,3)
40 FOR I = 1 TO 5     'nested loop for week 1 table
50       FOR J = 1 TO 3
60             READ W1(I,J)
70       NEXT J
80 NEXT I
90  FOR I = 1 TO 5     'nested loop for week 2 table
100      FOR J = 1 TO 3
110            READ W2(I,J)
120      NEXT J
130 NEXT I
140 FOR J = 1 TO 3     'loop for the list of rates
150       READ R(J)
160 NEXT J
170 FOR I = 1 TO 5     'nested loop for calculations
180      LET G = 0
190      FOR J = 1 TO 3
```

```
200              LET A(I,J) = W1(I,J) + W2(I,J)    'sums both weeks components
210              LET G = G + A(I,J)*R(J)            'accumulates piecework rate
220      NEXT J                                     'times number produced
230      PRINT USING "WORKER ##       GROSS WAGE   $###.## "; I,G
240 NEXT I
250 DATA 200,100,20, 150,125,30, 320,75,15, 275,100,15,100,200,10
260 DATA 185,110,22, 160,115,25, 275,100,30, 275,90,20,150,150,10
270 DATA .25,.35,.50
299 END

RUN
WORKER   1      GROSS WAGE   $190.75
WORKER   2      GROSS WAGE   $189.00
WORKER   3      GROSS WAGE   $232.50
WORKER   4      GROSS WAGE   $221.50
WORKER   5      GROSS WAGE   $195.00
```

Line 30 in Program 12.13 provides the necessary dimensioning for each of the two tables. The output for week 1 is designated Table W1, and the output for week 2 is Table W2. Note the dimensioning for Table A. The values in this table are developed further on in the program, and, since they are to be stored, dimensioning prior to their creation is necessary. Table W1 is read in with a nested FOR/NEXT loop (lines 40–80). Table W2 is read in with a nested FOR/NEXT loop (lines 90–130). The piecework rates are in the list designated R and are read in with a single FOR/NEXT loop (lines 140–160).

Within the nested FOR/NEXT loops (lines 170–240), the following calculations occur: Within the inner loop (lines 190–220), line 200 accumulates the number of units each worker produced by component for 2 weeks and stores the sum in Table A; in line 210 the gross wage for each worker is calculated by multiplying the total number of units of each component produced, $A(I,J)$, by the piecework rate, $R(J)$, for each component.

Below are the step-by-step calculations carried out for worker 1. Assume that line 190 has been executed, and $I = 1$, and $J = 1$.

line 200: $A(1,1) = W(1,1) + W2(1,1) = 200 + 185 = 385$

line 210: $G = G + A(I,J)*R(J) = 0 + A(1,1)*R(1)$

$G = 0 + 385*.25 = 96.25$

The NEXT J brings us to $I = 1$, $J = 2$,

line 200: $A(1,2) = W1(1,2) + W2(1,2) = 100 + 110 = 210$

line 210: $G = 96.25 + A(1,2)*R(2) = 96.25 + 210*.35$

$G = 96.25 + 73.5 = 169.75$

The NEXT J brings us to $I = 1$, $J = 3$,

line 200: $A(1,3) = W1(1,3) + W2(1,3) = 20 + 22 = 42$

line 210: $G = 169.75 + A(1,3)*R(3) = 169.75 + 42*.50$

$G = 169.75 + 21 = 190.75$

After $J = 3$, line 230 is executed, causing the results for worker 1 to be printed out. The execution of line 240, the NEXT I, starts the process over again, but this time for $I = 2$, the second worker. Note how line 180 reinitializes G at zero before starting the next worker. This process ensures that the accumulation for G starts at zero for each worker.

String data can be assigned to subscripted variables in the same way that we assign numeric data to them. This works for both one-dimensional arrays and two-dimensional arrays. Examples of subscripted string variables are shown in Table 12.5. As we saw with numeric data values, appropriate dimensioning is also required for string data in lists and tables. Table 12.6 shows examples of the dimension statement for string variables.

Program 12.14 provides an example of the subscripted string variable concepts just described. This program reads and stores the array MO$ for the 12 months of the year.

**TABLE 12.5**  Subscripted String Variables

| VARIABLE NOTATION | EXPLANATION |
|---|---|
| B$(1) | A subscripted variable for a string data item to be placed in a one-dimensional array B$, location 1. |
| DIV$(35) | A subscripted variable for a string data item to be placed in a one-dimensional array DIV$, location 35. |
| ID1$(I) | A subscripted variable for a string data item to be placed in a one-dimensional array ID1$, in location I. |
| CO$(1,6) | A subscripted variable for a string data item to be placed in a two-dimensional array CO$, row 1, column 6. |
| MONTH$(12,12) | A subscripted variable for a string data item to be placed in a two-dimensional array MONTH$, row 12, column 12. |
| SIZE$(I,J) | A subscripted variable for a string data item to be placed in a two-dimensional array SIZE$, row I, column J. |

**TABLE 12.6**  Examples of the Dimension Statement—String Variables

| STATEMENT | EXPLANATION |
|---|---|
| 1. 25 DIM B$(45) | The maximum number of storage locations for the variable B$ is 45 items, or 46 if you include the location B$(0). |
| 2. 45 DIM D$(35), KT$(60), M01$(42) | Multiple data lists or arrays can be dimensioned within a single DIM statement. |
| 3. 50 DIM C$(15,8) | The maximum number of storage locations for the table variable C$ is 15 rows and 8 columns, or 16 rows and 9 columns if you include the zero row and zero column. |
| 4. 55 DIM G$(20,60), TT3$(50,3) | Several tables can be dimensioned within a single DIM statement. |
| 5. 60 DIM MO$(35,20), F1$(40) | Tables and lists can be dimensioned within a single DIM statement. |

Line 10 is the appropriate dimension statement for this array. Once the string data items are read by line 20, line 25 causes each string to be printed out. The FOR/NEXT loop in lines 55–65 causes the string array data items to be printed out in reverse order. Note line 55,

55 FOR I = 12 TO 1 STEP −1

which starts the loop at the array index of 12. The loop index of *I* steps down by 1, and this causes the months to be printed with DECEMBER (*I* = 12), NOVEMBER (*I* = 11), and so on, down to JANUARY (*I* = 1).

## PROGRAM 12.14   Reading, Printing, and Storing with Subscripted String Variables

```
10 DIM MO$(12)
15 FOR I = 1 TO 12     'loop to read and print each month
20      READ MO$(I)
25      PRINT MO$(I),
30 NEXT I
35 PRINT
40 DATA JANUARY, FEBRUARY, MARCH, APRIL, MAY, JUNE
45 DATA JULY, AUGUST, SEPTEMBER, OCTOBER, NOVEMBER, DECEMBER
50 PRINT
55 FOR I = 12 TO 1 STEP -1  'loop to print out in reverse sequence
60      PRINT MO$(I),       'subscripted string data
65 NEXT I
99   END

RUN
JANUARY       FEBRUARY      MARCH        APRIL         MAY
JUNE          JULY          AUGUST       SEPTEMBER     OCTOBER
NOVEMBER      DECEMBER

DECEMBER      NOVEMBER      OCTOBER      SEPTEMBER     AUGUST
JULY          JUNE          MAY          APRIL         MARCH
FEBRUARY      JANUARY
```

Case 12.6, using Program 12.15, illustrates how one-dimensional subscripted string variables are handled.

## CASE 12.6

**Problem**   **Generation of Quarterly Production Report**
A company with monthly production data would like to have a report printed that groups production figures by quarters.

**Data Input**      The monthly production data is as follows:

| MONTH | PRODUCTION |
|---|---|
| January | 1,500 |
| February | 1,200 |
| March | 1,750 |
| April | 1,600 |
| May | 1,550 |
| June | 1,350 |
| July | 1,400 |
| August | 1,750 |
| September | 1,600 |
| October | 1,250 |
| November | 1,300 |
| December | 1,500 |

**Process/Formulas**   A repetitive FOR/NEXT loop process is to be used, with the months as string data items being assigned to a subscripted string array and with the production data items being assigned to a numeric array. A nested FOR/NEXT loop process is to be used to produce the desired report.

**Output**      A typical quarterly output has the following format:

```
QUARTER NUMBER 1
    MONTH           PRODUCTION
-----------------------------

    JANUARY         1,500 UNITS
    FEBRUARY        1,200 UNITS
    MARCH           1,750 UNITS
```

---

## PROGRAM 12.15   Case 12.6, Production Report, Subscripted String Variables

```
10 REM CASE 12.6, PRODUCTION REPORT BY QUARTER
15 REM PROGRAMMER- (name of person)   DATE- mm/dd/yy
17 REM     VARIABLE LIST-
18 REM        F1$,F2$,F3$,F4$ = FORMATS
19 REM        I=LOOP INDEX
21 REM        MO$(I)=MONTH
23 REM        PROD(I)=PRODUCTION
25 REM -------------------------------------------
30 DIM MO$(12), PROD(12)
40 FOR I = 1 TO 12                'loop to enter data for
50     READ MO$(I), PROD(I)       'each month and production
60 NEXT I
70 DATA JANUARY,1500, FEBRUARY,1200, MARCH,1750
80 DATA APRIL,1600, MAY,1550, JUNE,1350
90 DATA JULY,1400, AUGUST,1750, SEPTEMBER,1600
100 DATA OCTOBER,1250, NOVEMBER,1300, DECEMBER,1500
```

```
110 LET F1$ = " QUARTER NUMBER"
120 LET F2$ = "   MONTH          PRODUCTION"
130 LET F3$ = " --------------------------"
140 LET F4$ = " \              \   #,###   UNITS
150 FOR I = 1 TO 4        'nested loop for each quarter
160        PRINT F1$; I
170        PRINT F2$
180        PRINT F3$
190        FOR J = 1 TO 3
200            PRINT USING F4$; MO$(3*(I-1)+J, PROD(3*(I-1)+J)
210        NEXT J
220        PRINT
230 NEXT I
240 END

RUN
 QUARTER NUMBER 1
   MONTH          PRODUCTION
 --------------------------
   JANUARY        1,500   UNITS
   FEBRUARY       1,200   UNITS
   MARCH          1,750   UNITS

 QUARTER NUMBER 2
   MONTH          PRODUCTION
 --------------------------
   APRIL          1,600   UNITS
   MAY            1,550   UNITS
   JUNE           1,350   UNITS

 QUARTER NUMBER 3
   MONTH          PRODUCTION
 --------------------------
   JULY           1,400   UNITS
   AUGUST         1,750   UNITS
   SEPTEMBER      1,600   UNITS

 QUARTER NUMBER 4
   MONTH          PRODUCTION
 --------------------------
   OCTOBER        1,250   UNITS
   NOVEMBER       1,300   UNITS
   DECEMBER       1,500   UNITS
```

Note that line 50 reads in data for the string variable array, MO$, as well as for the numeric variable array PROD. By dimensioning MO$, we can use MO$(6) to refer to the sixth month, which will be printed out as June. Note how the expressions in the parentheses in line 200 print the $J$th month in the $I$th quarter. Thus, for example, the second month in the third quarter corresponds to $J = 2$ and $I = 3$ and $3*(I - 1) + J = 8$, which is August, the eighth month of the year.

Case 12.7, using Program 12.16, also illustrates both numeric and string data in one-dimensional arrays.

## CASE 12.7

**Problem**

**Grade Determination Program**

In a certain course, three class exams and one final exam are given. A student's final average for the term is based on the average of the three class-exam grades averaged in with the final-exam grade. A letter grade of A, B+, B, C+, C, D+, D, or F is also given. We wish to write a program to read the student's name, class-exam grades, and final-exam grade and to print a table with the student's name, final average for the term, and letter grade. A letter grade of A is given to those whose term average is at least 90, a B+ is given to those whose term average is at least 85 and less than 90, and so forth. There are 10 students in the class. We also wish to print the number of people receiving each of the grades.

**Data Input**

The names and numeric grades of each student are as follows:

| NAME | 3 EXAM GRADES | | | FINAL EXAM |
|---|---|---|---|---|
| J.SAMBORN | 65 | 76 | 80 | 90 |
| P.FISHMAN | 70 | 81 | 95 | 93 |
| E.GOLD | 76 | 84 | 68 | 78 |
| A.EINSTEIN | 98 | 97 | 90 | 95 |
| B.WEIN | 86 | 88 | 89 | 89 |
| S.LACHS | 77 | 76 | 80 | 73 |
| M.FALIG | 81 | 84 | 90 | 80 |
| R.HERMAN | 58 | 74 | 67 | 54 |
| B.GILA | 70 | 75 | 78 | 79 |
| J.LYNN | 70 | 74 | 65 | 68 |

The letter grades are A, B+, B, C+, C, D+, D, and F.

**Process/Formulas**

A FOR/NEXT loop process is to assign the letter grades to a subscripted string array. A FOR/NEXT loop will process the numeric grades for each student to calculate a final average for the term. This average is found by averaging the grades of the three class exams with the grade of the final exam. Decision testing compares the term average with a cut off (see problem description) to generate a numeric code of 1 to 8, which corresponds to each letter grade. A match of this code to the subscripted string array will cause the correct letter grade to be printed. A count is to be kept of the number of students receiving each letter grade.

**Output**

The output should look like that presented below:

```
NAME            TERM AVERAGE        GRADE
J.SAMBORN           81.83             B
P.FISHMAN           87.50             B+
E.GOLD              77.00             C+
A.EINSTEIN          95.00             A
B.WEIN              88.33             B+
S.LACHS             75.33             C+
M.FALIG             82.50             B
R.HERMAN            60.17             D
B.GILA              76.67             C+
J.LYNN              68.83             D+
```

```
GRADE       NUMBER
  A           1
  B+          2
  B           2
  C+          3
  C           0
  D+          1
  D           1
  F           0
```

. . . . . . . . . . . . . . . . . . . . . . . . . . . . . . . . .

## PROGRAM 12.16    Case 12.7, Grading Program

```
10 REM CASE 12.7, GRADING PROGRAM
15 REM PROGRAMMER- (name of person)   DATE- mm/dd/yy
16 REM     VARIABLE LIST-
17 REM        A=AVERAGE SCORE
18 REM        F=GRADE OF FINAL EXAM
19 REM        F$,F0$,F1$,F2$=FORMATS
20 REM        G1,G2,G3=SCORE FOR EACH EXAM
21 REM        G$(I)=LETTER GRADE
22 REM        N(I)=# OF STUDENTS RECEIVING EACH GRADE
23 REM        N$=NAME
24 REM        X=INTEGER TO IDENTIFY GRADE
25 REM -------------------------------------------------       `
40 DIM N(8),G$(8)
50 FOR I = 1 TO 8     'enter letter grades
60     READ G$(I)
70     DATA A,B+,B,C+,C,D+,D,F
80     LET N(I)=0                 'initialize N list to 0
90 NEXT I
94 LET F0$ = "NAME           TERM AVERAGE       GRADE"
95 LET F $ = "\             \      ###.##         \ \"
96 LET F1$ = "GRADE       NUMBER"
97 LET F2$ = "  \   \        ##"
100 PRINT F0$
110 FOR I =1 TO 10  'loop for 10 students
120     READ N$,G1,G2,G3,F
130     LET A=((G1+G2+G3)/3+F)2       'calculate average
140     IF A>=90 THEN 240             'test to determine letter grade
150     IF A>=85 THEN 250
160     IF A>=80 THEN 260
170     IF A>=75 THEN 270
180     IF A>=70 THEN 280
190     IF A>=65 THEN 290
200     IF A>=60 THEN 300
210        LET X = 8
215        GOTO 360
240           LET X = 1
245           GOTO 360
250              LET X = 2
255              GOTO 360
260                 LET X = 3
```

```
265                     GOTO 360
270                   LET X = 4
275                   GOTO 360
280                     LET X = 5
285                   GOTO 360
290                       LET X = 6
295                     GOTO 360
300                         LET X = 7
360          LET N(X)=N(X)+1
370        PRINT USING F$; N$,A,G$(X)
380 NEXT I
385 PRINT
390 PRINT "GRADE      NUMBER"
400 FOR I = 1 TO 8     'loop to print grade results
410       PRINT USING F2$; G$(I), N(I)
420 NEXT I
430 DATA J.SAMBORN,65,76,80,90, P.FISHMAN,70,81,95,93, E.GOLD,76,84,68,78
450 DATA A.EINSTEIN,98,97,90,95, B.WEIN,86,88,89,89, S.LACHS,77,76,80,73
470 DATA M.FALIG 81,84,90,80, R.HERMAN,58,74,67,54, B.GILA,70,75,78,79
490 DATA J.LYNN 70,74,65,68
499  END


RUN
NAME           TERM AVERAGE       GRADE
J.SAMBORN          81.83            B
P.FISHMAN          87.50            B+
E.GOLD             77.00            C+
A.EINSTEIN         95.00            A
B.WEIN             88.33            B+
S.LACHS            75.33            C+
M.FALIG            82.50            B
R.HERMAN           60.17            D
B.GILA             76.67            C+
J.LYNN             68.83            D+


GRADE      NUMBER
  A           1
  B+          2
  B           2
  C+          3
  C           0
  D+          1
  D           1
  F           0
```

In Program 12.16, an array G$ contains each of the possible grades A, B+, B, C+, C, D+, D, and F. Similarly, the array $N$ will contain the number of students receiving each grade. Thus, G$(3) = B and N(3) = the number of students receiving a B, and so on. Therefore, if the average is, say, at least 80 and under 85, the computer branches to line 260 where $X$ is set to 3. Then, the computer branches to line 360 where N(X) or N(3) increases by 1 and then prints the name of the student, the final average for the term, and G$(X) or G$(3), which is B. The values of the array G$ were read in at the beginning of the program (lines 50–90), and the initial zero values of the array $N$ were also set to zero within these lines.

Instead of reading the values of the array G$, we could have written

LET G$(1) = ''A''
LET G$(2) = ''B + ''
LET G$(3) = ''B''

and so on.

Where Cases 12.6 and 12.7 used a subscripted variable that took the form of a one-dimensional array, the next case illustrates how a two-dimensional string table can be developed.

## CASE 12.8

**Problem**  **String Table Lookup for Name Matching**
A college would like to print the names of all male seniors and female juniors to invite to a social gathering. A program will examine a student data list to print out the names of those students having the desired characteristics.

**Data Input**  The string data items to be processed are as follows:

| NAME | YEAR | SEX |
|------|------|-----|
| SAM CHERA | SR | M |
| GEORGE ROBBIN | FR | M |
| TOBY WOLF | SO | F |
| DEBBY FRANK | JR | F |
| MARK HANNAN | JR | M |
| SOL MENSH | SO | M |
| MARK GANCHROW | SR | M |
| FAY HOCH | JR | F |
| MARJORIE LEE | SR | F |

**Process/Formulas**  Two nested FOR/NEXT loops will be used. The first set of loops will read and store the string data items as a table. The second set of loops will produce an output table so that the names, year in school, and sex appear as columns rather than as separate rows of data. Another FOR/NEXT loop uses decision testing to carry out the task of matching the items in the table with the characteristics required by the problem, that is, male seniors and female juniors.

**Output**  The output should show three columns containing the original student names, their year in school, and their sex, followed by a listing of those students to be invited to the social function.

Program 12.17 was written for Case 12.8. A table N$ was created that stores the relevant information for each student (name, year, sex).

Note how the data in lines 260–300, grouped as nine names, followed by nine class-year designations, and then nine sex classifications, are reformed when read and stored as a table of nine rows and three columns (lines 50–90). This is done by using the variable N$(J,I) to assign each data item the row index J (1 to 9), and the column index I (1 to 3).

To output the information in this table with the names going down the first column rather than across the first row, we reverse the FOR/NEXT loops as shown in lines 120–170. There the J loop is first, followed by the I loop. This change causes the output to appear as three columns; name, year, and sex. The FOR/NEXT in lines 220–250 is used to look up the original data table to match males with seniors, and females with juniors. Logical IF/THEN statements in that loop search the data table to find a match and then print out the names of the students who fulfill the requirements.

**PROGRAM 12.17   Case 12.8, Matching with Subscripted String Table Data**

```
10 REM CASE 12.8, STRING TABLE LOOKUP-PRINTING THE NAMES OF PEOPLE
12 REM              TO INVITE TO A SOCIAL GATHERING
14 REM PROGRAMMER- (name of person)   DATE- mm/dd/yy
16 REM     VARIABLE LIST-
17 REM          I,J=LOOP INDICES
18 REM          N$(I,1)=NAME
20 REM          N$(I,2)=YEAR
22 REM          N$(I,3)=SEX
24 REM -----------------------------------
30 DIM N$(9,3)
50 FOR I = 1 TO 3     'read in- 3 rows by 9 columns
60     FOR J = 1 TO 9
70          READ N$(J,I)
80     NEXT J
90 NEXT I
100 REM **PRINT ALL STUDENTS AND THEIR STATUS**
110 PRINT "NAME","YEAR","SEX"
120 FOR J = 1 TO 9       'print out- 9 rows by 3 columns
130     FOR I = 1 TO 3
140          PRINT N$(J,I),
150     NEXT I
160     PRINT
170 NEXT J
180 PRINT
190 REM ** PRINT STUDENTS WITH CORRECT STATUS:   **
200 REM **       MALE & SR, FEMALE & JR          **
210 PRINT "THE SELECTED STUDENTS:"
220 FOR J = 1 TO 9
230     IF N$(J,3) ="M" AND N$(J,2) = "SR" THEN PRINT N$(J,1)
240     IF N$(J,3) ="F" AND N$(J,2) = "JR" THEN PRINT N$(J,1)
250 NEXT J
260 DATA SAM CHERA, GEORGE ROBBIN, TOBY WOLF
270 DATA DEBBY FRANK, MARK HANNAN, SOL MENSH
280 DATA MARK GANCHROW, FAY HOCH, MARJORIE LEE
290 DATA SR,FR,SO,JR,JR,SO,SR,JR,SR
300 DATA M,M,F,F,M,M,M,F,F
310 END
```

```
RUN
NAME              YEAR      SEX
SAM CHERA         SR        M
GEORGE ROBBIN     FR        M
TOBY WOLF         SO        F
DEBBY FRANK       JR        F
MARK HANNAN       JR        M
SOL MENSH         SO        M
MARK GANCHROW     SR        M
FAY HOCH          JR        F
MARJORIE LEE      SR        F

THE SELECTED STUDENTS:
SAM CHERA
DEBBY FRANK
MARK GANCHROW
FAY HOCH
```

Program 12.18, as it applies to Case 12.9, illustrates how a computer program can create graphic displays in the form of a histogram or bar chart. A string lookup that, in response to a screen menu, matches a data input to a character stored in a one-dimensional string array is also illustrated.

## CASE 12.9

**Problem**

**Graphics: Bar Chart Creation**
It is desired to develop graphs in the form of bar charts for company data. Such computer-generated graphics can be created using FOR/NEXT loops in a conversational program.

**Data Input**

Three possible user-selected display characters ( = , *, and #) are to be read and stored in a string array. The actual data to be graphed is entered interactively with the user specifying the following: the number of bars in the graph, the data values for each bar, the display output character for the bars, and the heading for the graph. In addition, the user can choose to create another graph.

**Process/Formulas** READ/DATA are to be used to assign the three display characters to a string array. Data values are stored in an array as they are entered in response to an INPUT query. A FOR/NEXT loop causes a menu to be displayed showing the display characters that can be selected for the output. A repetitive nested FOR/NEXT loop process is to be used. The length of the bars in the chart is set by the size of the data values. If a data value is $20 million, for example, the length of the bar is 20 characters. Each bar is made up of a character previously selected ( = , or *, or #).

**Output**

A bar chart output could look like this:

```
HOW MANY BARS IN YOUR GRAPH? 2
ENTER 2 DATA VALUES
  1 ? 24
  2 ? 15
```

```
FOR YOUR GRAPH SELECT AN OUTPUT CHARACTER
1    =
2    *
3    #
ENTER CHOICE: 1, 2, OR 3? 3
ENTER A HEADING IF DESIRED? EMPLOYEES (000'S)

              EMPLOYEES (000'S)

DIVISION 1 :#########################: 24

DIVISION 2 :###############: 15

DO YOU WISH TO CREATE ANOTHER GRAPH (YES OR NO)?
```

Program 12.18 shows the kind of program that will perform the tasks specified by Case 12.9. The user must interactively supply the following information in response to program-generated display questions: the number of bars in the graph (line 80), the data values for each bar (lines 100–140), which of the display characters ( = , *, or #) to use from a menu (lines 150–190), the heading for the graph (line 200), and if another graph is to be created (lines 340–360).

The program segment, lines 240–330, produces the plot of the bar chart in response to the user's entries. The output of Program 12.18 reflects the user's creation of two bar charts. One chart shows company sales plotted for each division. The other chart shows a plot of the number of units produced (production) for five divisions of the company. Each bar chart has a different string for output display.

## PROGRAM 12.18   Case 12.9, Bar Chart Preparation

```
10 REM CASE 12.9, GRAPHICS: BAR CHART CREATION
12 REM PROGRAMMER- (name of person)   DATE- mm/dd/yy
14 REM     VARIABLE LIST-
16 REM         A=CHOICE 1,2,3  A & I = LOOP INDICES
18 REM         C$(I)=SYMBOL "=","*","#"
19 REM         D(I)=DATA VALUE UP TO 15 CHARACTERS
20 REM         N=# OF BARS IN THE GRAPH
22 REM         H$=HEADING
26 REM         Y$="YES" OR "NO"
28 REM -----------------------------------
30 DIM C$(3),D(15)
50 READ C$(1), C$(2), C$(3)    'store string characters for output display
70 DATA "=","*","#"
80 INPUT "HOW MANY BARS IN YOUR GRAPH"; N
100 PRINT "ENTER";N; " DATA VALUES"
110 FOR I = 1 TO N               'loop to enter data values
120       PRINT I;
```

```
130       INPUT D(I)
140 NEXT I
150 PRINT "FOR YOUR GRAPH SELECT AN OUTPUT CHARACTER"
160 FOR A = 1 TO 3              'loop to print menu
170       PRINT A;TAB(10);C$(A)
180 NEXT A
190 INPUT "ENTER CHOICE: 1, 2, OR  3"; A
200 INPUT "ENTER A HEADING IF DESIRED"; H$
210 PRINT
240 PRINT TAB(16);H$
250 PRINT
260 FOR I = 1 TO N              'loop to print bars
270       PRINT "DIVISION";I;":";
280       FOR P = 1 TO D(I)
290             PRINT C$(A);
300       NEXT P
320       PRINT ":";D(I)
330 NEXT I
335 PRINT
340 INPUT "DO YOU WISH TO CREATE ANOTHER GRAPH (YES OR NO)"; Y$
360 IF Y$ = "YES" THEN 80
390 END


RUN
HOW MANY BARS IN YOUR GRAPH? 4
ENTER  4  DATA VALUES
 1 ? 15
 2 ? 22
 3 ? 18
 4 ? 30
FOR YOUR GRAPH SELECT AN OUTPUT CHARACTER
 1        =
 2        *
 3        #
ENTER CHOICE: 1, 2, OR 3? 2
ENTER A HEADING IF DESIRED? COMPANY SALES-MILLIONS $ 3RD QUARTER

              COMPANY SALES-MILLIONS $ 3RD QUARTER
DIVISION 1 :***************: 15
DIVISION 2 :**********************: 22
DIVISION 3 :******************: 18
DIVISION 4 :******************************: 30

DO YOU WISH TO CREATE ANOTHER GRAPH (YES OR NO)? YES
HOW MANY BARS IN YOUR GRAPH?  5
ENTER  5  DATA VALUES
 1 ? 12
 2 ? 16
 3 ? 18
 4 ? 23
 5 ? 30
FOR YOUR GRAPH SELECT AN OUTPUT CHARACTER
 1        =
 2        *
 3        #
```

```
ENTER CHOICE: 1, 2, OR 3? 1
ENTER A HEADING IF DESIRED? PRODUCTION BY DIVISION (000'S UNITS)

              PRODUCTION BY DIVISION (000'S UNITS)

DIVISION 1 :============: 12
DIVISION 2 :================: 16
DIVISION 3 :==================: 18
DIVISION 4 :======================: 23
DIVISION 5 :=============================: 30

DO YOU WISH TO CREATE ANOTHER GRAPH (YES OR NO)? NO
```

## Array Subscripts

As described earlier in the chapter, the dimension statement is used to specify how much storage space should be reserved for an array. Without a dimension statement, the value of the array subscripts goes from 0 to a maximum of 10. Using the dimension statement enables us to increase the maximum value of an array subscript beyond 10.

PC/Microsoft BASIC provides a means of specifying the lower bounds of the subscripts for all the arrays in a program. To declare that the arrays start at either 0 or 1 requires the use of the OPTION BASE keywords. The general form of the declaration statement is:

line # OPTION BASE n

where *n* is either 0 or 1. For example, the statement

5 OPTION BASE 1

will cause *all* arrays in a program to begin with the subscript of 1. This applies to both lists and tables. When used in a program, the OPTION BASE statement must come before any dimension statement. Without an OPTION BASE statement, the computer sets *n* at 0. Thus, without the OPTION BASE statement DIM X(20) actually reserves 21 positions for variable X, namely X(0), X(1), X(2), . . . , X(20).

## SUMMARY

This chapter introduced the concept of numeric and string subscripted variables. Such variables identify individual storage locations. The subscripting process can be accomplished within a single FOR/NEXT loop if the data consists of a list, or within nested FOR/NEXT loops if the data forms a table.

Each type of subscripted variable may also be given values directly with READ/DATA, INPUT, or LET statements. To reserve more than ten storage spaces for subscripted variables, dimensioning is necessary. The DIM statement is used to dimension both lists and tables of data. The OPTION BASE statement provides a means to specify a lower bound for all array subscripts.

## BASIC VOCABULARY SUMMARY

| Statement | Purpose | Examples |
|-----------|---------|----------|
| DIM B(n)<br>DIM D$(n) | Specifies the maximum* (n) number of one-dimensional array values for numeric or string data, and sets storage space required. | 40 DIM B(35)<br>60 DIM D$(60) |
| DIM TB(i,j)<br>DIM DC$(I,J) | Specifies the maximum* (i,j) number of two-dimensional array values for numeric or string data, and sets storage space required where i is the maximum* number of rows and j the maximum* number of columns. | 20 DIM TB(20,15)<br>30 DIM CD$(12,60) |
| OPTION BASE n | Specifies the minimum value n, 0 or 1, for all array subscripts. | 5 OPTION BASE 1 |

## EXERCISES

### Review Questions

**12.1**  The program below is to read and store a string list and a numeric list, each containing 25 items. Correct all the errors you may find.

```
10 DIM NM$25,NUM(20)
20 FOR 1 TO 30
30      READ NUM(I), NM$(J)
40 NEXT 1
50 DATA A, 1, B, 2, C, 3, D, 4, E, 5
50 DATA F, 6, G, 7, H, 8, I, 9, J, 10
50 DATA K, 11, L, 12, M, 13, N, 14, 0, 15
50 DATA P, 16, Q, 17, R, 18, S, 19, T, 20
50 DATA U, 21, V, 22, W, 23, X, 24, Y, 25
99 END
```

The next four exercises relate to Program 12.5, which is shown below:

```
10 REM CASE 12.2, COMPUTING THE MARKET VALUE OF AN INVESTMENT PORTFOLIO
15 REM PROGRAMMER- (name of person)  DATE- mm/dd/yy
16 REM    VARIABLE LIST-
17 REM       A$,B$ = FORMATS
19 REM       I=# OF STOCK AND LOOP INDEX
```

---

*Maximum is increased by one if you include a zero subscript, row, or column.

```
20 REM          N(I)=# OF SHARES
21 REM          P(I)=MARKET PRICE
22 REM           T=TOTAL CURRENT VALUE
25 REM ---------------------------------
30 DIM N(15),P(15)
32 LET A$ = "STOCK      # SHARES      MARKET PRICE"
34 LET B$ = " ##         ###          $ ##"
40 PRINT A$
50 LET T=0
60 FOR I = 1 TO 12
70    READ N(I)
80 NEXT I
90 FOR I = 1 TO 12
100    READ P(I)
110 NEXT I
120 FOR I = 1 TO 12
130    PRINT USING B$;I,N(I),P(I)
140    LET T = T+N(I)*P(I)
150 NEXT I
160 FOR I= 1 TO 40
170    PRINT "-";
180 NEXT I
190 PRINT
200 PRINT USING "    PORTFOLIO VALUE   $$###,### ";T
210 DATA 300,400,500,900,300,500,500,100,800,100,400,800
220 DATA 50,42,32,5,31,17,77,98,52,49,80,83
230 END

RUN
STOCK      # SHARES      MARKET PRICE
   1         300           $ 50
   2         400           $ 42
   3         500           $ 32
   4         900           $  5
   5         300           $ 31
   6         500           $ 17
   7         500           $ 77
   8         100           $ 98
   9         800           $ 52
  10         100           $ 49
  11         400           $ 80
  12         800           $ 83
----------------------------------------
    PORTFOLIO VALUE    $263,300
```

**12.2**  a. What would Program 12.5 do if lines 110 and 120 were omitted?

b. What would Program 12.5 do if lines 80 and 90 were omitted?

c. How can we get the program to work without lines 80, 90, 110, and 120 by changing the DATA statements in lines 210 and 220?

**12.3**  Revise Program 12.5 (shown above) for Case 12.2 to add a column showing the current value (current market value = # shares × market price per share) for each stock and to total this column. A listing of the output takes this form:

| STOCK | # SHARES | MARKET PRICE | CURRENT MARKET VALUE |
|-------|----------|--------------|----------------------|
| 1 | 300 | $ 50 | $15,000 |
| 2 | 400 | $ 42 | $16,800 |
| 3 | 500 | $ 32 | $16,000 |
| 4 | 900 | $  5 | $ 4,500 |
| 5 | 300 | $ 31 | $ 9,300 |
| 6 | 500 | $ 17 | $ 8,500 |
| 7 | 500 | $ 77 | $38,500 |
| 8 | 100 | $ 98 | $ 9,800 |
| 9 | 800 | $ 52 | $41,600 |
| 10 | 100 | $ 49 | $ 4,900 |
| 11 | 400 | $ 80 | $32,000 |
| 12 | 800 | $ 83 | $66,400 |

------------------------------------------------------

                      PORTFOLIO VALUE   $263,300

**◆ 12.4**  Suppose that the purchase prices for the 12 stocks listed in Program 12.5 (shown above) are as follows: $46, $40, $30, $8, $30, $27, $87, $108, $42, $49, $69, and $80. Revise the program to produce output that shows for each stock the purchase price and the net gain or loss (net gain or loss = number of shares × (market price − purchase price)). The bottom line of the output should show the total gain or loss for the entire portfolio.

A listing of the output takes this form:

| STOCK | # SHARES | MARKET PRICE | PUR. PRICE | GAIN/LOSS |
|-------|----------|--------------|------------|-----------|
| 1 | 300 | $ 50 | $ 46 | -$1,200 |
| 2 | 400 | $ 42 | $ 40 | -$800 |
| 3 | 500 | $ 32 | $ 30 | -$1,000 |
| 4 | 900 | $  5 | $  8 | $2,700 |
| 5 | 300 | $ 31 | $ 30 | -$300 |
| 6 | 500 | $ 17 | $ 27 | $5,000 |
| 7 | 500 | $ 77 | $ 87 | $5,000 |
| 8 | 100 | $ 98 | $108 | $1,000 |
| 9 | 800 | $ 52 | $ 42 | -$8,000 |
| 10 | 100 | $ 49 | $ 49 | $0 |
| 11 | 400 | $ 80 | $ 69 | -$4,400 |
| 12 | 800 | $ 83 | $ 80 | -$2,400 |

------------------------------------------------------

              PORTFOLIO GAIN/LOSS        -$4,400

**12.5**  Revise Program 12.5 (shown above), for Case 12.2 so that the DATA statements (lines 210 and 220) for the number of shares and market price are as follows:

210 DATA 300,50,400,42,500,32,900,5,300,31,500,17
220 DATA 500,77,100,98,800,52,100,49,400,80,800,83

**12.6**  What will the following program print as output?

```
10 DIM X(10)
15 FOR I = 1 TO 10 STEP 2
20    READ X(I)
25    LET X(I + 1) = 10 − I
30 NEXT I
35 FOR N = 1 TO 10
```

```
40     PRINT X(N);X(X(N))
45 NEXT N
50 DATA 4,7,2,6,3
55 END
```

**12.7** For the following program,
  a. What will the program print as output?
  b. What will the program print as output if the RESTORE statement in line 55 is omitted?

```
10 DIM B(2,4)
20 FOR I = 1 TO 2
30    FOR J = 1 TO 4
40         READ B(I,J)
50    NEXT J
55    RESTORE
60 NEXT I
70 DATA 1,3,5,7,9,11,13,15,17,19,21,23
80 PRINT B(1,3),B(2,1),B(1,4),B(B(1,1),B(1,2))
90 END
```

**12.8** a. What does the statement 10 OPTION BASE 1 specify?
  b. What does the statement 10 OPTION BASE 0 specify?

**12.9** Revise and run the program below with an OPTION BASE statement so that all arrays in the program will start with the subscripts of 1.

```
10 DIM N$(10), Q(10)
20 FOR I = 0 TO 4
30     READ N$(I), Q(I)
40 NEXT I
50 DATA A, 21, B, 32, C, 43, D, 54, E, 65
60 FOR I = 0 TO 4
70     PRINT I, N$(I), Q(I)
80 NEXT I
99 END
```

```
RUN
0          A          21
1          B          32
2          C          43
3          D          54
4          E          65
```

## Programming Activities

**12.10** **Purpose** To store two numeric data lists.

**Problem** Using the data on four separate manufacturing plants, shown below, write and run a program that will treat the data as separate lists and derive the column totals for each year.

**Data**  1989 data: 2,400, 3,000, 2,500, 3,000
1990 data: 2,900, 3,100, 3,000, 3,200

**Output**  Your output should have this format:

```
        UNITS PRODUCED
        --------------
PLANT       1989        1990
-----       ----        ----
  1         2,400       2,900
  2         3,000       3,100
  3         2,500       3,000
  4         3,000       3,200
        --------------------------
TOTAL      10,900      12,200
```

♦ **12.11**  **Purpose**  To store data into three data lists, one string and the other two numeric.

**Problem**  Write and run a program that will treat the data below as three separate lists and derive the column totals for each year.

**Data**  Plant data: Ave. A, Ave. B, Crosstown, West Side
1989 data: 2,400, 3,000, 2,500, 3,000
1990 data: 2,900, 3,100, 3,000, 3,200

**Output**  Your output should have this format:

```
        UNITS PRODUCED
        --------------
PLANT       1989        1990
-----       ----        ----
Ave. A      2,400       2,900
Ave. B      3,000       3,100
Crosstown   2,500       3,000
West Side   3,000       3,200
        --------------------------
TOTAL      10,900      12,200
```

**12.12**  **Purpose**  To read data into two lists, one string and the other numeric.

**Problem**  The XYZ Company has five salespersons. They are listed below with the amount of goods each sold last month. Write and run a program to compute the commissions on their sales (commissions = 10% × sales), and derive the totals for sales and commissions.

**Data**  Treat the names and the amount sold as separate lists.

| SALESPERSON | AMOUNT SOLD |
|---|---|
| JULIE SHANA | $12,000 |
| JAY JOSHUA | 17,500 |
| SHIRLEY EFRAM | 14,500 |
| AL BENNET | 18,250 |
| ARI LEE | 16,250 |

**Output**   Your output should have this format:

```
SALESPERSON        AMOUNT SOLD    COMMISSION
-------------------------------------------
JULIE SHANA        $12,000        $1,200
JAY JOSHUA         17,500         $1,750
SHIRLEY EFRAM      14,500         $1,450
AL BENNET          18,250         $1,825
ARI LEE            16,250         $1,625
-------------------------------------------
TOTALS             $78,500        $7,850
```

**12.13**   **Purpose**   To read data into a string data list and a numeric data list.

**Problem**   In order to prepare a budget for next year, the ARCO Company estimates that each of its sales regions will show a growth in sales of more than 8½ percent over this year's sales. Write and run a program that will derive the estimate for next year's sales for each region (estimated sales = this year's sales × (1.0 + growth percent)).

**Data**   Treat the region names and this year's sales as separate lists.

| REGION | SALES (MILLION $) |
|--------|-------------------|
| Northern | $4.65 |
| Central | 5.23 |
| Western | 2.81 |
| Midwest | 9.67 |
| Eastern | 3.56 |
| Southern | 8.89 |

**Output**   Your output should have this format:

```
REGION     SALES (MILL.$)    ESTIMATED SALES
--------------------------------------------
Northern      $ 4.65           $ 5.05
Central       $ 5.23           $ 5.67
Western       $ 2.81           $ 3.05
Midwest       $ 9.67           $10.49
Eastern       $ 3.56           $ 3.86
Southern      $ 8.89           $ 9.65
```

**12.14**   **Purpose**   To read into a single numeric data table.

**Problem**   Using the data on four manufacturing plants shown below, write and run a program that will treat the data as a table (4 × 2) and derive the column totals for each year, the row totals for each plant, and the grand total.

**Data**

| PLANT | UNITS PRODUCED | |
|-------|------|------|
|       | 1989 | 1990 |
| 1 | 2,400 | 2,900 |
| 2 | 3,000 | 3,100 |
| 3 | 2,500 | 3,000 |
| 4 | 3,000 | 3,200 |

**Output**   Your output should have this format:

```
              UNITS PRODUCED
              --------------
    PLANT     1989      1990      TOTAL
    -----     ----      ----      -----
      1       2,400     2,900     5,300
      2       3,000     3,100     6,100
      3       2,500     3,000     5,500
      4       3,000     3,200     6,200
    ----------------------------------------
    TOTALS   10,000    12,200    23,100
```

♦ **12.15**   **Purpose**   To read two two-dimensional arrays of numeric data.

**Problem**   Below is two weeks of production data for five workers. Write and run a program that will treat the data as two separate tables (5 × 3) and derive the following information:

a. The row totals for each worker.
b. The column totals for each component.
c. A third table combining week 1 and week 2 that has row and column totals.
d. A grand total for all the units produced for each table.

**Data**

| | WEEK 1 COMPONENTS | | | WEEK 2 COMPONENTS | | |
|---|---|---|---|---|---|---|
| WORKER | A | B | C | A | B | C |
| 1 | 200 | 100 | 20 | 185 | 110 | 22 |
| 2 | 150 | 125 | 30 | 160 | 115 | 25 |
| 3 | 320 | 75 | 15 | 275 | 100 | 30 |
| 4 | 275 | 100 | 15 | 275 | 90 | 20 |
| 5 | 100 | 200 | 10 | 150 | 150 | 10 |

**Output**   Your output should have this format:

```
WEEK ONE
--------
WORKER     A          B          C        # UNITS
-----------------------------------------------------
      1    200        100        20         320
      2    150        125        30         305
      3    320         75        15         410
      4    275        100        15         390
      5    100        200        10         310
-----------------------------------------------------
TOTALS   1,045       600        90        1,735


WEEK TWO
--------
WORKER     A          B          C        # UNITS
-----------------------------------------------------
      1    185        110        22         317
      2    160        115        25         300
      3    275        100        30         405
      4    275         90        20         385
      5    150        150        10         310
-----------------------------------------------------
TOTALS   1,045       565       107        1,717
```

```
TWO WEEK AGGREGATION
--------------------
WORKER      A           B           C       # UNITS
-----------------------------------------------------
   1       385         210          42        637
   2       310         240          55        605
   3       595         175          35        815
   4       550         190          35        775
   5       250         350          20        620
-----------------------------------------------------
TOTALS   2,090       1,165         197       3,452
```

♦ **12.16**   **Purpose**   To read a one-dimensional numeric array and a two-dimensional numeric array.

**Problem**   Below are the prices at which four models of minicomputers are sold. Also shown are the number of units sold by the five salespersons selling these products. Write and run a program that will store this information and generate the total dollar volume for each salesperson (total dollar volume = price per unit × number of units sold). Also have the program derive the total dollar sales volume for *all* the salespersons.

**Data**   Treat the price list as a 1 × 4 array and the units sold as a 5 × 4 table.

| MODEL | 1 | 2 | 3 | 4 |
|-------|---|---|---|---|
| PRICE | $10,000 | $12,500 | $17,200 | $20,000 |

| | NUMBER OF UNITS SOLD THIS MONTH, BY MODEL | | | |
|-------------|---|---|---|---|
| SALESPERSON | 1 | 2 | 3 | 4 |
| 1 | 6 | 8 | 2 | 1 |
| 2 | 5 | 4 | 3 | 1 |
| 3 | 7 | 6 | 1 | 2 |
| 4 | 3 | 9 | 5 | 0 |
| 5 | 4 | 2 | 4 | 3 |

**Output**   Your output should have this format:

```
SALESPERSON     TOTAL DOLLAR VOLUME
---------------------------------------
     1          $214,400.00
     2          $171,600.00
     3          $202,200.00
     4          $228,500.00
     5          $193,800.00
---------------------------------------
GRAND TOTAL   $1,010,500.00
```

**12.17**   **Purpose**   To read a one-dimensional string array and a two-dimensional numeric array.

**Problem**   The data table (6 × 4) below shows the sales (in millions of dollars) for each division of the XYZ Company for the first six months. Write and run a program to do the following:
a. Read in and store this information.
b. Output the data for the first quarter (months 1–3).
c. Output the data for the second quarter (months 4–6).

d. Output the data for divisions 2, 3, and 4.

e. Output the data for divisions 1 and 3.

f. Output the data for months January and June.

g. Provide total sales by each quarter for all divisions.

**Data**

| MONTH | DIVISION SALES (MILLION $) | | | |
|---|---|---|---|---|
| | 1 | 2 | 3 | 4 |
| Jan. | 2.1 | 3.2 | 1.8 | .9 |
| Feb. | 2.0 | 2.7 | 1.4 | .8 |
| March | 1.7 | 3.1 | 1.5 | .6 |
| April | 2.3 | 3.3 | 1.7 | .7 |
| May | 1.8 | 3.0 | 1.9 | .9 |
| June | 1.4 | 3.1 | 2.0 | .9 |

**Output**   Your output should have this format:

```
b.                   DIVISION
    MONTH      1    2    3    4
    JAN.      2.1  3.2  1.8  0.9
    FEB.      2.0  2.7  1.4  0.8
    MARCH     1.7  3.1  1.5  0.6


c.                   DIVISION
    MONTH      1    2    3    4
    APRIL     2.3  3.3  1.7  0.7
    MAY       1.8  3.0  1.9  0.9
    JUNE      1.4  3.1  2.0  0.9


d.                 DIVISION
    MONTH      2    3    4
    JAN.      3.2  1.8  0.9
    FEB.      2.7  1.4  0.8
    MARCH     3.1  1.5  0.6
    APRIL     3.3  1.7  0.7
    MAY       3.0  1.9  0.9
    JUNE      3.1  2.0  0.9


e.                 DIVISION
    MONTH      1         3
    JAN.      2.1       1.8
    FEB.      2.0       1.4
    MARCH     1.7       1.5
    APRIL     2.3       1.7
    MAY       1.8       1.9
    JUNE      1.4       2.0


f.                   DIVISION
    MONTH      1    2    3    4
    JAN.      2.1  3.2  1.8  0.9
    JUNE      1.4  3.1  2.0  0.9


g. TOTALS BY          DIVISION
    QUARTER    1    2    3    4
    FIRST     5.8  9.0  4.7  2.3
    SECOND    5.5  9.4  5.6  2.5
```

● ● ● ● ● ● **12.18** **Purpose** To read two one-dimensional numeric arrays that are used for lookup.

**Problem** Write and run a program that reads in an employee's name; the number of his or her dependents; the number of hours that he or she worked during the week; the hourly rate that applies; and a code number of 0, 1, or 2 to indicate that the employee carries no insurance, insurance for himself or herself only, or insurance for the family, respectively.

Have the computer calculate the employee's wages. This is calculated by the number of hours × the hourly rate if the number of hours worked is 40 hours or less. If the number of hours worked is greater than 40, the employee should receive 1½ times the hourly rate for the additional hours above 40. The taxes deducted from the wages should be according to the following table:

| NUMBER OF DEPENDENTS | PERCENT DEDUCTED |
|---|---|
| 0 | 28 |
| 1 | 26 |
| 2 | 24 |
| 3 | 22 |
| 4 | 20 |
| 5 | 18 |
| 6 | 16 |
| 7 or more | 14 |

The insurance deducted should be according to the following table:

| CODE | MEANING | AMOUNT DEDUCTED |
|---|---|---|
| 0 | No insurance | $ 0 |
| 1 | Insurance for self only | 5 |
| 2 | Insurance for family | 10 |

Set up an array for the tax deduction percents and an array for the amount to be deducted for insurance. Use the number of dependents and the code as subscript indices. When the coded data is processed, the values (percent deducted and amount deducted) associated with the code are looked up in the array and then used as part of the program's computations.

**Data** Along with the information given above (tax deductions and insurance deductions), use the following data for the program:

| EMPLOYEE | DEPENDENTS | HOURS WORKED | HOURLY RATE | INSURANCE CODE |
|---|---|---|---|---|
| K.GRIBETZ | 0 | 37 | $8.50 | 1 |
| G.LANDA | 2 | 42 | 7.75 | 2 |
| E. FROMEN | 1 | 40 | 7.10 | 2 |
| J.HILLER | 0 | 47 | 7.50 | 1 |
| Y.DAHAN | 8 | 45 | 7.80 | 0 |
| G.MARK | 4 | 50 | 8.50 | 1 |
| D.CHILL | 2 | 40 | 8.00 | 1 |
| J.TUCHMAN | 5 | 42 | 8.60 | 2 |
| N.MEISEL | 7 | 38 | 7.25 | 2 |
| S.KLEIN | 0 | 41 | 8.80 | 0 |

**Output**   Your output should include column totals as shown in this format:

```
                                 TAX      INSURANCE
          EMPLOYEE   GROSS WAGES  DEDUCTED  DEDUCTED   NET PAY
          -----------------------------------------------------
          K.GRIBETZ    $314.50     $88.06    $5.00    $221.44
          G.LANDA      $333.25     $79.98   $10.00    $243.27
          E.FROMEN     $284.00     $73.84   $10.00    $200.16
          J.HILLER     $378.75    $106.05    $5.00    $267.70
          Y.DAHAN      $370.50     $51.87    $0.00    $318.63
          G.MARK       $467.50     $93.50    $5.00    $369.00
          D.CHILL      $320.00     $76.80    $5.00    $238.20
          J.TUCHMAN    $369.80     $66.56   $10.00    $293.24
          M.MEISEL     $275.50     $38.57   $10.00    $226.93
          S.KLEIN      $365.20    $102.26    $0.00    $262.94
          -----------------------------------------------------
          TOTALS     $3,479.00    $777.49   $60.00  $2,641.51
```

# CHAPTER 13

## ARITHMETIC FUNCTIONS AND STRING FUNCTIONS

Upon completing this chapter, you will be able to do the following:

- Understand the use and purpose of stored library functions.
- Create programs that incorporate such arithmetic functions as RND, SQR, INT, ABS, and SGN.
- Discuss the meaning and purpose of computer simulation.
- Understand the use and purpose of string functions.
- Create programs that incorporate such string functions as LEN, LEFT$, RIGHT$, and MID$.
- Use string functions in a program to provide for data entry checking.
- Explain the purpose and use of ASCII codes and the CHR$ function.
- Define a function using the DEF statement.

In this chapter we examine several types of functions. One type are those that are called *stored library functions*. These include trigonometric functions, logarithmic functions, square roots, and so forth. Stored library functions are used to manipulate numeric data. Another group of functions, *string functions,* handle nonnumeric data. String functions enable us to perform operations on string data. For example, we can determine how long a string data item is; or we can take apart a string data item from the left end, the right end, or the middle. Other string functions to be described include ASC, CHR$, SPACE$, and STRING$. We will also see how it is possible to access and set the date and time by using the DATE$ and TIME$ statements. Toward the end of this chapter, we show how the programmer can develop his or her own functions by defining them using the DEF statement.

## STORED LIBRARY FUNCTIONS

There are a number of mathematical operations that the computer can be directed to perform without the individual user or programmer having to write detailed instructions for those operations. For example, we can get the absolute value of a number directly without giving the computer detailed instructions. Such operations are possible because of stored library functions included in the BASIC language. They are summarized below in Table 13.1. The (X) in the function references a value, or *argument,* passed to the function by a LET, READ, or INPUT statement, or a value placed into the parentheses.

We will confine our immediate attention to the last five functions in Table 13.1.

**TABLE 13.1** Stored Library Functions

| FUNCTION | DESCRIPTION |
| --- | --- |
| SIN(X) | The trigonometric sine function. |
| COS(X) | The trigonometric cosine function. |
| TAN(X) | The trigonometric tangent function. |
| ATN(X) | The trigonometric arctangent function. |
| LOG(X) | The natural logarithm function. |
| EXP(X) | $e$ raised to $X$ power. |
| INT(X) | The greatest integer less than or equal to $X$. |
| SGN(X) | The sign of $X$. |
| ABS(X) | Absolute value of $X$. |
| SQR(X) | The square root of $X$. |
| RND | Random number between 0 and 1. |

## The Integer Function

The INT function (integer function) assigns the greatest integer that is less than or equal to its argument. For example,

| X | INT(X) |
|---|---|
| 5 | 5 |
| 7.2 | 7 |
| 6.9 | 6 |
| 0.5 | 0 |
| −2.3 | −3 |
| −1.7 | −2 |
| −.4 | −1 |
| 10E−3 | 0 |

Note that INT(6.9) = 6. The number is not rounded. It is truncated. Note also the INT(−2.3) = −3, since −3 is the greatest integer less than or equal to −2.3.

## The Sign Function

The SGN function (sign function) gives three possible values: −1, 0, or +1. If $X > 0$, SGN(X) = 1; if $X = 0$, SGN(X) = 0; and if $X < 0$, SGN(X) = −1.

| X | SGN(X) |
|---|---|
| 5 | +1 |
| −5.7 | −1 |
| 1.0 | +1 |
| 0.5 | +1 |
| 0 | 0 |
| −4 | −1 |
| −1 | −1 |
| 10E−3 | +1 |

## The Absolute Value Function

The ABS function (absolute value function) returns the number in the parentheses without any sign. If $X >= 0$, ABS(X) = X; if $X < 0$, ABS(X) = −1 * X.

| X | ABS(X) |
|---|---|
| −4.8 | 4.8 |
| 0 | 0 |
| 5.1 | 5.1 |
| −.5 | .5 |
| 1.1 | 1.1 |
| 10E−3 | 10E−3 |

Note that SGN(X) * ABS(X) = X for any X.

### The Square Root Function

The SQR function (square root function) gives the positive square root of the number or variable in the parentheses. The value in the parentheses should be positive, although some systems will allow negative numbers but ignore their sign. Programs 13.1 and 13.2 summarize the INT, SGN, ABS, and SQR functions. In Program 13.1 the square roots of negative numbers were not printed since the SQR function of a negative number generates an error message on IBM Microsoft BASIC.

## PROGRAM 13.1   Stored Library Functions

```
10 PRINT "NUMBER","INTEGER","SIGN","ABS.VALUE","SQ.ROOT"
20 READ A,B,C,D,E,F
30 PRINT A, INT(A), SGN(A), ABS(A), SQR(A)
40 PRINT B, INT(B), SGN(B), ABS(B), SQR(B)
50 PRINT C, INT(C), SGN(C), ABS(C), SQR(C)
60 PRINT D, INT(D), SGN(D), ABS(D), SQR(D)
70 PRINT E, INT(E), SGN(E), ABS(E), "-"
80 PRINT F, INT(F), SGN(F), ABS(F), "-"
100 DATA 2, 1.44, .08, 0, -10.6, -5.1
199 END
```

```
RUN
NUMBER          INTEGER         SIGN        ABS.VALUE       SQ.ROOT
 2               2               1           2               1.414214
 1.44            1               1           1.44            1.2
 .08             0               1           .08             .2828427
 0               0               0           0               0
-10.6           -11             -1           10.6            -
-5.1            -6              -1           5.1             -
```

The parentheses may enclose a single variable, a constant, or an expression. The parentheses may also enclose another function, as illustrated in Program 13.2.

## PROGRAM 13.2   Function of Functions

```
10 READ X,Y,Z
12 DATA 5,-1.7,.4
14 PRINT "original data values:",X,Y,Z
16 PRINT
20 PRINT "function of a function:",INT(SGN(ABS(X))), ABS(INT(Y)), SGN(INT(Z))
30 END
```

```
RUN
original data values:        5             -1.7            .4

function of a function:      1              2              0
```

Note that in line 20 of Program 13.2, one of the things we wish to print is the absolute value of the integer of variable $Y$ ($Y = -1.7$) that yields the result 2.

A practical application of the INT function is when we want to *round* a number *to the nearest* integer or tenth. We can use the INT function to accomplish this, as shown in Program 13.3.

## PROGRAM 13.3 Rounding Numbers

```
10 READ A,B,C,D,E
15 DATA 2.58, 3.46, 4.71, 5.18, 9.26
20 PRINT "ROUNDING TO THE NEAREST WHOLE NUMBER"
25 LET A0 = INT(A+.5)
30 LET B0 = INT(B+.5)
35 LET C0 = INT(C+.5)
40 LET D0 = INT(D+.5)
45 LET E0 = INT(E+.5)
50 PRINT A,B,C,D,E
51 PRINT A0, B0, C0, D0, E0
55 PRINT
60 PRINT "ROUNDING TO THE NEAREST TENTH"
65 LET A1 = INT((A+.05)*10)/10
70 LET B1 = INT((B+.05)*10)/10
75 LET C1 = INT((C+.05)*10)/10
80 LET D1 = INT((D+.05)*10)/10
85 LET E1 = INT((E+.05)*10)/10
95 PRINT A,B,C,D,E
96 PRINT A1,B1,C1,D1,E1
100 END

RUN
ROUNDING TO THE NEAREST WHOLE NUMBER
 2.58          3.46          4.71          5.18          9.26
 3             3             5             5             9

ROUNDING TO THE NEAREST TENTH
 2.58          3.46          4.71          5.18          9.26
 2.6           3.5           4.7           5.2           9.3
```

Note that when we round a number to the nearest whole number, we add 1/2 or .5 to it and take the INT function of the sum. For example, to round off 4.71 to the nearest whole number, we add .5 to 4.71 giving 5.21, and when we take the INT function of 5.21 we get 5. To round off 9.26 to the nearest whole number, we add .5 to 9.26 giving 9.76, and when we take INT of 9.76 we get 9. To round a number to the nearest tenth, we just add .05 to the number, multiply the sum by 10, take the INT function of that product, and then divide by 10. For example, to round 3.46 to the nearest tenth, we get $3.46 + .05 = 3.51$, $3.51 \times 10 = 35.1$, INT(35.1) = 35, and 35/10 = 3.5.

Another program that rounds numbers to the nearest whole number and uses the SGN, INT, and ABS functions is given in Program 13.4. Note that the intermediate values are given as well. Programs 13.3 and 13.4 work for both positive and negative numbers.

## PROGRAM 13.4    Rounding Numbers Using SGN, INT, and ABS Functions

```
5 PRINT "   X           SGN(X)      INT(ABS(X)+.5)   NEAREST WHOLE NUMBER"
10 READ X
15     LET S=SGN(X)            'find the sign of the data item
20     LET R=INT(ABS(X)+.5)    'round to nearest whole number
25     LET N=S*R               'return the sign to the original data item
30     PRINT X,S,R,N
35     DATA -1.6,-5.4,7.5
36 GOTO 10
40 END


RUN
   X          SGN(X)     INT(ABS(X)+.5)    NEAREST WHOLE NUMBER
 -1.6           -1            2                  -2
 -5.4           -1            5                  -5
  7.5            1            8                   8
```

Program 13.5, based on Case 13.1, makes use of the SQR function.

## CASE 13.1

**Problem**         **Inventory Analysis—Economic Order Quantity**
Using the formulas given below, a program can be written that determines the optimum number of units to be ordered that will minimize a firm's total inventory costs.

**Data Input**      The data is to be entered interactively for the numeric values of $C$, $R$, $S$, and $I$ as defined below. Test the program using $C = \$2.00$, $R = 4,000$ units, $S = \$15.00$, and $I = 10\%$.

**Process/Formulas** Two useful formulas for inventory analysis and control are:

$$(1)\ Q_O = \sqrt{\frac{2RS}{IC}} \qquad \text{and} \qquad (2)\ T_{\min} = \sqrt{2RISC}$$

where

$Q_O$ = the optimum order quantity or the number of units to order that will minimize the firm's total inventory costs; also referred to as the *economic order quantity* (EOQ)

$C$ = the total cost of a single unit

$R$ = the number of units required per year

$S$ = the cost of placing a single order

$I$ = the inventory carrying costs which are a percentage figure based on the value of the average inventory

$T_{\min}$ = the minimum total cost for carrying and ordering $Q_O$.

Using a simple logic sequence, appropriate input queries, and the formulas for inventory analysis and control, a conversational program can be written to derive the outputs shown below.

**Output**

The output should look like this:

```
*****INVENTORY ANALYSIS PROGRAM*****
WHAT IS THE COST OF A SINGLE UNIT? 2
HOW MANY UNITS ARE REQUIRED FOR THE YEAR? 4000
WHAT IS THE COST OF PLACING AN ORDER? 15
WHAT IS THE PERCENTAGE OF THE AVERAGE INVENTORY VALUE
THAT IS FOR CARRYING COSTS? .10


          *****INVENTORY ANALYSIS REPORT*****
THE OPTIMUM ORDER QUANTITY, EOQ IS    775 UNITS PER ORDER
MINIMUM TOTAL COST FOR ORDERING AND CARRYING EOQ    $154.92
THE ABOVE RESULTS ARE BASED ON THE FOLLOWING:
A COST PER UNIT OF    $2.00
NUMBER OF UNITS REQUIRED 4,000 UNITS
A COST OF PLACING AN ORDER OF   $15
A CARRYING COST PERCENT OF AVG. INVENTORY VALUE   10%
```

Program 13.5 carries out the computation of $Q_O$ and $T_{min}$. The values entered for $C$, $R$, $S$, and $I$ are \$2.00, 4,000 units, \$15.00, and 10%, respectively.

Look at lines 80 and 85 in the program. Formulas (1) and (2) require a square root operation; these two lines and the LET statements in them carry out the evaluation required by using the SQR function.

## PROGRAM 13.5   Case 13.1, Economic Order Quantity

```
5 REM CASE 13.1 INVENTORY ANALYSIS-ECONOMIC ORDER QUANTITY
10 REM PROGRAMMER- (name of person)  DATE-mm/dd/yy
15 REM      VARIABLE LIST-
20 REM         C=UNIT COST
22 REM         I=CARRYING COST (%)
23 REM         Q=OPTIMUM ORDER QUANTITY
24 REM         R=UNITS REQUIRED/YEAR
25 REM         S=ORDER COST
30 REM         T=TOTAL COST
32 REM -----------------------------------------
35 PRINT "*****INVENTORY ANALYSIS PROGRAM*****"
40 INPUT "WHAT IS THE COST OF A SINGLE UNIT"; C
45 INPUT "HOW MANY UNITS ARE REQUIRED FOR THE YEAR"; R
50 INPUT "WHAT IS THE COST OF PLACING AN ORDER ; S
55 PRINT "WHAT IS THE PERCENTAGE OF THE AVERAGE INVENTORY VALUE"
60 INPUT "THAT IS FOR CARRYING COSTS"; I
65 REM *** COMPUTE EOQ AND T-MIN ***
80 LET Q=SQR(2*R*S/(I*C))       'use square root function to find Q
85 LET T=SQR(2*R*I*S*C)         'use square root function to find T
90 PRINT
95 PRINT TAB(12);"*****INVENTORY ANALYSIS REPORT*****"
100 PRINT USING "THE OPTIMUM ORDER QUANTITY, EOQ IS #,### UNITS PER ORDER";Q
105 PRINT USING "MINIMUM TOTAL COST FOR ORDERING AND CARRYING EOQ  $$#,###.##";T
110 PRINT "THE ABOVE RESULTS ARE BASED ON THE FOLLOWING:"
115 PRINT USING "A COST PER UNIT OF $$###.##";C
```

```
120 PRINT USING "NUMBER OF UNITS REQUIRED #,### UNITS";R
125 PRINT USING "A COST OF PLACING AN ORDER OF $$###";S
130 PRINT USING "A CARRYING COST PERCENT OF AVG. INVENTORY VALUE ###%";I*100
135 PRINT
140 END

RUN
*****INVENTORY ANALYSIS PROGRAM*****
WHAT IS THE COST OF A SINGLE UNIT? 2
HOW MANY UNITS ARE REQUIRED FOR THE YEAR? 4000
WHAT IS THE COST OF PLACING AN ORDER? 15
WHAT IS THE PERCENTAGE OF THE AVERAGE INVENTORY VALUE
THAT IS FOR CARRYING COSTS? .10


          *****INVENTORY ANALYSIS REPORT*****
THE OPTIMUM ORDER QUANTITY, EOQ IS    775 UNITS PER ORDER
MINIMUM TOTAL COST FOR ORDERING AND CARRYING EOQ    $154.92
THE ABOVE RESULTS ARE BASED ON THE FOLLOWING:
A COST PER UNIT OF     $2.00
NUMBER OF UNITS REQUIRED 4,000 UNITS
A COST OF PLACING AN ORDER OF    $15
A CARRYING COST PERCENT OF AVG. INVENTORY VALUE   10%
```

## The Random Number Function

The RND function (random number function) generates a random number between 0 and 1. A random number is a number selected at random. Imagine the computer as having a round card with a spinner at the center and a scale going from 0 to 1 around the edge of the card. When the RND function is used, the spinner spins, the number to which the spinner points is recorded, and RND takes that value. Thus, every number between 0 and 1 has an equal chance of being selected each time the RND function is used. (In reality there is no spinner inside the computer, but a description of the actual method used to generate random numbers is beyond the scope of this book.) This function is useful when it is necessary to create artificial data.

Random numbers will be generated from the same starting point each time this function is used. Observe the two runs of Program 13.6.

## PROGRAM 13.6   RND Function

```
10 FOR N = 1 TO 5
15    PRINT RND, RND    'gives the same sequence for each run
20 NEXT N
45 END

RUN
 .7151002       .683111
 .4821425       .9992938
 .6465093       .1322918
 .3692191       .5873315
 .1345934       .9348853
```

```
RUN
 .7151002      .683111
 .4821425      .9992938
 .6465093      .1322918
 .3692191      .5873315
 .1345934      .9348853
```

Each of the output results has the same sequence of random numbers. If different sets of random numbers are desired for each program run, the RANDOMIZE statement must be used preceding the RND function in the program. This statement provides an initial starting value for the computer's random number generator. The RANDOMIZE statement has several forms. One form is

line # RANDOMIZE

It causes the execution of the program to halt and requests an input value in response to the following query:

Random number seed ($-32768$ to $32767$)?

A response in the range indicated results in the resumption of the program's execution. Different seeds produce different random numbers. If the same seed is chosen, the same sequence of random numbers will be produced.

Another form of the RANDOMIZE statement is

line # RANDOMIZE n

where $n$ is an integer value placed after RANDOMIZE. The placement of this value eliminates the random number seed message and response described above. A different number results in a new sequence of random numbers. If the same number is chosen, the same sequence of random numbers will be produced.

The third form of the RANDOMIZE statement is

line # RANDOMIZE TIMER

It places the TIMER function at the end of the statement. This form is the most practical because it provides a new random number seed for each program run without the seed query. It also assumes you will not want your program to duplicate the prior number sequence at some later point in time.

Examples of the different forms of the RANDOMIZE statement are shown in Program 13.7. Observe lines 14, 42, and 70:

14 RANDOMIZE

42 RANDOMIZE 9

70 RANDOMIZE TIMER

Examine the output of each of the three program runs. When the seed is entered as 8 and then as 3 in the first two runs, different random numbers result. When the seed of 3 is repeated in the last run, the same set of numbers occur. Line 42 will continue to generate the same numbers each time the program is run as long as $n = 9$. Line 70 will cause a new sequence of numbers each time the program is run.

## PROGRAM 13.7  RND Function and Different Forms of the RANDOMIZE Statement

```
10 PRINT "---------- USING RANDOMIZE "
14 RANDOMIZE              'a response is needed for the seed each run
18 FOR N = 1 TO 5
22    PRINT RND;     'number sequence is different for each run
26 NEXT N              'if the seed is changed
30 PRINT
34 PRINT
38 PRINT "---------- USING RANDOMIZE n"
42 RANDOMIZE 9            'no response is needed for the seed each run
46 FOR N = 1 TO 5
50    PRINT RND;     'number sequence is the same for each run
54 NEXT N
58 PRINT
62 PRINT
66 PRINT "---------- USING RANDOMIZE TIMER"
70 RANDOMIZE TIMER     'no response is needed for the seed each run
74 FOR N = 1 TO 5
78    PRINT RND;     'number sequence is different for each run
82 NEXT N
99 END

RUN
---------- USING RANDOMIZE
Random number seed (-32768 to 32767)? 8
 .2545374  .451457  .8101  7.346545E-02  .7029858
---------- USING RANDOMIZE n
 .6675926  .6555285  .7431739  1.337956E-02  .5408362

---------- USING RANDOMIZE TIMER
 .5242563  .7992828  4.567544E-02  .2795809  9.611394E-02


RUN
---------- USING RANDOMIZE
Random number seed (-32768 to 32767)? 3
 .2226008  .5941419  .2414202  .2013799  5.361749E-02 <--- new numbers

---------- USING RANDOMIZE n
 .6675926  .6555285  .7431739  1.33956E-02  .5408362  <--- same numbers as
                                                           before n = 9


---------- USING RANDOMIZE TIMER
 .2664285  .307141  .3189756  .0690554  .8995654    <--- new numbers


RUN
---------- USING RANDOMIZE
Random number seed (-32768 to 32767)? 3              <--- same seed 3
 .2226008  .5941419  .2414202  .2013799  5.361749E-02 <--- same numbers

---------- USING RANDOMIZE n
 .6675926  .6555285  .7431739  1.337956E-02  .5408362 <--- same numbers as
                                                           before n = 9

---------- USING RANDOMIZE TIMER
 .9681191  .2333191  .4466917  .9671572  .3615101    <--- new numbers
```

Because the RND function generates numbers *between* 0 and 1, it is necessary to use the following procedure if *exact* limits and integer output are required.

If the range of values desired is from low (*L*) to high (*H*), inclusive, then the RND function could be used in an expression like this:

INT((D + 1)*RND + L)

where *D* is equal to the difference or range between the integers *H* and *L*. For example, if random integers from 10 to 20, inclusive, had to be generated, an appropriate statement would be:

40 LET R = INT(11*RND + 10)

Since RND function generates numbers between 0 and 1, or from .000001 to .999999, then 11*RND will produce values from .000011 to 10.999989. By adding 10 to this range, we have values from 10.000011 to 20.999989. The integer part of this range is from 10 to 20, which is the desired range of values.

Program 13.8 in lines 40–55 shows how the above procedure can be used to produce random numbers as integer values. Note how each run produces not only the desired range of values but also a completely different sequence as well because of line 20.

---

**PROGRAM 13.8   Generating Integer Values Using INT((D + 1)*RND + L)**

```
10 REM A=INTEGER, FROM 0 TO 9
12 REM B=INTEGER, FROM 1 TO 10
14 REM C=INTEGER, FROM 10 TO 20
16 REM D=INTEGER, FROM 25 TO 100
18 REM ---------------------------------------
20 RANDOMIZE TIMER
25 PRINT "A:0-9", "B:1-10", "C:10-20", "D:25-100"
30 PRINT "----------------------------------------------------"
35 FOR I=1 TO 15
40     LET A=INT(10*RND)        'integers 0 through 9
45     LET B=INT(10*RND+1)      'integers 1 through 10
50     LET C=INT(11*RND+10)     'integers 10 through 20
55     LET D=INT(76*RND+25)     'integers 25 through 100
60     PRINT A,B,C,D
65 NEXT I
70 END
```

```
RUN
A:0-9           B:1-10          C:10-20         D:25-100
--------------------------------------------------------
  0               4               19              65
  3               2               19              84
  1               4               16              58
  9               3               20              86
  4               8               20              28
  2               4               10              93
  7               9               18              87
  4               5               15              48
  7               9               10              59
  9               1               16              87
```

```
4              1              14             58
8              5              19             42
2              6              16             64
3              4              17             90
3              2              16             39
```

```
RUN
A:0-9          B:1-10         C:10-20        D:25-100
--------------------------------------------------------
7              2              12             83
1              5              14             30
5              6              12             32
9              4              16             54
4              6              13             43
1              3              18             72
8              10             15             37
4              7              20             65
7              6              16             28
6              6              17             56
9              1              14             92
4              7              12             67
9              2              15             96
5              3              13             84
8              1              11             39
```

Case 13.2 requires a program using numbers that are generated by the RND function.

- - - - - - - - - - - - - - - - - - - - - - - - - - - - - - - - - - - - - -

## CASE 13.2

**Problem**          **Generating Random Inspection Times**
In order to check the quality of a product coming off its assembly line, the National Electronics Company quality control department examines samples of output twice a day. One inspection is in the morning between 9 A.M. and 12:59 P.M. The other is in the afternoon between 1 P.M. and 5:59 P.M. The times that the samples are taken each day are selected at random. A program is to be written to generate the daily inspection times by a random process.

**Data Input**       The data values required are computer generated using the RND function.

**Process/Formulas** A simple logic sequence, the RND function and the RANDOMIZE statement are to be used to produce integer values from 9–12, 1–5, and 0–60. A program can be written to derive the output shown below.

**Output**           Output follows this format:

```
**********INSPECTION TIMES**********

        MORNING TIME 11:54

        AFTERNOON TIME 4:26
```

- - - - - - - - - - - - - - - - - - - - - - - - - - - - - - - - - - - - - -

Program 13.9 shows how the inspection times can be randomly obtained for the quality control department. The program generates the hours and minutes for each time interval by using the RND functions in lines 35–50.

## PROGRAM 13.9   Case 13.2, Random Inspection Times

```
10 REM CASE 13.2, RANDOMIZE INSPECTION TIMES
15 REM PROGRAMMER- (name of person)  DATE - mm/dd/yy
16 REM     VARIABLE LIST-
17 REM        H1=A.M. HOUR
18 REM        H2=P.M. HOUR
19 REM        M1=A.M. MINUTE
20 REM        M2=P.M. MINUTE
25 REM -----------------------------------
30 RANDOMIZE TIMER
35 LET H1=INT(4*RND+9)        '9 a.m.-12 noon
40 LET M1=INT(60*RND)         '0-59 a.m. minutes
45 LET H2=INT(5*RND+1)        '1 p.m.-5 p.m.
50 LET M2=INT(60*RND)         '0-59 p.m. minutes
54 PRINT
55 PRINT     "**********INSPECTION TIMES**********"
57 PRINT
60 PRINT USING "   MORNING TIME ##:##";H1,M1
65 PRINT
70 PRINT USING "   AFTERNOON TIME ##:##";H2,M2
75 END

RUN

**********INSPECTION TIMES**********

   MORNING TIME 11:19

   AFTERNOON TIME 3:41
```

Case 13.3 also requires the generation of random numbers.

· · · · · · · · · · · · · · · · · · · · · · · · · · · · · · · · · · · · · ·

## CASE 13.3

**Problem**      **Generating a Randomly Assigned Vacation Schedule**
A manager must plan the vacation schedules for six employees. Each employee is entitled to one week out of six designated vacation weeks. Because the manager does not want to give anyone preferential treatment in the assignment of vacation weeks, a computer program is needed that will randomly schedule each of the six employees to one of the six available weeks.

**Data Input**      The data values are employee names.

**Process/Formulas**  A repetitive FOR/NEXT loop process is to be used, with the employees' names being assigned to a subscripted array. A nested FOR/NEXT loop process that includes a random number function to generate integers from 1–6 is used to scramble the six weeks of vacation. A new array is developed that shows in which week each one of the employees is to take a vacation.

**Output**  The output follows this format:

```
EMPLOYEE     VACATION WEEK
-------------------------
ALICE            2
BEN              3
CHARLES          4
DORIS            6
EDNA             5
FRED             1
```

Program 13.10 shows how a list of six numbers, 1–6, representing the six vacation weeks, can be scrambled. The employee names are read into the array N$(I) by lines 30–40. A random number, X, from 1–6 is picked by line 60. Once a number, X, is picked, it is processed through the FOR/NEXT loop (lines 65–100). The following tasks are performed within this loop.

Line 70 tests to see if a particular week number has been picked before by checking for a −9 in the array location R(I). If a −9 is found, the program will go on to the NEXT I, or R(2). If the number in the array has not already been picked, is it equal to the random number X? If it is not equal to X, the program keeps searching for the value of R(I) equal to X. Once found, the value of X is assigned by line 85 to the array V(C). A −9 is placed into the location R(I) so that duplicates in the vacation schedule do not occur. Once all six week numbers have been randomly picked from the array R(I), transferred to the array V(C), and replaced in R(I) by −9's, the program continues to the FOR/NEXT loop in lines 115–125, which causes the vacation schedule to be printed out.

## PROGRAM 13.10   Case 13.3, A Randomly Assigned Vacation Schedule

```
5 REM CASE 13.3 ESTABLISHING A RANDOMLY ASSIGNED VACATION SCHEDULE
9 REM PROGRAMMER- (name of person)  DATE - mm/dd/yy
11 REM      VARIABLE LIST-
12 REM          C=COUNTER
13 REM          N$(I)=EMPLOYEE NAME
14 REM          R(I)=VACATION WEEK 1-6
17 REM          V(C)=SCRAMBLED VACATION WEEK ARRAY
19 REM          X=RANDOM NUMBER
21 REM ------------------------------------------------
25 RANDOMIZE TIMER
30 FOR I = 1 TO 6                    'loop to read in employee names
35     READ N$(I)
36     LET R(I) = I                  'an array for vacation weeks 1-6
40 NEXT I
```

```
45 DATA ALICE, BEN, CHARLES
46 DATA DORIS, EDNA, FRED
50 LET C=0
55 FOR N = 1 TO 100                      'loop to perform scrambling
60    LET X=INT(6*RND+1)                 'pick X randomly from 1 - 6
65    FOR I= 1 TO 6                      'loop to analyze each number X
70        IF R(I)= -9 THEN 100           'has number been picked before?
75            IF R(I)<>X THEN 100        'search to see if X is in  R(I).
80                LET C=C+1               'count when replacing I with X
85                LET V(C)=X              'assign random number X to array V
90                LET R(I)= -9           'assign a -9 into array R
95                    IF C=6 THEN 110    'exit loop when all six numbers
100   NEXT I                                  'have been randomly scrambled
105 NEXT N
110 PRINT "EMPLOYEE     VACATION WEEK"
112 PRINT "------------------------"
115 FOR C= 1 TO 6                        'loop to print out employee
120    PRINT N$(C), V(C)                     'name and vacation week
125 NEXT C
199 END


RUN
EMPLOYEE     VACATION WEEK
------------------------
ALICE            4
BEN              1
CHARLES          5
DORIS            6
EDNA             2
FRED             3
```

## Computer Simulation

Random numbers in the form of data values are useful when there is a need to carry out a *simulation*. Simulation is a technique applied to many business problems where, for example, it may be too costly to construct and test a new system or to market a new product. Thus, a computer model that mimics the behavior of the system is created, with data inputs supplied by using an appropriate random number function. Simulation is also used when it is impractical to perform direct experimentation (for example, a simulated space launching or war games) or when a process is too slow (for example, ecology or forestry).

An example of a simple computer simulation is given by Program 13.11. This program simulates the tossing of a pair of dice using the RND function to produce integer values from 1–6. It prints the outcomes of 10 tosses of a red and blue die and the sum of both dice.

### PROGRAM 13.11    Simulating Tossing a Pair of Dice

```
10 REM SIMULATING TOSSING A PAIR OF DICE
20 RANDOMIZE TIMER
30 PRINT "RED DIE", "BLUE DIE", "TOTAL"
40 FOR I=1 TO 10
```

```
50      LET R=INT(6*RND+1)      'generate a number from 1-6 (red die)
60      LET B=INT(6*RND+1)      'generate a number from 1-6 (blue die)
70      PRINT R,B,R+B
80 NEXT I
90 END

RUN
RED DIE         BLUE DIE        TOTAL
  4               4               8
  5               3               8
  4               6              10
  5               3               8
  6               2               8
  1               1               2
  3               2               5
  5               3               8
  5               1               6
  1               3               4
```

Another simulation application is provided by Case 13.4. (A much larger illustration of a simulation application can be found in Chapter 16, Case Problem II, Process Simulation.)

## CASE 13.4

**Problem**

**Simulating Customer Traffic History**
The manager at a bank branch wishes to analyze the flow of customer traffic by simulating for a five-day period the number of arrivals between the hours of 9 A.M. and 3 P.M. From past experience it has been observed that during any one hour there can be from 10–20 customers taken care of in the branch. To help with the analysis, a simulation program was written to create an artificial history of five working days, each six hours long.

**Data Input**

The data values for 10–20 customers are to be generated by a RND function for six hours per day over a five-day period.

**Process/Formulas**

A nested FOR/NEXT loop process is to be used. The outer loop will act as the five days; the inner loop will serve as the six hours per day. A RND function to produce values from 10–20 is placed in the inner loop.

**Output**

The output for a typical day's simulation follows this format:

```
DAY 1           HOUR            NUMBER OF CUSTOMERS
-----------------------------------------------------
                  1                     17
                  2                     13
                  3                     14
                  4                     14
                  5                     20
                  6                     20
```

Program 13.12 produces the simulated history of five days for the situation described in Case 13.4. Line 75 in that program is responsible for the generation of the data to correspond to the 10–20 customers arriving during any one-hour period.

## PROGRAM 13.12    Case 13.4, Customer Traffic History Simulation

```
10 REM CASE 13.4, SIMULATING CUSTOMER TRAFFIC HISTORY
15 REM   PROGRAMMER- (name of person)  DATE - mm/dd/yy
20 REM      VARIABLE LIST-
25 REM         C=INTEGER, FROM 10 TO 20
26 REM         D=LOOP INDEX, FROM 1 TO 5, FOR DAYS
27 REM         H$=HEADING, K$=FORMAT
28 REM         L$=DASHED LINE
30 REM         T=LOOP INDEX, FROM 1 TO 6 FOR HOURS
35 REM --------------------------------------------------
40 RANDOMIZE TIMER
45 LET H$= "DAY #     HOUR     NUMBER OF CUSTOMERS"
50 LET L$= "-----------------------------------"
52 LET K$= "          #               ##   "
55 FOR D = 1 TO 5                  'loop for five days
60     PRINT USING H$; D
65     PRINT L$
70     FOR T = 1 TO 6              'loop for six hours
75         LET C = INT(11*RND+10)  'generates values from 10-20
80         PRINT USING K$;T,C
85     NEXT T
90     PRINT
95 NEXT D
100 END
```

```
DAY 1     HOUR     NUMBER OF CUSTOMERS
-----------------------------------
          1              16
          2              17
          3              12
          4              16
          5              17
          6              15

DAY 2     HOUR     NUMBER OF CUSTOMERS
-----------------------------------
          1              16
          2              14
          3              13
          4              17
          5              20
          6              15
```

```
DAY 3     HOUR       NUMBER OF CUSTOMERS
------------------------------------------
            1              11
            2              20
            3              15
            4              20
            5              20
            6              11

DAY 4     HOUR       NUMBER OF CUSTOMERS
------------------------------------------
            1              18
            2              13
            3              10
            4              16
            5              10
            6              19

DAY 5     HOUR       NUMBER OF CUSTOMERS
------------------------------------------
            1              17
            2              11
            3              16
            4              13
            5              16
            6              14
```

## STRING FUNCTIONS

### LEN, LEFT$, RIGHT$, and MID$

To perform operations on string items, there exists a group of string functions that are found in most dialects of the BASIC language. These functions are summarized in Table 13.2.

In the functions listed in Table 13.2, the string items can be an ordinary string variable, a subscripted string variable, or an item in quotation marks, such as "MARCH." The value for *n* may be a numeric constant or variable. The same is true for the value of *p* in the MID$ function.

The LEN function measures the character length of a string. In the example that follows, the PRINT statement causes the length of the argument to be printed out.

10 LET N$ = "CALIFORNIA"

20 PRINT LEN(N$)

or

30 PRINT LEN("CALIFORNIA")

The number 10 will be printed by line 20 or 30.

**TABLE 13.2** String Functions

| FUNCTION | PURPOSE |
|---|---|
| LEN(string) | Returns the length or number of characters of the string argument. |
| LEFT$(string,n) | Returns the first n characters of the string argument. |
| RIGHT$(string,n) | Returns the last n characters of the string argument. |
| MID$(string,p,n) | Returns a substring of the string argument having a length n beginning with the position p in the string. |

The LEFT$ function returns the left, or first, part of a string item. The RIGHT$ function will return the right, or last, part of a string item. The examples that follow show both of these functions operating on the string item "NEW YORK."

    40 LET N$ = "NEW YORK"

    50 PRINT LEFT$(N$,3)

or

    60 PRINT LEFT$("NEW YORK",3)

    70 PRINT RIGHT$(N$,4)

or

    80 PRINT RIGHT$("NEW YORK",4)

Line 50 or 60 will print NEW, and line 70 or 80 will print YORK.

To obtain a middle part, or substring, of a string item requires the use of a function like the MID$ function. If N$ represents the string item "NEW YORK," to obtain the middle characters EW YO we would use this statement,

    80 PRINT MID$(N$,2,5)

which would return a substring of five characters in length starting with the second character in N$.

Program 13.13 illustrates the four string functions itemized in Table 13.2. Line 30 finds the length of each string using LEN(N$). Line 50 finds the left, middle, and right parts of each string using the functions LEFT$(N$,3), MID$(N$,2,5), and RIGHT$(N$,4), respectively.

**PROGRAM 13.13   String Functions**

```
5 PRINT     " STRING & LENGTH   LEFT PART    MIDDLE    RIGHT PART"
10 PRINT    "------------------------------------------------------"
15 LET F$= "\            \ ##      \      \      \      \      \      \"
20 FOR A = 1 TO 8
25     READ N$
30     LET L = LEN(N$)
50     PRINT USING F$; N$, L, LEFT$(N$,3), MID$(N$,2,5), RIGHT$(N$,4)
55 NEXT A
```

```
60 DATA CALIFORNIA, NEW YORK, ILLINOIS, MAINE
65 DATA NEBRASKA, NEW MEXICO, COLORADO, ALASKA
70 END

RUN
  STRING & LENGTH      LEFT PART    MIDDLE    RIGHT PART
  ------------------------------------------------------
CALIFORNIA     10         CAL        ALIFO       RNIA
NEW YORK        8         NEW        EW YO       YORK
ILLINOIS        8         ILL        LLINO       NOIS
MAINE           5         MAI        AINE        AINE
NEBRASKA        8         NEB        EBRAS       ASKA
NEW MEXICO     10         NEW        EW ME       XICO
COLORADO        8         COL        OLORA       RADO
ALASKA          6         ALA        LASKA       ASKA
```

Program 13.14, based on Case 13.5, illustrates the use of the string functions LEN, LEFT\$, RIGHT\$, and MID\$.

## CASE 13.5

**Problem**        **Changing the Order of Names**
An employee list contains names in first-name, last-name order. For example, Jack North, Sally Winter, Michael Worth, and so forth. A program is needed to take the original name list and change the order of the names.

**Data Input**     The data consists of the following list of seven names.

| | |
|---|---|
| Jack North | Bruce Bennett |
| Sally Winter | James Keenan |
| Michael Worth | Donald Rosen |
| Elaine Wine | |

**Process/Formulas** A nested FOR/NEXT loop is used to process each name. The length of each name is determined within the loop. By examining each name and finding where the space is between the first and last name, it is possible to split the whole name into two parts. The right part can then be moved to the left, and the left part to the right.

**Output**         The output should look as follows:

```
FIRST-LAST NAME                 LAST-FIRST NAME
------------------------------------------------
JACK NORTH                      NORTH, JACK
SALLY WINTER                    WINTER, SALLY
MICHAEL WORTH                   WORTH, MICHAEL
ELAINE WINE                     WINE, ELAINE
BRUCE BENNETT                   BENNETT, BRUCE
JAMES KEENAN                    KEENAN, JAMES
DONALD ROSEN                    ROSEN, DONALD
```

Program 13.14 performs the reversal of the name list required by Case 13.5. Line 60 finds the length of each name assigned to N$. To determine where the first and last names are in the string N$, the FOR/NEXT loop (lines 65–75) examines each character using the string function MID$(N$,P,1) in line 70 to locate the position of the blank space that separates the names. Once that position (P) is located, the name can be divided into two parts. Line 80 establishes the length of the last name, and line 85 establishes the length of the first name. Line 95 is needed to print out these names in the required last-name, first-name sequence.

## PROGRAM 13.14    Case 13.5, Name List Reversal Program

```
5 REM CASE 13.5, NAME LIST REVERSAL PROGRAM
8 REM   PROGRAMMER- (name of person)   DATE - mm/dd/yy
11 REM      VARIABLE LIST-
14 REM         A = NUMBER OF CHARACTERS TO THE RIGHT OF P (L - P)
15 REM         B = NUMBER OF CHARACTERS TO THE LEFT OF P (L - A)
17 REM         L = LENGTH OF N$
18 REM         N$ = NAME
20 REM         P = POSITION OF BLANK IN N$
28 REM --------------------------------------------------------
40 PRINT "FIRST-LAST NAME","LAST-FIRST NAME"
45 PRINT "---------------------------------------------"
50 FOR N = 1 TO 7
55     READ N$
60     LET L = LEN(N$)                        'finds length of each name
65     FOR P = 1 TO L
70        IF MID$(N$,P,1) = " " THEN 80 'find space in the middle of N$
75     NEXT P
80        LET A = L - P                       'determine length of last name
85        LET B = L - A                       'determine length of first name
90        PRINT N$," ",
95        PRINT RIGHT$(N$,A);", ";LEFT$(N$,B)   'print last-first name
100 NEXT N
105 DATA JACK NORTH,     SALLY WINTER
115 DATA MICHAEL WORTH,   ELAINE WINE
125 DATA BRUCE BENNETT,   JAMES KEENAN
135 DATA DONALD ROSEN
140 END

RUN
FIRST-LAST NAME                LAST-FIRST NAME
-------------------------------------------
JACK NORTH                     NORTH, JACK
SALLY WINTER                   WINTER, SALLY
MICHAEL WORTH                  WORTH, MICHAEL
ELAINE WINE                    WINE, ELAINE
BRUCE BENNETT                  BENNETT, BRUCE
JAMES KEENAN                   KEENAN, JAMES
DONALD ROSEN                   ROSEN, DONALD
```

The solution of Case 13.6 requires a program that uses both the MID$ function and RND function.

- - - - - - - - - - - - - - - - - - - - - - - - - - - - - - - - - -

## CASE 13.6

**Problem**     **Generating Security Passwords**

A standard computer security procedure for users of computer terminals involves the use of passwords. If a user wishes to gain access to the computer, there is a sign-on procedure that requires the user to enter a password that is verified by the system. Passwords may be randomly generated and distributed to users. They are generally from three to six characters in length, and many organizations that use passwords change them frequently. A program can be written that will generate passwords each time they are needed.

**Data Input**    The data values are the letters of the alphabet: ABCDEFGHIJKLMNOPQRSTUVWXYZ. The program is conversational with the user entering ''how many passwords needed'' and ''how many characters in each password.''

**Process/Formulas** A nested FOR/NEXT loop process is to be used. The outer loop sets the number of passwords that are requested, and the inner loop sets the number of characters in each password. To create each password, as many letters as required by the user are picked randomly from the alphabet string until a password is complete.

**Output**     A typical output has the following format:

```
HOW MANY PASSWORDS NEEDED? 6
HOW MANY CHARACTERS IN EACH PASSWORD? 3

PASSWORD 1 WZO
PASSWORD 2 ABP
PASSWORD 3 WGP
PASSWORD 4 PJC
PASSWORD 5 IIG
PASSWORD 6 PAN
```

- - - - - - - - - - - - - - - - - - - - - - - - - - - - - - - - - -

Program 13.15 generates the passwords for Case 13.6. The program uses the letters of the alphabet stored in P$ as the characters to make up each randomly generated password. By entering the number of passwords needed (N in line 180) and the length of each password (C in line 200), the nested loop (lines 220–290) can produce the desired results. Note that line 250 causes a random number (I = 1–26) to be picked. Each number corresponds to one of the 26 alphabet characters in P$. Using the MID$ function of line 260

    260 PRINT MID$(P$,I,1);

where P$ is the 26 alphabet letters, I is the position of the randomly picked letter, and 1 indicates that only one character will be printed out at a time. The printing continues until a password of *C* characters is produced.

## PROGRAM 13.15   Case 13.6, Password Generator Program

```
10 REM CASE 13.6, PASSWORD GENERATOR PROGRAM
15 REM PROGRAMMER- (name of person)    DATE- mm/dd/yy
20 REM      VARIABLE LIST-
22 REM          A, B= LOOP INDICES
25 REM          C=NUMBER OF CHARACTERS IN EACH PASSWORD
30 REM          N=NUMBER OF PASSWORDS NEEDED
35 REM          P$=ALPHABET
40 REM -------------------------------------------------
120 RANDOMIZE TIMER
140 LET P$ = "ABCDEFGHIJKLMNOPQRSTUVWXYZ"              'assign the alphabet to P$
180 INPUT "HOW MANY PASSWORDS NEEDED"; N
200 INPUT "HOW MANY CHARACTERS IN EACH PASSWORD "; C
210 PRINT
220 FOR A = 1 TO N                                     'loop for N passwords
230     PRINT "PASSWORD";A;
240     FOR B = 1 TO C                                 'loop for C characters
250         LET I = INT(26*RND + 1)                    'pick a number from 1-26
260         PRINT MID$(P$,I,1);                 'print one letter from the alphabet
270     NEXT B
280     PRINT
290 NEXT A
300 END


RUN
HOW MANY PASSWORDS NEEDED? 5
HOW MANY CHARACTERS IN EACH PASSWORD ? 4

PASSWORD 1 QGUE
PASSWORD 2 IOWW
PASSWORD 3 PCNN
PASSWORD 4 CJIK
PASSWORD 5 XZYP


RUN
HOW MANY PASSWORDS NEEDED? 4
HOW MANY CHARACTERS IN EACH PASSWORD ? 6

PASSWORD 1 LCFYSE
PASSWORD 2 OLCWDT
PASSWORD 3 DDMNRX
PASSWORD 4 BGGHYY


RUN
HOW MANY PASSWORDS NEEDED? 6
HOW MANY CHARACTERS IN EACH PASSWORD ? 3

PASSWORD 1 IGF
PASSWORD 2 HVQ
PASSWORD 3 RKH
PASSWORD 4 EVZ
PASSWORD 5 LAL
PASSWORD 6 YMJ
```

**Data Entry Checking**    It is important to check data as it is entered into a program before processing to prevent both output errors and possible syntax errors. With string functions we can build routines into the program that may check the length of a string item to see if it fits into the fixed space on a form or if the string item has certain characters in specific positions.

Program 13.16 below performs a data entry check on a Social Security number that is entered interactively in response to line 40. The purpose of the check is to ensure that each data item entered has all 11 characters. This check is performed using the LEN function in line 50:

50 IF LEN(SSN$) = 11 THEN 60

If SSN$ is too long or too short, the message in line 52 is displayed, instructing the program user to reenter the Social Security number.

---

**PROGRAM 13.16    Data Entry Checking with the LEN Function**

```
10 REM   DATA ENTRY CHECKING
20 FOR DE = 1 TO 3
40     INPUT "ENTER S.S. NUMBER IN THIS FORM: 123-45-6789 : ", SSN$
50         IF LEN(SSN$) = 11 THEN 60
52             PRINT SSN$; " **ENTERED INCORRECTLY, PLEASE REDO.**"
54     GOTO 40
60             PRINT "S.S. NO. ENTERED ";SSN$
65             PRINT
70 NEXT DE
99 END

RUN
ENTER S.S. NUMBER IN THIS FORM: 123-45-6789 : 111-22-3333
S.S. NO. ENTERED 111-22-3333

ENTER S.S. NUMBER IN THIS FORM: 123-45-6789 : 111-22-33333
111-22-33333 **ENTERED INCORRECTLY, PLEASE REDO.**
ENTER S.S. NUMBER IN THIS FORM: 123-45-6789 : 111-22-3333
S.S. NO. ENTERED 111-22-3333

ENTER S.S. NUMBER IN THIS FORM: 123-45-6789 : 111-22-33
111-22-33 **ENTERED INCORRECTLY, PLEASE REDO.**
ENTER S.S. NUMBER IN THIS FORM: 123-45-6789 : 111-22-3333
S.S. NO. ENTERED 111-22-3333
```

Another check that could have been built into Program 13.16 would use the MID$ function to ensure that characters in positions 4 and 7 were dashes. This might be done using a statement like

IF MID$(SSN$,4,1) AND MID$(SSN$,7,1) <> "-" THEN . . .

This type of data entry check is part of exercises 13.23–13.26.

In addition to the string functions just discussed, there are others that enable us to perform various programming tasks. Table 13.3 shows several of these functions followed by a brief description and program illustration.

**ASC and CHR$**   Each character on the keyboard, including the nonprinting characters such as backspace and return, is assigned a numeric code between 1 and 255 called the ASCII code. ASCII (pronounced "askey") stands for the American Standard Code for Information Interchange. The ASC function will return the ASCII code for any single character or for the first character in a string item. For example, ASC("N") returns a code of 78 and so does ASC(Nn5). Program 13.17 illustrates this ASC function.

---

**PROGRAM 13.17   Character and ASCII Code**

```
5 PRINT "CHARACTER AND ASCII CODE"
10 PRINT "N";ASC("N"), "n";ASC("n"),"5"; ASC("5"), "Nn5";ASC("Nn5")
15 READ X$, Y$, Z$, A$
20 DATA ?, @, *, ?@*
25 PRINT X$ ;ASC(X$), Y$ ;ASC(Y$), Z$; ASC(Z$), A$; ASC(A$)
30 END

RUN
CHARACTER AND ASCII CODE
N 78          n 110         5 53          Nn5 78
? 63          @ 64          * 42          ?@* 63
```

Table 13.4 (pp. 378–379) contains a complete list of the ASCII codes (in decimals) and their corresponding printable and nonprintable characters. These characters can be displayed using PRINT CHR$ (n), where *n* is the ASCII code.

Each of the characters can be entered from the keyboard by pressing and holding the Alt key and then pressing the digits for the ASCII code on the numeric keypad. Note, however, that some of the codes have special meaning to the BASIC program editor. BASIC uses its own interpretation for the codes and may not display the special character listed here.

**TABLE 13.3**   Other Functions

| FUNCTION | PURPOSE | EXAMPLES |
|---|---|---|
| ASC(string) | Returns the ASCII code number of the first character in the string. | 10 PRINT ASC("B") <br> 15 PRINT ASC(M$), ASC("ABC") |
| CHR$(code) | Converts code to a one-character string. | 20 PRINT CHR$(98) <br> 25 PRINT CHR$(NV) |
| SPACE$(n) | Returns *n* blank spaces. | 30 PRINT SPACE$(23) <br> 350 PRINT SPACE$(X) |
| STRING$(n,string) | Returns the first character in the string *n* times. | 40 PRINT STRING$(10,"*") <br> 45 PRINT STRING$(5,"E$") |

The CHR$ function will convert the ASCII code to the character. For example, CHR$(78) returns the capital letter *N*, while CHR$(110) returns a lowercase letter *n*. See Program 13.18 for examples of this function.

## PROGRAM 13.18   ASCII Code and Character

```
5 PRINT "ASCII CODE AND CHARACTER"
10 PRINT 78; CHR$(78), 110; CHR$(110), 53; CHR$(53)
11 READ A, B, C
12 DATA 63, 64, 42
15 PRINT A;CHR$(A), B;CHR$(B), C;CHR$(C)
20 END

RUN
ASCII CODE AND CHARACTER
 78 N            110 n          53 5
 63 ?            64 @           42 *
```

The CHR$ function has several uses. We can use the CHR$ function to print a quotation mark with PRINT CHR$(34) or to print a smiling face on the screen using PRINT CHR$(01). The CHR$ function can also be used to move the cursor on the screen using ASCII codes 28–31.

The codes with numbers 127 or higher are used for special symbols and graphic characters (see Table 13.4). Program 13.19 prints out some of these characters. However, not every printer can print out all of the characters shown in Table 13.4. Check your printer before using these codes to generate special characters.

## PROGRAM 13.19   ASCII Code and Graphics Characters

```
5 PRINT "ASCII CODE AND GRAPHICS CHARACTER"
6 PRINT
10 FOR CODE = 176 TO 223
20   PRINT CODE;" "; CHR$(CODE),   'some graphics character codes
30 NEXT CODE
40 END

RUN
ASCII CODE AND GRAPHICS CHARACTER

 176 ▒          177 ▓          178 ▓          179 │          180 ┤
 181 ╡          182 ╢          183 ╖          184 ╕          185 ╣
 186 ║          187 ╗          188 ╝          189 ╜          190 ╛
 191 ┐          192 └          193 ┴          194 ┬          195 ├
 196 ─          197 ┼          198 ╞          199 ╟          200 ╚
 201 ╔          202 ╩          203 ╦          204 ╠          205 ═
 206 ╬          207 ╧          208 ╨          209 ╤          210 ╥
 211 ╙          212 ╘          213 ╒          214 ╓          215 ╫
 216 ╪          217 ┘          218 ┌          219 █          220 ▄
 221 ▌          222 ▐          223 ▀
```

**TABLE 13.4** ASCII Codes and Characters

| ASCII VALUE | CHARACTER | ASCII VALUE | CHARACTER | ASCII VALUE | CHARACTER | ASCII VALUE | CHARACTER |
|---|---|---|---|---|---|---|---|
| 000 | (null) | 032 | (space) | 064 | @ | 096 | ` |
| 001 | ☺ | 033 | ! | 065 | A | 097 | a |
| 002 | ☻ | 034 | " | 066 | B | 098 | b |
| 003 | ♥ | 035 | # | 067 | C | 099 | c |
| 004 | ♦ | 036 | $ | 068 | D | 100 | d |
| 005 | ♣ | 037 | % | 069 | E | 101 | e |
| 006 | ♠ | 038 | & | 070 | F | 102 | f |
| 007 | (beep) | 039 | ' | 071 | G | 103 | g |
| 008 | ▫ | 040 | ( | 072 | H | 104 | h |
| 009 | (tab) | 041 | ) | 073 | I | 105 | i |
| 010 | (line feed) | 042 | * | 074 | J | 106 | j |
| 011 | (home) | 043 | + | 075 | K | 107 | k |
| 012 | (form feed) | 044 | , | 076 | L | 108 | l |
| 013 | (carriage return) | 045 | - | 077 | M | 109 | m |
| 014 | ♪ | 046 | . | 078 | N | 110 | n |
| 015 | ☼ | 047 | / | 079 | O | 111 | o |
| 016 | ► | 048 | 0 | 080 | P | 112 | p |
| 017 | ◄ | 049 | 1 | 081 | Q | 113 | q |
| 018 | ↕ | 050 | 2 | 082 | R | 114 | r |
| 019 | ‼ | 051 | 3 | 083 | S | 115 | s |
| 020 | ¶ | 052 | 4 | 084 | T | 116 | t |
| 021 | § | 053 | 5 | 085 | U | 117 | u |
| 022 | ▬ | 054 | 6 | 086 | V | 118 | v |
| 023 | ↨ | 055 | 7 | 087 | W | 119 | w |
| 024 | ↑ | 056 | 8 | 088 | X | 120 | x |
| 025 | ↓ | 057 | 9 | 089 | Y | 121 | y |
| 026 | → | 058 | : | 090 | Z | 122 | z |
| 027 | ← | 059 | ; | 091 | [ | 123 | { |
| 028 | (cursor right) | 060 | < | 092 | \ | 124 | ¦ |
| 029 | (cursor left) | 061 | = | 093 | ] | 125 | } |
| 030 | (cursor up) | 062 | > | 094 | ∧ | 126 | ~ |
| 031 | (cursor down) | 063 | ? | 095 | — | 127 | ⌂ |

**TABLE 13.4**  Continued

| ASCII VALUE | CHARACTER | ASCII VALUE | CHARACTER | ASCII VALUE | CHARACTER | ASCII VALUE | CHARACTER |
|---|---|---|---|---|---|---|---|
| 128 | Ç | 160 | á | 192 | ∟ | 224 | α |
| 129 | ü | 161 | í | 193 | ⊥ | 225 | β |
| 130 | é | 162 | ó | 194 | ⊤ | 226 | Γ |
| 131 | â | 163 | ú | 195 | ⊦ | 227 | π |
| 132 | ä | 164 | ñ | 196 | – | 228 | Σ |
| 133 | à | 165 | Ñ | 197 | + | 229 | σ |
| 134 | å | 166 | ª | 198 | ⊧ | 230 | μ |
| 135 | ç | 167 | º | 199 | ⊪ | 231 | τ |
| 136 | ê | 168 | ¿ | 200 | ⊔ | 232 | Φ |
| 137 | ë | 169 | ⌐ | 201 | ⊩ | 233 | θ |
| 138 | è | 170 | ¬ | 202 | ⊥ | 234 | Ω |
| 139 | ï | 171 | ½ | 203 | ⊤ | 235 | δ |
| 140 | î | 172 | ¼ | 204 | ⊩ | 236 | ∞ |
| 141 | ì | 173 | ¡ | 205 | = | 237 | ∅ |
| 142 | Ä | 174 | « | 206 | ⊹ | 238 | ε |
| 143 | Å | 175 | » | 207 | ⊥ | 239 | ∩ |
| 144 | É | 176 | ░ | 208 | ⊥ | 240 | ≡ |
| 145 | æ | 177 | ▒ | 209 | ⊤ | 241 | ± |
| 146 | Æ | 178 | ▓ | 210 | ⊤ | 242 | ≥ |
| 147 | ô | 179 | │ | 211 | ⊔ | 243 | ≤ |
| 148 | ö | 180 | ┤ | 212 | ⊦ | 244 | ⌠ |
| 149 | ò | 181 | ╡ | 213 | ⊦ | 245 | ⌡ |
| 150 | û | 182 | ╢ | 214 | ⊤ | 246 | ÷ |
| 151 | ù | 183 | ╖ | 215 | ⊹ | 247 | ≈ |
| 152 | ÿ | 184 | ╕ | 216 | ⊹ | 248 | ° |
| 153 | Ö | 185 | ╣ | 217 | ⌐ | 249 | ● |
| 154 | Ü | 186 | ║ | 218 | ⌐ | 250 | • |
| 155 | ¢ | 187 | ╗ | 219 | █ | 251 | √ |
| 156 | £ | 188 | ╝ | 220 | ▄ | 252 | ⁿ |
| 157 | ¥ | 189 | ╜ | 221 | ▌ | 253 | ² |
| 158 | Pt | 190 | ╛ | 222 | ▐ | 254 | ■ |
| 159 | ƒ | 191 | ┐ | 223 | ▀ | 255 | (blank 'FF') |

**SPACE$**  If we wanted to print or skip 10 spaces, we could enclose 10 spaces within quotation marks (PRINT `` `` '') and print that, or, more conveniently, we can use SPACE$(10). Observe line 20 in Program 13.20. The function SPACE$(I) outputs *I* blank spaces between the two special characters « ».

---

**PROGRAM 13.20   The SPACE$ Function**

```
10 FOR I=1 TO 10
20     PRINT CHR$(174);SPACE$(I);CHR$(175)
30 NEXT I
40 END

RUN
« »
«  »
«   »
«    »
«     »
«      »
«       »
«        »
«         »
«          »
```

---

**STRING$**  The STRING$ function allows us to easily generate a string of *n* copies of a particular character. For example, STRING$(5,``N'') will return NNNNN or five Ns. Another form of the STRING$ function is STRING$(n,X$), which will return *n* copies of the first character of the string variable X$. This concept is shown in lines 10 and 30 of Program 13.21.

---

**PROGRAM 13.21   The STRING$ Function**

```
10 PRINT STRING$(12,"-")            'print out a dash 12 times
20 LET X$="ABC"
30 PRINT STRING$(4,X$)              'print out first character of ABC 4 times
40 END

RUN
------------
AAAA
```

---

**DATE$ and TIME$**  Both the date and time can be programmed either as a variable or as a statement.

As a variable, we can have the date and time represented as

variable$ = DATE$
variable$ = TIME$

As a statement, we can have the date and time represented as

line # DATE$ = variable$
line # TIME$ = variable$

The following remarks relate to date and time variables and statements. The DATE$ variable returns the current date as set by DOS in the form mm-dd-yy where mm is the month, dd is the day 01 to 31, and yy is the year. In Program 13.22, DOS sets the current date as March 5, 1990 when booting the machine, and that date appears as the first line of output as a result of line 10.

Similarly, the TIME$ variable in line 10 returns the current time as set by DOS in the form hh:mm:ss where hh is the hours, mm is the minutes, and ss is the seconds. This is also shown in the first line of output as result of line 10.

The current date may also be set by the statement DATE$ = v$ where v$ is a string variable or expression in any one of the following forms: mm-dd-yy or mm/dd/yy. The month and day may also be one digit, and the year may be two digits. The DATE$ as output, however, will always be in the form of mm-dd-yy. Observe line 20 in Program 13.22. The year must be in the range 1980 to 2079. If only two digits are given for the year, they will set to 19 if the year is at least 80 or to 20 if the year is less than 80.

The current time may also be set by the statement TIME$ = v$ where v$ is a string variable or expression in the form hh:mm:ss. The minutes and seconds may be omitted but not the hours. The hours may be one or two digits as required, but even 15 minutes past midnight must be set as TIME$ = ''0:15''. The TIME$ statement is shown in line 35 of Program 13.22.

Both the date and time can be entered interactively. In Program 13.22 this is shown by line 55 where the date is assigned to D$ and the time to T$. Lines 60 and 65, the DATE$ and TIME$ statements, respectively, enable the date and time to be printed out using lines 75 and 85.

## PROGRAM 13.22    Date and Time Variables and Statements

```
10 PRINT "TODAY'S DATE AND TIME ARE: "; DATE$, TIME$    'from the computer
20 DATE$ ="4/3/91"                              'assigns the date
25 PRINT "THE DATE IS:   ";DATE$
35 TIME$ ="1:2:3"                               'assigns the time
40 PRINT "THE TIME IS:   ";TIME$
50 REM --USING INPUT TO ENTER DATE AND TIME--
55 INPUT "WHAT IS THE DATE AND TIME";D$, T$
60 DATE$ = D$
65 TIME$ = T$
75 PRINT "THE DATE IS:   ";DATE$
85 PRINT "THE TIME IS:   ";TIME$
90 END

RUN
TODAY'S DATE AND TIME ARE: 03-05-1990    05:34:22
THE DATE IS:   04-03-1991
THE TIME IS:   01:02:03
WHAT IS THE DATE AND TIME? 2/3/91, 6:35
THE DATE IS: 02-03-1991
THE TIME IS: 06:35:00
```

## COMBINING STORED LIBRARY AND STRING FUNCTIONS

Different functions can be combined in a program to create unusual displays. Program 13.23 illustrates these ideas.

### PROGRAM 13.23  Plotting a SIN Curve Using SIN, INT, and SPACE$ Functions

```
5 REM PLOTTING A SIN CURVE USING SPACE$
10 FOR X= 0 TO 9 STEP .25
20      LET A = SIN(X)
30      LET B = 30 + INT(20*A)
40      PRINT SPACE$(B);"*"          'the SPACE$ function plots SIN(X)
50 NEXT X
60 END

RUN
                             *
                               *
                                *
                                 *
                                  *
                                   *
                                    *
                                    *
                                   *
                                  *
                               *
                             *
                           *
                         *
                       *
                     *
                    *
                   *
                  *
                  *
                  *
                   *
                     *
                       *
                         *
                           *
                             *
                                *
                                  *
                                    *
                                     *
                                     *
                                    *
                                 *
                              *
                            *
```

Note that the trigonometric SIN function (line 20) and an INT function (line 30) can be used with a SPACE$ function (line 40) to produce the plot of a SIN curve. The FOR statement in line 10 of the program provides the data needed for the argument X of the SIN function. The B value derived by the LET statement in line 30 is used as the argument for the SPACE$ function in line 40.

Case 13.7 and Program 13.24 further illustrate how several functions can create interesting output displays.

## CASE 13.7

**Problem**

**A Demonstration Program**

A computer store wants a demonstration program developed that will have the store name appear to dance across the screen.

**Data Input**

The data values required will be generated internally by the program.

**Process/Formulas**

A FOR/NEXT loop process is to be used. The loop variable will provide the argument for the COS(X). To round the values of the COS(X) function for plotting, an INT function is used. To space the output on the screen, a SPACE$ function is required. A special character (» store name «) on each side of the store name will be displayed using the CHR$ function.

**Output**

A typical output has the following format:

```
                    » THE COMPUTER STORE «
                   » THE COMPUTER STORE «
                  » THE COMPUTER STORE «
                 » THE COMPUTER STORE «
                » THE COMPUTER STORE «
               » THE COMPUTER STORE «
              » THE COMPUTER STORE «
             » THE COMPUTER STORE «
            » THE COMPUTER STORE «
           » THE COMPUTER STORE «
```

The dancing effect desired for Case 13.7 is achieved by Program 13.24. This program uses a COS(X) function (line 30) with a SPACE$ function (line 50) to cause the output display to dance across the screen with the string item "THE COMPUTER STORE." The FOR/NEXT loop in lines 70 and 80 causes the output display to slow down so that the desired display effect is produced. Increasing the output display for a longer time requires that the upper limit of the FOR statement in line 70 to be increased.

## PROGRAM 13.24   Case 13.7, Store Demonstration Program

```
10 REM CASE 13.7 STORE DEMONSTRATION PROGRAM
15 REM   PROGRAMMER- (name of person)  DATE- mm/dd/yy
16 REM      VARIABLE LIST-A1,B1,X,S
17 REM           A1=COS FUNCTION
18 REM           B1=INTEGER FOR SPACE$ FUNCTION
19 REM           X,S=LOOP INDICES
20 REM -------------------------------------------
25 FOR X=0 TO 8 STEP .2
30     LET A1=COS(X)
40     LET B1=25 + INT(15*A1)
50     PRINT SPACE$(B1); CHR$(175);" THE COMPUTER STORE "; CHR$(174)
70     FOR S= 1 to 50                    'the FOR/NEXT slows down the screen  display
80     NEXT S
90 NEXT X
100 END
```

```
RUN
                                » THE COMPUTER STORE «
                               » THE COMPUTER STORE «
                              » THE COMPUTER STORE «
                             » THE COMPUTER STORE «
                            » THE COMPUTER STORE «
                           » THE COMPUTER STORE «
                          » THE COMPUTER STORE «
                         » THE COMPUTER STORE «
                        » THE COMPUTER STORE «
                       » THE COMPUTER STORE «
                      » THE COMPUTER STORE «
                     » THE COMPUTER STORE «
                    » THE COMPUTER STORE «
                   » THE COMPUTER STORE «
                  » THE COMPUTER STORE «
                  » THE COMPUTER STORE «
                  » THE COMPUTER STORE «
                  » THE COMPUTER STORE «
                   » THE COMPUTER STORE «
                    » THE COMPUTER STORE «
                     » THE COMPUTER STORE «
                      » THE COMPUTER STORE «
                       » THE COMPUTER STORE «
                        » THE COMPUTER STORE «
                         » THE COMPUTER STORE «
                          » THE COMPUTER STORE «
                           » THE COMPUTER STORE «
                            » THE COMPUTER STORE «
                             » THE COMPUTER STORE «
                              » THE COMPUTER STORE «
                               » THE COMPUTER STORE «
                                » THE COMPUTER STORE «
                                 » THE COMPUTER STORE «
                                 » THE COMPUTER STORE «
                                 » THE COMPUTER STORE «
                                 » THE COMPUTER STORE «
                                » THE COMPUTER STORE «
                               » THE COMPUTER STORE «
                              » THE COMPUTER STORE «
                             » THE COMPUTER STORE «
                            » THE COMPUTER STORE «
```

## THE *DEF* STATEMENT

The DEF statement allows the programmer to define functions. For example, suppose you are interested in the amount of money that would be on deposit if $100 were invested at 6 percent compounded annually after *n* years for $n = 1, 5, 10$, and 20. We would use the compound interest formula described in Chapter 3, under "Basic Variables."

$$A = P(1 + r)^n$$

Without the DEF statement we could write Program 13.25.

## PROGRAM 13.25   Compound Interest without DEF

```
10 READ P,R
15 PRINT P*(1+R)^1, P*(1+R)^5, P*(1+R)^10, P*(1+R)^20
20 DATA 100,.06
25 END

RUN
 106            133.8225        179.0847        320.7132
```

With the DEF statement, we could write Program 13.26.

## PROGRAM 13.26   Compound Interest with DEF

```
10 READ P,R
15 DEF FNA(N)=P*(1+R)^N                'define a function
20 PRINT FNA(1), FNA(5), FNA(10), FNA(20)    'evaluate with values of N
25 DATA 100,.06
30 END

RUN
 106          133.8225        179.0847      320.7132
```

The statement on line 15 defines the function of the *dummy* variable *N*. It is not necessary for the variable *N* to have been previously given a value. Line 20 then prints the values of the function for the values of the numbers in parentheses. That is, FNA(1) assigns the value of 1 to *N* and evaluates the function on line 15.

The form of the DEF statement is

line # DEF FNvn(Arg) = expression

**TABLE 13.5** Examples of the DEF Statement

| STATEMENT | EXPLANATION |
|---|---|
| 1.  20 DEF FNCIRC(D) = 3.141*D | Defines the numeric function FNCIRC, which calculates the circumference of a circle with diameter $D$. |
| 2.  40 DEF FNLN(A,X) = A + 5*X | Defines the numeric function FNLN, which calculates the value of the expression using two arguments. |
| 3.  60 DEF FNB\$(NM\$) = RIGHT\$(NM\$,5) | Defines the string function FNB\$, which operates on the string expression. |

The *vn* is a valid variable name, numeric or string. The function type is declared by whether the name given is numeric or string. The *Arg* is the argument that is any variable name. Normally this variable would appear in the expression to the right of the equal sign. Table 13.5 shows examples of the DEF statement.

## A DEF Caution

Be sure the expression (string or numeric) matches the function type, or else a "Type mismatch" error will occur.

If we were to replace line 15 in Program 13.26 with

15 DEF FNA(P) = P * (1 + R) ^ N

and variable $N$ were given a value of 5 by the addition of line 16, LET N = 5, then line 20 would print the amount on deposit after 5 years if \$1, \$5, \$10, and \$20 were deposited at 6 percent interest compounded annually. Note that all we changed was the variable in parentheses, and now we are defining a function of $P$, the principal, rather than a function of $N$, the number of years. Program 13.27 defines a function FNR (line 5) that rounds a number to the nearest hundredth or penny and also defines a function FNA (line 15) to calculate the interest amount. Note how line 20 prints a function of a function.

## PROGRAM 13.27   Rounding with DEF

```
5 DEF FNR(X)=INT((X+.005)*100)/100   'defines a rounding function
10 READ P,R
15 DEF FNA(N)=P*(1+R)^N               'defines a function
20 PRINT FNR(FNA(1)), FNR(FNA(5)), FNR(FNA(10)), FNR(FMA(20))
25 DATA 100,.06
30 END

RUN
 106            133.82          179.08          320.71
```

## SUMMARY

There are several stored library functions in the BASIC language including SIN, COS, TAN, ATN, LOG, EXP, INT, SGN, ABS, SQR, and RND. Using the RND function, it is possible to design computer simulations.

String operations can be performed on string items by using the functions LEN, LEFT$, RIGHT$, and MID$. Other string functions that perform useful operations include ASC, CHR$, SPACE$, and STRING$. The time and date can be expressed as variables or as statements using TIME$ and DATE$.

In addition, you can define your own specialized functions using the DEF statement.

## BASIC VOCABULARY SUMMARY

| Function | Purpose | Examples |
|---|---|---|
| ABS(X) | Returns the absolute value of $X$ (without a sign) | 5 PRINT ABS(5*($-7$)), ABS(NUM) |
| INT(X) | Returns the largest integer that is less than or equal to $X$. | 10 PRINT INT(35.42)<br>15 LET J = INT(NUM2) |
| RND | Returns a random number between 0 and 1. | 15 PRINT RND |
| SGN(X) | Returns the sign of $X$: 1 if $X > 0$, $-1$ if $X < 0$, and 0 if $X = 0$. | 20 PRINT SGN($-2.45$)<br>22 LET B = SGN(NUM4) |
| SQR(X) | Returns the square root of $X$, where $X >= 0$. | 25 PRINT SQR(25)<br>30 LET X = SQR(NUMS) |
| LEN(string) | Returns the length or number of characters of the string. | 90 PRINT LEN(WD$)<br>85 PRINT LEN("WORDS") |
| LEFT$(string,n) | Returns the first $n$ characters of the string. | 80 PRINT LEFT$(W$,3)<br>75 PRINT LEFT$("NAMES",2) |
| RIGHT$(string,n) | Returns the last $n$ characters of the string. | 70 PRINT RIGHT$(C$,6)<br>65 LET C$ = RIGHT$("ROME",2) |
| MID$(string,p,n) | Returns a substring of the string with length $n$ starting from position $p$. | 60 PRINT MID$(D$,3,5)<br>55 PRINT MID$("AX234",2,3) |
| ASC(string) | Returns the ASCII code number of the first character in the string. | 10 PRINT ASC("C")<br>15 PRINT ASC(W$), ASC("XYZ") |
| CHR$(code) | Converts code to a one-character string. | 20 PRINT CHR$(66)<br>25 PRINT CHR$(D) |
| SPACE$(n) | Returns $n$ blank spaces. | 30 PRINT SPACE$(16)<br>35 PRINT SPACE$(J) |
| STRING$(n,string) | Returns the first character in the string $n$ times. | 40 PRINT STRING$ (12,"+")<br>45 PRINT STRING$ (4,GE$) |

| Statement | Purpose | Examples |
|-----------|---------|----------|
| RANDOMIZE | Seeds the random number generator. Requires a numeric response between $-32768$ and 32767. | 5 RANDOMIZE |
| RANDOMIZE n | Seeds the random number generator without a prompt. A seed, *n*, is supplied to produce a different sequence of numbers. If not changed, each program run gives the same sequence of random numbers. | 7 RANDOMIZE 23 |
| RANDOMIZE TIMER | Seeds the random number generator without a prompt. | 10 RANDOMIZE TIMER |
| DATE$ | Sets the value of the string variable as the date, mm-dd-yy. | 15 DATE$ = A$ |
| TIME$ | Sets the value of the string variable as the time, hh:mm:ss. | 20 TIME$ = B$ |
| DEF FNvn(Arg) | Defines and names a user-specified function, either numeric or string. | 40 DEF FNA(X) = 10 + 5*X<br>50 DEF FNB$(M$) = LEFT$(M$,4) |

## EXERCISES

### Review Questions

**13.1** What value is assigned to the variables shown below?
   a. LET P = INT($-61.49$)       e. LET X = SGN($-51.3$)
   ◆ b. LET C = INT(2*31.2 + .9)     f. LET M = SQR(225) + INT(46/3)
   ◆ c. LET W = SQR(.16)         ◆ g. LET R = ABS($-45.01$)
   d. LET Y = INT(SQR(.25))

**13.2** What are the values of INT(X), SGN(X), and ABS(X) if X is
   a. $-10E-3$?
   b. $-10E3$?

**13.3** What value is assigned to V7 in line 80?

   50 LET M = .6
   60 LET B = 2
   70 LET A = 7
   80 LET V7 = 10 * INT(M + B + A*.30)

**13.4** What will the following program cause to be printed?

   10 READ X, Y, Z
   15 PRINT ABS(X), SGN(Y + Z), INT(Y)

20 PRINT ABS(SGN(INT(X)))
25 PRINT INT(ABS(SGN(X)))
30 DATA −4.1, 7.8, −7.8
35 END

**13.5** What is the range of values in each case below:

a. LET R = 10*RND
♦ b. LET X = RND*2.5
c. LET L = − .5*RND
♦ d. LET T = INT(10*RND)

e. LET B9 = INT(RND*5*1)
♦ f. LET C2 = INT(50 + 101*RND)
g. LET K4 = INT(21*RND) + 60

**13.6** What will each of the following statements do?

a. 10 RANDOMIZE
b. 20 RANDOMIZE 35
c. 30 RANDOMIZE TIMER

**13.7** Suppose the National Electronics Company (Case 13.2) is operating on an overtime schedule that is, from 8 A.M. to 12:59 P.M. and from 1 P.M. to 8:59 P.M. Revise Program 13.9 (shown below) to take these changes into account.

```
10 REM CASE 13.2, RANDOMIZE INSPECTION TIMES
15 REM PROGRAMMER- (name of person)   DATE - mm/dd/yy
16 REM     VARIABLE LIST-H1,M1,H2,M2
17 REM          H1=A.M.HOUR
18 REM          M1=A.M.MINUTE
19 REM          H2=P.M.HOUR
20 REM          M2-P.M.MINUTE
25 REM -------------------------------
30 RANDOMIZE TIMER
35 LET H1=INT(4*RND+9)
40 LET M1=INT(60*RND)
45 LET H2=INT(5*RND+1)
50 LET M2=INT(60*RND)
54 PRINT
55 PRINT       "**********INSPECTION TIMES**********"
57 PRINT
60 PRINT USING "  MORNING TIME ##:##";H1,M1
65 PRINT
70 PRINT USING "  AFTERNOON TIME ##:##";H2,M2
75 END
```

**13.8** What will each of the following statements return if

C$ = ''ANY CITY, U.S.A 12345''

a. 5 PRINT LEN(C$)
♦ b. 10 PRINT LEFT$(C$,8)
c. 15 PRINT RIGHT$(C$,5)

♦ d. 20 PRINT MID$(C$,10,6)
e. 25 PRINT MID$(C$,3,1); MID$(C$,8,1)
f. 30 PRINT RIGHT$(C$,12), LEFT$(C$,8)

**13.9** What will the following program cause to be printed?

10 PRINT ASC(''a''), ASC(''B''), ASC(''z''), ASC(''Bb4'')
15 READ X$, Y$, Z$, A$
20 DATA #, &, %, + =-
25 PRINT ASC(X$), ASC(Y$), ASC(Z$), ASC(A$)
30 END

**13.10** What will the following program cause to be printed?

```
12 FOR A = 1 TO 6
15      READ CN
20      PRINT CHR$(CN);
25 NEXT A
26 DATA 83, 109, 105, 108, 101, 46
30 END
```

**13.11** What will the following program cause to be printed?

```
10 FOR I=1 TO 10
20      PRINT SPACE$(5);CHR$(195);STRING$(10,CHR$(196));CHR$(180)
30 NEXT I
40 END
```

**13.12** Given the following program:

```
 5 DATA 1,2,3,4
10 READ A,B,C,X
15 DEF FNA(X) = A*X+B^2+C
20 PRINT FNA(1),FNA(A),FNA(B),FNA(C),FNA(X)
25 END
```

What will it print

a. With the current line 15?
b. If line 15 is changed to 15 DEF FNA(A) = A*X+B^2+C?
c. If line 15 is changed to 15 DEF FNA(B) = A*X+B^2+C?
d. If line 15 is changed to 15 DEF FNA(C) = A*X+B^2+C?
e. If line 15 is changed to 15 DEF FNA(D) = A*X+B^2+C?

**13.13** How would you change a modification of Program 13.26 (shown below) to print the amount on deposit after 5 years if $100 is deposited at 6%, 7%, 8%, and 8 1/2%? Change only lines 15 and 20.

```
10 READ P,R,N
15 DEF FNA(N)=P*(1+R)^N
20 PRINT FNA(1), FNA(5), FNA(10), FNA(20)
25 DATA 100,.06,5
30 END
```

## Programming Activities

**13.14** **Purpose** To use the INT function.

**Problem** Write and run a program to round numbers off to the nearest thousandth.

**Data** 4.8921, 5.6548, 1.9876, 9.852479

**Output** Your output should have this format:

```
Number          Rounded
 4.8291           4.829
 5.6548           5.655
 1.9876           1.988
 9.852479         9.852
```

**13.15**   **Purpose**   To use the INT function.

**Problem**   Write and run a program that determines whether a number is even or odd.

**Data**   11, 16, 13, 45, 72

**Output**   Your output should have this format:

```
11 IS AN ODD NUMBER
16 IS AN EVEN NUMBER
13 IS AN ODD NUMBER
45 IS AN ODD NUMBER
72 IS AN EVEN NUMBER
```

♦ **13.16**   **Purpose**   To use the INT and RND functions and the RANDOMIZE TIMER statement.

**Problem**   Your club has sold 500 raffle tickets numbered from 001 to 500. Write and run a program to randomly select the first, second, and third prize-winning numbers.

**Data**   Generated internally.

**Output**   A typical output should have this format:

```
              Winning Number
1ST Prize      185
2ND Prize      213
3RD Prize       91
```

**13.17**   **Purpose**   To use the RND function and the RANDOMIZE TIMER statement.

**Problem**   Using an appropriate loop structure, write and run a program to simulate the tossing of a coin 10 times. Each time the program is run, it should produce a different set of outcomes.

**Data**   Generated internally.

**Output**   Your output should have this appearance:

```
TOSS NUMBER              OUTCOME
     1                      H
     2                      H
     3                      T
     . . .                  . . .
    10                      H
```

Assume H = heads, and T = tails.

**13.18**   **Purpose**   To use the RND function and RANDOMIZE TIMER statement.

**Problem**   Using an appropriate loop structure, write and run a program to simulate the tossing of three coins a total of 100 times. Accumulate the number of times heads comes up 0, 1, 2, or 3 times. Each time the program is run, it should produce a different set of outcomes.

**Data**   Generated internally.

**Output**   Your output should have this appearance:

```
NUMBER OF HEADS          NUMBER OF TIMES
        0                      14
        1                      35
        2                      36
        3                      15
                              ---
                              100
```

**13.19**   **Purpose**   To use the INT and RND functions and the RANDOMIZE TIMER statement.

**Problem**   Using an appropriate loop structure with decision testing, design an interactive computer game. The game requires that the player must guess a random number from 1 to 100 picked by the computer. After each guess, the player is informed to go higher or lower. Upon guessing the random number, the player is given the number of guess attempts. If more than nine tries were needed, the player is given a "poor rating"; for four to nine tries, the player is given an "average rating"; and for three or fewer tries, an "excellent rating." Each time the program is run, it should select a different number between 1 and 100.

**Data**   Generated internally and by user response.

**Output**   A typical output may have this appearance:

```
PICK A NUMBER 1 TO 100
WHAT IS YOUR GUESS? 50

PICK A HIGHER NUMBER, WHAT IS YOUR GUESS? 75

PICK A LOWER NUMBER, WHAT IS YOUR GUESS? 60

PICK A HIGHER NUMBER, WHAT IS YOUR GUESS? 62

CONGRATULATIONS-YOU GUESSED IT
# OF TRIES 4  RATING: AVERAGE
```

**13.20**   **Purpose**   To use the INT and RND functions and the RANDOMIZE TIMER statement.

**Problem**   Using an appropriate loop structure with decision testing, design a computer simulation. The Always-Have-a-Room Motel Co., Inc., has motels in nine locations:

| | |
|---|---|
| Atlanta, Ga. | New York, N.Y. |
| Baltimore, Md. | Raleigh, N.C. |
| Boston, Mass. | Richmond, Va. |
| Jacksonville, Fla. | Washington, D.C. |
| Miami, Fla. | |

A person phones for a reservation in a certain city. Depending on the number of persons in the party, there may or may not be a vacancy. If there is no vacancy, the caller is told the two closest cities to the desired location—one north of it and the other south of it.* The program should simulate 20 telephone calls. Assume that a call for each of the nine cities is equally likely (a one-ninth probability for each). Each time the program is run, it should produce a different set of outcomes.

**Data**   Treat the nine city locations given above as a subscripted string array. All of the other data for the program is generated internally, using a random number function. This function is used to simulate the city desired by the caller (1–9), the number of people in the party (1–6), and whether or not there is a vacancy.

Use the following information (based on historical data) to simulate the number of persons in the party and whether or not there is a vacancy:

| IF THE NUMBER OF PERSONS IS: | THE PROBABILITY OF *NO* VACANCY IS: |
| --- | --- |
| 1 | .30 |
| 2 | .40 |
| 3 | .50 |
| 4 to 6 | .60 |

**Output**   Your printed output might look like this (an illustration only):

```
          CITY       NUMBER IN   VACANCY   NEAREST OTHER
 CALL     DESIRED    PARTY       YES/NO    CITIES

  1       NYC          5           No      XYZ and ABC
 ----     -------    ---------   -------   -------------
 ----     -------    ---------   -------   -------------
 ----     -------    ---------   -------   -------------
  20      -------    ---------   -------   -------------
```

**13.21**   **Purpose**   To use the string functions LEN, LEFT$, RIGHT$, and MID$.

**Problem**   Write and run a program that will take your name and, using the appropriate string functions, print out the following:
a. The length of the string.
b. The first three characters of the name.
c. The last four characters of the name.
d. The last two characters of the first name, and the first three characters of the last name.
e. The two initials.

**Data**   Your name.

**Output**   A typical output may have this format:

```
Your Name...   11    You       me..      ur Nam     Y.N.
```

---

*This list of cities is not in any geographical sequence. Consult a map or atlas for the correct location of each one.

**13.22** **Purpose** To use the string functions LEN and MID$.

**Problem** Using an appropriate loop structure, write and run an interactive program that takes a name as a string and prints it out in reverse order.

**Data** Your name.

**Output** A typical output may have this format:

```
ENTER A NAME?   J. A. Student

tnedutS .A .J
```

**13.23** **Purpose** To use the LEN function for data entry checking.

**Problem** Using an appropriate loop structure and decision testing, write and run a program segment that will check if addresses are too long to fit on an output form. The character limit on the printed form is 20 characters for the city, state, and zip code. If an item is too long, a message should be printed out to shorten or abbreviate the address.

**Data** Use these addresses:

COLUMBUS, OHIO 43210             DENTON, TEXAS 90216
HOUSTON, TEXAS 77004             BOULDER, COLORADO 80309
ALBANY, NEW YORK 11222           YOUR ADDRESS, AND ZIP
CHICAGO, ILLINOIS 60680

**Output** Your output should have this format:

```
COLUMBUS, OHIO  43210       TOO LONG-SHORTEN OR ABBREV.
HOUSTON, TEXAS  77004       TOO LONG-SHORTEN OR ABBREV.
ALBANY, NEW YORK  11222     TOO LONG-SHORTEN OR ABBREV.
CHICAGO, ILLINOIS  60680    TOO LONG-SHORTEN OR ABBREV.
DENTON, TEXAS  90216
BOULDER, COLORADO  80309    TOO LONG-SHORTEN OR ABBREV.
```

♦ **13.24** **Purpose** To use the LEN function for data entry checking.

**Problem** Using an appropriate loop structure and decision testing, write and run a program to check that the zip codes of addresses are all five characters in length. For any zip code not five characters, the program causes a message to be printed that the zip code is "too long" or "too short."

**Data** Use the following data in your program, plus your own location.

Columbus, Ohio 43210          Houston, Texas 770004
Denton, Texas 0216            Boulder, Colorado 80309
Albany, New York 1222         Chicago, Illinois 60680

**Output** Your output should have this format:

```
COLUMBUS   OHIO       43210
HOUSTON    TEXAS      770004   ZIP CODE TOO LONG
DENTON     TEXAS      0216     ZIP CODE TOO SHORT
BOULDER    COLORADO   80309
ALBANY     NEW YORK   1222     ZIP CODE TOO SHORT
CHICAGO    ILLINOIS   60680
```

**13.25**  **Purpose**  To use the LEN and MID$ functions for data entry checking.

**Problem**  Using a nested FOR/NEXT loop structure and decision testing, write and run a program to check if a name does not have a blank space between the first name and the last name. Whenever such a name is found, a message "No blank in name—error" should be printed out.

**Data**  To test your program use these data items:

MICHAEL WORTH     JACK NORTH
ELAINE WINE       SALLY WINTER
C.COLUMBUS        ME.TARZAN
A.EINSTEIN

**Output**  Your output should have this format:

```
MICHAEL WORTH
ELAINE WINE
C.COLUMBUS   <--- NO BLANK IN NAME-ERROR
A.EINSTEIN   <--- NO BLANK IN NAME-ERROR
JACK NORTH
SALLY WINTER
ME.TARZAN    <--- NO BLANK IN NAME-ERROR
```

**13.26**  **Purpose**  To use the LEN and MID$ functions for data entry checking.

**Problem**  Using a loop structure and decision testing, write and run a program that examines telephone numbers to check the following:
a. Each number is eight characters.
b. Each number has the dash in the fourth character position.
If the number is not correctly formed a message should be printed indicating it is wrong.

**Data**  To test your program use these numbers: 225-8854, 526-53688, 55-42751, 351-942, 8291-942, 632-6110, 9906921, and your own number.

**Output**  Your output should have this format:

```
225-8854          IS AN O.K. NUMBER
526-53688         MISSING - /OR NOT 8 CHAR.
55-42751          MISSING - /OR NOT 8 CHAR.
351-942           MISSING - /OR NOT 8 CHAR.
8291-942          MISSING - /OR NOT 8 CHAR.
632-6110          IS AN O.K. NUMBER
9906921           MISSING - /OR NOT 8 CHAR.
990-6392          IS AN O.K. NUMBER
```

**13.27**  **Purpose**  To use the EXP, INT, SPACE$, CHR$ functions for plotting.

**Problem**  Using a loop structure, write and run a program that will display a plot of the EXP(X) function. Use the statement

LET B = INT(EXP(X)).

**Data**  To test your program use $X = 2$ to 4 STEP .15

**Output** Your output should display the ASCII character 249 and have this appearance.

• • • • • • **13.28** **Purpose** To use the LOG, INT, SPACE$, CHR$ functions for plotting.

**Problem** Using a loop structure, write and run a program that will display a plot of the LOG(X) function. Use the statement

LET B = INT(24*LOG(X))

**Data** To test your program use $X = 2$ to 20.

**Output** Your output should display the ASCII character 223 and have this appearance:

• • • • • • **13.29** **Purpose** To use the SPACE$, STRING$, and CHR$ functions for graphics displays.

**Problem** Using a loop structure, write and run a program that will display the figure below. The sides are five lines, the space between the two sides is thirty spaces.

**Data** Use the ASCII codes required.

**Output**    Your output should display the ASCII character 205 for horizontal lines and 186 for the vertical lines and should use the appropriate ASCII characters for the corners. The display should have this appearance:

**13.30**    **Purpose**    To use the STRING$ and CHR$ functions for graphics displays.

**Problem**    Using a loop structure, write and run a program that will display the bar chart shown below.

**Data**    Use the following data:

| Division | 1 | 2 | 3 | 4 |
|----------|----|----|----|----|
| Year 1 | 10 | 13 | 11 | 25 |
| Year 2 | 15 | 22 | 18 | 30 |

**Output**    Your output should display the ASCII character 219 for the horizontal bars. The display should have this appearance:

```
DIV. 1 Y1 ██████████
DIV. 1 Y2 ███████████████

DIV. 2 Y1 █████████████
DIV. 2 Y2 ██████████████████████

DIV. 3 Y1 ███████████
DIV. 3 Y2 ██████████████████

DIV. 4 Y1 █████████████████████████
DIV. 4 Y2 ██████████████████████████████
```

# SORTING
# NUMERIC AND
# ALPHABETIC DATA

Upon completing this chapter, you will be able to do the following:

- Understand how a computer can be programmed to sort large lists of data items.
- Explain how a selection sort works with numeric and nonnumeric data.
- Explain how a bubble sort works with numeric and nonnumeric data.
- Create a sorting program that includes the use of the SWAP statement.

It is frequently necessary to sort a data list or an array — that is, to arrange numbers of an array in ascending or descending order or to put alphabetic strings in alphabetic order. In this chapter, we study several sorting programs for both numeric and alphabetic data. The concepts used in these programs will enable you to write your own sorting programs.

## FINDING THE SMALLEST DATA VALUE

Given a data list of five values (1, 7, 6, 0, 3), how can a program find the minimum or smallest of the values? Observe how Program 14.1 accomplishes the task. Lines 10–20 read the data list in line 80 into the array $A$. Line 30 assigns the first value of the array $A(1)$ to the variable $S$. Lines 35–60 compare variable $S$ with the 2nd–5th data values in the array $A$. If any value of $A(I)$ is smaller than $S$, that value is then assigned to $S$ by line 50. When the FOR/NEXT loop is completed, the program causes the computer to print out the smallest data value, which happens to be 0.

## PROGRAM 14.1   Finding the Smallest Data Value

```
10 FOR I = 1 TO 5
15     READ A(I)
17     PRINT A(I);
20 NEXT I
25 PRINT
30 LET S=A(1)
35 FOR I = 2 TO 5
40     IF A(I) >= S THEN 60
50         LET S=A(I)
60 NEXT I
65 PRINT
70 PRINT "smallest value is ";S
80 DATA 1,7,6,0,3
90 END

RUN
 1 7 6 0 3

smallest value is 0
```

Although Program 14.1 found the smallest value in a data list, we might want to sort a data list from low to high or from high to low and have the results printed. Such sorting is the subject of the next sections in this chapter. There you will see how we can build upon Program 14.1 to do various sorting tasks.

Before first pass

| A | X | B | S |
|---|---|---|---|
| 1 | 1E10 | * | * |
| 7 | | * | |
| 6 | | * | |
| 0 | | * | |
| 3 | | * | |

After first pass

| A | X | B | S |
|---|---|---|---|
| 1 | 0 | 0 | 4 |
| 7 | | * | |
| 6 | | * | |
| 1E10 | | * | |
| 3 | | * | |

After second pass

| A | X | B | S |
|---|---|---|---|
| 1E10 | 1 | 0 | 1 |
| 7 | | 1 | |
| 6 | | * | |
| 1E10 | | * | |
| 3 | | * | |

After third pass

| A | X | B | S |
|---|---|---|---|
| 1E10 | 3 | 0 | 5 |
| 7 | | 1 | |
| 6 | | 3 | |
| 1E10 | | * | |
| 1E10 | | * | |

After fourth pass

| A | X | B | S |
|---|---|---|---|
| 1E10 | 6 | 0 | 3 |
| 7 | | 1 | |
| 1E10 | | 3 | |
| 1E10 | | 6 | |
| 1E10 | | * | |

After fifth pass

| A | X | B | S |
|---|---|---|---|
| 1E10 | 7 | 0 | 2 |
| 1E10 | | 1 | |
| 1E10 | | 3 | |
| 1E10 | | 6 | |
| 1E10 | | 7 | |

**FIGURE 14.1**   Illustration of Program 14.2

The symbol * means not yet defined.

## NUMERIC SORTING—THE SELECTION SORT

Suppose array *A* contains five numbers in a random order, and we would like to sort them in ascending order and put them into array *B*. Program 14.2 accomplishes this by repeated selection of the smallest element in array *A*. Once the smallest element of *A* is found, it is replaced with a very large number so that it will not be selected again. Figure 14.1 illustrates how this program works.

## PROGRAM 14.2   The Selection Sort

```
5 PRINT "Original Data Values: ";
10 FOR I = 1 TO 5
15      READ A(I)
20      PRINT A(I);
22 NEXT I
23 PRINT
27 FOR I=1 TO 5
30      LET X= 1E+10
35      FOR J=1 TO 5
40            IF A(J)>=X THEN 65
50                  LET X=A(J)   'remember the smallest
60                  LET S=J      'remember the index
65      NEXT J
70      LET B(I)=X
80      LET A(S)=1E+10           'set A(S) = a very big number
85 NEXT I
87 PRINT "Sorted Data Values:   ";
90 FOR I = 1 TO 5
95      PRINT B(I);
100 NEXT I
105 DATA 1,7,6,0,3
110 END

RUN
Original Data Values: 1 7 6 0 3
Sorted Data Values:   0 1 3 6 7
```

Note that the inner loop (lines 35–65) determines the smallest value. The loop lets *X* be equal to the smallest value and lets *S* be equal to the index, that is, equal to the position in the array of the smallest element just found.

## NUMERIC SORTING—THE BUBBLE SORT

The bubble sort is a much more efficient method of sorting than the selection sort. Although Program 14.3 accomplishes the same thing as Program 14.2 and uses the same data, it requires only one array, the original one, and it takes less time to process. Figure 14.2 illustrates how Program 14.3 works.

```
Before 1st switch          1      7      6      0      3
After 1st switch           1      6      7      0      3
After 2nd switch           1      6      0      7      3
After 3rd switch           1      0      6      7      3
After 4th switch           0      1      6      7      3
After 5th switch           0      1      6      3      7
After 6th switch           0      1      3      6      7
```

**FIGURE 14.2**  Illustration of Program 14.3

## PROGRAM 14.3   The Bubble Sort

```
5 PRINT "Original Data Values: ";
10 FOR I = 1 TO 5
15     READ A(I)
17     PRINT A(I);
20 NEXT I
23 PRINT
25 FOR I= 2 TO 5
30     LET J=I
35     IF A(J)>=A(J-1) THEN 65
40     SWAP A(J), A(J-1)
50     LET J=J-1
60     IF J>=2 THEN 35
65 NEXT I
67 PRINT "Sorted Data Values:    ";
70 FOR I= 1 TO 5
75     PRINT A(I);
80 NEXT I
85 DATA 1,7,6,0,3
90 END

RUN
Original Data Values:   1  7  6  0  3
Sorted Data Values:     0  1  3  6  7
```

This routine is called the bubble sort because the smaller numbers ''bubble'' their way up to the surface by repeated switches with the numbers preceding them.

In Chapter 5 we described how the SWAP statement can be used to exchange the values of two variables (see Programs 5.6 and 5.7, for example). It was also pointed out that the SWAP statement is useful when writing sorting programs. Note how the SWAP statement in line 40 of Program 14.3 makes it easy to exchange the values of two variables A(J) and A(J − 1). Without using the SWAP statement, we would need three LET statements to perform the same task. The current SWAP statement of

40 SWAP A(J), A(J − 1)

has the LET equivalency of

37 LET D = A(J)
39 LET A(J) = A(J − 1)
41 LET A(J − 1) = D

Case 14.1 illustrates a bubble sort for numeric data.

. . . . . . . . . . . . . . . . . . . . . . . . . . . . . . . . . . .

## CASE 14.1

**Problem**

**Car Pool Zip Code Sort**

A large manufacturing company asked its employees who were interested in forming car pools to submit their names and addresses (with zip codes) to the personnel office. Nearly 500 employees responded. A computer program sorted the last four digits of the supplied zip codes and prepared a list for the employees to use in forming their car pools.

**Data Input**

The program is to be tested using the following data items:

| NAME | ADDRESS | ZIP CODE |
|------|---------|----------|
| Name 1 | Add-1 | 7504 |
| Name 2 | Add-2 | 7501 |
| Name 3 | Add-3 | 6811 |
| Name 4 | Add-4 | 7504 |
| Name 5 | Add-5 | 6812 |
| Name 6 | Add-6 | 7501 |
| Name 7 | Add-7 | 6811 |
| Name 8 | Add-8 | 6799 |

**Process/Formulas**

A repetitive FOR/NEXT loop process is to be used with the data items placed into three subscripted array lists. A nested FOR/NEXT loop containing a comparison test for the zip codes with appropriate swapping performs the required sorting.

**Output**

The output will show the sorted zip codes along with the corresponding name and address. It should look like this:

```
ZIP CODE        NAME            ADDRESS
---------------------------------------
  6799          NAME 8          ADD-8
  6811          NAME 3          ADD-3
  6811          NAME 7          ADD-7
  6812          NAME 5          ADD-5
  7501          NAME 6          ADD-6
  7501          NAME 2          ADD-2
  7504          NAME 4          ADD-4
  7504          NAME 1          ADD-1
```

. . . . . . . . . . . . . . . . . . . . . . . . . . . . . . . . . . .

## PROGRAM 14.4    Case 14.1, Car Pool List Using Numeric Bubble Sort

```
10 REM CASE 14.1, CAR POOL LIST USING NUMERIC BUBBLE SORT
12 REM PROGRAMMER-(name of person)   DATE- mm/dd/yy
14 REM      VARIABLE LIST-
15 REM          A$=ADDRESS
16 REM          I,J,P=INDICES
17 REM          N=NUMBER OF DATA ITEMS
18 REM          N$=NAME
```

```
19 REM             Z=ZIP CODE
20 REM ------------------------------------------
30 DIM N$(10),A$(10),Z(10)
40 LET N=8
50 FOR I = 1 TO N
60     READ N$(I),A$(I),Z(I)
70 NEXT I
80 DATA NAME 1,ADD-1,7504,NAME 2,ADD-2,7501
90 DATA NAME 3,ADD-3,6811,NAME 4,ADD-4,7504
100 DATA NAME 5,ADD-5,6812,NAME 6,ADD-6,7501
110 DATA NAME 7,ADD-7,6811,NAME 8,ADD-8,6799
120 REM SORT OF ZIP CODES FOLLOWS:
130 FOR I = 1 TO N-1
140     FOR J = 1 TO N-1
150         IF Z(J+1)>Z(J) THEN 190
160             SWAP Z(J), Z(J+1)     'SWAP zip codes
170             SWAP N$(J), N$(J+1)   'SWAP names
180             SWAP A$(J), A$(J+1)   'SWAP addresses
190     NEXT J
200 NEXT I
205 PRINT
210 PRINT "CAR POOL LIST SORTED BY ZIP CODE"
215 PRINT
220 PRINT "ZIP CODE","NAME","ADDRESS"
225 PRINT "----------------------------------"
230 FOR P = 1 TO N
240     PRINT Z(P),N$(P),A$(P)
250 NEXT P
260 END


RUN

CAR POOL LIST SORTED BY ZIP CODE

ZIP CODE        NAME            ADDRESS
----------------------------------
 6799           NAME 8          ADD-8
 6811           NAME 3          ADD-3
 6811           NAME 7          ADD-7
 6812           NAME 5          ADD-5
 7501           NAME 6          ADD-6
 7501           NAME 2          ADD-2
 7504           NAME 4          ADD-4
 7504           NAME 1          ADD-1
```

Program 14.4 not only sorts the numeric zip codes but also maintains the names and addresses that go along with the sorted zip codes. Otherwise, the end result would be a sorted zip code list of little value to those wanting to form a car pool.

As each zip code value in the array Z is sorted and its position in the array is changed, so is the position of the name N$ and the address A$. For example, the lowest zip code is 6799 in position Z(8), along with ''Name 8'' in N$(8), and ''Add-8'' in A$(8). When the value 6799 in Z(8) is switched into a new position Z(J), the associated items in N$(8)

and A$(8) must also be switched into N$(J) and A$(J), respectively. These switches of the items associated with the zip code are accomplished by the following program statements:

170 SWAP N$(J), N$(J + 1)
180 SWAP A$(J), A$(J + 1)

Once the sort is completed, the program will output—in ascending order—the zip code, name, and address list. Lines 230–250 in Program 14.4 will cause the output listing shown.

Before going on to the next topic of alphabetic sorting, let us examine the following statements in Program 14.4:

150 IF Z(J + 1) > Z(J) THEN 190
160 SWAP Z(J), Z(J + 1)

These sort the zip code values. Two values are tested at a time: one in the J + 1 position of the array Z and the other in the J position of the array Z. If the value in the J + 1 position is greater than the value in the J position, no further processing of the values occurs. But if the value in the J + 1 position is *not* greater than the value in the J position, lines 160–180 are executed. The purpose of line 160 is to change the positions of the zip codes putting the smaller value in the position of the larger value and vice versa; the purpose of lines 170 and 180 is to swap the positions of the corresponding names and addresses.

## ALPHABETIC SORTING

Just as we were able to sort numeric arrays, we can also sort alphabetic arrays. Program 14.5 puts seven names into alphabetic order using a bubble-sort technique.

## PROGRAM 14.5   Alphabetic Bubble Sort

```
5 PRINT "Original List:"
15 FOR I = 1 TO 7
25      READ N$(I)
35      PRINT N$(I)
45 NEXT I
55 DATA JULIE,JOSHUA,EFRAM,BENNET,ARI,ISAAC,ELIZABETH
65 PRINT
75 FOR I = 2 TO 7
85      LET J=I
95      IF N$(J) >= N$(J-1) THEN 135
105            SWAP N$(J), N$(J-1)
115            LET J = J-1
125            IF J>=2 THEN 95
135 NEXT I
145 PRINT "Sorted List:"
155 FOR I = 1 TO 7
165      PRINT N$(I)
```

```
175 NEXT I
185 END

RUN
Original List:
JULIE
JOSHUA
EFRAM
BENNET
ARI
ISAAC
ELIZABETH

Sorted List:
ARI
BENNET
EFRAM
ELIZABETH
ISAAC
JOSHUA
JULIE
```

A problem may involve several alphabetic lists the require sorting. Case 14.2 presents such a situation.

· · · · · · · · · · · · · · · · · · · · · · · · · · · · · · · · · · · · · ·

## CASE 14.2

**Problem**      **Sorting Mailing Lists To Eliminate Duplicates**
A catalog mail-order company has purchased two mailing lists. They may contain duplicate names. The lists are not in alphabetic order. To reduce mailing costs, the lists are to be sorted and merged. Any duplicate names are to be deleted.

**Data Input**      To test the program, the following two lists will be used:

| LIST 1 | LIST 2 |
|--------|--------|
| XYZ | CBA |
| JKL | BMD |
| LMN | PDQ |
| CBA | XXX |
| YYY | XYA |
| ABC | LMN |
| AAA | BBB |
| XXX | ZZZ |
| EFG | GFE |

**Process/Formulas**   A repetitive FOR/NEXT loop process is to be used, with both data lists stored in a single array.

**Output**      The output will show two newly sorted lists. The first list contains all the items of both lists without the duplicates. The second list contains the duplicates that were removed from the original data lists. A count of the items in both lists will also be provided as shown below:

```
# OF ITEMS IN LIST 15      # OF DUPLICATES 3

NEW LIST        DUPLICATES
--------------------------
AAA             CBA
ABC             LMN
BBB             XXX
BMD
CBA
EFG
GFE
JKL
LMN
PDQ
XXX
XYA
XYZ
YYY
ZZZ
```

---

## PROGRAM 14.6   Case 14.2, Mailing List Using Alphabetic Sort

```
10 REM CASE 14.2, MAILING LIST USING ALPHABETIC SORT
11 REM   PROGRAMMER- (name of person)  DATE - mm/dd/yy
12 REM     VARIABLE LIST-
13 REM          N=TOTAL # OF ITEMS IN BOTH LISTS
14 REM          C=# OF ITEMS IN FINAL LIST
15 REM          D=# OF DUPLICATES IN LIST
16 REM          I,J,M = INDICES
17 REM          N$=MAILING LIST
18 REM          X$=DUPLICATE LIST
19 REM -------------------------------------------
20 DIM N$(20),X$(20)
25 REM INITIALIZE COUNTERS
30 LET D=0
35 LET C=0
40 LET N=18
45 FOR I = 1 TO N
50     READ N$(I)              'read in both lists
55 NEXT I
60 DATA XYZ,JKL,LMN,CBA,YYY,ABC,AAA,XXX,EFG
65 DATA CBA,BMD,PDQ,XXX,XYA,LMN,BBB,ZZZ,GFE
70 REM SORT BOTH LISTS
75 FOR I = 1 TO N-1
80     FOR J= 1 TO N-1
85          IF N$(J+1)>N$(J) THEN 95
90               SWAP N$(J), N$(J+1)
95     NEXT J
```

```
100 NEXT I
105 REM TEST FOR DUPLICATES
110 FOR M= 1 TO N
115    IF N$(M)=N$(M+1) THEN 135
120       LET C=C+1          'count items in the lists
125       LET N$(C)=N$(M)
130       GOTO 145
135          LET D=D+1      'count duplicates in both lists
140          LET X$(D)=N$(M+1)
145 NEXT M
150 PRINT "# OF ITEMS IN LIST";C; "      # OF DUPLICATES";D
155 PRINT
160 PRINT "NEW LIST","DUPLICATES"
165 PRINT "-------------------------"
170 FOR M=1 TO C
175    PRINT N$(M),X$(M)
180 NEXT M
185 END

RUN
# OF ITEMS IN LIST 15      # OF DUPLICATES 3

NEW LIST         DUPLICATES
-------------------------
AAA              CBA
ABC              LMN
BBB              XXX
BMD
CBA
EFG
GFE
JKL
LMN
PDQ
XXX
XYA
XYZ
YYY
ZZZ
```

In Program 14.6, the two lists are read in and stored as a single list in the array N$. This process is accomplished by lines 45–55. A bubble sort of the alphabetic list is then performed by lines 75–100.

Once both lists are sorted into a single list, a test for duplicates is performed by the program section lines 110–145. If a duplicate is found; that is, if line

115 IF N$(M) = N$(M + 1) THEN 135

is true, the duplicate is removed from the list and placed into a new array designated X$. This placement of duplicates into the new array is performed by line 140.

140 LET X$(D) = N$(M + 1)

The final phase of the program prints out the new list and any duplicates found. This task is performed by lines 170–180.

Numeric arrays can be sorted and alphabetic arrays can be put in alphabetic order using the bubble-sort and selection-sort techniques.

## BASIC VOCABULARY SUMMARY

| Statement | Purpose | Examples |
|---|---|---|
| IF/THEN line # | Transfers control to other lines after a test relationship is evaluated. | 20 IF A(J) >= X THEN 60<br>40 IF Z(J+1) > Z(J) THEN 90<br>70 IF N$(J) >= N$(J−1) THEN 160 |
| LET | Assigns numeric values or character strings to variables, from the right side of the equal sign (=) to the left side. | 10 LET J = J−1<br>20 LET D = D + 1<br>30 LET X$(D) = N$(M+1) |
| SWAP | Causes contents of variable on the right to be exchanged with variable on the left. | 25 SWAP A(J), A(J−1)<br>35 SWAP N$(J), N$(J−1) |

## EXERCISES

### Review Questions

◆ **14.1**  Prepare a diagram similar to Figure 14.1 for the data 0, 8, 9, 3, 2.

◆ **14.2**  Prepare a diagram similar to Figure 14.2 for the data 0, 8, 9, 3, 2.

◆ **14.3**  Prepare a diagram similar to Figure 14.1, in which the data is still 1, 7, 6, 0, 3 but is sorted in descending order instead.

### Programming Activities

**14.4**  **Purpose**  To do a numeric selection sort.

**Problem**  Write and run a program to sort a set of numeric data values (shown below) in descending order.

**Data**  11, 17, 16, 10, 30

**Output**  Your output should have this format:

```
Original Data Values: 11 17 16 10 30
Sorted Data Values:   30 17 16 11 10
```

**14.5** **Purpose** To do a numeric bubble sort.

**Problem** Write and run a program to sort a set of numeric data values (shown below) in descending order.

**Data** 55, 61, 60, 50, 74, 35, 42

**Output** Your output should have this format:

```
Original Data Values: 55 61 60 50 74 35 42
Sorted Data Values:   74 61 60 55 50 42 35
```

**14.6** **Purpose** To do a string selection sort.

**Problem** Write and run a program to sort a set of data values (shown below) in an alphabetic array.

**Data** January, February, March, April, May, June, July

**Output** Your output should have this format:

```
Sorted List:
 April
 February
 January
 July
 June
 March
 May
```

**14.7** **Purpose** To do a numeric sort.

**Problem** Write and run a program to carry out the first step in the reconciliation of a checking account by putting the cancelled checks into a sort sequence from low to high numbers. Use the data shown below.

**Data** 1108, 1102, 1098, 1100, 1095, 1110, 1107, 1097, 1104, 1105, 1094

**Output** Your output should have this format:

```
Sorted Check Numbers
      1094
      1095
       • • •
      1110
```

**14.8** **Purpose** To do a numeric sort and find any missing numbers.

**Problem** Write and run a program to carry out the first step in the reconciliation of a checking account by putting the cancelled checks into a sort sequence from low to high numbers; any missing checks are noted by check number. Use the data shown below.

**Data** 1108, 1102, 1098, 1100, 1095, 1110, 1107, 1097, 1104, 1105, 1094

**Output** Your output should have this format:

```
Sorted Check Numbers
      1094
      1095
      check 1096 missing
```

```
1097
+  +  +
check 1109 missing
1110
```

**14.9**    **Purpose**  To do a numeric sort on one of two data lists.

**Problem**  The Town Food Stores, Inc., has 13 stores in its chain. Yesterday's sales for each store are given below. Write and run a program that outputs the data shown below in descending order (from high to low), according to the amount of sales. Store numbers should also be outputted alongside the sales data.

**Data**

| STORE | SALES | STORE | SALES |
|---|---|---|---|
| 1 | $3,696 | 2 | $4,281 |
| 3 | 5,650 | 4 | 6,969 |
| 5 | 3,854 | 6 | 4,955 |
| 7 | 5,724 | 8 | 1,695 |
| 9 | 7,864 | 10 | 1,947 |
| 11 | 4,417 | 12 | 5,092 |
| 13 | 2,611 | | |

**Output**  Your output should have this format:

```
SALES                          STORE #
--------------------------------
$ 7,864                           9
$ 6,969                           4
    +  +  +                     +  +  +
$ 1,695                           8
```

**14.10**   **Purpose**  To do a numeric sort on one of two data lists.

**Problem**  For the regional sales data below, write and run a program that will sort sales in ascending order from low to high.

**Data**

| REGION | SALES (MILLION $) |
|---|---|
| Northeast | $20 |
| Atlantic | 25 |
| South | 18 |
| Central | 16 |
| Southwest | 23 |
| West | 28 |
| Pacific | 26 |

**Output**  Your output should have this format:

```
REGION                     SALES(MILLION $)
-------------------------------------------
CENTRAL                            $ 16
SOUTH                              $ 18
   +  +  +                         +  +  +
WEST                               $ 28
```

**14.11**   **Purpose**  To do a numeric sort on one of two data lists.

**Problem**  For the regional sales data below, write and run a program that will sort sales in descending order (from high to low).

| Data | REGION | SALES (MILLION $) |
|---|---|---|
| | Northeast | $20 |
| | Atlantic | 25 |
| | South | 18 |
| | Central | 16 |
| | Southwest | 23 |
| | West | 28 |
| | Pacific | 26 |

**Output**   Your output should have this format:

```
REGION                          SALES(MILLION $)
----------------------------------------
WEST                                 $ 28
PACIFIC                              $ 26
 ◆  ◆  ◆                              ◆  ◆  ◆
CENTRAL                              $ 16
```

**14.12**   **Purpose**   To do a string sort on one of two data lists.

**Problem**   For the regional sales data below, write and run a program that will alphabetize each region.

| Data | REGION | SALES (MILLION $) |
|---|---|---|
| | Northeast | $20 |
| | Atlantic | 25 |
| | South | 18 |
| | Central | 16 |
| | Southwest | 23 |
| | West | 28 |
| | Pacific | 26 |

**Output**   Your output should have this format:

```
REGION                          SALES(MILLION $)
----------------------------------------
ATLANTIC                             $ 25
CENTRAL                                16
 ◆  ◆  ◆                              ◆  ◆  ◆
WEST                                   28
```

**◆ 14.13**   **Purpose**   To do a string sort after combining three data lists.

**Problem**   Write and run a program that will alphabetize all the data shown below into a single list without any duplicates. (Hint: See Program 14.6.)

| Data | LIST 1 | LIST 2 | LIST 3 |
|---|---|---|---|
| | XYZ | CBA | XYZ |
| | JKL | BMD | MNO |
| | LMN | PDQ | BBC |
| | CBA | XXX | BBB |
| | YYY | XYA | XXX |
| | ABC | LMN | ZXY |
| | AAA | BBB | BMD |
| | XXX | ZZZ | |
| | EFG | GFE | |

**Output**   Your output should have this format:

```
NEW LIST

    AAA

    ABC

    BBB

    •   •   •

    ZXY

    ZZZ
```

# CHAPTER 15

# SEQUENTIAL AND RANDOM ACCESS DATA FILES

Upon completing this chapter, you will be able to do the following:

- Place data into a separate data file.
- Understand the difference between sequential access and random access.
- Create a sequential access file.
- Develop a program that incorporates a sequential access file.
- Create a random access file.
- Prepare a program that uses a random access file.

Up to this point, we have seen that each program has had its own set of data and data lines as an integral part of the program.

In this chapter we will see how it is possible to place data into a separate and distinct storage entity called a *data file*. Such files are typical of information systems where data is stored and retrieved as the situation requires. Once we have data in a file, any of numerous programs can then use it as though it were part of the program.

The process by which files are placed on diskettes is described in the sections that follow.

## FILE ACCESS

A file consists of related items or records. Files are typically stored external to the computer in secondary, or auxiliary, storage devices. Such devices make use of magnetic tapes, disks, and drums to actually retain the data files.

Once a file has been stored, data retrieval will depend on what type of storage device was used. In general, there are two methods for accessing data on files. If retrieval is done from magnetic tape storage, the method is called *sequential access*. With this method, data on the magnetic tape must be read from the beginning of the tape to search for the particular item of data required.

In contrast is the second method called *direct access*, also referred to as *random access*. This is used when retrieval is done from disk storage. Any particular item of data can be directly obtained whenever it is needed—without searching through each item from the beginning of the file.

We will examine the storage and access of data by first looking at sequential access and then at random access files.

## SEQUENTIAL ACCESS FILES

The statements that are used for sequential file operations using IBM Microsoft BASIC are described next.

### Statements Used

**OPEN**   The OPEN statement takes the following form:

Line # OPEN ''I'' or ''O'' or ''A'', #N, ''File Name''

''I'' indicates we will be inputting data from a file; ''O'' indicates that we will be outputting data to the beginning of a file (and in the process, destroying what was already there); and ''A'' indicates that we will be outputting data to the end of an existing file, thereby preserving its contents.

Note that if the "File Name" *does not* exist and we use the "O" (output) or "A" (append), the OPEN statement will create a file with that "File Name"; but if "I" (input) is used, an error message "File not found" (error number 53) will appear.

The *N* is a number associated with the specific file for reference as well as for directing file items to a buffer storage area in memory until the file is closed (see discussion on CLOSE below).

Specific examples of the form of the OPEN statement follow:

```
For output: 15 OPEN "O", #1, "NAMES"
            20 OPEN "O", #2, "INVENTORY"
 For input: 15 OPEN "I", #1, "NAMES"
            20 OPEN "I", #2, "INVENTORY"
For appending: 15 OPEN "A", #1, "NAMES"
            20 OPEN "A", #2, "INVENTORY"
```

If you are working in disk drive A, and want the OPEN statement to carry out operations directed for disk drive B, you precede the file name with the drive label; for example,

```
15 OPEN "O", #1, "B:NAMES"
20 OPEN "I", #2, "B:INVENTORY"
30 OPEN "A", #2, "B:SALES"
```

◆ **Keyboard Tip**    To save keystrokes, you can enter the keyword OPEN by typing the combination of Alt plus O to cause OPEN to display.

**PRINT # and WRITE #**    The PRINT # statement has the following form:

Line # PRINT #N, data item 1; data item 2; . . . ; data item n

The PRINT # statement writes data to the file referenced in the buffer storage as #N. Embedded commas are needed to separate strings, so they can be read by a program; semicolons are needed to separate numeric variables. Specific examples of the form of the PRINT # statement follow:

```
40 PRINT #1, A$; ","; B$
50 PRINT #2, N; A; XY1
60 PRINT #3, TOT; NUM; ","; DIV$
```

The PRINT # statement can also be used with the USING option to control the format of the file. You can see examples of this statement and listings of the file contents by looking at Programs 15.1 and 15.6. Specific examples of the PRINT #N, USING statement follow:

```
50 PRINT #2, USING " ##  $$#,###  ##.##"; N, A, XY1
```

or

```
60 LET FT$ = " ##  $$#,###  ##.##"
70 PRINT #2, USING FT$; N, A, XY1
```

You can see an example of this statement and a listing of the file contents by looking at Program 15.7. For more examples of the possible USING options that can be used to format the file, refer to Chapter 6, "Formatting Output."

An alternate way to write data to a sequential file uses the WRITE # statement, which has the following form:

Line # WRITE #N, data item 1, data item 2, . . . , data item n

The WRITE # statement differs from the PRINT # statement in that it places comma separators between data items as they are written to the file without your having to include them with the PRINT # statement. Also, string items have quotation marks placed around them when written to the file. Specific examples of this statement follow:

    40 WRITE #1, A$, B$
    50 WRITE #2, N, A, XY1
    60 WRITE #3, TOT, NUM, DIV$

You can see examples of this statement and listings of the file contents by looking at Programs 15.3 and 15.5.

**INPUT #**    The INPUT # statement has the following form:

Line # INPUT #N, Variable List

The INPUT# statement reads data from the sequential file into the program using a variable list that agrees with the type of data in the file. Specific examples of this statement follow:

    60 INPUT #1, A$, B$
    70 INPUT #2, N, A, X1
    80 INPUT #3, Y$, A, B$

See also line 20 of Program 15.2, and lines 65 and 70 of Program 15.4.

**CLOSE**    The CLOSE statement has the following form:

Line # CLOSE #N

Every open statement should have a matching close statement processed before the program is completed. The CLOSE statement ensures that the data file is saved for future use. The N is the optional buffer number and usually corresponds to the OPEN N. A CLOSE without an N will close all OPEN files. Specific examples of this statement follow:

    100 CLOSE
    110 CLOSE #1
    120 CLOSE #1,#2

## Creating a Sequential Access File

If we have sales information for five years, as shown below, we could create a file to save such information.

**XYZ CO. – SALES DATA**

| Year | Millions of Dollars |
|------|---------------------|
| 1987 | 10.3 |
| 1988 | 11.4 |
| 1989 | 12.6 |
| 1990 | 13.7 |
| 1991 | 12.8 |

Program 15.1 shows how the sequential file SALESF is created using the OPEN, PRINT #, and CLOSE statements described above. In general, a file listing, as shown in Program 15.1b, is obtained when in the system mode rather than in BASIC. To leave BASIC and enter the system mode, you need to type the command SYSTEM. This command will cause the drive prompt, >, to be displayed. Any file can be shown on the screen by entering after the prompt the word TYPE followed by the file name. The file will display on the screen. That is,

A>TYPE FILENAME

For example, to get the listing of the file SALESF in Program 15.1, assuming we are in drive A, we type after the A>

A>type salesf

(either lowercase or uppercase is acceptable) followed by pressing the Enter key and the file is displayed on the screen. To output the file that is on the screen to paper, use the Shift and Print Screen combination of keys for IBM PCs, or just PRINT SCREEN for IBM PS/1 and 2s. If the file is in drive B and you have the A>, then enter

A>TYPE B:FILENAME

For a listing from drive B use

B>TYPE FILENAME

Further on in this chapter we will see how it is possible to list a file by using a program (see Program 15.14) to do the task rather than by using system commands.

---

**PROGRAM 15.1   Creating a Data File – Program (a) and File Listing (b)**

```
a.   10 REM CREATING A SEQUENTIAL ACCESS FILE
     20 OPEN "O",#1,"SALESF"
     30 FOR I=1 TO 5
     40    READ Y,S
     45    PRINT #1,Y;",";S        'print to salesf file #1
     50 NEXT I
     60 DATA 1987,10.3, 1988,11.4, 1989,12.6
     70 DATA 1990,13.7, 1991,12.8
     80 CLOSE
     90 END
```

b.  SALESF file

```
1987 , 10.3
1988 , 11.4
1989 , 12.6
1990 , 13.7
1991 , 12.8
```

---

## Reading from a Sequential Access File

To make use of, or gain access to, a sequential data file, we use the appropriate BASIC statements in a program, that is, the OPEN and INPUT # statements described above.

Program 15.2 reads each line, one at a time, and then prints out the entire contents of the previously created file, SALESF (Program 15.1b).

## PROGRAM 15.2  Reading the Contents of a Data File

```
10 OPEN "I",#1,"SALESF"
15 PRINT "YEAR","SALES(MILL.$)"
20 INPUT #1,Y,S              'read from salesf file #1
25     PRINT Y,S
30 GOTO 20
45 CLOSE
99 END

RUN
YEAR            SALES(MILL.$)
 1987              10.3
 1988              11.4
 1989              12.6
 1990              13.7
 1991              12.8
Input past end in 20
```

In the program (line 20), the data list variables $Y$ and $S$ correspond to the type of data in the file SALESF, that is, numeric data for both year and sales. Note that line 25 (PRINT Y, S) is merely the way the programmer wants to have $Y$ and $S$ outputted. If only the sales data were desired as output, this could have been obtained by 25 PRINT S. Also note that without line 30 (GOTO 20), only the first line of the data file SALESF would be outputted. This is because of the sequential nature of the file process being used. The contents of the file are read from the first line, line by line, until there is no more data, as indicated by the "Input past end in 20" error message that appears after the output.

Rather than have your program output end with the "Input past end" error message, you can put an end of file test into your program. This is done by using the EOF function. Its form is

EOF(file #N)

where the file #N being tested is placed into the parentheses. Used with an IF/THEN statement and placed before the file INPUT #N statement, a program segment to test for the end of the file looks like this:

```
30 IF EOF(1) THEN 998
40 INPUT #1, A, B, N$
998 CLOSE
999 END
```

The EOF function returns a $-1$ if the condition is true and there is no more file data and a 0 (zero) if the end of the file has not been reached. Program 15.4 shows this test in line 55.

When working with files, it is possible to read data from several files. All that is required is additional file INPUT statements in the program. This reading from several files is illustrated in Case 15.1.

## CASE 15.1

**Problem**

**Sales Report Generation Using Two Sequential Files**

The XYZ Company has sales data for the years 1987–1991 in a file named SALESF. Below are the total sales for the industry group of which the XYZ Company is a member. Using both sets of data, a report is needed that shows company sales as a percent of industry sales for the years 1987–1991.

**Data Input**

A previously created company data file SALESF and a set of industry data are as follows:

| XYZ CO. | | INDUSTRY SALES DATA | |
|---|---|---|---|
| Year | Sales (Mill. $) | Year | Millions of $ |
| 1987 | 10.3 | 1987 | 150.6 |
| 1988 | 11.4 | 1988 | 175.2 |
| 1989 | 12.6 | 1989 | 203.0 |
| 1990 | 13.7 | 1990 | 230.8 |
| 1991 | 12.8 | 1991 | 254.5 |

**Process/Formulas**  Using a FOR/NEXT loop and appropriate file operation statements, create a new sequential file INDSF. In a single program, access both the SALESF and INDSF files to produce a report as shown below. Company sales as a percent of industry sales are found by using the formula Percent = (company sales/industry sales) $\times$ 100. This program will use a FOR/NEXT loop structure that includes an EOF test for each of the files being read into the program. See Figure 15.1.

**Output**

The sales report output should look like this:

```
             XYZ CO,       INDUSTRY
 YEAR        SALES          SALES          % OF IND,
------------------------------------------------------
 1987       $10,30        $150,6            6,84%
 1988       $11,40        $175,2            6,51%
 1989       $12,60        $203,0            6,21%
 1990       $13,70        $230,8            5,94%
 1991       $12,80        $254,5            5,03%
------------------------------------------------------
```

Program 15.3 creates the new file INDSF, called for in Case 15.1. Note the use of line 45, WRITE #1, N, D, as the alternate to a PRINT # statement for placing data into a file. The listing of this file is shown below the program. Program 15.4 reads from the previously created data file SALESF (Program 15.1b) and the new file INDSF. Lines 65 and 70 obtain the data needed from the two files. The end of file tests are performed by lines 55 and 60. By using both files, this program generates the required output, as diagrammed in Figure 15.1.

## PROGRAM 15.3   Creating INDSF Sequential File (a) and File Listing (b)

a.
```
10 REM CREATING A SEQUENTIAL ACCESS FILE
20 OPEN "O",#1,"INDSF"          'open the file #1
30 FOR I= 1 TO 5
40     READ N,D
45     WRITE #1, N, D           'write data to file #1 using
50 NEXT I                       'commas to separate items
60 DATA 1987,150.6, 1988,175.2, 1989,203.0
70 DATA 1990,230.8, 1991,254.5
80 CLOSE
90 END
```

b. INDSF file
```
    1987, 150.6
    1988, 175.2
    1989, 203
    1990, 230.8
    1991, 254.5
```

## PROGRAM 15.4   Case 15.1, Reading Several Sequential Data Files in One Program

```
2 REM CASE 15.1, READING SEVERAL SEQUENTIAL DATA FILES IN ONE PROGRAM
6 REM   PROGRAMMER- (name of person)   DATE- mm/dd/yy
8 REM      VARIABLE LIST-
10 REM         D=INDUSTRY SALES
11 REM         F$=FORMAT
12 REM         N=YEAR IN INDSF FILE
14 REM         S=SALES
16 REM         Y=YEAR IN SALESF FILE
17 REM         YR=LOOP INDEX
18 REM -----------------------------------
20 OPEN "I",#1,"SALESF"
25 OPEN "I",#2,"INDSF"
30 PRINT    "           XYZ CO.     INDUSTRY                 "
35 PRINT    " YEAR        SALES        SALES      % OF IND."
40 LET F$= "  ####      $##.##       $###.#       ##.##%"
45 PRINT STRING$(45,"-")
50 FOR YR = 1 TO 20
55     IF EOF(1) THEN 85                    'end of file test
60     IF EOF(2) THEN 85                    'end of file test
```

```
65              INPUT #1,Y,S                        'reading from file #1
70              INPUT #2,N,D                        'reading from file #2
75          PRINT USING F$; N,S,D,(S/D)*100
80 NEXT YR
85 CLOSE
90 PRINT STRING$(50,"-")
95 END
```

```
RUN
           XYZ CO.       INDUSTRY
   YEAR    SALES         SALES      % OF IND.
   -----------------------------------------
   1987    $10.30        $150.6        6.84%
   1988    $11.40        $175.2        6.51%
   1989    $12.60        $203.0        6.21%
   1990    $13.70        $230.8        5.94%
   1991    $12.80        $254.5        5.03%
   -----------------------------------------
```

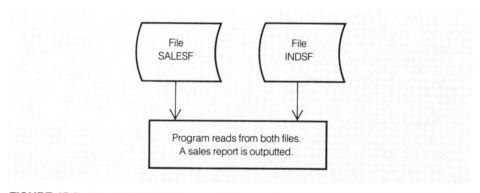

**FIGURE 15.1**   Case 15.1, XYZ Company, Diagram of Files and Programs

## Writing to a Sequential Access File

In addition to reading from a sequential file in a program, it is also possible to take the results of a program and have them placed into a sequential file. To transfer program results to a sequential file requires the PRINT # statement or WRITE # statement described earlier.

Case 15.2 illustrates the use of several sequential data files generated by different programs.

## CASE 15.2

**Problem**

**Payroll Report Generation Using Two Sequential Files**

The Ajax Company has an employee payroll file named MASTER. The file structure contains each employee's name, Social Security number, number of dependents, and wage rate per hour. A second file named HOURS contains each employee's Social Security number and the number of hours worked during the week.

Each week a payroll report for management is generated by a program named RE-PORT. This program makes use of the contents of the two files. The program REPORT also transfers to a file named GROSS the net pay (gross pay minus deductions) of each employee. A summary pay report is required by management. This task is accomplished by using a program named SEGROS.

Refer to Figure 15.2 for an illustration of the relationship between the various files and programs used in this case.

**Data Input**
Data input consists of two previously created company data files, MASTER and HOURS. Each MASTER record includes name, Social Security number, number of dependents, and hourly wage. Each HOURS record includes an employee's number and hours worked during a week. The data for the MASTER and the HOURS files is as follows:

| | MASTER | | | HOURS | |
|---|---|---|---|---|---|
| Name | Soc. Sec. No. | Depen-dents | Rate | Soc. Sec. No. | Worked |
| J. STING | 012345679 | 2 | $8.50 | 012345679 | 40 |
| B. O'HARA | 089012349 | 3 | $9.25 | 089012349 | 35 |
| M. BENNETT | 056789019 | 1 | $7.75 | 056789019 | 37 |
| J. LAKE | 023456789 | 5 | $5.75 | 023456789 | 40 |
| B. FARRONE | 090123459 | 4 | $8.00 | 090123459 | 30 |
| C. ERICSON | 067890129 | 3 | $7.00 | 067890129 | 32 |

**Process/Formulas**
In a single program, access both the MASTER and HOURS files to produce a report as shown below. To find the net pay, use the following formulas:

Net pay = gross pay − deductions
Gross pay = wage rate × hours worked
Tax deductions = percent × gross pay

The tax deduction percent is based on the number of dependents, as given by the following information:

| NUMBER OF DEPENDENTS | DEDUCTION FROM GROSS |
|---|---|
| 1 | 10% |
| 2 | 9% |
| 3 | 8% |
| 4 | 7% |
| 5 or more | 6% |

A second program will use the output of the first program to generate a summary pay report using a FOR/NEXT loop process and appropriate file operations. This second program will derive the average hours worked by dividing the total of all hours worked by the number of workers during the week. In addition, the total gross pay of all workers for the week will be derived.

**Output**
The payroll report output should look like this:

```
           AJAX CO. WEEKLY PAYROLL REPORT

     NAME         SOC.SEC.NO.    GROSS PAY      NET PAY
     -----------------------------------------------------------
     J. STING      012345679      $340.00       $309.40
     B. O'HARA     089012349      $323.75       $297.85
     M. BENNETT    056789019      $286.75       $258.08
     J. LAKE       023456789      $230.00       $216.20
     B. FARRONE    090123459      $240.00       $223.20
     C. ERICSON    067890129      $224.00       $206.08

          ***PAYROLL REPORT COMPLETED***
```

A new file called GROSS is created from the REPORT program with each record of the new file having the format: name, number of hours worked, and gross pay. The summary report output should look like this:

```
EMPLOYEE, HOURS WORKED THIS WEEK, GROSS PAYROLL

     NAME           HOURS WORKED        GROSS PAY
-------------------------------------------------------
   J. STING             40              $340.00
   B. O'HARA            35              $323.75
   M. BENNETT           37              $286.75
   J. LAKE              40              $230.00
   B. FARRONE           30              $240.00
   C. ERICSON           32              $224.00
-------------------------------------------------------
   AVERAGE HOURS WORKED THIS WEEK   35.7
   TOTAL GROSS PAY THIS WEEK   $1,644.50

      SUMMARY GROSS PAY REPORT COMPLETED
```

Figure 15.2 is a diagram of the files and programs in Case 15.2. It shows the two files, MASTER and HOURS, and the new file, GROSS. The contents for this file are derived from the REPORT program.

Programs 15.5 and 15.6 create the sequential access files MASTER and HOURS, respectively. Note how the MASTER file listing for Program 15.5 shows quotes around the first two string items. This is a result of using the WRITE # statement in the program

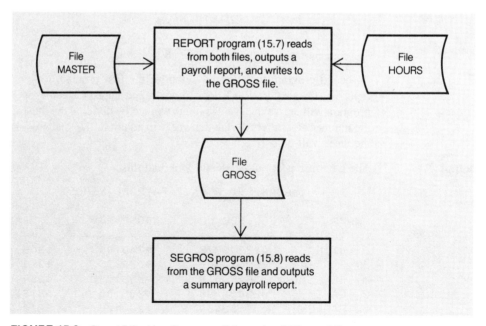

**FIGURE 15.2**  Case 15.2, Ajax Company, Schematic of Files and Programs

shown as line 50. Because of this statement, the file contents are also compressed, without spaces between items, as contrasted with files using the PRINT # statement.

---

**PROGRAM 15.5   Case 15.2, MASTER Sequential File (a) and File Listing (b)**

a.
```
   10 REM CASE 15.2, AJAX COMPANY, CREATING MASTER SEQUENTIAL FILE
   15 REM PROGRAMMER- (name of person)  DATE- mm/dd/yy
   16 REM     VARIABLE LIST-
   17 REM          D=# OF DEPENDENTS
   18 REM          N$=EMPLOYEE NAME
   19 REM          P=WAGE PER HOUR FOR EACH PERSON
   20 REM          S$=EMPLOYEE NO.
   21 REM          I=LOOP INDEX
   25 REM ---------------------------------------------
   30 REM CREATING A SEQUENTIAL ACCESS FILE
   35 OPEN "O",#1,"MASTER"
   40 FOR I = 1 TO 6
   45    READ N$,S$,D,P
   50    WRITE #1, N$, S$, D, P          'write to master file #1
   55 NEXT I
   60 DATA J. STING, 012345679, 2, 8.50
   65 DATA B. O'HARA, 089012349, 3, 9.25
   70 DATA M. BENNETT, 056789019, 1, 7.75
   75 DATA J. LAKE, 023456789, 5, 5.75
   80 DATA B. FARRONE, 090123459, 4, 8.00
   85 DATA C. ERICSON, 067890129, 3, 7.00
   90 CLOSE
   95 END
```

b. MASTER file
```
"J. STING","012345679",2,8.5
"B. O'HARA","089012349",3,9.25
"M. BENNETT","056789019",1,7.75
"J. LAKE","023456789",5,5.75
"B. FARRONE","090123459",4,8
"C. ERICSON","067890129",3,7
```

---

**PROGRAM 15.6   Case 15.2, HOURS Sequential File (a) and File Listing (b)**

a.
```
   10 REM CASE 15.2, AJAX COMPANY, CREATING HOURS SEQUENTIAL FILE
   15 REM  PROGRAMMER- (name of person)  DATE - mm/dd/yy
   16 REM     VARIABLE LIST-
   17 REM          H=HOURS WORKED PER WEEK
   18 REM          S$=EMPLOYEE NO.
   19 REM          I=LOOP INDEX
   20 REM -------------------------------------
   30 REM CREATING A SEQUENTIAL ACCESS FILE
   35 OPEN "O",#1,"HOURS"
   40 FOR I= 1 TO 6
```

```
45      READ S$,H
50      WRITE #1, S$, H           'write to HOURS file #1
55 NEXT I
60 DATA 012345679,40
65 DATA 089012349,35
70 DATA 056789019,37
75 DATA 023456789,40
80 DATA 090123459,30
85 DATA 067890129,32
90 CLOSE
95 END
```

b. HOURS file

```
"012345679",40
"089012349",35
"056789019",37
"023456789",40
"090123459",30
"067890129",32
```

The files, MASTER and HOURS (from Programs 15.5 and 15.6, respectively), are then used by Program 15.7 (REPORT) to generate the weekly payroll report.

Line 125 of Program 15.7 generates the contents of the GROSS file with the PRINT USING option and a format in line 87 of

LET G$ = "\        \ , ## , ###.##"

This format includes a comma between items to provide for item separation when the file record is created. Note the listing of the file below the program as a direct result of the PRINT #3, USING G$; N$, H, G in line 125.

This GROSS file is then used by Program 15.8 (SEGROS) to provide management with a summary payroll report.

---

## PROGRAM 15.7 Case 15.2, REPORT Program (a) and GROSS File Listing (b)

```
a.  2 REM CASE 15.2, AJAX COMPANY, REPORT AND GROSS FILE LISTING
    4 REM PROGRAMMER- (name of person)   DATE - mm/dd/yy
    6 REM      VARIABLE LIST-
    8 REM          D=# OF DEPENDENTS
    9 REM          F$, G$=FORMATS
   10 REM          G=GROSS WAGE
   12 REM          H=HOURS WORKED PER WEEK
   14 REM          N$=EMPLOYEE NAME
   16 REM          P=WAGE RATE PER HOUR
   18 REM          S$=EMPLOYEE NO.
   20 REM          T=TAX DEDUCTION FROM GROSS
   21 REM          I,A=LOOP INDICES
   22 REM -------------------------------------
   30 OPEN "I",#1,"MASTER"
   35 OPEN "I",#2,"HOURS"
   40 OPEN "O",#3,"GROSS"
   45 FOR I= 1 TO 5
```

```
50      READ T(I)              'read tax rates
55 NEXT I
60 DATA .10,.09,.08,.07,.06
65 REM ** GENERATE REPORT
70 PRINT SPACE$(10);"AJAX CO. WEEKLY PAYROLL REPORT"
75 PRINT
80 PRINT      " NAME          EMPLOYEE NO.    GROSS PAY      NET PAY"
85 LET F$ =   " \          \       \          \      $###.##       $###.##"
87 LET G$ =   " \          \ , ##   , ###.##"
90 PRINT STRING$(55,"-")
95 FOR A= 1 TO 6
100      INPUT #1,N$,S$,D,P                'read from file #1
105      INPUT #2,S$,H                     'read from file #2
110      LET G=P*H
115      IF D>4 THEN LET D = 5
120          PRINT USING F$; N$,S$,G,G-G*T(D)
125          PRINT #3,USING G$; N$, H, G   'print output to file #3
130 NEXT A
135 PRINT
140 PRINT SPACE$(10);"***PAYROLL REPORT COMPLETED***"
145 CLOSE #1,#2,#3
150 END

RUN
         AJAX CO. WEEKLY PAYROLL REPORT

   NAME          EMPLOYEE NO.    GROSS PAY      NET PAY
   -------------------------------------------------------
   J. STING        012345679      $340.00        $309.40
   B. O'HARA       089012349      $323.75        $297.85
   M. BENNETT      056789019      $286.75        $258.08
   J. LAKE         023456789      $230.00        $216.20
   B. FARRONE      090123459      $240.00        $223.20
   C. ERICSON      067890129      $224.00        $206.08

         ***PAYROLL REPORT COMPLETED***
```

b. GROSS file

```
   J. STING     , 40 , 340.00
   B. O'HARA    , 35 , 323.75
   M. BENNETT   , 37 , 286.75
   J. LAKE      , 40 , 230.00
   B. FARRONE   , 30 , 240.00
   C. ERICSON   , 32 , 224.00
```

---

## PROGRAM 15.8   Case 15.2, Ajax Company, SEGROS Program

```
10 REM CASE 15.2, AJAX COMPANY, GENERATE OUTPUT BASED ON THE GROSS FILE
12 REM   PROGRAMMER- (name of person)   DATE- mm/dd/yy
14 REM      VARIABLE LIST-
15 REM         F$ = FORMAT
17 REM         G=GROSS PAY
18 REM         H=HOURS WORKED PER WEEK
```

```
19 REM          N$=EMPLOYEE NAME
20 REM          P=TOTAL GROSS PAY
21 REM          W=TOTAL HOURS
22 REM          I=LOOP INDEX
25 REM -----------------------------------------
30 OPEN "I",#1,"GROSS"
35 PRINT "EMPLOYEE, HOURS WORKED THIS WEEK, GROSS PAYROLL"
40 PRINT
45 PRINT    "   NAME          HOURS WORKED     GROSS PAY"
50 LET F$= "  \            \         ##            $###.##"
55 PRINT STRING$(43,"-")
60 LET W=0
65 LET P=0
70 FOR I=1 TO 6
75     INPUT #1,N$,H,G            'read from gross file #1
80     PRINT USING F$;N$,H,G
85     LET W=W+H
90     LET P=P+G
95 NEXT I
100 PRINT STRING$(43,"-")
105 PRINT USING "AVERAGE HOURS WORKED THIS WEEK  ##.# ";W/6
110 PRINT USING "TOTAL GROSS PAY THIS WEEK $$#,###.##";P
115 PRINT
120 PRINT SPACE$(10);"SUMMARY GROSS PAY REPORT COMPLETED"
125 CLOSE #1
130 END


RUN
EMPLOYEE, HOURS WORKED THIS WEEK, GROSS PAYROLL

    NAME          HOURS WORKED     GROSS PAY
-------------------------------------------
    J. STING          40           $340.00
    B. O'HARA         35           $323.75
    M. BENNETT        37           $286.75
    J. LAKE           40           $230.00
    B. FARRONE        30           $240.00
    C. ERICSON        32           $224.00
-------------------------------------------
AVERAGE HOURS WORKED THIS WEEK  35.7
TOTAL GROSS PAY THIS WEEK  $1,644.50

        SUMMARY GROSS PAY REPORT COMPLETED
```

Case 15.3, which follows, also demonstrates the advantages of using sequential files.

· · · · · · · · · · · · · · · · · · · · · · · · · · · · · · · ·

## CASE 15.3

**Problem**    **Stock Purchase Plan Using Two Input Files and One Output File**
The Atlantic Specialty Company conducts a stock purchase plan for its employees. Each month the employee contributes a part of his or her salary toward the purchase of Atlantic Specialty stock. The company will purchase full (not fractional) shares of the company

stock with the employee's contribution, based on the current market value of the shares. The company will also keep a record for each employee of the number of shares owned and any dollar balance left. To carry out the stock purchase plan and to keep track of all relevant information, a program and several data files are used.

**Data Input**

The data consists of two files, a previously created company data file, CONTR, and an updated monthly file, as well as the current price per share which is INPUT when the program is run. Each CONTR record contains an employee name and the monthly dollar contribution to the stock purchase plan. Each monthly file record contains the employee name, the number of shares the employee has already purchased, and any dollar balance in his or her account.

**Process/Formulas**

In a single program, access both the contribution (CONTR) and the current monthly file to determine each employee's current stock purchase situation. To update each monthly file and each employee's situation, the current price per share of the stock being purchased is entered into the program interactively. Figures 15.3 and 15.4 outline the process.

**Output**

The output consists of a new monthly file that becomes the input file for the next monthly update. See Figures 15.7 and 15.8. Each file shows the employee's name, number of shares, and residual amount for investment in the next month. At each monthly update, the processing program has the following input query and printed output:

```
WHAT IS CURRENT PRICE PER SHARE? 100

NO. OF SHARES PURCHASED = 4

NO. OF SHARES OWNED = 612

CURRENT TOTAL DOLLAR BALANCE = 220
```

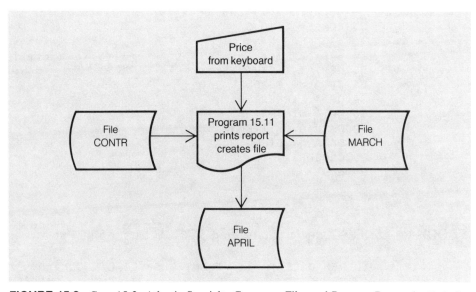

**FIGURE 15.3**  Case 15.3, Atlantic Specialty Company, Files and Program Run at the End of March

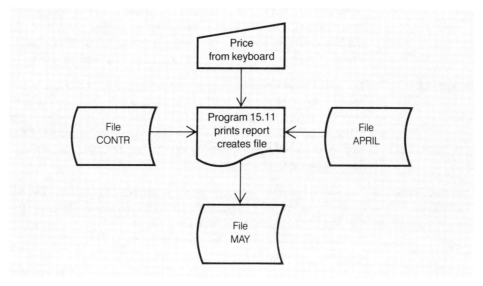

**FIGURE 15.4** Case 15.3, Atlantic Specialty Company, Files and Program Run at the End of April

## PROGRAM 15.9   Case 15.3, Creating CONTR Sequential File

```
10 REM CASE 15.3, ATLANTIC SPECIALTY COMPANY, CREATING
12 REM          CONTRIBUTION SEQUENTIAL FILE
14 REM   PROGRAMMER- (name of person)  DATE- mm/dd/yy
16 REM      VARIABLE LIST-
18 REM          C=AMOUNT CONTRIBUTED EACH MONTH
20 REM          N$=EMPLOYEE NAME
21 REM          I=LOOP INDEX
22 REM ----------------------------------------
30 OPEN "O",#1,"CONTR"
35 FOR I= 1 TO 5
40     READ N$,C
45     PRINT #1,N$;",";C          'print to contr file #1
50 NEXT I
55 DATA M. TENDLER, 50
60 DATA L.ROSS, 60
65 DATA G.WIND, 40
70 DATA A. RITTER, 70
75 DATA M.GOTEL , 30
80 CLOSE
85 END
```

## PROGRAM 15.10   Case 15.3, Creating MARCH Sequential File

```
10 REM CASE 15.3, ATLANTIC SPECIALTY COMPANY, CREATING MARCH
12 REM                    SEQUENTIAL FILE
14 REM   PROGRAMMER- (name of person) DATE- mm/dd/yy
16 REM      VARIABLE LIST-
```

```
18 REM            B=AMOUNT OF MONEY LEFT OVER
20 REM            M$=EMPLOYEE NAME
22 REM            S=# OF SHARES OWNED AS OF MARCH 1
23 REM            I=LOOP INDEX
24 REM ---------------------------------------------
30 OPEN "O",#1,"MARCH"
35 FOR I= 1 TO 5
40    READ M$,S,B
45    PRINT #1,M$;",";S;",";B      'print to march file #1
50 NEXT I
55 DATA M.TENDLER, 146, 70
60 DATA L.ROSS, 45, 30
65 DATA G.WIND, 67, 90
70 DATA A.RITTER, 250, 130
75 DATA M.GOTEL, 100, 50
80 CLOSE
85 END
```

The data input to Program 15.11 consists of two sequential files (CONTR and MARCH) and one number (price per share) entered as input from the keyboard. The first data file, CONTR, shown in Figure 15.5, contains each employee's name, followed by the amount contributed each month. The second data file, MARCH, shown in Figure 15.6, contains each employee's name followed by the number of shares owned as of March 1 and the amount of money that is left over from the previous stock purchase. The current price per share is input from the keyboard when Program 15.11 is run.

The program combines the information from both files and the price per share of the stock to create a file shown in Figure 15.7 called APRIL, which is identical in structure to the MARCH file but contains the updated information. Program 15.11 also prints a report that contains the number of shares purchased this month, the number of shares owned by each employee, and the total amount of money in each employee's account.

```
                M. TENDLER, 50
                L.ROSS, 60
                G.WIND, 40
                A.RITTER, 70
                M.GOTEL, 30
```

**FIGURE 15.5**  Case 15.3, Atlantic Specialty Company, Data File CONTR

```
                M.TENDLER, 146, 70
                L.ROSS, 45, 30
                G.WIND, 67, 90
                A.RITTER, 250, 130
                M.GOTEL, 100, 50
```

**FIGURE 15.6**  Case 15.3, Atlantic Specialty Company, Data File MARCH

```
M.TENDLER,  147,  20
L.ROSS,     45,  90
G.WIND,     68,  30
A.RITTER,  252,   0
M.GOTEL,    100,  80
```

**FIGURE 15.7** Case 15.3, Atlantic Specialty Company, Data File APRIL

Normally, the MARCH file would not be created by Program 15.10 but rather by a program such as 15.11, which would read the FEBRUARY and CONTR files to create the MARCH file.

## PROGRAM 15.11   Case 15.3, Stock Purchase Plan Program, March

```
2 REM CASE 15.3, ATLANTIC SPECIALTY COMPANY
4 REM              STOCK PURCHASE PROGRAM
6 REM   PROGRAMMER- (name of person)  DATE- mm/dd/yy
8 REM      VARIABLE LIST-
10 REM          B=AMOUNT OF MONEY LEFT OVER
12 REM          B1=TOTAL AMOUNT OF MONEY LEFT OVER
14 REM          C=AMOUNT CONTRIBUTED
16 REM          M$=EMPLOYEE NAME FROM MONTHLY FILE
18 REM          N=# OF SHARES PURCHASED THIS MONTH BY AN EMPLOYEE
20 REM          N$=EMPLOYEE NAME FROM CONTR FILE
22 REM          N1=TOTAL # OF SHARES PURCHASED THIS MONTH
24 REM          P=CURRENT PRICE PER SHARE
26 REM          S=# OF SHARES OWNED BY EACH EMPLOYEE
28 REM          S1=TOTAL # OF SHARES OWNED
29 REM          I=LOOP INDEX
30 REM -------------------------------------------------------------
35 OPEN "I", #1,"CONTR"
40 OPEN "I", #2,"MARCH"
45 OPEN "O", #3,"APRIL"
50 INPUT "WHAT IS CURRENT PRICE PER SHARE"; P
55 LET S1=0
60 LET B1=0
65 LET N1=0
70 FOR I= 1 TO 5
75     INPUT #1,N$,C          'read from contr file #1
80     INPUT #2,M$,S,B        'read from march file #2
85     LET B=B+C              'calc. total amount available for purchase
90     LET N=INT(B/P)         'calc. no. shares purchased this month
95     LET N1=N1+N            'accumulate no. shares purchased this month
100    LET S=S+N              'calc. new no. shares owned
105    LET S1=S1+S            'accumulate total no. shares owned
110    LET B=B-N*P            'calc. new balance
115    LET B1=B1+B            'accumulate total of all available balances
120    PRINT #3,M$,",",";S;",";B    'print to april file #3
125 NEXT I
```

```
130 CLOSE #1,#2,#3
135 PRINT "NO, OF SHARES PURCHASED =";N1
140 PRINT "NO, OF SHARES OWNED =";S1
145 PRINT "CURRENT TOTAL DOLLAR BALANCE= ";B1
150 END

RUN
WHAT IS CURRENT PRICE PER SHARE? 100
NO, OF SHARES PURCHASED = 4
NO, OF SHARES OWNED = 612
CURRENT TOTAL DOLLAR BALANCE= 220
```

The file MARCH (Figure 15.6) indicates that M. Tendler currently owns 146 shares of stock and has a balance of $70. This month he is contributing $50 (see Figure 15.5, the file CONTR), and the current price per share is $100. Therefore, the company purchases one additional share for M. Tendler for $100, and file APRIL shown in Figure 15.7 indicates that M. Tendler now owns 147 shares and has a balance of $20; that is, $70 from last month + $50 current contribution − $100 for the one share purchased = $20.

When the month of May arrives, the CONTR file (Figure 15.5) is combined with the APRIL file (Figure 15.7) and the current price per share ($80) to create a MAY file (Figure 15.8). To carry out this processing, the original program (15.11) is revised by changing lines 40 and 45. This revised program and output are shown as Program 15.12. Each month a similar revision of the program is required to read from the file for the current month to write the file for the next month.

```
M.TENDLER,  147,  70
L.ROSS,   46,  70
G.WIND,   68,  70
A.RITTER,  252,  70
M.GOTEL,  101,  30
```

**FIGURE 15.8** Case 15.3, Atlantic Specialty Company, Data File MAY

## PROGRAM 15.12   Case 15.3, Stock Purchase Plan Program, April

```
2 REM CASE 15,3, ATLANTIC SPECIALTY COMPANY,
4 REM              STOCK PURCHASE PROGRAM
6 REM   PROGRAMMER- (name of person)  DATE- mm/dd/yy
8 REM      VARIABLE LIST-
10 REM      B=AMOUNT OF MONEY LEFT OVER
12 REM      B1=TOTAL AMOUNT OF MONEY LEFT OVER
14 REM      C=AMOUNT CONTRIBUTED
16 REM      M$=EMPLOYEE NAME FROM MONTHLY FILE
18 REM      N=# OF SHARES PURCHASED THIS MONTH BY AN EMPLOYEE
20 REM      N$=EMPLOYEE NAME FROM CONTR FILE
22 REM      N1=TOTAL # OF SHARES PURCHASED THIS MONTH
24 REM      P=CURRENT PRICE PER SHARE
26 REM      S=# OF SHARES OWNED BY EACH EMPLOYEE
```

```
28 REM         S1=TOTAL # OF SHARES OWNED
30 REM --------------------------------------------------
35 OPEN "I", #1, "CONTR"
40 OPEN "I", #2, "APRIL"
45 OPEN "O", #3, "MAY"
50 INPUT "WHAT IS CURRENT PRICE PER SHARE";P
55 LET S1=0
60 LET B1=0
65 LET N1=0
70 FOR I= 1 TO 5
75     INPUT #1,N$,C               'read from contr file #1
80     INPUT #2,M$,S,B             'read from April file #2
85     LET B=B+C                   'calc. total amount available for purchase
90     LET N=INT (B/P)             'calc. no. shares purchased this month
95     LET N1=N1+N                 'accumulate no. shares purchased this month
100    LET S=S+N                   'calc. new no. shares owned
105    LET S1=S1+S                 'accumulate total no. shares owned
110    LET B=B-N*P                 'calc. new balance
115    LET B1=B1+B                 'accumulate total of all available balances
120    PRINT #3,M$;",";S;",";B     'print to may file #3
125 NEXT I
130 CLOSE #1,#2,#3
135 PRINT "NO. OF SHARES PURCHASED =";N1
140 PRINT "NO. OF SHARES OWNED =";S1
145 PRINT "CURRENT TOTAL DOLLAR BALANCE= ";B1
150 END

RUN
WHAT IS CURRENT PRICE PER SHARE? 80
NO. OF SHARES PURCHASED = 2
NO. OF SHARES OWNED = 614
CURRENT TOTAL DOLLAR BALANCE= 310
```

The advantage of using files in this case illustration is evident, since it demonstrates how large amounts of data can be manipulated without using DATA statements. Having the program create a file that can be used as input when the program is run the next time avoids much effort and eliminates the possibilities of errors in repeating the data entry.

## Appending Data to a Sequential Access File

Once a sequential file has been created, it is possible to add, or append, records to it. This is easily done by using an OPEN statement with a file specification of "A" rather than "O", as described earlier. This "A" specification places data at the end of an existing file. Suppose we have the file called "CUSTF" as shown in Figure 15.9. A simple program has been created, Program 15.13, to add items to this file each time there is a new customer's name and address. This program makes use of the LINE INPUT statement discussed in Chapter 4. First observe line 20 of the program

20 OPEN "A",#1,"CUSTF"

that indicates data will be appended to the file CUSTF. The statement

35 LINE INPUT "CUSTOMER NAME & ADDRESS "; NA$

```
MCS CO, SANTA CLARA, CA 95051
CAC CORP, PHOENIX, AZ 85080
PM CO, SEATTLE, WA 98104
MW CO, CHICAGO, IL 60614
FSW CO, CAMBRIDGE, MA 02142
```

**FIGURE 15.9**   Customer Name and Address File CUSTF

allows us to enter from the keyboard an entire line of characters (up to a maximum of 255 characters) that includes commas typically found in an address without confusing the computer should those commas separate data items. In Program 15.13 we will enter only two new data items as an illustration. This is done after RUN in the program.

## PROGRAM 15.13    Appending Data to a Sequential File

```
10 REM APPENDING TO A SEQUENTIAL ACCESS FILE
20 OPEN"A",#1,"CUSTF"          'append to the file #1
30 FOR I= 1 TO 2
35    LINE INPUT "CUSTOMER NAME & ADDRESS  "; NA$   'enter from keyboard
45    PRINT #1, NA$                    'print to end of file #1
50 NEXT I
55 CLOSE
85 END

RUN
CUSTOMER NAME & ADDRESS   PCD CO, NEW YORK, NY   10006
CUSTOMER NAME & ADDRESS   C&M CO, WASHINGTON, DC 20017
```

To confirm that the original data file CUSTF has been added to, going from five to seven items, Program 15.14 was written. This program will list out the contents of the CUSTF data file making use of a new statement, LINE INPUT #, shown in line 50.

The form of this statement is

line # LINE INPUT #N, SV$

where the N corresponds to the file number for the OPEN file, and SV$ is a string variable that corresponds to the data item in the data file that is being accessed. With the LINE INPUT statement, an entire line of characters (up to a maximum of 255 characters) including commas can be read from a sequential file into a string variable. Examples of this statement follow:

40 LINE INPUT #1, A$
50 LINE INPUT #2, Names$
60 LINE INPUT #3, DIV$

## PROGRAM 15.14 Listing Data from a Sequential File Using LINE INPUT #

```
10 REM LISTING A SEQUENTIAL ACCESS FILE
20 OPEN "I",#1,"CUSTF"
30 FOR I= 1 TO 10
40     IF EOF(1) THEN 80          'check for end-of-file
50     LINE INPUT #1, NA$          'reads from file #1
60     PRINT NA$
70 NEXT I
80 CLOSE
90 END

RUN
MCS CO. SANTA CLARA, CA 95051
CAC CORP. PHOENIX, AZ 85080
PM CO. SEATTLE, WA 98104
MW CO. CHICAGO, IL 60614
FSW CO. CAMBRIDGE, MA 02142
PCD CO. NEW YORK, NY 10006
C&M CO. WASHINGTON, DC 20017
```

Observe that the output of the program has all seven records, thus confirming our ability to append data to a file as shown in Program 15.13.

## RANDOM ACCESS FILES

With sequential files, it is not possible to read an item from the middle of a file without first reading everything else before it. Random access files make it possible to read directly any item desired. We can also write to, or update, any item in the file. This is done by specifying the record in the file we are interested in.

Random access files are handled with the five statements described next and with the CLOSE statement previously discussed with sequential files.

### Statements Used

**OPEN**   The OPEN statement allows the program to read or write to a random access file. It also assigns a buffer to the file or an area of storage in the memory to hold input or output records. The OPEN statement can be used in two forms for random input and output to a file. One form of the statement is

Line # OPEN ''R'', #N, ''File Name'', rl

where ''R'' stands for random access, #N is the file reference number, followed by the filename, and the rl equals the length of the records with a maximum of 32,767 characters. Specific examples of this form of the OPEN statement are

20 OPEN ''R'', #1, ''CUSTF1'', 100
30 OPEN ''R'', #2, ''FILEA'', 8

The second form of the statement is

Line # OPEN "File Name" AS #N LEN = rl

This second form does not specify what type of file is being used, "A", "O", "I", or "R." It then defaults to a random access file type. Specific examples of this file type statement are

20 OPEN "CUSTF1" AS #1 LEN = 100
30 OPEN "FILEA" AS #2 LEN = 8

In Line 10 of Program 15.16, FILEA is opened as a random access file using buffer #1, and LEN = 8 tells the computer that each record will contain 8 bytes, or characters, of information. Without LEN = 8, the computer will assume a default length of 128 bytes, or characters.

**FIELD**   The FIELD statement tells the computer how each record is divided into separate fields. Each field of a record contains a piece of information. The FIELD statement has the form

Line # FIELD #N, flwl AS svl$, . . . , flwn AS svn$

where #N is the file reference number, flwl is the width of the field assigned to the string variable svl$, and so on, depending on how the record of each file is formatted. A typical FIELD statement could look like this, for example:

30 FIELD #1, 30 AS SSN$, 40 AS NM$, 15 AS TELN$

It allocates 30 positions in the random file buffer to the string variable SSN$, the next 40 positions to the string variable NM$, and then 15 positions to the string variable TELN$.

Line 20 in Program 15.15 offers the following example of a FIELD statement:

20 FIELD #1, 2 AS A$, 6 AS B$

This line says that the file using buffer #1 has 2 fields; the first, with a length of 2, is called A$ and the second, with a length of 6, is called B$. The names must always be string variables. (See Figure 15.10.) The actual placement of data into the random file buffer is done by the LSET and RSET statements described next.

**LSET and RSET**   To put data into the random access file requires either the LSET or RSET statements followed by a PUT statement. When we want to place data into a file field in a left-justified position, we use LSET (left set). For a right-justified placement into a file field, we use RSET (right set). The form for these two statements is

Line # LSET sv$ = stex$
Line # RSET sv$ = stex$

where the string expression on the right of the equal sign is assigned to the string variable on the left of the equal sign. These variables have been previously defined in the FIELD statement. Following is a specific example:

20 LSET NM$ = P$
30 RSET SSN$ = R$

where lines 20 and 30 assign string data items to field positions NM$ and SSN$, respectively.

Program 15.15 uses these statements:

50 LSET A$ = MKI$(N)
60 LSET B$ = C$

Line 50 says to convert the numeric integer variable N into a string using MKI$(N) and to set that equal to buffer variable A$.

Line 60 sets C$ directly into buffer variable B$, since it is already a string variable.

Note that MKI$ converts an integer, nondecimal number to a two-character string. To convert a single-precision number, six digits with decimals, to a four-character string, use MKS$. MKD$ will convert a double-precision number, sixteen digits with decimals, to an eight-character string.

## PROGRAM 15.15 Writing to a Random Access Disk File

```
10 OPEN "R", #1, "FILEA", 8          'open a random access file
20 FIELD #1, 2 AS A$, 6 AS B$
30 FOR I=1 TO 5
40     READ N,C$
50     LSET A$ = MKI$(N)       'left justify in the field
60     LSET B$ = C$            'left justify in the field
70     PRINT N, C$
80     PUT #1, I               'write to the random file #1
90 NEXT I
100 CLOSE
110 DATA 25,BLUE, 20,RED, 30,YELLOW
120 DATA 10,GREEN, 16,BROWN
130 END

RUN
 25         BLUE
 20         RED
 30         YELLOW
 10         GREEN
 16         BROWN
```

**PUT** The PUT statement takes the buffer variable contents and writes (puts) them into the file in the specified record. It has the form

Line # PUT #N, num

where #N is the file that was opened, and num is the record number for the record to be written into the file. Thus line 80 in Program 15.15 is

80 PUT #1, I

which puts the contents of A$ and B$ into the $I$th record of file FILEA.

Figure 15.10 shows how each data list (N, C$) in Program 15.15 will be assigned to a record of the file FILEA in a left-justified position.

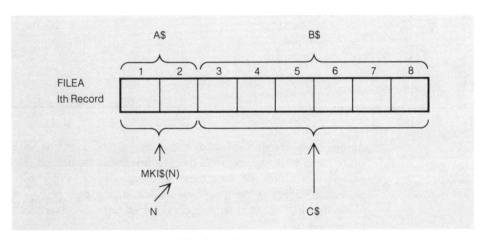

**FIGURE 15.10**   Random Access File Operations

**GET**   The GET statement reads (gets) the information from a particular record in a file and puts it into the buffer variables. It has the form

Line # GET #N, num

where #N is the file that was opened, and num is the number of the record to be read from the file. Thus line 50 in Program 15.16 is

50 GET #1, I

The GET statement reads the information from the Ith record of file FILEA and puts it into the buffer variables A$ and B$.

To print out A$ as a number, we must first convert it with the CVI function into an integer. B$ can be printed out directly.

Note that CVI will convert a two-byte string to an integer. To convert a four-byte string to a single-precision number, we use CVS. CVD will convert an eight-byte string to a double-precision number. Each byte stores a single character.

## PROGRAM 15.16   Reading from a Random Access Disk File by Direct Access

```
10 OPEN "FILEA" AS #1 LEN = 8
20 FIELD #1, 2 AS A$, 6 AS B$
25 FOR N = 1 TO 10
30     READ I
40     IF I=-99 THEN 80
50         GET #1, I                    'get a record from file #1
60         PRINT I; CVI(A$); B$
70 NEXT N
80 CLOSE
85 DATA 3,2,5,4,1,-99
90 END

RUN
 3  30 YELLOW
 2  20 RED
 5  16 BROWN
 4  10 GREEN
 1  25 BLUE
```

### Reading from a Random Access File

As has been already explained, to retrieve a record or line with sequential files, the entire file is read, starting from the first line, until the desired record is located. With a random access disk file we retrieve a record without having to pass through all of the preceding records in the file. Thus random access disk storage increases the speed of processing file information and provides us with direct access to a specified record when needed.

In order to access a data record from a random disk file, we use a GET statement that has the general form

line # GET # file number, I

where I is the number of a data record.

This process of direct (or random) access is shown in Program 15.16 above. The program does not search the entire disk for the desired array contents of FILEA. Instead the computer is directed to access through the GET statement in line 50 the *I*th record as instructed by line 30 READ I. Thus when I = 3, the third record 30 YELLOW is retrieved without a complete search through the file, FILEA.

Because it provides data retrieval faster than sequential access, random access has found wide application in business systems dealing with customers' inquiries. This type of system is used by organizations that typically receive requests for information over the phone. Examples include people requesting information from

**1.** Public utility companies about bills—gas, electric, or telephone.

**2.** Insurance companies about policies.

**3.** Airlines about reservations and flight information.

**4.** Banks about checking or savings accounts.

Fast retrieval and access to stored information is also a characteristic of many information systems. Many inventory systems are based on locating items in a hurry or checking to see if an item is in stock. Random access makes such systems a reality.

The case that follows is a rather simple illustration of the disk file concepts described so far.

## CASE 15.4

**Problem**

**Bank Credit Checking, Random Access File Processing**

Many banks provide their checking account customers with overdraft privileges of varying amounts. The range of privileges associated with checking plus may be from $500 to $2,000, depending on the individual. Since a bank may have thousands of accounts, a random access system for credit inquiries is desired to minimize delay when a transaction takes place. For such a system, two programs will be needed. The first program will be a Disk File Record Entry Program that will enter such items as the customer's account number, name, and credit limit to a disk file. The second program will be a conversational one that, upon entry of the customer's account number, will directly access the appropriate disk file and output the desired record. We can call this second program a Random Access Credit Check Program. See Figure 15.11, which is a flowchart illustrating how the bank credit checking procedure works.

**Data Input**

A previously created company random file, CREDIT, is used with each record containing a customer's account number, name, and credit limit. A keyboard entry of the customer's account number is used to retrieve a customer's record.

**Process/Formulas**

A single program using appropriate random access operations retrieves a credit record in response to a keyboard entry. Figure 15.11 shows this process. The program is designed to allow the data entry user to continue entering account numbers until he or she is ready to terminate the program.

**Output**

The output consists of a screen display showing the customer's account number, name, and credit limit. This results from a response to an input query requesting an account number. The query and display have this format:

```
TO ACCESS AN ACCOUNT FOR CREDIT CHECKING
ENTER THE ACCOUNT NUMBER.
WHAT IS THE ACCOUNT NUMBER?   538

ACCOUNT NUMBER: 538
NAME         : FRED KEENAN
CREDIT LIMIT  $ 2000

DO YOU WISH ANOTHER CREDIT CHECK (Y = YES, N = NO)? N

****** CREDIT CHECK COMPLETED ******
```

Programs 15.17 and 15.18 illustrate what is needed to satisfy Case 15.4. Figure 15.11 shows a system flowchart. The Disk File Record Entry Program (Program 15.17) writes

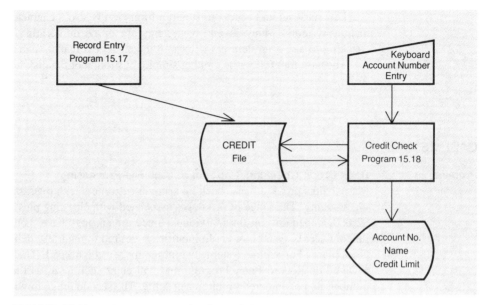

**FIGURE 15.11**   System Flowchart for Case 15.4

to file CREDIT data first read into the program by line 40 READ A,P$,N. Note that the PUT statement,

65 PUT #1, A

uses the record number A, which is the checking account number. This is important because we wish to access from the disk by this number. Therefore, we have to write the initial data to the disk using the same number as the record number.

Also notice that the output of the program consists of the data assigned to the disk and an additional line 134 IRA MORGAN 500. This last line of output results from a "TEST ON ACCESS" included in the program to see if the data has gotten to the disk and is retrievable. The test is found in line 110, GET #1, 134, which requests that the record with account number 134 be directly accessed. It is then printed out by line 120.

## PROGRAM 15.17   Case 15.4, Random Access Disk File Record Entry Program

```
2 REM CASE 15.4, BANK CREDIT CHECKING, RANDOM ACCESS FILE
4 REM   PROGRAMMER- (name of person)   DATE - mm/dd/yy
6 REM      VARIABLE LIST-
8 REM         A=CHECKING ACCOUNT NO.
10 REM        C$=STRING CONVERTED FROM NUMERICAL NO.
12 REM        L$=STRING CONVERTED FROM NUMERICAL NO.
14 REM        N=CREDIT LIMIT
16 REM        N$=ACCOUNT NAME
18 REM        P$=ACCOUNT NAME
19 REM        I=LOOP INDEX
20 REM ------------------------------------------------
25 OPEN "CREDIT" AS #1 LEN =24
30 FIELD #1, 3 AS C$, 14 AS N$, 7 AS L$
```

```
35 FOR I = 1 TO 4
40     READ A,P$,N
45     PRINT USING "      ###    \            \    $$##,###,##";A,P$,N
50     LSET C$ = MKI$(A)
55     LSET N$ = P$
60     LSET L$ = MKS$(N)
65     PUT #1, A
70 NEXT I
75 DATA 691, ELAINE ROBBINS, 1500
80 DATA 538, FRED KEENAN, 2000
85 DATA 134, IRA MORGAN, 500
90 DATA 369, LINDA COHEN, 1000
95 PRINT
100    REM TEST ON ACCESS
110    GET #1, 134
120    PRINT CVI(C$); N$; CVS(L$)
130 CLOSE
140 END

RUN
    691    ELAINE ROBBINS    $1,500,00
    538    FRED KEENAN       $2,000,00
    134    IRA MORGAN          $500,00
    369    LINDA COHEN       $1,000,00

134 IRA MORGAN     500
```

In order to retrieve data from the file CREDIT we can use a direct Random Access Credit Check Program as shown in Program 15.18. This is a conversational program with the user entering only the account through line 60,

> 60 INPUT "WHAT IS THE ACCOUNT NUMBER"; C

The GET statement in line 70

> 70 GET #1, C

uses the account number, $C$, to locate the desired record and bring it into the program so that it can be outputted by the PRINT statements in lines 90–110. If an account number not in the file is entered, say 678, the output for that number may be nonsense values. This is the case of GIGO; garbage in garbage out.

---

## PROGRAM 15.18    Case 15.4, Random Access Credit Check Program

```
2 REM CASE 15.4, BANK CREDIT CHECKING, RANDOM ACCESS FILE
4 REM   PROGRAMMER- (name of person)   DATE- mm/dd/yy
6 REM      VARIABLE LIST-
8 REM         C=ACCOUNT NUMBER
10 REM        C$=FIRST FIELD IN RECORD, ACCOUNT NUMBER
12 REM        N$=SECOND FIELD IN RECORD, NAME
14 REM        L$=LAST FIELD IN RECORD, CREDIT LIMIT
```

```
16 REM            Y$="YES" OR "NO"
18 REM -------------------------------------------------
20 OPEN "CREDIT" AS #1 LEN = 24
30 FIELD #1, 3 AS C$, 14 AS N$, 7 AS L$
40 PRINT "TO ACCESS AN ACCOUNT FOR CREDIT CHECKING"
50 PRINT "ENTER THE ACCOUNT NUMBER."
60 INPUT "WHAT IS THE ACCOUNT NUMBER"; C
70      GET #1,C
80      PRINT
90      PRINT "ACCOUNT NUMBER:"; CVI (C$)
100     PRINT "NAME          :"; N$
110     PRINT "CREDIT LIMIT  $"; CVS(L$)
120     PRINT
130     INPUT "DO YOU WISH ANOTHER CREDIT CHECK (Y = YES, N = NO)"; Y$
160 IF Y$ = "Y" OR Y$ = "y" THEN 60
170 PRINT
180 PRINT "****** CREDIT CHECK COMPLETED ******"
190 CLOSE
200 END


RUN
TO ACCESS AN ACCOUNT FOR CREDIT CHECKING
ENTER THE ACCOUNT NUMBER.
WHAT IS THE ACCOUNT NUMBER? 538

ACCOUNT NUMBER: 538
NAME          : FRED KEENAN
CREDIT LIMIT  $ 2000

DO YOU WISH ANOTHER CREDIT CHECK (Y = YES, N = NO)? y
WHAT IS THE ACCOUNT NUMBER? 369

ACCOUNT NUMBER: 369
NAME          : LINDA COHEN
CREDIT LIMIT  $ 1000

DO YOU WISH ANOTHER CREDIT CHECK (Y = YES, N = NO)? y
WHAT IS THE ACCOUNT NUMBER? 134

ACCOUNT NUMBER: 134
NAME          : IRA MORGAN
CREDIT LIMIT  $ 500

DO YOU WISH ANOTHER CREDIT CHECK (Y = YES, N = NO)? Y
WHAT IS THE ACCOUNT NUMBER? 691

ACCOUNT NUMBER: 691
NAME          : ELAINE ROBBINS
CREDIT LIMIT  $ 1500

DO YOU WISH ANOTHER CREDIT CHECK (Y = YES, N = NO)? N

****** CREDIT CHECK COMPLETED ******
```

## SUMMARY

This chapter introduces the concepts of sequential access files and random access files. For efficiency, such files are usually placed in auxiliary storage so that they can be used by many programs. Before a program can use data in a file, the file must be created and saved as a separate entity. File operations make use of the OPEN and CLOSE statements. To obtain data from a sequential file, an INPUT file statement is used. To write data to a sequential file, a PRINT or WRITE file statement is used. To access data in a random disk file, we use a GET statement. To write data onto the disk and into a random access file, we use a PUT statement.

## BASIC VOCABULARY SUMMARY

| Statement | Purpose | Examples |
|---|---|---|
| OPEN<br>(Alt + O key) | Allows for input or output to a file. It uses the following specifications: For sequential files, "O" for output, "I" for input, "A" to append; for random files, "R" for random input or output. Without a specification, the random mode is assumed. | 15 OPEN ''O'', #1, ''NAMES''<br>20 OPEN ''I'', #2, ''INVENTORY''<br>30 OPEN ''A'', #2, ''SALES''<br>20 OPEN ''R'', #1, ''CUSTF1'', 100<br>30 OPEN ''FILEA'' AS #2 LEN = 8 |
| PRINT # | Writes data sequentially to a file. If data is to be read later by a program, semicolons separate items and string items must have a comma in quotation marks between them. | 40 PRINT #1, A$; '','' ; B$<br>50 PRINT #2, N; A; XY1 |
| WRITE # | Writes data sequentially to a file. So that the file can be read later by a program, it places string items in quotation marks and inserts commas between items. | 40 WRITE #1, A$, B$<br>50 WRITE #2, N, A, XY$ |
| INPUT # | Reads data items from a sequential file into a program. | 60 INPUT #1, B$, M$<br>70 INPUT #2, N, A, XY$ |
| CLOSE | Ends the input and output to and from a file. It ensures that file contents are saved for future use. | 100 CLOSE<br>100 CLOSE #1<br>100 CLOSE #1, #2, #3 |
| LINE INPUT# | Reads an entire line (up to a maximum of 255 characters), ignoring delimiters (commas and semicolons) from a sequential file into a string variable. | 40 LINE INPUT #1, A$<br>50 LINE INPUT #2, NAMES$<br>60 LINE INPUT #3, DIV$ |

| FIELD | Allocates the space for variables in a random file buffer. | 20 FIELD #1, 20 AS A\$,16 AS B\$ |
| LSET<br>RSET | Moves data into a random file buffer in preparation for a PUT (into a file) statement. LSET left justifies in the field; RSET right justifies. | 20 LSET NM\$ = P\$<br>30 RSET SSN\$ = R\$<br>40 LSET G\$ = MKS\$(TOT)<br>50 RSET N\$ = MKI\$(CT) |
| PUT | Writes a record from a random file buffer to a random file. | 90 PUT #1, A<br>95 PUT #2, 3542 |
| GET | Reads a record from a random file to a random buffer. | 40 GET #1, A<br>50 GET #2, 3542 |

| Function | Purpose | Examples |
| --- | --- | --- |
| EOF(n) | Indicates an end of file condition. It returns $-1$ (true) if end of file has been reached; 0 if it has not. | 30 IF EOF(1) THEN 180<br>40 IF EOF(1) THEN CLOSE |
| MKI\$(ie)<br>MKS\$(spe)<br>MKD\$(dpe) | For random file operations, converts numeric type values to string type values. The $ie =$ integer expression, $spe =$ single-precision expression, and $dpe =$ double-precision expression. | 50 LSET N\$ = MKS\$(P)<br>60 LSET K\$ = MKI\$(TT)<br>70 RSET A\$ = MKD\$(SUM)<br>80 LET N\$ = MKI \$(B%)<br>85 LET A\$ = MKS \$(E!)<br>90 LET G\$ = MKD \$(H#) |
| CVI(S2\$)<br>CVS(S4\$)<br>CVD(S8\$) | For random file operations, converts string variable types to numeric variable types. The S2\$ is a 2-byte string that is converted to an integer. The S4\$ is a 4-byte string that is converted to a single-precision number. The S8\$ is an 8-byte string that is converted to a double-precision number. | 50 LET M = CVI(P\$)<br>60 LET K = CVS(A\$)<br>70 LET L = CVD(UM\$)<br>80 PRINT CVI(B\$); CVD(NM\$) |

## EXERCISES

### Review Questions

**15.1** Correct any errors in each of the following statements:
 a. 15 OPEN #2, ''FILE2'', ''O''
 ♦ b. 20 OPEN ''#1'', A, FILE3
 c. 30 OPEN ''O'' or ''I'', #4
 ♦ d. 40 OPEN ''R'', #2, FILE \$, LENGTH = 25
 e. 50 OPEN R AS #3, 45

**15.2** Correct any errors in each of the following statements:
  a. 10 PRINT #1 A$ ;,; C$
◆ b. 20 PRINT #2 '',''X; Y, Z
  c. 30 WRITE #1 A$, '';'', B$
◆ d. 40 WRITE #2 N,'';'',M,'';'',O

**15.3** Write an appropriate FIELD statement for each of the following records:
  a. Inventory part number with 10 characters, part description with 15 characters, and warehouse storage bin location with 8 characters.
  b. Names with 20 characters, street address with 25 characters, city and state with 30 characters, and zip code with 5 characters.

**15.4** For each of the records given above in exercise 15.3. Write an appropriate OPEN statement in both statement formats.

**15.5** A program starting with the statement 20 OPEN ''O'', #2, ''FILEB'' should have either a _____ or _____ statement to place data into FILEB.

**15.6** The three random file functions to:
  a. Convert string variables types to numeric values are _____, _____, and _____.
  b. Convert numeric type values to string type values are _____, _____, and _____.

**15.7** To position data items in a random file record requires either the _____ or _____ statement.

**15.8** The following sequential file creation program is incomplete in what ways?

```
20 OPEN "O","FILE4"
30 FOR I = 1 TO 2
40     READ A,B,C
45     PRINT #1,A;",";B;",";C
50 NEXT I
60 DATA 77,103,88,114,81,126
70 DATA 90,137,99,128,86,142
90 END
```

**15.9** The following random file creation program is incomplete in what ways?

```
10 FIELD #2, 5 AS C$, 10 AS D$
15 FOR I=1 TO 6
20     READ B$, M
25     LSET C$ = M
30     LSET D$ = B$
35     PRINT B$, M
40 NEXT I
45 CLOSE
50 DATA JAN,, 12, FEB,, 10, MARCH, 9
55 DATA APRIL, 16, MAY, 14, JUNE 10
60 END
```

Programming Activities

♦ **15.10** **Purpose** To create a sequential data file.

**Problem** Write and run a program creating a sequential data file using the PRINT # statement. After it has been created, list it out.

**Data** Use the following data:

| PLANT | UNITS PRODUCED |
|-------|----------------|
| 1 | 3,400 |
| 2 | 4,200 |
| 3 | 2,800 |
| 4 | 3,100 |
| 5 | 4,000 |
| 6 | 5,500 |

**Output** Your file listing should look like this:

```
B>type unitf
1 , 3400
2 , 4200
3 , 2800
4 , 3100
5 , 4000
6 , 5500
```

**15.11** **Purpose** To create a sequential data file.

**Problem** Write and run a program creating a sequential data file using the WRITE # statement. After it has been created, list it out.

**Data** Use the following data:

| STOCK | PRICE |
|-------|-------|
| ATT | $ 25 |
| CBS | $157 |
| EXXON | $ 46 |
| GNMOT | $ 80 |
| GTE | $ 37 |
| IBM | $125 |
| XEROX | $ 55 |

**Output** Your file listing should look like this:

```
B>type pricef
"ATT",25
"CBS",157
"EXXON",46
"GNMOT",80
"GTE",37
"IBM",125
"XEROX",55
```

**15.12** **Purpose** To create a sequential data file.

**Problem** Write and run a program creating a sequential data file using the WRITE # statement. After it has been created, list it out.

**Data**   Use the following data:

| CITY | HIGH TEMPERATURE (°F) | |
| | Yesterday | A Year Ago |
| --- | --- | --- |
| Boston | 65 | 61 |
| New York | 72 | 69 |
| Washington, D.C. | 71 | 68 |
| Denver | 49 | 55 |
| Los Angeles | 83 | 88 |
| Honolulu | 79 | 79 |
| Phoenix | 101 | 100 |

**Output**   Your file listing should look like this:

```
B>type tempf
"BOSTON",65,61
"NEW YORK",72,69
"WASHINGTON, D.C.",71,68
"DENVER",49,55
"LOS ANGELES",83,88
"HONOLULU",79,79
"PHOENIX",101,100
```

♦ **15.13**   **Purpose**   To read a sequential data file and process it.

**Problem**   Write and run a program that uses a previously created sequential data file (see exercise 15.10). For the data given below, derive the total units produced for all six plants and the average production (total/six) for the six plants.

**Data**   Use the following data:

| PLANT | UNITS PRODUCED |
| --- | --- |
| 1 | 3,400 |
| 2 | 4,200 |
| 3 | 2,800 |
| 4 | 3,100 |
| 5 | 4,000 |
| 6 | 5,500 |

**Output**   Your output should look like this:

```
PLANT                    UNITS PRODUCED
---------------------------------------
  1                            3,400
  2                            4,200
  3                            2,800
  4                            3,100
  5                            4,000
  6                            5,500
---------------------------------------
TOTAL                         23,000
AVERAGE                        3,833
```

**15.14** **Purpose** To read a sequential data file and process it.

**Problem** Write and run a program that uses a previously created sequential data file (see exercise 15.10). For the data given below, derive the total cost, total revenue, and net revenue for each plant, where

Total cost = number of units produced × unit cost ($3)
Total revenue = number of units produced × unit price ($5.50)
Net Revenue = total revenue − total cost

Direct the program to place the plant number, total cost, total revenue, and net revenue into a separate file. List out the contents of this file.

**Data** Use the following data. Unit cost is $3.00 per item, and unit price is $5.50 per item.

| PLANT | UNITS PRODUCED | PLANT | UNITS PRODUCED |
|-------|----------------|-------|----------------|
| 1 | 3,400 | 4 | 3,100 |
| 2 | 4,200 | 5 | 4,000 |
| 3 | 2,800 | 6 | 5,500 |

**Output** Your program output should look like this:

| PLANT | TOTAL COST | TOTAL REVENUE | NET REVENUE |
|-------|------------|---------------|-------------|
| 1 | $10,200 | $18,700 | $ 8,500 |
| 2 | $12,600 | $23,100 | $10,500 |
| 3 | $ 8,400 | $15,400 | $ 7,000 |
| 4 | $ 9,300 | $17,050 | $ 7,750 |
| 5 | $12,000 | $22,000 | $10,000 |
| 6 | $16,500 | $30,250 | $13,750 |

Your file listing should look like this:

```
B>type totalf
1,10200,18700,8500
2,12600,23100,10500
3,8400,15400,7000
4,9300,17050,7750
5,12000,22000,10000
6,16500,30250,13750
```

**15.15** **Purpose** To access a sequential data file.

**Problem** Write and run a program that accesses a sequential data file using the LINE INPUT # statement. Do this for the output file of exercise 15.14.

**Data** Use the file data for exercise 15.14.

**Output** Your program output should look like this:

```
1,10200,18700,8500
2,12600,23100,10500
3,8400,15400,7000
4,9300,17050,7750
5,12000,22000,10000
6,16500,30250,13750
```

**15.16** **Purpose** To read two sequential data files, process them, and output the results to another file.

**Problem** a. For the data given below, create two separate sequential data files (see exercise 15.11), one for price, the other for shares.

b. Write and run a program that uses these two files to derive for each stock the market value (price × number of shares). Direct the program to place output results exactly as printed by the program into another file. Use the PRINT # USING statement to do this.

c. Write and run a program that takes the output file just produced (part b) using the LINE INPUT # statement and prints out its contents.

**Data** Use the following data:

| STOCK | PRICE | NO. OF SHARES |
|-------|-------|---------------|
| ATT   | $ 25  | 5,000 |
| CBS   | $157  | 4,500 |
| EXXON | $ 46  | 2,500 |
| GNMOT | $ 80  | 6,000 |
| GTE   | $ 37  | 2,000 |
| IBM   | $125  | 1,200 |
| XEROX | $ 55  | 1,500 |

**Output** There are two outputs, one for each program in parts b and c. Your program and file output should both look like this:

```
STOCK:ATT     NO. SHARES 5,000   PRICE    $25   MARKET VALUE   $125,000
STOCK:CBS     NO. SHARES 4,500   PRICE   $157   MARKET VALUE   $706,500
STOCK:EXXON   NO. SHARES 2,500   PRICE    $46   MARKET VALUE   $115,000
STOCK:GNMOT   NO. SHARES 6,000   PRICE    $80   MARKET VALUE   $480,000
STOCK:GTE     NO. SHARES 2,000   PRICE    $37   MARKET VALUE    $74,000
STOCK:IBM     NO. SHARES 1,200   PRICE   $125   MARKET VALUE   $150,000
STOCK:XEROX   NO. SHARES 1,500   PRICE    $55   MARKET VALUE    $82,500
```

♦ **15.17** **Purpose** To append data to a sequential data file.

**Problem** For the first group of data (1) given below, create a sequential data file. Write and run a single program that first appends the additional data items (2) and then outputs the appended data file using the WRITE # statement.

**Data** Use the following data:

(1) DIV A,400,15      (2) DIV E,380,13
    DIV B,500,23          DIV F,450,25
    DIV C,430,20          DIV G,300,21
    DIV D,330,30

**Output** Your file output should look like this:

```
"DIV A",400,15
"DIV B",500,23
"DIV C",430,20
"DIV D",330,30
"DIV E",380,13
"DIV F",450,25
"DIV G",300,21
```

•  •  •  •  •  ◆ **15.18**    **Purpose**  To access a sequential data file and process the information interactively.

**Problem**  For the airline flight schedule given below, create a sequential data file. Write and run a program that is conversational in design to display the flight schedule when a menu number is entered, 1= Monday, 2= Tuesday, and so forth.

**Data**  Use the following data:

**747'S FROM NEW YORK TO GENEVA AND ZURICH**

| Day of Week | Leaves New York | Arrives Geneva | Arrives Zurich |
|---|---|---|---|
| Mo/Th/Sa/Su | 7:10 P.M. | 7:30 A.M. | 9:00 A.M. |
| | 10:05 P.M. | (nonstop) | 10:40 A.M. |
| Tu/We/Fr | 8:50 P.M. | 9:10 A.M. | 10:40 A.M. |

**Output**  Your data file output should look like this:

```
MO/TH/SA/SU      7:10 P.M.      7:30 A.M.         9:00 A.M.
MO/TH/SA/SU     10:05 P.M.     (NONSTOP)         10:40 A.M.
TU/WE/FR         8:50 P.M.      9:10 A.M.         10:40 A.M.
```

A typical interactive session could look like this:

```
RUN
ENTER THE DAY OF THE WEEK FOR SCHEDULE INFORMATION:
1. MONDAY    2. TUESDAY   3. WEDNESDAY   4. THURSDAY
5. FRIDAY    6. SATURDAY  7. SUNDAY      8. QUIT

DAY NUMBER PLEASE: 1, 2, 3, 4, 5, 6, 7, OR 8 TO QUIT? 3

DAY OF WEEK      LEAVES N.Y.   ARRIVES GENEVA   ARRIVES ZURICH
-------------------------------------------------------------
TU/WE/FR         8:50 P.M.        9:10 A.M.        10:40 A.M.

ENTER THE DAY OF THE WEEK FOR SCHEDULE INFORMATION:
1. MONDAY    2. TUESDAY   3. WEDNESDAY   4. THURSDAY
5. FRIDAY    6. SATURDAY  7. SUNDAY      8. QUIT

DAY NUMBER PLEASE: 1, 2, 3, 4, 5, 6, 7 OR 8 TO QUIT? 7

DAY OF WEEK      LEAVES N.Y.   ARRIVES GENEVA   ARRIVES ZURICH
-------------------------------------------------------------
MO/TH/SA/SU      7:10 P.M.        7:30 A.M.         9:00 A.M.
MO/TH/SA/SU     10:05 P.M.     (NONSTOP)          10:40 A.M.

ENTER THE DAY OF THE WEEK FOR SCHEDULE INFORMATION:
1. MONDAY    2. TUESDAY   3. WEDNESDAY   4. THURSDAY
5. FRIDAY    6. SATURDAY  7. SUNDAY      8. QUIT

DAY NUMBER PLEASE: 1, 2, 3, 4, 5, 6, OR 8 TO QUIT? 8
```

•  •  •  •  •  •  • **15.19**    **Purpose**  To access two sequential data files and process the information interactively.

**Problem**  For the airline flight schedule given below, create two sequential data files, one for Seattle and one for Portland. Write and run a program that is conversational in design to display the flight schedule when the departure city is entered along with the destination city.

**Data**  Use the following data:

| TO | FLT # | LEAVES | REMARKS |
|---|---|---|---|
| | | **From Seattle** | |
| Auckland | 815 | 11:45 P.M. | 707 Tu/Su |
| Tokyo | 891/831 | 8:00 A.M. | 707/747 Daily |
| Singapore | 893/841 | 7:35 P.M. | 747/707 Mo/We/Fr |
| Manila | 893/841 | 7:35 P.M. | 707/747 Tu/Th/Sa/Su |
| Sydney | 893/811 | 7:35 P.M. | 707 Mo |
| Melbourne | 895 | 8:00 P.M. | 707/747 We/Sa |
| | | **From Portland** | |
| Sydney | 893/811 | 6:10 P.M. | 707/Su/Mo/Tu 707/747/We/Th/Fr/Sa |
| Tokyo | 891/831 | 9:15 A.M. | 707/747 Daily |
| Singapore | 893/841 | 6:10 P.M. | 707/747 Mo/We/Fr |
| Manila | 893/841 | 6:10 P.M. | 707/747 Tu/Th/Sa/Su |

Test your program with the following departures and destinations.

| | |
|---|---|
| Seattle, Tokyo | Seattle, Melbourne |
| Seattle, Auckland | Seattle, Manila |
| Portland, Manila | Seattle, Sydney |
| Portland, Tokyo | Seattle, Sydney |
| Portland, Manila | Seattle, Sydney |
| Seattle, Auckland | Portland, Sydney |
| Seattle, Melbourne | Seattle, Manila |

See what happens if you enter Portland, Auckland.

**Output**  Your data files should look like this:

```
File 1
AUCKLAND     815          11:45 P.M.   707       TU/SU
TOKYO        891/831      8 A.M.       707/747   DAILY
SINGAPORE    893/841      7:35 P.M.    747/707   MO/WE/FR
MANILA       893/841      7:35 P.M.    707/747   TU/TH/SA/SU
SYDNEY       893/811      7:35 P.M.    707       MO
MELBOURNE    895          8 P.M.       707/747   WE/SA

File 2
SYNDEY       893/811      6:10 P.M.    707       SU/MO/TU
                                       707/747   WE/TH/FR/SA
TOKYO        891/831      9:15 A.M.    707/747   DAILY
SINGAPORE    893/841      6:10 P.M.    707/747   MO/WE/FR
MANILA       893/841      6:10 P.M.    707/747   TU/TH/SA/SU
```

A typical interactive session could look like this:

```
FLIGHT INFORMATION IS AVAILABLE FROM: SEATTLE-
  TO: AUCKLAND, TOKYO, SINGAPORE, MANILA, SYDNEY, AND MELBOURNE

FLIGHT INFORMATION IS AVAILABLE FROM: PORTLAND-
  TO: SYDNEY, TOKYO, SINGAPORE, AND MANILA
```

```
TO STOP PROCESSING ENTER S, S FOR EACH RESPONSE
ENTER DEPARTURE CITY (PORT OR SEA)? SEA
ENTER DESTINATION CITY (FIRST 3 CHARACTERS)? SYD
----------------------------------------------------------------
                         FLT #    LEAVES    REMARKS
----------------------------------------------------------------
FROM:SEATTLE- TO: SYDNEY  893/811  7:35 P.M. 707 MO
----------------------------------------------------------------


ENTER DEPARTURE CITY (PORT OR SEA)? PORT
ENTER DESTINATION CITY (FIRST 3 CHARACTERS)? SIN
----------------------------------------------------------------
                         FLT #    LEAVES    REMARKS
----------------------------------------------------------------
FROM:PORTLAND- TO: SINGAPORE 893/841 6:10P.M. 707/747    MO/WE/FR
----------------------------------------------------------------


ENTER DEPARTURE CITY (PORT OR SEA)? S
ENTER DESTINATION CITY (FIRST 3 CHARACTERS)? S
```

**15.20** **Purpose** To create a large sequential data file and retrieve the file information interactively.

**Problem** Below are amounts, due dates, rates, and yields for a new bond issue. Treat this information as a data file. Write a conversational program that, when the due date is inputted, will print out the amount, rate, and yield for that date.

**Data** Use the following data:

| AMOUNT | DUE | RATE | YIELD |
|---|---|---|---|
| $ 290,000 | 1996 | 10.25% | 7.25% |
| 315,000 | 1997 | 10.25 | 7.50 |
| 335,000 | 1998 | 10.25 | 7.75 |
| 355,000 | 1999 | 10.25 | 8.00 |
| 385,000 | 2000 | 10.25 | 8.20 |
| 410,000 | 2001 | 10.25 | 8.35 |
| 440,000 | 2002 | 10.25 | 8.45 |
| 470,000 | 2003 | 10.25 | 8.60 |
| 505,000 | 2004 | 10.25 | 8.70 |
| 540,000 | 2005 | 10.25 | 8.85 |
| 580,000 | 2006 | 10.00 | 9.00 |
| 620,000 | 2007 | 10.00 | 9.10 |
| 665,000 | 2008 | 10.00 | 9.25 |
| 710,000 | 2009 | 10.00 | 9.40 |
| 755,000 | 2010 | 10.00 | 9.60 |
| 810,000 | 2011 | 10.00 | 9.75 |
| 1,005,000 | 2012 | 10.00 | 9.90 |

Test your program by inputting these dates: 1996, 1999, 2000, 1997, 2002, 1998, 2011. See what happens if you enter 1990 or 2020.

**Output** The lines in your data file should look like this:

```
290000   1996   10.25   7.25
315000   1997   10.25   7.50
335000   1998   10.25   7.75
```

```
355000   1999   10.25   8.00
385000   2000   10.25   8.20
410000   2001   10.25   8.35
  . . .  . . .  . . . .  . . . .
810000   2011   10.00   9.75
1005000  2012   10.00   9.90
```

A typical interactive session could look like this:

```
ENTER DUE DATE AS A FOUR DIGIT NUMBER, OR S TO STOP: 2001
AMOUNT    DUE    RATE%   YIELD%
$410000   2001   10.25    8.35%

ENTER DUE DATE AS A FOUR DIGIT NUMBER, OR S TO STOP: 2010

AMOUNT    DUE    RATE%   YIELD%
$755000   2010   10.00    9.60%

ENTER DUE DATE AS A FOUR DIGIT NUMBER, OR S TO STOP: S
```

**15.21**  **Purpose**  To create a random data file and process it with another program.

**Problem**  Write and run a program that creates a random access data file for the data given below. Create a program that will access and output the information in that file.

**Data**  Use the following data:

| PLANT | UNITS PRODUCED |
|-------|----------------|
| 1 | 3,400 |
| 2 | 4,200 |
| 3 | 2,800 |
| 4 | 3,100 |
| 5 | 4,000 |
| 6 | 5,500 |

**Output**  Your output should look like this:

```
PLANT 1   UNITS PRODUCED 3,400
PLANT 2   UNITS PRODUCED 4,200
PLANT 3   UNITS PRODUCED 2,800
PLANT 4   UNITS PRODUCED 3,100
PLANT 5   UNITS PRODUCED 4,000
PLANT 6   UNITS PRODUCED 5,500
```

**15.22**  **Purpose**  To create a random data file and test it within the same program.

**Problem**  Write and run a program that creates a random access data file for the data given below. As part of your program, have a test segment to check if the data has been successfully written to the disk file.

**Data**  Use the following data:

| DIVISION | MANAGER'S NAME | TELEPHONE NUMBER |
|----------|----------------|------------------|
| 1 | Stan Stern | 633–5550 |
| 2 | Allan Price | 711–2345 |
| 3 | Liz Kent | 355–9876 |
| 4 | Jack Baker | 632–6110 |

Use the division number as the record number. Do not have the division number as part of the file; the record has only two fields, a name and a telephone number.

**Output**    Your output should look like this:

```
ENTER A DIVISION NUMBER? 3
  3       LIZ KENT        355-9876
ENTER A DIVISION NUMBER? 1
  1       STAN STERN      633-5550
```

**15.23    Purpose**   To create a random access file and retrieve the information interactively.

**Problem**   For the airline flight schedule given below, create a random access data file. Write and run a program that is conversational in design to display the flight schedule when a flight number is entered.

**Data**    Use the following data:

| FLIGHT NUMBER | LEAVE | ARRIVE | MEALS |
|---|---|---|---|
| 985 | 7:10 A.M. | 9:13 A.M. | Breakfast |
| 201 | 9:10 A.M. | 11:17 A.M. | Snack |
| 327 | 12:10 P.M. | 2:11 P.M. | Lunch |
| 817 | 3:00 P.M. | 5:17 P.M. | Snack |
| 123 | 5:00 P.M. | 7:03 P.M. | Dinner |

**Output**    A typical interactive session could look like this:

```
ENTER A FLIGHT NUMBER: 201
  NO.        LEAVE            ARRIVE          MEALS
  201         9:10 A.M.        11:17 A.M.      SNACK
DO YOU WISH TO CONTINUE (Y = YES, N = NO)? Y

ENTER A FLIGHT NUMBER: 817
  NO.        LEAVE            ARRIVE          MEALS
  817         3 P.M.           5:17 P.M.       SNACK
DO YOU WISH TO CONTINUE (Y = YES, N = NO)? N
```

**15.24    Purpose**   To create a random access file and retrieve the information interactively with two separate programs.

**Problem**   a. For the part numbers and current inventory given below, create a random access data file.

b. Write and run a program that is interactive in design to display the current inventory for a part after the part number has been entered.

c. Write and run a program that will subtract from current inventory the order-size amounts shown below. The part number and order size are entered as input data. If there is insufficient inventory to cover the order, that condition should be printed out.

**Data**    Use the following data for parts a and c of the problem:

a.    **PART NUMBER**         **CURRENT INVENTORY**
    3241                         250
    1345                          75
    1432                         125
    4321                          75
    3311                          80

| c. | Part number: | 3241 | 1345 | 1432 | 4321 | 3311 |
|----|--------------|------|------|------|------|------|
|    | Order size:  | 175  | 80   | 100  | 50   | 100  |

**Output**    Your output for parts b and c of the problem could look like this:

b.    
```
ENTER A PART NUMBER: 4321
PART 4321  CURR. INV. 75
DO YOU WISH TO CONTINUE (Y = YES, N = NO)? Y

ENTER A PART NUMBER: 1345
PART 1345  CURR. INV. 75

DO YOU WISH TO CONTINUE (Y = YES, N = NO)? N
```

c.    
```
ENTER A PART NUMBER AND ORDER SIZE AS ####,###: 1432,100

PART NUMBER   CURR.INV.   ORDER SIZE   END.INV.
   1432          125          100         25

DO YOU WISH TO CONTINUE (Y = YES, N = NO)? Y

ENTER A PART NUMBER AND ORDER SIZE AS ####,###: 3311,100
ORDER IS GREATER THAN CURRENT INVENTORY ....

DO YOU WISH TO CONTINUE (Y = YES, N = NO)? N
```

# CASE APPLICATION PROBLEMS AND PROGRAMMING PROJECTS

Upon completing this chapter, you will be able to do the following:

- Understand the techniques of structure design.
- Discuss the concept of modularity.
- Plan and develop a large program as a solution of a project problem.
- See how a program can solve a problem related to production decision making.
- See how a program can be used to carry out a Monte Carlo simulation.
- Write a large program that could create a billing system, an inventory control system, a payroll system, a tax deduction analyzer, or a repetitive typing–word processing system.

In previous chapters the case illustration programs were usually limited to less than 50 lines of code, or about one page in length. Because of their limited size, these programs were easy for one person to code, test, and document. Typically though, application programs are much longer and more involved than what we have seen so far. In this chapter we illustrate programs for several longer and more involved case applications. The chapter begins with some structured design ideas that can help you develop a plan for carrying out the larger programming projects that conclude the chapter.

## STRUCTURED DESIGN

Structured design can be viewed as a collection of guidelines and techniques that can help you, the program designer, produce a better product. Because larger problems are typically more complex and involved, you need to reduce the complexity to manageable proportions. One approach to breaking up a problem into smaller pieces involves following a top-down design approach.

### Top-Down Design

After you have been given a large, complex problem and before you begin coding, a plan, or strategy, is needed so that you can carry out the project successfully. Top-down design is a planning strategy that involves reducing large, complex problems into smaller, less complex ones. Figure 16.1 illustrates how this need to simplify can be approached.

At stage 1 is the stated problem, with its need for a program. At stage 2 you establish a main program followed by three *modules* or functions. These modules correspond to the three program segments that relate to data input, computations and processing, and output. Within each of these modules are additional extensions in the form of other modules, as shown in stage 3. This last stage is often referred to as a *hierarchy chart* or *structure chart*. It is a convenient way to show the overall design of a program and is useful as part of the documentation for a project.

### Modularity

Each module you write can be considered a small program within a larger program. For example, a subroutine may be a module.

As you look ahead at the solutions to Case Problems I and II, you will note that subroutines are utilized to carry out the major functions of data entry, computation and processing, and output. Figure 16.2 provides a subroutine structure chart for Case Problem I.

A major benefit of programming with modules is that it is easy to test and debug each module as it is completed. Errors can be detected and corrected before the whole program is completed. Early error detection improves the overall quality of the final program. After all, a small amount of program code in the form of a module is easier to review and examine than several hundred lines of program code all at one time. Also, by knowing

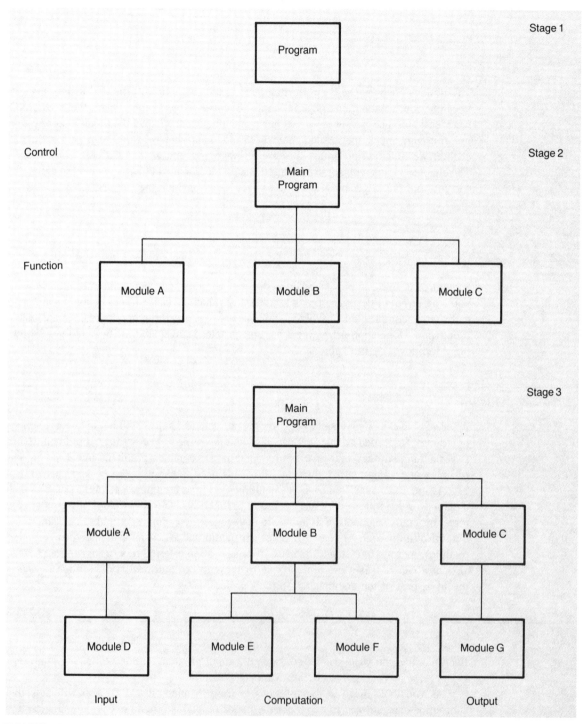

**FIGURE 16.1** Development Stages Leading to a Structure Chart

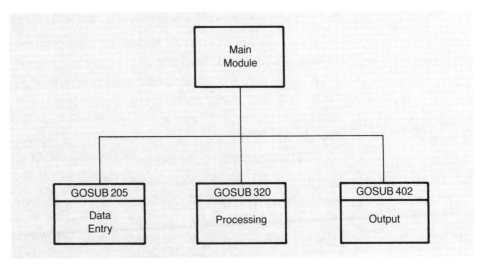

**FIGURE 16.2**   Case I, Subroutine Structure Chart

ahead of time what each module is to be used for, a project can be divided up among several programmers so that a team approach to the overall project is possible.

## Program Development

Before you begin any of the programming projects in this chapter, create a structure chart. This chart should have the general appearance of stage 3 in Figure 16.1, with various tasks labeled in each module box. This gives you a plan of attack for your coding and testing. If your main program is a series of subroutine calls as in the program solutions for Case Problems I and II, they can be easily coded and tested as a single unit. From there you can proceed to add modules to the program, one at a time, testing each task and changing what is required. By doing this, you can clean up any problems along the way, rather than all at once. In the end, this approach helps to make the final program a bug-free quality product.

Observe that the programs for Case Problems I and II each have a large number of lines for internal documentation in the form of REM statements or comments. Your final project programs should have a similar amount of documentation.

## CASE PROBLEM I, PRODUCTION DECISION MAKING

To determine how much of an item should be produced when its production is not continuous but in batches, an employee can use a computer program to find which batch size is the most profitable. In this case problem, the number of batches to produce is based on total expected profit, which is the average profit that can be obtained given the probability of a demand and multiplying it by the profit for that demand. The total is obtained by summing up each of the expected profits for each demand. Symbolically, this can be written as

$$EP = \Sigma(P(D) \times \text{profit of } D)$$

where $EP$ is expected profit, $\Sigma$ is sum of, and $P(D)$ is probability of demand ($D$).

Program 16.1 is based on the following relevant facts:

**1.** A company can make one, two, three, four, or five batches of a chemical a day.

**2.** The daily demand varies from zero to five or more batches.

**3.** The company gains $3,000 for each batch sold and loses $3,500 for each batch made but not sold.

**4.** Actual sales for the last 10 days were five, seven, one, zero, two, three, three, one, one, and four batches.

The program, using the above information, does the following:

**1.** Estimates the probability of demand based on the 10 days' sales data.

**2.** Calculates and prints out the profits and expected profits for each day for each production level (that is, one, two, three, four, and five batches).

**3.** Determines the most profitable number of batches to be produced based on the total expected profit found for each batch size.

## PROGRAM 16.1    Case Problem I, Production Decision Making

```
10 REM ***CASE PROBLEM 1 - PRODUCTION DECISION MAKING ***
15 REM PROGRAMMER- (name of person) DATE- mm/dd/yy
20 REM
25 REM           ***PROGRAM DESCRIPTION ***
30 REM
35 REM ***THIS PROGRAM WILL DETERMINE HOW MUCH OF AN ITEM
40 REM ***SHOULD BE PRODUCED WHEN PRODUCTION OF THAT ITEM IS
45 REM ***IN BATCHES RATHER THAN A CONTINUOUS PROCESS.
50 REM ***THE PROGRAM BELOW DOES THE FOLLOWING:
55 REM ***   CALCULATES THE ESTIMATED PROBABILITY OF DEMAND
60 REM ***   CALCULATES PROFITS AND EXPECTED PROFITS
65 REM ***   PRINTS OUT PROFITS AND EXPECTED PROFITS
70 REM ***   DETERMINES THE MOST PROFITABLE NUMBER OF
75 REM ***   BATCHES TO BE PRODUCED BASED ON EXPECTED PROFIT.
80 REM
85 REM   *** VARIABLE DESCRIPTION ***
90 REM
100 REM   A- THE DEMAND
105 REM   B- THE LOOP VARIABLE ON BATCHES PRODUCED
110 REM   F$,F1$,F2$,F3$- PRINT USING FORMATS
115 REM   I - LOOP INDEX
120 REM   J - THE LOOP VARIABLE ON BATCHES DEMANDED
125 REM   K - THE BATCHES PRODUCED
130 REM   P - THE PROFIT
135 REM   Q - THE BEST PROFIT SO FAR
140 REM   T - THE TOTAL EXPECTED PROFIT
145 REM   X - THE PROBABILITY OF DEMAND ARRAY
150 REM -----------------------------------
155 REM
160 REM   *** MAIN PROGRAM ROUTINE ***
165 REM
170       GOSUB 205 'Subroutine for data entry & initialization
175       GOSUB 320 'Subroutine for computations & processing
180       GOSUB 402 'Subroutine for output display
185       GOTO 995 'goto end when completed
```

```
190 REM
195 REM    *** SUBROUTINE FOR DATA ENTRY & INITIALIZATION ***
200    REM
205    FOR A = 0 TO 5              'initialize demand counts to zero
210         LET X(A) = 0
215    NEXT A
220 REM
225    FOR I = 1 TO 10
230         READ A                 'read past demand for last 10 days
235         DATA 5,7,1,0,2,3,3,1,1,4
240         IF A > 5 THEN LET A = 5 'if demand is more than 5, set A = 5
245              LET X(A)=X(A)+1     'count occurrence of demand
250    NEXT I
255    REM
260    FOR J = 0 TO 5              'derive probabilities of demand
265         LET X(J) = X(J)/10
270    NEXT J
275    REM
280        RETURN
285 REM
290 REM    ***  SUBROUTINE FOR COMPUTATIONS AND PROCESSING   ***
295 REM
300 REM     FORM OUTER LOOP ON BATCHES PRODUCED USING VARIABLE B
305 REM       INITIALIZE TOTAL EXPECTED PROFIT T TO ZERO
310 REM      FORM INNER LOOP ON BATCHES DEMANDED
315 REM
320  FOR B = 1 TO 5                    'outer loop on batches produced
325    LET T(B) = 0              'set total expected profit to zero
330    FOR J = 0 TO 5            'inner loop on demand
335     LET P(B,J) = 3000 * B   'profit when B is prod. & demand is J & J >=B
340     IF J > B THEN 350 'is demand greater than or = to amt produced?
345        LET P(B,J) = 3000 * J - 3500 * (B-J) 'calculate loss
350        LET T(B) = T(B) + P(B,J) * X(J)
355    NEXT J
360    IF Q > T(B) THEN 375  'compare expected profit with profit so far
365      LET Q = T(B)
370      LET K = B              'save in K best no. of batches produced
375  NEXT B
380 REM
385      RETURN
390 REM
395 REM *** SUBROUTINE TO PRINT OUT CALCULATED RESULTS ***
400 REM
402    LET F$ = "   DEMAND     PROB.      PROFIT    EXPECTED   PROFIT"
405    LET F1$ = "     ##        .##       $$###,###       $$###,###"
410    LET F2$ = "            TOTAL EXPECTED PROFIT    $$###,###"
412    LET F3$ = STRING$(54,"-")
415 REM
420  FOR B = 1 TO 5
425      PRINT "NO. OF BATCHES TO BE MADE";B
430      PRINT F3$
435      PRINT F$
440      REM
445      FOR J = 0 TO 5
450            PRINT USING F1$;J,X(J), P(B,J), P(B,J)*X(J)
455      NEXT J
460      REM
465      PRINT F3$
470      PRINT USING F2$;T(B)
475      PRINT
480  NEXT B
```

```
482      PRINT "THE MOST PROFITABLE NO. OF BATCHES TO BE MADE IS ";K
485 REM
490      PRINT
495      PRINT
500     RETURN
995 END

RUN
```

NO. OF BATCHES TO BE MADE  1
--------------------------------------------------------

| DEMAND | PROB. | PROFIT | EXPECTED PROFIT |
|--------|-------|--------|-----------------|
| 0 | .10 | -$3,500 | -$350 |
| 1 | .30 | $3,000 | $900 |
| 2 | .10 | $3,000 | $300 |
| 3 | .20 | $3,000 | $600 |
| 4 | .10 | $3,000 | $300 |
| 5 | .20 | $3,000 | $600 |

--------------------------------------------------------

```
        TOTAL EXPECTED PROFIT    $2,350
```

NO. OF BATCHES TO BE MADE  2
--------------------------------------------------------

| DEMAND | PROB. | PROFIT | EXPECTED PROFIT |
|--------|-------|--------|-----------------|
| 0 | .10 | -$7,000 | -$700 |
| 1 | .30 | -$500 | -$150 |
| 2 | .10 | $6,000 | $600 |
| 3 | .20 | $6,000 | $1,200 |
| 4 | .10 | $6,000 | $600 |
| 5 | .20 | $6,000 | $1,200 |

--------------------------------------------------------

```
        TOTAL EXPECTED PROFIT    $2,750
```

NO. OF BATCHES TO BE MADE  3
--------------------------------------------------------

| DEMAND | PROB. | PROFIT | EXPECTED PROFIT |
|--------|-------|--------|-----------------|
| 0 | .10 | -$10,500 | -$1,050 |
| 1 | .30 | -$4,000 | -$1,200 |
| 2 | .10 | $2,500 | $250 |
| 3 | .20 | $9,000 | $1,800 |
| 4 | .10 | $9,000 | $900 |
| 5 | .20 | $9,000 | $1,800 |

--------------------------------------------------------

```
        TOTAL EXPECTED PROFIT    $2,500
```

NO. OF BATCHES TO BE MADE  4
--------------------------------------------------------

| DEMAND | PROB. | PROFIT | EXPECTED PROFIT |
|--------|-------|--------|-----------------|
| 0 | .10 | -$14,000 | -$1,400 |
| 1 | .30 | -$7,500 | -$2,250 |
| 2 | .10 | -$1,000 | -$100 |
| 3 | .20 | $5,500 | $1,100 |
| 4 | .10 | $12,000 | $1,200 |
| 5 | .20 | $12,000 | $2,400 |

--------------------------------------------------------

```
        TOTAL EXPECTED PROFIT    $950
```

```
NO. OF BATCHES TO BE MADE  5
--------------------------------------------------------
   DEMAND    PROB.        PROFIT    EXPECTED PROFIT
     0        .10      -$17,500        -$1,750
     1        .30      -$11,000        -$3,300
     2        .10       -$4,500          -$450
     3        .20        $2,000           $400
     4        .10        $8,500           $850
     5        .20       $15,000         $3,000
--------------------------------------------------------

          TOTAL EXPECTED PROFIT       -$1,250

THE MOST PROFITABLE NO. OF BATCHES TO BE MADE IS 2
```

## CASE PROBLEM II. PROCESS SIMULATION

Computer simulation is useful for management planning and analysis of certain kinds of operations. This case problem uses Monte Carlo simulation to examine the processing of mail bags in a mail order department.

Monte Carlo simulation is a technique that generates artificial outcomes that represent the process being examined. The technique requires that the process being studied have probabilistic outcomes. From such information, outcomes can be predicted by random sampling instructions included in the computer program. The results obtained can then be analyzed in terms of the management decisions that must be made.

Program 16.2 is designed to carry out a Monte Carlo simulation. The program is based on these relevant facts:

1. A mail order department has two employees who process bags of mail. The bags are delivered during the night for processing that begins at 9 A.M. the next morning.

2. It takes an employee one hour to process the contents of one mail bag.

3. At the end of the day, any unprocessed mail bags are left for processing on the next day.

4. Each employee works seven hours a day, five days a week.

5. Over the last 50 days, the distribution of the number of bags arriving has been as follows:

| NUMBER OF BAGS ARRIVING | RELATIVE FREQUENCY | CUMULATIVE FREQUENCY |
|---|---|---|
| 12 | .13 | .13 |
| 13 | .22 | .35 |
| 14 | .26 | .61 |
| 15 | .30 | .91 |
| 16 | .06 | .97 |
| 17 | .03 | 1.00 |
|  | 1.00 |  |

*Note*: The relative frequency represents the probability distribution. For example, 13 percent of the time 12 bags were received, 22 percent of the time 13 bags were received, and so on. The cumulative frequency was obtained by adding each successive relative frequency value. Thus, for example, the cumulative frequency for 13 bags is .13 + .22 = .35, which represents the probability that 13 or fewer bags have arrived. These values are used in Program 16.2 to do the random sampling of outcomes (number of bags arriving).

The purpose of the simulation is to help answer these questions:

**1.** How many mail bags can arrive each day over a 50-day period?

**2.** How many mail bags remain unprocessed each day over a 50-day period?

**3.** On the average, how many bags arrive each day?

**4.** On the average, how many bags are unprocessed each day?

**5.** Out of 50 days, on how many days were mail bags unprocessed?

The output of the computer simulation generates answers to these questions. Management can then decide whether to (a) hire additional employees, (b) put the present employees on overtime, or (c) maintain the present operation.

## PROGRAM 16.2 Case Problem II, Process Simulation

```
10   REM   *** CASE PROBLEM II - PROCESS SIMULATION
15   REM        PROGRAMMER- (name of person) DATE- mm/dd/yy
20   REM
25   REM   *** PROGRAM DESCRIPTION ***
30   REM
35   REM  ** THIS PROGRAM WILL DO A MONTE CARLO SIMULATION OF A MAIL ORDER
40   REM  ** DEPARTMENT PROCESSING OPERATION. THE PROGRAM SIMULATES HOW MANY
45   REM  ** MAIL BAGS ARRIVE EACH DAY; THE NUMBER OF MAIL
50   REM  ** BAGS THAT REMAIN UNPROCESSED EACH DAY; THE
55   REM  ** AVERAGE NUMBER OF MAIL BAGS THAT ARRIVE EACH
60   REM  ** DAY; THE AVERAGE NUMBER UNPROCESSED EACH DAY
65   REM  ** AND THE TOTAL NUMBER OF DAYS THAT THERE WERE
70   REM  ** UNPROCESSED MAIL BAGS.
75   REM
80   REM          **VARIABLE LIST **
100  REM
105  REM    A IS THE ACCUMULATION OF BAGS DELIVERED
110  REM    B IS THE NUMBER SET TO BAGS DELIVERED
115  REM    C IS THE CAPACITY TO PROCESS MAIL BAGS
120  REM    E IS THE NUMBER OF WORKERS PRESENT
125  REM    D REPRESENTS DAY NUMBER IN FIFTY DAY PERIOD
130  REM    I SERVES AS A COUNTER
135  REM    L IS THE TOTAL NUMBER OF BAGS UNPROCESSED
140  REM    N IS A RANDOM NUMBER FUNCTION
145  REM    P IS THE TOTAL NUMBER OF BAGS TO BE PROCESSED
150  REM    U IS THE NUMBER OF BAGS UNPROCESSED FOR EACH DAY
155  REM    Y IS THE NUMBER OF DAYS THERE ARE UNPROCESSED BAGS
160  REM  -------------------------------------------------
165  REM
170  REM          *** MAIN PROGRAM ROUTINE ***
175  REM
180  REM
185        GOSUB 225 'subroutine for data entry & initialization
190        GOSUB 280 'subroutine for processing & computations
195        GOSUB 400 'subroutine for output display
200        GOTO 505  'goto end when completed
205  REM
```

```
210 REM
215 REM   *** SUBROUTINE FOR DATA ENTRY & INITIALIZATION ***
220 REM
225      DIM B(100), P(100), U(100)
230      LET A = 0      'accumulation of bags is set to zero
235      LET L = 0      'total number of bags unprocessed at start, set to zero
240      LET U(1) = 0 'number of bags unprocessed, day 1, set to zero
245      LET Y = 0      'number of days with unprocessed bags, at start, set to zero
250      LET E = 2      'employees set at 2
255      LET C = E * 7 'capactiy = no. employees x 7 bags per day
260         RETURN
265 REM
270 REM *** SUBROUTINE FOR PROCESSING & COMPUTATIONS ***
275 REM
280   RANDOMIZE TIMER
285   FOR D = 1 TO 50
290   LET N = RND                        'pick a random number & then
295   IF N <= 1.0 THEN LET B(D) = 17     'test the number picked
300   IF N <= .97 THEN LET B(D) = 16
305   IF N <= .91 THEN LET B(D) = 15
310   IF N <= .61 THEN LET B(D) = 14
315   IF N <= .35 THEN LET B(D) = 13
320   IF N <= .13 THEN LET B(D) = 12
325     LET A = A + B(D)                 'accumulate # bags delivered
330     LET  P(D) = B(D)+U(D-1)          'total = delivered + unprocessed from previous day
335     IF P(D) > C THEN 350             'is total bags to be processed > capacity
340       LET U(D) = 0                   'if enough capacity, unprocessed is set to zero
345       GOTO 365
350         LET U(D) = P(D) - C          'unprocessed = total bags to be proc. - capacity
355         LET L = L + U(D)             'total number of unprocessed bags
360         LET Y = Y + 1                'count of days there are unproc. bags
365 NEXT D
375      RETURN
380 REM
385 REM
390 REM     ***     SUBROUTINE TO PRINT OUT RESULTS    ***
395 REM
400 LET F$= "DAY       # MAIL BAGS     TOTAL # BAGS     NUMBER        MAILBAGS"
405 LET F0$="NUMBER    DELIVERED     TO BE PROCESSED   PROCESSED    UNPROCESSED"
410 LET F1$="  ##          ###            ###           ###          ## "
415 LET F2$="  TOTALS      ###                                       ### "
420 LET F3$="  AVERAGES   ##.##                                      ##.#"
422 PRINT F$
424 PRINT F0$
425 PRINT  STRING$(70,"-")
430 REM
435  FOR D= 1 TO 50
440         IF P(D) > C THEN 455
445             PRINT USING F1$; D,B(D),P(D),P(D),U(D)
450            GOTO 460
455               PRINT USING F1$;D,B(D),P(D),C,U(D)
460  NEXT D
465 REM
470        PRINT STRING$(70,"-")
475        PRINT USING F2$;A,L
480        PRINT USING F3$;A/50,L/50
485        PRINT
490        PRINT "OUT OF 50 DAYS";Y; "DAYS HAD MAIL UNPROCESSED"
495         RETURN
500 REM
505 END
```

| RUN DAY NUMBER | # MAIL BAGS DELIVERED | TOTAL # BAGS TO BE PROCESSED | NUMBER PROCESSED | MAILBAGS UNPROCESSED |
|---|---|---|---|---|
| 1 | 15 | 15 | 14 | 1 |
| 2 | 14 | 15 | 14 | 1 |
| 3 | 13 | 14 | 14 | 0 |
| 4 | 15 | 15 | 14 | 1 |
| 5 | 15 | 16 | 14 | 2 |
| 6 | 12 | 14 | 14 | 0 |
| 7 | 14 | 14 | 14 | 0 |
| 8 | 16 | 16 | 14 | 2 |
| 9 | 16 | 18 | 14 | 4 |
| 10 | 15 | 19 | 14 | 5 |
| 11 | 14 | 19 | 14 | 5 |
| 12 | 12 | 17 | 14 | 3 |
| 13 | 12 | 15 | 14 | 1 |
| 14 | 15 | 16 | 14 | 2 |
| 15 | 13 | 15 | 14 | 1 |
| 16 | 15 | 16 | 14 | 2 |
| 17 | 15 | 17 | 14 | 3 |
| 18 | 12 | 15 | 14 | 1 |
| 19 | 15 | 16 | 14 | 2 |
| 20 | 15 | 17 | 14 | 3 |
| 21 | 13 | 16 | 14 | 2 |
| 22 | 13 | 15 | 14 | 1 |
| 23 | 14 | 15 | 14 | 1 |
| 24 | 13 | 14 | 14 | 0 |
| 25 | 13 | 13 | 13 | 0 |
| 26 | 15 | 15 | 14 | 1 |
| 27 | 15 | 16 | 14 | 2 |
| 28 | 12 | 14 | 14 | 0 |
| 29 | 13 | 13 | 13 | 0 |
| 30 | 16 | 16 | 14 | 2 |
| 31 | 13 | 15 | 14 | 1 |
| 32 | 15 | 16 | 14 | 2 |
| 33 | 13 | 15 | 14 | 1 |
| 34 | 13 | 14 | 14 | 0 |
| 35 | 15 | 15 | 14 | 1 |
| 36 | 15 | 16 | 14 | 2 |
| 37 | 16 | 18 | 14 | 4 |
| 38 | 15 | 19 | 14 | 5 |
| 39 | 13 | 18 | 14 | 4 |
| 40 | 16 | 20 | 14 | 6 |
| 41 | 16 | 22 | 14 | 8 |
| 42 | 15 | 23 | 14 | 9 |
| 43 | 13 | 22 | 14 | 8 |
| 44 | 16 | 24 | 14 | 10 |
| 45 | 12 | 22 | 14 | 8 |
| 46 | 15 | 23 | 14 | 9 |
| 47 | 14 | 23 | 14 | 9 |
| 48 | 13 | 22 | 14 | 8 |
| 49 | 13 | 21 | 14 | 7 |
| 50 | 13 | 20 | 14 | 6 |

| TOTALS | 704 | | | 156 |
|---|---|---|---|---|
| AVERAGES | 14.08 | | | 3.1 |

OUT OF 50 DAYS 42 DAYS HAD MAIL BAGS UNPROCESSED

## Project I, Design of a Computerized Billing System

**Background**   The G&E Power Co., Inc., is a public utility that wants to set up a computerized billing system. You have been asked to design a program to meet their needs. Your program will be a prototype for handling two types of customers. Customer 1 pays all bills on time. Customer 2 fails to pay bills on time. Even though only two customers are being billed here, the program must ultimately be able to handle several thousand customers.

**Program Test Data**   The following information is to be used to test the program:

| CUSTOMER NAME/ADDRESS | ACCT. NO. | METER READINGS | | | | |
| | | Gas (Cu. Ft.) | | Elec. (kWh) | | |
| | | Begin | End | Begin | End | Mo. |
| Your Name | Soc. Sec. No. | 1000 | 1500 | 300 | 400 | Jan. |
| Your Address | | 1500 | 2000 | 400 | 500 | Feb. |
| | | 2000 | 2400 | 500 | 625 | Mar. |
| | | 2400 | 2800 | 625 | 700 | Apr. |
| Mr. Bill Due | 999–00–6666 | 1200 | 1400 | 180 | 210 | Jan. |
| Smogville, | | 1400 | 1650 | 210 | 290 | Feb. |
| USA | | 1650 | 2000 | 290 | 350 | Mar. |
| | | 2000 | 2400 | 350 | 400 | Apr. |

Four months of test data are to be used so that the logic of the program can be checked. This is necessary because of the warning notices that are printed out when bills are not paid (see below).

**Computational Information**   Rates and taxes are as follows:

| | |
|---|---|
| Gas | $.10 (10¢) per cu. ft. |
| Electricity | $.03 (3¢) per kWh (kilowatt-hour) |
| Taxes | 6 percent of total bill each month |

Each month a bill is sent to each customer, based on the following simple computation:

$$\text{Total without taxes} = \text{gas total} + \text{electric total}$$
$$= \text{no. of cu. ft.} \times \text{gas rate} + \text{no. kWh} \times \text{electric rate}$$
$$\text{Amount due} = (\text{total without taxes}) + (\text{total} \times \text{tax rate})$$

**Program Operation**   Each month, the meter readings for each customer are fed as data into the computer. The name, address, identification (account) number, and rates are already available as part of the program.

**Output Requirements**   The following printed output is desired: the present balance due, showing the month and dollar amount for gas and electricity; the usage for each item; the customer's name, address, and account number; any previous balance due; the taxes; and the total amount due. All of this output should appear as a billing statement. The form it should take is shown below.

If the customer is in arrears, one of the following notices must be printed on the statement:

**1.** First notice (no payment received after two months of service)

> Warning—No payment for two months.
> Your next notice will be for a cutoff
> of gas and electricity. Pay up now.

**2.** Second notice (no payment received after three months of service)

> Your gas and electricity have been cut off.
> Service will be restored when full payment
> is made of the amount due.

For a four-month period, your billing system should consist of a billing statement for each (two) customer for each month and one of the two notices described above, if appropriate. Remember that customer 1 pays all bills on time and customer 2 does not pay any bills. These facts should be built into your program so that the warning notices can be tested.

The output format below is based on a single monthly statement and warning notice.

```
------------------------------------------------------------
            **** G&E POWER COMPANY ****
               - MONTHLY STATEMENT-
------------------------------------------------------------
NAME:  MR. BILL DUE    DATE: APR. 1, 1990
ADDRESS: SMOGVILLE, USA
ACCOUNT NUMBER:  999-00-666
MONTH:  MAR.


------------------------------------------------------------
GAS        ELEC.    GAS         ELEC.       TOTAL
(CU. FT.)(KWH)      AMOUNT      AMOUNT      AMOUNT      TAX
        USAGE
------------------------------------------------------------
  350         60      $35.00      $1.80      $36.80   $2.21
------------------------------------------------------------
TOTAL AMOUNT INCLUDING TAX = 39.01

PREVIOUS BALANCE:    51.20
AMOUNT DUE FOR MAR.  39.01
TOTAL AMOUNT DUE:    90.21

------------------------------------------------------------
**** WARNING NOTICE ****

YOUR GAS AND ELECTRICITY HAVE BEEN CUT OFF. SERVICE
WILL BE RESTORED WHEN FULL PAYMENT IS MADE OF THE
AMOUNT DUE.
------------------------------------------------------------
```

**Documentation**   Include a structure chart with your program. Have a program title, programmer name, date, summary, and variable list as internal documentation. Use REM statements and comments to explain relevant segments of the program.

## Project II, Inventory Control System

**Background**   Your firm, Top Knotch Management Consultants Inc., Jamaica, New York 11439, has been hired by the Good Toy Co., Inc., Fun and Games Street, Any City, USA 10000 to write an inventory system program for their 1,000 different products. The final program is one that will allow an inventory clerk at the end of each day to merely inform the computer via a keyboard of the number of units of each product sold during the day. Such reporting of daily sales by product will provide a constant inventory updating for each product.

When the inventory of any particular item reaches a specified low point, new goods will be ordered to replenish the stock. These new orders are called the EOQ (economic order quantity). All new orders shall arrive on or before the inventory level of the products reaches zero. Figure 16.3 shows how a typical system works for *each* product.

**Programming Assignment**   You have been asked to write the prototype program for one of the products kept in the inventory. This program is to be conversational in design. Data is entered by means of INPUT statements.

The product is a small above ground swimming pool 12 feet in diameter that has an item number 738. It sells for $198 and has a purchase price of $100 from the wholesaler (Wet Pool Co., Inc., Lakeville, USA 20000). The pool can be ordered only in 50-unit lots. Reordering is required when inventory reaches 20 percent of the order size (EOQ). There are 25 units now in stock.

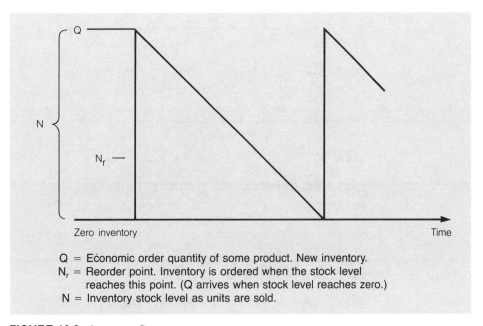

$Q$ = Economic order quantity of some product. New inventory.
$N_r$ = Reorder point. Inventory is ordered when the stock level
reaches this point. ($Q$ arrives when stock level reaches zero.)
$N$ = Inventory stock level as units are sold.

**FIGURE 16.3**   Inventory System

**Generating Sales Data**   To test the program, data for daily sales for the product is obtained by using two predefined BASIC functions, RND and INT. These functions together will generate random numbers from 0 to 10. For example:

```
 5 RANDOMIZE TIMER
10 FOR I = 1 TO 10
20     PRINT INT(11*RND),
30 NEXT I
99 END
```

The 10 numbers generated will represent sales data for each of the 10 days.

**Program and Output Requirements**   The Good Toy Co., Inc., would like this program to accomplish the following:

**1.** The program should "ask" the clerk the item number, description of the item sold from inventory, and the number of units sold during the day.

**2.** The program should result in the following printouts:
   a. Current inventory *after* the clerk inputs the desired information.
   b. A summary table of the day-by-day inventory for the product at the end of each five-day week. This table should show the total number of units sold and the dollar value of these sales, both day by day and for the whole week.
   c. When the reorder point, $N_r$, is reached, a warning that informs the clerk of this situation.
   d. An order form (when the reorder point is reached) that contains the supplier's address, the purchaser's address, the date of the order, the number of units being ordered, the item number, the item description, the retail unit cost, and the total retail cost of the order.

The output below is based on using five days of test data.

```
----------------------------------------------------
ITEM NO.  738 SMALL ROUND POOL

UNITS SOLD TODAY      CURRENT INVENTORY
----------------------------------------------------
 5                        20
----------------------------------------------------


----------------------------------------------------
ITEM NO.  738 SMALL ROUND POOL

UNITS SOLD TODAY      CURRENT INVENTORY
----------------------------------------------------
 5                        15
----------------------------------------------------


----------------------------------------------------
ITEM NO.  738 SMALL ROUND POOL

UNITS SOLD TODAY      CURRENT INVENTORY
----------------------------------------------------
 4                        11
----------------------------------------------------
```

```
----------------------------------------------------
ITEM NO.  738 SMALL ROUND POOL

UNITS SOLD TODAY     CURRENT INVENTORY
----------------------------------------------------
  9                        2
----------------------------------------------------


----------------------------------------------------
      WARNING NOTICE - REORDER POINT IS REACHED
      *******************************************
----------------------------------------------------
              ORDER FORM

FROM:  GOOD TOY CO., INC.           DATE:  /  /
       FUN AND GAMES ST.
       ANY CITY, U.S.A 10000

TO:   WET POOL CO., INC., LAKEVILLE, USA 20000
----------------------------------------------------
ITEM NUMBER 738
ITEM DESCRIPTION:  SMALL ROUND POOL

ORDER SIZE      UNIT COST     TOTAL COST OF THE ORDER
----------------------------------------------------
   50           $100.00        $5,000.00
----------------------------------------------------
ITEM NO.  738  SMALL ROUND POOL

UNITS SOLD TODAY     CURRENT INVENTORY
----------------------------------------------------
  1                       51
----------------------------------------------------


----------------------------------------------------
      WEEKLY REPORT - ITEM NO. 738 SMALL ROUND POOL
----------------------------------------------------
         TOTAL NO.    INVENTORY       TOTAL VALUE
         UNITS SOLD   AT END          OF SALES
----------------------------------------------------
DAY 1      5             20           $   990
DAY 2      5             15           $   990
DAY 3      4             11           $   792
DAY 4      9              2           $1,782
DAY 5      1             51           $   198
----------------------------------------------------
TOTALS    24                          $4,752
----------------------------------------------------
```

**Documentation**   Include a structure chart with your program. Have a program title, programmer name, date, summary, and variable list as internal documentation. Use REM statements and comments to explain relevant segments of the program.

**Background** The Alpha Co, Inc., wants to set up a computerized payroll accounting system that will be able to handle up to 30 employees. You have been hired to write a computer program to do the weekly payroll. Initially, you will write a test program for only two employees (see below).

**Pertinent Information** Each employee will have a record containing the following items of information:

1. Identification number (Social Security number)
2. Name
3. Number of dependents
4. Hourly wage
5. Pay information:
   a. Gross earnings
   b. Federal income tax and state income tax
   c. Social Security tax
   d. Net earnings
6. Year to date: all information in item 5 above

A paycheck is printed out for each employee each week. Along with the paycheck, the employee gets a stub detailing the information in items 5 and 6 above.

Weekly time cards are processed for each employee to obtain his or her gross pay (hours worked × hourly wage).

### Computational Requirements

1. To prepare the paychecks, the federal income tax to be withheld is computed as follows:
   a. The tax base is determined by subtracting from gross earnings $30 times the number of dependents.
   b. The amount to be withheld is computed from the following table:

   **IF THE AMOUNT OF THE TAX BASE IS:**

   | Over | But not over | The federal income tax to be withheld is: | | |
   |------|-------------|------|------|------|
   | $ 0 | $100 | | 14% | of excess over | $ 0 |
   | 100 | 200 | $ 14 + | 15% | | 100 |
   | 200 | 300 | 29 + | 16% | | 200 |
   | 300 | 400 | 45 + | 17% | | 300 |
   | 400 | 800 | 62 + | 19% | | 400 |
   | 800 | | 138 + | 22% | | 800 |

2. To prepare the paychecks, the state income tax to be withheld is computed on the basis of the following table:

   **IF THE GROSS WAGE IS:**

   | Over | But not over | The state tax to be withheld is: | | |
   |------|-------------|------|------|------|
   | $ 0 | $100 | | 2% | of excess over | $ 0 |
   | 100 | 300 | $2 + | 3% | | 100 |
   | 300 | 500 | 8 + | 4% | | 300 |
   | 500 | | 16 + | 5% | | 500 |

3. Social security tax is 10.8 percent of gross earnings, not to exceed $1,080 in any one year.

4. Overtime wages are at 1½ times the hourly wage for more than 35 hours worked in one week.

5. Net earnings (the amount of the check) equals gross earnings minus federal and state taxes plus the Social Security contribution.

6. Before writing the checks, pay-period figures should be added to year-to-date figures.

**Computer Output**   For each employee, for *each* week, the program should generate printouts of the following:

1. A company record for each employee having all of the six items listed under "Pertinent Information."

2. A paycheck for each employee showing name, identification number, company name, week 1 or 2, and the net wage.

3. A check stub having all of the items 5 and 6 listed under "Pertinent Information."

The output below is an example of what is required. It shows the results for the first week for one employee.

```
PLEASE ENTER THE DATE (i.e. mm/dd/yy)? 10/12/90
-------------------------------------------------------
-------------------------------------------------------
¦¦        THE ALPHA CO., INC.                        ¦¦
¦¦        PERTINENT INFORMATION                      ¦¦
-------------------------------------------------------


EMPLOYEE I.D. NUMBER:  113526400
EMPLOYEE NAME:  JOHN SMITH
RATE PER HOUR:   14
NUMBER OF DEPENDENTS:   1


DATE       HOURS     GROSS      FEDERAL    STATE    FICA    NET
           WORKED    EARNINGS   TAX        TAX      TAX     EARNINGS
-----------------------------------------------------------------------
10/12/90    42       $637.00    $101.33    $22.85   $68.80  $444.02

              YEAR TO DATE TOTALS
-----------------------------------------------------------------------
                     $637.00    $101.33    $22.85   $190.51 $444.02
-----------------------------------------------------------------------


-----------------------------------------------------------------------
              THE ALPHA CO., INC.
                                                   10/12/90

PAY TO THE ORDER OF: JOHN SMITH                 EXACTLY $444.02

BETA BANK OF AMERICA
JAMAICA, N.Y.  11439

                                          ----------------------
                                          AUTHORIZED SIGNATURE

-----------------------------------------------------------------------
```

```
WEEK 1
----------------------------------------------------------------

EMPLOYEE I.D. NUMBER:  113526400
EMPLOYEE NAME:  JOHN SMITH
RATE PER HOUR:   14
NUMBER OF DEPENDENTS:  1


DATE        HOURS      GROSS       FEDERAL     STATE     FICA      NET
            WORKED     EARNINGS    TAX         TAX       TAX       EARNINGS
----------------------------------------------------------------
10/12/90    42        $637.00     $101.33     $22.85    $68.80    $444.02

                YEAR TO DATE TOTALS
----------------------------------------------------------------
                      $637.00     $101.33     $22.85    $190.51   $444.02
----------------------------------------------------------------
```

**Program Test Data**  The following information for two employees is to be used to test the program:

| NAME | I.D. NUMBER (SOC. SEC. NO.) | NUMBER OF DEPENDENTS | WAGE/ HOUR | HOURS WORKED WEEK 1 | WEEK 2 |
|------|------------------------------|----------------------|-----------|---------------------|--------|
| Your name | Your number | 1 | $14 | 42 | 35 |
| Any worker | 111–88–9669 | 4 | 7 | 35 | 32 |

**Documentation**  Include a structure chart with your program. Have a program title, programmer name, date, summary, and variable list as internal documentation. Use REM statements and comments to explain relevant segments of the program.

## Project IV, Tax Deduction Analyzer

**Background**  Each year at tax time, *Form 1040*, the U.S. Individual Income Tax Return, is filed by millions of taxpayers. In many cases a Schedule A—Itemized Deductions is also filed with the form 1040. This schedule has the following categories, each with examples:

1. Medical and dental expenses—medicines and drugs, doctors, dentists, nurses, hospitals, insurance premiums, transportation, and other.

2. Taxes—state and local income, real estate, and other.

3. Interest expense—home mortgage interest and investment and personal interest.

4. Contributions—cash and other.

5. Casualty and theft losses—theft, fire, vandalism, and so forth.

6. Miscellaneous deductions.

Typically when preparing this schedule, an individual places a code (1–6), corresponding to the categories given above, next to the relevant entries in his or her checkbook register. Then the actual dollar amounts of those items that have been coded are posted to corresponding deduction categories that have been set up on an accounting spread sheet.

After itemizing expenditures for the entire year in this manner, each of the deduction classifications is totaled. These totals are then placed onto the Form 1040.

**Programming Assignment**   Write an interactive program that will enable a taxpayer to enter expenditures for each of the six categories given above. Here's how the program should work. Based on each relevant item in his or her checkbook register for the entire year, the taxpayer would enter the code for the expenditures and the amount expended. The program would sort out all of the items by expenditure classification and provide dollar totals for each of the six deduction groupings. In addition, the program should find the percentage of the dollar total of all deductions for each classification. A count of the items in each group should also be part of the program.

**Computer Output**   Output should consist of all expenditures that have been entered, grouped by classification. A summary of all six classifications should have an output format such as the one below:

| DEDUCTION TYPE | TOTAL | PERCENT | ITEM COUNT |
|---|---|---|---|
| 1. MEDICAL & DENTAL | $510 | 19.84 | 2 |
| 2. TAXES | $830 | 32.30 | 2 |
| 3. INTEREST | $550 | 21.40 | 2 |
| 4. CONTRIBUTIONS | $255 | 9.92 | 2 |
| 5. LOSSES | $200 | 7.78 | 2 |
| 6. MISCELLANEOUS | $225 | 8.75 | 2 |
| ------------------------------------------------------------ | | | |
| TOTAL | $2,570 | 100.00 | 12 |

**Program Test Data**   In order to test this program, a test data generation program, such as the one below, can be used to provide appropriate test data.

```
10 REM TEST DATA GENERATION PROGRAM FOR PROJECT IV
15 RANDOMIZE TIMER
20 LET FM$= "## ##   $$### !"
25 PRINT  "TEST DATA FORM IS - CHECK #  CODE (1-6)  EXPENDITURE"
30 PRINT
35 FOR D = 1 TO 50
40      PRINT USING FM$; D,INT(6*RND+1), INT(500*RND+1),
45 NEXT D
50 END
```

```
RUN
TEST DATA FORMAT IS - CHECK #  CODE (1-6)  EXPENDITURE

 1   3   $385!  2   6   $186!  3   5   $397!  4   2   $405!  5   6   $368!
 6   6   $364!  7   6   $490!  8   1   $351!  9   4   $442! 10   6    $55!
11   6   $496! 12   3   $480! 13   3   $241! 14   1   $480! 15   6   $432!
16   5   $426! 17   6   $471! 18   2   $495! 19   2   $  7! 20   1    $81!
21   2   $161! 22   6   $339! 23   6   $378! 24   3   $345! 25   4   $405!
26   1   $386! 27   3   $394! 28   5   $375! 29   4   $123! 30   5   $389!
31   3   $352! 32   6   $336! 33   4   $300! 34   3   $238! 35   3   $244!
36   4   $151! 37   4   $246! 38   4   $202! 39   6    $6! 40   4   $252!
41   3   $338! 42   5   $186! 43   3   $270! 44   3   $327! 45   4   $274!
46   1   $475! 47   2   $114! 48   3    $73! 49   3   $324! 50   4   $490!
```

**Documentation**   Include a structure chart with your program. Have a program title, programmer name, date, summary, and variable list as internal documentation. Use REM statements and comments to explain relevant segments of the program.

## Project V, Repetitive Typing or Word Processing

**Background**   *Boilerplate,* as a word processing term, means that a new document has been created by combining documents or parts of documents. Such document preparation is typical of legal contracts, wills, and other such lengthy written items.

**Program Requirements**   Develop a word processing program that will create boilerplate. Specifically what is desired is the creation of a home owners' insurance policy that is based on the loss coverage an individual wants to have.

The HomeOwners Insurance Company will provide coverage for any or all of 16 different personal property loss categories shown below:

1. Fire or lightning
2. Windstorm or hail
3. Explosion
4. Riot or civil commotion
5. Aircraft
6. Vehicles
7. Smoke
8. Vandalism or malicious mischief
9. Theft
10. Falling objects
11. Weight of ice, snow, or sleet
12. Collapse of a building or any part of a building
13. Water from broken plumbing
14. Steam from broken heating systems
15. Frozen heating or air-conditioning systems
16. Breakage of glass

Not all home owners may want all 16 areas of coverage since the cost of a policy increases with the number of categories covered. Provide the document preparer with an interactive menu from which areas (1–16) of policy coverage can be chosen.

**Program Outputs**   The output should consist of a fixed opening statement, followed by the item categories the policy will cover. For example, if only three categories are covered, the output may look like this:

```
     PERSONAL PROPERTY COVERAGE

  We insure for direct loss to property caused by

  1.    Smoke
  2.    Theft
  3.    Falling objects
```

Also provide the user with an interactive menu option to generate multiple copies (1, 2, or 3 . . .) of the final policy document. An example of a sample session and output is as follows:

```
RUN
PRESENTED BELOW IS A LIST OF ITEMS YOU CAN SELECT FOR THE POLICY

1. FIRE OR LIGHTNING
2. WINDSTORM OR HAIL
3. EXPLOSION
4. RIOT OR CIVIL COMMOTION
5. AIRCRAFT
6. VEHICLES
7. SMOKE
8. VANDALISM OR MALICIOUS MISCHIEF
9. THEFT
10. FALLING OBJECTS
11. WEIGHT OF ICE OR SNOW OR SLEET
12. COLLAPSE OF A BUILDING
13. WATER FROM BROKEN PLUMBING
14. STEAM FROM BROKEN HEATING SYSTEMS
15. FROZEN HEATING OR AIR CONDITIONING SYSTEMS
16. BREAKAGE OF GLASS

CHOOSE FROM THE COVERAGE LISTED ABOVE.
HOW MANY ITEMS DO YOU WANT TO ENTER INTO THE POLICY
(PLEASE TYPE THE NUMBER e.g. 1, 2, . . .,  16)   3

PLEASE TYPE IN THE ITEM NUMBER OF EACH ITEM THAT
YOU DESIRE TO GO INTO YOUR POLICY ONE AT A TIME

ITEM NUMBER 3

ITEM NUMBER 5

ITEM NUMBER 9

HOW MANY COPIES OF YOUR POLICY WOULD YOU LIKE?   1

*************************************************************

           PERSONAL PROPERTY COVERAGE

WE INSURE FOR DIRECT LOSS OF PROPERTY CAUSED BY THE FOLLOWING:

1. EXPLOSION
2. AIRCRAFT
3. THEFT

*************************************************************
```

**Data for the Program**    Test your program using the categories for the eight different policies given below.

| POLICY | COVERAGE CATEGORIES | | | | | | | |
|--------|---|---|---|---|---|---|---|---|
| 1 | 1 | 3 | 5 | | | | | |
| 2 | 1 | 2 | 4 | 7 | 8 | | | |
| 3 | 1 | 2 | 5 | 7 | 9 | 11 | | |
| 4 | 1 | 3 | 4 | 6 | 9 | 10 | | |
| 5 | 1 | 2 | 4 | 7 | 9 | 10 | 13 | |
| 6 | 1 | 2 | 4 | 7 | 8 | 11 | 12 | 15 |
| 7 | 1 | 3 | 5 | 7 | 9 | 10 | 12 | 14 |
| 8 | 1 | 3 | 5 | 7 | 8 | 11 | 13 | 15 | 16 |

**Documentation**    Include a structure chart with your program. Have a program title, programmer name, date, summary, and variable list as internal documentation. Use REM statements and comments to explain relevant segments of the program.

# SUMMARY OF MICROCOMPUTER COMMANDS

The following commands are used when working with BASIC. As shown, these commands are typed outside of your program, followed by pressing the Enter key.

| BASIC Command | Purpose and Example |
|---|---|
| AUTO | Automatically numbers lines by increments of 10 as program is entered. Ctrl + Break terminates this command. Alt + A.<br>AUTO<br>AUTO 20,10 numbers with increments of 10 beginning with line 20. |
| CLS | Clears the screen.<br>CLS |
| CONT | Continues the program execution after a pause or break. Function key F5.<br>CONT |
| DELETE | Erases lines in a program. Alt + D.<br>DELETE 10−40 erases the lines 10−40 inclusive. |
| FILES | Displays all the files on the current drive.<br>FILES<br>FILES ''B:'' displays files on drive indicated, in this case drive B. |
| KEY | Can deactivate and activate the function key display line on the bottom of the screen. Function key F9.<br>KEY OFF turns off the display.<br>KEY ON turns on the display. |
| KILL | Erases programs or files.<br>KILL''HW1.BAS'' erases the file HW1.BAS from the current drive.<br>KILL''B:HW2.BAS'' erases the file HW2.BAS from the drive indicated, in this case drive B. |
| LIST | Displays a listing of all program lines. Function key F1.<br>LIST<br>LIST 20−80 lists the lines indicated, in this case lines 20−80 inclusive. |
| LLIST | Sends to the printer a hard copy listing of all program lines.<br>LLIST<br>LLIST 20−80 prints a listing of the lines indicated, in this case lines 20−80 inclusive.<br>The letter L followed by the function key F1 also performs an LLIST. |

| | |
|---|---|
| LOAD | Loads a program into memory, LOAD''PrgName''. Function key F3. |
| | LOAD ''HW1'' loads the program HW1 from the current drive. |
| | LOAD ''B:HW2'' loads the program HW2 from the drive indicated, in this case drive B. |
| NEW | Erases current program from memory. |
| | NEW |
| RENUM | Renumbers lines of the entire program by increments of 10. |
| | RENUM |
| | RENUM 20,5 renumbers the entire program by increments of 5 starting with line 20. |
| RUN | Executes the current program in memory. Function key F2. |
| | RUN |
| SAVE | Saves the program in memory, SAVE''PrgName''. Function key F4. |
| | SAVE''HW1'' saves to the current drive. |
| | SAVE''B:HW2'' saves to the drive indicated, in this case drive B. |
| SYSTEM | Returns to DOS from BASIC. The DOS prompt, >, appears. |
| | SYSTEM |

The following commands are used when working with DOS. As shown, these commands are typed after a DOS prompt, A>, B>, or C>, followed by pressing the Enter key.

| DOS Command | Purpose and Example |
|---|---|
| CLS | Clears the screen. |
| | A>CLS |
| COPY | Enables you to copy one program or file. |
| | A>COPY A:HW1.BAS B: copies the program or file from drive A to drive B. |
| | B>COPY B:EX5C9.BAS A: copies the program or file from drive B to drive A. |
| DISKCOPY | Enables you to make copy of a complete diskette onto another diskette having the same size and format specifications. (See FORMAT below.) |
| | A>DISKCOPY A: B: causes the contents of a diskette in drive A to be copied to a ''target'' diskette in drive B. |
| | *Caution: DISKCOPY automatically destroys all original contents on the target disk.* |

DIR

Displays all the files in the current directory of the current drive. The display is vertical scrolling down the left side of the screen.

A>DIR

A>DIR /W causes the display to go horizontally across the screen. *W* stands for ''wide.''

A>DIR /P causes the display to pause when the screen is full. Pressing any key will continue the display. *P* stands for ''pause.''

A>DIR B: displays all the files in the directory of drive B.

ERASE

Erases a program or a file.

A>ERASE HW1.BAS causes the program in drive A to be erased.

A>ERASE B:EX23C7.BAS causes the program in drive B to be erased.

B>ERASE B:PRO3C4.BAS causes the program in drive B to be erased.

FORMAT

Prepares a diskette for use. *Note:* Since there are different types of diskettes (5.25 inches, 3.5 inches, single-sided, double-sided, and so forth) as well as drives, there are a variety of ways to format a diskette. You should refer to the documentation that came with the system you are using.

A>FORMAT B: formats a 5.25-inch diskette in drive B.

C>FORMAT A: /F:720 formats a 3.5-inch, 720KB diskette in 1.44MB drive A.

*Caution: Formatting destroys all data/information on the disk.*

RENAME

Changes the name of a program or file.

A>RENAME PROG1.BAS TO EXER3.BAS changes the name of the program PROG1 to EXER3 on drive A.

A>RENAME B:HW1.BAS TO EXER3.BAS changes the name of the program HW1 to EXER3 on drive B.

B>RENAME A:EX8.BAS TO PR3.BAS changes the name of the program EX8 to PR3 on drive A.

## APPENDIX B

# SOME COMMON *BASIC*
# ERROR MESSAGES

When an error is detected, your program will stop running and an error message will be displayed. Below is a list with examples of some of the most common error messages you will encounter. A complete list of error messages can be found in the various editions of the manual entitled *IBM BASIC Reference*. In the examples shown below, comments to help describe the error have been inserted in each program using either REM remarks or the ' character.

| Error Message (and Error Number) | Meaning and Example |
|---|---|
| Division by zero (11) | Occurs when trying to divide an expression by zero, or when raising zero to a negative power. |

```
5   REM ** Division by zero **
10 FOR N =1 TO 5
20      LET X = 7*(1.1)^N/(N-1)  'when N=1, N-1=0
30      PRINT N, X
40 NEXT N
90 END

RUN
Division by zero
   1   1.701412E+38
   2   8.47
   3   4.6585
   4   3.416234
   5   2.818393
```

| | |
|---|---|
| FOR without NEXT (26) | Occurs when a FOR statement does not have a matching NEXT statement. (See also NEXT without FOR, shown below.) |

```
10 FOR D = 1 TO 20
20        PRINT "-"
25 REM
30 REM ** a FOR without a NEXT **
99 END

RUN
FOR without NEXT in 10
```

| | |
|---|---|
| Missing operand (22) | Occurs when expression is incomplete. |

```
5  REM ** A missing operand**
10 READ A, B, C
20 DATA 47, 19, 17
30 LET X = (A+B)
```

```
35 LET Y =                          'the RHS is missing something
40 PRINT A, B, C, X, Y
90 END

RUN
Missing operand in 35
```

NEXT without FOR
(1)

Occurs when a NEXT statement does not have a matching FOR statement. (See also FOR without NEXT shown above.)

```
10 REM ** a NEXT without FOR**
15 REM
20       PRINT "-"
30 NEXT D
99 END

RUN
-
NEXT without FOR in 30
```

Out of data
(4)

Occurs when a READ statement tries to read more data than is in the DATA statements.

```
5 REM ** Out of data**
10 FOR D = 1 TO 6    'process six data values; only four in line 40
15       READ MN$
20       PRINT MN$
30 NEXT D
40 DATA jan, feb, march, april
99 END

RUN
jan
feb
march
april
Out of DATA in 15
```

RETURN without GOSUB
(3)

Occurs when a RETURN statement does not have a prior GOSUB statement.

```
5  REM ** A RETURN without A GOSUB**
10 READ NM$
20 DATA JACK, JILL, SALLY, SAM
30 PRINT NM$
50 REM --- subroutine ----- 'missing a line, say 40 GOSUB 60 and a
60 FOR D = 1 TO 20              'line 45 GOTO 90
70       PRINT "-";
80 NEXT D
85 RETURN
90 END

RUN
JACK
-------------------
RETURN without GOSUB in 85
```

Syntax error
(2)

Occurs in several ways—when a line has a misspelled keyword or command, unmatched parenthesis, incorrect sequence of characters, or incorrect punctuation. Also, when the data in a DATA statement does not match the type (string or numeric) of the variable type in a READ statement. Can occur when a reserved word, such as commands, keywords, statements, functions, and operator names, is used as a variable name. Note that the line containing the syntax error will be displayed by the computer.

```
5  REM ** syntax errors **
10 FOUR D = 1 TO 20   'misspelled keyword
20         PRINT "-";
30 NEXT D
99 END

RUN
Syntax error in 10

10 FOUR D = 1 TO 20   'misspelled keyword


5  REM ** A Syntax Error **
10 READ A, B, C, D
20 DATA 17, 36, 21, 13
30 LET X = (A + B) / (C - D   'a missing parenthesis
40 PRINT A, B, C, D, X
90 END

RUN
Syntax error in 30

30 LET X = (A + B) / (C - D   'missing parenthesis


5  REM ** Syntax Error **
10 READ TO         'TO is a reserved word
20         PRINT TO
25 GOTO 10
30 DATA 27, 43, 29, 86
35 DATA 25, 13, 54, 37
40 END

RUN
Syntax error in 10

10 READ TO            'TO is a reserved word
```

Type mismatch
(13)

Occurs when a string item is expected and not a numeric item, or when a numeric item is expected and not a string item.

```
5 REM ** A Type mismatch **
10 READ M$, YR
20 DATA FEB, 1990
30 PRINT USING " ####  \   \ "; M$, YR         'should be \   \ ####
99 END

RUN
Type mismatch in 30
```

```
5  REM ** A Type mismatch**
6  LET H = "XYZ COMPANY"  'assigning a string to a numeric
10 PRINT H$
99 END

RUN
Type mismatch in 6
```

Undefined line number
(8)

Occurs when a line that does not exist in the program is referred to by a statement or command.

```
5 REM ** Undefined line number **
30 READ B
40        PRINT B
50 GOTO 10   'the transfer should be to 30 not 10
60 DATA 127, 243, 329, 286, 195
70 DATA 215, 103, 354, 237, 311
80 END

RUN
 127
Undefined line number in 50
```

## APPENDIX C

# SUMMARY OF ALT (ALTERNATE) KEY FUNCTIONS

To type an entire BASIC keyword or command with a single keystroke, hold down the Alt (alternate) key and press one of the alphabetic keys shown below.

| KEY | *BASIC* KEYWORD OR COMMAND | CHAPTER REFERENCE |
|-----|------|------|
| A | AUTO | 2 |
| D | DELETE | 2 |
| E | ELSE | 8 |
| F | FOR | 11 |
| G | GOTO | 7 |
| I | INPUT | 4 |
| L | LOCATE | 2 |
| N | NEXT | 11 |
| O | OPEN | 15 |
| P | PRINT | 2 |
| R | RUN | 2 |
| T | THEN | 8 |
| U | USING | 6 |

# ANSWERS AND SOLUTIONS
# TO SELECTED EXERCISES

# Chapter 2

**2.1**  a. 20 PRINT ''EARNINGS FOR 3RD QUARTER''
b. 30 PRINT ,''DIVISION'', ,''SALES''
c. 40 PRINT ''NAME'',''S.S.#'',''DATE OF BIRTH'',''NO. OF DEP.''

**2.4**  a. .00528    c. 4,680,000.    e. 75,310,000,000.
b. .000000153    d. .0341791    f. − .0123658

**2.7**  Numerical solutions:
a. 1/7    c. − 19    e. 1 1/2    g. − 240
b. 15 4/7    d. 80    f. 20    h. 360

**2.9**
```
 5 PRINT "ANY STUDENT'S NAME"
10 PRINT "124 UNIVERSITY PL."
15 PRINT "ANY TOWN, ANY STATE   ZIP CODE"
20 PRINT "COURSE IS - BUS 10"
99 END

RUN
ANY STUDENT'S NAME
124 UNIVERSITY PL.
ANY TOWN, ANY STATE   ZIP CODE
COURSE IS - BUS 10
```

**2.12**
```
10 PRINT "SALES","TAX","TOTAL"
12 PRINT "-------------------------------------------------"
15 PRINT "$";5,"$";5*.05,"$";5+5*.05
20 PRINT "$";10,"$";10*.05,"$";10+10*.05
25 PRINT "$";15,"$";15*.05,"$";15+15*.05
99 END

RUN
SALES          TAX             TOTAL
------------------------------------------------
$ 5            $ 0.25          $ 5.25
$ 10           $ 0.5           $ 10.5
$ 15           $ 0.75          $ 15.75
```

**2.17**  Expressions have the following values:
a. 5    b. 3    c. 27    d. 11

**2.20**
```
 1 REM THIS PROGRAM FINDS THE AREA OF A TRIANGLE.
 2 REM NOTE THE USE OF COMPUTATIONAL PRINT.
 5 PRINT "BASE","HEIGHT","AREA"
10 PRINT 5,7,5*7/2
15 PRINT 10.5,6.2,10.5*6.2/2
20 PRINT 100,78;100*78/2
99 END

RUN
BASE           HEIGHT         AREA
 5              7              17.5
 10.5           6.2            32.55
 100            78             3900
```

## Chapter 3

**3.4** $(2*R*C/(U*P))^\wedge.50$

**3.6** 69
304

**3.11** a.
```
 1  PRINT "A","B","C"
 5  READ A,B,C
10 DATA 1
12 DATA 2,3
15 PRINT A,B,C
16 PRINT
22 PRINT "X","Y","Z"
25 READ X,Y,Z
30 PRINT X,Y,Z
99 END

RUN
A                 B                 C
 1                2                 3

X                 Y                 Z
Out of data in 25
```

**3.14**
```
10 PRINT "SALES","TAX","TOTAL"
15 DATA 5,10,15
20 READ S1,S2,S3
25 PRINT S1,S1*.05,S1+S1*.05
30 PRINT S2,S2*.05,S2+S2*.05
35 PRINT S3,S3*.05,S3+S3*.05
99 END

RUN
SALES           TAX           TOTAL
 5              .25           5.25
10              .5            10.5
15              .75           15.75
```

## Chapter 4

**4.7**
```
10 REM THIS PROGRAM SHOWS THAT THE SUM OF DEVIATIONS
11 REM ABOUT THE MEAN IS ZERO.
25 READ X1,X2,X3,X4,X5
26 PRINT "THE MEAN IS: ";(X1 + X2 + X3 + X4 + X5)/5
28 INPUT "ENTER THE COMPUTED VALUE OF THE MEAN: ", U
30 PRINT "THE SUM OF THE DEVIATION ABOUT THE MEAN IS: ";
35 PRINT (X1-U)+(X2-U)+(X3-U)+(X4-U)+(X5-U)
40 DATA 5,-3,7,8,-2
99 END

RUN
THE MEAN IS: -3
ENTER THE COMPUTED VALUE OF THE MEAN: 3
THE SUM OF THE DEVIATION ABOUT THE MEAN IS: 0
```

**4.9**
```
25 REM UNITED COMPUTER COMPANY
30 INPUT "ENTER 4 SALESPERSONS NAMES: ", N1$, N2$, N3$, N4$
35 INPUT "ENTER THE AMOUNT SOLD FOR EACH PERSON: ", S1,S2,S3,S4
40 READ W,P
45 DATA 1000, .015
50 PRINT "SALESPERSON","AMOUNT SOLD", "SALARY"
55 PRINT N1$,S1, W+P*S1
```

```
60 PRINT N2$,S2, W+P*S2
65 PRINT N3$,S3, W+P*S3
70 PRINT N4$,S4, W+P*S4
75 END
```

---

## Chapter 5

**5.3**
```
10 READ A,B,C,D
15 DATA 1,2
20 LET X=A+B
25 LET A=X^B/C*A-5          '<---
30 LET B=X+A               '<---
35 DATA 4,5,6
40 PRINT A,B,C,X
45 END

RUN
-2,75          ,25          4          3
```

**5.4**
```
10 READ A,B,C,D
15 DATA 1,2
20 LET X=A+B
25 LET B=X+A
30 LET A=X^B/C*A-5
35 DATA 4,5,6
40 PRINT A,B,C,X
45 END

RUN
15,25          4          4          3
```

**5.8**
```
5   REM PROGRAM TO FIND TOTAL PROFITS, TOTAL PROFITS = TOTAL
10  REM REVENUE - TOTAL COST, WHERE T=TOTAL PROFITS, P=PRICE
15  REM PER UNIT, C=COST PER UNIT, U=# UNITS SOLD AND BOUGHT
20  REM T1=TOTAL REV. (P*U), AND T2=TOTAL COST (C*U).
30  READ P,C,U
40  LET T1=P*U        '<----total revenue
50  LET T2=C*U        '<----total cost
60  LET T=T1-T2       '<----total profit
70  PRINT "TOTAL PROFIT REPORT"
75  PRINT
80  PRINT "NUMBER OF UNITS SOLD";U
85  PRINT "PRICE PER UNIT";P,"COST PER UNIT";C
86  PRINT "TOTAL REVENUE";T1
90  PRINT "LESS TOTAL COST";T2
95  PRINT "---------------------------------------------"
100 PRINT "TOTAL PROFIT";T
150 DATA 10,6,50,225
199 END

RUN
TOTAL PROFIT REPORT

NUMBER OF UNITS SOLD 225
PRICE PER UNIT 10              COST PER UNIT 6,5
TOTAL REVENUE 2250
LESS TOTAL COST 1462,5
---------------------------------------------
TOTAL PROFIT 787,5
```

**5.15**
```
10 READ F,R,N
20 DATA 300000,0,15,5
30 LET P=F/(1+R)^N
35 PRINT "FUTURE AMOUNT IS $"; F
36 PRINT "ANNUAL RATE OF INTEREST IS"; R*100;"%"
```

```
37 PRINT "TIME PERIOD IS ";N;"YEARS"
40 PRINT "THE PRESENT VALUE IS $";P
50 END

RUN
FUTURE AMOUNT IS $ 300000
ANNUAL RATE OF INTEREST IS 15 %
TIME PERIOD IS   5  YEARS
THE PRESENT VALUE IS $ 149153
```

**5.22**
```
10 LINE INPUT "ENTER EMPLOYEE NAME "; N$
15 INPUT "ENTER NUMBER OF HOURS WORKED AND RATE", H,R
20 LET L$="-----------------------------------------------------------------"
25 PRINT L$
30 PRINT "EMPLOYEE","SALARY";"FED. TAX","S.S TAX","NET SALARY"
35 PRINT L$
40 LET S=H*R
45 LET F=.2*S
50 LET S1=.05478*S
55 LET N1=S-(F+S1)
60 PRINT N$,S,F,S1,N1
65 PRINT L$
70 END
RUN
ENTER EMPLOYEE NAME  Brown, A.
ENTER NUMBER OF HOURS WORKED AND RATE 37, 4.50
-----------------------------------------------------------------
EMPLOYEE      SALARY       FED. TAX      SS. TAX      NET SALARY
-----------------------------------------------------------------
Brown, A.     166.5          33.3        9.120869     124.0791
-----------------------------------------------------------------
```

## Chapter 6

**6.2**  b. Line 30 should have a string format, "\      \", not a numeric format.

d. Line 70 of the format is missing a backslash, \.

**6.7**
```
10 LET A$= "NAME              RATE     HOURS       SALARY"
15 LET B$= "\               \ ##.##   ##.#        ###.##"   '<---
20 READ N$,R,H
30 PRINT A$
40 PRINT USING B$; N$, R, H, H*R
41 READ N$, R, H                      'new lines: 41-47, 51,52
43 PRINT USING B$; N$, R, H, H*R
45 READ N$; R, H
47 PRINT USING B$; N$, R, H, H*R
50 DATA "I.GREEN", 20.53, 40.5
51 DATA "M.HEIGH", 10.45, 35
52 DATA "D.HIMBER", 30.79, 22.28
60 END

RUN
NAME         RATE      HOURS       SALARY
I.GREEN      20.53     40.5        831.47
M.HEIGH      10.45     35.0        365.75
D.HIMBER     30.79     22.3        686.00
```

**6.12**
```
5  LET FT$="###.#         ###.#          #,###.#"
10 PRINT "BASE","HEIGHT","AREA"
15 READ B1,H1,B2,H2,B3,H3
16 LET A1=B1*H1/2
17 LET A2=B2*H2/2
18 LET A3=B3*H3/2
20 PRINT USING FT$; B1,H1,A1
25 PRINT USING FT$; B2,H2,A2
```

```
30 PRINT USING FT$, B3,H3,A3
35 DATA 5,7,10.5,6.2,100,78
99 END

RUN
BASE            HEIGHT          AREA
  5.0             7.0           17.5
 10.5             6.2           32.6
100.0            78.0        3,900.0
```

**6.18**
```
25 LET F$="       \              \         $##,###        $#,###.##"
30 LET L$="       ------------------------------------------------"
35 PRINT  "    SALESPERSON        AMOUNT SOLD          SALARY"
40 READ SP1$, SP2$, SP3$, SP4$
45 PRINT L$
50 READ S1,P1,W1,S2,P2,W2,S3,P3,W3,S4,P4,W4
55 LET SA1=W1+P1*S1
60 LET SA2=W2+P2*S2
65 LET SA3=W3+P3*S3
70 LET SA4=W4+P4*S4
75 PRINT USING F$; SP1$,S1,SA1
80 PRINT USING F$; SP2$,S2,SA2
85 PRINT USING F$; SP3$,S3,SA3
90 PRINT USING F$; SP4$,S4,SA4
95 PRINT L$
100 DATA M. Worth, K. Gray, S. Legan, B. Hinz
105 DATA 13600,.015,1000,22000,.015,1000
106 DATA 9800,.015,1000,24500,.015,1000
110 END

RUN
     SALESPERSON        AMOUNT SOLD          SALARY
     ------------------------------------------
       M. Worth           $13,600        $1,204.00
       K. Gray            $22,000        $1,330.00
       S. Legan           $ 9,800        $1,147.00
       B. Hinz            $24,500        $1,367.50
     ------------------------------------------
```

**6.22**
```
25 INPUT "WHAT IS THE NUMBER OF YEARS"; N#
30 INPUT "WHAT IS THE ANNUAL INTEREST RATE (.dd)"; R#
35 INPUT "WHAT IS THE FUTURE AMOUNT OWED"; F#
40 LET PV#=F#/(1+R#)^N#
45 PRINT
50 PRINT USING "N = ## YEARS R = .##   F = $$#,###,###";N#,R#,F#
55 PRINT USING "THE PRESENT VALUE IS $$#,###,###.##"; PV#
60 END

RUN
WHAT IS THE NUMBER OF YEARS?  5
WHAT IS THE ANNUAL INTEREST RATE (.dd)?  .15
WHAT IS THE FUTURE AMOUNT OWED?  300000

N = 5 YEARS  R = .15   F = $300,000
THE PRESENT VALUE IS    $149,153.03
```

## Chapter 7

**7.1**   a. The program would loop infinitely, printing out the same first line of results.

b. Only the first line of output would result.

**7.7**   b. Variable $S$ would always be set equal to zero, and the last column of output would have the values of $X$. The heading is repeated each time.

e. Only the heading and the first line of output result. The computer would not say ''Out of data''.

i. Same as e.

j. The variable *S* would not accumulate. Since *S* is equal to zero, the values in the last column of output would be zero.

```
7.14  25 LET F$ = "\            \     $###,###        $#,###,##"
      30 PRINT "SALESPERSON","AM'T SOLD","SALARY+COMM."
      35 PRINT "-----------","---------","------------"
      40 READ SP$,A
      50    LET SC = 1000 + .015*A
      55    PRINT USING F$; SP$, A, SC
      60 GOTO 40
      62 DATA   M. WORTH,13500, K. GRAY,21000
      63 DATA   S. LEGAN,9600, B. HINZ,24400
      65 END

      RUN
      SALESPERSON      AM'T SOLD     SALARY+COMM.
      -----------      ---------     ------------
      M. WORTH          $13,500       $1,202.50
      K. GRAY           $21,000       $1,315.00
      S. LEGAN          $ 9,600       $1,144.00
      B. HINZ           $24,400       $1,366.00
      Out of DATA in 40
```

## Chapter 8

8.2  a. The output would not change.

b. Omitting line 80 would not cause the output to change, because *A* is greater than *B*. If *A* were less than *B*, both the *B* and *A* values would be printed out, each on a separate line.

8.7  The data value 999 would be processed in lines 60, 65, and 70. An additional line of output results with these values: 999 and 998001. The column totals become 1021 and 998121.

```
8.15  10 REM CASE 8.3, IDENTIFYING ELIGIBILITY FOR RETIREMENT
      15 REM PROGRAMMER- (name of person)  DATE - mm/dd/yy
      16 REM    VARIABLE LIST - A,N,S,Y
      17 REM       A=EMPLOYEE'S AGE
      18 REM       N=EMPLOYEE NO.
      19 REM       S=EMPLOYEE'S SALARY
      20 REM       Y=YEARS EMPLOYED WITH THE COMPANY
      25 REM ----------------------------------------
      26 LET T1=0                        '<---- number processed = 0
      27 LET T2=0                        '<---- number eligible = 0
      28 PRINT " AGE    YEARS    SALARY    NUMBER"
      30 READ N,A,Y,S
      35    IF N=0 THEN 104
      36       LET T1=T1 + 1             'Count number processed <---
      40       IF A>=65 THEN 65          'at least 65 years old
      45          IF Y>=30 THEN 65       'worked at least 30 years
      50             IF A>60 THEN 75     'over 60 years old
      55                IF A>55 THEN 85  'over 55 years old
      60 GOTO 30
      65    PRINT USING " ##     ##    $###,###    ####  "; A, Y, S, N
      66    LET T2 = T2 + 1              'Count eligible employees <---
      70 GOTO 30
      75    IF Y>25 THEN 65              'over 60 years old & worked at least 25   years
```

```
80 GOTO 55
85    IF Y>=20 THEN 95        'over 55 years old & worked at least 20 years
90 GOTO 30
95    IF S>=30000 THEN 65     'over 55 & 20+ years & $30,000+ salary
100 GOTO 30
104 PRINT
105 PRINT USING "TOTAL NUMBER OF EMPLOYEES PROCESSED ####";T1 '<--
106 PRINT USING "TOTAL NUMBER OF ELIGIBLE EMPLOYEES  ####";T2 '<--
110 DATA 1234,40,5,12500,  1235,61,25,15000
120 DATA 1236,56,21,30000, 1237,71,15,18000
130 DATA 1238,62,19,41000,  1239,59,30,11000
140 DATA 1240,20,10,10000,  1241,56,22,29000
150 DATA 1242,57,18,31000,  1243,62,24,35000
160 DATA 0,0,0,0
999 END

RUN

AGE    YEARS   SALARY    NUMBER
 61     25     $15,000    1235
 56     21     $30,000    1236
 71     15     $18,000    1237
 59     30     $11,000    1239
 62     24     $35,000    1243

TOTAL NUMBER OF EMPLOYEES PROCESSED    10
TOTAL NUMBER OF ELIGIBLE EMPLOYEES      5
```

**8.24**
```
10 LET N=0
15 LET S=0
16 PRINT "DATA VALUES";
20 READ A
30    IF A=-999 THEN 70
31        PRINT USING " ###";A;
40        LET N=N+1
50        LET S=S+A
60 GOTO 20
70 LET M=S/N
75 PRINT
80 PRINT USING "THE AVERAGE IS ###.##";M
90 DATA 25,15,70,15,20,25,30,35,40,-999
100 END

RUN
DATA VALUES   25   15   70   15   20   25   30   35   40
THE AVERAGE IS   30.56
```

**8.29**
```
40 PRINT    " DIVISION      JAN.       FEB.       MAR."
45 PRINT    "--------------------------------------------------"
47 LET FT$= "\          \  $#,###     $#,###     $#,###"
50 LET A=0
60 LET B=0
70 LET C=0
80 READ D$, J, F, M
90    IF D$= "EOD" THEN 150
100        PRINT USING FT$;D$, J, F, M
110        LET A=A+J
120        LET B=B+F
130        LET C=C+M
140 GOTO 80
150 PRINT "--------------------------------------------------"
160 PRINT USING FT$; "TOTALS", A,B,C
180 DATA WEST,1000,750,750, SOUTH,1200,800,1000
190 DATA NORTH,1200,500,1200, EAST,1500,1050,950
200 DATA EOD, 0, 0, 0
210 END
```

```
RUN
DIVISION        JAN.            FEB.            MAR.
------------------------------------------------------
WEST            $1,000      $   750      $   750
SOUTH           $1,200      $   800      $1,000
NORTH           $1,200      $   500      $1,200
EAST            $1,500      $1,050      $   950
------------------------------------------------------
TOTALS          $4,900      $3,100      $3,900
```

## Chapter 9

**9.4**   b. 
```
10 LET I=1
15 ON 2*I GOTO 40,20,30     '<---Part b.
20 PRINT "IS",
25 GOTO 45
30 PRINT "EASY"
35 GOTO 45
40 PRINT "PROGRAMMING",
45 LET I=I+1
50 IF I<=3 THEN 15
55 END

RUN
IS              IS              IS
```

**9.5**   b. 
```
10 READ X
12     IF X = -99 THEN 99
15         ON X GOTO 30,20,50,40,10     '<---9.5 b
20             PRINT X; "TWO"
25 GOTO 10
30     PRINT X; "ONE"
35 GOTO 10
40     PRINT X; " FOUR"
45 GOTO 10
50     PRINT X;  " THREE"
55 GOTO 10
60 DATA 3, 1, 4, 2, 1.4, 2.8, 3.5, 2.2, 5
70 DATA -99
99 END

RUN
 3 THREE
 1 ONE
 4 FOUR
 2 TWO
 1.4 ONE
 2.8 THREE
 3.5 FOUR
 2.2 TWO
```

**9.6**
```
5 PRINT "ACCOUNT NUMBER      MONTHS NO PAYMENT       ACTION TO BE TAKEN"
6 PRINT "-----------------------------------------------------------------"
10 READ N,M
12 IF N=-999 THE 190
15          PRINT USING "      ####                   ##              "; N,M,
40          IF M>= 4 THEN 100
50              ON M+1 GOTO 55,60,80,80
55                  PRINT "NONE"
56          GOTO 10
60              PRINT "GENTLE REMINDER"
70          GOTO 10
80              PRINT "STRONG REMINDER"
```

```
90              GOTO 10
100                PRINT LAWYER'S LETTER"
110             GOTO 10
120             DATA 2370,2,3542,3,2372,0,8282,1,3838,4
130             DATA 2182,8,1352,5,1519,1,2315,2,1820,0
131             DATA -999,0
190             END

RUN
ACCOUNT NUMBER        MONTHS NO PAYMENT        ACTION TO BE TAKEN
----------------------------------------------------------------
    2370                   2                    STRONG REMINDER
    3542                   3                    STRONG REMINDER
    2372                   0                    NONE
    8282                   1                    GENTLE REMINDER
    3838                   4                    LAWYER'S LETTER
    2182                   8                    LAWYER'S LETTER
    1352                   5                    LAWYER'S LETTER
    1519                   1                    GENTLE REMINDER
    2315                   2                    STRONG REMINDER
    1820                   0                    NONE
```

---

## Chapter 11

```
11.3    10 READ A, B, C
        15 FOR I=A TO B/C STEP C*A
        20     PRINT I;
        25 NEXT I
        30 DATA 1,10,1
        35 END

        RUN
         1  2  3  4  5  6  7  8  9  10
```

```
11.7  10 REM CASE 11.1, ANALYZING FOOD CHAIN SALES
      25 REM ---------------------------------
      27    LET GC = 0        '<----
      29    LET GT = 0        '<----
      30 FOR I= 1 TO 3
      40     LET C=0
      50     LET T=0
      60     PRINT "REGION";I;
      70     READ A
      80        IF A=-99 THEN 130      'test for the end of each DATA list
      90            LET C = C+1        'count the items
      95            LET GC = GC+1      '<---
      100           LET T = T+A        'accumulate A values
      105           LET GT = GT+A      '<---
      110           PRINT A;
      120     GOTO 70
      130        LET AVE = T/C        'calculate the average
      132        PRINT TAB(35);
      135        PRINT USING "TOTAL    ###    AVERAGE   ##.##"; T;AVE
      140        PRINT
      150 NEXT I
      152        LET AVE3=GT/GC        '<---
      153        PRINT TAB(28);"---------------    --------------------" '<---
      154        PRINT TAB(29);        '<----
      156        PRINT USING " GRAND TOTAL ###    3 REGION AVERAGE ##.##";GT;AVE3
      160 DATA 40,20,50,60,-99
      170 DATA 50,40,55,35,70,65,-99
      180 DATA 35,46,25,-99
      190 END
```

```
RUN
REGION 1   40   20   50   60              TOTAL 170   AVERAGE 42.50

REGION 2   50   40   55   35   70   65   TOTAL 315   AVERAGE 52.50

REGION 3   35   46   25                   TOTAL 106   AVERAGE 35.33
                                          ---------------   -----------------
                                          GRAND TOTAL 591   3 REGION AVERAGE 45.46
```

**11.14**
```
  5 LET F$= "   ###                "
 10 PRINT   "ITEM      BEGINNING INVEN.   UNITS SOLD   ENDING INV."
 20 PRINT   "-------------------------------------------------------"
 50 FOR I = 1 TO 3
 60     READ B,U
 70          LET E=B-U
 80          PRINT USING F$;I,B,U,E
 90 NEXT I
100 DATA 250,40,700,75,600 280
110 END
```

```
RUN
ITEM       BEGINNING INVEN.    UNITS SOLD   ENDING INV.
-------------------------------------------------------
   1            250                 40           210
   2            700                 75           625
   3            600                280           320
```

**11.20**
```
 40 PRINT        " DIVISION        SALES        % OF TOTAL    "
 50 PRINT        "--------------------------------------------------"
 55 LET FT$ = " \               \     ##,##          #,##      "
 60 LET A=0
 70 LET B=0
 90 FOR I = 1 TO 4
100      READ D$,S
110      LET A=A+S
120 NEXT I
125 RESTORE
130 FOR I = 1 TO 4
140      READ D$, S
150      LET P=S/A
160      LET B=B+P
170      PRINT USING FT$;D$, S, P
180 NEXT I
190 PRINT "---------------------------------------------------"
200 PRINT USING FT$; " TOTALS", A,B
210 DATA WEST, 2.85, SOUTH,7.62
220 DATA NORTH,3.57, EAST 2.81
230 END
```

```
RUN
DIVISION        SALES        % OF TOTAL
---------------------------------------
  WEST          2.85            0.17
  SOUTH         7.62            0.45
  NORTH         3.57            0.21
  EAST          2.81            0.17
---------------------------------------
  TOTALS       16.85            1.00
```

**11.29**
```
 10 FOR I =1 TO 10
 15     FOR J=1 TO 10
 20          LET X = 0
 30          IF I = J THEN 40
 32          IF I+J = 11 THEN 40
 35               GOTO 45
 40                   LET X = 1
```

```
45                        PRINT X;
50        NEXT J
55        PRINT
60 NEXT I
65 END

RUN

1  0  0  0  0  0  0  0  0  1
0  1  0  0  0  0  0  0  1  0
0  0  1  0  0  0  0  1  0  0
0  0  0  1  0  0  1  0  0  0
0  0  0  0  1  1  0  0  0  0
0  0  0  0  1  1  0  0  0  0
0  0  0  1  0  0  1  0  0  0
0  0  1  0  0  0  0  1  0  0
0  1  0  0  0  0  0  0  1  0
1  0  0  0  0  0  0  0  0  1
```

# Chapter 12

**12.11**
```
  5 LET T1=0
  8 LET T2=0
 10 PRINT ," UNITS PRODUCED"
 20 PRINT," --------------"
 30 PRINT "PLANT","1989","1990"
 40 PRINT "-----","----","----"
 50 DIM Y(4),X(4)
 52 FOR I=1 TO 4
 54     READ P$(I)
 56 NEXT I
 60 FOR I=1 TO 4
 70     READ Y(I)
 80 NEXT I
 90 FOR I=1 TO 4
 95     READ X(I)
100 NEXT I
105 DATA Ave. A, Ave. B, Crosstown, West Side
110 DATA 2400,3000,2500,3000
120 DATA 2900,3100,3000,3200
130 LET TI=0
140 LET T2=0
150 FOR I=1 TO 4
160     LET T1=T1+Y(I)
170     LET T2=T2+X(I)
180     PRINT USING "\            \ #,###          #,###";P$(I), Y(I),   X(I)
190 NEXT I
200 PRINT            "---------------------------------"
210 PRINT USING      "  TOTAL  ##,###      ##,###";T1,T2
220 END

RUN
             UNITS PRODUCED
             --------------
PLANT     1989              1990
-----     ----              ----
Ave. A    2,400            2,900
Ave. B    3,000            3,100
Crosstown 2,500            3,000
West Side 3,000            3,200
---------------------------------
  TOTAL  10,900           12,200
```

```
12.15 16 LET F$="   #,###        "
      18 LET H$="  WORKER          A            B            C         # UNITS"
      19 LET L$="----------------------------------------------------------------------"
      20 REM TOTAL UNITS PRODUCED
      25 DIM W1(5,3),W2(5,3)
      30 FOR I=1 TO 5
      35     FOR J=1 TO 3
      40         READ W1(I,J)
      45     NEXT J
      50 NEXT I
      55 FOR I=1 TO 5
      60     FOR J=1 TO 3
      65         READ W2(I,J)
      70     NEXT J
      75 NEXT I
      80 FOR I=1 TO 5
      85     LET B(I)=0
      90     LET C(I)=0
      95     LET RT(I)=0
      100     FOR J=1 TO 3
      105         LET B(I)=B(I)+W1(I,J)
      110         LET C(I)=C(I)+W2(I,J)
      115         LET RT(I)=B(I)+C(I)          'COMBINED ROW TOTALS
      120         LET T3(I,J)=W1(I,J) + W2(I,J)  'COMBINE TABLE W1 + W2
      125     NEXT J
      130 NEXT I
      135 PRINT "WEEK ONE"
      140 PRINT "--------"
      145 PRINT H$
      148 PRINT L$
      150 FOR I=1 TO 5
      155     PRINT USING F$;I,
      160     FOR J=1 TO 3
      165         PRINT USING F$;W1(I,J),
      170     NEXT J
      175     PRINT USING F$;B(I)
      180 NEXT I
      185 FOR J=1 TO 3
      190     LET D(J)=0
      195     LET E(J)=0
      200     LET F(J)=0      'NEW COL. TOTALS
      205     FOR I=1 TO 5
      210         LET D(J)=D(J)+W1(I,J)
      215         LET E(J)=E(J)+W2(I,J)
      220         LET F(J)=D(J)+E(J)     'NEW COL. TOTALS
      225     NEXT I
      230 NEXT J
      240     PRINT L$
      255 PRINT "TOTALS",
      260 LET G1=0
      265 FOR J=1 TO 3
      270     PRINT USING F$;D(J);
      275     LET G1=G1+D(J)
      280 NEXT J
      285 PRINT USING F$;G1
      295 PRINT
      300 PRINT "WEEK TWO"
      305 PRINT "--------"
      310 PRINT H$
      312 PRINT L$
      315 FOR I=1 TO 5
      320     PRINT USING F$; I,
      325     FOR J=1 TO 3
      330         PRINT USING F$;W2(I,J),
      335     NEXT J
      340     PRINT USING F$;C(I)
      345 NEXT I
```

```
355     PRINT L$
370 PRINT "TOTALS",
375 LET G2=0
380 FOR J1 TO 3
385     PRINT USING F$;E(J),
390     LET G2=G2+E(J)
395 NEXT J
400 PRINT USING F$;G2
410 DATA 200,100,20,150,125,30,320,75,15,275,100,15
415 DATA 100,200,10,185,110,22,160,115,25,275,100,30
420 DATA 275,90,20,150,150,10
450 PRINT
500 PRINT "TWO WEEK AGGREGATION"
505 PRINT "--------------------"
510 PRINT H$
512 PRINT L$
515 FOR I=1 TO 5
520     PRINT USING F$;I,
525     FOR J=1 TO 3
530         PRINT USING F$;T3(I,J),
535     NEXT J
540     PRINT USING F$;RT(I)
545 NEXT I
555 PRINT L$
570 PRINT "TOTALS",
580 FOR J=1 TO 3
585     PRINT USING F$;F(J),
595 NEXT J
600 PRINT USING F$;G1+G2
825 END

RUN
WEEK ONE
--------
```

| WORKER | A | B | C | # UNITS |
|--------|------|-----|-----|---------|
| 1 | 200 | 100 | 20 | 320 |
| 2 | 150 | 125 | 30 | 305 |
| 3 | 320 | 75 | 15 | 410 |
| 4 | 275 | 100 | 15 | 390 |
| 5 | 100 | 200 | 10 | 310 |
| TOTALS | 1,045 | 600 | 90 | 1,735 |

```
WEEK TWO
--------
```

| WORKER | A | B | C | # UNITS |
|--------|------|-----|-----|---------|
| 1 | 185 | 110 | 22 | 317 |
| 2 | 160 | 115 | 25 | 300 |
| 3 | 275 | 100 | 30 | 405 |
| 4 | 275 | 90 | 20 | 385 |
| 5 | 150 | 150 | 10 | 310 |
| TOTALS | 1,045 | 565 | 107 | 1,717 |

```
TWO WEEK AGGREGATION
--------------------
```

| WORKER | A | B | C | # UNITS |
|--------|------|-----|-----|---------|
| 1 | 385 | 210 | 42 | 637 |
| 2 | 310 | 240 | 55 | 605 |
| 3 | 595 | 175 | 45 | 815 |
| 4 | 550 | 190 | 35 | 775 |
| 5 | 250 | 350 | 20 | 620 |
| TOTALS | 2,090 | 1,165 | 197 | 3,452 |

```
12.16   5   REM TOTAL DOLLAR SALES OF MINICOMPUTERS
        10  PRINT "SALESPERSON      TOTAL DOLLAR VOLUME"
        15  PRINT "-----------------------------------"
        20  DIM S(5,4)
        25  LET G=0
        30  FOR J=1 TO 4
        40      READ P(J)
        50  NEXT J
        60  FOR I=1 TO 5
        70  LET T(I)=0
        80  FOR J=1 TO 4
        90      READ S(I,J)
        100     LET T(I)=S(I,J)*P(J)+T(I)
        120 NEXT J
        140     PRINT USING "      #          $$###,###.##";I,T(I)
        145     LET G=G+T(I)
        160 NEXT I
        170 PRINT "-----------------------------------"
        175 PRINT USING "   GRAND TOTAL      $$#,###,###.##";G
        900 DATA 10000, 12500, 17200, 20000
        950 DATA 6,8,2,1,5,4,3,1,7,6,1,2,3,9,5,0,4,2,4,3
        999 END

        RUN
        SALESPERSON     TOTAL DOLLAR VOLUME
        -----------------------------------
            1               $214,400.00
            2               $171,600.00
            3               $202,200.00
            4               $228,500.00
            5               $193,800.00
        -----------------------------------
        GRAND TOTAL       $1,010,500.00
```

## Chapter 13

**13.1** b. 63        c. .4        g. 45.01

**13.5** b. Between zero and 2.5, excluding 0 and 2.5

d. From zero to 9, inclusive

f. From 50 to 150, inclusive

**13.8** b. ANY CITY        d. U.S.A

```
13.16 10 REM PICKING RANDOM NUMBERS FROM 001 TO 500
      12 PRINT "  Winning Number"
      13 RANDOMIZE TIMER
      15 FOR P = 1 TO 3
      20     READ P$
      25     LET WN=INT(500*RND+1)
      30     PRINT P$;"PRIZE",WN
      40 NEXT P
      45 DATA "1ST", "2ND", "3RD"
      99 END

      RUN
        Winning Number
      1ST PRIZE    315
      2ND PRIZE    219
      3RD PRIZE    262
```

```
13.24 10 FOR C=1 TO 6
      15     READ C$,S$,Z$
      17     PRINT C$,S$,Z$,
      20     LET L=LEN(Z$)
      25     IF L=5 THEN PRINT
```

```
30      IF L<5 THEN PRINT "ZIP CODE TOO SHORT"
45      IF L>5 THEN PRINT "ZIP CODE TOO LONG"
50 NEXT C
55 DATA COLUMBUS,OHIO,43210,HOUSTON,TEXAS,770004
60 DATA DENTON,TEXAS,0216,BOULDER,COLORADO,80309
65 DATA ALBANY,NEW YORK,1222,CHICAGO,ILLINOIS,60680
70 END

RUN
COLUMBUS      OHIO          43210
HOUSTON       TEXAS         770004      ZIP CODE TOO LONG
DENTON        TEXAS         0216        ZIP CODE TOO SHORT
BOULDER       COLORADO      80309
ALBANY        NEW YORK      1222        ZIP CODE TOO SHORT
CHICAGO       ILLINOIS      60680
```

## Chapter 14

**14.1** Before first pass

| | $A$ | $X$ | $B$ | $S$ |
|---|---|---|---|---|
| | 0 | 1E10 | * | * |
| | 8 | | * | |
| | 9 | | * | |
| | 3 | | * | |
| | 2 | | * | |

After first pass

| | $A$ | $X$ | $B$ | $S$ |
|---|---|---|---|---|
| | 1E10 | 0 | 0 | 1 |
| | 8 | | * | |
| | 9 | | * | |
| | 3 | | * | |
| | 2 | | * | |

After second pass

| | $A$ | $X$ | $B$ | $S$ |
|---|---|---|---|---|
| | 1E10 | 2 | 0 | 5 |
| | 8 | | 2 | |
| | 9 | | * | |
| | 3 | | * | |
| | 1E10 | * | | |

After third pass

| | $A$ | $X$ | $B$ | $S$ |
|---|---|---|---|---|
| | 1E10 | 3 | 0 | 4 |
| | 8 | | 2 | |
| | 9 | | 3 | |
| | 1E10 | | * | |
| | 1E10 | | * | |

After fourth pass

| | $A$ | $X$ | $B$ | $S$ |
|---|---|---|---|---|
| | 1E10 | 8 | 0 | 2 |
| | 1E10 | | 2 | |
| | 9 | | 3 | |
| | 1E10 | | 8 | |
| | 1E10 | | * | |

After fifth pass

| | $A$ | $X$ | $B$ | $S$ |
|---|---|---|---|---|
| | 1E10 | 9 | 0 | 3 |
| | 1E10 | | 2 | |
| | 1E10 | | 3 | |
| | 1E10 | | 8 | |
| | 1E10 | | 9 | |

*means not yet defined

**14.2**

| | | | | | |
|---|---|---|---|---|---|
| Before 1st switch | 0 | 8 | 9 | 3 | 2 |
| After 1st switch | 0 | 8 | 3 | 9 | 2 |
| After 2nd switch | 0 | 3 | 8 | 9 | 2 |
| After 3rd switch | 0 | 3 | 8 | 2 | 9 |
| After 4th switch | 0 | 3 | 2 | 8 | 9 |
| After 5th switch | 0 | 2 | 3 | 8 | 9 |

**14.3**

| | *A* | *X* | *B* | *S* |
|---|---|---|---|---|
| Before first pass | 1 | $-1E10$ | * | * |
| | 7 | | * | |
| | 6 | | * | |
| | 0 | | * | |
| | 3 | | * | |
| After first pass | *A* | *X* | *B* | *S* |
| | 1 | 7 | 7 | 2 |
| | $-1E10$ | | * | |
| | 6 | | * | |
| | 0 | | * | |
| | 3 | | * | |
| After second pass | *A* | *X* | *B* | *S* |
| | 1 | 6 | 7 | 3 |
| | $-1E10$ | | 6 | |
| | $-1E10$ | | * | |
| | 0 | | * | |
| | 3 | | * | |
| After third pass | *A* | *X* | *B* | *S* |
| | 1 | 3 | 7 | 3 |
| | $-1E10$ | | 6 | |
| | $-1E10$ | | 3 | |
| | 0 | | * | |
| | $-1E10$ | | * | |
| After fourth pass | *A* | *X* | *B* | *S* |
| | $-1E10$ | 1 | 7 | 1 |
| | $-1E10$ | | 6 | |
| | $-1E10$ | | 3 | |
| | 0 | | 1 | |
| | $-1E10$ | | * | |
| After fifth pass | *A* | *X* | *B* | *S* |
| | $-1E10$ | 0 | 7 | 0 |
| | $-1E10$ | | 6 | |
| | $-1E10$ | | 3 | |
| | $-1E10$ | | 1 | |
| | $-1E10$ | | 0 | |

**14.13** Revisions to Program 14.6 that are needed:

```
20 DIM N$(30),X$(30)    '<——change dim
40 LET N=25             '<——change let from 8 to 25
68 DATA XYZ,MNO,BBC,BBB,XXX,ZXY,BMD '<——add data
```

*means not yet defined

## Chapter 15

**15.1**   b. 20 OPEN ''A'', #1, ''FILE3''

d. 40 OPEN ''R'', #2, ''FILE$'',25

**15.2**   b. 20 PRINT #2, X; Y; Z

d. 40 WRITE #2, N, M, O

**15.10**
```
10 REM EX 15-10 FILE CREATION
20 OPEN "O",#1,"UNITF"
30 FOR I = 1 TO 6
40     READ P,U
50       PRINT #1,P;",";U
60 NEXT I
70 DATA 1,3400, 2,4200, 3,2800
80 DATA 4,3100, 5,4000, 6,5500
90 CLOSE
100 END

A:\>UNITF
1 , 3400
2 , 4200
3 , 2800
4 , 3100
5 , 4000
6 , 5500
```

**15.13**
```
10 REM EX 15-13
20 LET T=0
30 OPEN "I",#1,"UNITF"
40 PRINT "PLANT    UNITS PRODUCED"
50 PRINT "-----------------------"
60 FOR I = 1 TO 6
70      INPUT #1, P, U
80      LET T = T + U
90      PRINT USING " ##     ##,###";P,U
100 NEXT I
110 LET I = I - 1
120 PRINT "-----------------------"
130 PRINT USING "TOTAL     ##,###"; T
140 PRINT USING "AVERAGE    #,###"; T/I
150 CLOSE
160 END

RUN
PLANT    UNITS PRODUCED
-----------------------
   1        3,400
   2        4,200
   3        2,800
   4        3,100
   5        4,000
   6        5,500
-----------------------
TOTAL      23,000
AVERAGE     3,833
```

**15.17**
```
10 REM EX 15-17A FILE CREATION
20 OPEN "O",#1,"FILEA"
30 FOR I = 1 TO 4
40     READ D$, A, B
50      WRITE #1,D$, A, B
60 NEXT I
70 DATA DIV A, 400,15, DIV B, 500,23
```

```
80 DATA DIV C, 430,20, DIV D, 330,30
95 CLOSE
100 END

A:\>TYPE FILEA
"DIV A",400,15
"DIV B",500,23
"DIV C",430,20
"DIV D",330,30

10 REM EX 15-17B FILE APPEND & OUTPUT
15 OPEN "A",#1,"FILEA"
20 FOR I = 1 TO 3
25      READ D$, A, B
30      WRITE #1,D$, A, B
35 NEXT I
40 DATA DIV E, 380,13, DIV F, 450,25
45 DATA DIV G, 300,21
50 CLOSE
55 OPEN "I", #1, "FILEA"
60 FOR I = 1 TO 7
65      INPUT #1, D$
70      PRINT D$
75      NEXT I
80 CLOSE
85 END

RUN
"DIV A",400,15
"DIV B",500,23
"DIV C",430,20
"DIV D",330,30
"DIV E",380,13
"DIV F",450,25
"DIV G",300,21
```

15.18  a. 
```
10 REM EX 15-18A FILE CREATION 747 SCHEDULE
15 OPEN "O",#1,"SCHED"
20 FOR I = 1 TO 3
35      READ S$
30      PRINT #1,S$
35      PRINT S$
40 NEXT I
45 DATA "MO/TH/SA/SU     7:10 P.M.    7:30 A.M.    9:00 A.M."
50 DATA "MO/TH/SA/SU    10:05 P.M.    (NON STOP) 10:40 A.M."
55 DATA "TU/WE/FR        8:50 P.M.    9:10 A.M.   10:40 A.M."
60  CLOSE #1
65  END

RUN
MO/TH/SA/SU        7:10 P.M.      7:30 A.M.       9:00 A.M.
MO/TH/SA/SU       10:05 P.M.      (NON STOP)     10:40 A.M.
TU/WE/FR           8:50 P.M.      9:10 A.M.      10:40 A.M.

A:\>TYPE SCHED
MO/TH/SA/SU        7:10 P.M.      7:30 A.M.       9:00 A.M.
MO/TH/SA/SU       10:05 P.M.      (NON STOP)     10:40 A.M.
TU/WE/FR           8:50 P.M.      9:10 A.M.      10:40 A.M.
```

b. 
```
10 REM EX 15-18B ACCESSING OF SCHEDULE FILE
15 DIM S$(10)
20 OPEN "I",#1,"SCHED"
25 FOR I = 1 TO 3
30      INPUT #1,S$(I)
40 NEXT I
45 CLOSE #1
```

```
50 LET H$= "DAY OF WEEK    LEAVES N.Y.    ARRIVES GENEVA    ARRIVES ZURICH"
55 PRINT "ENTER THE DAY OF THE WEEK FOR SCHEDULE INFORMATION:";
60      PRINT "1. MONDAY  2. TUESDAY    3. WEDNESDAY  4. THURSDAY"
65      PRINT "5. FRIDAY  6. SATURDAY   7. SUNDAY     8. QUIT"
66      PRINT
70      INPUT "DAY NUMBER PLEASE 1, 2, 3, 4, 5, 6, 7, OR 8 TO QUIT"; DN
75      PRINT
80 ON DN GOTO 85, 115, 115, 85, 115, 85, 85, 140
85         PRINT H$
90         PRINT STRING$(60,"-")
95         PRINT S$(1)
100        PRINT S$(2)
105        PRINT
110 GOTO 55
115     PRINT H$
120     PRINT STRING$(60,"-")
125     PRINT S$(3)
130     PRINT
135 GOTO 55
140 END


RUN
ENTER THE DAY OF THE WEEK FOR SCHEDULE INFORMATION:
1. MONDAY    2. TUESDAY    3. WEDNESDAY    4. THURSDAY
5. FRIDAY    6. SATURDAY  7. SUNDAY       8. QUIT

DAY NUMBER PLEASE:  1, 2, 3, 4, 5, 6, 7, OR 8 TO QUIT?  2

DAY OF WEEK    LEAVES N.Y.    ARRIVES GENEVA    ARRIVES ZURICH
------------------------------------------------------------
TU/WE/FR       8:50 P.M.      9:10 A.M.         10:40 A.M.

ENTER THE DAY OF THE WEEK FOR SCHEDULE INFORMATION:
1. MONDAY    2. TUESDAY    3. WEDNESDAY    4. THURSDAY
5. FRIDAY    6. SATURDAY  7. SUNDAY       8. QUIT

DAY NUMBER PLEASE: 1, 2, 3, 4, 5, 6, 7, OR 8 TO QUIT?  4

DAY OF WEEK    LEAVES N.Y.    ARRIVES GENEVA    ARRIVES ZURICH
------------------------------------------------------------
MO/TH/SA/SU    7:10 P.M.      7:30 A.M.         9:00 A.M.
MO/TH/SA/SU    10:05 P.M.     (NON STOP)        10:40 A.M.

ENTER THE DAY OF THE WEEK FOR SCHEDULE INFORMATION:
1. MONDAY    2. TUESDAY    3. WEDNESDAY    4. THURSDAY
5. FRIDAY    6. SATURDAY  7. SUNDAY       8. QUIT

DAY NUMBER PLEASE: 1, 2, 3, 4, 5, 6, 7, OR 8 TO QUIT?  8
```

# INDEX